THE SEAGULL READER

Plays

Second Edition

W. W. Norton & Company, Inc., also publishes

THE SEAGULL READER: STORIES, Second Edition

•

THE SEAGULL READER: POEMS, Second Edition

•

THE SEAGULL READER: ESSAYS, Second Edition

THE SEAGULL READER

Plays

Second Edition

edited by Joseph Kelly

College of Charleston

W. W. Norton & Company, Inc. • New York • London

W. W. Norton & Company has been independent since its founding in 1923, when William Warder Norton and Mary D. Herter Norton first published lectures delivered at the People's Institute, the adult education division of New York City's Cooper Union. The Nortons soon expanded their program beyond the Institute, publishing books by celebrated academics from America and abroad. By mid-century, the two major pillars of Norton's publishing program—trade books and college texts—were firmly established. In the 1950s, the Norton family transferred control of the company to its employees, and today—with a staff of four hundred and a comparable number of trade, college, and professional titles published each year—W. W. Norton & Company stands as the largest and oldest publishing house owned wholly by its employees.

Manufacturing by Haddon Craftsmen, Inc. / RR Donnelley.
Book design by Chris Welch.
Production manager: Jane Searle.

Library of Congress Cataloging-in-Publication Data

The seagull reader. Plays / edited by Joseph Kelly. — 2nd. ed.
    p. cm.
Includes bibliographical references.

ISBN 978-0-393-93324-6 (pbk.)

    1. Drama—Collections.   2. Drama—History and criticism.   I. Kelly, Joseph,
1962–

PN6112.S36 2008
808.82—dc22

2008035523

W. W. Norton & Company, Inc., 500 Fifth Avenue, New York, N.Y. 10110-0017
www.wwnorton.com

W. W. Norton & Company Ltd., Castle House, 75/76 Wells Street,
London W1T 3QT

2 3 4 5 6 7 8 9 0

Contents

*

Acknowledgments

I thank Peter Simon, Kurt Wildermuth, Marian Johnson, and Conor Sullivan, all at W. W. Norton, for their great help in putting together this volume. Every book is a collaboration; the Seagull Readers, more than most.

Along with the publisher, I thank the following for their assistance during various stages of this project:

John Aber (College of Mount Saint Joseph); Timothy Adams (West Virginia University); Jay Adler (Los Angeles Southwest College); Elizabeth Ann Altruda (Middlesex County College); Leslie Antonette (East Stroudsburg University); Thomas Austenfeld (Drury College); Paul Aviles (Onondaga Community College); Leslie G. Bailey (Saint Martin's College); Raymond L. Baubles, Jr. (Western Connecticut State University); Terrell Beck (University of Wisconsin at La Crosse); G. R. Benzinger (Duquesne University); David Bergman (Towson University); Michael Berndt (University of Minnesota); Stephen Bernstein (University of Michigan at Flint); Martin Bickman (University of Colorado); Eric Birdsall (University of Akron); George Bishop (D'Youville College); Jonathan Blake (Worcester State College); Elvina Boliek (Georgia Southern University); Anthony Boyle (State University of New York at Potsdam); Jenny Brantley (University of Wisconsin at River Falls); Edward H. Brodie, Jr. (University of South Carolina); Stuart C. Brown (New Mexico State University); Donna Burney (Howard Payne University); Rex Burns (University of Colorado at Denver); John Carlson (Waldolf College); William Carpenter (College of the Atlantic); Tom Chandler (Bryant College); Lisa Chen; Kevin Clark (California Polytechnic State University at San Luis Obispo); Patricia Clark (Grand Valley State University); Bruce Clarke (Texas Tech University); Joseph Rocky Clavito (Northwestern State University); Gina Claywell (Murray State University); Gerald Concannon (Massachusetts Maritime Academy); Thomas F. Connolly (Suffolk University); Seamus Cooney (Western Michigan University); Ruth L. Copp (Saginaw Valley State University and Northwood University); Denise Coulter (Atlantic Community College); Karen Cox (Bronx Community College); Carolyn M. Craft (Longwood College); Virginia Crank (Rock Valley College); A. C. Crosland (University of South Carolina, Spartanburg); Koos Daley (Adams State College); Debbie Danowski (Sacred Heart University); Robert Darling (Keuka College); Charles L. Darr (University of Pittsburgh at Johnstown); Adam Brooke Davis (Truman State University); Cathy Day (Minnesota State University); Louise Dibble; John Dick (The University of Texas at El Paso); Paul B. Diehl (University of Iowa); Marylynne Diggs (Clark College); William Doreski (Keene University); Gregory Eiselein (Kansas State University); S. K. Eisiminger (Clemson University); B. L. Farley (Ocean County Community College); Shir Filler (North County Community College); Sharon S. Fong (University of Nevada at Las Vegas); Marilyn Fontane (St. Louis College of Pharmacy); Chris Forhan (Trident Technical College); Kyle Friedow (Kent State University); Robert Fuhrel (Community College of Southern Nevada); David Galef (University of Mississippi); Victoria Gaydosik (Southwestern Oklahoma State University); Amy Getty (Augustana College); Robert L. Giron (Montgomery College); Len Gougeon (University of Scranton); George Greenlee (Missouri Southern State College); Charles Grogg (Santa Barbara City College); Amanda Gulla (New York University); Carol Hardin (Western Oregon University); Pamela S. Hardman; Clarinda Harris (Towson University); Muriel Harris (Purdue University); Lois Head (St. Cloud State University); John Healy (Baker University); Michael Hennessy (Southwest Texas State University); Walter J. Hickey (Pacific Bell Prep); John Hildebidle (Massachusetts Institute of Technology); Mark Hochberg (Juniata College); Charles Hood (Antelope Valley College); Shari Horner (Shippensburg University); George Hudson (Colgate University); Jefferson Hunter (Smith College); Kathleen Jacquette (State University of New York at Farmingdale); James D. Johnson (Humboldt State University); Linda Karlen (Oakton Community College);

Deborah A. Kearney (California State University, Sacramento);
Robert Johnson (Midwestern State University); Bruce W. Jorgenson
(Brigham Young University); Richard Kelly; Christopher B.
Kennedy (Duke University); Brian Gordon Kennelly (Webster University); De'Lara Khalili; David Kidd (Norfolk Academy); Millie M.
Kidd (Mount Saint Mary's College, Los Angeles); Herbert W. Kitson (University of Pittsburgh at Titusville); Linda Kittell (Washington State University); Steve Klepetar (Saint Cloud State University);
Diane Koenig (Columbia-Greene Community College); Leonard
Kress (Owens Community College); Stanley Krohmer (Grand Valley State University); Brigitte LaPresto (Pikeville College); Emily
Law; Joy Leasure (New York University); Dennis Leavens (Truman
State University); Michael Leddy (Eastern Illinois University); Dennis Lynch (Elgin Community College); James L. Machor (Kansas
State University); Chris Mackowski (University of Pittsburgh at
Bradford); Michael Mattison (University of Massachusetts at
Amherst); David Mazel (Adams State College); J. L. McClure
(Kirkwood Community College); David McCordick (University of
Wisconsin); Douglas J. McMillan (East Carolina University); David
Melzer (Florida State University); G. Douglas Meyers (University of
Texas at El Paso); Patricia Meyers (Grand Canyon University);
Charles W. Mignon (University of Nebraska at Lincoln); Ruth
Misheloff (Borough of Manhattan Community College/City University of New York); James J. Mooney (Immacula College); Deborah Murray (Kansas State University); Mike Mutschelknaus (Saint
Mary's University of Minnesota); Lisa Nakamura (Sonoma State
University); Ruth Newberry (Duquesne University); Rolf Norgaard
(University of Colorado at Boulder); Barry H. Novick (The College of New Jersey); Stephen O'Neill (Bucks County Community
College); Angela M. Pellettiere (New York University); Diane Penrod (Rowan University); Barry Phillips (College of Public and
Community Service); Brian R. Plant (Mary Baldwin College);
Donna Potts (Kansas State University); Gordon M. Pradl (New
York University); Diane Putnam (Cabrillo College); Mark Putnam
(Northwestern College); David Rachels (Virginia Military Institute); Stacey A. Rannik (Paradise Valley Community College);
Steven L. Reagles (Bethany Lutheran College); Jason Rosenblatt
(Georgetown University); Robert E. Rubin (Wright State Univer-

sity); Marsha Rutter (Southwestern College); Carol de Saint Victor (University of Iowa); David Schelhaas (Dordt College); Ana Schnellman (Lindenwood University); Barbara Goldstein Scott (New York University); Craig L. Shurtleff (Illinois Central College); Shirley Simpson (Nicholls State University); Elliott L. Smith; Adam Sorkin (Penn State Delaware County); Jamieson Spencer (Saint Louis Community College at Florissant Valley); Karen Stewart (Beloit College); Kip Strasma (Illinois Central College); Anthony Stubbs (Iowa Lakes Community College); Timothy Stump; Carolyn P. Sturm (Valley College); Debra Sutton (Jefferson College); Dan K. Thorpe (College of DuPage); Maurice Tome (New York University); Mary Troy (University of Missouri—St. Louis); Sandra Varone (Brookdale Community College); Mark Vinz (Moorhead State University); Suzanne Waldenberger (Pima County Community College); Ronald G. Walker (Western Illinois University); Heidemarie Z. Weidner (Tennessee Technological University); David Winn (Hunter College, City University of New York); Alan Zhang (Darton College).

Note on Dates

After each play, we cite the date of composition on the left; where possible, we cite the date of first production on the right.

INTRODUCTION

✳

What Is Drama?

Even if you have never read a play before, you have probably
spent your life absorbing the skills necessary to read one.
Anyone who has grown up going to the movies and watching television learned the common language of drama long ago.
When your pulse races during a tense scene in a movie, or when you
laugh at a pratfall in a sitcom, you're responding as you should
when you read a play: exercising your best judgment of character,
following and reacting to the manipulations of plot, and staying
alert to underlying meanings.

As if by instinct, you most likely react to drama with the "correct" emotions. These reactions don't happen accidentally, of course.
Directors, scriptwriters, and playwrights avidly study human nature, and they use their knowledge of instinctual responses to push
emotional buttons. For example, they count on your responding in
a particular way when you see a child in danger, in a different way
when you see an attractive person disrobing by candlelight. But instinct is only half the story; many of your responses are shaped not
by your instincts but by **dramatic conventions**—devices, phrases,
or actions that have, over time, become so common that their
meaning is immediately apparent. Without knowing it, you've in-

ternalized dozens of dramatic conventions. When you hear a violin playing in a minor key on a movie sound track, you, like most people, probably feel melancholy. That's not so much instinct at work as a learned response, even if you are not consciously aware of it. You don't need to *know* you've been conditioned to feel sad when you hear a violin in the background for your emotions to respond "correctly." The process is automatic.

Dramatic Conventions Then and Now

While familiar dramatic conventions produce responses automatically (or nearly so), unfamiliar ones can seem strange and can interfere with your emotional responses. If you've ever struggled through Shakespeare or puzzled over Sophocles, your confusion might have resulted from unfamiliar conventions. The use of a **chorus**—in ancient-Greek theater, a group of singers and dancers who participate in or comment on the action—is a good example. When you first read Greek tragedy, the chorus's pronouncements can seem odd— unrealistic and alienating. Once you absorb the rules of this particular dramatic convention, however, the strangeness disappears.

Contemporary dramas don't use choruses, unless they're self-consciously, perhaps ironically, borrowing the ancient device. But the conventions of long-ago theater have modern counterparts. What these now-strange conventions accomplished for their audiences are accomplished today by other means, conventions that contemporary audiences feel perfectly comfortable with and interpret without even noticing. One such convention is the "voiceover" narration common in movies. The voiceover would no doubt strike someone completely unfamiliar with film or television as a very odd convention. Where, after all, is that voice *coming from*? Whose voice is it? And where, exactly, is the speaking supposed to be occurring? To the person asking questions such as these, the voiceover would be just as strange as the Greek chorus is to you today.

By learning about some of the older conventions of drama, and keeping in mind that contemporary forms of cultural expression have their own peculiar conventions, you should be able to overcome many of the difficulties inherent in reading plays written for past societies, even ones that have long since perished.

Cultural Context

Another possible confusion when reading plays written in the past has to do with cultural differences between you—reader (or theatergoer)—and the characters inhabiting the play (and the playwright who created those characters). In all the plays reprinted in this book, the characters struggle with questions that remain pertinent: What is the meaning of existence? What constitutes a good life? How can men and women get along? Why must children contest their parents? Why is there suffering and injustice? As universal as these questions may be, however, the ways they are presented, and the assumptions that guide the characters' actions and words as they seek to answer them, are often rooted in a specific time and place—in a **cultural context**—that can seem unfamiliar and confusing now. But just as frequent exposure to dramatic conventions can make them seem more and more familiar, so too learning about the time and place in which a play was written can help you respond to the work in a more direct and meaningful way.

Take an example from Shakespeare's *Hamlet*. Near the end of act 2, his fellow students Rosencrantz and Guildenstern inform Prince Hamlet about the late difficulties of a traveling group of tragic actors. In subsequent scenes, Hamlet digresses on the proper way to perform a play. Though the whole issue of acting troupes occupies hundreds of lines, it is so tangential to the main line of the play's action that modern directors, looking for places to cut this long play, often dispense with them altogether. To modern readers, Hamlet's long speeches on acting may prove confusing or, worse, intrusive and boring. But to Shakespeare's contemporaries, the lines must have made perfect sense, as a reference to a particular theatrical controversy with which they were all familiar.

Theaters like the Globe, which Shakespeare co-owned and where most of his plays were performed, dominated theatrical London until about 1600, when a more exclusive type of theater developed. The Globe was an open-air structure in which people from different social classes took in popular entertainments that mixed verbiage with physicality and were performed entirely by men and boys. In the alternative, private type of theater, the venues were smaller and enclosed. Admission was expensive, so the clientele tended to exclude the lower orders. Because the actors were children, the plays tended to be less raucous and bawdy (a company of boys could hardly have acted many scenes in a play like *Hamlet*); and they were seen as more erudite than the lowbrow affairs Shakespeare wrote. So the strange digressions about theater in the second and third acts of *Hamlet* can be seen as Shakespeare's contribution to the bitter dispute among competing acting companies.

Henrik Ibsen's *A Doll House* provides another type of cultural dissonance between an older play—this one from nineteenth-century Europe—and contemporary readers. The plot hinges on a bit of contractual fraud that most readers today find fairly trivial. Whenever I teach the play, my students wonder why the characters make such a fuss about a course of events that would pretty well meet their own ethical standards. To feel any of the tension Ibsen meant you to feel, you have to understand how important public reputation was to a business career at the time, and how even a small slip could ruin a reputation.

Throughout this book, I keep footnotes to a minimum, but I use them to explain cultural differences like these, which would otherwise make the plays harder to understand.

Page versus Stage

Unlike a short story or a novel, a play is written not primarily for *reading*, but instead as the guiding text for *performing* onstage. When reciting lines, actors provide all sorts of physical cues—facial expressions and body language and tone of voice—that make the words more understandable, that deliver to their audience a thousand subtleties latent in the written words. For example:

> MAN: I'm through with everything here. I want peace. I want to see if somewhere there is something left in life with charm and grace. Do you know what I'm talking about?
> WOMAN: No. I only know that I love you.
> MAN: That's your misfortune.
> WOMAN: If you go, where shall I go? What shall I do?
> MAN: Frankly, my dear, I don't give a damn.

Once you reached the last line, you might have realized that this dialogue comes from the last scene of Victor Fleming's film *Gone With the Wind* (1939), where Rhett Butler (Clark Gable) abandons a sobbing Scarlett O'Hara (Vivien Leigh) on the staircase of their mansion. If you've seen the film, you can probably conjure images of Gable and Leigh, he delivering his lines with cold disdain, she delivering hers with panicked desperation. But if you *haven't* seen the movie, you might wonder, reading the lines above, what all the fuss has been about—why some people claim that the final scene of *Gone With the Wind* is one of the most powerful and memorable movie endings they've ever seen. Without the actors' intonations and gestures, without the sets and lighting, without dozens of contextual cues, the dialogue can seem dry.

Although plays can be enjoyed and studied as texts, fundamentally they are written guides for other artists—directors, actors, set designers, and many others—to create artistic performances. When you read a play on the page, those other artists are not present to help you imagine all aspects of the performance, as they would be if you saw the play performed. Therefore, your imagination needs to be fully engaged when you read—at every turn, you essentially decide how you would stage the play if you were the director.

After you've read a play once, you should try to see it performed—not as a *substitute* for your reading, of course, but as a *supplement*. It is not likely that you will have the chance to see a live performance of one of these plays during the time that you're studying it, but if you do, be sure to go. Probably, your library will have recordings of some productions, and you will find it very helpful to watch them. Watching the lines being brought to life often reveals subtleties of meaning barely perceptible in the text. This is especially true of Shakespeare. I often show my students scenes from Franco Zeffirelli's 1990 film adaptation of *Hamlet* (starring Mel Gibson, Glenn Close, and Helena Bonham Carter), and only then do they realize that Polonius is something of a fool, understand how betrayed Hamlet feels by Ophelia, and recognize the barely submerged sexual tension between Hamlet and his mother. But even more recent plays—plays with characters whose speech patterns are closer to our own, or with detailed stage directions—become more accessible when experienced in performance.

Perhaps more important, a performance helps you see that the very act of putting a play into action involves interpretation and analysis on the part of the director, the actors, and every other artist involved in the production—activities very similar to your own interpretative and analytical work when you read the play on the page and form a version in your mind's eye. Each production of a play, even one that follows the text to the letter, differs from every other production, and the differences among productions reveal interesting differences of opinions about the play's meanings.

Before you can fully appreciate the differences among performances, though, you need to understand what is familiar, the elements common to all drama. Let's turn to those elements now.

The Parts of a Play

Analysis means "a breaking down into parts." You do this whenever you come out of a movie arguing with your friends about one thing or another—did the main character deserve what he got? did you like or dislike so-and-so? and other questions of that nature. To answer those questions, you analyze the film, meaning you break it into parts and scrutinize these parts in some detail.

People have been breaking plays down into parts for over two thousand years. Aristotle, a Greek philosopher of the fourth century B.C.E., wrote the first great work of literary criticism, *Poetics*, not long after Sophocles wrote *Oedipus the King*. In fact, the *Poetics* drew on *Oedipus* for most of its examples. Aristotle invented the first list of parts to drama: spectacle, (moral) character, plot, diction, melody, and thought. Over the centuries, these have been modified somewhat, but most discussions of dramatic form owe a debt to Aristotle's acute analysis of Greek theater.

Plot

The **plot** is the sequence of things that happen in a play. Generally, a play acts out a story before the eyes of its audience, so that people in the audience feel as though they are witnessing the events. (Some specialized forms of drama, such as Samuel Beckett's extremely minimal monologues, do not work this way, but those genres are beyond the scope of this book.) And so a play includes all the elements you expect of a story:

1. it begins in some state of **equilibrium**, which is stable and often (though not necessarily) more or less pleasant;
2. a **conflict** is introduced into this state of equilibrium by some event (the **complication**);
3. over the course of the play, the conflict grows in a sequence of events (**rising action**);
4. the conflict comes to a head (the **climax**), which ends the conflict;
5. the climactic event brings about a sequence of consequences (**falling action**);
6. finally, the plot reaches its **resolution**, a concluding situation that rests in another state of equilibrium, though the condition of the characters is probably different than it was at the story's beginning.

These elements constitute just about any plot. The story in nearly every mainstream movie, television drama, short story, novel, narrative poem, or play can be broken down into these parts.

Let's take a simple fairy tale for an example, say the story of the Three Little Pigs. The initial state of equilibrium exists when the story begins, with the three pigs building and moving into their houses of straw, sticks, and brick. Everything is stable at this point in the story. But this initial condition of stability is disrupted by the arrival of a wolf, who threatens to eat the pigs. This event is the complication, because it introduces into the story a conflict: pig versus wolf.

Conflict can always be expressed as one force struggling against another. Sometimes these forces are people: in *Hamlet*, Hamlet struggles against Claudius; in *A Doll House*, Nora opposes Helmer. Sometimes the "forces" battle within one character: Hamlet fights against his own tendency to overanalyze the situation and procrastinate rather than act; Nora fights against her own motherly instincts. And as the preceding examples make clear, typically several conflicts occur in any play.

Most plays don't devote much time to the original state of things before the complication. They tend to begin **in media res** (literally, "in the midst of things"), after the action has started, the complication has occurred, and the conflict is in its beginning stages. Typically, a dramatist will provide some sort of background information in the opening scene to give viewers an understanding of the early stages of the plot. This information is called **exposition.**

The rising action depicts the escalating struggle of the conflict. In our example, the rising action plays out in the huffs and puffs of the wolf. He threatens the first pig, then blows down the house of straw; but this pig escapes to the house of sticks, and the wolf renews his threats and blows down that house too. The rising action is often compared to the slope of a mountain, and you've probably seen graphs of plots in the shape of a pyramid:

This metaphor is apt. As the play moves toward the climax, the conflict grows more and more acute, and so the audience tends to feel more and more anxiety about the outcome.

The climax of the Three Little Pigs is that scene in which the wolf fails to blow down the brick house and resorts to climbing down the inside of the chimney. The clever pigs, of course, have a hot cauldron on the fire, and the wolf gets cooked or, in less gruesome versions, runs away. No matter the version, the wolf clearly won't come back any time soon; the pigs have won the struggle. The climax has resolved the conflict. One side wins, so to speak, and the other side loses. You can speak in terms of a contest even when the conflict happens within one character, as if two impulses or sides within that character are fighting for control. At the climax, one impulse or side "wins" and the other "loses."

The falling action is the sequence of events that cascade in consequence of the climax. In movies and television dramas, the falling action tends to be very brief, but in plays it often occupies a fairly substantial portion of the drama. The Three Little Pigs contains practically no falling action. Once the pigs win, the wolf disappears without further incident. You're launched immediately into the res-olution: that final situation in which order and stability are restored. Usually, the fairy tale ends with a scene depicting the "happy ever after" of the pigs as they dance around, feast, and live the high life in their brick house.

In most of the plays in this book, the resolution is a state consid-erably less attractive than the original state of equilibrium. The characters enjoy no happy ever after. That's because most of these plays either are tragedies, which tend to depict the fall of the main character, or owe a debt to tragedy. We'll talk more about tragedy a little further below.

Character

A **character**, of course, is a person on the stage, a personage being acted for the audience. Time has proven character to be the element of drama that distinguishes great plays from the rest. Plays that rely on interesting plots but superficial characters often become popular for a short time, but they burn out quickly and are forgotten. An entire genre of drama, the **well-made play** of the nineteenth cen-tury, exploited the crowd-pleasing elements of plot, like surprise revelations and dramatic climaxes—while purposely neglecting to develop memorable characters. The formulaic nature of Hollywood **genre** movies—westerns, crime films, horror movies, the *Rambo* se-ries, and so on—makes them the modern versions of plot-driven drama. Some movies made in these genres rise above the others and join the ranks of classic films, but they always do so by add-ing depth of character to their exciting plots. In fact, fascinating characters enable even plays, television shows, and films with straightforward or simple plots to live beyond their first seasons or initial releases. Obviously, the best combinations wed interesting plots to interesting characters, but of the two, character seems more important.

You analyze characters in a play much the same way you analyze people in life. At first, you react to them spontaneously. Gradually, as each character acts, speaks, and develops (or doesn't develop), you modify your first impression to create a more complex sense of each character's nature. Throughout, you should trust your instincts, but be open to new information and new impressions. Be cautious about personal likes and dislikes—you might hate redheads, for instance, for no good (or a very personal) reason, and thus fail to sympathize with a character with whom the playwright intends you to sympathize. As long as you're mindful of your prejudices and idiosyncrasies, you'll probably have little trouble judging characters. Of all parts of analysis, analyzing characters will come most naturally.

At the most basic level, you should determine which characters you like and which you dislike. As in real life, characters tend to be a mixture of good and bad, but, typically, the play will lead you to sympathize with some over others—to wish them well and feel sorry for them when they suffer. Such characters are called **sympathetic characters.** Characters with whom you are not meant to sympathize are called **unsympathetic characters.** Sometimes, a play will ask you to do more than sympathize. In fact, according to Aristotle, tragedy works only if the play gets you to **identify** with the protagonist. To identify with a character is to imagine yourself in the character's place.

No one can call your responses to characters wrong, but you should cultivate an ability to justify your spontaneous reactions. Rather than merely judging characters—saying you like this person or dislike that one—try to explain why you have made these judgments. Again, your reasons may be the same as they would be in real life. As you watch a play, all sorts of things influence your spontaneous impressions: the costumes, the actors' body language and **diction**, and so on. If you're reading the play, you have fewer cues. You will be able to judge the characters mostly by what they say and do, and also by how the other characters react to them. So the process of analyzing characters, while fairly easy, might require you to slow down and become conscious of how your affinities have been manipulated by the writer. You might keep in mind these very simple questions: Why do I like so-and-so? What is it about so-and-so that rubs me the wrong way? Simple questions like these will lead to sophisticated answers about character.

You should also note certain roles played by characters. Every play, if it has a conflict, will have a **protagonist.** The protagonist is the character that the play focuses on—logically enough, it is Hamlet in *Hamlet* and Oedipus in *Oedipus the King*. Though the protagonist is usually a good person, it does not have to be (it is not sufficient to define *protagonist* as "the good guy"). In most plays, the protagonist faces some physical or psychological challenge, and the play dramatizes his or her grappling with that challenge. If the protagonist struggles against another character, that character is called the **antagonist**.

Generally, the struggle (or conflict) causes some change in the protagonist. Any character who changes through the course of the play is called a **dynamic character**. A character who does not change is called a **static character**. A static character may be so two-dimensional, even one-dimensional, that it is called a **stock character**, as if the playwright just rummaged around in the stockroom to find a character to perform a particular function. The gravediggers in *Hamlet* might be called stock characters—in this case, witty stereotypes of the working class, often found in Elizabethan plays.

Spectacle

Spectacle was Aristotle's term for what the audience sees—the play as a physical reality. We might amplify this category to include all the material aspects of the play, including the **set**, costumes, **props**, music, sound effects, and so on. These elements contribute much to your experience of a play. Think, for example, of scenery. The lights come up on a deserted stage. You see nothing but the setting—*Before is the Salesman's house. We are aware of towering, angular shapes behind it, surrounding it on all sides. . . . As more light appears, we see a solid vault of apartment houses around the small, fragile-seeming home.* Thus Arthur Miller describes the set of *Death of a Salesman*. The set is designed to make you feel constricted, even claustrophobic, almost as if the characters are living inside prison walls. You might not even realize this intellectually, but the set can have this emotional effect on you.

Thus the spectacle establishes the atmosphere for the play. The production manipulates your attitude and mood. Essentially, as a viewer, you are told how to regard the action you are about to see. A good production uses spectacle to communicate to you on a non-verbal level, and you begin "interpreting" the spectacle before you even hear any words. Your gut reacts to it.

To a large extent, then, *reading* a play rather than *viewing* it puts you at a disadvantage. When you read a play, of course, you have to picture the scene in your mind, so the process is somewhat lengthened. For plays as old as those of Sophocles and Shakespeare, that imaginative work puts you on a level playing field with the original audiences. The older playwrights don't provide elaborate directions for how to set the scenes because their theaters didn't use much scenery or costuming. You have to pay careful attention to the dialogue, which is often encumbered by descriptions of the setting and the weather. These verbal cues enable you, like the plays' original audiences, to visualize the spectacle.

Contemporary plays, of course, often use fairly elaborate scenery, which you won't see if you just read the plays. But the play texts tend to give detailed descriptions of that scenery, usually at the very beginning. In fact, by reading contemporary plays you might have an advantage over theatergoers, because playwrights often go beyond mere description and actually interpret sets for you. For example, Lorraine Hansberry describes the set of *A Raisin in the Sun* like this: the *"furnishings . . . have clearly had to accommodate the living of too many people for too many years—and they are tired. Still, we can see that at some time, a time probably no longer remembered by the family (except perhaps for MAMA), the furnishings of this room were actually selected with care and love and even hope—and brought to this apartment and arranged with taste and pride. That was a long time ago. . . . [Now, w]eariness has, in fact, won in this room."* No matter how talented the set designer is, audiences can hardly see all that Hansberry says "we can see." In this case, the *reader* of the play has a much sharper understanding than the *theatergoer.*

Music can help to create atmosphere in the theater and a mood in the viewer. Reading a text cannot re-create in you the physical reaction you might have to music, but usually you can approximate the experience intellectually. And sometimes the playwright will tell you flat out how the sound should affect you, as Arthur Miller does.

The spectacle necessarily raises another important element in drama: symbolism.

Symbolism

A **symbol** is a thing that represents something else. It might represent an object or objects, or it might represent an idea or a set of ideas. Some things, usually things in the natural world, seem to carry the same symbolic meaning in just about any culture. The sunrise will probably call to mind birth or beginning no matter where you go, just as the sunset seems to naturally represent death or ending. The general meaning is the same in Bali as it is in Belgium. Ferocious predators might symbolize evil in many different cultures. A dense forest might symbolize the unknown. Having such broad applicability makes something a **universal symbol**. For example, Hamlet contemplates a skull in act 5; for many cultures (Hamlet's included), a human skull is a natural reminder of human mortality.

Other things and objects carry meaning only in a particular culture. In any culture acquainted with Christianity, for example, the cross represents Jesus' crucifixion, his redemption of humanity, and all the religious sects that believe in his divinity. But if you erected a cross in some distant town whose inhabitants had never heard of the Christian Gospels, the villagers might hang their laundry from it, never thinking they were dishonoring someone's god. A cross would have no symbolic meaning for them; it carries meaning only within the context of cultures familiar with Christianity. Rather than being universal, the symbol has a meaning that is agreed on by a particular group of people. It is a **conventional symbol.**

Sometimes, the symbolic meanings of conventional symbols have obviously been contrived by particular people. The regalia of clubs and political organizations are good examples. A new baseball franchise in Arizona chooses "Diamondbacks" for its name, and suddenly this Major League team is symbolized by a rattlesnake. A committee adopts the flag sewn by Betsy Ross, and thereafter the Stars and Stripes symbolizes a nation.

But most conventional symbols have anonymous genealogies. It is impossible to say who created them, as though they simply arose out of their cultures. Who can say when apple pie came to symbolize the values of Middle America? Who decided that the American Midwest would represent wholesomeness and honesty, while the

West would symbolize rugged individualism? Show anyone who grew up in American culture a picture of John Wayne on a horse in a Texas landscape, and that person will understand the symbolism. In fact, many people around the globe would recognize it too, for the icon of the cowboy, and the notions of self-reliance and freedom (and violence) that he represents, is one of America's cultural exports, courtesy of Hollywood. But show the same picture to a farmer in rural China, and he might see just a man on a horse. Richard Nixon's face represents, to a great many Americans, the personification of political dishonesty, but to a Latvian it might be just another face. No one person or committee decided that these images would convey symbolic meaning in American culture; nevertheless, they do. And outside that culture and its global ripple effects they are meaningless. In the opening sequence of *Oedipus the King*, Creon returns from a visit to the oracle wearing on his head a wreath made of laurel branches. To the typical contemporary reader, this object is meaningless. But any Greek citizen in antiquity would have recognized the laurel crown as an indication that Creon's trip was something of a victory or triumph. He was bringing good news.

A **literary symbol** is a thing that represents something else only within a particular work of literature. Outside the work, the thing does not mean what it does inside the work. A literary symbol, then, is authored neither by nature nor by a culture, but by a writer. As with a conventional symbol, when you take a literary symbol out of its original context, it stops being a symbol. For example, you will see that a bird in *Trifles* symbolizes something, but only within the context of the play. Its significance was invented by Susan Glaspell, and outside the play a bird would not carry the same meaning.

How do you recognize that an object in a play is not just its literal self but also represents something else? Identifying literary symbols is an art, but a few tricks will help you hone your interpretive skills. If a play title refers to an object, for example, you can be pretty sure the object symbolizes something. Pay careful attention, then, to the fence in *Fences*. By calling attention to the fence through his title, Wilson tips us off to its importance. On your first reading of the play you should be asking yourself, What could the fence represent? Meanwhile, watch for textual references to it. Repeated references are another good indication that something has symbolic significance.

No foolproof way exists, though, to recognize immediately which objects are symbolic and which are not. Again, trust your instincts. If you find your attention drawn to an object, if you suspect that something might have more than literal significance, you're probably right. The text will guide you to its literary symbols. Even if Wilson had called his play *The Tragedy of Troy Maxson*, you still could figure out that the fence is symbolic, because the characters draw your attention to it.

After you've identified a potential symbol, you still have the tougher task of figuring out what the symbol represents. You might have to read scenes or passages a few times until an idea comes to you. Usually, a symbol represents an abstraction: love, death, dreams, hope, and so on.

Trust your gut, but be prepared to revise your gut feelings. If you try to interpret an object symbolically and it doesn't seem to work, maybe you were wrong. As Sigmund Freud reportedly put it, "Sometimes a cigar is just a cigar." Maybe the object is not a symbol. Or maybe you were wrong about what the object represents. Keep revising and refining your idea until you have it right—until your interpretation of the symbol's meaning and importance fits your sense of the play as a whole.

Tragedy

Everything we've considered so far applies to plays in general. But now we need to focus on one particular genre of plays: **tragedy**. *Oedipus, Hamlet, Death of a Salesman*, and *Fences* are tragedies, and many other plays in this collection share some elements of tragedy. So an understanding of how tragedy affects plot and character will prove useful in much of your reading here.

The plot of tragedy follows the general pattern of all plots, but some aspects of plot are unique to tragedy. Tragedy always begins with the protagonist in a state of **prosperity**. Sometimes, you can take this term literally—the character is rich, well liked, and admired, a figure of some prominence in the community. Other times, especially in modern plays, the character displays a metaphoric "prosperity" based on a different measure of success. For example, at the beginning of *Fences*, Troy Maxson, despite his modest economic status, enjoys stature among his friends and relations. He is a success in their eyes, even a leader among them.

The conflict in a tragedy usually occurs between the protagonist and some larger force, like the gods or fate in Greek tragedy, or like a social imperative in modern plays. This force is so powerful that it overwhelms the protagonist, who nonetheless gains nobility in the struggle. For example, in *Fences*, Troy defies the insults and indignities that segregation imposed on African Americans. He is doomed to fail, but in his determined attempt he anticipates the civil rights activists of the 1960s.

The conflict reaches its breaking point at the climax, and in tragedy the climax always enacts a **reversal**. In the plainest terms, the hero's original prosperity turns into poverty. In Greek tragedy, this is a literal reversal: Oedipus, king of Thebes at the play's beginning, becomes a beggar by the play's end. But for works from other ages, these terms apply figuratively: after the reversal, the protagonist somehow falls from his or her metaphorical prosperity. At the play's end, the protagonist has a lower status than at the beginning, having lost something crucial to that earlier success and happiness.

The falling action of tragedy typically reveals that the protagonist has gained some self-understanding. Aristotle called this element **recognition** and considered it crucial to tragedy. Tragic heroes must face up to their own complicity in reversal. They have to take responsibility for the events that bring them to the point of poverty.

The term **tragic hero** merits some explanation. The protagonist in a tragedy is, by definition, a tragic hero. But over the ages such protagonists have tended to share certain character traits. For example, tragic heroes generally have been drawn from the higher classes—even from royalty, as in *Oedipus the King* and *Hamlet*. This exalted status ensures that audiences view the heroes as, in some ways, larger, even better, than themselves, and their fates as more important than ordinary people's fates. In the modern world, especially in democratic societies, this imbalance seems anachronistic, even offensive, so dramatists convey largeness of character in other ways. In *Fences*, for example, Troy transcends his job as a sanitation worker by carrying himself like the sports hero he once was. He fills the stage when he walks onto it.

The audience must admire the hero to some extent, whatever his or her faults, for a tragedy to work properly. Viewers must feel **pity** as they watch the hero go from a position above them to a position below them. They must feel sorry for the hero. And so the character's final state of poverty must appear out of proportion. The punishment cannot fit the crime. If the plot depicted a wicked person (someone visibly worse than the audience) receiving just deserts, viewers probably would feel satisfaction rather than pity or sorrow.

Still, the protagonist must have earned some punishment. The tragic hero cannot be a saint, someone too good and exalted to make a mistake. High school textbooks often label this aspect of the hero a tragic "flaw," and they typically identify overweening pride (or **hubris**) as the most common tragic flaw. These ideas derive from Aristotle's *Poetics*, but they are a bit too loosely translated and are too reductive to describe complex heroes. It would be a mistake, for example, to try to figure out Hamlet's "flaw" merely because a tragic hero "must" have one. Instead, think of the proverb "To err is human." The tragic hero must be as imperfect, perhaps as full of contradictions, as any human being.

If the hero were a god or good beyond reason, the audience would not be able to identify with the hero, and this sense of identification lies at the heart of tragedy. Viewers must be able to see themselves in the hero, to think that they are not all that different from the hero, to recognize shared human traits in even a large or exalted character. Not many people will identify with a saint; but most people will identify with a character who is mostly but not entirely good, because that is how they think of themselves. Once people put themselves in the hero's shoes, they can experience the second of the tragic emotions, what Aristotle somewhat grandly called **terror.**

After first pitying the hero, viewers realize that they, who are not fundamentally different from the hero, can or do share the character's fate; that they are, in fact, pitying themselves. And it should be a bit terrifying to contemplate suffering the same fate as the hero, to realize that the hero's struggle could be your own, and to conclude that a massive reversal of fortune may be part of the human condition.

You might wonder why anyone would go to a tragedy if seeing one just leads to feelings of pity and terror. Who would pay money to experience those emotions? The answer is a bit elusive. Aristotle thought tragedies were valuable, even popular, because they not only make people feel pity and terror, but they ultimately flush those emotions out of people. It is almost as if tragedies inoculate viewers against the effects of those emotions in real life. This purgation is sometimes called **catharsis**. But whatever the reason, throughout history audiences have enjoyed watching, and vicariously experiencing, tragic events onstage.

Comedy

Comedy's popularity presents no such mystery. As a genre or subgenre, however, comedy is much more difficult to describe and define than tragedy (Aristotle's thoughts on the subject are lost to the ages). Everyone can recognize a comedy when they see one, and perhaps the common understanding of the term is the best—a comedy is a play that makes people laugh a lot. Just as tragedy elicits feelings of pity and terror in viewers, so comedy must make viewers happy. And just as tragedy makes viewers experience (at least vicariously) the difficulties and frailties of the human condition, so comedy celebrates humanity in all its sloppy, raucous, robust fertility.

The comedic plot is generally the reverse of the tragic plot: the protagonist begins in a state of relative poverty and ends in a state of prosperity. But these terms must be taken even more metaphorically than they are in tragedy, because the "poverty" often consists of nothing more than the protagonist's feelings of loneliness or emptiness in not having a mate. That is certainly the case in the thousands of **romantic comedies** that have been forever popular (*The Importance of Being Earnest* is a good example). You might describe the standard plot reductively but pretty accurately as *Boy is alone; boy meets girl; boy is separated from girl; boy and girl reunite.* (For many contemporary examples, substitute *boy* for *girl* or *girl* for *boy* as necessary.) While tragedies often end in death, romantic comedies usually end in betrothal or marriage, a symbol of human renewal and fecundity.

This description is not meant to trivialize comedy. The most famous comedies of all time, including Shakespeare's, basically tell boy-meets-girl stories. The genius of such plays resides never in the plot itself, but in the playwright's handling of the characters. Ingenuity enables comedians to still delight and entertain audiences as they tell the same basic story time and time again.

Major Moments in the History of Theater

I mentioned above that the conventions of theater have changed throughout the ages, and that the strange conventions of long-past civilizations might make it harder to enjoy reading these plays. What follows here is a very brief discussion of the types of theater represented in this volume. You should not take it as a comprehensive history—nor even an outline of theater history. I focus only on the contexts of the plays in this book: eight nearly discrete points in a timeline. I've skipped everything between those points, even the evolutionary connections between the different epochs. But this sketch should help you appreciate the plays. I recommend that you read it through from beginning to end now, then return to an individual section when (before, after, while) you read the corresponding play.

Greek Theater

The Greeks invented drama. Johnny Depp and Angelina Jolie and Will Smith earn millions today because of what the Greeks did twenty-five centuries ago. This is not to say Greek theater much resembled movies. Drama grew out of religious festivals devoted to the worship of Dionysus, the god of wine. Raised to the pantheon of gods fairly late in Greek history, Dionysus was a social leveler. His rites first became popular in Athens during the antiaristocratic reign of Peisistratus (d. 527 B.C.E.), so drama, from its very beginnings, was linked to democratic traditions. In ecstatic dances and songs, choruses took on the identities of historical figures (soldiers of Argos, for example) and satyrs. They sometimes retold traditional epic stories in song, but they did not dramatize the events.

Spoken dialogue became possible after a man named Thespis (sixth century B.C.E.), from whose name comes the word *thespian*, added an actor to these choral dances and songs. The earliest tragedy (by Aeschylus, 525–456 B.C.E.) includes three choruses, who dance and sing for 603 of 1,073 lines. In performances, an actor playing a character would give speeches that interacted with the chorus's songs. When Aeschylus added a second actor to subsequent plays, the songs and speeches began to dramatize stories. Having two actors enabled Aeschylus to introduce conflicts between people, and conflict is the essential element of plot. So drama as the playing out of a story really began with Aeschylus. Sophocles (ca. 496–406 B.C.E.) added a third actor and was thus able to increase the complexities of the stories. He retained the chorus, but diminished its role to a supporting function, such as representing the people (the citizens of Thebes, in *Oedipus the King*); and he used its songs to punctuate the action, commenting on and sometimes interpreting for the audience what the characters do and say. In *Oedipus*, the chorus sings only 317 lines out of 1,530. The performance focuses not on the lyric songs, but on the story unfolded by the characters.

Greek plays were performed during daytime in immense, outdoor amphitheaters, with semicircular rows of stone bleachers rising up hillsides. These theaters could seat up to fifteen thousand spectators—as many people as can fit into sports arenas today. At the base of the bleachers was a circular floor, the **orchestra**, where the chorus danced and sang its odes. Behind this level space stood a slightly raised, uncurtained stage area, where the actors performed in front of a wooden facade. The actors could change costumes in a backstage area behind the facade. They made their entrances through doors in this structure—a door might represent, for example, the entrance to a palace, as it does in *Oedipus*. Sophocles introduced painted scenery to the stage, but otherwise these productions employed no sets.

The actors could use their voices expressively thanks to the theaters' incredible acoustics. Even in the largest theaters, whispers could project into the audience. As an undergraduate, I went on a school trip to Greece, where we visited the theater at Epidarus, one of the best-preserved Greek amphitheaters. I sat in the very back row and looked down on my teacher, who stood on a stone that marked the exact center of the theater. I could barely see his face. He removed from his pocket a bus ticket, a flimsy thing about as thick as the tissue paper we stuff in gift boxes. When he tore this little piece of paper in half, I could barely see the thing in his fingers, but I could hear it rip. Such subtleties, of volume and vocal tone, will of course be lost when you read a play, so you'll have to imagine how each speech should be delivered.

The size of the Greek theaters made it impossible for actors to use anything but the grandest gestures. Actors today—on television, in movies, and even in smaller theaters—can communicate through facial expressions, like raised eyebrows or slight frowns, but these expressions would be lost in theaters the size of sports arenas. So Greek actors wore large masks, carved and painted with realistic faces, that could be seen even from the back rows of the theaters. These masks provided one way for the audience to distinguish one character from another (remember, only three actors played all the roles in Sophocles' plays; Sophocles expanded the repertoire of dramatic masks). Because these masks were stiff, the actors had to rely on their voices and the words themselves to convey subtleties of emotion and attitude. So a *reader* (as opposed to a *viewer*) might find it relatively easy to imagine the characters' emotions. Because the playwrights couldn't rely on the actors' facial expressions to convey emotions, they put a lot of emotional cues into the texts. Contemporary plays sometimes read much flatter than ancient-Greek plays, because actors now perform the work of those cues.

Even so, contemporary audiences tend to find Greek drama a bit stiff, even boring. That's because contemporary culture is dominated by the visual. If something dramatic happens, people want to *see* it. They're much more interested in watching people *do* something than in listening to them *talk* about something. Even when they read fiction—consuming through the eyes, but not in the same visual way movies are consumed—the text must involve them vicariously in the action, to make them feel as though they are part of what's happening.

Greek culture was much more aural. Greek drama, then, unfolds in verbal exchanges. Not much *happens*. While a lot of blood spills in *Oedipus*, it spills offstage, away from the audience's eyes, and is reported by messengers. And the real drama of the play doesn't reside in the bloody scenes anyway—it's in the verbal battles between Oedipus and Creon and Tiresias. This convention can be a barrier to modern readers, but because you come to the play prepared, you should be able to bypass the problem.

No doubt some conventions of ancient Greek drama have been lost forever. But the ones I've discussed should help you approximate in your imagination what Sophocles wanted his audience to experience when they saw *Oedipus* performed.

Elizabethan Theater

The term *Elizabethan* refers to the first Queen Elizabeth of England, who ruled from 1558 to 1603. During her reign, England rose to the level of superpower among the nations of Europe, and London was the continent's largest city, a sprawling, gangly octopus of narrow, filthy streets, bustling docksides, grand palaces, lively bars, spectacular churches, and a vibrant mix of European tongues and English dialects.

Some of Shakespeare's contemporaries—more learned men like Ben Jonson—were influenced by Roman drama (itself indebted to Greek theater), but for the most part early Elizabethan theater was a homegrown phenomenon. Entertainers performed modest scenes from wagons at fairs or, sometimes, in the banquet halls of the rich. But those dramatists hardly seem related to the energetic, industrious, and glamorous London play companies in Shakespeare's time. Theater struck London in the 1580s as suddenly as movies hit America in the 1920s and television did in the 1950s. Coming out of nowhere, it completely reshaped the cultural landscape.

The theaters and the life surrounding them were seen as disreputable. Onstage and offstage, actors and playwrights excited the public with the prospect of love affairs, villainy, and swordplay. People from all social levels came together in audiences to witness murder, mayhem, and sex. (Because women were not allowed to act, boys in drag played all the female roles.) The phenomenon seemed uncontrollable, and governmental figures feared the effects on the people. When the Puritans came to power, in 1642, they closed the theaters outright rather than try to moralize them. You might think of the theatrical explosion in Elizabethan England as the Internet revolution of its day. In each case, a new medium becomes immensely popular and seems able to democratically influence politics and, perhaps, undermine morals. In Shakespeare's chaotic, raucous world, theater companies were every bit as entrepreneurial as today's dotcoms. They schemed against each other, stole each other's talent, and jealously guarded their material. Fortunes were made nearly overnight, especially by those who built the theater buildings. (Fortunes were also lost nearly overnight, especially when the Puritans closed the theaters.)

Shakespeare's Globe theater was built on the south side of the River Thames in 1599. *Hamlet* most likely was first played in this theater, probably around 1600. The theater was shaped like a doughnut. Its empty center was open to the sky and contained no seats; like the Greeks, the Elizabethans performed plays only during the daytime. The common people, or **groundlings,** each paid a penny, or about a day's wage, to enter this yard, where they stood and chewed their sausages and watched the action onstage. The stage, uncurtained though canopied with an elaborate roof, stood on five-foot-high trestles and jutted into this open-air space, so the players would have been acting practically in the midst of the groundlings, their feet in the faces of the poor. People who could afford more expensive tickets (about three pence) sat in the tiers of roofed seats that made up the outside of the doughnut. All together, these audiences represented a broad range of London's one hundred thousand citizens, from nobility down to artisans and shopkeepers. As many as three thousand people could fit in the theater at once, making it large by contemporary standards but much more intimate than the Greek theaters.

At the back of the stage stood a facade with, perhaps, three curtained doors that led into the backstage area, or **tiring-house.** Above these doors were box seats for wealthy spectators, making the stage almost a "theater-in-the-round." The actors also appeared in these boxes during some rare scenes, like the famous balcony scene in *Romeo and Juliet*. A trapdoor in the stage enabled actors to suddenly appear or disappear, as, for example, when playing the ghost in the first act of *Hamlet*.

The Elizabethans used few props and, like the Greeks, little to no scenery, so audiences had to imagine the setting from clues given in the dialogue. Despite similarities like this, Elizabethans experienced the theater very differently than did the Greeks. The Elizabethan actors' physical proximity to the groundlings more than likely led to a fair amount of give-and-take between the two sides. The play texts sometimes call for characters to whisper confidences to the audience about the other characters, and playwrights seem to have expected actors to interact with the audience almost the way stand-up comics "play to" their audiences today. In the last act of *Hamlet*, for example, the gravediggers certainly played to the groundlings, who must have delighted while their counterparts onstage outwitted their betters.

You will probably find *Hamlet* more immediately interesting than *Oedipus*, because it employs nearly contemporary plot conventions. The action might seem a bit tame to a reader conditioned by superhero films and kung-fu movies, but the play is still fairly busy. In fact, the multiple scene changes and time shifts, the swords drawn and people killed onstage would all have seemed quite dizzying to an ancient Athenian.

But you will also find more speeches than you are used to. Contemporary dialogue tends to sound close to natural speech—with informal vocabulary, rough grammar, clipped sentences—to provide the illusion of reality. In real life, people generally don't talk to each other in paragraphs; one interlocutor hardly completes a sentence before the other speaker responds. Some dialogue in *Hamlet* doesn't work this way. Even in the midst of informal exchanges, like Hamlet's famous harangue of Ophelia, the characters go on much longer than people would in real life. This is not to say Shakespeare had a bad ear for real conversation (the dialogue in the opening scene will sound remarkably "real" even to contemporary ears). It is just that Elizabethan audiences tolerated much longer exchanges without any insult to their sense of reality. Indeed, Elizabethan audiences tolerated much longer stretches of sustained drama, for the actors didn't pause between scenes and acts. Scene and act numbers were added by later editors, not by Shakespeare.

Nineteenth-Century Middle-Class Theater

Henrik Ibsen's *A Doll House* was staged in a new type of theater that corresponded (more or less) to what most people today think of when they hear the word *theater*. With the advent of good artificial lighting, first gas and later electric, the theater became a decidedly indoor activity. People attended the theater at night, to fill their leisure hours. Actors no longer performed in the midst of the audience—they acted in a space removed from the theater seats, as if an invisible fourth wall separated them from the audience. Curtains could be drawn to close the stage from view, enabling theater companies to divide one scene from another and change sets. The sets became far more elaborate and important than in Shakespeare's day, and set designers took full advantage of innovations in engineering to create special effects. In general, the *spectacle* of the theater became nearly as important as the actors. Sometimes, it even overwhelmed the actors, as when, for example, in productions of *Ben Hur*, an epic set in ancient Rome, live horses on treadmills recreated chariot races on stage.

The nineteenth-century theater also sharply divided audiences according to economic status. The music hall variety show catered to the lower classes, who watched, cheered, and heckled these performances in penny theaters—cheap, no-frills playhouses with tables and chairs that ran perpendicular to the stage. People could drink, facing each other, with the show going on to the left or right, over their shoulders. Other theaters—the ones we are concerned with here—catered to the middle class. They used the auditorium seating still in use today: rows of individual seats facing a stage, which was usually crowned by what came to be known as the **proscenium arch**. The seats sported cushions, which encouraged audiences to be more passive than those in the music halls were (or than the groundlings in Shakespeare's Globe theater had been). Going to a play began to resemble your experience today—you pay for your ticket, find your seat, settle back in the darkness, then quietly witness what happens on the lighted stage.

The new style of theater separated audiences from the actors decisively. Actors no longer confided in the audience with knowing winks or clever asides. Watching scenes played out in elaborate sets and with authentic costumes, audiences began to feel like flies on the wall, eavesdropping on real life. They lost themselves in the drama—forgot they were in a theater at all. Thus the current custom of studied silence in the audience established itself in these theaters. To make noise was considered impolite. It disturbed the illusion of reality.

In general, nineteenth-century theater demanded a much higher degree of realism than had been present in either Greek or Elizabethan drama. In plays like *A Doll House* and (to a degree) Oscar Wilde's *The Importance of Being Earnest*, theatergoers expected to see people like themselves moving about in rooms that resembled their own houses. And the style of acting grew progressively less exaggerated, quieter, and more subtle.

Audiences still demanded to be entertained, however, and most of the plays that thrilled the middle class then would probably be called "melodramatic" today. Most popular of all were the well-made plays, a tradition that Ibsen reacted against with his serious social dramas and that Wilde made fun of with his highly unserious social comedy.

The Provincetown Players

By the early twentieth century, Broadway in New York City had become the established center of theater in America, and most of the productions there could be described as well-made plays. These plays often made a lot of money, but they seemed superficial and lightweight to a coterie of disaffected intellectuals, many of whom lived in New York's Greenwich Village. It was a heady time for radical thinkers, and the Village was full of revolutionaries who challenged the inherited social institutions (like monogamous marriage) and the inherited economic structures and political structures of American society. These progressives firmly opposed, for example, the exclusion of women from politics (women still could not vote in America) and the near-exclusion of women from higher education and the professions. From the art of painting to the art of politics, these bohemian artists and activists were ready to remake the world.

They came largely from the middle and upper-middle classes, but repudiated the paths provided for them by their social status—jobs as lawyers or stockbrokers or doctors for the men, roles as socialites for the women—to pursue what they saw as more vital and meaningful lives. As one member of the group, Susan Glaspell, put it, "Most of us were from families who had other ideas—who wanted to make money, played bridge, voted the Republican ticket, went to church, thinking one should be like everyone else." Glaspell's husband, George Cook, came from a wealthy, stolid Iowa family, whom he shocked by divorcing two wives; the second divorce freed him up to marry Glaspell.

Cook and Glaspell (among others) established a new kind of theater that was decidedly uncommercial. They didn't care whether the typical Broadway audience was interested. They set about writing and staging plays they were interested in seeing: theater that would examine and interpret the national character and present to audiences intelligent plays regardless of commercial concerns.

In summers, Glaspell, Cook, and a number of their friends would escape the heat of New York City and gather in the fishing village of Provincetown, Massachusetts, where they could rent cheap cottages and discuss their ideas late into the night. In 1915, Cook converted a small warehouse on a fishing wharf into a crude theater, and the group of New Yorkers wrote some short plays to present to themselves—a fairly informal and certainly uncommercial beginning for what would blossom into the Provincetown Players, an amateur troupe of actors with a bona fide theater in New York City. Their notion of theater was purposely stripped-down: gone were the elaborate sets and the spectacle of nineteenth-century tradition. The focus was on character. This serious, intellectual theater scorned easy entertainment, and it helped produce America's first acknowledged great dramatist: Eugene O'Neill.

Because the Provincetown Players scorned spectacle, you won't be missing too much visually by reading rather than viewing Glaspell's play *Trifles*. You will lose, of course, the actors' interpretations of their lines (which you should try to imagine). Glaspell wrote her play for an intimate theater in which the slightest gesture on stage could be seen by the audience. Consequently, a fair amount of subtlety was conveyed by the actors. The trend toward realistic dialogue and gesture that dominated the nineteenth century was extended even further.

Contemporary American Theater

Unsurprisingly, theater companies like the Provincetown Players never became hugely popular. They cultivated a sophisticated, perhaps even elite, audience. Meanwhile, Broadway chugged merrily along. In the 1920s, the kind of theater that Glaspell was reacting against grew even more successful. Nevertheless, its days were numbered, because live theater faced the challenge of a new medium— movies—that easily outdid the best spectacles and well-made plots that the commercial theaters produced. After the 1920s, plays would never again occupy the central cultural role they enjoyed in previous centuries, because they could never hope to compete with the popularity of movies—which drew from not only the lower classes, but also the middle classes. After the stock market crash of 1929, live theater declined.

The stories and characters on the American stage during the Great Depression exposed and diagnosed problems in modern society, much the way that Henrik Ibsen did in *A Doll House*, which examines the limitations of the domestic role assigned women by the expanding middle class. Glaspell's *Trifles* helped bring this tradition of serious, realistic drama to America, where it reached its peak of importance in the 1930s.

Going into the 1940s, serious American theater was still influenced by old traditions, and plays tended toward the style popularized by Ibsen. Arthur Miller cut against this tradition, experimenting with new techniques, some of which he borrowed from the film industry, which in turn had borrowed from the melodramatic drama vilified by Ibsen and Glaspell. For example, the music in *Death of a Salesman* resembles a movie sound track, with different instruments and themes complimenting the action on the stage. And while the scenes with Ben are not exactly **flashbacks**, they do seem to be influenced by the narrative technique of film.

One important change that Miller participated in had to do with the actors. The new style of acting was called **method acting**. In 1947, Elia Kazan established the Actors Studio to train actors in "the method," which relied less on stock gestures and more on subtleties like facial and tonal expression. This style encouraged actors to draw on their own emotional memories in embodying their roles, to *become* their characters and let their bodies act in a natural, almost unconscious manner. Some of the most successful actors to come out of the 1940s and 1950s, such as Marlon Brando and Paul Newman, made their names in conjunction with Kazan. When Miller's play debuted on Broadway in 1949, Kazan was the director.

Nevertheless, Miller never drifted too far from the realism pioneered by Ibsen, and both his and Lorraine Hansberry's successes on Broadway probably demonstrate more continuity than change in the history of drama. Someone who watched Ibsen's plays in the 1870s would probably feel pretty much at home going to a New York theater in the 1950s. The position of the audience, for example, had changed hardly at all in eighty years. Theater-goers still sat in the dark in comfortable, ticketed seats, politely quiet and passive, witnessing the events as if looking through an invisible fourth wall.

Regional Theaters

Though August Wilson has certainly found success on Broadway, it might be more appropriate to associate him with the regional theater movement. Regional theaters have grown in cities all across North America, and they vary so widely that it is difficult to generalize about them. Often, they're subsidized by cadres of patrons— private individuals who donate money to keep the theaters afloat. So they typically do not depend on developing a viable commercial market for live theater.

This type of funding would seem to make theater the domain of the wealthier classes of society. But the regional theaters tend to customize their repertoires to the needs and interests of their local populations, and they usually cut against the economic grain—bringing theater to groups excluded by the highbrow nature of most contemporary theater. Many regional theaters have specific missions, like the Kuntu Repertory Theater at the University of Pittsburgh, which is committed to educating audiences about the black experience and moving them to social action.

Because they are uncommercial, regional theaters do not often produce theatrical spectaculars. Typically, their plays take place in single settings, so that only one set has to be built for each production. A contemporary work derived from that world, *Fences* employs no difficult or arcane theatrical conventions.

Conclusion

After all of this prefatory material, it would be easy to lose sight of an important goal in reading these plays: to have fun. Ultimately, increasing your reading pleasure is the purpose of this introduction. You should enjoy reading these plays (your level of enjoyment being a good index of your level of understanding), just as your teacher and I delight in introducing you to plays that we continue to enjoy reading.

THE SEAGULL READER

Plays

Second Edition

Sophocles
496?–406? B.C.E.

OEDIPUS THE KING

The ancient Athenians who saw Oedipus the King *first performed
would have gone into the theater knowing the outline of Oedipus's
story: The king and queen of Thebes, Laïos and Iocaste, had a son.
When they asked one of the oracles at Delphi to prophesy about this
boy, the oracle told them that their son would kill his father. So
Laïos gave the infant to a shepherd, who was supposed to destroy
him. The shepherd pinned the child's ankles together and left him
on a remote hillside. A peasant from Corinth found the boy, rescued
him, and brought him back to the king and queen of that city,
who, having no child of their own, adopted him. That child was
Oedipus.*

*As a young man, not knowing his true origins, Oedipus met
Laïos on a road. Both were driving chariots, and neither would
yield the right of way. Laïos's attendant killed one of Oedipus's
horses, enraging Oedipus, who killed both the attendant and his
own father, Laïos.*

*Not long after that, Thebes was beseiged by the Sphinx, a mon-
ster with the body of a lion and the head of a woman. The Sphinx
would ask travelers a riddle, and when they could not answer it,
she would eat them. Oedipus boldly went out to face the monster
and was challenged with this question: what walks on four legs
in the morning, two legs in the afternoon, and three legs in the
evening? He answered that man does—meaning that a human being crawls on all fours as an infant, walks upright as an adult, and
leans on a cane in old age. In despair over Oedipus's success, the
Sphinx jumped off a cliff to its death.*

*The people of Thebes were so grateful and so impressed by Oedi-
pus's courage and ability, they made him king. He married the
widowed queen, Iocaste, his own mother. They had four children,
Polyneices, Eteocles, Antigone, and Ismene. But later, during a
plague, Oedipus's true parentage was revealed, Iocaste killed herself,
and Oedipus, driven mad by the knowledge that Iocaste was his*

mother, blinded himself and left his native city to wander as a beggar.

Sophocles changed the story in some places and added a number of elements. For example, Oedipus's initial anxiety about sleeping with his mother (and Iocaste's response to his anxieties) may be Sophocles' addition to or at least his amplification of the story. This anxiety inspired Sigmund Freud's great interest in the myth and his coining of the term Oedipus complex (in his Interpretation of Dreams [1900]).

Sophocles almost certainly did not intend a psychological interpretation of his play—at least not consciously. In its original context, the play's concerns are more obvious, especially its treatment of politics (the obligations of a citizen and a ruler to his city) and religion (the role of the gods in the lives of humans). So the political and religious history of Athens will help you understand the play.

Oedipus the King probably was first performed in 430 B.C.E., when Sophocles was about sixty-five. For a generation, the city-state of Athens had enjoyed unparalleled prestige and influence in the Greek world, as it expanded its political dominion and championed its self-consciously superior civic institutions. But in the year before Sophocles wrote Oedipus, Athens was shaken to its foundations. The city of Sparta had invaded Attica, the region of Greece attached to Athens. Refugees filled Athens; the crowded people suffered plagues for the next few years (the opening scene of this play would have seemed all too close to home to Sophocles' audience). Thebes and Corinth allied themselves with Sparta against Athens. Though Oedipus was reared in Corinth and ruled Thebes, Sophocles' audience would have recognized in him the traits that Athenians liked to see in themselves—respect for practical experience, trust in logical reasoning, and decisiveness of action. Apparently, Sophocles meant for Oedipus to embody the prototypical Athenian. As you read, you might consider Sophocles' insights into this character type. Does Sophocles blame Athens for its crises? Does he criticize the Athenian "character"?

The theological questions in the play were topics of fiery debate in Sophocles' Athens. The great intellectual explosion in this century, which produced thinkers such as Socrates and Plato, Pericles and Euripides, brought with it a conflict between free thought and religion. *Apollo's oracles at Delphi were the central religious institution among the Greek cities, and their influence dominated policy and manners. The younger generation of Athenians included free thinkers who openly attacked the prophets' claim to unique knowledge, even going so far as to suggest that the prophets were frauds. That suggestion threatened the whole structure of the Greek pantheon. The conflict between fate and free will, then, had an immediate urgency for Sophocles' audience.*

These issues are more than historical curiosities. Indeed, Sophocles' play, despite its antiquity, remains amazingly topical. In this post-Darwinian age, we ask ourselves some of the same religious and political questions that the ancient Athenians asked themselves.

Oedipus the King*

PERSONS REPRESENTED:

OEDIPUS	MESSENGER
A PRIEST	SHEPHERD OF LAÏOS
CREON	SECOND MESSENGER
TEIRESIAS	CHORUS OF THEBAN ELDERS
IOCASTE	

THE SCENE: *Before the palace of Oedipus, King of Thebes. A central door and two lateral doors open onto a platform which runs the length of the façade. On the platform, right and left, are altars; and three steps lead down into the "orchestra," or chorus-ground. At the beginning of the action these steps are crowded by suppliants who have brought branches and chaplets of olive leaves and who lie in various attitudes of despair.* OEDIPUS *enters.*

PROLOGUE[1]

OEDIPUS: My children, generations of the living
  In the line of Kadmos,[2] nursed at his ancient hearth:

---

* Translated by Dudley Fitts and Robert Fitzgerald.
  1. Introductory scene that establishes the setting, conflict, themes, and main characters of the play.
  2. Or Cadmus, legendary founder of Thebes.

Why have you strewn yourselves before these altars
In supplication, with your boughs and garlands?
The breath of incense rises from the city   5
With a sound of prayer and lamentation.
                                    Children,
I would not have you speak through messengers,
And therefore I have come myself to hear you—
I, Oedipus, who bear the famous name.
[*To a* PRIEST.] You, there, since you are eldest in the company,   10
Speak for them all, tell me what preys upon you,
Whether you come in dread, or crave some blessing:
Tell me, and never doubt that I will help you
In every way I can; I should be heartless
Were I not moved to find you suppliant here.   15
PRIEST: Great Oedipus, O powerful King of Thebes!
You see how all the ages of our people
Cling to your altar steps: here are boys
Who can barely stand alone, and here are priests
By weight of age, as I am a priest of God,   20
And young men chosen from those yet unmarried;
As for the others, all that multitude.
They wait with olive chaplets in the squares,
At the two shrines of Pallas,[3] and where Apollo
Speaks in the glowing embers.
                              Your own eyes   25
Must tell you: Thebes is tossed on a murdering sea
And cannot lift her head from the death surge.
A rust consumes the buds and fruits of the earth;
The herds are sick; children die unborn,
And labor is vain. The god of plague and pyre   30
Raids like detestable lightning through the city,
And all the house of Kadmos is laid waste,
All emptied, and all darkened: Death alone
Battens[4] upon the misery of Thebes.
You are not one of the immortal gods, we know;   35

3. Athena, goddess of wisdom.
4. Fattens.

Yet we have come to you to make our prayer
As to the man surest in mortal ways
And wisest in the ways of God. You saved us
From the Sphinx, that flinty singer, and the tribute
We paid to her so long; yet you were never   40
Better informed than we, nor could we teach you:
It was some god breathed in you to set us free.

Therefore, O mighty King, we turn to you:
Find us our safety, find us a remedy,
Whether by counsel of the gods or men.   45
A king of wisdom tested in the past
Can act in a time of troubles, and act well.
Noblest of men, restore
Life to your city! Think how all men call you
Liberator for your triumph long ago;   50
Ah, when your years of kingship are remembered,
Let them not say *We rose, but later fell*—
Keep the State from going down in the storm!
Once, years ago, with happy augury,[5]
You brought us fortune; be the same again!   55
No man questions your power to rule the land:
But rule over men, not over a dead city!
Ships are only hulls, citadels are nothing,
When no life moves in the empty passageways.
OEDIPUS: Poor children! You may be sure I know   60
All that you longed for in your coming here.
I know that you are deathly sick; and yet,
Sick as you are, not one is as sick as I.
Each of you suffers in himself alone
His anguish, not another's; but my spirit   65
Groans for the city, for myself, for you.
I was not sleeping, you are not waking me.
No, I have been in tears for a long while
And in my restless thought walked many ways.
In all my search, I found one helpful course,   70

---

5. Oedipus saved Thebes by solving the riddle of the Sphinx.

And that I have taken: I have sent Creon,
Son of Menoikeus, brother of the Queen,
To Delphi, Apollo's place of revelation,
To learn there, if he can,
What act or pledge of mine may save the city.   75
I have counted the days, and now, this very day,
I am troubled, for he has overstayed his time.
What is he doing? He has been gone too long.
Yet whenever he comes back, I should do ill
To scant whatever duty God reveals.   80

PRIEST: It is a timely promise. At this instant
   They tell me Creon is here.

OEDIPUS: O Lord Apollo!
   May his news be fair as his face is radiant!

PRIEST: It could not be otherwise: he is crowned with bay,
   The chaplet is thick with berries.

OEDIPUS: We shall soon know;   85
   He is near enough to hear us now.
      [*Enter* CREON.]
                              O Prince:
   Brother: son of Menoikeus:
   What answer do you bring us from the god?

CREON: A strong one. I can tell you, great afflictions
   Will turn out well, if they are taken well.   90

OEDIPUS: What was the oracle? These vague words
   Leave me still hanging between hope and fear.

CREON: Is it your pleasure to hear me with all these
   Gathered around us? I am prepared to speak,
   But should we not go in?

OEDIPUS: Let them all hear it.   95
   It is for them I suffer, more than for myself.

CREON: Then I will tell you what I heard at Delphi.

   In plain words
   The god commands us to expel from the land of Thebes
   An old defilement we are sheltering.   100
   It is a deathly thing, beyond cure;
   We must not let it feed upon us longer.

OEDIPUS: What defilement? How shall we rid ourselves of it?
CREON: By exile or death, blood for blood. It was
    Murder that brought the plague-wind on the city.   105
OEDIPUS: Murder of whom? Surely the god has named him?
CREON: My lord: long ago Laïos was our king,
    Before you came to govern us.
OEDIPUS: I know;
    I learned of him from others; I never saw him.
CREON: He was murdered; and Apollo commands us now   110
    To take revenge upon whoever killed him.
OEDIPUS: Upon whom? Where are they? Where shall we find a clue
    To solve that crime, after so many years?
CREON: Here in this land, he said.
                  If we make enquiry,
    We may touch things that otherwise escape us.   115
OEDIPUS: Tell me: Was Laïos murdered in his house,
    Or in the fields, or in some foreign country?
CREON: He said he planned to make a pilgrimage.
    He did not come home again.
OEDIPUS: And was there no one,
    No witness, no companion, to tell what happened?   120
CREON: They were all killed but one, and he got away
    So frightened that he could remember one thing only.
OEDIPUS: What was that one thing? One may be the key
    To everything, if we resolve to use it.
CREON: He said that a band of highwaymen attacked them,   125
    Outnumbered them, and overwhelmed the King.
OEDIPUS: Strange, that a highwayman should be so daring—
    Unless some faction here bribed him to do it.
CREON: We thought of that. But after Laïos' death
    New troubles arose and we had no avenger.   130
OEDIPUS: What troubles could prevent your hunting down the
    killers?
CREON: The riddling Sphinx's song
    Made us deaf to all mysteries but her own.
OEDIPUS: Then once more I must bring what is dark to light.
    It is most fitting that Apollo shows,   135
    As you do, this compunction for the dead.

You shall see how I stand by you, as I should,
To avenge the city and the city's god,
And not as though it were for some distant friend,
But for my own sake, to be rid of evil.   140
Whoever killed King Laïos might—who knows?—
Decide at any moment to kill me as well.
By avenging the murdered king I protect myself.

Come, then, my children: leave the altar steps,
Lift up your olive boughs!
      One of you go   145
And summon the people of Kadmos to gather here.
I will do all that I can; you may tell them that. [*Exit a* PAGE.]
So, with the help of God,
We shall be saved—or else indeed we are lost.
PRIEST: Let us rise, children. It was for this we came,   150
 And now the King has promised it himself.
 Phoibos has sent us an oracle; may he descend
 Himself to save us and drive out the plague.
  [*Exeunt* OEDIPUS *and* CREON *into the palace by the central door.
  The* PRIEST *and the* SUPPLIANTS *disperse. After a short pause the*
  CHORUS *enters the orchestra.*]

PÁRODOS[1]
CHORUS: [*Strophe 1.*] What is God singing in his profound
 Delphi of gold and shadow?
 What oracle for Thebes, the sunwhipped city?   155

Fear unjoints me, the roots of my heart tremble.

Now I remember, O Healer, your power, and wonder:
Will you send doom like a sudden cloud, or weave it
Like nightfall of the past?   160

Speak, speak to us, issue of holy sound:
Dearest to our expectancy: be tender!

---

1. Entrance of the chorus. The chorus moves in one direction while chanting the strophe
and reverses its direction during the antistrophe.

[*Antistrophe 1.*] Let me pray to Athenê, the immortal daughter
    of Zeus,
And to Artemis her sister
Who keeps her famous throne in the market ring,   165
And to Apollo, bowman at the far butts[2] of heaven—

O gods, descend! Like three streams leap against
The fires of our grief, the fires of darkness;
Be swift to bring us rest!

As in the old time from the brilliant house   170
Of air you stepped to save us, come again!

[*Strophe 2.*] Now our afflictions have no end,
Now all our stricken host lies down
And no man fights off death with his mind;

The noble plowland bears no grain,   175
And groaning mothers cannot bear—

See, how our lives like birds take wing,
Like sparks that fly when a fire soars,
To the shore of the god of evening.

[*Antistrophe 2.*] The plague burns on, it is pitiless,   180
Though pallid children laden with death
Lie unwept in the stony ways,

And old gray women by every path
Flock to the strand about the altars

There to strike their breasts and cry   185
Worship of Phoibos[3] in wailing prayers:
Be kind, God's golden child!

---

2. Places where shooting is practiced.   3. Or Phoebus, Apollo.
Zeus: king of the gods. *Artemis:* moon god-
dess, often depicted as a virgin huntress.

[*Strophe 3.*] There are no swords in this attack by fire,
No shields, but we are ringed with cries.

Send the besieger plunging from our homes   190
Into the vast sea-room of the Atlantic
Or into the waves that foam eastward of Thrace—

For the day ravages what the night spares—

Destroy our enemy, lord of the thunder!
Let him be riven by lightning from heaven!   195

[*Antistrophe 3.*] Phoibos Apollo, stretch the sun's bowstring,
That golden cord, until it sing for us,
Flashing arrows in heaven!
                          Artemis, Huntress,
Race with flaring lights upon our mountains!

O scarlet god, O golden-banded brow,   200
O Theban Bacchos in a storm of Maenads,[4]
     [*Enter* OEDIPUS.]
Whirl upon Death, that all the Undying hate!
Come with blinding torches, come in joy!

SCENE I

OEDIPUS: Is this your prayer? It may be answered. Come,
    Listen to me, act as the crisis demands.   205
    And you shall have relief from all these evils.

    Until now I was a stranger to this tale,
    As I had been a stranger to the crime.
    Could I track down the murderer without a clue?
    But now, friends,   210
    As one who became a citizen after the murder,
    I make this proclamation to all Thebans:
    If any man knows by whose hand Laïos, son of Labdakos,

---

4. Priestesses or followers of Bacchos, or Bacchus, god of wine and fertility.

Met his death, I direct that man to tell me everything,
No matter what he fears for having so long withheld it.   215
Let it stand as promised that no further trouble
Will come to him, but he may leave the land in safety.

Moreover: If anyone knows the murderer to be foreign,
Let him not keep silent: he shall have his reward from me.
However, if he does conceal it; if any man   220
Fearing for his friend or for himself disobeys this edict,
Hear what I propose to do:

I solemnly forbid the people of this country,
Where power and throne are mine, ever to receive that man
Or speak to him, no matter who he is, or let him   225
Join in sacrifice, lustration, or in prayer.
I decree that he be driven from every house,
Being, as he is, corruption itself to us: the Delphic
Voice of Zeus has pronounced this revelation.
Thus I associate myself with the oracle   230
And take the side of the murdered king.

As for the criminal, I pray to God—
Whether it be a lurking thief, or one of a number—
I pray that that man's life be consumed in evil and
    wretchedness.
And as for me, this curse applies no less   235
If it should turn out that the culprit is my guest here,
Sharing my hearth.
                        You have heard the penalty.
I lay it on you now to attend to this
For my sake, for Apollo's, for the sick
Sterile city that heaven has abandoned.   240
Suppose the oracle had given you no command:
Should this defilement go uncleansed for ever?
You should have found the murderer: your king,
A noble king, had been destroyed!
                        Now I,
Having the power that he held before me,   245

Having his bed, begetting children there
Upon his wife, as he would have, had he lived—
Their son would have been my children's brother,
If Laïos had had luck in fatherhood!
(But surely ill luck rushed upon his reign)—   250
I say I take the son's part, just as though
I were his son, to press the fight for him
And see it won! I'll find the hand that brought
Death to Labdakos' and Polydoros' child,
Heir of Kadmos' and Agenor's line.   255
And as for those who fail me,
May the gods deny them the fruit of the earth,
Fruit of the womb, and may they rot utterly!
Let them be wretched as we are wretched, and worse!

For you, for loyal Thebans, and for all   260
Who find my actions right, I pray the favor
Of justice, and of all the immortal gods.
CHORAGOS:[1] Since I am under oath, my lord, I swear
I did not do the murder, I cannot name
The murderer. Might not the oracle   265
That has ordained the search tell where to find him?
OEDIPUS: An honest question. But no man in the world
Can make the gods do more than the gods will.
CHORAGOS: There is one last expedient—
OEDIPUS: Tell me what it is.
Though it seem slight, you must not hold it back.   270
CHORAGOS: A lord clairvoyant to the lord Apollo,
As we all know, is the skilled Teiresias.
One might learn much about this from him, Oedipus.
OEDIPUS: I am not wasting time:
Creon spoke of this, and I have sent for him—   275
Twice, in fact; it is strange that he is not here.
CHORAGOS: The other matter—that old report—seems useless.
OEDIPUS: Tell me. I am interested in all reports.
CHORAGOS: The King was said to have been killed by highway-men.

1. Leader of the chorus.

OEDIPUS: I know. But we have no witnesses to that.   280
CHORAGOS: If the killer can feel a particle of dread,
    Your curse will bring him out of hiding!
OEDIPUS: No.
    The man who dared that act will fear no curse.
    [*Enter the blind seer* TEIRESIAS, *led by a* PAGE.]
CHORAGOS: But there is one man who may detect the criminal.
    This is Teiresias, this is the holy prophet   285
    In whom, alone of all men, truth was born.
OEDIPUS: Teiresias: seer: student of mysteries,
    Of all that's taught and all that no man tells,
    Secrets of Heaven and secrets of the earth:
    Blind though you are, you know the city lies   290
    Sick with plague; and from this plague, my lord,
    We find that you alone can guard or save us.
    Possibly you did not hear the messengers?
    Apollo, when we sent to him,
    Sent us back word that this great pestilence   295
    Would lift, but only if we established clearly
    The identity of those who murdered Laïos.
    They must be killed or exiled.
                      Can you use
    Birdflight or any art of divination
    To purify yourself, and Thebes, and me   300
    From this contagion? We are in your hands.
    There is no fairer duty
    Than that of helping others in distress.
TEIRESIAS: How dreadful knowledge of the truth can be
    When there's no help in truth! I knew this well,   305
    But made myself forget. I should not have come.
OEDIPUS: What is troubling you? Why are your eyes so cold?
TEIRESIAS: Let me go home. Bear your own fate, and I'll
    Bear mine. It is better so: trust what I say.
OEDIPUS: What you say is ungracious and unhelpful   310
    To your native country. Do not refuse to speak.
TEIRESIAS: When it comes to speech, your own is neither
      temperate
    Nor opportune. I wish to be more prudent.

OEDIPUS: In God's name, we all beg you—
TEIRESIAS: You are all ignorant.
No; I will never tell you what I know. 315
Now it is my misery; then, it would be yours.
OEDIPUS: What! You do know something, and will not tell us?
You would betray us all and wreck the State?
TEIRESIAS: I do not intend to torture myself, or you.
Why persist in asking? You will not persuade me. 320
OEDIPUS: What a wicked old man you are! You'd try a stone's
Patience! Out with it! Have you no feeling at all?
TEIRESIAS: You call me unfeeling. If you could only see
The nature of your own feelings . . .
OEDIPUS: Why,
Who would not feel as I do? Who could endure 325
Your arrogance toward the city?
TEIRESIAS: What does it matter!
Whether I speak or not, it is bound to come.
OEDIPUS: Then, if "it" is bound to come, you are bound to
tell me.
TEIRESIAS: No, I will not go on. Rage as you please.
OEDIPUS: Rage? Why not!
And I'll tell you what I think: 330
You planned it, you had it done, you all but
Killed him with your own hands: if you had eyes,
I'd say the crime was yours, and yours alone.
TEIRESIAS: So? I charge you, then,
Abide by the proclamation you have made: 335
From this day forth
Never speak again to these men or to me;
You yourself are the pollution of this country.
OEDIPUS: You dare say that! Can you possibly think you have
Some way of going free, after such insolence? 340
TEIRESIAS: I have gone free. It is the truth sustains me.
OEDIPUS: Who taught you shamelessness? It was not your craft.
TEIRESIAS: You did. You made me speak. I did not want to.
OEDIPUS: Speak what? Let me hear it again more clearly.
TEIRESIAS: Was it not clear before? Are you tempting me? 345
OEDIPUS: I did not understand it. Say it again.

TEIRESIAS: I say that you are the murderer whom you seek.

OEDIPUS: Now twice you have spat out infamy. You'll pay for it!

TEIRESIAS: Would you care for more? Do you wish to be really
    angry?

OEDIPUS: Say what you will. Whatever you say is worthless.   350

TEIRESIAS: I say you live in hideous shame with those
  Most dear to you. You cannot see the evil.

OEDIPUS: It seems you can go on mouthing like this for ever.

TEIRESIAS: I can, if there is power in truth.

OEDIPUS: There is:
  But not for you, not for you,   355
  You sightless, witless, senseless, mad old man!

TEIRESIAS: You are the madman. There is no one here
  Who will not curse you soon, as you curse me.

OEDIPUS: You child of endless night! You cannot hurt me
  Or any other man who sees the sun.   360

TEIRESIAS: True: it is not from me your fate will come.
  That lies within Apollo's competence,
  As it is his concern.

OEDIPUS: Tell me:
  Are you speaking for Creon, or for yourself?

TEIRESIAS: Creon is no threat. You weave your own doom.   365

OEDIPUS: Wealth, power, craft of statesmanship!
  Kingly position, everywhere admired!
  What savage envy is stored up against these,
  If Creon, whom I trusted, Creon my friend,
  For this great office which the city once   370
  Put in my hands unsought—if for this power
  Creon desires in secret to destroy me!

  He has bought this decrepit fortune-teller, this
  Collector of dirty pennies, this prophet fraud—
  Why, he is no more clairvoyant than I am!
                               Tell us: 375
  Has your mystic mummery ever approached the truth?
  When that hellcat the Sphinx was performing here,
  What help were you to these people?
  Her magic was not for the first man who came along:

It demanded a real exorcist. Your birds— 380
What good were they? or the gods, for the matter of that?
But I came by,
Oedipus, the simple man, who knows nothing—
I thought it out for myself, no birds helped me!
And this is the man you think you can destroy, 385
That you may be close to Creon when he's king!
Well, you and your friend Creon, it seems to me,
Will suffer most. If you were not an old man,
You would have paid already for your plot.

CHORAGOS: We cannot see that his words or yours 390
Have been spoken except in anger, Oedipus,
And of anger we have no need. How can God's will
Be accomplished best? That is what most concerns us.

TEIRESIAS: You are a king. But where argument's concerned
I am your man, as much a king as you. 395
I am not your servant, but Apollo's.
I have no need of Creon to speak for me.

Listen to me. You mock my blindness, do you?
But I say that you, with both your eyes, are blind:
You cannot see the wretchedness of your life, 400
Nor in whose house you live, no, nor with whom.
Who are your father and mother? Can you tell me?
You do not even know the blind wrongs
That you have done them, on earth and in the world below.
But the double lash of your parents' curse will whip you 405
Out of this land some day, with only night
Upon your precious eyes.
Your cries then—where will they not be heard?
What fastness of Kithairon[2] will not echo them?
And that bridal-descant of yours—you'll know it then, 410
The song they sang when you came here to Thebes
And found your misguided berthing.
All this, and more, that you cannot guess at now,
Will bring you to yourself among your children.

2. Mountain range between Corinth and Thebes.

Be angry, then. Curse Creon. Curse my words.   415
I tell you, no man that walks upon the earth
Shall be rooted out more horribly than you.
OEDIPUS: Am I to bear this from him?—Damnation
   Take you! Out of this place! Out of my sight!
TEIRESIAS: I would not have come at all if you had not asked me.   420
OEDIPUS: Could I have told that you'd talk nonsense, that
   You'd come here to make a fool of yourself, and of me?
TEIRESIAS: A fool? Your parents thought me sane enough.
OEDIPUS: My parents again!—Wait: who were my parents?
TEIRESIAS: This day will give you a father, and break your heart.   425
OEDIPUS: Your infantile riddles! Your damned abracadabra!
TEIRESIAS: You were a great man once at solving riddles.
OEDIPUS: Mock me with that if you like; you will find it true.
TEIRESIAS: It was true enough. It brought about your ruin.
OEDIPUS: But if it saved this town?
TEIRESIAS: [*To the* PAGE.] Boy, give me
   your hand.   430
OEDIPUS: Yes, boy; lead him away.
                              —While you are here
   We can do nothing. Go; leave us in peace.
TEIRESIAS: I will go when I have said what I have to say.
   How can you hurt me? And I tell you again:
   The man you have been looking for all this time,   435
   The damned man, the murderer of Laïos,
   That man is in Thebes. To your mind he is foreign-born,
   But it will soon be shown that he is a Theban,
   A revelation that will fail to please.
                              A blind man,
   Who has his eyes now; a penniless man, who is rich now;   440
   And he will go tapping the strange earth with his staff
   To the children with whom he lives now he will be
   Brother and father—the very same; to her
   Who bore him, son and husband—the very same
   Who came to his father's bed, wet with his father's blood.   445

   Enough. Go think that over.
   If later you find error in what I have said,

You may say that I have no skill in prophecy.
[*Exit* TEIRESIAS, *led by his* PAGE, OEDIPUS *goes into the palace.*]

ODE I
CHORUS: [*Strophe 1.*] The Delphic stone of prophecies
    Remembers ancient regicide   450
    And a still bloody hand.
    That killer's hour of flight has come.
    He must be stronger than riderless
    Coursers of untiring wind,
    For the son of Zeus armed with his father's thunder   455
    Leaps in lightning after him;
    And the Furies[1] follow him, the sad Furies.

[*Antistrophe 1.*] Holy Parnassos[2] peak of snow
    Flashes and blinds that secret man.
    That all shall hunt him down: 460
    Though he may roam the forest shade
    Like a bull gone wild from pasture
    To rage through glooms of stone.
    Doom comes down on him; flight will not avail him;
    For the world's heart calls him desolate,   465
    And the immortal Furies follow, for ever follow.

[*Strophe 2.*] But now a wilder thing is heard
    From the old man skilled at hearing Fate in the wingbeat of
      a bird.
    Bewildered as a blown bird, my soul hovers and cannot find
    Foothold in this debate, or any reason or rest of mind.   470
    But no man ever brought—none can bring
    Proof of strife between Thebes' royal house,
    Labdakos' line, and the son of Polybos;
    And never until now has any man brought word
    Of Laïos' dark death staining Oedipus the King.   475

---

1. Supernatural avengers.   2. Mountain on which the oracle at Delphi is located.

[*Antistrophe 2.*] Divine Zeus and Apollo hold
Perfect intelligence alone of all tales ever told;
And well though this diviner works, he works in his own
    night;
No man can judge that rough unknown or trust in second
    sight,
For wisdom changes hands among the wise.   480
Shall I believe my great lord criminal
At a raging word that a blind old man let fall?
I saw him, when the carrion woman faced him of old,
Prove his heroic mind! These evil words are lies.

SCENE II

CREON: Men of Thebes: 485
    I am told that heavy accusations
    Have been brought against me by King Oedipus.

    I am not the kind of man to bear this tamely.

    If in these present difficulties
    He holds me accountable for any harm to him   490
    Through anything I have said or done—why, then,
    I do not value life in this dishonor.
    It is not as though this rumor touched upon
    Some private indiscretion. The matter is grave.
    The fact is that I am being called disloyal   495
    To the State, to my fellow citizens, to my friends.
CHORAGOS: He may have spoken in anger, not from his mind.
CREON: But did you not hear him say I was the one
    Who seduced the old prophet into lying?
CHORAGOS: The thing was said; I do not know how seriously.   500
CREON: But you were watching him! Were his eyes steady?
    Did he look like a man in his right mind?
CHORAGOS: I do not know.
    I cannot judge the behavior of great men.
    But here is the King himself.
        [*Enter* OEDIPUS.]
OEDIPUS: So you dared come back.

Why? How brazen of you to come to my house,   505
You murderer!
                    Do you think I do not know
That you plotted to kill me, plotted to steal my throne?
Tell me, in God's name: am I coward, a fool,
That you should dream you could accomplish this?
A fool who could not see your slippery game?   510
A coward, not to fight back when I saw it?
You are the fool, Creon, are you not? hoping
Without support or friends to get a throne?
Thrones may be won or bought: you could do neither.

CREON: Now listen to me. You have talked; let me talk, too.   515
    You cannot judge unless you know the facts.

OEDIPUS: You speak well: there is one fact; but I find it hard
    To learn from the deadliest enemy I have.

CREON: That above all I must dispute with you.

OEDIPUS: That above all I will not hear you deny.   520

CREON: If you think there is anything good in being stubborn
    Against all reason, then I say you are wrong.

OEDIPUS: If you think a man can sin against his own kind
    And not be punished for it, I say you are mad.

CREON: I agree. But tell me: what have I done to you?   525

OEDIPUS: You advised me to send for that wizard, did you not?

CREON: I did. I should do it again.

OEDIPUS: Very well. Now tell me:
    How long has it been since Laïos—

CREON: What of Laïos?

OEDIPUS: Since he vanished in that onset by the road?

CREON: It was long ago, a long time.

OEDIPUS: And this prophet,   530
    Was he practicing here then?

CREON: He was; and with honor, as now.

OEDIPUS: Did he speak of me at that time?

CREON: He never did;
    At least, not when I was present.

OEDIPUS: But . . . the enquiry?
    I suppose you held one?

CREON: We did, but we learned nothing.

OEDIPUS: Why did the prophet not speak against me then?   535
CREON: I do not know; and I am the kind of man
   Who holds his tongue when he has no facts to go on.
OEDIPUS: There's one fact that you know, and you could tell it.
CREON: What fact is that? If I know it, you shall have it.
OEDIPUS: If he were not involved with you, he could not say   540
   That it was I who murdered Laïos.
CREON: If he says that, you are the one that knows it!—
   But now it is my turn to question you.
OEDIPUS: Put your questions. I am no murderer.
CREON: First, then: You married my sister?
OEDIPUS: I married your sister.   545
CREON: And you rule the kingdom equally with her?
OEDIPUS: Everything that she wants she has from me.
CREON: And I am the third, equal to both of you?
OEDIPUS: That is why I call you a bad friend.
CREON: No. Reason it out, as I have done.   550
   Think of this first: Would any sane man prefer
   Power, with all a king's anxieties,
   To that same power and the grace of sleep?
   Certainly not I.
   I have never longed for the king's power—only his rights.   555
   Would any wise man differ from me in this?
   As matters stand, I have my way in everything
   With your consent, and no responsibilities.
   If I were king, I should be a slave to policy.

   How could I desire a scepter more   560
   Than what is now mine—untroubled influence?
   No, I have not gone mad; I need no honors,
   Except those with the perquisites I have now.
   I am welcome everywhere; every man salutes me,
   And those who want your favor seek my ear,   565
   Since I know how to manage what they ask.
   Should I exchange this ease for that anxiety?
   Besides, no sober mind is treasonable.
   I hate anarchy
   And never would deal with any man who likes it.   570

Test what I have said. Go to the priestess
At Delphi, ask if I quoted her correctly.
And as for this other thing: if I am found
Guilty of treason with Teiresias,
Then sentence me to death! You have my word   575
It is a sentence I should cast my vote for—
But not without evidence!
                              You do wrong
When you take good men for bad, bad men for good.
A true friend thrown aside—why, life itself
Is not more precious!
                              In time you will know this well: 580
For time, and time alone, will show the just man,
Though scoundrels are discovered in a day.

CHORAGOS: This is well said, and a prudent man would
    ponder it.
Judgments too quickly formed are dangerous.

OEDIPUS: But is he not quick in his duplicity?   585
    And shall I not be quick to parry him?
    Would you have me stand still, hold my peace, and let
    This man win everything, through my inaction?

CREON: And you want—what is it, then? To banish me?

OEDIPUS: No, not exile. It is your death I want,   590
    So that all the world may see what treason means.

CREON: You will persist, then? You will not believe me?

OEDIPUS: How can I believe you?

CREON: Then you are a fool.

OEDIPUS: To save myself?

CREON: In justice, think of me.

OEDIPUS: You are evil incarnate.

CREON: But suppose that you are
    wrong?   595

OEDIPUS: Still I must rule.

CREON: But not if you rule badly.

OEDIPUS: O city, city!

CREON: It is my city, too!

CHORAGOS: Now, my lords, be still. I see the Queen,
    Iocastê, coming from her palace chambers;

And it is time she came, for the sake of you both.   600
This dreadful quarrel can be resolved through her.
   [*Enter* IOCASTE.]
IOCASTE: Poor foolish men, what wicked din is this?
  With Thebes sick to death, is it not shameful
  That you should rake some private quarrel up?
  [*To* OEDIPUS.] Come into the house.
                —And you, Creon, go
     now: 605
  Let us have no more of this tumult over nothing.
CREON: Nothing? No, sister: what your husband plans for me
  Is one of two great evils: exile or death.
OEDIPUS: He is right.
             Why, woman I have caught him squarely
  Plotting against my life.
CREON: No! Let me die   610
  Accurst if ever I have wished you harm!
IOCASTE: Ah, believe it, Oedipus!
  In the name of the gods, respect this oath of his
  For my sake, for the sake of these people here!
CHORAGOS: [*Strophe 1.*] Open your mind to her, my lord. Be
    ruled by her, I beg you!   615
OEDIPUS: What would you have me do?
CHORAGOS: Respect Creon's word. He has never spoken like
    a fool,
  And now he has sworn an oath.
OEDIPUS: You know what you ask?
CHORAGOS: I do.
OEDIPUS: Speak on, then.
CHORAGOS: A friend so sworn should not be baited so,
  In blind malice, and without final proof.   620
OEDIPUS: You are aware, I hope, that what you say
  Means death for me, or exile at the least.
CHORAGOS: [*Strophe 2.*] No, I swear by Helios,[1] first in Heaven!
    May I die friendless and accurst,
  The worst of deaths, if ever I meant that!   625

---

1. The sun god.

It is the withering fields
That hurt my sick heart:
Must we bear all these ills,
And now your bad blood as well?
OEDIPUS: Then let him go. And let me die, if I must,   630
  Or be driven by him in shame from the land of Thebes.
  It is your unhappiness, and not his talk,
  That touches me.
              As for him—
  Wherever he goes, hatred will follow him.
CREON: Ugly in yielding, as you were ugly in rage!   635
  Natures like yours chiefly torment themselves.
OEDIPUS: Can you not go? Can you not leave me?
CREON: I can.
  You do not know me; but the city knows me,
  And in its eyes I am just, if not in yours.   [*Exit* CREON.]
CHORAGOS: [*Antistrophe 1.*] Lady Locastê, did you not ask the
    King to go to his chambers?   640
IOCASTE: First tell me what has happened.
CHORAGOS: There was suspicion without evidence; yet it rankled
  As even false charges will.
IOCASTE: On both sides?
CHORAGOS: On both.
IOCASTE: But what was said?
CHORAGOS: Oh let it rest, let it be done with!
  Have we not suffered enough?   645
OEDIPUS: You see to what your decency has brought you:
  You have made difficulties where my heart saw none.
CHORAGOS: [*Antistrophe 2.*] Oedipus, it is not once only I have
    told you—
  You must know I should count myself unwise
  To the point of madness, should I now forsake you—   650
        You, under whose hand,
           In the storm of another time,
        Our dear land sailed out free.
        But now stand fast at the helm!
IOCASTE: In God's name, Oedipus, inform your wife as well: 655
  Why are you so set in this hard anger?

OEDIPUS: I will tell you, for none of these men deserves
  My confidence as you do. It is Creon's work,
  His treachery, his plotting against me.
IOCASTE: Go on, if you can make this clear to me.   660
OEDIPUS: He charges me with the murder of Laïos.
IOCASTE: Has he some knowledge? Or does he speak from hearsay?
OEDIPUS: He would not commit himself to such a charge,
  But he has brought in that damnable soothsayer
  To tell his story.
IOCASTE: Set your mind at rest.   665
  If it is a question of soothsayers, I tell you
  That you will find no man whose craft gives knowledge
  Of the unknowable.

                  Here is my proof:

An oracle was reported to Laïos once
(I will not say from Phoibos himself, but from   670
His appointed ministers, at any rate)
That his doom would be death at the hands of his own son—
His son, born of his flesh and of mine!

Now, you remember the story: Laïos was killed
By marauding strangers where three highways meet;   675
But his child had not been three days in this world
Before the King had pierced the baby's ankles
And left him to die on a lonely mountainside.

Thus, Apollo never caused that child
To kill his father, and it was not Laïos' fate   680
To die at the hands of his son, as he had feared.
This is what prophets and prophecies are worth!
Have no dread of them.
                  It is God himself
Who can show us what he wills, in his own way.
OEDIPUS: How strange a shadowy memory crossed my mind,   685
  Just now while you were speaking: it chilled my heart.
IOCASTE: What do you mean? What memory do you speak of?

OEDIPUS: If I understand you, Laïos was killed
  At a place where three roads meet.
IOCASTE: So it was said;
  We have no later story.
OEDIPUS: Where did it happen?   690
IOCASTE: Phokis, it is called: at a place where the Theban Way
  Divides into the roads toward Delphi and Daulia.
OEDIPUS: When?
IOCASTE: We had the news not long before you came
  And proved the right to your succession here.
OEDIPUS: Ah, what net has God been weaving for me?   695
IOCASTE: Oedipus! Why does this trouble you?
OEDIPUS: Do not ask me yet.
  First, tell me how Laïos looked, and tell me
  How old he was.
IOCASTE: He was tall, his hair just touched
  With white; his form was not unlike your own.
OEDIPUS: I think that I myself may be accurst   700
  By my own ignorant edict.
IOCASTE: You speak strangely.
  It makes me tremble to look at you, my King.
OEDIPUS: I am not sure that the blind man cannot see.
  But I should know better if you were to tell me—
IOCASTE: Anything—though I dread to hear you ask it.   705
OEDIPUS: Was the King lightly escorted, or did he ride
  With a large company, as a ruler should?
IOCASTE: There were five men with him in all: one was a
    herald,
  And a single chariot, which he was driving.
OEDIPUS: Alas, that makes it plain enough!
                        But who—   710
  Who told you how it happened?
IOCASTE: A household servant,
  The only one to escape.
OEDIPUS: And is he still
  A servant of ours?
IOCASTE: No; for when he came back at last
  And found you enthroned in the place of the dead king,

He came to me, touched my hand with his, and begged   715
That I would send him away to the frontier district
Where only the shepherds go—
As far away from the city as I could send him.
I granted his prayer; for although the man was a slave,
He had earned more than this favor at my hands.   720
OEDIPUS: Can he be called back quickly?
IOCASTE: Easily.
   But why?
OEDIPUS: I have taken too much upon myself
   Without enquiry; therefore I wish to consult him.
IOCASTE: Then he shall come.
                                    But am I not one also
To whom you might confide these fears of yours?   725
OEDIPUS: That is your right; it will not be denied you,
   Now least of all; for I have reached a pitch
   Of wild foreboding. Is there anyone
   To whom I should sooner speak?

Polybos of Corinth is my father.   730
My mother is a Dorian: Meropê.
I grew up chief among the men of Corinth
Until a strange thing happened—
Not worth my passion, it may be, but strange.

At a feast, a drunken man maundering in his cups   735
Cries out that I am not my father's son!

I contained myself that night, though I felt anger
And a sinking heart. The next day I visited
My father and mother, and questioned them. They stormed,
Calling it all the slanderous rant of a fool;   740
And this relieved me. Yet the suspicion
Remained always aching in my mind;
I knew there was talk; I could not rest;
And finally, saying nothing to my parents,
I went to the shrine at Delphi.   745
The god dismissed my question without reply;

He spoke of other things.
                                 Some were clear,
Full of wretchedness, dreadful, unbearable:
As, that I should lie with my own mother, breed
Children from whom all men would turn their eyes;   750
And that I should be my father's murderer.

I heard all this, and fled. And from that day
Corinth to me was only in the stars
Descending in that quarter of the sky,
As I wandered farther and farther on my way   755
To a land where I should never see the evil
Sung by the oracle. And I came to this country
Where, so you say, King Laïos was killed.

I will tell you all that happened there, my lady.

There were three highways   760
Coming together at a place I passed;
And there a herald came towards me, and a chariot
Drawn by horses, with a man such as you describe
Seated in it. The groom leading the horses
Forced me off the road at his lord's command;   765
But as this charioteer lurched over towards me
I struck him in my rage. The old man saw me
And brought his double goad down upon my head
As I came abreast.
                          He was paid back, and more!
Swinging my club in this right hand I knocked him   770
Out of his car, and he rolled on the ground.
                                              I killed him.
I killed them all.
Now if that stranger and Laïos were—kin,
Where is a man more miserable than I?
More hated by the gods? Citizen and alien alike   775
Must never shelter me or speak to me—
I must be shunned by all.

And I myself
Pronounced this malediction upon myself!

Think of it: I have touched you with these hands,
These hands that killed your husband. What defilement!   780

Am I all evil, then? It must be so,
Since I must flee from Thebes, yet never again
See my own countrymen, my own country,
For fear of joining my mother in marriage
And killing Polybos, my father.
                                                Ah.   785
If I was created so, born to this fate,
Who could deny the savagery of God?

O holy majesty of heavenly powers!
May I never see that day! Never!
Rather let me vanish from the race of men   790
Than know the abomination destined me!
CHORAGOS: We too, my lord, have felt dismay at this.
    But there is hope: you have yet to hear the shepherd.
OEDIPUS: Indeed, I fear no other hope is left me.
IOCASTE: What do you hope from him when he comes?
OEDIPUS: This much: 795
    If his account of the murder tallies with yours,
    Then I am cleared.
IOCASTE: What was it that I said
    Of such importance?
OEDIPUS: Why, "marauders," you said,
    Killed the King, according to this man's story.
    If he maintains that still, if there were several,   800
    Clearly the guilt is not mine: I was alone.
    But if he says one man, singlehanded, did it,
    Then the evidence all points to me.
IOCASTE: You may be sure that he said there were several;
    And can he call back that story now? He cannot.   805
    The whole city heard it as plainly as I.

But suppose he alters some detail of it:
He cannot ever show that Laïos' death
Fulfilled the oracle: for Apollo said
My child was doomed to kill him; and my child—   810
Poor baby!—it was my child that died first.

No. From now on, where oracles are concerned,
I would not waste a second thought on any.
OEDIPUS: You may be right.
                              But come: let someone go
For the shepherd at once. This matter must be settled.   815
IOCASTE: I will send for him.
I would not wish to cross you in anything:
And surely not in this.—Let us go in. [*Exeunt into the
    palace.*]

ODE II

CHORUS: [*Strophe 1.*] Let me be reverent in the ways of right,
    Lowly the paths I journey on;   820
    Let all my words and actions keep
    The laws of the pure universe
    From highest Heaven handed down.
    For Heaven is their bright nurse,
    Those generations of the realms of light;   825
    Ah, never of mortal kind were they begot,
    Nor are they slaves of memory, lost in sleep:
    Their Father is greater than Time, and ages not.

    [*Antistrophe 1.*] The tyrant is a child of Pride
    Who drinks from his great sickening cup   830
    Recklessness and vanity,
    Until from his high crest headlong
    He plummets to the dust of hope.
    That strong man is not strong.
    But let no fair ambition be denied;   835
    May God protect the wrestler for the State
    In government, in comely policy,
    Who will fear God, and on His ordinance wait.

[*Strophe 2.*] Haughtiness and the high hand of disdain
Tempt and outrage God's holy law;   840
And any mortal who dares hold
No immortal Power in awe
Will be caught up in a net of pain:
The price for which his levity is sold.
Let each man take due earnings, then,   845
And keep his hands from holy things,
And from blasphemy stand apart—
Else the crackling blast of heaven
Blows on his head, and on his desperate heart;
Though fools will honor impious men,   850
In their cities no tragic poet sings.

[*Antistrophe 2.*] Shall we lose faith in Delphi's obscurities,
We who have heard the world's core
Discredited, and the sacred wood
Of Zeus at Elis praised no more?   855
The deeds and the strange prophecies
Must make a pattern yet to be understood.
Zeus, if indeed you are lord of all,
Throned in light over night and day,
Mirror this in your endless mind: 860
Our masters call the oracle
Words on the wind, and the Delphic vision blind!
Their hearts no longer know Apollo,
And reverence for the gods has died away.

SCENE III
    [*Enter* IOCASTE.]
IOCASTE: Princes of Thebes, it has occurred to me   865
    To visit the altars of the gods, bearing
    These branches as a suppliant, and this incense.
    Our King is not himself: his noble soul
    Is overwrought with fantasies of dread,
    Else he would consider   870
    The new prophecies in the light of the old.
    He will listen to any voice that speaks disaster,

And my advice goes for nothing. [*She approaches the altar.*]
                                    To you, then, Apollo,
Lycean[1] lord, since you are nearest, I turn in prayer.
Receive these offerings, and grant us deliverance   875
From defilement. Our hearts are heavy with fear
When we see our leader distracted, as helpless sailors
Are terrified by the confusion of their helmsman.
    [*Enter* MESSENGER.]
MESSENGER: Friends, no doubt you can direct me:
    Where shall I find the house of Oedipus,   880
    Or, better still, where is the King himself?
CHORAGOS: It is this very place, stranger; he is inside.
    This is his wife and mother of his children.
MESSENGER: I wish her happiness in a happy house,
    Blest in all the fulfillment of her marriage.   885
IOCASTE: I wish as much for you: your courtesy
    Deserves a like good fortune. But now, tell me:
    Why have you come? What have you to say to us?
MESSENGER: Good news, my lady, for your house and your
    husband.
IOCASTE: What news? Who sent you here?
MESSENGER: I am from Corinth.   890
    The news I bring ought to mean joy for you,
    Though it may be you will find some grief in it.
IOCASTE: What is it? How can it touch us in both ways?
MESSENGER: The word is that the people of the Isthmus
    Intend to call Oedipus to be their king.   895
IOCASTE: But old King Polybos—is he not reigning still?
MESSENGER: No. Death holds him in his sepulchre.
IOCASTE: What are you saying? Polybos is dead?
MESSENGER: If I am not telling the truth, may I die myself.
IOCASTE: [*To a* MAIDSERVANT.] Go in, go quickly; tell this to
    your master.   900

    O riddlers of God's will, where are you now!
    This was the man whom Oedipus, long ago,

---

1. Of Lycia, an ancient region in Asia Minor.

Feared so, fled so, in dread of destroying him—
But it was another fate by which he died.
    [*Enter* OEDIPUS.]
OEDIPUS: Dearest Iocastê, why have you sent for me?   905
IOCASTE: Listen to what this man says, and then tell me
  What has become of the solemn prophecies.
OEDIPUS: Who is this man? What is his news for me?
IOCASTE: He has come from Corinth to announce your father's
  death!
OEDIPUS: Is it true, stranger? Tell me in your own words.   910
MESSENGER: I cannot say it more clearly: the King is dead.
OEDIPUS: Was it by treason? Or by an attack of illness?
MESSENGER: A little thing brings old men to their rest.
OEDIPUS: It was sickness, then?
MESSENGER: Yes, and his many years.
OEDIPUS: Ah!   915
  Why should a man respect the Pythian hearth, or
  Give heed to the birds that jangle above his head?
  They prophesied that I should kill Polybos.
  Kill my own father; but he is dead and buried.
  And I am here—I never touched him, never,   920
  Unless he died of grief for my departure,
  And thus, in a sense, through me. No. Polybos
  Has packed the oracles off with him underground.
  They are empty words.
IOCASTE: Had I not told you so?
OEDIPUS: You had; it was my faint heart that betrayed me.   925
IOCASTE: From now on never think of those things again.
OEDIPUS: And yet—must I not fear my mother's bed?
IOCASTE: Why should anyone in this world be afraid,
  Since Fate rules us and nothing can be foreseen?
  A man should live only for the present day.   930

  Have no more fear of sleeping with your mother:
  How many men, in dreams, have lain with their
    mothers!
  No reasonable man is troubled by such things.
OEDIPUS: That is true; only—

If only my mother were not still alive!   935
But she is alive. I cannot help my dread.
IOCASTE: Yet this news of your father's death is wonderful.
OEDIPUS: Wonderful. But I fear the living woman.
MESSENGER: Tell me, who is this woman that you fear?
OEDIPUS: It is Meropê, man; the wife of King Polybos.   940
MESSENGER: Meropê? Why should you be afraid of her?
OEDIPUS: An oracle of the gods, a dreadful saying.
MESSENGER: Can you tell me about it or are you sworn to silence?
OEDIPUS: I can tell you, and I will.

Apollo said through his prophet that I was the man   945
Who should marry his own mother, shed his father's blood
With his own hands. And so, for all these years
I have kept clear of Corinth, and no harm has come—
Though it would have been sweet to see my parents again.
MESSENGER: And is this the fear that drove you out of
     Corinth?   950
OEDIPUS: Would you have me kill my father?
MESSENGER: As for that
You must be reassured by the news I gave you.
OEDIPUS: If you could reassure me, I would reward you.
MESSENGER: I had that in mind, I will confess: I thought
I could count on you when you returned to Corinth.   955
OEDIPUS: No: I will never go near my parents again.
MESSENGER: Ah, son, you still do not know what you are
     doing—
OEDIPUS: What do you mean? In the name of God tell me!
MESSENGER:—If these are your reasons for not going home.
OEDIPUS: I tell you, I fear the oracle may come true.   960
MESSENGER: And guilt may come upon you through your
     parents?
OEDIPUS: That is the dread that is always in my heart.
MESSENGER: Can you not see that all your fears are groundless?
OEDIPUS: How can you say that? They are my parents, surely?
MESSENGER: Polybos was not your father.
OEDIPUS: Not my father?   965
MESSENGER: No more your father than the man speaking
     to you.

OEDIPUS: But you are nothing to me!

MESSENGER: Neither was he.

OEDIPUS: Then why did he call me son?

MESSENGER: I will tell you:
    Long ago he had you from my hands, as a gift.

OEDIPUS: Then how could he love me so, if I was not his?   970

MESSENGER: He had no children, and his heart turned to you.

OEDIPUS: What of you? Did you buy me? Did you find me by
    chance?

MESSENGER: I came upon you in the crooked pass of Kithairon.

OEDIPUS: And what were you doing there?

MESSENGER: Tending my flocks.

OEDIPUS: A wandering shepherd?

MESSENGER: But your savior, son, that day.   975

OEDIPUS: From what did you save me?

MESSENGER: Your ankles should tell
    you that.

OEDIPUS: Ah, stranger, why do you speak of that childhood
    pain?

MESSENGER: I cut the bonds that tied your ankles together.

OEDIPUS: I have had the mark as long as I can remember.

MESSENGER: That was why you were given the name you bear.[1]   980

OEDIPUS: God! Was it my father, or my mother who did it?
    Tell me!

MESSENGER: I do not know. The man who gave you to me
    Can tell you better than I.

OEDIPUS: It was not you that found me, but another?

MESSENGER: It was another shepherd gave you to me.   985

OEDIPUS: Who was he? Can you tell me who he was?

MESSENGER: I think he was said to be one of Laïos' people.

OEDIPUS: You mean the Laïos who was king here years ago?

MESSENGER: Yes; King Laïos; and the man was one of his
    herdsmen.

OEDIPUS: Is he still alive? Can I see him?

MESSENGER: These men here   990
    Know best about such things.

---

1. The name *Oedipus* means "swollen foot."

OEDIPUS: Does anyone here
  Know this shepherd that he is talking about?
  Have you seen him in the fields, or in the town?
  If you have, tell me. It is time things were made plain.
CHORAGOS: I think the man he means is that same shepherd   995
  You have already asked to see. Iocastê perhaps
  Could tell you something.
OEDIPUS: Do you know anything
  About him, Lady? Is he the man we have summoned?
  Is that the man this shepherd means?
IOCASTE: Why think of him?
  Forget this herdsman. Forget it all.   1000
  This talk is a waste of time.
OEDIPUS: How can you say that.
  When the clues to my true birth are in my hands?
IOCASTE: For God's love, let us have no more questioning!
  Is your life nothing to you?
  My own is pain enough for me to bear.   1005
OEDIPUS: You need not worry. Suppose my mother a slave,
  And born of slaves: no baseness can touch you.
IOCASTE: Listen to me, I beg you: do not do this thing!
OEDIPUS: I will not listen; the truth must be made known.
IOCASTE: Everything that I say is for your own good!
OEDIPUS: My own
   good   1010
  Snaps my patience, then; I want none of it.
IOCASTE: You are fatally wrong! May you never learn who
   you are!
OEDIPUS: Go, one of you, and bring the shepherd here.
  Let us leave this woman to brag of her royal name.
IOCASTE: Ah, miserable!   1015
  That is the only word I have for you now.
  That is the only word I can ever have. [*Exit into the palace.*]
CHORAGOS: Why has she left us, Oedipus? Why has she gone
  In such a passion of sorrow? I fear this silence:
  Something dreadful may come of it.
OEDIPUS: Let it come!   1020
  However base my birth, I must know about it.

The Queen, like a woman, is perhaps ashamed
To think of my low origin. But I
Am a child of Luck; I cannot be dishonored.
Luck is my mother; the passing months, my brothers,   1025
Have seen me rich and poor.
                                        If this is so,
How could I wish that I were someone else?
How could I not be glad to know my birth?

ODE III

CHORUS: [*Strophe.*] If ever the coming time were known
    To my heart's pondering,   1030
    Kithairon, now by Heaven I see the torches
    At the festival of the next full moon,
    And see the dance, and hear the choir sing
    A grace to your gentle shade:
    Mountain where Oedipus was found,   1035
    O mountain guard of a noble race!
    May the god who heals us lend his aid,
    And let that glory come to pass
    For our king's cradling-ground.

    [*Antistrophe.*] Of the nymphs that flower beyond the years,   1040
    Who bore you, royal child,
    To Pan of the hills or the timberline Apollo,
    Cold in delight where the upland clears,
    Or Hermês for whom Kyllenê's heights are piled?[1]
    Or flushed as evening cloud,   1045
    Great Dionysos, roamer of mountains,
    He—was it he who found you there,
    And caught you up in his own proud
    Arms from the sweet god-ravisher
    Who laughed by the Muses' fountains?[2]   1050

1. Mount Kyllene, his birthplace, is sacred to Hermes, a multifaceted god. *Nymphs:* maiden goddesses who live in nature. *Pan:* god of pastures, flocks, and shepherds.

2. The Muses, sister goddesses, dwelled near fountains on Mount Helicon. *Dionysos:* Or Dionysus, also known as Bacchos/Bacchus, here posited as having taken Oedipus from Oedipus's "mother," a nymph.

SCENE IV

OEDIPUS: Sirs: though I do not know the man,
  I think I see him coming, this shepherd we want:
  He is old, like our friend here, and the men
  Bringing him seem to be servants of my house.
  But you can tell, if you have ever seen him.   1055
    [*Enter* SHEPHERD *escorted by servants.*]
CHORAGOS: I know him, he was Laïos' man. You can trust him.
OEDIPUS: Tell me first, you from Corinth: is this the shepherd
  We were discussing?
MESSENGER: This is the very man.
OEDIPUS: [*To* SHEPHERD.] Come here. No, look at me. You
    must answer
  Everything I ask.—You belonged to Laïos: 1060
SHEPHERD: Yes: born his slave, brought up in his house.
OEDIPUS: Tell me: what kind of work did you do for him?
SHEPHERD: I was a shepherd of his, most of my life.
OEDIPUS: Where mainly did you go for pasturage?
SHEPHERD: Sometimes Kithairon, sometimes the hills near-by.   1065
OEDIPUS: Do you remember ever seeing this man out there?
SHEPHERD: What would he be doing there? This man?
OEDIPUS: This man standing here. Have you ever seen him
    before?
SHEPHERD: No. At least, not to my recollection.
MESSENGER: And that is not strange, my lord. But I'll refresh   1070
  His memory: he must remember when we two
  Spent three whole seasons together, March to September,
  On Kithairon or thereabouts. He had two flocks:
  I had one. Each autumn I'd drive mine home
  And he would go back with his to Laïos' sheepfold.—   1075
  Is this not true, just as I have described it?
SHEPHERD: True, yes; but it was all so long ago.
MESSENGER: Well, then: do you remember, back in those days,
  That you gave me a baby boy to bring up as my own?
SHEPHERD: What if I did? What are you trying to say?   1080
MESSENGER: King Oedipus was once that little child.
SHEPHERD: Damn you, hold your tongue!

OEDIPUS: No more of that!
It is your tongue needs watching, not this man's.
SHEPHERD: My King, my Master, what is it I have done wrong?
OEDIPUS: You have not answered his question about the boy.   1085
SHEPHERD: He does not know . . . He is only making
      trouble . . .
OEDIPUS: Come, speak plainly, or it will go hard with you.
SHEPHERD: In God's name, do not torture an old man!
OEDIPUS: Come here, one of you; bind his arms behind him.
SHEPHERD: Unhappy king! What more do you wish to learn?   1090
OEDIPUS: Did you give this man the child he speaks of?
SHEPHERD: I did.
      And I would to God I had died that very day,
OEDIPUS: You will die now unless you speak the truth.
SHEPHERD: Yet if I speak the truth, I am worse than dead.
OEDIPUS: Very well; since you insist upon delaying—   1095
SHEPHERD: No! I have told you already that I gave him the
      boy.
OEDIPUS: Where did you get him? From your house? From
      somewhere else?
SHEPHERD: Not from mine, no. A man gave him to me.
OEDIPUS: Is that man here? Do you know whose slave he was?
SHEPHERD: For God's love, my King, do not ask me any more!   1100
OEDIPUS: You are a dead man if I have to ask you again.
SHEPHERD: Then . . . Then the child was from the palace of
      Laïos.
OEDIPUS: A slave child? or a child of his own line?
SHEPHERD: Ah, I am on the brink of dreadful speech!
OEDIPUS: And I of dreadful hearing. Yet I must hear.   1105
SHEPHERD: If you must be told, then . . .
                                          They said it was
      Laïos' child;
      But it is your wife who can tell you about that.
OEDIPUS: My wife!—Did she give it to you?
SHEPHERD: My lord, she did.
OEDIPUS: Do you know why?
SHEPHERD: I was told to get rid of it.

OEDIPUS: An unspeakable mother!

SHEPHERD: There had been
    prophecies . . .   1110

OEDIPUS: Tell me.

SHEPHERD: It was said that the boy would kill his own father.

OEDIPUS: Then why did you give him over to this old man?

SHEPHERD: I pitied the baby, my King,
    And I thought that this man would take him far away   1115
    To his own country.

                        He saved him—but for what a fate!
    For if you are what this man says you are,
    No man living is more wretched than Oedipus.

OEDIPUS: Ah God!
    It was true!

            All the prophecies!

                        —Now,   1120
    O Light, may I look on you for the last time!
    I, Oedipus,
    Oedipus, damned in his birth, in his marriage damned,
    Damned in the blood he shed with his own hand! [*He rushes
        into the palace.*]

ODE IV

CHORUS: [*Strophe 1.*] Alas for the seed of men.   1125

    What measure shall I give these generations
    That breathe on the void and are void
    And exist and do not exist?

    Who bears more weight of joy
    Than mass of sunlight shifting in images,   1130
    Or who shall make his thought stay on
    That down time drifts away?

    Your splendor is all fallen.

    O naked brow of wrath and tears,
    O change of Oedipus!   1135

I who saw your days call no man blest—
Your great days like ghósts góne.

[*Antistrophe 1.*] That mind was a strong bow.

Deep, how deep you drew it then, hard archer,
At a dim fearful range,   1140
And brought dear glory down!

You overcame the stranger—
The virgin with her hooking lion claws—
And though death sang, stood like a tower
To make pale Thebes take heart.   1145

Fortress against our sorrow!

True king, giver of laws,
Majestic Oedipus!
No prince in Thebes had ever such renown,
No prince won such grace of power.   1150

[*Strophe 2.*] And now of all men ever known
Most pitiful is this man's story:
His fortunes are most changed, his state
Fallen to a low slave's
Ground under bitter fate.   1155

O Oedipus, most royal one!
The great door that expelled you to the light
Gave at night—ah, gave night to your glory:
As to the father, to the fathering son.

All understood too late.   1160

How could that queen whom Laïos won,
The garden that he harrowed at his height,
Be silent when that act was done?

[*Antistrophe 2.*] But all eyes fail before time's eye,
All actions come to justice there.   1165
Though never willed, though far down the deep past,
Your bed, your dread sirings,
Are brought to book at last.

Child by Laïos doomed to die,
Then doomed to lose that fortunate little death,   1170
Would God you never took breath in this air
That with my wailing lips I take to cry:

For I weep the world's outcast.

I was blind, and now I can tell why:
Asleep, for you had given ease of breath   1175
To Thebes, while the false years went by.

ÉXODOS[1]
    [*Enter, from the palace,* SECOND MESSENGER.]
SECOND MESSENGER: Elders of Thebes, most honored in this
    land,
    What horrors are yours to see and hear, what weight
    Of sorrow to be endured, if, true to your birth,
    You venerate the line of Labdakos!   1180
    I think neither Istros nor Phasis, those great rivers,
    Could purify this place of the corruption
    It shelters now, or soon must bring to light—
    Evil not done unconsciously, but willed.

    The greatest griefs are those we cause ourselves.   1185
CHORAGOS: Surely, friend, we have grief enough already;
    What new sorrow do you mean?
SECOND MESSENGER: The Queen is dead.
CHORAGOS: Iocastê? Dead? But at whose hand?
SECOND MESSENGER: Her own.
    The full horror of what happened you cannot know,

---

1. The final scene, which includes the chorus's exit.

For you did not see it; but I, who did will tell you   1190
As clearly as I can how she met her death.

When she had left us,
In passionate silence, passing through the court,
She ran to her apartment in the house,
Her hair clutched by the fingers of both hands.   1195
She closed the doors behind her; then, by that bed
Where long ago the fatal son was conceived—
That son who should bring about his father's death—
We heard her call upon Laïos, dead so many years,
And heard her wail for the double fruit of her marriage,   1200
A husband by her husband, children by her child.

Exactly how she died I do not know:
For Oedipus burst in moaning and would not let us
Keep vigil to the end: it was by him
As he stormed about the room that our eyes were
    caught.   1205
From one to another of us he went, begging a sword.
Cursing the wife who was not his wife, the mother
Whose womb had carried his own children and himself.
I do not know: it was none of us aided him,
But surely one of the gods was in control!   1210
For with a dreadful cry
He hurled his weight, as though wrenched out of himself,
At the twin doors: the bolts gave, and he rushed in.
And there we saw her hanging, her body swaying
From the cruel cord she had noosed about her neck.   1215
A great sob broke from him, heartbreaking to hear,
As he loosed the rope and lowered her to the ground.

I would blot out from my mind what happened next!
For the King ripped from her gown the golden brooches
That were her ornament, and raised them, and plunged
    them down   1220
Straight into his own eyeballs, crying, "No more,
No more shall you look on the misery about me,

The horrors of my own doing! Too long you have known
The faces of those whom I should never have seen,
Too long been blind to those for whom I was searching!   1225
From this hour, go in darkness!" And as he spoke,
He struck at his eyes—not once, but many times;
And the blood spattered his beard,
Bursting from his ruined sockets like red hail.

So from the unhappiness of two this evil has sprung.   1230
A curse on the man and woman alike. The old
Happiness of the house of Labdakos
Was happiness enough: where is it today?
It is all wailing and ruin, disgrace, death—all
The misery of mankind that has a name—   1235
And it is wholly and for ever theirs.
CHORAGOS: Is he in agony still? Is there no rest for him?
SECOND MESSENGER: He is calling for someone to lead him to
      the gates
So that all the children of Kadmos may look upon
His father's murderer, his mother's—no,   1240
I cannot say it!
                  And then he will leave Thebes.
Self-exiled, in order that the curse
Which he himself pronounced may depart from the house.
He is weak, and there is none to lead him,
So terrible is his suffering.
                              But you will see: 1245
Look, the doors are opening; in a moment
You will see a thing that would crush a heart of stone.
      [*The central door is opened;* OEDIPUS, *blinded, is led in.*]
CHORAGOS: Dreadful indeed for men to see.
Never have my own eyes
Looked on a sight so full of fear.   1250

Oedipus!
What madness came upon you, what daemon
Leaped on your life with heavier
Punishment than a mortal man can bear?

No: I cannot even   1255
  Look at you, poor ruined one.
  And I would speak, question, ponder,
  If I were able. No.
  You make me shudder.
OEDIPUS: God.   God.   1260
  Is there a sorrow greater?
  Where shall I find harbor in this world?
  My voice is hurled far on a dark wind.
  What has God done to me?
CHORAGOS: Too terrible to think of, or to see.   1265
OEDIPUS: [*Strophe 1.*] O cloud of night,
  Never to be turned away: night coming on,
  I cannot tell how: night like a shroud!

  My fair winds brought me here.
                                   O God. Again
  The pain of the spikes where I had sight,   1270
  The flooding pain
  Of memory, never to be gouged out.
CHORAGOS: This is not strange.
  You suffer it all twice over, remorse in pain,
  Pain in remorse.   1275
OEDIPUS: [*Antistrophe 1.*] Ah dear friend
Are you faithful even yet, you alone?
  Are you still standing near me, will you stay here,
  Patient, to care for the blind?
                                 The blind man!
  Yet even blind I know who it is attends me,   1280
  By the voice's tone—
  Though my new darkness hide the comforter.
CHORAGOS: Oh fearful act!
  What god was it drove you to rake black
  Night across your eyes?   1285
OEDIPUS: [*Strophe 2.*] Apollo. Apollo. Dear
  Children, the god was Apollo.
  He brought my sick, sick fate upon me.
  But the blinding hand was my own!

How could I bear to see   1290
   When all my sight was horror everywhere?
CHORAGOS: Everywhere; that is true.
OEDIPUS: And now what is left?
   Images? Love? A greeting even,
   Sweet to the senses? Is there anything?   1295
   Ah, no, friends: lead me away.
   Lead me away from Thebes.
                                    Lead the great wreck
   And hell of Oedipus, whom the gods hate.
CHORAGOS: Your fate is clear, you are not blind to that.
   Would God you had never found it out!   1300
OEDIPUS: [*Antistrophe 2.*] Death take the man who unbound
   My feet on that hillside
   And delivered me from death to life! What life?
   If only I had died,
   This weight of monstrous doom   1305
   Could not have dragged me and my darlings down.
CHORAGOS: I would have wished the same.
OEDIPUS: Oh never to have come here
   With my father's blood upon me! Never
   To have been the man they call his mother's husband!   1310
   Oh accurst! Oh child of evil,
   To have entered that wretched bed—
                                    the selfsame one!
   More primal than sin itself, this fell to me.
CHORAGOS: I do not know how I can answer you.
   You were better dead than alive and blind.   1315
OEDIPUS: Do not counsel me any more. This punishment
   That I have laid upon myself is just.
   If I had eyes,
   I do not know how I could bear the sight
   Of my father, when I came to the house of Death,   1320
   Or my mother: for I have sinned against them both
   So vilely that I could not make my peace
   By strangling my own life.
                                    Or do you think my children,
   Born as they were born, would be sweet to my eyes?

Ah never, never! Nor this town with its high walls,   1325
Nor the holy images of the gods.
                              For I,
Thrice miserable—Oedipus, noblest of all the line
Of Kadmos, have condemned myself to enjoy
These things no more, by my own malediction
Expelling that man whom the gods declared   1330
To be a defilement in the house of Laïos.
After exposing the rankness of my own guilt,
How could I look men frankly in the eyes?
No, I swear it,
If I could have stifled my hearing at its source,   1335
I would have done it and made all this body
A tight cell of misery, blank to light and sound:
So I should have been safe in a dark agony
Beyond all recollection.
                              Ah Kithairon!
Why did you shelter me? When I was cast upon you,   1340
Why did I not die? Then I should never
Have shown the world my execrable birth.

Ah Polybos! Corinth, city that I believed
The ancient seat of my ancestors: how fair
I seemed, your child! And all the while this evil   1345
Was cancerous within me!
                              For I am sick
In my daily life, sick in my origin.

O three roads, dark ravine, woodland and way
Where three roads met: you, drinking my father's blood,
My own blood, spilled by my own hand: can you remember   1350
The unspeakable things I did there, and the things
I went on from there to do?
                              O marriage, marriage!
The act that engendered me, and again the act
Performed by the son in the same bed
                              Ah, the net
Of incest, mingling fathers, brothers, sons,   1355

With brides, wives, mothers: the last evil
That can be known by men: no tongue can say
How evil!

       No. For the love of God, conceal me
Somewhere far from Thebes; or kill me; or hurl me
Into the sea, away from men's eyes for ever.   1360

Come, lead me. You need not fear to touch me.
Of all men, I alone can bear this guilt.
    [*Enter* CREON.]
CHORAGOS: We are not the ones to decide; but Creon here
    May fitly judge of what you ask. He only
    Is left to protect the city in your place.   1365
OEDIPUS: Alas, how can I speak to him? What right have I
    To beg his courtesy whom I have deeply wronged?
CREON: I have not come to mock you, Oedipus,
    Or to reproach you, either.
                 [*To* ATTENDANTS.]—You, standing
      there:
    If you have lost all respect for man's dignity,   1370
    At least respect the flame of Lord Helios:
    Do not allow this pollution to show itself
    Openly here, an affront to the earth
    And Heaven's rain and the light of day. No, take him
    Into the house as quickly as you can.   1375
    For it is proper
    That only the close kindred see his grief.
OEDIPUS: I pray you in God's name, since your courtesy
    Ignores my dark expectation, visiting
    With mercy this man of all men most execrable: 1380
    Give me what I ask—for your good, not for mine.
CREON: And what is it that you would have me do?
OEDIPUS: Drive me out of this country as quickly as may be
    To a place where no human voice can ever greet me.
CREON: I should have done that before now—only,   1385
    God's will had not been wholly revealed to me.
OEDIPUS: But his command is plain: the parricide
    Must be destroyed. I am that evil man.

CREON: That is the sense of it, yes; but as things are,
   We had best discover clearly what is to be done.   1390
OEDIPUS: You would learn more about a man like me?
CREON: You are ready now to listen to the god.
OEDIPUS: I will listen. But it is to you
   That I must turn for help. I beg you, hear me.

   The woman in there—   1395
   Give her whatever funeral you think proper:
   She is your sister.
            —But let me go, Creon!
   Let me purge my father's Thebes of the pollution
   Of my living here, and go out to the wild hills,
   To Kithairon, that has won such fame with me,   1400
   The tomb my mother and father appointed for me,
   And let me die there, as they willed I should.
   And yet I know
   Death will not ever come to me through sickness
   Or in any natural way: I have been preserved   1405
   For some unthinkable fate. But let that be.

   As for my sons, you need not care for them.
   They are men, they will find some way to live.
   But my poor daughters, who have shared my table,
   Who never before have been parted from their father—   1410
   Take care of them, Creon; do this for me.
   And will you let me touch them with my hands
   A last time, and let us weep together?
   Be kind, my lord,
   Great prince, be kind!
            Could I but touch them,   1415
   They would be mine again, as when I had my eyes.
     [*Enter* ANTIGONE *and* ISMENE, *attended.*]
   Ah, God!
   Is it my dearest children I hear weeping?
   Has Creon pitied me and sent my daughters?
CREON: Yes, Oedipus: I knew that they were dear to you   1420
   In the old days, and know you must love them still.

OEDIPUS: May God bless you for this—and be a friendlier
  Guardian to you than he has been to me!

  Children, where are you?
  Come quickly to my hands: they are your brother's—   1425
  Hands that have brought your father's once clear eyes
  To this way of seeing—
                     Ah dearest ones,
  I had neither sight nor knowledge then, your father
  By the woman who was the source of his own life!
  And I weep for you—having no strength to see
    you—,   1430
  I weep for you when I think of the bitterness
  That men will visit upon you all your lives.
  What homes, what festivals can you attend
  Without being forced to depart again in tears?
  And when you come to marriageable age,   1435
  Where is the man, my daughters, who would dare
  Risk the bane that lies on all my children?
  Is there any evil wanting? Your father killed
  His father; sowed the womb of her who bore him;
  Engendered you at the fount of his own existence!   1440
  That is what they will say of you.

                                Then, whom
  Can you ever marry? There are no bridegrooms for you,
  And your lives must wither away in sterile dreaming.

  O Creon, son of Menoikeus!
  You are the only father my daughters have,   1445
  Since we, their parents, are both of us gone for ever.
  They are your own blood: you will not let them
  Fall into beggary and loneliness;
  You will keep them from the miseries that are mine!
  Take pity on them; see, they are only children,   1450
  Friendless except for you. Promise me this,
  Great Prince, and give me your hand in token of it.
    [CREON *clasps his right hand.*]

Children:
I could say much, if you could understand me,
But as it is, I have only this prayer for you: 1455
Live where you can, be as happy as you can—
Happier, please God, than God has made your father!
CREON: Enough. You have wept enough. Now go within.
OEDIPUS: I must; but it is hard.
CREON: Time eases all things.
OEDIPUS: But you must promise—
CREON: Say what you desire.   1460
OEDIPUS: Send me from Thebes!
CREON: God grant that I may!
OEDIPUS: But since God hates me . . .
CREON: No, he will grant your
    wish.
OEDIPUS: You promise?
CREON: I cannot speak beyond my knowledge.
OEDIPUS: Then lead me in.
CREON: Come now, and leave your children.
OEDIPUS: No! Do not take them from me!
CREON: Think no longer   1465
    That you are in command here, but rather think
    How, when you were, you served your own destruction.
        [*Exeunt into the house all but the* CHORUS; *the* CHORAGOS
        chants directly to the audience.]
CHORAGOS: Men of Thebes: look upon Oedipus.

    This is the king who solved the famous riddle
    And towered up, most powerful of men.   1470
    No mortal eyes but looked on him with envy,
    Yet in the end ruin swept over him.

    Let every man in mankind's frailty
    Consider his last day; and let none
    Presume on his good fortune until he find   1475
    Life, at his death, a memory without pain.

ca. 430 B.C.E.

William Shakespeare
1564–1616

HAMLET

Sometime in the late 1580s, William Shakespeare, then in his early twenties, traveled the muddy roads that connected the picturesque country town of Stratford-on-Avon to England's metropolis, the London of Queen Elizabeth. No one knows how Shakespeare made his living in Stratford, nor why he left. But most Shakespeare scholars believe he joined an acting company in London and learned the business of theater from the bottom up. When he started writing plays, Shakespeare broke the mold—playwrights were typically men of much higher education. His plays were undeniably popular, but to those in polite English society, Shakespeare and his fans were somewhat lowbrow.

As he did for many of his plays, Shakespeare borrowed the story for Hamlet. *At least four hundred years old when Shakespeare adapted it, the story of* Hamlet *had its roots in Norse legend. Its earliest written version was nearly a hundred years old by 1600, when Shakespeare based his play on another Elizabethan* Hamlet, *perhaps by John Kyd. Staged in the late 1580s, this first version had helped popularize the genre known as* **revenge tragedy**, *which is roughly equivalent to today's action thriller. In the typical revenge tragedy, the main character commits acts of terrible violence to avenge some murdered relative. Catering to unsophisticated tastes, the revenge tragedy fills the stage with bloody bodies.*

Shakespeare's Hamlet, *too, ends in carnage, but in other respects it differs from its immediate predecessor and from the earlier versions of the Hamlet story. In the previous incarnations, for example, Claudius's regicide is well known, not a secret, and Ophelia is indubitably Hamlet's mistress. This organic quality to the Hamlet story—its changing and growing in each new telling—probably accounts for the many inconsistencies in Shakespeare's version. In act 3, for example, Hamlet spies on Claudius and leaves him praying, then goes directly to Gertrude's chamber, where he thinks he finds Claudius hiding. The play presents dozens of such problems,* which seem to derive from Shakespeare's rewriting of an existing tale for his own purposes, purposes that in some ways contradict the conventions of the revenge tragedy.

The most important of these changes involves Hamlet's character—and audiences' responses to it. Shakespeare's audience would have known Hamlet's basic story, and they would have expected Hamlet to be a swashbuckling hothead. They would have been surprised by the brooding, introspective character Shakespeare gave them. Even so, Hamlet's long delays, apparently, did not much affect them. Not until the Romantic period, in the early 1800s, did critics remark on Hamlet's slow execution of revenge. The Romantics, perhaps seeing themselves in Shakespeare's hero, attributed his procrastinating to a fatal introspection, which drains his will of energy for action. In the twentieth century, after the advent of Freud's theories of human psychology, critics added an Oedipal complex to Hamlet's problems. Some contemporary readers hear in Hamlet's ravings what would become the angst of the existential philosophers. You should consider for yourself why Hamlet takes so long to act and what his delays mean.

How the play is staged can radically change your interpretation of such issues. For example, is Hamlet's madness real or fake? Of course, he tells Horatio in the first act that he will pretend to be mad, but this plot device might have been one of those awkward holdovers from Shakespeare's sources. There, the feigned madness protects Hamlet from Claudius's suspicions; it doesn't seem to have that effect here, nor does Hamlet seem too careful to hide his enmity for Claudius. Consider his treatment of Ophelia in act 3: does he rave so angrily because her sudden, inexplicable coldness has driven him to the edge of sanity, or because he knows she's a pawn in a plot against himself? Franco Zeffirelli's 1990 film adaptation of Hamlet presents the second version: Hamlet secretly watches Polonius manipulate Ophelia, and so he knows she's in league with her father and the king. Mel Gibson's Hamlet, though distraught, is clearly sane.

In making the story of Hamlet his own, Shakespeare created a huge, linguistically rich drama, one that addresses themes too complex and varied to fit within a conventional telling of the same story. He crafted a protagonist large enough—spiritually, intellectu-

ally, emotionally—to continue fascinating audiences four hundred years later. Whether you see yourself in that character, become engrossed in his predicament and his contradictory responses to it, or find some other route into the play's many inner chambers, Hamlet *should leave you feeling as though you've witnessed an expansion of the theater's possibilities. When the Danish prince tells his friend Horatio that "There are more things in heaven and earth . . . / Than are dreamt of in your philosophy" (1.5.165–66), his wisdom about life could easily apply to the work in which he appears.*

Hamlet

CHARACTERS

CLAUDIUS, *King of Denmark*
HAMLET, *son of the former and nephew to the present King*
POLONIUS, *Lord Chamberlain*
HORATIO, *friend of Hamlet*
LAERTES, *son of Polonius*
VOLTEMAND
CORNELIUS
ROSENCRANTZ
GUILDENSTERN } *courtiers*
OSRIC
A GENTLEMAN
A PRIEST

MARCELLUS
BERNARDO } *officers*
FRANCISCO, *a soldier*
REYNALDO, *servant to Polonius*
PLAYERS
TWO CLOWNS, *gravediggers*
FORTINBRAS, *Prince of Norway*
A NORWEGIAN CAPTAIN
ENGLISH AMBASSADORS
GERTRUDE, *Queen of Denmark, and mother of Hamlet*
OPHELIA, *daughter of Polonius*
GHOST OF HAMLET'S FATHER

LORDS, LADIES, OFFICERS, SOLDIERS, SAILORS, MESSENGERS, AND ATTENDANTS

SCENE: *The action takes place in or near the royal castle of Denmark at Elsinore.*

ACT I
SCENE 1

A guard station atop the castle. Enter BERNARDO *and* FRANCISCO, *two sentinels.*

BERNARDO: Who's there?

FRANCISCO: Nay, answer me. Stand and unfold yourself.

BERNARDO: Long live the king!

FRANCISCO: Bernardo?

BERNARDO: He. 5

FRANCISCO: You come most carefully upon your hour.

BERNARDO: 'Tis now struck twelve. Get thee to bed, Francisco.

FRANCISCO: For this relief much thanks. 'Tis bitter cold,
 And I am sick at heart.

BERNARDO: Have you had quiet guard?

FRANCISCO: Not a mouse stirring. 10

BERNARDO: Well, good night.
 If you do meet Horatio and Marcellus,
 The rivals[1] of my watch, bid them make haste.
  [*Enter* HORATIO *and* MARCELLUS.]

FRANCISCO: I think I hear them. Stand, ho! Who is there?

HORATIO: Friends to this ground.

MARCELLUS: And liegemen to the Dane.[2] 15

FRANCISCO: Give you good night.

MARCELLUS: O, farewell, honest soldier!
 Who hath relieved you?

FRANCISCO: Bernardo hath my place.
 Give you good night.   [*Exit* FRANCISCO.]

MARCELLUS: Holla, Bernardo!

BERNARDO: Say—
 What, is Horatio there?

HORATIO: A piece of him.

BERNARDO: Welcome, Horatio. Welcome, good Marcellus. 20

HORATIO: What, has this thing appeared again tonight?

BERNARDO: I have seen nothing.

MARCELLUS: Horatio says 'tis but our fantasy,
 And will not let belief take hold of him
 Touching this dreaded sight twice seen of us. 25
 Therefore I have entreated him along
 With us to watch the minutes of this night,

---

1. Companions.   2. The king of Denmark, also called
"Denmark," as in line 48 of this scene.

That if again this apparition come,
He may approve[3] our eyes and speak to it.
HORATIO: Tush, tush, 'twill not appear.
BERNARDO:　　　　　　　　　　　Sit down awhile,　　　30
 And let us once again assail your ears,
 That are so fortified against our story,
 What we have two nights seen.
HORATIO:　　　　　　　　　　　Well, sit we down.
 And let us hear Bernardo speak of this.
BERNARDO: Last night of all,　　　　　　　　　　35
 When yond same star that's westward from the pole[4]
 Had made his course t' illume that part of heaven
 Where now it burns, Marcellus and myself,
 The bell then beating one—
  [*Enter* GHOST.]
MARCELLUS: Peace, break thee off. Look where it comes again.　　40
BERNARDO: In the same figure like the king that's dead.
MARCELLUS: Thou art a scholar; speak to it, Horatio.
BERNARDO: Looks 'a[5] not like the king? Mark it, Horatio.
HORATIO: Most like. It harrows me with fear and wonder.
BERNARDO: It would be spoke to.
MARCELLUS:　　　　　　　　　　Speak to it, Horatio.　　45
HORATIO: What art thou that usurp'st this time of night
 Together with that fair and warlike form
 In which the majesty of buried Denmark
 Did sometimes march? By heaven I charge thee, speak.
MARCELLUS: It is offended.
BERNARDO:　　　　　　　See, it stalks away.　　　　50
HORATIO: Stay. Speak, speak. I charge thee, speak.
         [*Exit* GHOST.]
MARCELLUS: 'Tis gone and will not answer.
BERNARDO: How now, Horatio! You tremble and look pale.
 Is not this something more than fantasy?
 What think you on't?　　　　　　　　　　　　55
HORATIO: Before my God, I might not this believe

---

3. Confirm the testimony of.　　　　5. He.
4. Polestar.

Without the sensible[6] and true avouch
Of mine own eyes.

MARCELLUS: Is it not like the king?

HORATIO: As thou art to thyself.
Such was the very armor he had on   60
When he the ambitious Norway combated.
So frowned he once when, in an angry parle,[7]
He smote the sledded Polacks on the ice.
'Tis strange.

MARCELLUS: Thus twice before, and jump[8] at this dead hour,
With martial stalk hath he gone by our watch.   65

HORATIO: In what particular thought to work I know not,
But in the gross and scope of mine opinion,
This bodes some strange eruption to our state.

MARCELLUS: Good now, sit down, and tell me he that knows,
Why this same strict and most observant watch   70
So nightly toils the subject[9] of the land,
And why such daily cast of brazen cannon
And foreign mart for implements of war;
Why such impress of shipwrights, whose sore task
Does not divide the Sunday from the week.   75
What might be toward that this sweaty haste
Doth make the night joint-laborer with the day?
Who is't that can inform me?

HORATIO: That can I.
At last, the whisper goes so. Our last king,
Whose image even but now appeared to us,   80
Was as you know by Fortinbras of Norway,
Thereto pricked on by a most emulate pride,
Dared to the combat; in which our valiant Hamlet
(For so this side of our known world esteemed him)
Did slay this Fortinbras; who by a sealed compact   85
Well ratified by law and heraldry,
Did forfeit, with his life, all those his lands
Which he stood seized of,[1] to the conqueror;

6. Perceptible.   9. People.
7. Parley, debate.   1. Possessed.
8. Precisely.

Against the which a moiety competent[2]
Was gagéd[3] by our king; which had returned   90
To the inheritance of Fortinbras,
Had he been vanquisher; as, by the same covenant
And carriage of the article designed,
His fell to Hamlet. Now, sir, young Fortinbras,
Of unimprovéd[4] mettle hot and full,   95
Hath in the skirts of Norway here and there
Sharked up a list of lawless resolutes
For food and diet to some enterprise
That hath a stomach in't; which is no other,
As it doth well appear unto our state,   100
But to recover of us by strong hand
And terms compulsatory, those foresaid lands
So by his father lost; and this, I take it,
Is the main motive of our preparations,
The source of this our watch, and the chief head   105
Of this post-haste and romage[5] in the land.
BERNARDO: I think it be no other but e'en so.
Well may it sort[6] that this portentous figure
Comes arméd through our watch so like the king
That was and is the question of these wars.   110
HORATIO: A mote[7] it is to trouble the mind's eye.
In the most high and palmy state of Rome,
A little ere the mightiest Julius fell,
The graves stood tenantless, and the sheeted dead
Did squeak and gibber in the Roman streets;   115
As stars with trains of fire, and dews of blood,
Disasters in the sun; and the moist star,[8]
Upon whose influence Neptune's empire stands,
Was sick almost to doomsday with eclipse.
And even the like precurse[9] of feared events,   120
As harbingers preceding still the fates

2. Portion of similar value.   6. Chance.
3. Pledged.   7. Speck of dust.
4. Unproved.   8. The moon.
5. Stir.   9. Precursor.

And prologue to the omen coming on,
Have heaven and earth together demonstrated
Unto our climatures[1] and countrymen.
    [*Enter* GHOST.]
But soft, behold, lo where it comes again!   125
I'll cross it though it blast me.—Stay, illusion.
    [*It spreads (its) arms.*]
If thou hast any sound or use of voice,
Speak to me.
If there be any good thing to be done,
That may to thee do ease, and grace to me,   130
Speak to me.
If thou art privy to thy country's fate,
Which happily foreknowing may avoid,
O, speak!
Or if thou hast uphoarded in thy life   135
Extorted treasure in the womb of earth,
For which, they say, you spirits oft walk in death,
    [*The cock crows.*]
    Speak of it. Stay, and speak. Stop it, Marcellus.
MARCELLUS: Shall I strike at it with my partisan?[2]
HORATIO: Do, if it will not stand.
BERNARDO: 'Tis here.
HORATIO: 'Tis here.   140
MARCELLUS: 'Tis gone.   [*Exit* GHOST.]
    We do it wrong, being so majestical,
    To offer it the show of violence;
    For it is as the air, invulnerable,
    And our vain blows malicious mockery.   145
BERNARDO: It was about to speak when the cock crew.
HORATIO: And then it started like a guilty thing
    Upon a fearful summons. I have heard
    The cock, that is the trumpet to the morn;
    Doth with his lofty and shrill-sounding throat   150
    Awake the god of day, and at his warning,
    Whether in sea or fire, in earth or air,

---

1. Regions.   2. Halberd.

Th' extravagant and erring[3] spirit hies
To his confine; and of the truth herein
This present object made probation.[4]   155
MARCELLUS: It faded on the crowing of the cock.
  Some say that ever 'gainst that season comes
  Wherein our Savior's birth is celebrated,
  This bird of dawning singeth all night long,
  And then, they say, no spirit dare stir abroad,   160
  The nights are wholesome, then no planets strike,
  No fairy takes,[5] nor witch hath power to charm,
  So hallowed and so gracious is that time.
HORATIO: So have I heard and do in part believe it.
  But look, the morn in russet mantle clad   165
  Walks o'er the dew of yon high eastward hill.
  Break we our watch up, and by my advice
  Let us impart what we have seen tonight
  Unto young Hamlet, for upon my life
  This spirit, dumb to us, will speak to him.   170
  Do you consent we shall acquaint him with it,
  As needful in our loves, fitting our duty?
MARCELLUS: Let's do't, I pray, and I this morning know
  Where we shall find him most conveniently.   [*Exeunt.*]

SCENE 2

A chamber of state. Enter KING CLAUDIUS, QUEEN GERTRUDE,
HAMLET, POLONIUS, LAERTES, VOLTEMAND, CORNELIUS *and other
members of the court.*

KING: Though yet of Hamlet our dear brother's death
  The memory be green, and that it us befitted
  To bear our hearts in grief, and our whole kingdom
  To be contracted in one brow of woe,
  Yet so far hath discretion fought with nature   5
  That we with wisest sorrow think on him,
  Together with remembrance of ourselves.
  Therefore our sometime sister, now our queen,

3. Wandering out of bounds.   5. Enchants.
4. Proof.

Th' imperial jointress[1] to this warlike state,
Have we, as 'twere with a defeated joy, 10
With an auspicious and a dropping eye,
With mirth in funeral, and with dirge in marriage,
In equal scale weighing delight and dole,
Taken to wife; nor have we herein barred
Your better wisdoms, which have freely gone 15
With this affair along. For all, our thanks.
Now follows that you know young Fortinbras,
Holding a weak supposal of our worth,
Or thinking by our late dear brother's death
Our state to be disjoint and out of frame, 20
Colleaguéd with this dream of his advantage,
He hath not failed to pester us with message
Importing the surrender of those lands
Lost by his father, with all bonds of law,
To our most valiant brother. So much for him. 25
Now for ourself, and for this time of meeting,
Thus much the business is: we have here writ
To Norway, uncle of young Fortinbras—
Who, impotent and bedrid, scarcely hears
Of this his nephew's purpose—to suppress 30
His further gait[2] herein, in that the levies,
The lists, and full proportions are all made
Out of his subject; and we here dispatch
You, good Cornelius, and you, Voltemand,
For bearers of this greeting to old Norway, 35
Giving to you no further personal power
To business with the king, more than the scope
Of these dilated[3] articles allow.
Farewell, and let your haste commend your duty.

CORNELIUS: ⎱ In that, and all things will we show our duty. 40
VOLTEMAND: ⎰
KING: We doubt it nothing, heartily farewell.

---

1. A widow who holds a *jointure*, or life
interest, in the estate of her deceased husband.

2. Progress.

3. Fully expressed.

[Exeunt VOLTEMAND *and* CORNELIUS.]

And now, Laertes, what's the news with you?
You told us of some suit. What is't, Laertes?
You cannot speak of reason to the Dane
And lose your voice. What wouldst thou beg, Laertes,   45
That shall not be my offer, not thy asking?
The head is not more native to the heart,
The hand more instrumental[4] to the mouth,
Than is the throne of Denmark to thy father.
What wouldst thou have, Laertes?

LAERTES: My dread lord,   50
Your leave and favor to return to France,
From whence, though willingly, I came to Denmark
To show my duty in your coronation,
Yet now I must confess, that duty done,
My thoughts and wishes bend again toward France,   55
And bow them to your gracious leave and pardon.

KING: Have you your father's leave? What says Polonius?

POLONIUS: He hath, my lord, wrung from me my slow leave
By laborsome petition, and at last
Upon his will I sealed my hard consent.   60
I do beseech you give him leave to go.

KING: Take thy fair hour, Laertes. Time be thine,
And thy best graces spend it at thy will.
But now, my cousin[5] Hamlet, and my son—

HAMLET: [*Aside.*] A little more than kin, and less than kind.   65

KING: How is it that the clouds still hang on you?

HAMLET: Not so, my lord. I am too much in the sun.

QUEEN: Good Hamlet, cast thy nighted color off,
And let thine eye look like a friend on Denmark.
Do not for ever with thy vailéd lids[6]   70
Seek for thy noble father in the dust.
Thou know'st 'tis common—all that lives must die,
Passing through nature to eternity.

HAMLET: Ay, madam, it is common.

4. Serviceable.   6. Lowered eyes.
5. Used here as a general term of kinship.

QUEEN: If it be,
    Why seems it so particular with thee?   75
HAMLET: Seems, madam? Nay, it is. I know not "seems."
    'Tis not alone my inky cloak, good mother,
    Nor customary suits of solemn black,
    Nor windy suspiration of forced breath,
    No, nor the fruitful river in the eye,   80
    Nor the dejected havior[7] of the visage,
    Together with all forms, moods, shapes of grief,
    That can denote me truly. These indeed seem,
    For they are actions that a man might play,
    But I have that within which passes show—   85
    These but the trappings and the suits of woe.
KING: 'Tis sweet and commendable in your nature, Hamlet,
    To give these mourning duties to your father,
    But you must know your father lost a father,
    That father lost, lost his, and the survivor bound   90
    In filial obligation for some term
    To do obsequious sorrow. But to persever[8]
    In obstinate condolement is a course
    Of impious stubbornness. 'Tis unmanly grief.
    It shows a will most incorrect to heaven,   95
    A heart unfortified, a mind impatient,
    An understanding simple and unschooled.
    For what we know must be, and is as common
    As any the most vulgar thing to sense,
    Why should we in our peevish opposition   100
    Take it to heart? Fie, 'tis a fault[9] to heaven,
    A fault against the dead, a fault to nature,
    To reason most absurd, whose common theme
    Is death of fathers, and who still hath cried,
    From the first corse[1] till he that died today,   105
    "This must be so." We pray you throw to earth
    This unprevailing woe and think of us
    As of a father, for let the world take note

7. Appearance.   9. Insult.
    8. Persevere. *Obsequious:* Suited for fu-   1. Corpse.
neral obsequies, or ceremonies.

You are the most immediate[2] to our throne,
And with no less nobility of love   110
Than that which dearest father hears his son
Do I impart toward you. For your intent
In going back to School in Wittenberg,
It is most retrograde[3] to out desire,
And we beseech you, bend you to remain   115
Here in the cheer and comfort of our eye,
Our chiefest courtier, cousin, and our son
QUEEN: Let not they mother lose her prayers, Hamlet.
   I pray thee stay with us, go not to Wittenberg.
HAMLET: I shall in all my best obey you madam.   120
KING: Why, 'tis a loving and a fair reply.
   Be as ourself in Denmark. Madam, come.
   This gentle and unforced accord of Hamlet
   Sits smiling to my heart, in grace whereof,
   No jocund health that Denmark drinks today   125
   But the great cannon to the clouds shall tell,
   And the king's rouse the heaven shall bruit[4] again,
   Respeaking earthly thunder. Come away.
                    [*Flourish. Exeunt all but* HAMLET.]
HAMLET: O, that this too too solid flesh would melt,
   Thaw, and resolve itself into a dew,   130
   Or that the Everlasting had not fixed
   His canon[5] 'gainst self-slaughter. O God, God,
   How weary, stale, flat, and unprofitable
   Seem to me all the uses of this world!
   Fie on't, ah, fie, 'tis an unweeded garden   135
   That grows to seed. Things rank and gross in nature
   Possess it merely.[6] That it should come to this,
   But two months dead, nay, not so much, not two.
   So excellent a king, that was to this
   Hyperion to a satyr,[7] so loving to my mother,   140

2. Next in line.
3. Contrary.
4. Echo. *Rouse:* carousal.
5. Law.

6. Entirely.
7. In Greek mythology, a lecherous creature, half man and half goat, in contrast to
Hyperion, a god.

That he might not beteem[8] the winds of heaven
Visit her face too roughly. Heaven and earth,
Must I remember? Why, she would hang on him
As if increase of appetite had grown
By what it fed on, and yet, within a month—   145
Let me not think on't. Frailty, thy name is woman—
A little month, or ere those shoes were old
With which she followed my poor father's body
Like Niobe,[9] all tears, why she, even she—
O God, a beast that wants discourse of reason   150
Would have mourned longer—married with my uncle,
My father's brother, but no more like my father
Than I to Hercules.[1] Within a month,
Ere yet the salt of most unrighteous tears
Had left the flushing in her gallèd eyes,   155
She married. O, most wicked speed, to post
With such dexterity to incestuous sheets!
It is not, nor it cannot come to good.
But break my heart, for I must hold my tongue.
    [*Enter* HORATIO, MARCELLUS, *and* BERNARDO.]
HORATIO: Hail to your lordship!
HAMLET: I am glad to see you well.   160
    Horatio—or I do forget myself.
HORATIO: The same, my lord, and your poor servant ever.
HAMLET: Sir, my good friend, I'll change[2] that name with you.
    And what make you from Wittenberg, Horatio?
    Marcellus?   165
MARCELLUS: My good lord!
HAMLET: I am very glad to see you. [*To* BERNARDO.] Good
    even, sir.—
    But what, in faith, make you from Wittenberg?
HORATIO: A truant disposition, good my lord.
HAMLET: I would not hear your enemy say so,   170
    Nor shall you do my ear that violence

8. Permit.
9. In Greek mythology, Niobe was
turned to stone while weeping over the
death of her fourteen children.

1. The demigod Hercules was noted for
his strength and a series of spectacular
labors.
2. Exchange.

To make it truster of your own report
Against yourself. I know you are no truant.
But what is you affair in Elsinore?
We'll teach you to drink deep ere you depart.   175
HORATIO: My lord, I came to see your father's funeral.
HAMLET: I prithee do not mock me, fellow-student,
  I think it was to see my mother's wedding.
HORATIO: Indeed, my lord, it followed hard upon.
HAMLET: Thrift, thrift, Horatio. The funeral-baked meats   180
  Did coldly furnish forth the marriage tables.
  Would I had met my dearest[3] foe in heaven
  Or ever I had seen that day, Horatio!
  My father—methinks I see my father.
HORATIO: Where, my lord?
HAMLET: In my mind's eye, Horatio.   185
HORATIO: I saw him once, 'a was a goodly king.
HAMLET: 'A was a man, take him for all in all,
  I shall not look upon his like again.
HORATIO: My lord, I think I saw him yesternight.
HAMLET: Saw who?   190
HORATIO: My lord, the king your father.
HAMLET: The king my father?
HORATIO: Season your admiration[4] for a while
  With an attent ear till I may deliver[5]
  Upon the witness of these gentlemen
  This marvel to you.
HAMLET: For God's love, let me hear!   195
HORATIO: Two nights together had these gentlemen,
  Marcellus and Bernardo, on their watch
  In the dead waste and middle of the night
  Been thus encountered. A figure like your father,
  Arméd at point exactly, cap-a-pe,[6]   200
  Appears before them, and with solemn march
  Goes slow and stately by them. Thrice he walked
  By their oppressed and fear-surpriséd eyes

3. Bitterest.
4. Moderate your wonder.
5. Relate. *Attent:* attentive.
6. From head to toe. *Exactly:* completely.

Within his truncheon's[7] length, whilst they, distilled
Almost to jelly with the act of fear,   205
Stand dumb and speak not to him. This to me
In dreadful secrecy impart they did,
And I with them the third night kept the watch,
Where, as they had delivered, both in time,
Form of the thing, each word made true and good,   210
The apparition comes. I knew your father.
These hands are not more like.

HAMLET: But where was this?

MARCELLUS: My lord, upon the platform where we watch.

HAMLET: Did you not speak to it?

HORATIO: My lord, I did,
But answer made it none. Yet once methought   215
It lifted up it head and did address
Itself to motion, like as it would speak;
But even then the morning cock crew loud,
And at the sound it shrunk in haste away
And vanished from our sight.

HAMLET: 'Tis very strange.   220

HORATIO: As I do live, my honored lord, 'tis true,
And we did think it writ down in our duty
To let you know of it.

HAMLET: Indeed, sirs, but
This troubles me. Hold you the watch tonight?

ALL: We do, my lord.

HAMLET: Armed, say you?

ALL: Armed, my lord.   225

HAMLET: From top to toe?

ALL: My lord, from head to foot.

HAMLET: Then saw you not his face.

HORATIO: O yes, my lord, he wore his beaver[8] up.

HAMLET: What, looked he frowningly?

HORATIO: A countenance more in sorrow than in anger.   230

HAMLET: Pale or red?

HORATIO: Nay, very pale.

---

7. His baton of office.   8. His helmet's visor.

HAMLET: And fixed his eyes upon you?
HORATIO: Most constantly.
HAMLET: I would I had been there.
HORATIO: It would have much amazed you.
HAMLET: Very like.
   Stayed it long?   235
HORATIO: While one with moderate haste might tell a hundred.
BOTH: Longer, longer.
HORATIO: Not when I saw't.
HAMLET: His beard was grizzled, no?
HORATIO: It was as I have seen it in his life,
   A sable silvered.
HAMLET: I will watch tonight.   240
   Perchance 'twill walk again.
HORATIO: I warr'nt it will.
HAMLET: If it assume my noble father's person,
   I'll speak to it though hell itself should gape[9]
   And bid me hold my peace. I pray you all,
   If you have hitherto concealed this sight,   245
   Let it be tenable[1] in your silence still,
   And whatsomever else shall hap tonight,
   Give it an understanding but no tongue.
   I will requite your loves. So fare you well.
   Upon the platform 'twixt eleven and twelve   250
   I'll visit you.
ALL: Our duty to your honor.
HAMLET: Your loves, as mine to you. Farewell.
                       [*Exeunt all but* HAMLET.]
  My father's spirit in arms? All is not well.
  I doubt[2] some foul play. Would the night were come!
  Till then sit still, my soul. Foul deeds will rise,   255
  Though all the earth o'erwhelm them, to men's eyes.
                             [*Exit.*]

9. Open (its mouth) wide.   2. Suspect.
1. Held.

SCENE 3
The dwelling of POLONIUS. *Enter* LAERTES *and* OPHELIA.

LAERTES: My necessaries are embarked. Farewell.
   And, sister, as the winds give benefit
   And convoy is assistant,[1] do not sleep,
   But let me hear from you.
OPHELIA: Do you doubt that?
LAERTES: For Hamlet, and the trifling of his favor,   5
   Hold it a fashion and a toy in blood,
   A violet in the youth of primy[2] nature,
   Forward, not permanent, sweet, not lasting,
   The perfume and suppliance of a minute,
   No more.
OPHELIA: No more but so?
LAERTES: Think it no more.   10
   For nature crescent[3] does not grow alone
   In thews and bulk, but as this temple[4] waxes
   The inward service of the mind and soul
   Grows wide withal. Perhaps he loves you now,
   And now no soil nor cautel[5] doth besmirch   15
   The virtue of his will, but you must fear,
   His greatness weighted,[6] his will is not his own,
   For he himself is subject to his birth.
   He may not, as unvalued persons do,
   Carve for himself, for on his choice depends   20
   The safety and health of this whole state,
   And therefore must his choice be circumscribed
   Unto the voice[7] and yielding of that body
   Whereof he is the head. Then if he says he loves you,
   It fits your wisdom so far to believe it   25
   As he in his particular act and place
   May give his saying deed,[8] which is no further

---

1. Means of transport is available.
2. Of the spring.
3. Growing.
4. Body.
5. Deceit.

6. Rank considered.
7. Assent.
8. *May give . . . deed:* can do what he promises (that is, marry Ophelia).

Than the main voice of Denmark goes withal.
Then weigh what loss your honor may sustain
If with too credent ear you list[9] his songs,   30
Or lose your heart, or your chaste treasure open
To his unmastered importunity.
Fear it, Ophelia, fear it, my dear sister,
And keep you in the rear of your affection,
Out of the shot and danger of desire.   35
The chariest[1] maid is prodigal enough
If she unmask her beauty to the moon.
Virtue itself scapes not calumnious strokes.
The canker galls the infants[2] of the spring
Too oft before their buttons be disclosed,[3]   40
And in the morn and liquid dew of youth
Contagious blastments[4] are most imminent.
Be wary then; best safety lies in fear.
Youth to itself rebels, though none else near.
OPHELIA: I shall the effect of this good lesson keep   45
  As watchman to my heart. But, good my brother,
  Do not as some ungracious pastors do,
  Show me the steep and thorny way to heaven,
  Whiles like a puffed and reckless libertine
  Himself the primrose path of dalliance treads   50
  And recks not his own rede.[5]
LAERTES: O, fear me not.
    [*Enter* POLONIUS.]
  I stay too long. But here my father comes.
  A double blessing is a double grace;
  Occasion smiles upon a second leave.
POLONIUS: Yet here, Laertes? Aboard, aboard, for shame!   55
  The wind sits in the shoulder of your sail,
  And you are stayed for. There—my blessing with thee,
  And these few precepts in thy memory
  Look thou character.[6] Give thy thoughts no tongue,

---

9. Too credulous an ear you listen to.   4. Blights.
1. Most circumspect.   5. Heeds not his own advice.
2. The rose caterpillar injures the shoots.   6. Write.
3. Before the buds blossom.

Nor any unproportioned thought his act.   60
Be thou familiar, but by no means vulgar.
Those friends thou hast, and their adoption tried,
Grapple them unto thy soul with hoops of steel;
But do not dull[7] thy palm with entertainment
Of each new-hatched, unfledged comrade. Beware   65
Of entrance to a quarrel, but being in,
Bear't that th' opposéd[8] may beware of thee.
Give every man thy ear, but few thy voice;[9]
Take each man's censure, but reserve thy judgment.
Costly thy habit as thy purse can buy,   70
But not expressed in fancy; rich not gaudy,
For the apparel oft proclaims the man,
And they in France of the best rank and station
Are of a most select and generous chief[1] in that.
Neither a borrower nor a lender be,   75
For loan oft loses both itself and friend,
And borrowing dulls th' edge of husbandry.
This above all, to thine own self be true,
And it must follow as the night the day
Thou canst not then be false to any man.   80
Farewell. My blessing season this in thee!
LAERTES: Most humbly do I take my leave, my lord.
POLONIUS: The time invests you. Go, your servants tend.[2]
LAERTES: Farewell, Ophelia, and remember well
　What I have said to you.
OPHELIA:　　　　　　　　'Tis in my memory locked,   85
　And you yourself shall keep the key of it.
LAERTES: Farewell.   [*Exit.*]
POLONIUS: What is't, Ophelia, he hath said to you?
OPHELIA: So please you, something touching the Lord Hamlet.
POLONIUS: Marry, well bethought.   90
　'Tis told me he hath very oft of late
　Given private time to you, and you yourself
　Have of your audience been most free and bounteous.

7. Make callous.　　　　　　　　1. Eminence.
8. Conduct it so that the opponent.　2. Await.
9. Approval.

If it be so—as so 'tis put on me,
And that in way of caution—I must tell you,   95
You do not understand yourself so clearly
As it behooves my daughter and your honor.
What is between you? Give me up the truth.
OPHELIA: He hath, my lord, of late made many tenders
  Of his affection to me.   100
POLONIUS: Affection? Pooh! You speak like a green girl,
  Unsifted in such perilous circumstance.
  Do you believe his tenders, as you call them?
OPHELIA: I do not know, my lord, what I should think.
POLONIUS: Marry, I will teach you. Think yourself a baby   105
  That you have ta'en these tenders for true pay
  Which are not sterling. Tender yourself more dearly,
  Or (not to crack the wind of the poor phrase,
  Running it thus) you'll tender me a fool.
OPHELIA: My lord, he hath importuned me with love   110
  In honorable fashion.
POLONIUS: Ay, fashion you may call it. Go to, go to.
OPHELIA: And hath given countenance[3] to his speech, my lord,
  With almost all the holy vows of heaven.
POLONIUS: Ay, springes to catch woodcocks.[4] I do know,   115
  When the blood burns, how prodigal the soul
  Lends the tongue vows. These blazes, daughter,
  Giving more light than heat, extinct in both
  Even in their promise, as it is a-making,
  You must not take for fire. From this time   120
  Be something scanter of your maiden presence.
  Set your entreatments[5] at a higher rate
  Than a command to parle. For Lord Hamlet,
  Believe so much in him that he is young,
  And with a larger tether may he walk   125
  Than may be given you. In few, Ophelia,
  Do not believe his vows, for they are brokers,[6]
  Not of that dye which their investments[7] show,

3. Confirmation.
4. Snares to catch gullible birds.
5. Negotiations before a surrender.
6. Panderers.
7. Garments.

But mere implorators[8] of unholy suits,
Breathing like sanctified and pious bawds,   130
The better to beguile. This is for all:
I would not, in plain terms, from this time forth
Have you so slander any moment leisure
As to give words or talk with the Lord Hamlet.
Look to't, I charge you. Come your ways.   135
OPHELIA: I shall obey, my lord.   [*Exeunt.*]

SCENE 4
The guard station. Enter HAMLET, HORATIO *and* MARCELLUS.

HAMLET: The air bites shrewdly;[1] it is very cold.
HORATIO: It is a nipping and an eager[2] air.
HAMLET: What hour now?
HORATIO: I think it lacks of twelve.
MARCELLUS: No, it is struck.
HORATIO: Indeed? I heard it not.
    It then draws near the season   5
    Wherein the spirit held his wont to walk.
        [*A flourish of trumpets, and two pieces go off.*]
    What does this mean, my lord?
HAMLET: The king doth wake tonight and takes his rouse,
    Keeps wassail, and the swagg'ring up-spring[3] reels,
    And as he drains his draughts of Rhenish[4] down,   10
    The kettledrum and trumpet thus bray out
    The triumph of his pledge.
HORATIO: Is it a custom?
HAMLET: Ay, marry, is't,
    But to my mind, though I am native here
    And to the manner born, it is a custom   15
    More honored in the breach than the observance.
    This heavy-headed revel east and west
    Makes us traduced and taxed of other nations.
    They clepe[5] us drunkards, and with swinish phrase

8. Solicitors.   3. A German dance.
1. Sharply.   4. Rhine wine.
2. Keen.   5. Call.

Soil our addition,[6] and indeed it takes   20
From our achievements, though performed at height,
The pith and marrow of our attribute.[7]
So oft it chances in particular men,
That for some vicious mole of nature[8] in them,
As in their birth, wherein they are not guilty   25
(Since nature cannot choose his origin),
By their o'ergrowth of some complexion,
Oft breaking down the pales[9] and forts of reason,
Or by some habit that too much o'er-leavens
The form of plausive[1] manners—that these men,   30
Carrying, I say, the stamp of one defect,
Being nature's livery or fortune's star,
His virtues else, be they as pure as grace,
As infinite as man may undergo,
Shall in the general censure take corruption   35
From that particular fault. The dram of evil
Doth all the noble substance often doubt[2]
To his own scandal.
          [*Enter* GHOST.]
HORATIO: Look, my lord, it comes.
HAMLET: Angels and ministers of grace defend us!
Be thou a spirit of health or goblin damned,   40
Bring with thee airs from heaven or blasts from hell,
Be thy intents wicked or charitable,
Thou com'st in such a questionable[3] shape
That I will speak to thee. I'll call thee Hamlet,
King, father, royal Dane. O, answer me!   45
Let me not burst in ignorance, but tell
Why thy canonized[4] bones, hearséd in death,
Have burst their cerements;[5] why the sepulchre
Wherein we saw thee quietly inurned
Hath oped his ponderous and marble jaws   50

6. Reputation.
7. Honor.
8. Some natural, vice-related blemish.
9. Defensive palisade or fence.
1. Pleasing.

2. Extinguish.
3. Prompting question.
4. Buried in accordance with church canons.
5. Burial cloths.

To cast thee up again. What may this mean
That thou, dead corse, again in complete steel[6]
Revisits thus the glimpses of the moon,
Making night hideous, and we fools of nature
So horridly to shake our disposition   55
With thoughts beyond the reaches of our souls?
Say, why is this? wherefore? What should we do?
　　[GHOST *beckons*.]
HORATIO: It beckons you to go away with it,
　As if it some impartment[7] did desire
　To you alone.
MARCELLUS:　　　Look with what courteous action   60
　It waves you to a more removéd[8] ground.
　But do not go with it.
HORATIO:　　　　　No, by no means.
HAMLET: It will not speak; then I will follow it.
HORATIO: Do not, my lord.
HAMLET:　　　　　　Why, what should be the fear?
　I do not set my life at a pin's fee,[9]   65
　And for my soul, what can it do to that,
　Being a thing immortal as itself?
　It waves me forth again. I'll follow it.
HORATIO: What if it tempt you toward the flood, my lord,
　Or to the dreadful summit of the cliff   70
　That beetles[1] o'er his base into the sea,
　And there assume some other horrible form,
　Which might deprive your sovereignty of reason
　And draw you into madness? Think of it.
　The very place puts toys of desperation,[2]   75
　Without more motive, into every brain
　That looks so many fathoms to the sea
　And hears it roar beneath.
HAMLET:　　　　　　It wafts me still.
　Go on. I'll follow thee.
MARCELLUS: You shall not go, my lord.

---

6. Armor.
7. Communication.
8. Beckons you to a more distant.

9. Price.
1. Juts out.
2. Desperate fancies.

HAMLET: Hold off your hands.   80
HORATIO: Be ruled. You shall not go.
HAMLET: My fate cries out
  And makes each petty artere³ in this body
  As hardy as the Nemean lion's⁴ nerve.
  Still am I called. Unhand me, gentlemen.
  By heaven, I'll make a ghost of him that lets⁵ me.   85
  I say, away! Go on. I'll follow thee.
                              [*Exeunt* GHOST *and* HAMLET.]
HORATIO: He waxes desperate with imagination.
MARCELLUS: Let's follow. 'Tis not fit thus to obey him.
HORATIO: Have after. To what issue will this come?
MARCELLUS: Something is rotten in the state of Denmark.   90
HORATIO: Heaven will direct it.
MARCELLUS: Nay, let's follow him.
                                          [*Exeunt.*]

SCENE 5
  Near the guard station. Enter GHOST *and* HAMLET.

HAMLET: Whither wilt thou lead me? Speak. I'll go no further.
GHOST: Mark me.
HAMLET: I will.
GHOST: My hour is almost come,
  When I to sulph'rous and tormenting flames
  Must render up myself.
HAMLET: Alas, poor ghost!
GHOST: Pity me not, but lend thy serious hearing   5
  To what I shall unfold.
HAMLET: Speak. I am bound to hear.
GHOST: So art thou to revenge, when thou shalt hear.
HAMLET: What?
GHOST: I am thy father's spirit,
  Doomed for a certain term to walk the night,   10
  And for the day confined to fast¹ in fires,

3. Artery.   5. Hinders.
4. A mythological lion slain by Hercules.   1. Do penance.

Till the foul crimes done in my days of nature[2]
Are burnt and purged away. But that I am forbid
To tell the secrets of my prison house,
I could a tale unfold whose lightest word   15
Would harrow up thy soul, freeze thy young blood,
Make thy two eyes like stars start from their spheres,
Thy knotted and combinéd[3] locks to part,
And each particular hair to stand an end,
Like quills upon the fretful porpentine.[4]   20
But this eternal blazon[5] must not be
To ears of flesh and blood. List, list, O, list!
If thou didst every thy dear father love—
HAMLET: O God!
GHOST: Revenge his foul and most unnatural murder.   25
HAMLET: Murder!
GHOST: Murder most foul, as in the best it is,
   But this most foul, strange, and unnatural.
HAMLET: Haste me to know't, that I, with wings as swift
   As meditation or the thoughts of love,   30
   May sweep to my revenge.
GHOST: I find thee apt.
   And duller shouldst thou be than the fat weed
   That rots itself in ease on Lethe wharf,—[6]
   Wouldst thou not stir in this. Now, Hamlet, hear.
   'Tis given out that, sleeping in my orchard,   35
   A serpent stung me. So the whole ear of Denmark
   Is by a forgéd process[7] of my death
   Rankly abused. But know, thou noble youth,
   The serpent that did sting thy father's life
   Now wears his crown.
HAMLET: O my prophetic soul!   40
   My uncle!
GHOST: Ay, that incestuous, that adulterate beast,
   With witchcraft of his wits, with traitorous gifts—

2. That is, while I was alive.
3. Tangled.
4. Porcupine.
5. Description of eternity.

6. The asphodel that rots on the bank of Lethe, the river of forgetfulness in the classical underworld.
7. False report.

O wicked wit and gifts that have the power
So to seduce!—won to his shameful lust   45
The will of my most seeming virtuous queen.
O Hamlet, what a falling off was there,
From me, whose love was of that dignity
That it went hand in hand even with the vow
I made to her in marriage, and to decline[8]   50
Upon a wretch whose natural gifts were poor
To those of mine!
But virtue as it never will be moved,
Though lewdness court it in a shape of heaven,
So lust, though to a radiant angel linked,   55
Will sate itself in a celestial bed
And prey on garbage.
But soft, methinks I scent the morning air.
Brief let me be. Sleeping within my orchard,
My custom always of the afternoon,   60
Upon my secure hour thy uncle stole,
With juice of cursed hebona[9] in a vial,
And in the porches of my ears did pour
The leperous distilment, whose effect
Holds such an enmity with blood of man   65
That swift as quicksilver it courses through
The natural gates and alleys of the body,
And with a sudden vigor it doth posset[1]
And curd, like eager[2] droppings into milk,
The thin and wholesome blood. So did it mine,   70
And a most instant tetter barked about[3]
Most lazar-like[4] with vile and loathsome crust
All my smooth body.
Thus was I sleeping by a brother's hand
Of life, of crown, of queen at once dispatched,   75
Cut off even in the blossoms of my sin,
Unhouseled, disappointed, unaneled,[5]

8. Sink.
9. A poison.
1. Coagulate.
2. Acid. *Curd:* curdle.

3. Covered like bark. *Tetter:* a skin disease.
4. Leperlike.
5. Without having received the Eucharist, made a final confession, or been given last rites.

No reck'ning made, but sent to my account
With all my imperfections on my head.
O, horrible! O, horrible! most horrible!   80
If thou hast nature in thee, bear it not.
Let not the royal bed of Denmark be
A couch of luxury[6] and damnéd incest.
But howsomever thou pursues this act,
Taint not thy mind, nor let thy soul contrive   85
Against thy mother aught. Leave her to heaven,
And to those thorns that in her bosom lodge
To prick and sting her. Fare thee well at once.
The glowworm shows the matin[7] to be near,
And gins to pale his uneffectual fire.   90
Adieu, adieu, adieu. Remember me.   [*Exit.*]
HAMLET: O all you host of heaven! O earth! What else?
And shall I couple hell? O, fie! Hold, hold, my heart,
And you, my sinews, grow not instant old,
But bear me stiffly up. Remember thee?   95
Ay, thou poor ghost, whiles memory holds a seat
In this distracted globe.[8] Remember thee?
Yea, from the table[9] of my memory
I'll wipe away all trivial fond[1] records,
All saws of books, all forms, all pressures past   100
That youth and observation copied there,
And thy commandment all alone shall live
Within the book and volume of my brain,
Unmixed with baser matter. Yes, by heaven!
O most pernicious woman!   105
O villain, villain, smiling, damnéd villain!
My tables—meet it is I set it down
That one may smile, and smile, and be a villain.
At least I am sure it may be so in Denmark.
So, uncle, there you are. Now to my word:[2]   110
It is "Adieu, adieu. Remember me."
I have sworn't.

6. Lust.
7. Morning.
8. Skull.

9. Writing tablet.
1. Foolish.
2. For my motto.

[*Enter* HORATIO *and* MARCELLUS.]

HORATIO: My lord, my lord!

MARCELLUS: Lord Hamlet!

HORATIO: Heavens secure him!

HAMLET: So be it!

MARCELLUS: Illo, ho, ho, my lord!   115

HAMLET: Hillo, ho, ho, boy![3] Come, bird, come.

MARCELLUS: How is't, my noble lord?

HORATIO: What news, my lord?

HAMLET: O, wonderful!

HORATIO: Good my lord, tell it.

HAMLET: No, you will reveal it.

HORATIO: Not I, my lord, by heaven.

MARCELLUS: Nor I, my lord.   120

HAMLET: How say you then, would heart of man once think it?
   But you'll be secret?

BOTH: Ay, by heaven, my lord.

HAMLET: There's never a villain dwelling in all Denmark
   But he's an arrant knave.

HORATIO: There needs no ghost, my lord, come from the grave 125
   To tell us this.

HAMLET: Why, right, you are in the right,
   And so without more circumstance at all
   I hold it fit that we shake hands and part,
   You, as your business and desire shall point you,
   For every man hath business and desire   130
   Such as it is, and for my own poor part,
   Look you, I'll go pray.

HORATIO: These are but wild and whirling words, my lord.

HAMLET: I am sorry they offend you, heartily;
   Yes, faith, heartily.

HORATIO: There's no offence, my lord.   135

HAMLET: Yes, by Saint Patrick, but there is, Horatio,
   And much offence too. Touching this vision here,
   It is an honest ghost, that let me tell you.
   For your desire to know what is between us,

3. A falconer's cry.

O'ermaster't as you may. And now, good friends,   140
As you are friends, scholars, and soldiers,
Give me one poor request.
HORATIO: What is't, my lord? We will.
HAMLET: Never make known what you have seen tonight.
BOTH: My lord, we will not.
HAMLET: Nay, but swear't.
HORATIO: In faith,   145
My lord, not I.
MARCELLUS: Nor I, my lord, in faith.
HAMLET: Upon my sword.
MARCELLUS: We have sworn, my lord, already.
HAMLET: Indeed, upon my sword, indeed.
        [GHOST *cries under the stage.*]
GHOST: Swear.
HAMLET: Ha, ha, boy, say'st thou so? Art thou there,
        truepenny?[4]
        Come on. You hear this fellow in the cellarage.[5]   150
        Consent to swear.
HORATIO: Propose the oath, my lord.
HAMLET: Never to speak of this that you have seen,
        Swear by my sword.
GHOST: [*Beneath.*] Swear.
HAMLET: Hic et ubique?[6] Then we'll shift our ground.   155
        Come hither, gentlemen,
        And lay your hands again upon my sword.
        Swear by my sword
        Never to speak of this that you have heard.
GHOST: [*Beneath.*] Swear by his sword.   160
HAMLET: Well said, old mole! Canst work i' th' earth so fast?
        A worthy pioneer![7] Once more remove, good friends.
HORATIO: O day and night, but this is wondrous strange!
HAMLET: And therefore as a stranger give it welcome.
        There are more things in heaven and earth, Horatio,   165
        Than are dreamt of in your philosophy.

4. Trusty fellow.   6. Here and everywhere?
5. Below.   7. Soldier who digs trenches.

But come.
Here as before, never, so help you mercy,
How strange or odd some'er I bear myself
(As I perchance hereafter shall think meet   170
To put an antic[8] disposition on),
That you, at such times, seeing me, never shall,
With arms encumbered[9] thus, or this head-shake,
Or by pronouncing of some doubtful phrase,
As "Well, we know," or "We could, and if we would"   175
Or "If we list to speak," or "There be, and if they might"
Or such ambiguous giving out, to note
That you know aught of me—this do swear,
So grace and mercy at your most need help you.
GHOST: [*Beneath.*] Swear.   180
　　[*They swear.*]
HAMLET: Rest, rest, perturbéd spirit! So, gentlemen,
　With all my love I do commend me to you,
　And what so poor a man as Hamlet is
　May do t'express his love and friending[1] to you,
　God willing, shall not lack. Let us go in together,   185
　And still your fingers on your lips, I pray.
　The time is out of joint. O cursèd spite
　That ever I was born to set it right!
　Nay, come, let's go together.   [*Exeunt.*]

ACT II
SCENE 1
　The dwelling of POLONIUS. *Enter* POLONIUS *and* REYNALDO.

POLONIUS: Give him this money and these notes, Reynaldo.
REYNALDO: I will, my lord.
POLONIUS: You shall do marvellous wisely, good Reynaldo,
　Before you visit him, to make inquire[1]
　Of his behavior.
REYNALDO:　　　　My lord, I did intend it.   5

---

8. Mad.　　　　　　　　　　　1. Friendship.
9. Folded.　　　　　　　　　　1. Inquiry.

POLONIUS: Marry, well said, very well said. Look you, sir.
  Enquire me first what Danskers[2] are in Paris,
  And how, and who, what means, and where they keep,[3]
  What company, at what expense; and finding
  By this encompassment[4] and drift of question   10
  That they do know my son, come you more nearer
  Than your particular demands[5] will touch it.
  Take you as 'twere some distant knowledge of him,
  As thus, "I know his father and his friends,
  And in part him." Do you mark this, Reynaldo?   15
REYNALDO: Ay, very well, my lord.
POLONIUS: "And in part him, but," you may say, "not well,
  But if't be he I mean, he's very wild,
  Addicted so and so." And there put on him
  What forgeries you please; marry, none so rank[6]   20
  As may dishonor him. Take heed of that.
  But, sir, such wanton, wild, and usual slips
  As are companions noted and most known
  To youth and liberty.
REYNALDO: As gaming, my lord.
POLONIUS: Ay, or drinking, fencing, swearing,   25
  Quarrelling, drabbing[7]—you may go so far.
REYNALDO: My lord, that would dishonor him.
POLONIUS: Faith, no, as you may season it in the charge.[8]
  You must not put another scandal on him,
  That he is open to incontinency.[9]   30
  That's not my meaning. But breathe his faults so quaintly[1]
  That they may seem the taints of liberty,[2]
  The flash and outbreak of a fiery mind,
  A savageness in unreclaiméd[3] blood,
  Of general assault.[4]
REYNALDO: But, my good lord—   35

2. Danes.
3. Live.
4. Indirect means.
5. Direct questions.
6. Foul. *Forgeries:* lies.
7. Whoring.

8. Soften the accusation.
9. Sexual excess.
1. With delicacy.
2. Faults of freedom.
3. Untamed.
4. Touching everyone.

POLONIUS: Wherefore should you do this?

REYNALDO: Ay, my lord,
  I would know that.

POLONIUS: Marry, sir, here's my drift,
  And I believe it is a fetch of warrant.[5]
  You laying these slight sullies on my son,
  As 'twere a thing a little soiled wi' th' working,   40
  Mark you,
  Your party in converse,[6] him you would sound,
  Having ever seen in the prenominate[7] crimes
  The youth you breathe[8] of guilty, be assured
  He closes with you in this consequence,   45
  "Good sir," or so, or "friend," or "gentleman,"
  According to the phrase or the addition
  Of man and country.

REYNALDO: Very good, my lord.

POLONIUS: And then, sir, does 'a this—'a does—What was I
    about to say?
  By the mass, I was about to say something.   50
  Where did I leave?

REYNALDO: At "closes in the consequence."

POLONIUS: At "closes in the consequence"—ay, marry,
  He closes thus: "I know the gentleman.
  I saw him yesterday, or th' other day,   55
  Or then, or then, with such, or such, and as you say,
  There was 'a gaming, there o'ertook in's rouse,[9]
  There falling out at tennis," or perchance
  "I saw him enter such a house of sale,"
  Videlicet,[1] a brothel, or so forth.   60
  See you, now—
  Your bait of falsehood takes this carp of truth,
  And thus do we of wisdom and of reach,[2]
  With windlasses and with assays of bias,[3]
  By indirections find directions out;   65

5. Permissible trick.
6. Conversation.
7. Already named.
8. Speak.

9. Carousing.
1. Namely.
2. Ability.
3. Indirect tests.

So by my former lecture and advice
Shall you my son. You have me, have you not?
REYNALDO: My lord, I have.
POLONIUS: God b'wi' ye; fare ye well.
REYNALDO: Good my lord.
POLONIUS: Observe his inclination in yourself.   70
REYNALDO: I shall, my lord.
POLONIUS: And let him ply⁴ his music.
REYNALDO: Well, my lord.
POLONIUS: Farewell.   [*Exit* REYNALDO.]
    [*Enter* OPHELIA.]
            How now, Ophelia, what's the matter?
OPHELIA: O my lord, my lord, I have been so affrighted!
POLONIUS: With what, i' th' name of God?   75
OPHELIA: My lord, as I was sewing in my closet,⁵
  Lord Hamlet with his doublet all unbraced,⁶
  No hat upon his head, his stockings fouled,
  Ungartered and down-gyvéd⁷ to his ankle,
  Pale as his shirt, his knees knocking each other,   80
  And with a look so piteous in purport
  As if he had been looséd out of hell
  To speak of horrors—he comes before me.
POLONIUS: Mad for thy love?
OPHELIA: My lord, I do not know,
  But truly I do fear it.
POLONIUS: What said he?   85
OPHELIA: He took me by the wrist, and held me hard,
  Then goes he to the length of all his arm,
  And with his other hand thus o'er his brow,
  He falls to such perusal of my face
  As 'a would draw it. Long stayed he so.   90
  At last, a little shaking of mine arm,
  And thrice his head thus waving up and down,
  He raised a sigh so piteous and profound
  As it did seem to shatter all his bulk,⁸

4. Practice.
5. Chamber.
6. Jacket all unlaced.

7. Fallen down like fetters.
8. Body.

And end his being. That done, he lets me go, 95
And with his head over his shoulder turned
He seemed to find his way without his eyes,
For out adoors he went without their helps,
And to the last bended[9] their light on me.
POLONIUS: Come, go with me. I will go seek the king. 100
This is the very ecstasy of love,
Whose violent property fordoes[1] itself,
And leads the will to desperate undertakings
As oft as any passion under heaven
That does afflict our natures. I am sorry. 105
What, have you given him any hard words of late?
OPHELIA: No, my good lord, but as you did command
I did repel[2] his letters, and denied
His access to me.
POLONIUS:　　　That hath made him mad.
I am sorry that with better heed and judgment 110
I had not quoted[3] him. I feared he did but trifle,
And meant to wrack[4] thee; but beshrew my jealousy.
By heaven, it is as proper to our age
To cast beyond ourselves in our opinions
As it is common for the younger sort 115
To lack discretion. Come, go we to the king.
This must be known,[5] which being kept close, might move
More grief to hide than hate to utter love.
Come.　　　　　　　　　　　　　　　[Exeunt.]

SCENE 2

A public room. Enter KING, QUEEN, ROSENCRANTZ *and* GUILDEN-
STERN.

KING: Welcome, dear Rosencrantz and Guildenstern.
Moreover that[1] we much did long to see you,
The need we have to use you did provoke
Our hasty sending. Something have you heard

9. Directed.
1. Character destroys.
2. Refuse.
3. Observed.

4. Harm.
5. Revealed (to the king).
1. In addition to the fact that.

Of Hamlet's transformation—so call it,   5
Sith[2] nor th' exterior nor the inward man
Resembles that it was. What it should be,
More than his father's death, that thus hath put him
So much from th' understanding of himself,
I cannot deem of, I entreat you both   10
That, being of so young days[3] brought up with him,
And sith so neighbored to his youth and havior,[4]
That you vouchsafe your rest here in our court
Some little time, so by your companies
To draw him on to pleasures, and to gather   15
So much as from occasion you may glean,
Whether aught to us unknown afflicts him thus,
That opened lies within our remedy.
QUEEN: Good gentlemen, he hath much talked of you,
And sure I am two men there are not living   20
To whom he more adheres. If it will please you
To show us so much gentry[5] and good will
As to expend your time with us awhile
For the supply and profit of our hope,
Your visitation shall receive such thanks   25
As fits a king's remembrance.
ROSENCRANTZ: Both your majesties
Might, by the sovereign power you have of us,
Put your dread pleasures more into command
Than to entreaty.
GUILDENSTERN: But we both obey,
And here give up ourselves in the full bent[6]   30
To lay our service freely at your feet,
To be commanded.
KING: Thanks, Rosencrantz and gentle Guildenstern.
QUEEN: Thanks, Guildenstern and gentle Rosencrantz.
And I beseech you instantly to visit   35
My too much changed son. Go, some of you,
And bring these gentlemen where Hamlet is.

2. Since.   5. Courtesy.
3. From childhood.   6. Completely.
4. Behavior. *Neighbored:* closely allied.

GUILDENSTERN: Heavens make our presence and our practices
  Pleasant and helpful to him!
QUEEN: Ay, amen!
          [*Exeunt* ROSENCRANTZ *and* GUILDENSTERN.]
      [*Enter* POLONIUS.]
POLONIUS: Th' ambassadors from Norway, my good lord,   40
  Are joyfully returned.
KING: Thou still⁷ hast been the father of good news.
POLONIUS: Have I, my lord? I assure you, my good liege,
  I hold my duty as I hold my soul,
  Both to my God and to my gracious king;   45
  And I do think—or else this brain of mine
  Hunts not the trail of policy⁸ so sure
  As it hath used to do—that I have found
  The very cause of Hamlet's lunacy.
KING: O, speak of that, that do I long to hear.   50
POLONIUS: Give first admittance to th' ambassadors.
  My news shall be the fruit⁹ to that great feast.
KING: Thyself do grace to them, and bring them in.
                              [*Exit* POLONIUS.]
  He tells me, my dear Gertrude, he hath found
  The head and source of all your son's distemper.   55
QUEEN: I doubt it is no other but the main,
  His father's death and our o'erhasty marriage.
KING: Well, we shall sift¹ him.
      [*Enter Ambassadors* (VOLTEMAND *and* CORNELIUS) *with*
      POLONIUS.]
                              Welcome, my good friends,
  Say, Voltemand, what from our brother Norway?
VOLTEMAND: Most fair return of greetings and desires.   60
  Upon our first,² he sent out to suppress
  His nephew's levies, which to him appeared
  To be a preparation 'gainst the Polack,³
  But better looked into, he truly found
  It was against your highness, whereat grieved,   65

7. Ever.   1. Examine.
8. Statecraft.   2. That is, first appearance.
9. Dessert.   3. King of Poland.

That so his sickness, age, and impotence
Was falsely borne in hand, sends out arrests[4]
On Fortinbras, which he in brief obeys,
Receives rebuke from Norway, and in fine,
Makes vow before his uncle never more   70
To give th' assay[5] of arms against your majesty.
Whereon old Norway, overcome with joy,
Gives him three thousand crowns in annual fee,
And his commission to employ those soldiers,
So levied as before, against the Polack,   75
With an entreaty, herein further shown, [*Gives* CLAUDIUS *a*
    paper.]
That it might please you to give quiet pass[6]
Through your dominions for this enterprise,
On such regards of safety and allowance
As therein are set down.

KING: It likes[7] us well,   80
And at our more considered time[8] we'll read,
Answer, and think upon this business.
Meantime we thank you for your well-took[9] labor.
Go to your rest; at night we'll feast together.
Most welcome home!   [*Exeunt* AMBASSADORS.]
POLONIUS: This business is well ended.   85
My liege and madam, to expostulate[1]
What majesty should be, what duty is,
Why day is day, night night, and time is time,
Were nothing but to waste night, day, and time.
Therefore, since brevity is the soul of wit,   90
And tediousness the limbs and outward flourishes,[2]
I will be brief. Your noble son is mad.
Mad call I it, for to define true madness,
What is't but to be nothing else but mad?
But let that go.

---

4. Orders to stop. *Falsely borne in hand:*
deceived.
  5. Trial.
  6. Safe conduct.
  7. Pleases.

8. Time for more consideration.
9. Successful.
1. Discuss.
2. Adornments.

QUEEN: More matter with less art.   95
POLONIUS: Madam, I swear I use no art at all.
  That he is mad, 'tis true: 'tis true 'tis pity,
  And pity 'tis 'tis true. A foolish figure,
  But farewell it, for I will use no art.
  Mad let us grant him, then, and now remains   100
  That we find out the cause of this effect,
  Or rather say the cause of this defect,
  For this effect defective comes by cause.
  Thus it remains, and the remainder thus.
  Perpend.[3]   105
  I have a daughter—have while she is mine—
  Who in her duty and obedience, mark,
  Hath given me this. Now gather, and surmise.
  "To the celestial, and my soul's idol, the most beautified
    Ophelia."—That's an ill phrase, a vile phrase, "beautified"   110
    is a vile phrase. But you shall hear. Thus:
  "In her excellent white bosom, these, etc."
QUEEN: Came this from Hamlet to her?
POLONIUS: Good madam, stay awhile. I will be faithful.
  "Doubt thou the stars are fire,   115
    Doubt that the sun doth move;
  Doubt truth to be a liar;
    But never doubt I love.
  O dear Ophella, I am ill at these numbers.[4] I have not art
    to reckon my groans, but that I love thee best, O most   120
    best, believe it. Adieu.
  Thine evermore, most dear lady, whilst this machine[5] is to
    him, Hamlet."
  This in obedience hath my daughter shown me,
  And more above, hath his solicitings,   125
  As they fell out by time, by means, and place,
  All given to mine ear.
KING: But how hath she
  Received his love?
POLONIUS: What do you think of me?

3. Consider.
4. Verses.
5. Body.

KING: As of a man faithful and honorable.

POLONIUS: I would fain prove so. But what might you think,   130
    When I had seen this hot love on the wing.
    (As I perceived it, I must tell you that,
    Before my daughter told me), what might you,
    Or my dear majesty your queen here, think,
    If I had played the desk or table-book,   135
    Or given my heart a winking, mute and dumb,
    Or looked upon this love with idle sight,[6]
    What might you think? No, I went round[7] to work,
    And my young mistress thus I did bespeak:
    "Lord Hamlet is a prince out of thy star.[8]   140
    This must not be." And then I prescripts[9] gave her,
    That she should lock herself from his resort,
    Admit no messengers, receive no tokens.
    Which done, she took[1] the fruits of my advice;
    And he repelled, a short tale to make,   145
    Fell into a sadness, then into a fast,
    Thence to a watch,[2] thence into a weakness,
    Thence to a lightness, and by this declension,
    Into the madness wherein now he raves,
    And all we mourn for.

KING: Do you think 'tis this?   150

QUEEN: It may be, very like.

POLONIUS: Hath there been such a time—I would fain know
    that—
    That I have positively said "Tis so,"
    When it proved otherwise?

KING: Not that I know.

POLONIUS: [*Pointing to his head and shoulder.*] Take this from
    this, if this be otherwise.   155
    If circumstances lead me, I will find
    Where truth is hid, though it were hid indeed
    Within the centre.[3]

---

6. If he had remained silent and kept the information to himself.
   7. Directly.
   8. Beyond your sphere.

9. Orders
1. Followed.
2. An insomnia.
3. Of the earth.

KING: How may we try it further?

POLONIUS: You know sometimes he walks four hours together
 Here in the lobby.

QUEEN: So he does, indeed.   160

POLONIUS: At such a time I'll loose⁴ my daughter to him.
 Be you and I behind an arras⁵ then.
 Mark the encounter. If he love her not,
 And be not from his reason fall'n thereon,
 Let me be no assistant for a state,   165
 But keep a farm and carters.

KING: We will try it.

 [*Enter* HAMLET *reading a book.*]

QUEEN: But look where sadly the poor wretch comes
 reading.

POLONIUS: Away, I do beseech you both away,
 I'll board⁶ him presently.   [*Exeunt* KING *and* QUEEN.]
                    O, give me leave.
 How does my good Lord Hamlet?   170

HAMLET: Well, God-a-mercy.

POLONIUS: Do you know me, my lord?

HAMLET: Excellent well, you are a fishmonger.

POLONIUS: Not I, my lord.

HAMLET: Then I would you were so honest a man.   175

POLONIUS: Honest, my lord?

HAMLET: Ay, sir, to be honest as this world goes, is to be one
 man picked out of ten thousand.

POLONIUS: That's very true, my lord.

HAMLET: For if the sun breed maggots in a dead dog, being a   180
 god kissing carrion⁷—Have you a daughter?

POLONIUS: I have, my lord.

HAMLET: Let her not walk i' th' sun. Conception is a blessing,
 but as your daughter may conceive—friend, look to't.

POLONIUS: How say you by that? [*Aside.*] Still harping on my   185
 daughter. Yet he knew me not at first. 'A said I was a fish-
 monger. 'A is far gone. And truly in my youth I suffered

---

4. Let loose.
5. Tapestry.
6. Accost.

7. The Elizabethans believed that sunshine on dead flesh produced maggots.

much extremity for love. Very near this. I'll speak to him again.—What do you read, my lord?

HAMLET: Words, words, words.   190

POLONIUS: What is the matter, my lord?

HAMLET: Between who?

POLONIUS: I mean the matter that you read, my lord.

HAMLET: Slanders, sir; for the satirical rogue says here that old men have grey beards, that their faces are wrinkled, their   195
eyes purging thick amber and plum-tree gum, and that they have a plentiful lack of wit, together with most weak hams[8]—all which, sir, though I most powerfully and potently believe, yet I hold it not honesty to have it thus set down, for yourself, sir shall grow old as I am, if like a crab   200
you could go backward.

POLONIUS: [Aside.] Though this be madness, yet there is method in't.—Will you walk out of the air, my lord?

HAMLET: Into my grave?

POLONIUS: [Aside.] Indeed, that's out of the air. How pregnant   205
sometime his replies are! a happiness that often madness hits on, which reason and sanity could not so prosperously be delivered of. I will leave him, and suddenly contrive the means of meeting between him and my daughter.—My honorable lord. I will most humbly take my leave of you.   210

HAMLET: You cannot take from me anything that I will more willingly part withal—except my life, except my life, except my life.

[Enter GUILDENSTERN and ROSENCRANTZ.]

POLONIUS: Fare you well, my lord.

HAMLET: These tedious old fools!   215

POLONIUS: You go to seek the Lord Hamlet. There he is.

ROSENCRANTZ: [To POLONIUS.] God save you, sir!

[Exit POLONIUS.]

GUILDENSTERN: My honored lord!

ROSENCRANTZ: My most dear lord!

HAMLET: My excellent good friends! How dost thou,
Guildenstern?   220

8. Limbs.

Ah, Rosencrantz! Good lads, how do you both?

ROSENCRANTZ: As the indifferent[9] children of the earth.

GUILDENSTERN: Happy in that we are not over-happy;
On Fortune's cap we are not the very button.[1]

HAMLET: Not the soles of her shoe?   225

ROSENCRANTZ: Neither, my lord.

HAMLET: Then you live about her waist, or in the middle of
her favors?

GUILDENSTERN: Faith, her privates[2] we.

HAMLET: In the secret parts of Fortune? O, most true, she is a   230
strumpet.[3] What news?

ROSENCRANTZ: None, my lord, but that the world's grown
honest.

HAMLET: Then is doomsday near. But your news is not true.
Let me question more in particular. What have you, my   235
good friends, deserved at the hands of Fortune, that she
sends you to prison hither?

GUILDENSTERN: Prison, my lord?

HAMLET: Denmark's a prison.

ROSENCRANTZ: Then is the world one.   240

HAMLET: A goodly one, in which there are many confines,
wards[4] and dungeons. Denmark being one o' th' worst.

ROSENCRANTZ: We think not so, my lord.

HAMLET: Why then 'tis none to you; for there is nothing
either good or bad, but thinking makes it so. To me it is a   245
prison.

ROSENCRANTZ: Why then your ambition makes it one. 'Tis
too narrow for your mind.

HAMLET: O God, I could be bounded in a nutshell and count
myself a king of infinite space, were it not that I have bad   250
dreams.

GUILDENSTERN: Which dreams indeed are ambition; for the very
substance of the ambitious is merely the shadow of a dream.

HAMLET: A dream itself is but a shadow.

9. Ordinary.   3. Prostitute.
1. That is, on top.   4. Cells.
2. Ordinary citizens, but also private
parts (sexual organs).

ROSENCRANTZ: Truly, and I hold ambition of so airy and light   255
   a quality that it is but a shadow's shadow.

HAMLET: Then are our beggars bodies, and our monarchs and
   outstretched heroes the beggars' shadows. Shall we to th'
   court? for, by my fay,[5] I cannot reason.

BOTH: We'll wait upon you.   260

HAMLET: No such matter. I will not sort[6] you with the rest of
   my servants; for to speak to you like an honest man, I am
   most dreadfully attended. But in the beaten way of friendship, what make you at Elsinore?

ROSENCRANTZ: To visit you, my lord; no other occasion.   265

HAMLET: Beggar that I am, I am even poor in thanks, but I
   thank you; and sure, dear friends, my thanks are too dear a
   halfpenny.[7] Were you not sent for? Is it your own inclining?
   Is it a free visitation? Come, come, deal justly with me.
   Come, come, nay speak.   270

GUILDENSTERN: What should we say, my lord?

HAMLET: Anything but to th' purpose. You were sent for, and
   there is a kind of confession in your looks, which your
   modesties have not craft enough to color. I know the good
   king and queen have sent for you.   275

ROSENCRANTZ: To what end, my lord?

HAMLET: That you must teach me. But let me conjure you by
   the rights of our fellowship, by the consonancy of our
   youth, by the obligation of our ever-preserved love, and by
   what more dear a better proposer can charge you withal, be   280
   even and direct with me whether you were sent for or no.

ROSENCRANTZ: [*Aside to* GUILDENSTERN.] What say you?

HAMLET: [*Aside.*] Nay, then, I have an eye of you.—If you love
   me, hold not off.

GUILDENSTERN: My lord, we were sent for.   285

HAMLET: I will tell you why; so shall my anticipation prevent
   your discovery,[8] and your secrecy to the king and queen
   moult no feather. I have of late—but wherefore I know
   not—lost all my mirth, forgone all custom of exercises; and

5. Faith.   7. Not worth a halfpenny.
6. Include.   8. Disclosure.

indeed it goes so heavily with my disposition, that this 290
goodly frame the earth seems to me a sterile promontory,
this most excellent canopy the air, look you, this brave
o'er-hanging firmament, this majestical roof fretted[9] with
golden fire, why it appeareth nothing to me but a foul and
pestilent congregation of vapors. What a piece of work is a 295
man, how noble in reason, how infinite in faculties, in
form and moving, how express[1] and admirable in action,
how like an angel in apprehension, how like a god: the
beauty of the world, the paragon of animals. And yet to
me; what is this quintessence of dust? Man delights not me, 300
nor woman neither, though by your smiling you seem to
say so.

ROSENCRANTZ: My lord, there was no such stuff in my thoughts.

HAMLET: Why did ye laugh, then, when I said "Man delights
not me"? 305

ROSENCRANTZ: To think, my lord, if you delight not in man,
what lenten entertainment the players shall receive from
you. We coted[2] them on the way, and hither are they coming to offer you service.

HAMLET: He that plays the king shall be welcome—his 310
majesty shall have tribute of me; the adventurous knight
shall use his foil and target; the lover shall not sigh gratis;
the humorous[3] man shall end his part in peace; the clown
shall make those laugh whose lungs are tickle o' th' sere;[4]
and the lady shall say her mind freely, or the blank verse 315
shall halt for't. What players are they?

ROSENCRANTZ: Even those you were wont to take such delight
in, the tragedians of the city.

HAMLET: How chances it they travel? Their residence,[5] both in
reputation and profit, was better both ways. 320

ROSENCRANTZ: I think their inhibition comes by the means of
the late innovation.

9. Ornamented with fretwork.
1. Well built.
2. Passed. *Lenten entertainment:* scanty reception.
3. Eccentric. *Foil and target:* sword and shield.
4. Easily set off.
5. Permanent or home theater.

HAMLET: Do they hold the same estimation they did when I was in the city? Are they so followed?

ROSENCRANTZ: No, indeed, are they not.   325

HAMLET: How comes it? Do they grow rusty?

ROSENCRANTZ: Nay, their endeavor keeps in the wonted pace; but there is, sir, an eyrie of children, little eyases,[6] that cry out on the top of question,[7] and are most tyrannically clapped for't. These are now the fashion, and so berattle the   330
common stages (so they call them) that many wearing rapiers are afraid of goose quills[8] and dare scarce come thither.

HAMLET: What, are they children? Who maintains 'em? How are they escoted?[9] Will they pursue the quality no longer   335
than they can sing? Will they not say afterwards, if they should grow themselves to common players (as it is most like, if their means are no better), their writers do them wrong to make them exclaim against their own succession?[1]

ROSENCRANTZ: Faith, there has been much todo on both sides;   340
and the nation holds it no sin to tarre[2] them to controversy. There was for a while no money bid for argument,[3] unless the poet and the player went to cuffs[4] in the question.

HAMLET: Is't possible?

GUILDENSTERN: O, there has been much throwing about of   345
brains.

HAMLET: Do the boys carry it away?

ROSENCRANTZ: Ay, that they do, my lord. Hercules and his load too.[5]

HAMLET: It is not very strange, for my uncle is King of Den-   350
mark, and those that would make mouths[6] at him while

---

6. Little hawks; an allusion to the boy-actor companies that rivaled the Globe theater.

7. With a loud, high delivery.

8. Many noblemen fear the pens of satirical writers.

9. Supported.

1. Future careers.

2. Urge.

3. Paid for a play plot.

4. Blows.

5. During one of his labors, Hercules assumed for a time the burden of the Titan Atlas, who supported the heavens on his shoulders. Also a reference to the effect on business at Shakespeare's theater, the Globe.

6. Sneer.

my father lived give twenty, forty, fifty, a hundred ducats apiece for his picture in little.[7] 'Sblood,[8] there is something in this more than natural, if philosophy could find it out.
    [*A flourish.*]

GUILDENSTERN: There are the players.   355

HAMLET: Gentlemen, you are welcome to Elsinore. Your hands. Come then, th' appurtenance of welcome is fashion and ceremony. Let me comply with you in this garb,[9] lest my extent[9] to the players, which I tell you must show fairly outwards should more appear like entertainment[1] than   360 yours. You are welcome. But my uncle-father and aunt-mother are deceived.

GUILDENSTERN: In what, my dear lord?

HAMLET: I am but mad north-north-west; when the wind is southerly I know a hawk from a handsaw.[2]   365
    [*Enter* POLONIUS.]

POLONIUS: Well be with you, gentlemen.

HAMLET: Hark you, Guildenstern—and you too—at each ear a hearer. That great baby you see there is not yet out of his swaddling clouts.[3]

ROSENCRANTZ: Happily he is the second time come to them,   370 for they say an old man is twice a child.

HAMLET: I will prophesy he comes to tell me of the players. Mark it.
    —You say right, sir, a Monday morning, 'twas then indeed.

POLONIUS: My lord, I have news to tell you.

HAMLET: My lord, I have news to tell you.   375
    When Roscius was an actor in Rome—[4]

POLONIUS: The actors are come hither, my lord.

HAMLET: Buzz, buzz.

POLONIUS: Upon my honor—

HAMLET: Then came each actor on his ass—   380

POLONIUS: The best actors in the world, either for tragedy,

---

7. Miniature.
8. By God's blood.
9. Fashion. *Comply with:* welcome.
1. Cordiality.
2. That is, I know a plasterer's tool from (perhaps) a hernshaw, or heron.

3. Wrappings for an infant.
4. Roscius was the most famous actor of classical Rome.

comedy, history, pastoral, pastoral-comical, historical-
pastoral, tragical-historical, tragical-comical-historical-
pastoral, scene individable, or poem unlimited. Seneca
cannot be too heavy nor Plautus too light. For the law of   385
writ and the liberty, these are the only men.[5]

HAMLET: O Jephtha, judge of Israel, what a treasure hadst
thou![6]

POLONIUS: What a treasure had he, my lord?

HAMLET: Why—
"One fair daughter, and no more,   390
The which he loved passing well."

POLONIUS: [*Aside.*] Still on my daughter.

HAMLET: Am I not i' th' right, old Jephtha?

POLONIUS: If you call me Jephtha, my lord, I have a daughter
that I love passing well.   395

HAMLET: Nay, that follows not.

POLONIUS: What follows then, my lord?

HAMLET: Why—
"As by lot, God wot"
and then, you know,   400
"It came to pass, as most like it was."
The first row of the pious chanson[7] will show you more,
for look where my abridgement comes.

[*Enter* the PLAYERS.]

You are welcome, masters; welcome, all—I am glad to
see thee well.—Welcome, good friends.—O, old friend!   405
Why thy face is valanced since I saw thee last. Com'st
thou to beard[8] me in Denmark?—What, my young lady
and mistress? By'r lady, your ladyship is nearer to heaven
than when I saw you last by the altitude of a chopine.[9]
Pray God your voice, like a piece of uncurrent gold, be   410

---

5. Seneca and Plautus were Roman writers of tragedy and comedy, respectively. The
"law of writ" refers to plays written according to classical rules; the "liberty," to those
written otherwise.

6. In the Bible, Jephtha asked God for
victory and vowed to sacrifice the first creature he encountered upon his return. His
only daughter became the victim of his vow.

7. Song. *Row:* stanza.

8. Defy. *Valanced:* Fringed (with a
beard).

9. The height of a woman's thick-soled
shoe.

not cracked within the ring.[1]—Masters, you are all welcome. We'll e'en to't like French falconers, fly at anything we see. We'll have a speech straight. Come give us
a taste of your quality,[2] come a passionate speech.

FIRST PLAYER: What speech, my good lord?   415

HAMLET: I heard thee speak me a speech once, but it was never
acted, or if it was, not above once, for the play, I remember,
pleased not the million; 'twas caviary to the general.[3] But it
was—as I received it, and others whose judgments in such
matters cried in the top of[4] mine—an excellent play, well   420
digested[5] in the scenes, set down with as much modesty as
cunning. I remember one said there were no sallets[6] in the
lines to make the matter savory, nor no matter in the
phrase that might indict the author of affectation, but
called it an honest method, as wholesome as sweet, and by   425
very much more handsome than fine. One speech in't I
chiefly loved. 'Twas Æneas' tale to Dido, and thereabout of
it especially where he speaks of Priam's slaughter.[7] If it live
in your memory, begin at this line—let me see, let me see:
   "The rugged Pyrrhus, like th' Hyrcanian beast"[8]—   430
'tis not so; it begins with Pyrrhus—
   "The rugged Pyrrhus, he whose sable arms,
   Black as his purpose, did the night resemble
   When he lay couchéd in th' ominous horse,[9]
   Hath now this dread and black complexion smeared   435
   With heraldry more dismal; head to foot
   Now is he total gules, horridly tricked[1]
   With blood of fathers, mothers, daughters, sons,
   Baked and impasted with the parching[2] streets,

1. *Pray God . . . ring:* a reference to the Elizabethan theatrical practice of us-ing boys to play women's roles; Hamlet hopes that this boy has not matured to the point at which his voice might change.
2. Trade.
3. Caviar to the masses.
4. Were weightier than.
5. Arranged.

6. Spicy passages.
7. In Virgil's *Aeneid*, Aeneas tells Dido, the queen of Carthage, about the fall of Troy. Here he describes Pyrrhus's killing of Priam, the aged king of Troy, also known (like his city) as Ilium.
8. Tiger.
9. That is, the Trojan horse.
1. Adorned. *Total gules:* completely red.
2. Burning. *Impasted:* crusted.

That lend a tyrannous and a damnéd light   440
To their lord's murder. Roasted in wrath and fire,
And thus o'er-sizéd with coagulate[3] gore,
With eyes like carbuncles, the hellish Pyrrhus
Old grandsire Priam seeks."
So proceed you.   445
POLONIUS: Fore God, my lord, well spoken, with good accent
    and good discretion.
FIRST PLAYER: "Anon he finds him[4]
    Striking too short at Greeks. His antique[5] sword,
    Rebellious[6] to his arm, lies where it falls,   450
    Repugnant to command. Unequal matched,
    Pyrrhus at Priam drives, in rage strikes wide.
    But with the whiff and wind of his fell sword
    Th' unnervéd father falls. Then senseless[7] Ilium,
    Seeming to feel this blow, with flaming top   455
    Stoops[8] to his base, and with a hideous crash
    Takes prisoner Pyrrhus' ear. For, lo! his sword,
    Which was declining[9] on the milky head
    Of reverend Priam, seemed i' th' air to stick.
    So as a painted tyrant Pyrrhus stood,   460
    And like a neutral to his will and matter,[1]
    Did nothing.
    But as we often see, against some storm,
    A silence in the heavens, the rack[2] stand still,
    The bold winds speechless, and the orb below   465
    As hush as death, anon the dreadful thunder
    Doth rend the region; so, after Pyrrhus' pause,
    A rouséd vengeance sets him new awork,[3]
    And never did the Cyclops' hammers fall
    On Mars's armor, forged for proof eterne,[4]   470
    With less remorse than Pyrrhus' bleeding sword

---

3. Clotted. *O'er-sizéd:* glued over.
4. That is, Pyrrhus finds Priam.
5. Which he used when young.
6. Unmanageable
7. Without feeling.
8. Falls.
9. About to fall.

1. Between his will and the fulfillment of it.
2. Clouds.
3. To work.
4. Mars, the Roman war god, had impenetrable armor made for him by the blacksmith god, Vulcan, and his assistants, the Cyclopes.

Now falls on Priam.
Out, out, thou strumpet, Fortune! All you gods,
In general synod take away her power,
Break all the spokes and fellies[5] from her wheel, 475
And bowl the round nave[6] down the hill of heaven
As low as to the fiends."

POLONIUS: This is too long.

HAMLET: It shall to the barber's with your beard.—Prithee
say on. He's for a jig,[7] or a tale of bawdry, or he sleeps. 480
Say on; come to Hecuba.[8]

FIRST PLAYER: "But who, ah woe! had seen the mobléd[9]
queen—"

HAMLET: "The mobléd queen"?

POLONIUS: That's good. "Mobléd queen" is good.

FIRST PLAYER: "Run barefoot up and down, threat'ning the
flames 485
With bisson rheum, a clout[1] upon that head
Where late the diadem stood, and for a robe,
About her lank and all o'er-teeméd loins.
A blanket, in the alarm of fear caught up—
Who this had seen, with tongue in venom steeped, 490
'Gainst Fortune's state[2] would treason have pronounced.
But if the gods themselves did see her then,
When she saw Pyrrhus make malicious sport
In mincing[3] with his sword her husband's limbs,
The instant burst of clamor that she made, 495
Unless things mortal move them not at all,
Would have made milch[4] the burning eyes of heaven,
And passion in the gods."

POLONIUS: Look whe'r[5] he has not turned his color, and has
tears in's eyes. Prithee no more. 500

HAMLET: 'Tis well. I'll have thee speak out the rest of this

5. Parts of the rim.
6. Roll the round hub.
7. A comic act.
8. Wife of Priam and queen of Troy. Her "loins" are described below as "o'erteemed" because of her celebrated fertility.

9. Muffled (in a hood).
1. With blinding tears, a cloth.
2. Government.
3. Cutting up.
4. Tearful (literally, milk-giving).
5. Whether.

soon.—Good my lord, will you see the players well bestowed?[6] Do you hear, let them be well used, for they are
the abstract[7] and brief chronicles of the time; after your
death you were better have a bad epitaph than their ill re-   505
port while you live.
POLONIUS: My lord, I will use them according to their desert.
HAMLET: God's bodkin,[8] man, much better. Use every man after his desert, and who shall 'scape whipping? Use them after your own honor and dignity. The less they deserve, the   510
more merit is in your bounty. Take them in.
POLONIUS: Come, sirs.
HAMLET: Follow him, friends. We'll hear a play tomorrow.
[*Aside to* FIRST PLAYER.] Dost thou hear me, old friend, can
you play "The Murder of Gonzago"?   515
FIRST PLAYER: Ay, my lord.
HAMLET: We'll ha't tomorrow night. You could for a need
study a speech of some dozen or sixteen lines which I
would set down and insert in't, could you not?
FIRST PLAYER: Ay, my lord.   520
HAMLET: Very well. Follow that lord, and look you mock him
not.   [*Exeunt* POLONIUS *and* PLAYERS.]
My good friends, I'll leave you till night. You are welcome
to Elsinore.
ROSENCRANTZ: Good my lord.   525
          [*Exeunt* ROSENCRANTZ *and* GUILDENSTERN.]
HAMLET: Ay, so God b'wi'ye. Now I am alone.
O, what a rogue and peasant slave am I!
Is it not monstrous that this player here,
But in a fiction, in a dream of passion,
Could force his soul so to his own conceit[9]   530
That from her working all his visage wanned;[1]
Tears in his eyes, distraction in his aspect[2]
A broken voice, and his whole function suiting
With forms to his conceit? And all for nothing,

6. Provided for.
7. Summary.
8. Dear body.

9. Imagination.
1. Grew pale.
2. Face.

For Hecuba!   535
What's Hecuba to him or he to Hecuba,
That he should weep for her? What would he do
Had he the motive and the cue for passion
That I have? He would drown the stage with tears,
And cleave the general ear with horrid speech,   540
Make mad the guilty, and appal the free,
Confound the ignorant, and amaze indeed
The very faculties of eyes and ears.
Yet I,
A dull and muddy-mettled rascal, peak³   545
Like John-a-dreams, unpregnant of⁴ my cause,
And can say nothing; no, not for a king
Upon whose property and most dear life
A damned defeat was made. Am I a coward?
Who calls me villain, breaks my pate across,   550
Plucks off my beard and blows it in my face,
Tweaks me by the nose, gives me the lie i' th' throat
As deep as to the lungs? Who does me this?
Ha, 'swounds,⁵ I should take it; for it cannot be
But I am pigeon-livered and lack gall⁶   555
To make oppression bitter, or ere this
I should 'a fatted all the region kites⁷
With this slave's offal. Bloody, bawdy villain!
Remorseless, treacherous, lecherous, kindless⁸ villain!
O, vengeance!   560
Why, what an ass am I! This is most brave,
That I, the son of a dear father murdered,
Prompted to my revenge by heaven and hell,
Must like a whore unpack⁹ my heart with words,
And fall a-cursing like a very drab,   565
A scullion! Fie upon't! foh!
About, my brains. Hum—I have heard
That guilty creatures sitting at a play,

---

3. Mope. *Muddy-mettled:* dull-spirited.   6. Bitterness.
4. Unenlivened by. *John-a-dreams:* a   7. Vultures of the area.
loafer.   8. Unnatural.
5. By God's wounds.   9. Relieve.

Have by the very cunning of the scene
Been struck so to the soul that presently   570
They have proclaimed[1] their malefactions;
For murder, though it have no tongue, will speak
With most miraculous organ. I'll have these players
Play something like the murder of my father
Before mine uncle. I'll observe his looks.   575
I'll tent him to the quick. If 'a do blench,[2]
I know my course. The spirit that I have seen
May be a devil, and the devil hath power
T' assume a pleasing shape, yea, and perhaps
Out of my weakness and my melancholy,   580
As he is very potent with such spirits,
Abuses me to damn me. I'll have grounds
More relative[3] than this. The play's the thing
Wherein I'll catch the conscience of the king.   [*Exit.*]

ACT III
SCENE 1

A room in the castle. Enter KING, QUEEN, POLONIUS, OPHELIA,
ROSENCRANTZ *and* GUILDENSTERN.

KING: And can you by no drift of conference[1]
  Get from him why he puts on this confusion,
  Grating so harshly all his days of quiet
  With turbulent and dangerous lunacy?
ROSENCRANTZ: He does confess he feels himself distracted,   5
  But from what cause 'a will by no means speak.
GUILDENSTERN: Nor do we find him forward to be sounded,[2]
  But with a crafty madness keeps aloof
  When we would bring him on to some confession
  Of his true state.
QUEEN: Did he receive you well?   10
ROSENCRANTZ: Most like a gentleman.

---

1. Admitted.   1. Line of conversation.
2. Turn pale. *Tent:* try.   2. Eager to be questioned.
3. Conclusive.

GUILDENSTERN: But with much forcing of his disposition.[3]

ROSENCRANTZ: Niggard of question, but of our demands[4]
  Most free in his reply.

QUEEN: Did you assay[5] him
  To any pastime?   15

ROSENCRANTZ: Madam, it so fell out that certain players
  We o'er-raught[6] on the way. Of these we told him,
  And there did seem in him a kind of joy
  To hear of it. They are here about the court,
  And as I think, they have already order   20
  This night to play before him.

POLONIUS: 'Tis most true,
  And he beseeched me to entreat your majesties
  To hear and see the matter.[7]

KING: With all my heart, and it doth much content me
  To hear him so inclined.   25
  Good gentlemen, give him a further edge,[8]
  And drive his purpose into these delights.

ROSENCRANTZ: We shall, my lord.

            [*Exeunt* ROSENCRANTZ *and* GUILDENSTERN.]

KING: Sweet Gertrude, leave us too,
  For we have closely sent for Hamlet hither,
  That he, as 'twere by accident, may here   30
  Affront[9] Ophelia.
  Her father and myself (lawful espials[1])
  Will so bestow ourselves that, seeing unseen,
  We may of their encounter frankly judge,
  And gather by him, as he is behaved,   35
  If't be th' affliction of his love or no
  That thus he suffers for.

QUEEN: I shall obey you.—
  And for your part, Ophelia, I do wish
  That your good beauties be the happy cause
  Of Hamlet's wildness. So shall I hope your virtues   40

---

3. Mood.
4. To our questions.
5. Tempt.
6. Passed.

7. Performance.
8. Sharpen his intention.
9. Confront.
1. Justified spies.

Will bring him to his wonted[2] way again,
To both your honors.
OPHELIA: Madam, I wish it may.

                                        [*Exit* QUEEN.]

POLONIUS: Ophelia, walk you here—Gracious,[3] so please you,
    We will bestow ourselves.—[*To* OPHELIA.] Read on this
    book,[4]
    That show of such an exercise may color[5]   45
    Your loneliness.—We are oft to blame in this,
    'Tis too much proved, that with devotion's visage
    And pious action we do sugar o'er
    The devil himself.
KING: [*Aside.*]   O, 'tis too true.
    How smart a lash that speech doth give my conscience!   50
    The harlot's cheek, beautied with plast'ring[6] art,
    Is not more ugly to the thing that helps it
    Than is my deed to my most painted word.
    O heavy burden!
POLONIUS: I hear him coming. Let's withdraw, my lord.   55

                    [*Exeunt* KING *and* POLONIUS.]

    [*Enter* HAMLET.]

HAMLET: To be, or not to be, that is the question:
    Whether 'tis nobler in the mind to suffer
    The slings and arrows of outrageous fortune,
    Or to take arms against a sea of troubles,
    And by opposing end them. To die, to sleep—   60
    No more; and by a sleep to say we end
    The heartache, and the thousand natural shocks
    That flesh is heir to. 'Tis a consummation
    Devoutly to be wished—to die, to sleep—
    To sleep, perchance to dream, ay there's the rub;   65
    For in that sleep of death what dreams may come
    When we have shuffled off this mortal coil[7]
    Must give us pause—there's the respect[8]

2. Usual.
3. Majesty.
4. Prayer book or devotional text.
5. Act of devotion may explain.

6. Thickly painted.
7. Turmoil.
8. Consideration.

That makes calamity of so long life.
For who would bear the whips and scorns of time,　　　70
Th' oppressor's wrong, the proud man's contumely,[9]
The pangs of despised love, the law's delay,
The insolence of office, and the spurns[1]
That patient merit of th' unworthy takes,
When he himself might his quietus[2] make　　　75
With a bare bodkin? Who would fardels[3] bear,
To grunt and sweat under a weary life,
But that the dread of something after death,
The undiscovered country, from whose bourn[4]
No traveller returns, puzzles the will,　　　80
And makes us rather bear those ills we have
Than fly to others that we know not of?
Thus conscience does make cowards of us all;
And thus the native[5] hue of resolution
Is sicklied o'er with the pale cast of thought,　　　85
And enterprises of great pitch and moment[6]
With this regard their currents turn awry
And lose the name of action.—Soft you now,
The fair Ophelia.—Nymph, in thy orisons[7]
Be all my sins remembered.
OPHELIA:　　　　　　　　Good my lord,　　　90
　How does your honor for this many a day?
HAMLET: I humbly thank you, well, well, well.
OPHELIA: My lord, I have remembrances of yours
　That I have longéd long to re-deliver.
　I pray you now receive them.
HAMLET:　　　　　　　　No, not I,　　　95
　I never gave you aught.
OPHELIA: My honored lord, you know right well you did,
　And with them words of so sweet breath composed

9. Insulting behavior.
1. Rejections.
2. Settlement, as in the paying off of a debt.
3. Burdens. *Bare bodkin:* an unsheathed dagger.

4. Boundary.
5. Natural.
6. Great height and importance.
7. Prayers.

As made the things more rich. Their perfume lost,
Take these again, for to the noble mind   100
Rich gifts wax[8] poor when givers prove unkind.
There, my lord.

HAMLET: Ha, ha! are you honest?[9]

OPHELIA: My lord?

HAMLET: Are you fair?   105

OPHELIA: What means your lordship?

HAMLET: That if you be honest and fair, your honesty should
admit no discourse to your beauty.

OPHELIA: Could beauty, my lord, have better commerce[1] than
with honesty?   110

HAMLET: Ay, truly, for the power of beauty will sooner transform honesty from what it is to a bawd than the force of
honesty can translate beauty into his likeness. This was
sometimes a paradox, but now the time gives it proof. I did
love you once.   115

OPHELIA: Indeed, my lord, you made me believe so.

HAMLET: You should not have believed me, for virtue cannot
so inoculate[2] our old stock but we shall relish of it. I loved
you not.

OPHELIA: I was the more deceived.   120

HAMLET: Get thee to a nunnery.[3] Why wouldst thou be a
breeder of sinners? I am myself indifferent[4] honest, but yet
I could accuse me of such things that it were better my
mother had not borne me: I am very proud, revengeful,
ambitious, with more offences at my beck[5] than I have   125
thoughts to put them in, imagination to give them shape,
or time to act them in. What should such fellows as I do
crawling between earth and heaven? We are arrant[6] knaves
all; believe none of us. Go thy ways to a nunnery. Where's
your father?   130

OPHELIA: At home, my lord.

8. Become.
9. Chaste.
1. Dealings.
2. Change by grafting.
3. Both a convent of nuns and, in Elizabethan slang, a brothel.

4. Moderately.
5. Command.
6. Thorough.

HAMLET: Let the doors be shut upon him, that he may play
the fool nowhere but in's own house. Farewell.

OPHELIA: O, help him, you sweet heavens!

HAMLET: If thou dost marry, I'll give thee this plague for thy
dowry: be thou as chaste as ice, as pure as snow, thou shalt
not escape calumny. Get thee to a nunnery, farewell. Or if
thou wilt needs marry, marry a fool, for wise men know
well enough what monsters[7] you make of them. To a nunnery, go, and quickly too. Farewell.

OPHELIA: Heavenly powers, restore him!

HAMLET: I have heard of your paintings, too, well enough.
God hath given you one face, and you make yourselves another. You jig, you amble, and you lisp;[8] you nickname
God's creatures, and make your wantonness your ignorance.[9] Go to, I'll no more on't, it hath made me mad. I say
we will have no more marriage. Those that are married already, all but one, shall live. The rest shall keep as they are.
To a nunnery, go. [Exit.]

OPHELIA: O, what a noble mind is here o'erthrown!
The courtier's, soldier's, scholar's, eye, tongue, sword,
Th' expectancy and rose[1] of the fair state,
The glass of fashion and the mould[2] of form,
Th' observed of all observers, quite quite down!
And I of ladies most deject and wretched,
That sucked the honey of his music[3] vows,
Now see that noble and most sovereign reason
Like sweet bells jangled, out of time and harsh;
That unmatched form and feature of blown[4] youth
Blasted with ecstasy. O, woe is me
T' have seen what I have seen, see what I see!
[Enter KING and POLONIUS.]

KING: Love! His affections do not that way tend,
Nor what he spake, though it lacked form a little,
Was not like madness. There's something in his soul

135
140
145
150
155
160

7. Horned because cuckolded.
8. Walk and talk affectedly.
9. Call things by pet names and then blame the affectation on ignorance.

1. The hope and ornament.
2. Model. *Glass:* mirror.
3. Musical.
4. Full-blown.

O'er which his melancholy sits on brood,[5]   165
And I do doubt the hatch and the disclose[6]
Will be some danger; which to prevent,
I have in quick determination
Thus set it down: he shall with speed to England
For the demand of our neglected tribute.   170
Haply the seas and countries different,
With variable objects, shall expel
This something-settled matter in his heart
Whereon his brains still beating puts him thus
From fashion of himself. What think you on't?   175
POLONIUS: It shall do well. But yet do I believe
The origin and commencement of his grief
Sprung from neglected love.—How now, Ophelia?
You need not tell us what Lord Hamlet said,
We heard it all.—My lord, do as you please,   180
But if you hold it fit, after the play
Let his queen-mother all alone entreat him
To show his grief. Let her be round[7] with him,
And I'll be placed, so please you, in the ear[8]
Of all their conference. If she find him not,[9]   185
To England send him; or confine him where
Your wisdom best shall think.
KING: It shall be so.
Madness in great ones must not unwatched go.

                                                        [*Exeunt.*]

SCENE 2
A public room in the castle. Enter HAMLET *and three of the*
PLAYERS.

HAMLET: Speak the speech, I pray you, as I pronounced it to
   you, trippingly on the tongue; but if you mouth it as many
   of our players do, I had as lief the town-crier spoke my

---

5. That is, like a hen.   8. Hearing.
6. Result. *Doubt:* fear.   9. Does not discover the cause of his be-
7. Direct.   havior.

lines. Nor do not saw the air too much with your hand thus, but use all gently, for in the very torrent, tempest, and as I may say, whirlwind of your passion, you must acquire and beget a temperance that may give it smoothness. O, it offends me to the soul to hear a robustious periwig-pated[1] fellow tear a passion to tatters, to very rags, to split the ears of the groundlings, who for the most part are capable of[2] nothing but inexplicable dumb shows and noise. I would have such a fellow whipped for o'erdoing Termagant. It out-herods Herod.[3] Pray you avoid it.

FIRST PLAYER: I warrant your honor.

HAMLET: Be not too tame neither, but let your own discretion be your tutor. Suit the action to the word, the word to the action, with this special observance, that you o'erstep not the modesty of nature; for anything so o'erdone is from[4] the purpose of playing, whose end both at the first, and now, was and is, to hold as 'twere the mirror up to nature, to show virtue her own feature, scorn her own image, and the very age and body of the time his form and pressure.[5] Now this overdone, or come tardy off, though it makes the unskilful[6] laugh, cannot but make the judicious grieve, the censure[7] of the which one must in your allowance o'erweigh a whole theatre of others. O, there be players that I have seen play—and heard others praise, and that highly—not to speak it profanely, that neither having th' accent of Christians, nor the gait of Christian, pagan, nor man, have so strutted and bellowed that I have thought some of nature's journeymen[8] had made men, and not made them well, they imitated humanity so abominably.

FIRST PLAYER: I hope we have reformed that indifferently[9] with us, sir.

305

310

315

320

325

330

335

1. A noisy bewigged.
2. That is, capable of understanding. *Groundlings:* the spectators in the cheapest area.
3. Termagant, an imaginary deity, and the biblical Herod were violent and loud stock characters in popular drama.

4. Contrary to.
5. His shape and likeness.
6. Ignorant.
7. Judgment.
8. Inferior craftsmen.
9. Somewhat.

HAMLET: O, reform it altogether. And let those that play
your clowns speak no more than is set down for them,
for there be of them that will themselves laugh, to set on
some quantity of barren[1] spectators to laugh too, though
in the meantime some necessary question of the play be   340
then to be considered. That's villainous, and shows a most
pitiful ambition in the fool that uses it. Go, make you
ready.

[*Exeunt* PLAYERS.]

[*Enter* POLONIUS, GUILDENSTERN, *and* ROSENCRANTZ.]

How now my lord? Will the king hear this piece of work?

POLONIUS: And the queen too, and that presently.   345

HAMLET: Bid the players make haste.   [*Exit* POLONIUS.]

Will you two help to hasten them?

ROSENCRANTZ: Ay, my lord.   [*Exeunt they two.*]

HAMLET: What, ho, Horatio!

[*Enter* HORATIO.]

HORATIO: Here, sweet lord, at your service.   350

HAMLET: Horatio, thou art e'en as just a man
As e'er my conversation coped[2] withal.

HORATIO: O my dear lord!

HAMLET: Nay, do not think I flatter,
For what advancement may I hope from thee,
That no revenue hast but thy good spirits   355
To feed and clothe thee? Why should the poor be flattered?
No, let the candied tongue lick absurd pomp,
And crook the pregnant[3] hinges of the knee
Where thrift[4] may follow fawning. Dost thou hear?
Since my dear soul was mistress of her choice   360
And could of men distinguish her election,
S'hath sealed thee for herself, for thou hast been
As one in suff'ring all that suffers nothing,
A man that Fortune's buffets and rewards
Hast ta'en with equal thanks; and blest are those   365
Whose blood and judgment are so well commingled

1. Dull-witted.   3. Quick to bend.
2. Encountered.   4. Profit.

That they are not a pipe[5] for Fortune's finger
To sound what stop[6] she please. Give me that man
That is not passion's slave, and I will wear him
In my heart's core, ay, in my heart of heart,   370
As I do thee. Something too much of this.
There is a play tonight before the king.
One scene of it comes near the circumstance
Which I have told thee of my father's death.
I prithee, when thou seest that act afoot,   375
Even with the very comment[7] of thy soul
Observe my uncle. If his occulted[8] guilt
Do not itself unkennel[9] in one speech,
It is a damnéd ghost that we have seen,
And my imaginations are as foul   380
As Vulcan's stithy. Give him heedful note,[1]
For I mine eyes will rivet to his face,
And after we will both our judgments join
In censure of his seeming.[2]
HORATIO: Well, my lord.
If 'a[3] steal aught the whilst this play in playing,   385
And 'scape detecting, I will pay[4] the theft.
    [*Enter Trumpets and Kettledrums,* KING, QUEEN, POLO-
    NIUS, OPHELIA, ROSENCRANTZ, GUILDENSTERN, *and other*
    LORDS *attendant.*]
HAMLET: They are coming to the play. I must be idle.
    Get you a place.
KING: How fares our cousin Hamlet?
HAMLET: Excellent, i' faith, of the chameleon's dish.[5] I eat the   390
    air, promise-crammed. You cannot feed capons so.
KING: I have nothing with this answer, Hamlet. These words
    are not mine.

---

5. Musical instrument.   2. Manner.
6. To play what note.   3. He.
7. Keenest observation.   4. Repay.
8. Hidden.   5. Chameleons were popularly believed
9. Break loose.   to eat nothing but air.
1. Careful attention. *Stithy:* smithy, forge.

HAMLET: No, nor mine now. [*To* POLONIUS.] My lord, you
    played once i' th' university, you say?   395

POLONIUS: That did I, my lord, and was accounted a good
    actor.

HAMLET: What did you enact?

POLONIUS: I did enact Julius Cæsar. I was killed i' th' Capitol;
    Brutus killed me.[6]   400

HAMLET: It was a brute part of him to kill so capital a calf
    there. Be the players ready?

ROSENCRANTZ: Ay, my lord, they stay upon your patience.[7]

QUEEN: Come hither, my dear Hamlet, sit by me.

HAMLET: No, good mother, here's metal more attractive.   405

POLONIUS: [*To the* KING.] O, ho! do you mark that?

HAMLET: Lady, shall I lie in your lap? [*Lying down at* OPHELIA'*s
    feet.*]

OPHELIA: No, my lord.

HAMLET: I mean, my head upon your lap?

OPHELIA: Ay, my lord.   410

HAMLET: Do you think I meant country matters?[8]

OPHELIA: I think nothing, my lord.

HAMLET: That's a fair thought to lie between maids' legs.

OPHELIA: What is, my lord?

HAMLET: Nothing.   415

OPHELIA: You are merry, my lord.

HAMLET: Who, I?

OPHELIA: Ay, my lord.

HAMLET: O God, your only jig-maker![9] What should a man
    do but be merry? For look you how cheerfully my mother   420
    looks, and my father died within's two hours.

OPHELIA: Nay, 'tis twice two months, my lord.

HAMLET: So long? Nay then, let the devil wear black, for I'll
    have a suit of sables.[1] O heavens! die two months ago, and

---

6. Perhaps an allusion to Shakespeare's
Julius Caesar, which dramatizes the assassi-
nation of Julius Caesar by Brutus and others.

7. Leisure. *Stay:* wait.

8. Here and elsewhere in this exchange
Hamlet intends some ribald double meanings.

9. Writer of comic scenes.

1. Fur; also, black.

not forgotten yet? Then there's hope a great man's memory   425
may outlive his life half a year, but by'r lady 'a must build
churches then, or else shall 'a suffer not thinking on, with
the hobby-horse, whose epitaph is "For O, for O, the
hobby-horse is forgot!"[2]

The trumpets sound. Dumb Show follows. Enter a KING
and a QUEEN *very lovingly; the* QUEEN *embracing him and
he her. She kneels, and makes show of protestation unto
him. He takes her up, and declines[3] his head upon her neck.
He lies him down upon a bank of flowers; she, seeing him
asleep, leaves him. Anon come in another man, takes off his
crown, kisses it, pours poison in the sleeper's ears, and leaves
him. The* QUEEN *returns, finds the* KING *dead, makes passionate action. The* POISONER *with some three or four come
in again, seem to condole with her. The dead body is carried
away. The* POISONER *woos the* QUEEN *with gifts; she seems
harsh awhile, but in the end accepts love.*

                                               [*Exeunt.*]

OPHELIA: What means this, my lord?   430
HAMLET: Marry, this is miching mallecho;[4] it means mischief.
OPHELIA: Belike this show imports the argument[5] of the play.
        [*Enter* PROLOGUE.]
HAMLET: We shall know by this fellow. The players cannot
        keep counsel; they'll tell all.
OPHELIA: Will 'a tell us what this show meant?   435
HAMLET: Ay, or any show that you will show him. Be not
        you ashamed to show, he'll not shame to tell you what it
        means.
OPHELIA: You are naught, you are naught. I'll mark[6] the play.
PROLOGUE: *For us, and for our tragedy,*   440
        Here stooping to your clemency,
        We beg your hearing patiently.   [*Exit.*]
HAMLET: Is this a prologue, or the posy[7] of a ring?
OPHELIA: 'Tis brief, my lord.

---

2. An Elizabethan ballad refrain. In traditional games and dances one of the characters was a man represented as riding a horse.
    3. Lays.

4. Sneaking crime.
5. Explains the plot.
6. Attend to. *Naught:* obscene.
7. Motto engraved inside.

HAMLET: As woman's love. 445

[*Enter the* PLAYER KING *and* QUEEN.]

PLAYER KING: *Full thirty times hath Phœbus' cart gone round*
    Neptune's salt wash and Tellus' orbéd ground,
    And thirty dozen moons with borrowed sheen[8]
    About the world have times twelve thirties been,
    Since love our hearts and Hymen did our hands 450
    Unite comutual in most sacred bands.[9]

PLAYER QUEEN: *So many journeys may the sun and moon*
    Make us again count o'er ere love be done!
    But woe is nie, you are so sick of late,
    So far from cheer and from your former state, 455
    That I distrust[1] you. Yet though I distrust,
    Discomfort you, my lord, it nothing must.
    For women's fear and love hold quantity,[2]
    In neither aught, or in extremity.[3]
    Now what my love is proof hath made you know, 460
    And as my love is sized,[4] my fear is so.
    Where love is great, the littlest doubts are fear;
    Where little fears grow great, great love grows there.

PLAYER KING: *Faith, I must leave thee, love, and shortly too;*
    My operant powers their functions leave[5] to do. 465
    And thou shalt live in this fair world behind,
    Honored, beloved, and haply one as kind
    For husband shalt thou—

PLAYER QUEEN: *O, confound the rest!*
    Such love must needs be treason in my breast.
    In second husband let me be accurst! 470
    None wed the second but who killed the first.

HAMLET: That's wormwood.

PLAYER QUEEN: *The instances[6] that second marriage move*

---

8. Light.

9. The speech contains several references to Greek and Roman mythology. Phoebus was the sun god; his chariot, or "cart," is the sun. Neptune was the sea god; his "salt wash" is the ocean. Tellus was an earth goddess; her "orbed ground" is Earth, or the globe. Hymen was the god of marriage. *Comutual:* mutually.

1. Fear for.

2. Agree in weight.

3. Without regard to too much or too little.

4. In size.

5. Cease. *Operant powers:* active forces.

6. Causes.

Are base respects⁷ of thrift, but none of love.
A second time I kill my husband dead,   475
When second husband kisses me in bed.
PLAYER KING: I do believe you think what now you speak,
But what we do determine oft we break.
Purpose is but the slave to memory,
Of violent birth, but poor validity;   480
Which now, like fruit unripe, sticks on the tree,
But fall unshaken when they mellow be.
Most necessary 'tis that we forget
To pay ourselves what to ourselves is debt.
What to ourselves in passion we propose,   485
The passion ending, doth the purpose lose.
The violence of either grief or joy
Their own enactures⁸ with themselves destroy.
Where joy most revels, grief doth most lament;
Grief joys, joy grieves, on slender accident.   490
This world is not for aye,⁹ nor 'tis not strange
That even our loves should with our fortunes change;
For 'tis a question left us yet to prove,
Whether love lead fortune, or else fortune love.
The great man down, you mark his favorite flies;   495
The poor advanced makes friends of enemies;
And hitherto doth love on fortune tend,
For who not needs shall never lack a friend,
And who in want a hollow¹ friend doth try,
Directly seasons him² his enemy.   500
But orderly to end where I begun,
Our wills and fates do so contrary run
That our devices³ still are overthrown;
Our thoughts are ours, their ends none of our own.
So think thou wilt no second husband wed,   505
But die thy thoughts when thy first lord is dead.
PLAYER QUEEN: Nor earth to me give food, nor heaven light,

---

7. Concerns.   1. False.
8. Actions.   2. Ripens him into.
9. Eternal.   3. Plans.

Sport and repose lock from me day and night,
To desperation turn my trust and hope,
An anchor's cheer[4] in prison be my scope,   510
Each opposite that blanks[5] the face of joy
Meet what I would have well, and it destroy,
Both here and hence[6] pursue me lasting strife,
If once a widow, ever I be wife!

HAMLET: If she should break it now!   515

PLAYER KING: *'Tis deeply sworn. Sweet, leave me here awhile.*
     My spirits grow dull, and fain I would beguile
     The tedious day with sleep. [*Sleeps.*]

PLAYER QUEEN: *Sleep rock thy brain,*
     And never come mischance between us twain!   [*Exit.*]

HAMLET: Madam, how like you this play?   520

QUEEN: The lady doth protest too much, methinks.

HAMLET: O, but she'll keep her word.

KING: Have you heard the argument? Is there no offence in't?

HAMLET: No, no, they do but jest, poison in jest; no offence i'
     th' world.   525

KING: What do you call the play?

HAMLET: "The Mouse-trap." Marry, how? Tropically.[7] This
     play is the image of a murder done in Vienna. Gonzago is
     the duke's name; his wife, Baptista. You shall see anon. 'Tis
     a knavish piece of work, but what of that? Your majesty,   530
     and we that have free souls, it touches us not. Let the galled
     jade wince, our withers are unwrung.[8]
     [*Enter* LUCIANUS.]
     This is one Lucianus, nephew to the king.

OPHELIA: You are as good as a chorus, my lord.

HAMLET: I could interpret between you and your love, if I   535
     could see the puppets dallying.

OPHELIA: You are keen, my lord, you are keen.

HAMLET: It would cost you a groaning to take off mine edge.

OPHELIA: Still better, and worse.

---

4. Anchorite's food.
5. Blanches.
6. In the next world.
7. Figuratively.

8 Let the horse with the sore back wince. Our shoulders are not chafed by the harness.

HAMLET: So you mistake your husbands.—Begin, murderer. 540
Leave thy damnable faces and begin. Come, the croaking
raven doth bellow for revenge.
LUCIANUS: *Thoughts black, hands apt, drugs fit, and time*
agreeing,
Confederate season,[9] else no creature seeing,
Thou mixture rank, of midnight weeds collected, 545
With Hecate's[1] ban thrice blasted, thrice infected,
Thy natural magic[2] and dire property
On wholesome life usurp immediately.
                              [*Pours the poison in his ears.*]
HAMLET: 'A poisons him i' th' garden for his estate. His name's
Gonzago. The story is extant, and written in very choice 550
Italian. You shall see anon how the murderer gets the love
of Gonzago's wife.
OPHELIA: The king rises.
HAMLET: What, frighted with false fire?
QUEEN: How fares my lord? 555
POLONIUS: Give o'er the play.
KING: Give me some light. Away!
POLONIUS: Lights, lights, lights!
                    [*Exeunt all but* HAMLET *and* HORATIO.]
HAMLET: Why; let the strucken deer go weep,
        The hart ungalléd[3] play. 560
    For some must watch while some must sleep;
        Thus runs the world away.
    Would not this, sir, and a forest of feathers[4]—if the rest of
    my fortunes turn Turk with[5] me—with two Provincial
    roses on my razed shoes, get me a fellowship in a cry[6] of 565
    players?
HORATIO: Half a share.
HAMLET: A whole one, I.
    For thou dost know, O Damon dear,[7]

9. Helpful time for the crime.
1. Classical goddess of witchcraft.
2. Native power.
3. Uninjured.
4. Plumes.

5. Turn against.
6. Partnership in a company.
7. *Damon:* a common name in ancient
lyric poetry. Also, a legendary friend.

This realm dismantled was   570
Of Jove[8] himself, and now reigns here
A very, very—peacock.
HORATIO: You might have rhymed.[9]
HAMLET: O good Horatio, I'll take the ghost's word for a
  thousand pound. Didst perceive?   575
HORATIO: Very well, my lord.
HAMLET: Upon the talk of the poisoning.
HORATIO: I did very well note him.
HAMLET: Ah, ha! Come, some music. Come, the recorders.
  For if the king like not the comedy.   580
  Why then, belike he likes it not, perdy.[1]
Come, some music.
  [*Enter* ROSENCRANTZ *and* GUILDENSTERN.]
GUILDENSTERN: Good my lord, vouchsafe me a word with
  you.
HAMLET: Sir, a whole history.   585
GUILDENSTERN: The king, sir—
HAMLET: Ay, sir, what of him?
GUILDENSTERN: Is in his retirement marvellous distempered.
HAMLET: With drink, sir?
GUILDENSTERN: No, my lord, with choler.[2]   590
HAMLET: Your wisdom should show itself more richer to
  signify this to the doctor, for for me to put him to his
  purgation[3] would perhaps plunge him into more
  choler.
GUILDENSTERN: Good my lord, put your discourse into some   595
  frame,[4] and start not so wildly from my affair.
HAMLET: I am tame, sir. Pronounce.
GUILDENSTERN: The queen your mother, in most great afflic-
  tion of spirit, hath sent me to you.
HAMLET: You are welcome.   600
GUILDENSTERN: Nay, good my lord, this courtesy is not of the
  right breed. If it shall please you to make me a wholesome[5]

8. Chief Roman god.
9. "Ass," for example, would have com-
pleted the rhyme.
1. *Par Dieu* (by God).
2. Bile.
3. Treatment with a laxative.
4. Speech into some order.
5. Reasonable.

answer, I will do your mother's commandment. If not, your
pardon and my return[6] shall be the end of my business.

HAMLET: Sir, I cannot. 605

ROSENCRANTZ: What, my lord?

hamlet: Make you a wholesome answer; my wit's diseased.
But, sir, such answer as I can make, you shall command, or
rather, as you say, my mother. Therefore no more, but to
the matter. My mother, you say— 610

ROSENCRANTZ: Then thus she says: your behavior hath struck
her into amazement and admiration.[7]

HAMLET: O wonderful son, that can so stonish[8] a mother! But
is there no sequel at the heels of his mother's admiration?
Impart. 615

ROSENCRANTZ: She desires to speak with you in her closet[9] ere
you go to bed.

HAMLET: We shall obey, were she ten times our mother. Have
you any further trade with us?

ROSENCRANTZ: My lord, you once did love me. 620

HAMLET: And do still, by these pickers and stealers.[1]

ROSENCRANTZ: Good my lord, what is your cause of distemper? You do surely bar the door upon your own liberty, if
you deny your griefs to your friend.

HAMLET: Sir, I lack advancement. 625

ROSENCRANTZ: How can that be, when you have the voice of
the king himself for your succession in Denmark?

HAMLET: Ay, sir, but "while the grass grows"—the proverb[2] is
something musty.

[*Enter the* PLAYERS *with recorders.*]

O, the recorders! Let me see one. To withdraw with you[3]— 630
why do you go about to recover the wind of me, as if you
would drive me into a toil?[4]

GUILDENSTERN: O my lord, if my duty be too bold, my love is
too unmannerly.

6. That is, to the queen.
7. Wonder.
8. Astonish.
9. Bedroom.
1. These hands.
2. The proverb ends "the horse starves."

3. Let me step aside.
4. The figure is from hunting. Hamlet asks why Guildenstern is attempting to get windward of him, as if he would drive him into a net.

HAMLET: I do not well understand that. Will you play upon   635
this pipe?[5]

GUILDENSTERN: My lord, I cannot.

HAMLET: I pray you.

GUILDENSTERN: Believe me, I cannot.

HAMLET: I do beseech you.   640

GUILDENSTERN: I know no touch of it,[6] my lord.

HAMLET: It is as easy as lying. Govern these ventages[7] with
your fingers and thumb, give it breath with your mouth,
and it will discourse most eloquent music. Look you, these
are the stops.   645

GUILDENSTERN: But these cannot I command to any utt'rance
of harmony. I have not the skill.

HAMLET: Why, look you now, how unworthy a thing you
make of me! You would play upon me, you would seem to
know my stops, you would pluck out the heart of my mys-   650
tery, you would sound[8] me from my lowest note to the top
of my compass;[9] and there is much music, excellent voice,
in this little organ, yet cannot you make it speak. 'Sblood,
do you think I am easier to be played on than a pipe? Call
me what instrument you will, though you can fret[1] me, you   655
cannot play upon me.

    [*Enter* POLONIUS.]

God bless you, sir!

POLONIUS: My lord, the queen would speak with you, and
presently.

HAMLET: Do you see yonder cloud that's almost in shape of a   660
camel?

POLONIUS: By th' mass, and 'tis like a camel indeed.

HAMLET: Methinks it is like a weasel.

POLONIUS: It is backed like a weasel.

HAMLET: Or like a whale.   665

POLONIUS: Very like a whale.

---

5. Recorder.
6. Have no ability.
7. Cover and uncover these holes, or
stops.
8. Play.

9. Range.
1 To annoy; also, to play a guitar or similar instrument using the "frets," or small
bars on the neck.

HAMLET: Then I will come to my mother by and by. [*Aside.*]
  They fool me to the top of my bent.[2]—I will come by and
  by.
POLONIUS: I will say so.   [*Exit.*]   670
HAMLET: "By and by" is easily said. Leave me, friends.
                     [*Exeunt all but* HAMLET.]
  'Tis now the very witching time of night,
  When churchyards yawn, and hell itself breathes out
  Contagion to this world. Now could I drink hot blood,
  And do such bitter business as the day   675
  Would quake to look on. Soft, now to my mother.
  O heart, lose not thy nature; let not ever
  The soul of Nero[3] enter this firm bosom.
  Let me be cruel, not unnatural;
  I will speak daggers to her, but use none.   680
  My tongue and soul in this be hypocrites—
  How in my words somever she be shent,[4]
  To give them seals[5] never, my soul, consent!   [*Exit.*]

SCENE 3

A room in the castle. Enter KING, ROSENCRANTZ *and* GUILDEN-
STERN.

KING: I like him not, nor stands it safe with us
  To let his madness range. Therefore prepare you.
  I your commission will forthwith dispatch,
  And he to England shall along with you.
  The terms of our estate[1] may not endure   5
  Hazard so near 's as doth hourly grow
  Out of his brows.
GUILDENSTERN: We will ourselves provide,[2]
  Most holy and religious fear[3] it is

2. Treat me as an utter fool.
3. Roman emperor who reputedly murdered his mother.
4. However much by my words she is
shamed.

5. Fulfillment in action.
1. Condition of the state.
2. Equip (for the journey).
3. Care.

To keep those many many bodies safe
That live and feed upon your majesty.   10
ROSENCRANTZ: The single and peculiar[4] life is bound
    With all the strength and armor of the mind
    To keep itself from noyance,[5] but much more
    That spirit upon whose weal[6] depends and rests
    The lives of many. The cess[7] of majesty   15
    Dies not alone, but like a gulf[8] doth draw
    What's near it with it. It is a massy[9] wheel
    Fixed on the summit of the highest mount,
    To whose huge spokes ten thousand lesser things
    Are mortised and adjoined,[1] which when it falls,   20
    Each small annexment, petty consequence,
    Attends[2] the boist'rous ruin. Never alone
    Did the king sigh, but with a general groan.
KING: Arm[3] you, I pray you, to this speedy voyage,
    For we will fetters put about this fear,   25
    Which now goes too free-footed.
ROSENCRANTZ: We will haste us.
                        [*Exeunt* ROSENCRANTZ *and* GUILDENSTERN.]
        [*Enter* POLONIUS.]
POLONIUS: My lord, he's going to his mother's closet.
    Behind the arras I'll convey myself
    To hear the process. I'll warrant she'll tax him home,[4]
    And as you said, and wisely was it said,   30
    'Tis meet that some more audience than a mother,
    Since nature makes them partial, should o'erhear
    The speech, of vantage.[5] Fare you well, my liege.
    I'll call upon you ere you go to bed,
    And tell you what I know.
KING: Thanks, dear my lord.   35
                                    [*Exit* POLONIUS.]

---

4. The individual and private.
5. Harm.
6. Welfare.
7. Cessation.
8. Whirlpool.
9. Massive.

1. Are attached.
2. Joins in.
3. Prepare.
4. Sharply. *Process:* proceedings.
5. From a position of vantage.

O, my offence is rank, it smells to heaven;
It hath the primal eldest curse[6] upon't,
A brother's murder. Pray can I not,
Though inclination be as sharp as will.
My stronger guilt defeats my strong intent,   40
And like a man to double business[7] bound,
I stand in pause where I shall first begin,
And both neglect. What if this cursèd hand
Were thicker than itself with brother's blood,
Is there not rain enough in the sweet heavens   45
To wash it white as snow? Whereto serves mercy
But to confront the visage of offence?
And what's in prayer but this twofold force,
To be forestallèd[8] ere we come to fall,
Or pardoned being down?[9] Then I'll look up.   50
My fault is past. But, O, what form of prayer
Can serve my turn? "Forgive me my foul murder"?
That cannot be, since I am still possessed
Of those effects[1] for which I did the murder—
My crown, mine own ambition, and my queen.   55
May one be pardoned and retain th' offence?[2]
In the corrupted currents of this world
Offence's gilded[3] hand may shove by justice,
And oft 'tis seen the wicked prize itself
Buys out the law. But 'tis not so above.   60
There is no shuffling; there the action[4] lies
In his true nature, and we ourselves compelled,
Even to the teeth and forehead of[5] our faults,
To give in evidence. What then? What rests?[6]
Try what repentance can. What can it not?   65
Yet what can it when one cannot repent?
O wretched state! O bosom black as death!

6. That is, of Cain (the biblical figure   2. That is, benefits of the offense.
who murdered his brother, Abel).   3. Bearing gold as a bribe.
    7. Two mutually opposed interests.   4. Legal case.
    8. Prevented (from sin).   5. Face-to-face with.
    9. Having sinned.   6. Remains.
    1. Gains.

O liméd[7] soul, that struggling to be free
Art more engaged! Help, angels! Make assay.
Bow, stubborn knees, and heart with strings of steel,   70
Be soft as sinews of the new-born babe.
All may be well. [*He kneels.*]
    [*Enter* HAMLET.]
HAMLET: Now might I do it pat,[8] now 'a is a-praying,
    And now I'll do't—and so 'a goes to heaven,
    And so am I revenged. That would be scanned.[9]   75
    A villain kills my father, and for that,
    I, his sole son, do this same villain send
    To heaven.
    Why, this is hire and salary, not revenge.
    'A took my father grossly, full of bread,[1]   80
    With all his crimes broad blown, as flush[2] as May;
    And how his audit stands who knows save heaven?
    But in our circumstance and course of thought
    'Tis heavy with him; and am I then revenged
    To take him in the purging of his soul,   85
    When he is fit and seasoned[3] for his passage?
    No.
    Up, sword, and know thou a more horrid hent.[4]
    When he is drunk, asleep, or in his rage,
    Or in th' incestuous pleasure of his bed,   90
    At game a-swearing, or about some act
    That has no relish[5] of salvation in't—
    Then trip him, that his heels may kick at heaven,
    And that his soul may be as damned and black
    As hell, whereto it goes. My mother stays.   95
    This physic[6] but prolongs thy sickly days.   [*Exit.*]
KING: [*Rising.*] My words fly up, my thoughts remain below.
    Words without thoughts never to heaven go.   [*Exit.*]

---

7. Caught as with birdlime.
8. Easily.
9. Calls for evaluation.
1. In a state of sin and without fasting.
2. Full-blown, as vigorous.

3. Ready.
4. Opportunity.
5. Flavor.
6. Medicine.

SCENE 4

The Queen's chamber. Enter QUEEN *and* POLONIUS.

POLONIUS: 'A will come straight. Look you lay home to[1] him.
  Tell him his pranks have been too broad[2] to bear with,
  And that your grace hath screen'd and stood between
  Much heat and him. I'll silence me even here.
  Pray you be round[3] with him.   5
HAMLET: [*Within.*] Mother, mother, mother!
QUEEN: I'll warrant you. Fear[4] me not.
  Withdraw, I hear him coming.
    [POLONIUS *goes behind the arras. Enter* HAMLET.]
HAMLET: Now, mother, what's the matter?
QUEEN: Hamlet, thou hast thy father much offended.   10
HAMLET: Mother, you have my father much offended.
HAMLET: Come, come, you answer with an idle tongue.
HAMLET: Go, go, you question with a wicked tongue.
QUEEN: Why, how now, Hamlet?
HAMLET: What's the matter now?
QUEEN: Have you forgot me?
HAMLET: No, by the rood,[5] not so.   15
  You are the queen, your husband's brother's wife,
  And would it were not so, you are my mother.
QUEEN: Nay, then I'll set those to you that can speak.
HAMLET: Come, come, and sit you down. You shall not budge.
  You go not till I set you up a glass[6]   20
  Where you may see the inmost part of you.
QUEEN: What wilt thou do? Thou wilt not murder me?
  Help, ho!
POLONIUS: [*Behind.*] What, ho! help!
HAMLET: [*Draws.*] How now, a rat?   25
  Dead for a ducat, dead![7] [*Kills* POLONIUS *with a pass
    through the arras.*]
POLONIUS: [*Behind.*] O, I am slain!

1. Be sharp with.   5. Cross.
2. Outrageous.   6. Mirror.
3. Direct forthright.   7. I bet a gold coin he's dead.
4. Doubt.

QUEEN: O me, what hast thou done?
HAMLET: Nay, I know not.
    Is it the king?
QUEEN: O, what a rash and bloody deed is this!   30
HAMLET: A bloody deed!—almost as bad, good mother,
    As kill a king and marry with his brother.
QUEEN: As kill a king?
HAMLET: Ay, lady, it was my word.
    [*Parting the arras.*] Thou wretched, rash, intruding fool,
        farewell!
    I took thee for thy better. Take thy fortune.   35
    Thou find'st to be too busy[8] is some danger.—
    Leave wringing of your hands. Peace, sit you down
    And let me wring your heart, for so I shall
    If it be made of penetrable stuff,
    If damnéd custom have not brazed it[9] so   40
    That it be proof and bulwark against sense.[1]
QUEEN: What have I done that thou dar'st wag thy tongue
    In noise so rude against me?
HAMLET: Such an act
    That blurs the grace and blush of modesty,
    Calls virtue hypocrite, takes off the rose   45
    From the fair forehead of an innocent love
    And sets a blister[2] there, makes marriage-vows
    As false as dicers' oaths. O, such a deed
    As from the body of contraction[3] plucks
    The very soul, and sweet religion makes   50
    A rhapsody of words. Heaven's face does glow
    O'er this solidity and compound mass[4]
    With heated visage, as against the doom[5]—
    Is thought-sick at the act.
QUEEN: Ay me, what act
    That roars so loud and thunders in the index?[6]   55
HAMLET: Look here upon this picture and on this,

8 Officious.
9. Plated it with brass.
1. Feeling. *Proof:* armor.
2. Brand.

3. The marriage contract.
4. Meaningless mass (Earth).
5. Judgment Day.
6. Table of contents.

The counterfeit presentment[7] of two brothers.
See what a grace was seated on this brow:
Hyperion's curls, the front[8] of Jove himself,
An eye like Mars, to threaten and command,   60
A station like the herald Mercury[9]
New lighted[1] on a heaven-kissing hill—
A combination and a form indeed
Where every god did seem to set his seal,
To give the world assurance of a man.   65
This was your husband. Look you now what follows.
Here is your husband, like a mildewed ear
Blasting[2] his wholesome brother. Have you eyes?
Could you on this fair mountain leave to feed,
And batten[3] on this moor? Ha! have you eyes?   70
You cannot call it love, for at your age
The heyday in the blood is tame, it's humble,
And waits upon the judgment, and what judgment
Would step from this to this? Sense sure you have
Else could you not have motion, but sure that sense   75
Is apoplexed[4] for madness would not err,
Nor sense to ecstacy was ne'er so thralled
But it reserved some quantity of choice
To serve in such a difference.[5] What devil was't
That thus hath cozened you at hoodman-blind?[6]   80
Eyes without feeling, feeling without sight,
Ears without hands or eyes, smelling sans[7] all,
Or but a sickly part of one true sense
Could not so mope.[8] O shame! where is thy blush?
Rebellious hell,   85
If thou canst mutine[9] in a matron's bones,
To flaming youth let virtue be as wax

7. Portrait.
8. Forehead.
9. A bearing like that of the messenger of the gods.
1. Newly alighted.
2. Infecting. *Ear:* of corn.
3. Fatten.

4. Paralyzed.
5. The power to choose between such different men.
6. Blindman's buff. *Cozened:* cheated.
7. Without.
8. Be stupid.
9. Commit mutiny.

And melt in her own fire. Proclaim no shame
When the compulsive ardor gives the charge,[1]
Since frost itself as actively doth burn,   90
And reason panders[2] will.
QUEEN: O Hamlet, speak no more!
   Thou turn'st my eyes into my very soul;
   And there I see such black and grainéd[3] spots
   As will not leave their tinct.[4]
HAMLET: Nay, but to live
   In the rank sweat of an enseaméd[5] bed,   95
   Stewed in curruption, honeying and making love
   Over the nasty sty—
QUEEN: O, speak to me no more!
   These words like daggers enter in my ears;
   No more, sweet Hamlet.
HAMLET: A murderer and a villain,
   A slave that is not twentieth part the tithe[6]   100
   Of your precedent lord, a vice[7] of kings,
   A cutpurse[8] of the empire and the rule,
   That from a shelf the precious diadem stole
   And put it in his pocket—
QUEEN: No more.   105
      [Enter GHOST.]
HAMLET: A king of shreds and patches—
   Save me and hover o'er me with your wings,
   You heavenly guards! What would your gracious figure?
QUEEN: Alas, he's mad.
HAMLET: Do you not come your tardy[9] son to chide,   110
   That lapsed in time and passion lets go by
   Th' important acting of your dread command?
   O, say!
GHOST: Do not forget. This visitation
   Is but to whet thy almost blunted purpose.   115

1. Attacks.
2. Pimps for.
3. Ingrained.
4. Lose their color.
5. Greasy.

6. One-tenth.
7. The "Vice" was a clown or buffoon in morality plays. *Precedent lord:* first husband.
8. Pickpocket.
9. Slow to act.

But look, amazement on thy mother sits.
O, step between her and her fighting soul!
Conceit[1] in weakest bodies strongest works.
Speak to her, Hamlet.

HAMLET: How is it with you, lady?

QUEEN: Alas, how is't with you,   120
That you do bend[2] your eye on vacancy,
And with th' incorporal[3] air do hold discourse?
Forth at your eyes your spirits wildly peep,
And as the sleeping soldiers in th' alarm,
Your bedded hairs like life in excrements[4]   125
Start up and stand an end. O gentle son,
Upon the heat and flame of thy distemper
Sprinkle cool patience. Whereon do you look?

HAMLET: On him, on him! Look you how pale he glares.
His form and cause conjoined,[5] preaching to stones,   130
Would make them capable.[6]—Do not look upon me,
Lest with this piteous action you convert
My stern effects.[7] Then what I have to do
Will want true color—tears perchance for blood.

QUEEN: To whom do you speak this?   135

HAMLET: Do you see nothing there?

QUEEN: Nothing at all, yet all that is I see.

HAMLET: Nor did you nothing hear?

QUEEN: No, nothing but ourselves.

HAMLET: Why, look you there. Look how it steals away.   140
My father, in his habit[8] as he lived!
Look where he goes even now out at the portal.

                                        [*Exit* GHOST.]

QUEEN: This is the very coinage[9] of your brain.
The bodiless creation ecstasy[1]
Is very cunning[2] in.

---

1. Imagination.   7. Deeds.
2. Turn.   8. Costume.
3. Incorporeal.   9. Invention.
4. Nails and hair.   1. Madness.
5. Working together.   2. Skilled.
6. Of responding.

HAMLET: Ecstasy?   145
   My pulse as yours doth temperately keep time,
   And makes as healthful music. It is not madness
   That I have uttered. Bring me to the test,
   And I the matter will re-word, which madness
   Would gambol³ from. Mother, for love of grace,   150
   Lay not that flattering unction⁴ to your soul,
   That not your trespass but my madness speaks.
   It will but skin and film the ulcerous place
   Whiles rank corruption, mining⁵ all within,
   Infects unseen. Confess yourself to heaven,   155
   Repent what's past, avoid what is to come.
   And do not spread the compost on the weeds,
   To make them ranker. Forgive me this my virtue,
   For in the fatness of these pursy⁶ times
   Virtue itself of vice must pardon beg,   160
   Yea, curb⁷ and woo for leave to do him good.
QUEEN: O Hamlet, thou hast cleft my heart in twain.
HAMLET: O, throw away the worser part of it,
   And live the purer with the other half.
   Good night—but go not to my uncle's bed.   165
   Assume a virtue, if you have it not.
   That monster custom⁸ who all sense doth eat,
   Of habits devil, is angel yet in this,
   That to the use of actions fair and good
   He likewise gives a frock or livery   170
   That aptly⁹ is put on. Refrain tonight,
   And that shall lend a kind of easiness
   To the next abstinence; the next more easy;
   For use almost can change the stamp of nature,
   And either curb the devil, or throw him out   175
   With wondrous potency. Once more, good night,
   And when you are desirous to be blest,
   I'll blessing beg of you. For this same lord

3. Shy away.   7. Bow.
4. Ointment.   8. Habit.
5. Undermining.   9. Easily.
6. Bloated.

I do repent; but heaven hath pleased it so,
To punish me with this, and this with me,   180
That I must be their scourge and minister.
I will bestow[1] him and will answer well
The death I gave him. So, again, good night.
I must be cruel only to be kind.
Thus bad begins and worse remains behind.   185
One word more, good lady.

QUEEN: What shall I do?

HAMLET: Not this, by no means, that I bid you do:
Let the bloat[2] king tempt you again to bed,
Pinch wanton[3] on your cheek, call you his mouse,
And let him, for a pair of reechy[4] kisses,   190
Or paddling in your neck with his damned fingers,
Make you to ravel[5] all this matter out,
That I essentially am not in madness,
But mad in craft. 'Twere good you let him know,
For who that's but a queen, fair, sober, wise,   195
Would from a paddock, from a bat, a gib,[6]
Such dear concernings hide? Who would so do?
No, in despite of sense and secrecy,
Unpeg the basket on the house's top,
Let the birds fly, and like the famous ape,   200
To try conclusions, in the basket creep
And break your own neck down.[7]

QUEEN: Be thou assured, if words be made of breath
And breath of life, I have no life to breathe
What thou hast said to me.   205

HAMLET: I must to England; you know that?

QUEEN: Alack,
I had forgot. 'Tis so concluded on.

HAMLET: There's letters sealed, and my two school-fellows,
Whom I will trust as I will adders fanged,

1. Dispose of.
2. Bloated.
3. Lewdly.
4. Foul.
5. Reveal.
6. Tomcat. *Paddock:* toad.

7. Apparently a reference to a now-lost fable in which an ape, finding a basket containing a cage of birds on a housetop, opens the cage. The birds fly away. The ape, thinking that if he were in the basket he too could fly, enters, jumps out, and breaks his neck.

They bear the mandate; they must sweep[8] my way   210
And marshal me to knavery. Let it work,
For 'tis the sport to have the enginer
Hoist with his own petard;[9] and't shall go hard
But I will delve[1] one yard below their mines
And blow them at the moon. O, 'tis most sweet   215
When in one line two crafts directly meet.
This man shall set me packing.
I'll lug the guts into the neighbor room.
Mother, good night. Indeed, this counsellor
Is now most still, most secret, and most grave,   220
Who was in life a foolish prating knave.
Come sir, to draw toward an end with you.
Good night, mother.
        [*Exit the* QUEEN. *Then exit* HAMLET *tugging* POLONIUS.]

ACT IV
SCENE 1

A room in the castle. Enter KING, QUEEN, ROSENCRANTZ *and*
GUILDENSTERN.

KING: There's matter in these sighs, these profound heaves,
    You must translate;[1] 'tis fit we understand them.
    Where is your son?
QUEEN: Bestow this place on us a little while.
            [*Exeunt* ROSENCRANTZ *and* GUILDENSTERN.]
    Ah, mine own lord, what have I seen tonight!   5
    KING: What, Gertrude? How does Hamlet?
QUEEN: Mad as the sea and wind when both contend
    Which is the mightier. In his lawless fit,
    Behind the arras hearing something stir,
    Whips out his rapier, cries "A rat, a rat!"   10
    And in this brainish apprehension[2] kills
    The unseen good old man.
KING: O heavy deed!

8. Prepare. *Mandate:* command.   1. Explain.
9. Blown up by his own bomb.   2. Insane notion.
1. Dig.

It had been so with us had we been there.
His liberty is full of threats to all—
To you yourself, to us, to every one.   15
Alas, how shall this bloody deed be answered?
It will be laid to us, whose providence[3]
Should have kept short, restrained, and out of haunt,[4]
This mad young man. But so much was our love,
We would not understand what was most fit;   20
But, like the owner of a foul disease,
To keep it from divulging, let it feed
Even on the pith of life. Where is he gone?
QUEEN: To draw apart the body he hath killed,
    O'er whom his very madness, like some ore   25
    Among a mineral of metals base,
    Shows itself pure: 'a weeps for what is done.
KING: O Gertrude, come away!
    The sun no sooner shall the mountains touch
    But we will ship him hence, and this vile deed   30
    We must with all our majesty and skill
    Both countenance and excuse. Ho, Guildenstern!
        [Enter ROSENCRANTZ and GUILDENSTERN.]
    Friends both, go join you with some further aid.
    Hamlet in madness hath Polonius slain,
    And from his mother's closet hath he dragged him.   35
    Go seek him out; speak fair, and bring the body
    Into the chapel. I pray you haste in this.
            [Exeunt ROSENCRANTZ and GUILDENSTERN.]
    Come, Gertrude, we'll call up our wisest friends
    And let them know both what we mean to do
    And what's untimely done;   40
    Whose whisper o'er the world's diameter,
    As level as the cannon to his blank,[5]
    Transports his poisoned shot—may miss our name,
    And hit the woundless air. O, come away!
    My soul is full of discord and dismay.   45
                                            [Exeunt.]

3. Prudence.   5. Mark. *Level:* direct.
4. Away from court.

SCENE 2
A passageway. Enter HAMLET.

HAMLET: Safely stowed.

ROSENCRANTZ *and* GUILDENSTERN: [*Within.*] Hamlet! Lord
   Hamlet!

HAMLET: But soft, what noise? Who calls on Hamlet? O, here
   they come.   5
   [*Enter* ROSENCRANTZ, GUILDENSTERN, *and* OTHERS.]

ROSENCRANTZ: What have you done, my lord, with the dead
   body?

HAMLET: Compounded it with dust, whereto 'tis kin.

ROSENCRANTZ: Tell us where 'tis, that we may take it thence
   And bear it to the chapel.   10

HAMLET: Do not believe it.

ROSENCRANTZ: Believe what?

HAMLET: That I can keep your counsel and not mine own.
   Besides, to be demanded of a sponge—what replication[1]
   should be made by the son of a king?   15

ROSENCRANTZ: Take you me for a sponge, my lord?

HAMLET: Ay, sir, that soaks up the king's countenance,[2] his rewards, his authorities. But such officers do the king best
   service in the end. He keeps them like an apple in the corner of his jaw, first mouthed to be last swallowed. When he 20
   needs what you have gleaned, it is but squeezing you and,
   sponge, you shall be dry again.

ROSENCRANTZ: I understand you not, my lord.

HAMLET: I am glad of it. A knavish speech sleeps in a foolish ear.

ROSENCRANTZ: My lord, you must tell us where the body is,   25
   and go with us to the king.

HAMLET: The body is with the king, but the king is not with
   the body.
   The king is a thing—

GUILDENSTERN: A thing, my lord!

HAMLET: Of nothing. Bring me to him. Hide fox, and all   30
   after.[3]   [*Exeunt.*]

1. Answer. *Demanded of:* questioned by.   3. Apparently a reference to a children's
2. Favor.   game like hide-and-seek.

SCENE 3

A room in the castle. Enter KING.

KING: I have sent to seek him, and to find the body.
   How dangerous is it that this man goes loose!
   Yet must not we put the strong law on him.
   He's loved of the distracted[1] multitude,
   Who like not in their judgment but their eyes,   5
   And where 'tis so, th' offender's scourge[2] is weighed,
   But never the offence. To bear all smooth and even,
   This sudden sending him away must seem
   Deliberate pause.[3] Diseases desperate grown
   By desperate appliance are relieved,   10
   Or not at all.
      [*Enter* ROSENCRANTZ, GUILDENSTERN, *and all the rest.*]
                 How now! what hath befall'n?
ROSENCRANTZ: Where the dead body is bestowed, my lord,
   We cannot get from him.
KING: But where is he?
ROSENCRANTZ: Without, my lord; guarded, to know[4] your
      pleasure.
KING: Bring him before us.
ROSENCRANTZ: Ho! bring in the lord.   15
      [*They enter with* HAMLET.]
KING: Now, Hamlet, where's Polonius?
HAMLET: At supper.
KING: At supper? Where?
HAMLET: Not where he eats, but where 'a is eaten. A certain
   convocation of politic worms are e'en[5] at him. Your worm   20
   is your only emperor for diet. We fat all creatures else to fat
   us, and we fat ourselves for maggots. Your fat king and your
   lean beggar is but variable service—two dishes, but to one
   table. That's the end.
KING: Alas, alas!   25

---

1. Confused.
2. Punishment.
3. That is, not an impulse.

4. Await.
5. Now. *Convocation of politic:* gathering
of scheming (or cunning).

HAMLET: A man may fish with the worm that hath eat of a
    king, and eat of the fish that hath fed of that worm.

KING: What dost thou mean by this?

HAMLET: Nothing but to show you how a king may go a
    progress through the guts of a beggar.   30

KING: Where is Polonius?

HAMLET: In heaven. Send thither to see. If your messenger
    find him not there, seek him i' th' other place yourself. But
    if, indeed, you find him not within this month, you shall
    nose[6] him as you go up the stairs into the lobby.   35

KING: [*To* ATTENDANTS.] Go seek him there.

HAMLET: 'A will stay till you come.

                                   [*Exeunt* ATTENDANTS.]

KING: Hamlet, this deed, for thine especial safety—
    Which we do tender, as we dearly[7] grieve
    For that which thou hast done—must sent thee hence   40
    With fiery quickness. Therefore prepare thyself.
    The bark is ready, and the wind at help,
    Th' associates tend, and everything is bent
    For England.

HAMLET: For England?

KING: Ay, Hamlet.

HAMLET: Good.

KING: So it is, if thou knew'st our purposes.   45

HAMLET: I see a cherub that sees them. But come, for
    England!
    Farewell, dear mother.

KING: Thy loving father, Hamlet.

HAMLET: My mother. Father and mother is man and wife,
    man and wife is one flesh. So, my mother. Come, for   50
    England.   [*Exit.*]

KING: Follow him at foot;[8] tempt him with speed aboard.
    Delay it not; I'll have him hence tonight.
    Away! for everything is sealed and done
                           [*Exeunt all but the* KING.]

6. Smell.
7. Deeply. *Tender:* consider.

8. Closely.

That else leans on th' affair. Pray you make haste.   55
And, England, if my love thou hold'st at aught—
As my great power thereof may give thee sense,[9]
Since yet thy cicatrice[1] looks raw and red
After the Danish sword, and thy free awe
Pays homage to us—thou mayst not coldly set[2]   60
Our sovereign process,[3] which imports at full
By letters congruing[4] to that effect
The present death of Hamlet. Do it, England,
For like the hectic[5] in my blood he rages,
And thou must cure me. Till I know 'tis done,   65
Howe'er my haps, my joys were ne'er begun.   [*Exit.*]

SCENE 4
Near Elsinore. Enter FORTINBRAS *with his army.*

FORTINBRAS: Go, captain, from me greet the Danish king.
    Tell him that by his license Fortinbras
    Craves the conveyance[1] of a promised march
    Over his kingdom. You know the rendezvous.
    If that his majesty would aught with us,   5
    We shall express our duty in his eye,[2]
    And let him know so.
CAPTAIN: I will do't, my lord.
FORTINBRAS: Go softly on.   [*Exeunt all but the* CAPTAIN.]
    [*Enter* HAMLET, ROSENCRANTZ, GUILDENSTERN, *and*
    OTHERS.]
HAMLET: Good sir, whose powers are these?
CAPTAIN: They are of Norway, sir.   10
HAMLET: How purposed, sir, I pray you?
CAPTAIN: Against some part of Poland.
HAMLET: Who commands them, sir?
CAPTAIN: The nephew to old Norway, Fortinbras.

9. Of its value.   4. Agreeing.
1. Scar.   5. Chronic fever.
2. Set aside.   1. Escort.
3. Mandate.   2. Presence.

HAMLET: Goes it against the main[3] of Poland, sir,   15
  Or for some frontier?
CAPTAIN: Truly to speak, and with no addition,[4]
  We go to gain a little patch of ground
  That hath in it no profit but the name.
  To pay five ducats,[5] five, I would not farm it;   20
  Nor will it yield to Norway or the Pole
  A ranker rate should it be sold in fee.[6]
HAMLET: Why, then the Polack never will defend it.
CAPTAIN: Yes, it is already garrisoned.
HAMLET: Two thousand souls and twenty thousand ducats   25
  Will not debate the question of this straw.
  This is th' imposthume[7] of much wealth and peace,
  That inward breaks, and shows no cause without
  Why the man dies. I humbly thank you, sir.
CAPTAIN: God b'wi'ye, sir.   [*Exit.*]
ROSENCRANTZ: Will't please you go, my lord?   30
HAMLET: I'll be with you straight. Go a little before.
                              [*Exeunt all but* HAMLET.]
  How all occasions do inform against me,
  And spur my dull revenge! What is a man,
  If his chief good and market[8] of his time
  Be but to sleep and feed? A beast, no more.   35
  Sure he that made us with such large discourse,[9]
  Looking before and after, gave us not
  That capability and godlike reason
  To fust[1] in us unused. Now, whether it be
  Bestial oblivion, or some craven scruple   40
  Of thinking too precisely on th' event[2]—
  A thought which, quartered, hath but one part wisdom
  And ever three parts coward—I do not know
  Why yet I live to say "This thing's to do,"
  Sith[3] I have cause, and will, and strength, and means,   45

3. Central part.   8. Occupation.
4. Exaggeration.   9. Ample reasoning power.
5. That is, in rent.   1. Grow musty.
6. Outright. *Ranker:* higher.   2. Outcome.
7. Abscess.   3. Since.

To do't. Examples gross as earth exhort me.
Witness this army of such mass and charge,[4]
Led by a delicate and tender prince,
Whose spirit, with divine ambition puffed,
Makes mouths at[5] the invisible event,   50
Exposing what is mortal and unsure
To all that fortune, death, and danger dare,
Even for an eggshell. Rightly to be great
Is not to stir without great argument,
But greatly to find quarrel in a straw   55
When honor's at the stake. How stand I then,
That have a father killed, a mother stained,
Excitements of my reason and my blood,
And let all sleep, while to my shame I see
The imminent death of twenty thousand men   60
That for a fantasy and trick of fame
Go to their graves like beds, fight for a plot
Whereon the numbers cannot try the cause,
Which is not tomb enough and continent
To hide the slain?[6] O, from this time forth,   65
My thoughts be bloody, or be nothing worth!   [*Exit.*]

SCENE 5

A room in the castle. Enter QUEEN, HORATIO *and a* GENTLEMAN.

QUEEN: I will not speak with her.
GENTLEMAN: She is importunate, indeed distract.
    Her mood will needs to be pitied.
QUEEN: What would she have?
GENTLEMAN: She speaks much of her father, says she hears
    There's tricks i' th' world, and hems, and beats her heart,   5
    Spurns enviously at straws,[1] speaks things in doubt
    That carry but half sense. Her speech is nothing,
    Yet the unshapéd use of it doth move

4. Expense.
5. Scorns.
6. The plot of ground involved is so
small that it cannot contain the number of

men involved in fighting or furnish burial
space for the number of those who will
die.
    1. Takes offense at trifles.

The hearers to collection;² they yawn at it,
And botch the words up fit to their own thoughts,   10
Which, as her winks and nods and gestures yield them,
Indeed would make one think there might be thought,
Though nothing sure, yet much unhappily.
HORATIO: 'Twere good she were spoken with, for she may strew
Dangerous conjectures in ill-breeding minds.   15
QUEEN: Let her come in.   [*Exit* GENTLEMAN.]
    [*Aside.*] To my sick soul, as sin's true nature is,
    Each toy seems prologue to some great amiss.³
    So full of artless jealousy is guilt,
    It spills itself in fearing to be spilt.   20
    [*Enter* OPHELIA *distracted.*]
OPHELIA: Where is the beauteous majesty of Denmark?
QUEEN: How now, Ophelia!
OPHELIA: [*Sings.*]
    How should I your true love know
      From another one?
    By his cockle hat and staff,⁴   25
      And his sandal shoon.⁵
QUEEN: Alas, sweet lady, what imports this song?
OPHELIA: Say you? Nay, pray you mark. [*Sings.*]
    He is dead and gone, lady,
      He is dead and gone;   30
    At his head a grass-green turf,
      At his heels a stone.
    O, ho!
QUEEN: Nay, but Ophelia—
OPHELIA: Pray you mark. [*Sings.*]
    White his shroud as the mountain snow—
    [*Enter* KING.]
QUEEN: Alas, look here, my lord.   35
OPHELIA: [*Sings.*]
    Larded all with sweet flowers;

2. To decipher her meaning.
3. Catastrophe. *Toy:* trifle.
4. Things associated with a pilgrimage.
5. Shoes.

    Which bewept to the grave did not go
      With true-love showers.

KING: How do you, pretty lady?

OPHELIA: Well, God dild[6] you! They say the owl was a baker's   40
    daughter. Lord, we know what we are, but know not what
    we may be. God be at your table!

KING: Conceit[7] upon her father.

OPHELIA: Pray let's have no words of this, but when they ask
    you what it means, say you this: [*Sings.*]   45
    Tomorrow is Saint Valentine's day,
      All in the morning betime,
    And I a maid at your window,
      To be your Valentine.

    Then up he rose, and donn'd his clo'es,   50
      And dupped the chamber-door,
    Let in the maid, that out a maid[8]
      Never departed more.

KING: Pretty Ophelia!

OPHELIA: Indeed, without an oath, I'll make an end on't.   55
    [*Sings.*]
    By Gis[9] and by Saint Charity,
      Alack, and fie for shame!
    Young men will do't, if they come to't;
      By Cock,[1] they are to blame.
    Quoth she "before you tumbled me,   60
      You promised me to wed."
    He answers:
    "So would I'a done, by yonder sun,
      An thou hadst not come to my bed."

KING: How long hath she been thus?   65

OPHELIA: I hope all will be well. We must be patient, but I
    cannot choose but weep to think they would lay him i'
    th' cold ground. My brother shall know of it, and so I
    thank you for your good counsel. Come, my coach! Good

6. Yield.
7. Thought.
8. Virgin. *Dupped:* opened.
9. Jesus.
1. God.

night, ladies, good night. Sweet ladies, good night, good   70
night.
                                                      [*Exit.*]
KING: Follow her close; give her good watch, I pray you.
                        [*Exeunt* HORATIO *and* GENTLEMAN.]
    O, this is the poison of deep grief; it springs
    All from her father's death, and now behold!
    O Gertrude, Gertrude!   75
    When sorrows come, they come not single spies,
    But in battalions: first, her father slain;
    Next, your son gone, and he most violent author
    Of his own just remove; the people muddied,[2]
    Thick and unwholesome in their thoughts and whispers   80
    For good Polonius' death; and we have done but greenly[3]
    In hugger-mugger[4] to inter him; poor Ophelia
    Divided from herself and her fair judgment,
    Without the which we are pictures, or mere beasts;
    Last, and as much containing as all these,   85
    Her brother is in secret come from France,
    Feeds on his wonder, keeps himself in clouds,
    And wants not buzzers[5] to infect his ear
    With pestilent speeches of his father's death,
    Wherein necessity, of matter beggared,[6]   90
    Will nothing stick our person to arraign[7]
    In ear and ear.[8] O my dear Gertrude, this,
    Like to a murd'ring piece,[9] in many places
    Gives me superfluous death.
        [*A noise within.*]
QUEEN: Alack, what noise is this?   95
KING: Attend!
    Where are my Switzers?[1] Let them guard the door.
    What is the matter?

2. Disturbed.
3. Without judgment.
4. Haste.
5. And doesn't lack scandal mongers. *Couds:* rumors, suspicions.
6. Short on facts.

7. Accuse. *Stick:* hesitate.
8. From both sides.
9. A cannon that fires grapeshot so as to kill as many soldiers as possible.
1. Swiss guards.

MESSENGER: Save yourself, my lord.
  The ocean, overpeering of his list,[2]
  Eats not the flats with more impiteous[3] haste   100
  Then young Laertes, in a riotous head,[4]
  O'erbears your officers. The rabble call him lord,
  And as the world were now but to begin,
  Antiquity forgot, custom not known,
  The ratifiers and props of every word,   105
  They cry "Choose we, Laertes shall be king."
  Caps, hands, and tongues, applaud it to the clouds,
  "Laertes shall be king, Laertes king."
QUEEN: How cheerfully on the false trail they cry![5]
      [A noise within.]
  O, this is counter,[6] you false Danish dogs!   110
KING: The doors are broke.
      [Enter LAERTES, with OTHERS.]
LAERTES: Where is this king?—Sirs, stand you all without.
ALL: No, let's come in.
LAERTES: I pray you give me leave.
ALL: We will, we will.
LAERTES: I thank you. Keep[7] the door.
                              [Exeunt his followers.]
                              O thou vile king,   115
  Give me my father!
QUEEN: Calmly, good Laertes.
LAERTES: That drop of blood that's calm proclaims me bastard,
  Cries cuckold to my father, brands the harlot
  Even here between the chaste unsmirchéd brow
  Of my true mother.
KING: What is the cause, Laertes,   120
  That thy rebellion looks so giant-like?
  Let him go, Gertrude. Do not fear[8] our person.
  There's such divinity doth hedge a king

2. Towering above its limits.   6. Backward.
3. Pitiless.   7. Guard.
4. With an armed band.   8. Fear for.
5. As if following the scent.

That treason can but peep to[9] what it would,
Acts little of his will. Tell me, Laertes.   125
Why thou art thus incensed. Let him go, Gertrude.
Speak, man.
LAERTES: Where is my father?
KING: Dead.
QUEEN: But not by him.
KING: Let him demand[1] his fill.
LAERTES: How came he dead? I'll not be juggled with.
To hell allegiance, vows to the blackest devil,   130
Conscience and grace to the profoundest pit!
I dare damnation. To this point I stand,
That both the worlds I give to negligence,[2]
Let come what comes, only I'll be revenged
Most throughly[3] for my father.   135
KING: Who shall stay you?
LAERTES: My will, not all the world's.
And for my means, I'll husband[4] them so well
They shall go far with little.
KING: Good Laertes,
If you desire to know the certainty
Of your dear father, is't writ in your revenge   140
That, swoopstake,[5] you will draw both friend and foe,
Winner and loser?
LAERTES: None but his enemies.
KING: Will you know them, then?
LAERTES: To his good friends thus wide I'll ope my arms,
And like the kind life-rend'ring pelican,[6]   145
Repast them with my blood.
KING: Why, now you speak
Like a good child and a true gentleman.
That I am guiltless of your father's death,

9. See over or through a barrier.
1. Question.
2. That I disregard this world and the next.
3. Thoroughly.
4. Manage.
5. Sweeping the board.
6. The pelican was believed to feed her young with her own blood.

And am most sensibly in grief for it,
It shall as level[7] to your judgment 'pear   150
As day does to your eye.
     [*A noise within*: "Let her come in."]
LAERTES: How now? What noise is that?
     [*Enter* OPHELIA.]
O, heat dry up my brains! tears seven times salt
Burn out the sense and virtue[8] of mine eye!
By heaven, thy madness shall be paid with weight   155
Till our scale turn the beam. O rose of May,
Dear maid, kind sister, sweet Ophelia!
O heavens! is't possible a young maid's wits
Should be as mortal as an old man's life?
Nature is fine[9] in love, and where 'tis fine   160
It sends some precious instances of itself
After the thing it loves.
OPHELIA: [*Sings.*]
     They bore him barefac'd on the bier;
          Hey non nonny, nonny, hey nonny;
     And in his grave rain'd many a tear—   165
Fare you well, my dove!
LAERTES: Hadst thou thy wits, and didst persuade revenge,
     It could not move thus.
OPHELIA: You must sing "A-down, a-down, and you call him
     a-down-a." O, how the wheel becomes it! It is the false   170
     steward, that stole his master's daughter.
LAERTES: This nothing's more than matter.
OPHELIA: There's a rosemary, that's for remembrance. Pray
     you, love, remember. And there is pansies, that's for
     thoughts.   175
LAERTES: A document[1] in madness, thoughts and remem-
     brance fitted.
OPHELIA: There's fennel for you, and columbines. There's rue
     for you, and here's some for me. We may call it herb of
     grace a Sundays. O, you must wear your rue with a differ-   180

---

7. Plain.   9. Refined.
8. The feeling and function.   1. Lesson

ence. There's a daisy. I would give you some violets,[2] but they withered all when my father died. They say 'a made a good end. [*Sings.*]
    For bonny sweet Robin is all my joy.

LAERTES: Thought and affliction, passion, hell itself,   185
  She turns to favor[3] and to prettiness.

OPHELIA: [*Sings.*]
    And will 'a not come again?
    And will 'a not come again?
      No, no, he is dead,
      Go to thy death-bed,   190
    He never will come again.

    His beard was as white as snow,
    All flaxen was his poll;[4]
      He is gone, he is gone,
      And we cast away moan: 195
    God-a-mercy on his soul!
And of all Christian souls, I pray God. God b'wi'you.
                                     [*Exit.*]

LAERTES: Do you see this, O God?

KING: Laertes, I must commune with your grief,
  Or you deny me right. Go but apart,   200
  Make choice of whom your wisest friends you will,
  And they shall hear and judge 'twixt you and me.
  If by direct or by collateral[5] hand
  They find us touched,[6] we will our kingdom give,
  Our crown, our life, and all that we call ours,   205
  To you in satisfaction; but if not,
  Be you content to lend your patience to us,
  And we shall jointly labor with your soul
  To give it due content.

LAERTES: Let this be so.
  His means of death, his obscure funeral—   210

---

2. Fennel symbolized flattery; columbines, ungratefulness; rue, grief; daisies, lies; and violets, loyalty.
3. Beauty.
4. Head.
5. Indirect.
6. By guilt.

No trophy, sword, nor hatchment,[7] o'er his bones,
No noble rite nor formal ostentation[8]—
Cry to be heard, as 'twere from heaven to earth,
That I must call't in question.

KING: So you shall;
And where th' offence is, let the great axe fall.   215
I pray you go with me.   [*Exeunt.*]

SCENE 6

Another room in the castle. Enter HORATIO *and a* GENTLEMAN.

HORATIO: What are they that would speak with me?

GENTLEMAN: Sea-faring men, sir. They say they have letters for
you.

HORATIO: Let them come in.   [*Exit* GENTLEMAN.]
I do not know from what part of the world   5
I should be greeted, if not from Lord Hamlet.
        [*Enter* SAILORS.]

SAILOR: God bless you, sir.

HORATIO: Let him bless thee too.

SAILOR: 'A shall, sir, an't please him. There's a letter for you,
sir—it came from th' ambassador that was bound for En-   10
gland—if your name be Horatio, as I am let to know[1]
it is.

HORATIO: [*Reads.*] "Horatio, when thou shalt have over-
looked[2] this, give these fellows some means[3] to the king.
They have letters for him. Ere we were two days old at sea,   15
a pirate of very warlike appointment[4] gave us chase. Finding ourselves too slow of sail, we put on a compelled valor,
and in the grapple I boarded them. On the instant they got
clear of our ship, so I alone became their prisoner. They
have dealt with me like thieves of mercy, but they knew   20
what they did; I am to do a good turn for them. Let the
king have the letters I have sent, and repair thou to me with

7. Coat of arms.   2. Read through.
8. Pomp.   3. Access.
1. Informed.   4. Equipment.

as much speed as thou wouldest fly death. I have words to
speak in thine ear will make thee dumb; yet are they much
too light for the bore of the matter.[5] These good fellows   25
will bring thee where I am. Rosencrantz and Guildenstern
hold their course for England. Of them I have much to tell
thee. Farewell.

　　　　　　　　　　　　　　He that thou knowest thine, Hamlet."
Come, I will give you way[6] for these your letters,   30
And do't the speedier that you may direct me
To him from whom you brought them.   [*Exeunt.*]

SCENE 7

Another room in the castle. Enter KING *and* LAERTES.

KING: Now must your conscience my acquittance seal,[1]
　　And you must put me in your heart for friend,
　　Sith you have heard, and with a knowing ear,
　　That he which hath your noble father slain
　　Pursued my life.
LAERTES:　　　　　　It well appears. But tell me   5
　　Why you proceeded not against these feats,
　　So criminal and so capital in nature,
　　As by your safety, greatness, wisdom, all things else,
　　You mainly were stirred up.
KING:　　　　　　　　　O, for two special reasons,
　　Which may to you, perhaps, seem much unsinewed,[2]   10
　　But yet to me th' are strong. The queen his mother
　　Lives almost by his looks, and for myself—
　　My virtue or my plague, be it either which—
　　She is so conjunctive[3] to my life and soul
　　That, as the star moves not but in his sphere,[4]   15
　　I could not but by her. The other motive,

---

5. A figure from gunnery, referring to
shot that is too small for the size of the
weapons to be fired.
　6. Means of delivery.
　1. Grant me innocent.
　2. Weak.

3. Closely joined.
　4. A reference to the Ptolemaic cosmol-
ogy, in which planets and stars were believed
to revolve in crystalline spheres concentri-
cally about Earth.

Why to a public count[5] I might not go,
Is the great love the general gender[6] bear him,
Who, dipping all his faults in their affection,
Work like the spring that turneth wood to stone,[7]   20
Convert his gyves[8] to graces; so that my arrows,
Too slightly timbered[9] for so loud a wind,
Would have reverted to my bow again,
But not where I had aimed them.

LAERTES: And so have I a noble father lost,   25
A sister driven into desp'rate terms,
Whose worth, if praises may go back again,
Stood challenger on mount of all the age
For her perfections.[1] But my revenge will come.

KING: Break not your sleeps for that. You must not think   30
That we are made of stuff so flat and dull
That we can let our beard be shook with danger,
And think it pastime. You shortly shall hear more.
I loved you father, and we love our self,
And that, I hope, will teach you to imagine—   35
    [*Enter a* MESSENGER *with letters.*]
How now? What news?

MESSENGER: Letters, my lord, from Hamlet.
These to your majesty; this to the queen.

KING: From Hamlet! Who brought them?

MESSENGER: Sailors, my lord, they say. I saw them not.
They were given me by Claudio; he received them   40
Of him that brought them.

KING: Laertes, you shall hear them.—
Leave us.   [*Exit* MESSENGER.]
[*Reads.*] "High and mighty, you shall know I am set naked
on your kingdom. Tomorrow shall I beg leave to see your
kingly eyes; when I shall, first asking your pardon there-   45

---

5. Reckoning.
6. Common people.
7. Certain English springs contain so much lime that a lime covering will be deposited on a log that sits in one of them long enough.

8. Shackles, that is, faults.
9. Shafted.
1. Challenged the world to match her perfections.

unto, recount the occasion of my sudden and more strange
return.

Hamlet."

What should this mean? Are all the rest come back?
Or is it some abuse,[2] and no such thing?   50
LAERTES: Know you the hand?
KING: 'Tis Hamlet's character.[3] "Naked"!
   And in a postscript here, he says "alone."
   Can you devise[4] me?
LAERTES: I am lost in it, my lord. But let him come.   55
   It warms the very sickness in my heart
   That I shall live and tell him to his teeth
   "Thus didest thou."
KING: If it be so, Laertes—
   As how should it be so, how otherwise?—
   Will you be ruled by me?
LAERTES: Ay, my lord,   60
   So you will not o'errule me to a peace.
KING: To thine own peace. If he be now returned,
   As checking at[5] his voyage, and that he means
   No more to undertake it, I will work him
   To an exploit now ripe in my device,   65
   Under the which he shall not choose but fall;
   And for his death no wind of blame shall breathe
   But even his mother shall uncharge[6] the practice
   And call it accident.
LAERTES: My lord, I will be ruled;
   The rather if you could devise it so   70
   That I might be the organ.[7]
KING: It falls right.
   You have been talked of since your travel much,
   And that in Hamlet's hearing, for a quality
   Wherein they say you shine. Your sum of parts
   Did not together pluck such envy from him   75

---

2. Trick.   5. Turning aside from.
3. Handwriting.   6. Not find villainy in.
4. Explain it to.   7. Instrument.

As did that one, and that, in my regard,
Of the unworthiest siege.[8]

LAERTES: What part is that, my lord?

KING: A very riband in the cap of youth,
  Yet needful too, for youth no less becomes
  The light and careless livery that it wears   80
  Than settled age his sables and his weeds,[9]
  Importing health and graveness. Two months since
  Here was a gentleman of Normandy.
  I have seen myself, and served against, the French,
  And they can[1] well on horseback, but this gallant   85
  Had witchcraft in't. He grew unto his seat,
  And to such wondrous doing brought his horse,
  As had he been incorpsed and demi-natured[2]
  With the brave beast. So far he topped my thought
  That I, in forgery[3] of shapes and tricks,   90
  Come short of what he did.

LAERTES: A Norman was't?

KING: A Norman.

LAERTES: Upon my life, Lamord.

KING: The very same.

LAERTES: I know him well. He is the brooch indeed
  And gem of all the nation.   95

KING: He made confession[4] of you,
  And gave you such a masterly report
  For art and exercise in your defence,[5]
  And for your rapier most especial,
  That he cried out 'twould be a sight indeed   100
  If one could match you. The scrimers[6] of their nation
  He swore had neither motion, guard, nor eye,
  If you opposed them. Sir, this report of his
  Did Hamlet so envenom with his envy
  That he could nothing do but wish and beg   105

8. Rank.
9. Dignified clothing.
1. Perform.
2. Shared a body and a nature.

3. Imagination.
4. Gave a report.
5. Skill in fencing.
6. Swordsmen.

Your sudden coming o'er, to play with you.
Now out of this—

LAERTES: What out of this, my lord?

KING: Laertes, was your father dear to you?
Or are you like the painting of a sorrow,
A face without a heart?

LAERTES: Why ask you this? 110

KING: Not that I think you did not love your father,
But that I know love is begun by time,
And that I see in passages of proof,[7]
Time qualifies the spark and fire of it.
There lives within the very flame of love 115
A kind of wick or snuff that will abate it,
And nothing is at a like goodness still,
For goodness, growing to a plurisy,[8]
Dies in his own too much.[9] That we would do,
We should do when we would; for this "would" changes, 120
And hath abatements and delays as many
As there are tongues, are hands, are accidents,
And then this "should" is like a spendthrift's sigh
That hurts by easing. But to the quick of th' ulcer—
Hamlet comes back; what would you undertake 125
To show yourself in deed your father's son
More than in words?

LAERTES: To cut his throat i' th' church.

KING: No place indeed should murder sanctuarize;[1]
Revenge should have no bounds. But, good Laertes,
Will you do this? Keep close within your chamber. 130
Hamlet returned shall know you are come home.
We'll put on those shall praise your excellence,
And set a double varnish[2] on the fame
The Frenchman gave you, bring you in fine[3] together,
And wager on your heads. He, being remiss,[4] 135

7. Tests of experience.
8. Fullness.
9. Excess.
1. Provide sanctuary for murder.

2. Gloss.
3. In short.
4. Careless.

Most generous, and free from all contriving,
Will not peruse[5] the foils, so that with ease,
Or with a little shuffling, you may choose
A sword unbated,[6] and in a pass of practice
Requite him for your father.
LAERTES: I will do't,   140
And for that purpose I'll anoint my sword.
I bought an unction of a mountebank
So mortal that but dip a knife in it,
Where it draws blood no cataplasm[7] so rare,
Collected from all simples[8] that have virtue   145
Under the moon, can save the thing from death
That is but scratched withal. I'll touch my point
With this contagion, that if I gall[9] him slightly,
It may be death.
KING: Let's further think of this,
Weigh what convenience both of time and means   150
May fit us to our shape. If this should fail,
And that our drift look[1] through our bad performance,
'Twere better not assayed. Therefore this project
Should have a back or second that might hold
If this did blast in proof.[2] Soft, let me see.   155
We'll make a solemn wager on your cunnings—
I ha't.
When in your motion you are hot and dry—
As make your bouts more violent to that end—
And that he calls for drink, I'll have prepared him   160
A chalice for the nonce, whereon but sipping,
If he by chance escape your venomed stuck,[3]
Our purpose may hold there.—But stay, what noise?
          [*Enter* QUEEN.]
QUEEN: One woe doth tread upon another's heel,
So fast they follow. Your sister's drowned, Laertes.   165
LAERTES: Drowned? O, where?

5. Examine.
6. Not blunted.
7. Poultice.
8. Herbs.

9. Scratch.
1. Intent become obvious.
2. Fail when tried.
3. Thrust.

QUEEN: There is a willow grows aslant the brook
   That shows his hoar leaves in the glassy stream.
   Therewith fantastic garlands did she make
   Of crowflowers, nettles, daisies, and long purples   170
   That liberal shepherds give a grosser[4] name,
   But our cold[5] maids do dead men's fingers call them.
   There on the pendent boughs her coronet weeds
   Clamb'ring to hang, an envious[6] sliver broke,
   When down her weedy trophies and herself   175
   Fell in the weeping brook. Her clothes spread wide,
   And mermaid-like awhile they bore her up,
   Which time she chanted snatches of old tunes,
   As one incapable[7] of her own distress,
   Or like a creature native and indued[8]   180
   Unto that element. But long it could not be
   Till that her garments, heavy with their drink,
   Pulled the poor wretch from her melodious lay
   To muddy death.
LAERTES: Alas, then she is drowned?
QUEEN: Drowned, drowned.   185
LAERTES: Too much of water hast thou, poor Ophelia,
   And therefore I forbid my tears; but yet
   It is our trick; nature her custom holds,
   Let shame say what it will. When these[9] are gone,
   The woman will be out. Adieu, my lord.   190
   I have a speech o' fire that fain would blaze
   But that this folly drowns it.   *[Exit.]*
KING: Let's follow, Gertrude.
   How much I had to do to calm his rage!
   Now fear I this will give it start again;
   Therefore let's follow.   *[Exeunt.]*   195

---

4. Coarser. *Liberal:* vulgar.   7. Unaware.
5. Chaste.   8. Habituated.
6. Malicious.   9. His tears.

ACT V
SCENE 1
A churchyard. Enter two CLOWNS.[1]

CLOWN: Is she to be buried in Christian burial when she wil-
fully seeks her own salvation?

OTHER: I tell thee she is. Therefore make her grave straight.
The crowner hath sat on her,[2] and finds it Christian
burial.   5

CLOWN: How can that be, unless she drowned herself in her
own defence?

OTHER: Why, 'tis found so.

CLOWN: It must be "se offendendo";[3] it cannot be else. For
here lies the point: if I drown myself wittingly, it argues an   10
act, and an act hath three branches— it is to act, to do, to
perform; argal,[4] she drowned herself wittingly.

OTHER: Nay, but hear you, Goodman Delver.

CLOWN: Give me leave. Here lies the water; good. Here stands
the man; good. If the man go to this water and drown him-   15
self, it is, will he, nill he, he goes—mark you that. But if
the water come to him and drown him, he drowns not
himself. Argal, he that is not guilty of his own death short-
ens not his own life.

OTHER: But is this law?   20

CLOWN: Ay, marry, is't; crowner's quest law.

OTHER: Will you ha' the truth on't? If this had not been a gen-
tlewoman, she should have been buried out o' Christian
burial.

CLOWN: Why, there thou say'st. And the more pity that great   25
folk should have count'nance[5] in this world to drown
or hang themselves more than their even-Christen.[6]
Come, my spade. There is no ancient gentlemen but
gard'ners, ditchers, and grave-makers. They hold up Adam's
profession.   30

---

1. Rustics.
2. Coroner held an inquest (below, "quest").
3. An error for *se defendendo*, "in self-
defense."

4. An error for *ergo*.
5. Approval.
6. Fellow Christians.

OTHER: Was he a gentleman?

CLOWN: 'A was the first that ever bore arms.

OTHER: Why, he had none.

CLOWN: What, art a heathen? How dost thou understand the
Scripture? The Scripture says Adam digged. Could he dig 35
without arms? I'll put another question to thee. If thou an-
swerest me not to the purpose, confess thyself—

OTHER: Go to.

CLOWN: What is he that builds stronger than either the mason,
the shipwright, or the carpenter? 40

OTHER: The gallows-maker, for that frame outlives a thousand
tenants.

CLOWN: I like thy wit well, in good faith. The gallows does
well. But how does it well? It does well to those that do ill.
Now thou dost ill to say the gallows is built stronger than 45
the church. Argal, the gallows may do well to thee. To't
again,⁷ come.

OTHER: Who builds stronger than a mason, a shipwright, or a
carpenter?

CLOWN: Ay tell me that, and unyoke.⁸ 50

OTHER: Marry, now I can tell.

CLOWN: To't.

OTHER: Mass, I cannot tell.

CLOWN: Cudgel thy brains no more about it, for your dull ass
will not mend his pace with beating. And when you are 55
asked this question next, say "a grave maker." The houses
he makes lasts till doomsday. Go, get thee in, and fetch me
a stoup⁹ of liquor.   [*Exit* OTHER CLOWN.]

        [*Enter* HAMLET *and* HORATIO *as* CLOWN *digs and sings.*]
        In youth, when I did love, did love,
            Methought it was very sweet, 60
        To contract the time for-a my behove,¹
            O, methought there-a was nothing-a meet.

HAMLET: Has this fellow no feeling of his business, that 'a
sings in grave-making?

---

7. Guess again.   9. Mug.
8. Finish the matter.   1. Advantage. *Contract:* shorten.

HORATIO: Custom hath made it in him a property of easiness.   65
HAMLET: 'Tis e'en so. The band of little employment hath the
   daintier sense.
CLOWN: [*Sings.*]
      But age, with his stealing steps,
         Hath clawed me in his clutch,
      And hath shipped me into the land,   70
         As if I had never been such. [*Throws up a skull.*]
HAMLET: That skull had a tongue in it, and could sing once.
   How the knave jowls[2] it to the ground, as if 'twere Cain's
   jawbone, that did the first murder! This might be the pate
   of a politician, which this ass now o'erreaches;[3] one that   75
   would circumvent God, might it not?
HORATIO: It might, my lord.
HAMLET: Or of a courtier, which could say, "Good morrow,
   sweet lord! How does thou, sweet lord?" This might be my
   Lord Such-a-one, that praised my Lord Such-a-one's horse,   80
   when 'a meant to beg it, might it not?
HORATIO: Ay, my lord.
HAMLET: Why, e'en so, and now my Lady Worm's, chapless,[4]
   and knock'd about the mazzard[5] with a sexton's spade.
   Here's fine revolution, an[6] we had the trick to see't. Did   85
   these bones cost no more the breeding but to play at
   loggets[7] with them? Mine ache to think on't.
CLOWN: [*Sings.*]
      A pick-axe and a spade, a spade,
         For and a shrouding sheet:
      O, a pit of clay for to be made   90
         For such a guest is meet. [*Throws up another skull.*]
HAMLET: There's another. Why may not that be the skull of a
   lawyer? Where be his quiddities now, his quillets, his cases,
   his tenures, and his tricks?[8] Why does he suffer this mad
   knave now to knock him about the sconce[9] with a dirty   95

---

2. Hurls.
3. Gets the better of.
4. Lacking a lower jaw.
5. Head.
6. Reversal of fortune, if.

7. Small pieces of wood thrown as part
of a game.
8. In this speech Hamlet lists legal terms
relating to property transactions.
9. Head.

shovel, and will not tell him of his action of battery? Hum! This fellow might be in's time a great buyer of land, with his statutes, his recognizances, his fines, his double vouchers, his recoveries. Is this the fine[1] of his fines, and the recovery of his recoveries, to have his fine pate full of fine dirt? Will his vouchers vouch him no more of his purchases, and double ones too, than the length and breadth of a pair of indentures?[2] The very conveyances of his lands will scarcely lie in this box, and must th' inheritor himself have no more, ha?

HORATIO: Not a jot more, my lord.

HAMLET: Is not parchment made of sheepskins?

HORATIO: Ay, my lord, and of calves' skins too.

HAMLET: They are sheep and calves which seek out assurance in that. I will speak to this fellow. Whose grave's this, sirrah?

CLOWN: Mine, sir. [*Sings.*]

  O, a pit of clay for to be made
    For such a guest is meet.

HAMLET: I think it be thine indeed, for thou liest in't.

CLOWN: You lie out on't, sir, and therefore 'tis not yours. For my part, I do not lie in't, yet it is mine.

HAMLET: Thou dost lie in't, to be in't and say it is thine. 'Tis for the dead, not for the quick;[3] therefore thou liest.

CLOWN: 'Tis a quick lie, sir; 'twill away again from me to you.

HAMLET: What man dost thou dig it for?

CLOWN: For no man, sir.

HAMLET: What woman, then?

CLOWN: For none neither.

HAMLET: Who is to be buried in't?

CLOWN: One that was a woman, sir; but, rest her soul, she's dead.

HAMLET: How absolute the knave is! We must speak by the card,[4] or equivocation will undo us. By the Lord, Horatio, this three years I have took note of it, the age is grown so

100

105

110

115

120

125

130

1. End.
2. Contracts.

3. Living.
4. Exactly. *Absolute:* literal.

picked[5] that the toe of the peasant comes so near the heel
of the courtier, he galls his kibe.[6] How long hast thou been
a grave-maker?

CLOWN: Of all the days i' th' year, I came to't that day that our
last King Hamlet overcame Fortinbras.   135

HAMLET: How long is that since?

CLOWN: Cannot you tell that? Every fool can tell that. It was
that very day that young Hamlet was born—he that is
mad, and sent into England.

HAMLET: Ay, marry, why was he sent into England?   140

CLOWN: Why, because 'a was mad. 'A shall recover his wits
there; or, if 'a do not, 'tis no great matter there.

HAMLET: Why?

CLOWN: 'Twill not be seen in him there. There the men are as
mad as he.   145

HAMLET: How came he mad?

CLOWN: Very strangely, they say.

HAMLET: How strangely?

CLOWN: Faith, e'en with losing his wits.

HAMLET: Upon what ground?   150

CLOWN: Why, here in Denmark. I have been sexton here, man
and boy, thirty years.

HAMLET: How long will a man lie i' th' earth ere he rot?

CLOWN: Faith, if 'a be not rotten before 'a die—as we have
many pocky[7] corses now-a-days that will scarce hold the   155
laying in—'a will last you some eight year or nine year. A
tanner will last you nine year.

HAMLET: Why he more than another?

CLOWN: Why, sir, his hide is so tanned with his trade that 'a
will keep out water a great while; and your water is a sore   160
decayer of your whoreson dead body. Here's a skull now
hath lien[8] you i' th' earth three and twenty years.

HAMLET: Whose was it?

CLOWN: A whoreson mad fellow's it was. Whose do you think
it was?   165

HAMLET: Nay, I know not.

5. Refined.
6. Rubs a blister on his heel.

7. Riddled with pox (syphilis).
8. Lain. *Whoreson:* bastard (figuratively).

CLOWN: A pestilence on him for a mad rogue! 'A poured a flagon of Rhenish on my head once. This same skull, sir, was, sir, Yorick's skull, the king's jester.

HAMLET: [*Takes the skull.*] This?   170

CLOWN: E'en that.

HAMLET: Alas, poor Yorick! I knew him, Horatio—a fellow of infinite jest, of most excellent fancy. He hath bore me on his back a thousand times, and now how abhorred in my imagination it is! My gorge[9] rises at it. Here hung those lips   175
that I have kissed I know not how oft. Where be your gibes now, your gambols, your songs, your flashes of merriment that were wont to set the table on a roar? Not one now to mock your own grinning? Quite chap-fall'n?[1] Now get you to my lady's chamber, and tell her, let her paint an inch   180
thick, to this favor[2] she must come. Make her laugh at that. Prithee, Horatio, tell me one thing.

HORATIO: What's that, my lord?

HAMLET: Dost thou think Alexander looked o' this fashion i' th' earth?   185

HORATIO: E'en so.

HAMLET: And smelt so? Pah! [*Throws down the skull.*]

HORATIO: E'en so, my lord.

HAMLET: To what base uses we may return, Horatio! Why may not imagination trace the noble dust of Alexander till 'a   190
find it stopping a bung-hole?

HORATIO: 'Twere to consider too curiously[3] to consider so.

HAMLET: No, faith, not a jot, but to follow him thither with modesty[4] enough, and likelihood to lead it. Alexander died, Alexander was buried, Alexander returneth to dust; the   195
dust is earth; of earth we make loam; and why of that loam whereto he was converted might they not stop a beer-barrel?

> Imperious Cæsar, dead and turned to clay,
> Might stop a hole to keep the wind away.   200
> O, that that earth which kept the world in awe

9. Throat.
1. Lacking a lower jaw.
2. Appearance.
3. Precisely.
4. Moderation.

Should patch a wall t'expel the winter's flaw![5]
But soft, but soft awhile! Here comes the king,
The queen, the courtiers.
    [*Enter* KING, QUEEN, LAERTES, *and the Corse with a* PRIEST
    and LORDS *attendant.*]
                            Who is this they follow?
And with such maiméd[6] rites? This doth betoken   205
The corse they follow did with desperate hand
Fordo its own life. 'Twas of some estate.[7]
Couch we[8] awhile and mark. [*Retires with* HORATIO.]
LAERTES: What ceremony else?[9]
HAMLET: That is Laertes, a very noble youth. Mark.   210
LAERTES: What ceremony else?
PRIEST: Here obsequies have been as far enlarged[1]
  As we have warranty. Her death was doubtful,
  And but that great command o'ersways the order,[2]
  She should in ground unsanctified been lodged   215
  Till the last trumpet. For charitable prayers,
  Shards, flints, and pebbles, should be thrown on her.
  Yet here she is allowed her virgin crants,[3]
  Her maiden strewments,[4] and the bringing home
  Of bell and burial.   220
LAERTES: Must there no more be done?
PRIEST: No more be done.
  We should profane the service of the dead
  To sing a requiem and such rest to her
  As to peace-parted souls.
LAERTES: Lay her i' th' earth,
  And from her fair and unpolluted flesh   225
  May violets spring! I tell thee, churlish priest,
  A minist'ring angel shall my sister be
  When thou liest howling.[5]
HAMLET: What, the fair Ophelia!

---

5. Gusty wind.
6. Abbreviated.
7. Rank. *Fordo:* destroy.
8. Conceal ourselves.
9. More.

1. Extended.
2. Usual rules.
3. Wreaths.
4. Flowers strewn on the grave.
5. In Hell.

QUEEN: Sweets to the sweet. Farewell! [*Scatters flowers.*]
  I hoped thou shouldst have been my Hamlet's wife.   230
  I thought thy bride-bed to have decked, sweet maid,
  And not t' have strewed thy grave.
LAERTES: O, treble woe
  Fall ten times treble on that curséd head
  Whose wicked deed thy most ingenious sense[6]
  Deprived thee of! Hold off the earth awhile,   235
  Till I have caught her once more in mine arms. [*Leaps into
    the grave.*]
  Now pile your dust upon the quick and dead,
  Till of this flat a mountain you have made
  T' o'er-top old Pelion or the skyish head
  Of blue Olympus.[7]   240
HAMLET: [*Coming forward.*] What is he whose grief
  Bears such an emphasis, whose phrase of sorrow
  Conjures[8] the wand'ring stars, and makes them stand
  Like wonder-wounded hearers? This is I,
  Hamlet the Dane. [HAMLET *leaps into the grave and they*   245
    grapple.]
LAERTES: The devil take thy soul!
HAMLET: Thou pray'st not well.
  I prithee take thy fingers from my throat,
  For though I am not splenitive[9] and rash,
  Yet have I in me something dangerous,
  Which let thy wisdom fear. Hold off thy hand.   250
KING: Pluck them asunder.
QUEEN: Hamlet! Hamlet!
ALL: Gentlemen!
HORATIO: Good my lord, be quiet.
    [*The* ATTENDANTS *part them, and they come out of the*
    grave.]
HAMLET: Why, I will fight with him upon this theme   255
  Until my eyelids will no longer wag.[1]
QUEEN: O my son, what theme?

6. Lively mind.   9. Hot-tempered.
7. Like Pelion, mountain in Greece.   1. Move.
8. Casts a spell on.

HAMLET: I loved Ophelia. Forty thousand brothers
  Could not with all their quantity of love
  Make up my sum. What wilt thou do for her?   260
KING: O, he is mad, Laertes.
QUEEN: For love of God, forbear[2] him.
HAMLET: 'Swounds, show me what th'owt do.
  Woo't[3] weep, woo't fight, woo't fast, woo't tear thyself,
  Woo't drink up eisel,[4] eat a crocodile?   265
  I'll do't. Dost come here to whine?
  To outface[5] me with leaping in her grave?
  Be buried quick with her, and so will I.
  And if thou prate of mountains, let them throw
  Millions of acres on us, till our ground,   270
  Singeing his pate against the burning zone,[6]
  Make Ossa[7] like a wart! Nay, an thou'lt mouth,
  I'll rant as well as thou.
QUEEN: This is mere madness;
  And thus awhile the fit will work on him.
  Anon, as patient as the female dove   275
  When that her golden couplets[8] are disclosed,
  His silence will sit drooping.
HAMLET: Hear you, sir.
  What is the reason that you use me thus?
  I loved you ever. But it is no matter.
  Let Hercules himself do what he may,   280
  The cat will mew, and dog will have his day.   *[Exit.]*
KING: I pray thee, good Horatio, wait upon[9] him.

                         [Exit HORATIO.]

  [*To* LAERTES.] Strengthen your patience in our last night's
    speech.
  We'll put the matter to the present push.[1]—
  Good Gertrude, set some watch over your son.—   285
  This grave shall have a living monument.

2. Bear with.
3. Will you.
4. Vinegar.
5. Get the best of.
6. Sky in the torrid zone.

7. Mountain in Greece.
8. Pair of eggs.
9. Attend.
1. Immediate trial.

An hour of quiet shortly shall we see;
Till then in patience our proceeding be.   [*Exeunt.*]

SCENE 2
A hall or public room. Enter HAMLET *and* HORATIO.

HAMLET: So much for this, sir; now shall you see the other.
    You do remember all the circumstance?
HORATIO: Remember it, my lord!
HAMLET: Sir, in my heart there was a kind of fighting
    That would not let me sleep. Methought I lay   5
    Worse than the mutines in the bilboes.[1] Rashly,
    And praised be rashness for it—let us know,
    Our indiscretion sometime serves us well,
    When our deep plots do pall; and that should learn[2] us
    There's a divinity that shapes our ends,   10
    Rough-hew them how we will—
HORATIO: That is most certain.
HAMLET: Up from my cabin,
    My sea-gown scarfed[3] about me, in the dark
    Groped I to find out them,[4] had my desire,
    Fingered their packet, and in fine[5] withdrew   15
    To mine own room again, making so bold,
    My fears forgetting manners, to unseal
    Their grand commission; where I found, Horatio—
    Ah, royal knavery!—an exact command,
    Larded[6] with many several sorts of reasons,   20
    Importing Denmark's health, and England's too,
    With, ho! such bugs and goblins in my life,[7]
    That on the supervise, no leisure bated,[8]
    No, not to stay the grinding of the axe,
    My head should be struck off.
HORATIO: Is't possible?   25

---

1. Mutineers in the stocks.
2. Teach. *Pall:* weaken and die.
3. Wrapped.
4. That is, Rosencrantz and Guildenstern.

5. Quickly. *Fingered:* stole.
6. Garnished.
7. Such dangers if I remained alive.
8. As soon as the commission was read, no pause allowed.

HAMLET: Here's the commission; read it at more leisure.
    But wilt thou hear now how I did proceed?
HORATIO: I beseech you.
HAMLET: Being thus benetted round with villainies,
    Ere I could make a prologue to my brains,   30
    They had begun the play. I sat me down,
    Devised a new commission, wrote it fair.[9]
    I once did hold it, as our statists[1] do,
    A baseness to write fair, and labored much
    How to forget that learning; but sir, now   35
    It did me yeoman's service. Wilt thou know
    Th' effect[2] of what I wrote?
HORATIO: Ay, good my lord.
HAMLET: An earnest conjuration[3] from the king,
    As England was his faithful tributary,
    As love between them like the palm might flourish,   40
    As peace should still her wheaten garland wear
    And stand a comma 'tween their amities[4]
    And many such like as's of great charge,[5]
    That on the view and knowing of these contents,
    Without debatement further more or less,   45
    He should those bearers put to sudden death,
    Not shriving-time allowed.[6]
HORATIO: How was this sealed?
HAMLET: Why, even in that was heaven ordinant,[7]
    I had my father's signet in my purse,
    Which was the model of that Danish seal,   50
    Folded the writ up in the form of th' other,
    Subscribed it, gave't th' impression,[8] placed it safely,
    The changeling[9] never known. Now, the next day
    Was our sea-fight, and what to this was sequent[1]
    Thou knowest already.   55

9. Legibly. *Devised:* made.
1. Politicians.
2. Contents.
3. Appeal.
4. And link their friendships.
  5. Important clauses beginning with "as";
also, asses bearing heavy burdens.

6. Without time for confession.
7. Operative.
8. Of the seal.
9. Alteration.
1. Followed.

HORATIO: So Guildenstern and Rosencrantz go to't.
HAMLET: Why, man, they did make love to this employment.
    They are not near my conscience; their defeat[2]
    Does by their own insinuation grow.
    'Tis dangerous when the baser nature comes   60
    Between the pass and fell incensèd points[3]
    Of mighty opposites.
HORATIO: Why, what a king is this!
HAMLET: Does it not, think thee, stand me now upon—
    He that hath killed my king and whored my mother,
    Popped in between th' election and my hopes,[4]   65
    Thrown out his angle[5] for my proper life,
    And with such coz'nage[6]—is't not perfect conscience
    To quit[7] him with this arm? And is't not to be damned
    To let this canker of our nature come
    In further evil?   70
HORATIO: It must be shortly known to him from England
    What is the issue of the business there.
HAMLET: It will be short; the interim is mine.
    And a man's life's no more than to say "one."
    But I am very sorry, good Horatio,   75
    That to Laertes I forgot myself;
    For by the image of my cause I see
    The portraiture of his. I'll court his favors.
    But sure the bravery[8] of his grief did put me
    Into a tow'ring passion.
HORATIO: Peace; who comes here?   80
    [*Enter* OSRIC.]
OSRIC: Your lordship is right welcome back to Denmark.
HAMLET: I humbly thank you, sir. [*Aside to* HORATIO.] Dost
    know this water-fly?
HORATIO: [*Aside to* HAMLET.] No, my good lord.
HAMLET: [*Aside to* HORATIO.] Thy state is the more gracious,   85
    for 'tis a vice to know him. He hath much land, and fertile.

2. Death. *Are not near:* do not touch.
3. That is, amidst dangerous swordplay.
4. Between the selection of the next king and Hamlet's desire for the throne.
5. Fishhook.
6. Trickery.
7. Repay.
8. Exaggerated display.

Let a beast be lord of beasts, and his crib shall stand at the king's mess. 'Tis a chough,[9] but as I say, spacious in the possession of dirt.

OSRIC: Sweet lord, if your lordship were at leisure, I should impart a thing to you from his majesty. 90

HAMLET: I will receive it, sir, with all diligence of spirit. Put your bonnet to his right use. 'Tis for the head.

OSRIC: I thank your lordship, it is very hot.

HAMLET: No, believe me, 'tis very cold; the wind is northerly. 95

OSRIC: It is indifferent[1] cold, my lord, indeed.

HAMLET: But yet methinks it is very sultry and hot for my complexion.[2]

OSRIC: Exceedingly, my lord; it is very sultry, as 'twere—I cannot tell how. My lord, his majesty bade me signify to you 100 that 'a has laid a great wager on your head. Sir, this is the matter—

HAMLET: I beseech you, remember. [*Moves him to put on his hat.*]

OSRIC: Nay, good my lord; for my ease, in good faith. Sir, here is newly come to court Laertes; believe me, an absolute 105 gentleman, full of most excellent differences,[3] of very soft society and great showing.[4] Indeed, to speak feelingly of him, he is the card or calendar of gentry, for you shall find in him the continent[5] of what part a gentleman would see. 110

HAMLET: Sir, his definement[6] suffers no perdition in you, though I know to divide him inventorially would dozy[7] th' arithmetic of memory, and yet but yaw[8] neither in respect of his quick sail. But in the verity of extolment, I take him to be a soul of great article, and his infusion[9] of such dearth 115 and rareness as, to make true diction of him, his semblage[1]

9. Jackdaw, a bird.
1. Moderately.
2. Temperament.
3. Qualities.
4. Good manners.
5. Sum total. *Calendar:* measure.

6. Description.
7. To examine him bit by bit would daze.
8. Steer wildly.
9. Great scope, and his nature.
1. To speak truly about him, his likeness.

is his mirror, and who else would trace him, his umbrage,[2]
nothing more.

OSRIC: Your lordship speaks most infallibly of him.

HAMLET: The concernancy,[3] sir? Why do we wrap the gentle-   120
man in our more rawer breath?[4]

OSRIC: Sir?

HORATIO: Is't not possible to understand in another tongue?
You will to't, sir, really.

HAMLET: What imports the nomination[5] of this gentleman?   125

OSRIC: Of Laertes?

HORATIO: [Aside.] His purse is empty already. All's golden
words are spent.

HAMLET: Of him, sir.

OSRIC: I know you are not ignorant—   130

HAMLET: I would you did, sir; yet, in faith, if you did, it would
not much approve me. Well, sir.

OSRIC: You are not ignorant of what excellence Laertes is—

HAMLET: I dare not confess that, lest I should compare[6] with
him in excellence; but to know a man well were to know   135
himself.

OSRIC: I mean, sir, for his weapon; but in the imputation[7] laid
on him by them, in his meed he's unfellowed.[8]

HAMLET: What's his weapon?

OSRIC: Rapier and dagger.   140

HAMLET: That's two of his weapons—but well.

OSRIC: The king, sir, hath wagered with him six Barbary
horses, against the which he has impawned,[9] as I take it, six
French rapiers and poniards, with their assigns, as girdle,
hangers,[1] and so. Three of the carriages, in faith, are very   145
dear to fancy,[2] very responsive to the hilts, most delicate
carriages, and of very liberal conceit.[3]

2. Would keep pace with him, his shadow.
3. Meaning.
4. Cruder words.
5. Naming.
6. That is, compare myself.
7. Reputation.

8. Unequaled in his excellence.
9. Staked.
1. Belts from which swords hang. *Assigns:* accessories.
2. Finely designed.
3. Intricately decorated. *Delicate:* well adjusted.

HAMLET: What call you the carriages?

HORATIO: [*Aside to* HAMLET.] I knew you must be edified by the margent[4] ere you had done.   150

OSRIC: The carriages, sir, are the hangers.

HAMLET: The phrase would be more germane to the matter if we could carry a cannon by our sides. I would it might be hangers till then. But on! Six Barbary horses against six French swords, their assigns, and three liberal conceited   155 carriages; that's the French bet against the Danish. Why is this all impawned, as you call it?

OSRIC: The king, sir, hath laid, sir, that in a dozen passes between yourself and him he shall not exceed you three hits; he hath laid on twelve for nine, and it would come to im-   160 mediate trial if your lordship would vouchsafe the answer.

HAMLET: How if I answer no?

OSRIC: I mean, my lord, the opposition of your person in trial.[5]

HAMLET: Sir, I will walk here in the hall. If it please his   165 majesty, it is the breathing time[6] of day with me. Let the foils be brought, the gentleman willing, and the king hold his purpose; I will win for him an I can. If not, I will gain nothing but my shame and the odd hits.

OSRIC: Shall I deliver you so?   170

HAMLET: To this effect, sir, after what flourish your nature will.

OSRIC: I commend my duty to your lordship.

HAMLET: Yours, yours. [*Exit* OSRIC.] He does well to commend it himself; there are no tongues else for's turn.

HORATIO: This lapwing runs away with the shell on his head.[7]   175

HAMLET: 'A did comply, sir, with his dug[8] before 'a sucked it. Thus has he, and many more of the same bevy that I know the drossy age dotes on, only got the tune of the time; and out of an habit of encounter, a king of yesty[9] collection which carries them through and through the most fanned   180

4. Marginal gloss.
5. Your participation in the contest.
6. Time for exercise.
7. The lapwing was thought to be so precocious that it could run immediately after

being hatched, even, as here, with bits of the shell still on its head.
8. Deal formally . . . with his mother's breast.
9. Yeasty.

and winnowed opinions; and do but blow them to their trial, the bubbles are out.

[*Enter a* LORD.]

LORD: My lord, his majesty commended him to you by young Osric, who brings back to him that you attend him in the hall. He sends to know if your pleasure hold to play with Laertes, or that you will take longer time.   185

HAMLET: I am constant to my purposes; they follow the king's pleasure. If his fitness speaks, mine is ready; now or whensoever, provided I be so able as now.

LORD: The king and queen and all are coming down.   190

HAMLET: In happy time.

LORD: The queen desires you to use some gentle entertainment[1] to Laertes before you fall to play.

HAMLET: She well instructs me.   [*Exit* LORD.]

HORATIO: You will lose this wager, my lord.   195

HAMLET: I do not think so. Since he went into France I have been in continual practice. I shall win at the odds. But thou wouldst not think how ill[2] all's here about my heart. But it's no matter.

HORATIO: Nay, good my lord—   200

HAMLET: It is but foolery, but it is such a kind of gaingiving[3] as would perhaps trouble a woman.

HORATIO: If your mind dislike anything, obey it. I will forestall their repair[4] hither, and say you are not fit.

HAMLET: Not a whit, we defy augury. There is special provi-   205
dence in the fall of a sparrow. If it be now, 'tis not to come;
if it be not to come, it will be now; if it be not now, yet it
will come. The readiness is all. Since no man of aught he
leaves knows, what is't to leave betimes? Let be.

[*A table prepared. Enter* TRUMPETS, DRUMS, *and* OFFICERS *with cushions;* KING, QUEEN, OSRIC *and* ATTENDANTS *with foils, daggers, and* LAERTES.]

KING: Come, Hamlet, come and take this hand from me. [*The*   210
KING *puts* LAERTES' *hand into* HAMLET'S.]

1. Cordiality.   3. Misgiving.
2. Uneasy.   4. Coming.

HAMLET: Give me your pardon, sir. I have done you wrong,
    But pardon 't as you are a gentleman.
    This presence[5] knows, and you must needs have heard,
    How I am punished with a sore distraction.
    What I have done   215
    That might your nature, honor, and exception[6]
    Roughly awake, I here proclaim was madness.
    Was't Hamlet wronged Laertes? Never Hamlet.
    If Hamlet from himself be ta'en away,
    And when he's not himself does wrong Laertes,   220
    Then Hamlet does it not, Hamlet denies it.
    Who does it then? His madness. If't be so,
    Hamlet is of the faction that is wronged;
    His madness is poor Hamlet's enemy.
    Sir, in this audience,   225
    Let my disclaiming from[7] a purposed evil
    Free[8] me so far in your most generous thoughts
    That I have shot my arrow o'er the house
    And hurt my brother.
LAERTES: I am satisfied in nature,
    Whose motive in this case should stir me most   230
    To my revenge. But in my terms of honor
    I stand aloof, and will no reconcilement
    Till by some elder masters of known honor
    I have a voice[9] and precedent of peace.
    To keep my name ungored.[1] But till that time   235
    I do receive your offered love like love,
    And will not wrong it.
HAMLET: I embrace it freely,
    And will this brother's wager frankly[2] play.
    Give us the foils. Come on.
LAERTES: Come, one for me.
HAMLET: I'll be your foil, Laertes. In mine ignorance   240

5. Company.
6. Resentment.
7. Denying of.
8. Absolve.

9. Authority.
1. Unshamed.
2. Without rancor.

Your skill shall, like a star i' th' darkest night,
Stick fiery off[3] indeed.

LAERTES: You mock me, sir.

HAMLET: No, by this hand.

KING: Give them the foils, young Osric. Cousin Hamlet,
You know the wager?

HAMLET: Very well, my lord;   245
Your Grace has laid the odds o' th' weaker side.

KING: I do not fear it, I have seen you both;
But since he is bettered[4] we have therefore odds.

LAERTES: This is too heavy; let me see another.

HAMLET: This likes me well. These foils have all a[5] length?   250
[They prepare to play.]

OSRIC: Ay, my good lord.

KING: Set me the stoups of wine upon that table.
If Hamlet give the first or second hit,
Or quit in answer of[6] the third exchange,
Let all the battlements their ordnance fire.   255
The king shall drink to Hamlet's better breath,
And in the cup an union[7] shall he throw,
Richer than that which four successive kings
In Denmark's crown have worn. Give me the cups,
And let the kettle[8] to the trumpet speak,   260
The trumpet to the cannoneer without,
The cannons to the heavens, the heaven to earth,
"Now the king drinks to Hamlet." Come, begin—
[Trumpets the while.]
And you, the judges, bear a wary eye.

HAMLET: Come on, sir.

LAERTES: Come, my lord.
[They play.]

HAMLET: One.

LAERTES: No.

HAMLET: Judgment?   265

3. Shine brightly.
4. Reported better.
5. The same. *Likes:* suits.

6. Or repay.
7. Pearl.
8. Kettledrum.

OSRIC: A hit, a very palpable hit.
> [*Drums, trumpets, and shot. Flourish; a piece goes off.*]
LAERTES: Well, again.
KING: Stay, give me drink. Hamlet, this pearl is thine.
> Here's to thy health. Give him the cup.
HAMLET: I'll play this bout first; set it by awhile.   270
> Come.
> [*They play.*]
> Another hit; what say you?
LAERTES: A touch, a touch, I do confess't.
KING: Our son shall win.
QUEEN: He's fat,[9] and scant of breath.
> Here, Hamlet, take my napkin, rub thy brows.   275
> The queen carouses to thy fortune, Hamlet.
HAMLET: Good madam!
KING: Gertrude, do not drink.
QUEEN: I will, my lord; I pray you pardon me.
KING: [*Aside.*] It is the poisoned cup; it is too late.   280
HAMLET: I dare not drink yet, madam; by and by.
QUEEN: Come, let me wipe thy face.
LAERTES: My lord, I'll hit him now.
KING: I do not think't.
LAERTES: [*Aside.*] And yet it is almost against my conscience.
HAMLET: Come, for the third, Laertes. You do but dally.   285
> I pray you pass[1] with your best violence;
> I am afeard you make a wanton of me.[2]
LAERTES: Say you so? Come on.
> [*They play.*]
OSRIC: Nothing, neither way.
LAERTES: Have at you now!   290
> [LAERTES *wounds* HAMLET: *then, in scuffling, they change*
> *rapiers, and* HAMLET *wounds* LAERTES.]
KING: Part them. They are incensed.
HAMLET: Nay, come again.
> [*The* QUEEN *falls.*]

---

9. Out of shape.   2. Trifle with me.
1. Attack.

OSRIC: Look to the queen there, ho!

HORATIO: They bleed on both sides. How is it, my lord?

OSRIC: How is't, Laertes?   295

LAERTES: Why, as a woodcock to mine own springe,[3] Osric.
    I am justly killed with mine own treachery.

HAMLET: How does the queen?

KING: She swoons to see them bleed.

QUEEN: No, no, the drink, the drink! O my dear Hamlet!
    The drink, the drink! I am poisoned. [*Dies.*]   300

HAMLET: O, villainy! Ho! let the door be locked.
    Treachery! seek it out.

LAERTES: It is here, Hamlet. Hamlet, thou art slain;
    No med'cine in the world can do thee good.
    In thee there is not half an hour's life.   305
    The treacherous instrument is in thy hand,
    Unbated[4] and envenomed. The foul practice
    Hath turned itself on me. Lo, here I lie,
    Never to rise again. Thy mother's poisoned.
    I can no more. The king, the king's to blame.   310

HAMLET: The point envenomed too?
    Then, venom, to thy work. [*Hurts the* KING.]

ALL: Treason! treason!

KING: O, yet defend me, friends. I am but hurt.[5]

HAMLET: Here, thou incestuous, murd'rous, damnéd Dane,   315
    Drink off this potion. Is thy union here?
    Follow my mother.
        [*The* KING *dies.*]

LAERTES: He is justly served.
    It is a poison tempered[6] by himself.
    Exchange forgiveness with me, noble Hamlet.
    Mine and my father's death come not upon thee,   320
    Nor thine on me! [*Dies.*]

HAMLET: Heaven make thee free of it! I follow thee.
    I am dead, Horatio. Wretched queen, adieu!
    You that look pale and tremble at this chance,[7]

---

3. Snare.   6. Mixed.
4. Unblunted.   7. Circumstance.
5. Wounded.

That are but mutes or audience to this act,   325
Had I but time, as this fell sergeant Death
Is strict in his arrest,[8] O, I could tell you—
But let it be. Horatio, I am dead:
Thou livest; report me and my cause aright
To the unsatisfied.[9]
HORATIO: Never believe it.   330
I am more an antique Roman than a Dane.[1]
Here's yet some liquor left.
HAMLET: As th'art a man,
Give me the cup. Let go. By heaven; I'll ha't.
O God, Horatio, what a wounded name,
Things standing thus unknown, shall live behind me!   335
If thou didst ever hold me in thy heart,
Absent thee from felicity awhile,
And in this harsh world draw thy breath in pain,
To tell my story.
    [A march afar off.]
                    What warlike noise is this?
OSRIC: Young Fortinbras, with conquest come from Poland,   340
To th' ambassadors of England gives
This warlike volley.
HAMLET: O, I die, Horatio!
The potent poison quite o'er-crows[2] my spirit.
I cannot live to hear the news from England,
But I do prophesy th' election lights
On Fortinbras. He has my dying voice.[3]   345
So tell him, with th' occurrents,[4] more and less,
Which have solicited[5]—the rest is silence. [Dies.]
HORATIO: Now cracks a noble heart. Good night, sweet
    prince,
And flights of angels sing thee to thy rest!   350
    [March within.]

8. Summons to court.   2. Overcomes.
9. Uninformed.   3. Support.
1. Horatio proposes to kill himself, as an   4. Circumstances.
ancient Roman might in similar circum-   5. Brought about this scene.
stances.

Why does the drum come hither?
　　[*Enter* FORTINBRAS, *with the* AMBASSADORS *and with drum,*
　　colors, and ATTENDANTS.]
FORTINBRAS: Where is this sight?
HORATIO:　　　　　　　　　　What is it you would see?
　　If aught of woe or wonder, cease your search.
FORTINBRAS: This quarry cries on havoc.[6] O proud death,
　　What feast is toward[7] in thine eternal cell　　　　　　　355
　　That thou so many princes at a shot
　　So bloodily hast struck?
AMBASSADORS:　　　　　　The sight is dismal;
　　And our affairs from England come too late.
　　The ears are senseless[8] that should give us hearing
　　To tell him his commandment is fulfilled,　　　　　　360
　　That Rosencrantz and Guildenstern are dead.
　　Where should we have our thanks?
HORATIO:　　　　　　　　　　Not from his[9] mouth,
　　Had it th' ability of life to thank you.
　　He never gave commandment for their death.
　　But since, so jump[1] upon this bloody question,　　　　365
　　You from the Polack wars, and you from England,
　　Are here arrived, give orders that these bodies
　　High on a stage be placéd to the view,
　　And let me speak to th' yet unknowing world
　　How these things came about. So shall you hear　　　370
　　Of carnal, bloody, and unnatural acts;
　　Of accidental judgments, casual[2] slaughters;
　　Of deaths put on by cunning and forced cause;
　　And, in this upshot,[3] purposes mistook
　　Fall'n on th' inventors' heads. All this can I　　　　375
　　Truly deliver.
FORTINBRAS:　　Let us haste to hear it,
　　And call the noblest to the audience.[4]

6. The game killed in the hunt proclaims
a slaughter.
7. In preparation.
8. Without sense of hearing.
9. That is, Claudius's.

1. Exactly.
2. Brought about by apparent accident.
3. Result.
4. Hearing.

For me, with sorrow I embrace my fortune.
I have some rights of memory[5] in this kingdom,
Which now to claim my vantage[6] doth invite me.   380
HORATIO: Of that I shall have also cause to speak,
    And from his mouth whose voice will draw on more.
    But let this same be presently performed,
    Even while men's minds are wild, lest more mischance
    On plots and errors happen.
FORTINBRAS: Let four captains   385
    Bear Hamlet like a soldier to the stage,
    For he was likely, had he been put on,[7]
    To have proved most royal; and for his passage
    The soldier's music and the rite of war
    Speak loudly for him.   390
    Take up the bodies. Such a sight as this
    Becomes the field, but here shows much amiss.
    Go, bid the soldiers shoot.
            [*Exeunt marching. A peal of ordinance shot off.*]

ca. 1600

Henrik Ibsen
1828–1906

A DOLL HOUSE

*Ibsen's early plays, beginning in 1850, were poetic, mythic, and ro-
mantic. But in the late 1860s he began writing in plain language
about the struggles of ordinary, middle-class people. Theatergoers
saw on the stage for the first time people just like themselves, who
talked as they did, dealt with the same issues they dealt with, and
lived the same kinds of lives. The people in the audience became the
subjects of the stories dramatized on stage. These plays are sometimes called "social dramas" because they tend to reveal defects in
society and the ways those defects hindered the individual's personal*

5. Succession.   7. Elected king.
6. Position.

growth. The route to the individual's full and unchained growth became Ibsen's most persistent theme, and A Doll House *represented the centerpiece of his realistic period.*

The rise of the middle class during this time intensified the subjection of women. Women of all classes exercised no political power in the European democracies until they gained the vote in the twentieth century. They had unequal rights in marriage: a husband owned what today would be joint property, and a wife surrendered property she owned even before marriage to her husband's absolute control. Women had unequal rights to divorce and risked losing their children if they pressed for a separation from even an abusive husband. And mainstream attitudes—often based on scientific mistakes, like the comparison of brain sizes between men and women— took for granted that women were mentally inferior to men.

Such attitudes, coupled with the middle class's fetish for home life, left few roles for women other than wife and mother and domestic ornament. Not until late in the nineteenth century could women attend university, and even then they rarely did so. They were systematically excluded from the professions, like medicine and law. Married middle-class women seldom worked outside their homes, so as not to embarrass their husbands. Unmarried middle-class women had very narrow career choices. Middle-class women generally were trained to perform subservient roles, learning, for example, to converse, to entertain, to play a musical instrument, to sketch (but not to paint with oils), to read French or Italian (but not Latin or Greek, the languages that prepared one for the professions), and so on.

As you might expect, many people, men and women alike, were dissatisfied with these conditions, so the "woman question" became a vital social issue. In 1869, John Stuart Mill's revolutionary book The Subjection of Women, *which argued that society ought to extend equal rights to women, was translated into German. Ibsen read the translation, and though he continued to believe that women were mentally inferior to men, he began to realize that both sexes held the right to individualism. And he recognized that Victorian society's compulsory domestication of women made it especially hard for them to fully realize their potential.*

Ironically, Ibsen did not consider himself a feminist. He saw his plays as chronicling the struggles of the individual—any individ-

*ual, man or woman, artist or schoolteacher, mythic hero or house-
wife—against the forces of banality, mediocrity, and philistinism.
Nora Helmer's story, in* A Doll House, *is one of these chronicles.*

*Nora is based on someone Ibsen knew. In 1869, by then a famous
playwright in his forties, he became a mentor to a twenty-year-old
writer named Laura Peterson, who lived in Copenhagen. Taken by
her personality, Ibsen called her "lark" and "songbird," and their
friendship grew even after Peterson married a poor schoolteacher in
Denmark. The husband fell ill and was advised to travel south to
warmer climates; Peterson secretly borrowed the money for the trip,
could not pay off the loan, and resorted to forging a note. She confided in Ibsen, who indignantly advised her to confess to her husband. But when she did confess, her husband, enraged, divorced
her. This cruel treatment broke the woman, who ended up in an
asylum. Laura Peterson's story—and the poor role he played in it—
affected Ibsen deeply.*

In the summer of 1878, he sent A Doll House *to Copenhagen,
where it was first produced. An immediate success, the play quickly
swept through Scandinavia, Germany, Finland, Poland, Russia,
Italy, and England. Audiences were attracted to Nora; some sympa-
thized with her, and others were revolted by her. The play constituted the biggest literary controversy of its generation, inspiring
ardent defenders and troubled detractors.*

*It also reinvented the theater. Realistic social drama would re-
main on the European stage for generations. In England, the great
playwright George Bernard Shaw considered himself the direct de-
scendent of Ibsen, and Shaw's social dramas dominated London's
theatrical tastes well into the twentieth century. To get a feel for this
"realism," you might contrast Ibsen's domestic drama with the plays
by Sophocles and Shakespeare, comparing the characters, the scope
of the stories, and the uses of language.*

*A good way to engage yourself in this play is to debate Nora's
choice. Did she do the right thing? What else might she have done?
Can you envision a marriage like hers today? You shouldn't need
much imagination to recognize similar cruxes in contemporary
lives—struggles between people's obligations to others, the impulse
to conform to middle-class standards of behavior, and individuals'
duties to themselves.*

A Doll House*

THE CHARACTERS

TORVALD HELMER, *a lawyer*   THE HELMERS' THREE SMALL
NORA, *his wife*   CHILDREN
DR. RANK   ANNE-MARIE, *their nurse*
MRS. LINDE   HELENE, *a maid*
NILS KROGSTAD, *a bank clerk*   A DELIVERY BOY

The action takes place in HELMER's *residence.*

ACT ONE

A comfortable room, tastefully but not expensively furnished. A door to the right in the back wall leads to the entryway; another to the left leads to HELMER's *study. Between these doors, a piano. Midway in the left-hand wall a door, and farther down a window. Near the window a round table with an armchair and a small sofa. In the right-hand wall, toward the rear, a door, and nearer the foreground a porcelain stove with two armchairs and a rocking chair beside it. Between the stove and the side door, a small table. Engravings on the walls. An* etagère[1] *with china figures and other small art objects; a small bookcase with richly bound books; the floor carpeted; a fire burning in the stove. It is a winter day.*

A bell rings in the entryway; shortly after we hear the door being unlocked. NORA *comes into the room, humming happily to herself; she is wearing street clothes and carries an armload of packages, which she puts down on the table to the right. She has left the hall door open; and through it a* DELIVERY BOY *is seen, holding a Christmas tree and a basket, which he gives to the* MAID *who let them in.*

NORA: Hide the tree well, Helene. The children mustn't get a glimpse of it till this evening, after it's trimmed. [*To the* DELIVERY BOY, *taking out her purse.*] How much?
DELIVERY BOY: Fifty, ma'am.
NORA: There's a crown. No, keep the change. [*The* BOY *thanks her*

---

*Translated by Rolf Fjelde.

1. Small piece of furniture with shelves for displaying small articles.

and leaves. NORA *shuts the door. She laughs softly to herself while taking off her street things. Drawing a bag of macaroons from her pocket, she eats a couple, then steals over and listens at her husband's study door.*] Yes, he's home. [*Hums again as she moves to the table right.*]

HELMER: [*From the study.*] Is that my little lark twittering out there?

NORA: [*Busy opening some packages.*] Yes, it is.

HELMER: Is that my squirrel rummaging around?

NORA: Yes!

HELMER: When did my squirrel get in?

NORA: Just now. [*Putting the macaroon bag in her pocket and wiping her mouth.*] Do come in, Torvald, and see what I've bought.

HELMER: Can't be disturbed. [*After a moment he opens the door and peers in, pen in hand.*] Bought, you say? All that there? Has the little spendthrift been out throwing money around again?

NORA: Oh, but Torvald, this year we really should let ourselves go a bit. It's the first Christmas we haven't had to economize.

HELMER: But you know we can't go squandering.

NORA: Oh yes, Torvald, we can squander a little now. Can't we? Just a tiny, wee bit. Now that you've got a big salary and are going to make piles and piles of money.

HELMER: Yes—starting New Year's. But then it's a full three months till the raise comes through.

NORA: Pooh! We can borrow that long.

HELMER: Nora! [*Goes over and playfully takes her by the ear.*] Are your scatterbrains off again? What if today I borrowed a thousand crowns, and you squandered them over Christmas week, and then on New Year's Eve a roof tile fell on my head, and I lay there—

NORA: [*Putting her hand on his mouth.*] Oh! Don't say such things!

HELMER: Yes, but what if it happened—then what?

NORA: If anything so awful happened, then it just wouldn't matter if I had debts or not.

HELMER: Well, but the people I'd borrowed from?

NORA: Them? Who cares about them! They're strangers.

HELMER: Nora, Nora, how like a woman! No, but seriously, Nora, you know what I think about that. No debts! Never borrow!

Something of freedom's lost—and something of beauty, too—
from a home that's founded on borrowing and debt. We've made
a brave stand up to now, the two of us; and we'll go right on like
that the little while we have to.

NORA: [*Going toward the stove.*] Yes, whatever you say, Torvald.

HELMER: [*Following her.*] Now, now, the little lark's wings mustn't
droop. Come on, don't be a sulky squirrel. [*Taking out his wallet.*]
Nora, guess what I have here.

NORA: [*Turning quickly.*] Money!

HELMER: There, see. [*Hands her some note.*] Good grief, I know how
costs go up in a house at Christmastime.

NORA: Ten—twenty—thirty—forty. Oh, thank you, Torvald; I can
manage no end on this.

HELMER: You really will have to.

NORA: Oh yes, I promise I will! But come here so I can show you
everything I bought. And so cheap! Look, new clothes for Ivar
here—and a sword. Here a horse and a trumpet for Bob. And a
doll and a doll's bed here for Emmy; they're nothing much, but
she'll tear them to bits in no time anyway. And here I have dress
material and handkerchiefs for the maids. Old Anne-Marie really
deserves something more.

HELMER: And what's in that package there?

NORA: [*With a cry.*] Torvald, no! You can't see that till tonight!

HELMER: I see. But tell me now, you little prodigal, what have you
thought of for yourself?

NORA: For myself? Oh, I don't want anything at all.

HELMER: Of course you do. Tell me just what—within reason—
you'd most like to have.

NORA: I honestly don't know. Oh, listen, Torvald—

HELMER: Well?

NORA: [*Fumbling at his coat buttons, without looking at him.*] If you
want to give me something, then maybe you could—you
could—

HELMER: Come on, out with it.

NORA: [*Hurriedly.*] You could give me money, Torvald. No more
than you think you can spare; then one of these days I'll buy
something with it.

HELMER: But Nora—

NORA: Oh, please, Torvald darling, do that! I beg you, please. Then I could hang the bills in pretty gilt paper on the Christmas tree. Wouldn't that be fun?

HELMER: What are those little birds called that always fly through their fortunes?

NORA: Oh yes, spendthrifts; I know all that. But let's do as I say, Torvald; then I'll have time to decide what I really need most. That's very sensible, isn't it?

HELMER: [*Smiling.*] Yes, very—that is, if you actually hung onto the money I give you, and you actually used it to buy yourself something. But it goes for the house and for all sorts of foolish things, and then I only have to lay out some more.

NORA: Oh, but Torvald—

HELMER: Don't deny it, my dear little Nora. [*Putting his arm around her waist.*] Spendthrifts are sweet, but they use up a frightful amount of money. It's incredible what it costs a man to feed such birds.

NORA: Oh, how can you say that! Really, I save everything I can.

HELMER: [*Laughing.*] Yes, that's the truth. Everything you can. But that's nothing at all.

NORA: [*Humming, with a smile of quiet satisfaction.*] Hm, if you only knew what expenses we larks and squirrels have, Torvald.

HELMER: You're an odd little one. Exactly the way your father was. You're never at a loss for scaring up money; but the moment you have it, it runs right out through your fingers; you never know what you've done with it. Well, one takes you as you are. It's deep in your blood. Yes, these things are hereditary, Nora.

NORA: Ah, I could wish I'd inherited many of Papa's qualities.

HELMER: And I couldn't wish you anything but just what you are, my sweet little lark. But wait; it seems to me you have a very— what should I call it?—a very suspicious look today—

NORA: I do?

HELMER: You certainly do. Look me straight in the eye.

NORA: [*Looking at him.*] Well?

HELMER: [*Shaking an admonitory finger.*] Surely my sweet tooth hasn't been running riot in town today, has she?

NORA: No. Why do you imagine that?

HELMER: My sweet tooth really didn't make a little detour through the confectioner's?

NORA: No, I assure you, Torvald—

HELMER: Hasn't nibbled some pastry?

NORA: No, not at all.

HELMER: Not even munched a macaroon or two?

NORA: No, Torvald, I assure you, really—

HELMER: There, there now. Of course I'm only joking.

NORA: [*Going to the table, right.*] You know I could never think of going against you.

HELMER: No, I understand that; and you *have* given me your word. [*Going over to her.*] Well, you keep your little Christmas secrets to yourself, Nora darling. I expect they'll come to light this evening, when the tree is lit.

NORA: Did you remember to ask Dr. Rank?

HELMER: No. But there's no need for that; it's assumed he'll be dining with us. All the same, I'll ask him when he stops by here this morning. I've ordered some fine wine. Nora, you can't imagine how I'm looking forward to this evening.

NORA: So am I. And what fun for the children, Torvald!

HELMER: Ah, it's so gratifying to know that one's gotten a safe, secure job, and with a comfortable salary. It's a great satisfaction, isn't it?

NORA: Oh, it's wonderful!

HELMER: Remember last Christmas? Three whole weeks before, you shut yourself in every evening till long after midnight, making flowers for the Christmas tree, and all the other decorations to surprise us. Ugh, that was the dullest time I've ever lived through.

NORA: It wasn't at all dull for me.

HELMER: [*Smiling.*] But the outcome *was* pretty sorry, Nora.

NORA: Oh, don't tease me with that again. How could I help it that the cat came in and tore everything to shreds.

HELMER: No, poor thing, you certainly couldn't. You wanted so much to please us all, and that's what counts. But it's just as well that the hard times are past.

NORA: Yes, it's really wonderful.

HELMER: Now I don't have to sit here alone, boring myself, and you don't have to tire your precious eyes and your fair little delicate hands—

NORA: [*Clapping her hands.*] No, is it really true, Torvald, I don't have to? Oh, how wonderfully lovely to hear! [*Taking his arm.*] Now I'll tell you just how I've thought we should plan things. Right after Christmas— [*The doorbell rings.*] Oh, the bell. [*Straightening the room up a bit.*] Somebody would have to come. What a bore!

HELMER: I'm not at home to visitors, don't forget.

MAID: [*From the hall doorway.*] Ma'am, a lady to see you—

NORA: All right, let her come in.

MAID: [*To* HELMER.] And the doctor's just come too.

HELMER: Did he go right to my study?

MAID: Yes, he did.

    [HELMER *goes into his room. The* MAID *shows in* MRS. LINDE, *dressed in traveling clothes, and shuts the door after her.*]

MRS. LINDE: [*In a dispirited and somewhat hesitant voice.*] Hello, Nora.

NORA: [*Uncertain.*] Hello—

MRS. LINDE: You don't recognize me.

NORA: No, I don't know—but wait, I think— [*Exclaiming.*] What! Kristine! Is it really you?

MRS. LINDE: Yes, it's me.

NORA: Kristine! To think I didn't recognize you. But then, how could I? [*More quietly.*] How you've changed, Kristine!

MRS. LINDE: Yes, no doubt I have. In nine—ten long years.

NORA: Is it so long since we met! Yes, it's all of that. Oh, these last eight years have been a happy time, believe me. And so now you've come in to town, too. Made the long trip in the winter. That took courage.

MRS. LINDE: I just got here by ship this morning.

NORA: To enjoy yourself over Christmas, of course. Oh, how lovely! Yes, enjoy ourselves, we'll do that. But take your coat off. You're not still cold? [*Helping her.*] There now, let's get cozy here by the stove. No, the easy chair there! I'll take the rocker here. [*Seizing her hands.*] Yes, now you have your old look again; it was only in that first moment. You're a bit more pale, Kristine—and maybe a bit thinner.

MRS. LINDE: And much, much older, Nora.

NORA: Yes, perhaps a bit older; a tiny, tiny bit; not much at all. [*Stopping short; suddenly serious.*] Oh, but thoughtless me, to sit here, chattering away. Sweet, good Kristine, can you forgive me?

MRS. LINDE: What do you mean, Nora?

NORA: [*Softly.*] Poor Kristine, you've become a widow.

MRS. LINDE: Yes, three years ago.

NORA: Oh, I knew it, of course; I read it in the papers. Oh, Kristine, you must believe me; I often thought of writing you then, but I kept postponing it, and something always interfered.

MRS. LINDE: Nora dear, I understand completely.

NORA: No, it was awful of me, Kristine. You poor thing, how much you must have gone through. And he left you nothing?

MRS. LINDE: No.

NORA: And no children?

MRS. LINDE: No.

NORA: Nothing at all, then?

MRS. LINDE: Not even a sense of loss to feed on.

NORA: [*Looking incredulously at her.*] But Kristine, how could that be?

MRS. LINDE: [*Smiling wearily and smoothing her hair.*] Oh, sometimes it happens, Nora.

NORA: So completely alone. How terribly hard that must be for you. I have three lovely children. You can't see them now; they're out with the maid. But now you must tell me everything—

MRS. LINDE: No, no, no, tell me about yourself.

NORA: No, you begin. Today I don't want to be selfish. I want to think only of you today. But there *is* something I must tell you, Did you hear of the wonderful luck we had recently?

MRS. LINDE: No, what's that?

NORA: My husband's been made manager in the bank, just think!

MRS. LINDE: Your husband? How marvelous!

NORA: Isn't it? Being a lawyer is such an uncertain living, you know, especially if one won't touch any cases that aren't clean and decent. And of course Torvald would never do that, and I'm with him completely there. Oh, we're simply delighted, believe me! He'll join the bank right after New Year's and start getting a huge salary and lots of commissions. From now on we can live quite differently—just as we want. Oh, Kristine, I feel so light and happy! Won't it be lovely to have stacks of money and not a care in the world?

MRS. LINDE: Well, anyway, it would be lovely to have enough for necessities.

NORA: No, not just for necessities, but stacks and stacks of money!

MRS. LINDE: [*Smiling.*] Nora, Nora, aren't you sensible yet? Back in school you were such a free spender.

NORA: [*With a quiet laugh.*] Yes, that's what Torvald still says. [*Shaking her finger.*] But "Nora, Nora" isn't as silly as you all think. Really, we've been in no position for me to go squandering. We've had to work, both of us.

MRS. LINDE: You too?

NORA: Yes, at odd jobs—needlework, crocheting, embroidery, and such—[*Casually.*] and other things too. You remember that Torvald left the department when we were married? There was no chance of promotion in his office, and of course he needed to earn more money. But that first year he drove himself terribly. He took on all kinds of extra work that kept him going morning and night. It wore him down, and then he fell deathly ill. The doctors said it was essential for him to travel south.

MRS. LINDE: Yes, didn't you spend a whole year in Italy?

NORA: That's right. It wasn't easy to get away, you know. Ivar had just been born. But of course we had to go. Oh, that was a beautiful trip, and it saved Torvald's life. But it cost a frightful sum, Kristine.

MRS. LINDE: I can well imagine.

NORA: Four thousand, eight hundred crowns it cost. That's really a lot of money.

MRS. LINDE: But it's lucky you had it when you needed it.

NORA: Well, as it was, we got it from Papa.

MRS. LINDE: I see. It was just about the time your father died.

NORA: Yes, just about then. And, you know, I couldn't make that trip out to nurse him. I had to stay here, expecting Ivar any moment, and with my poor sick Torvald to care for. Dearest Papa, I never saw him again, Kristine. Oh, that was the worst time, I've known in all my marriage.

MRS. LINDE: I know how you loved him. And then you went off to Italy?

NORA: Yes. We had the means now, and the doctors urged us. So we left a month after.

MRS. LINDE: And your husband came back completely cured?

NORA: Sound as a drum!

MRS. LINDE: But—the doctor?

NORA: Who?

MRS. LINDE: I thought the maid said he was a doctor, the man who came in with me.

NORA: Yes, that was Dr. Rank—but he's not making a sick call. He's our closest friend, and he stops by at least once a day. No, Torvald hasn't had a sick moment since, and the children are fit and strong, and I am, too. [*Jumping up and clapping her hands.*] Oh, dear God, Kristine, what a lovely thing to live and be happy! But how disgusting of me—I'm talking of nothing but my own affairs. [*Sits on a stool close by* KRISTINE, *arms resting across her knees.*] Oh, don't be angry with me! Tell me, is it really true that you weren't in love with your husband? Why did you marry him, then?

MRS. LINDE: My mother was still alive, but bedridden and helpless—and I had my two younger brothers to look after. In all conscience, I didn't think I could turn him down.

NORA: No, you were right there. But was he rich at the time?

MRS. LINDE: He was very well off, I'd say. But the business was shaky, Nora. When he died, it all fell apart, and nothing was left.

NORA: And, then—?

MRS. LINDE: Yes, so I had to scrape up a living with a little shop and a little teaching and whatever else I could find. The last three years have been like one endless workday without a rest for me. Now it's over, Nora. My poor mother doesn't need me, for she's passed on. Nor the boys, either; they're working now and can take care of themselves.

NORA: How free you must feel—

MRS. LINDE: No—only unspeakably empty. Nothing to live for now. [*Standing up anxiously.*] That's why I couldn't take it any longer out in that desolate hole. Maybe here it'll be easier to find something to do and keep my mind occupied. If I could only be lucky enough to get a steady job, some office work—

NORA: Oh, but Kristine, that's so dreadfully tiring, and you already look so tired. It would be much better for you if you could go off to a bathing resort.

MRS. LINDE: [*Going toward the window.*] I have no father to give me travel money, Nora.

NORA: [*Rising.*] Oh, don't be angry with me.

MRS. LINDE: [*Going to her.*] Nora dear, don't you be angry with me. The worst of my kind of situation is all the bitterness that's stored away. No one to work for, and yet you're always having to snap up your opportunities. You have to live; and so you grow selfish. When you told me the happy change in your lot, do you know I was delighted less for your sakes than for mine?

NORA: How so? Oh, I see. You think maybe Torvald could do something for you.

MRS. LINDE: Yes, that's what I thought.

NORA: And he will, Kristine! Just leave it to me; I'll bring it up so delicately—find something attractive to humor him with. Oh, I'm so eager to help you.

MRS. LINDE: How very kind of you, Nora, to be so concerned over me—doubly kind, considering you really know so little of life's burdens yourself.

NORA: I—? I know so little—?

MRS. LINDE: [*Smiling.*] Well, my heavens—a little needlework and such—Nora, you're just a child.

NORA: [*Tossing her head and pacing the floor.*] You don't have to act so superior.

MRS. LINDE: Oh?

NORA: You're just like the others. You all think I'm incapable of anything serious—

MRS. LINDE: Come now—

NORA: That I've never had to face the raw world.

MRS. LINDE: Nora dear, you've just been telling me all your troubles.

NORA: Hm! Trivia! [*Quietly.*] I haven't told you the big thing.

MRS. LINDE: Big thing? What do you mean?

NORA: You look down on me so, Kristine, but you shouldn't. You're proud that you worked so long and hard for your mother.

MRS. LINDE: I don't look down on a soul. But it *is* true: I'm proud—
and happy, too—to think it was given to me to make my
mother's last days almost free of care.

NORA: And you're also proud thinking of what you've done for your
brothers.

MRS. LINDE: I feel I've a right to be.

NORA: I agree. But listen to this, Kristine—I've also got something
to be proud and happy for.

MRS. LINDE: I don't doubt it. But whatever do you mean?

NORA: Not so loud. What if Torvald heard! He mustn't, not for anything in the world. Nobody must know, Kristine. No one but
you.

MRS. LINDE: But what is it, then?

NORA: Come here. [*Drawing her down beside her on the sofa.*] It's
true—I've also got something to be proud and happy for. I'm the
one who saved Torvald's life.

MRS. LINDE: Saved—? Saved how?

NORA: I told you about the trip to Italy. Torvald never would have
lived if he hadn't gone south—

MRS. LINDE: Of course; your father gave you the means—

NORA: [*Smiling.*] That's what Torvald and all the rest think, but—

MRS. LINDE: But—?

NORA: Papa didn't give us a pin. I was the one who raised the
money.

MRS. LINDE: You? That whole amount?

NORA: Four thousand, eight hundred crowns. What do you say to
that?

MRS. LINDE: But Nora, how was it possible? Did you win the lottery?

NORA: [*Disdainfully.*] The lottery? Pooh! No art to that.

MRS. LINDE: But where did you get it from then?

NORA: [*Humming, with a mysterious smile.*] Hmm, tra-la-la-la.

MRS. LINDE: Because you couldn't have borrowed it.

NORA: No? Why not?

MRS. LINDE: A wife can't borrow without her husband's consent.

NORA: [*Tossing her head.*] Oh, but a wife with a little business sense,
a wife who knows how to manage—

MRS. LINDE: Nora, I simply don't understand—

NORA: You don't have to. Whoever said I *borrowed* the money? I could have gotten it other ways. [*Throwing herself back on the sofa.*] I could have gotten it from some admirer or other. After all, a girl with my ravishing appeal—

MRS. LINDE: You lunatic.

NORA: I'll bet you're eaten up with curiosity, Kristine.

MRS. LINDE: Now listen here, Nora—you haven't done something indiscreet?

NORA: [*Sitting up again.*] Is it indiscreet to save your husband's life?

MRS. LINDE: I think it's indiscreet that without his knowledge you—

NORA: But that's the point: he mustn't know! My Lord, can't you understand? He mustn't ever know the close call he had. It was to *me* the doctors came to say his life was in danger—that nothing could save him but a stay in the south. Didn't I try strategy then! I began talking about how lovely it would be for me to travel abroad like other young wives; I begged and I cried; I told him please to remember my condition, to be kind and indulge me; and then I dropped a hint that he could easily take out a loan. But at that, Kristine, he nearly exploded. He said I was frivolous, and it was his duty as man of the house not to indulge me in whims and fancies—as I think he called them. Aha, I thought, now you'll just have to be saved—and that's when I saw my chance.

MRS. LINDE: And your father never told Torvald the money wasn't from him?

NORA: No, never. Papa died right about then. I'd considered bringing him into my secret and begging him never to tell. But he was too sick at the time—and then, sadly, it didn't matter.

MRS. LINDE: And you've never confided in your husband since?

NORA: For heaven's sake, no! Are you serious? He's so strict on that subject. Besides—Torvald, with all his masculine pride—how painfully humiliating for him if he ever found out he was in debt to me. That would just ruin our relationship. Our beautiful, happy home would never be the same.

MRS. LINDE: Won't you ever tell him?

NORA: [*Thoughtfully, half smiling.*] Yes—maybe sometime, years from now, when I'm no longer so attractive. Don't laugh! I only mean when Torvald loves me less than now, when he stops enjoying my dancing and dressing up and reciting for him. Then it might be wise to have something in reserve— [*Breaking off.*] How ridiculous! That'll never happen— Well, Kristine, what do you think of my big secret? I'm capable of something too, hm? You can imagine, of course, how this thing hangs over me. It really hasn't been easy meeting the payments on time. In the business world there's what they call quarterly interest and what they call amortization, and these are always so terribly hard to manage. I've had to skimp a little here and there, wherever I could, you know. I could hardly spare anything from my house allowance, because Torvald has to live well. I couldn't let the children go poorly dressed; whatever I got for them, I felt I had to use up completely—the darlings!

MRS. LINDE: Poor Nora, so it had to come out of your own budget, then?

NORA: Yes, of course. But I was the one most responsible, too. Every time Torvald gave me money for new clothes and such, I never used more than half; always bought the simplest, cheapest outfits. It was a godsend that everything looks so well on me that Torvald never noticed. But it did weigh me down at times, Kristine. It *is* such a joy to wear fine things. You understand.

MRS. LINDE: Oh, of course.

NORA: And then I found other ways of making money. Last winter I was lucky enough to get a lot of copying to do. I locked myself in and sat writing every evening till late in the night. Ah, I was tired so often, dead tired. But still it was wonderful fun, sitting and working like that, earning money. It was almost like being a man.

MRS. LINDE: But how much have you paid off this way so far?

NORA: That's hard to say, exactly. These accounts, you know, aren't easy to figure. I only know that I've paid out all I could scrape together. Time and again I haven't known where to turn. [*Smiling.*] Then I'd sit here dreaming of a rich old gentleman who had fallen in love with me—

MRS. LINDE: What! Who is he?

NORA: Oh, really! And that he'd died, and when his will was opened, there in big letters it said, "All my fortune shall be paid over in cash, immediately, to that enchanting Mrs. Nora Helmer."

MRS. LINDE: But Nora dear—who *was* this gentleman?

NORA: Good grief, can't you understand? The old man never existed; that was only something I'd dream up time and again whenever I was at my wits' end for money. But it makes no difference now; the old fossil can go where he pleases for all I care; I don't need him or his will—because now I'm free. [*Jumping up.*] Oh, how lovely to think of that, Kristine! Carefree! To know you're care-free, utterly carefree; to be able to romp and play with the chil-dren, and to keep up a beautiful, charming home—everything just the way Torvald likes it! And think, spring is coming, with big blue skies. Maybe we can travel a little then. Maybe I'll see the ocean again. Oh yes, it *is* so marvelous to live and be happy!
   [*The front doorbell rings.*]

MRS. LINDE: [*Rising.*] There's the bell. It's probably best that I go.

NORA: No, stay. No one's expected. It must be for Torvald.

MAID: [*From the hall doorway.*] Excuse me, ma'am—there's a gentle-man here to see Mr. Helmer, but I didn't know—since the doc-tor's with him—

NORA: Who is the gentleman?

KROGSTAD: [*From the doorway.*] It's me, Mrs. Helmer.
   [MRS. LINDE *starts and turns away toward the window.*]

NORA: [*Stepping toward him, tense, her voice a whisper.*] You? What is it? Why do you want to speak to my husband?

KROGSTAD: Bank business—after a fashion. I have a small job in the investment bank, and I hear now your husband is going to be our chief—

NORA: In other words, it's—

KROGSTAD: Just dry business, Mrs. Helmer. Nothing but that.

NORA: Yes, then please be good enough to step into the study. [*She nods indifferently as she sees him out by the hall door, then returns and begins stirring up the stove.*]

MRS. LINDE: Nora—who was that man?

NORA: That was a Mr. Krogstad—a lawyer.

MRS. LINDE: Then it really was him.

NORA: Do you know that person?

MRS. LINDE: I did once—many years ago. For a time he was a law clerk in our town.

NORA: Yes, he's been that.

MRS. LINDE: How he's changed.

NORA: I understand he had a very unhappy marriage.

MRS. LINDE: He's a widower now.

NORA: With a number of children. There now, it's burning. [*She closes the stove door and moves the rocker a bit to one side.*]

MRS. LINDE: They say he has a hand in all kinds of business.

NORA: Oh? That may be true; I wouldn't know. But let's not think about business. It's so dull.

[DR. RANK *enters from* HELMER's *study.*]

RANK: [*Still in the doorway.*] No, no, really—I don't want to intrude, I'd just as soon talk a little while with your wife. [*Shuts the door, then notices* MRS. LINDE.] Oh, beg pardon. I'm intruding here too.

NORA: No, not at all. [*Introducing him.*] Dr. Rank, Mrs. Linde.

RANK: Well now, that's a name much heard in this house. I believe I passed the lady on the stairs as I came.

MRS. LINDE: Yes, I take the stairs very slowly. They're rather hard on me.

RANK: Uh-hm, some touch of internal weakness?

MRS. LINDE: More overexertion, I'd say.

RANK: Nothing else? Then you're probably here in town to rest up in a round of parties?

MRS. LINDE: I'm here to look for work.

RANK: Is that the best cure for overexertion?

MRS. LINDE: One has to live, Doctor.

RANK: Yes, there's a common prejudice to that effect.

NORA: Oh, come on, Dr. Rank—you really do want to live yourself.

RANK: Yes, I really do. Wretched as I am, I'll gladly prolong my torment indefinitely. All my patients feel like that. And it's quite the same, too, with the morally sick. Right at this moment there's one of those moral invalids in there with Helmer—

MRS. LINDE: [*Softly.*] Ah!

NORA: Who do you mean?

RANK: Oh, it's a lawyer, Krogstad, a type you wouldn't know. His character is rotten to the root—but even he began chattering all-importantly about how he had to *live.*

NORA: Oh? What did he want to talk to Torvald about?

RANK: I really don't know. I only heard something about the bank.

NORA: I didn't know that Krog—that this man Krogstad had any-thing to do with the bank.

RANK: Yes, he's gotten some kind of berth down there. [*To* MRS. LINDE.] I don't know if you also have, in your neck of the woods, a type of person who scuttles about breathlessly, sniffing out hints of moral corruption, and then maneuvers his victim into some sort of key position where he can keep an eye on him. It's the healthy these days that are out in the cold.

MRS. LINDE: All the same, it's the sick who most need to be taken in.

RANK: [*With a shrug.*] Yes, there we have it. That's the concept that's turning society into a sanatorium.

[NORA, *lost in her thoughts, breaks out into quiet laughter and claps her hands.*]

RANK: Why do you laugh at that? Do you have any real idea of what society is?

NORA: What do I care about dreary old society? I was laughing at something quite different—something terribly funny. Tell me, Doctor—is everyone who works in the bank dependent now on Torvald?

RANK: Is that what you find so terribly funny?

NORA: [*Smiling and humming.*] Never mind, never mind! [*Pacing the floor.*] Yes, that's really immensely amusing: that we—that Torvald has so much power now over all those people. [*Taking the bag out of her pocket.*] Dr. Rank, a little macaroon on that?

RANK: See here, macaroons! I thought they were contraband here.

NORA: Yes, but these are some that Kristine gave me.

MRS. LINDE: What? I—?

NORA: Now, now, don't be afraid. You couldn't possibly know that Torvald had forbidden them. You see, he's worried they'll ruin my teeth. But hmp! Just this once! Isn't that so, Dr. Rank? Help yourself! [*Puts a macaroon in his mouth.*] And you too, Kristine. And I'll also have one, only a little one—or two, at the most. [*Walking about again.*] Now I'm really tremendously happy. Now there's just one last thing in the world that I have an enormous desire to do.

RANK: Well! And what's that?

NORA: It's something I have such a consuming desire to say so Torvald could hear.

RANK: And why can't you say it?

NORA: I don't dare. It's quite shocking.

MRS. LINDE: Shocking?

RANK: Well, then it isn't advisable. But in front of us you certainly can. What do you have such a desire to say so Torvald could hear?

NORA: I have such a huge desire to say—to hell and be damned!

RANK: Are you crazy?

MRS. LINDE: My goodness, Nora!

RANK: Go on, say it. Here he is.

NORA: [Hiding the macaroon bag.] Shh, shh, shh!

[HELMER comes in from his study, hat in hand, overcoat over his arm.]

NORA: [Going toward him.] Well, Torvald dear, are you through with him?

HELMER: Yes, he just left.

NORA: Let me introduce you—this is Kristine, who's arrived here in town.

HELMER: Kristine—? I'm sorry, but I don't know—

NORA: Mrs. Linde, Torvald dear. Mrs. Kristine Linde.

HELMER: Of course. A childhood friend of my wife's, no doubt?

MRS. LINDE: Yes, we knew each other in those days.

NORA: And just think, she made the long trip down here in order to talk with you.

HELMER: What's this?

MRS. LINDE: Well, not exactly—

NORA: You see, Kristine is remarkably clever in office work, and so she's terribly eager to come under a capable man's supervision and add more to what she already knows—

HELMER: Very wise, Mrs. Linde.

NORA: And then when she heard that you'd become a bank manager—the story was wired out to the papers—then she came in as fast as she could and— Really, Torvald, for my sake you can do a little something for Kristine, can't you?

HELMER: Yes, it's not at all impossible. Mrs. Linde, I suppose you're a widow?

MRS. LINDE: Yes.

HELMER: Any experience in office work?

MRS. LINDE: Yes, a good deal.

HELMER: Well, it's quite likely that I can make an opening for you—

NORA: [*Clapping her hands.*] You see, you see!

HELMER: You've come at a lucky moment, Mrs. Linde.

MRS. LINDE: Oh, how can I thank you?

HELMER: Not necessary. [*Putting his overcoat on.*] But today you'll have to excuse me—

RANK: Wait, I'll go with you. [*He fetches his coat from the hall and warms it at the stove.*]

NORA: Don't stay out long, dear.

HELMER: An hour; no more.

NORA: Are you going too, Kristine?

MRS. LINDE: [*Putting on her winter garments.*] Yes, I have to see about a room now.

HELMER: Then perhaps we can all walk together.

NORA: [*Helping her.*] What a shame we're so cramped here, but it's quite impossible for us to—

MRS. LINDE: Oh, don't even think of it! Good-bye, Nora dear, and thanks for everything.

NORA: Good-bye for now. Of course you'll be back this evening. And you too, Dr. Rank. What? If you're well enough? Oh, you've got to be! Wrap up tight now.

[*In a ripple of small talk the company moves out into the hall; children's voices are heard outside on the steps.*]

NORA: There they are! There they are! [*She runs to open the door. The children come in with their nurse,* ANNE-MARIE.] Come in, come in! [*Bends down and kisses them.*] Oh, you darlings—! Look at them, Kristine. Aren't they lovely!

RANK: No loitering in the draft here.

HELMER: Come, Mrs. Linde—this place is unbearable now for anyone but mothers.

[DR. RANK, HELMER, *and* MRS. LINDE *go down the stairs.* ANNE-MARIE *goes into the living room with the children.* NORA *follows, after closing the hall door.*]

NORA: How fresh and strong you look. Oh, such red cheeks you have! Like apples and roses. [*The children interrupt her throughout the following.*] And it was so much fun? That's wonderful. Really? You pulled both Emmy and Bob on the sled? Imagine, all together! Yes, you're a clever boy, Ivar. Oh, let me hold her a bit, Anne-Marie. My sweet little doll baby! [*Takes the smallest from the nurse and dances with her.*] Yes, yes, Mama will dance with Bob as well. What? Did you throw snowballs? Oh, if I'd only been there! No, don't bother, Anne-Marie—I'll undress them myself. Oh yes, let me. It's such fun. Go in and rest; you look half frozen. There's hot coffee waiting for you on the stove. [*The nurse goes into the room to the left.* NORA *takes the children's winter things off, throwing them about, while the children talk to her all at once.*] Is that so? A big dog chased you? But it didn't bite? No, dogs never bite little, lovely doll babies. Don't peek in the packages, Ivar! What is it? Yes, wouldn't you like to know. No, no, it's an ugly something. Well? Shall we play? What shall we play? Hide-and-seek? Yes, let's play hide-and-seek. Bob must hide first. I must? Yes, let me hide first. [*Laughing and shouting, she and the children play in and out of the living room and the adjoining room to the right. At last* NORA *hides under the table. The children come storming in, search, but cannot find her, then hear her muffled laughter, dash over to the table, lift the cloth up and find her. Wild shouting. She creeps forward as if to scare them. More shouts. Meanwhile, a knock at the hall door; no one has noticed it. Now the door half opens, and* KROGSTAD *appears. He waits a moment; the game goes on.*]

KROGSTAD: Beg pardon, Mrs. Helmer—

NORA: [*With a strangled cry, turning and scrambling to her knees.*] Oh! What do you want?

KROGSTAD: Excuse me. The outer door was ajar; it must be someone forgot to shut it—

NORA: [*Rising.*] My husband isn't home, Mr. Krogstad.

KROGSTAD: I know that.

NORA: Yes—then what do you want here?

KROGSTAD: A word with you.

NORA: With—? [*To the children, quietly.*] Go in to Anne-Marie. What? No, the strange man won't hurt Mama. When he's gone, we'll play some more. [*She leads the children into the room to the left and shuts the door after them. Then, tense and nervous.*] You want to speak to me?

KROGSTAD: Yes, I want to.

NORA: Today? But it's not yet the first of the month—

KROGSTAD: No, it's Christmas Eve. It's going to be up to you how merry a Christmas you have.

NORA: What is it you want? Today I absolutely can't—

KROGSTAD: We won't talk about that till later. This is something else. You do have a moment to spare, I suppose?

NORA: Oh yes, of course—I do, except—

KROGSTAD: Good. I was sitting over at Olsen's Restaurant when I saw your husband go down the street—

NORA: Yes?

KROGSTAD: With a lady.

NORA: Yes. So?

KROGSTAD: If you'll pardon my asking: wasn't that lady a Mrs. Linde?

NORA: Yes.

KROGSTAD: Just now come into town?

NORA: Yes, today.

KROGSTAD: She's a good friend of yours?

NORA: Yes, she is. But I don't see—

KROGSTAD: I also knew her once.

NORA: I'm aware of that.

KROGSTAD: Oh? You know all about it. I thought so. Well, then let me ask you short and sweet: is Mrs. Linde getting a job in the bank?

NORA: What makes you think you can cross-examine me, Mr. Krogstad—you, one of my husband's employees? But since you ask, you might as well know—yes, Mrs. Linde's going to be taken on at the bank. And I'm the one who spoke for her, Mr. Krogstad. Now you know.

KROGSTAD: So I guessed right.

NORA: [*Pacing up and down.*] Oh, one does have a tiny bit of influence, I should hope. Just because I am a woman, don't think it means that— When one has a subordinate position, Mr. Krogstad, one really ought to be careful about pushing somebody who—hm—

KROGSTAD: Who has influence?

NORA: That's right.

KROGSTAD: [*In a different tone.*] Mrs. Helmer, would you be good enough to use your influence on my behalf?

NORA: What? What do you mean?

KROGSTAD: Would you please make sure that I keep my subordinate position in the bank?

NORA: What does that mean? Who's thinking of taking away your position?

KROGSTAD: Oh, don't play the innocent with me. I'm quite aware that your friend would hardly relish the chance of running into me again; and I'm also aware now whom I can thank for being turned out.

NORA: But I promise you—

KROGSTAD: Yes, yes, yes, to the point: there's still time, and I'm advising you to use your influence to prevent it.

NORA: But Mr. Krogstad, I have absolutely no influence.

KROGSTAD: You haven't? I thought you were just saying—

NORA: You shouldn't take me so literally. I! How can you believe that I have any such influence over my husband?

KROGSTAD: Oh, I've known your husband from our student days. I don't think the great bank manager's more steadfast than any other married man.

NORA: You speak insolently about my husband, and I'll show you the door.

KROGSTAD: The lady has spirit.

NORA: I'm not afraid of you any longer. After New Year's, I'll soon be done with the whole business.

KROGSTAD: [*Restraining himself.*] Now listen to me, Mrs. Helmer. If necessary, I'll fight for my little job in the bank as if it were life itself.

NORA: Yes, so it seems.

KROGSTAD: It's not just a matter of income; that's the least of it. It's something else— All right, out with it! Look, this is the thing. You know, just like all the others, of course, that once, a good many years ago, I did something rather rash.

NORA: I've heard rumors to that effect.

KROGSTAD: The case never got into court; but all the same, every door was closed in my face from then on. So I took up those various activities you know about. I had to grab hold somewhere; and I dare say I haven't been among the worst. But now I want to drop all that. My boys are growing up. For their sakes, I'll have to win back as much respect as possible here in town. That job in the bank was like the first rung in my ladder. And now your husband wants to kick me right back down in the mud again.

NORA: But for heaven's sake, Mr. Krogstad, it's simply not in my power to help you.

KROGSTAD: That's because you haven't the will to—but I have the means to make you.

NORA: You certainly won't tell my husband that I owe you money?

KROGSTAD: Hm—what if I told him that?

NORA: That would be shameful of you. [*Nearly in tears.*] This secret—my joy and my pride—that he should learn it in such a crude and disgusting way—learn it from you. You'd expose me to the most horrible unpleasantness—

KROGSTAD: Only unpleasantness?

NORA: [*Vehemently.*] But go on and try. It'll turn out the worse for you, because then my husband will really see what a crook you are, and then you'll *never* be able to hold your job.

KROGSTAD: I asked if it was just domestic unpleasantness you were afraid of?

NORA: If my husband finds out, then of course he'll pay what I owe at once, and then we'd be through with you for good.

KROGSTAD: [*A step closer.*] Listen, Mrs. Helmer—you've either got a very bad memory, or else no head at all for business. I'd better put you a little more in touch with the facts.

NORA: What do you mean?

KROGSTAD: When your husband was sick, you came to me for a loan of four thousand, eight hundred crowns.

NORA: Where else could I go?

KROGSTAD: I promised to get you that sum—

NORA: And you got it.

KROGSTAD: I promised to get you that sum, on certain conditions. You were so involved in your husband's illness, and so eager to finance your trip, that I guess you didn't think out all the details. It might just be a good idea to remind you. I promised you the money on the strength of a note I drew up.

NORA: Yes, and that I signed.

KROGSTAD: Right. But at the bottom I added some lines for your father to guarantee the loan. He was supposed to sign down there.

NORA: Supposed to? He did sign.

KROGSTAD: I left the date blank. In other words, your father would have dated his signature himself. Do you remember that?

NORA: Yes, I think—

KROGSTAD: Then I gave you the note for you to mail to your father. Isn't that so?

NORA: Yes.

KROGSTAD: And naturally you sent it at once—because only some five, six days later you brought me the note, properly signed. And with that, the money was yours.

NORA: Well, then; I've made my payments regularly, haven't I?

KROGSTAD: More or less. But—getting back to the point—those were hard times for you then, Mrs. Helmer.

NORA: Yes, they were.

KROGSTAD: Your father was very ill, I believe.

NORA: He was near the end.

KROGSTAD: He died soon after?

NORA: Yes.

KROGSTAD: Tell me, Mrs. Helmer, do you happen to recall the date of your father's death? The day of the month, I mean.

NORA: Papa died the twenty-ninth of September.

KROGSTAD: That's quite correct; I've already looked into that. And now we come to a curious thing— [*Taking out a paper.*] which I simply cannot comprehend.

NORA: Curious thing? I don't know—

KROGSTAD: This is the curious thing: that your father co-signed the note for your loan three days after his death.

NORA: How—? I don't understand.

KROGSTAD: Your father died the twenty-ninth of September. But look. Here your father dated his signature October second. Isn't that curious, Mrs. Helmer? [NORA *is silent.*] Can you explain it to me? [NORA *remains silent.*] It's also remarkable that the words "October second" and the year aren't written in your father's hand, but rather in one that I think I know. Well, it's easy to understand. Your father forgot perhaps to date his signature, and then someone or other added it, a bit sloppily, before anyone knew of his death. There's nothing wrong in that. It all comes down to the signature. And there's no question about *that*, Mrs.

Helmer. It really *was* your father who signed his own name here, wasn't it?

NORA: [*After a short silence, throwing her head back and looking squarely at him.*] No, it wasn't. *I* signed Papa's name.

KROGSTAD: Wait, now—are you fully aware that this is a dangerous confession?

NORA: Why? You'll soon get your money.

KROGSTAD: Let me ask you a question—why didn't you send the paper to your father?

NORA: That was impossible. Papa was so sick. If I'd asked him for his signature, I also would have had to tell him what the money was for. But I couldn't tell him, sick as he was, that my husband's life was in danger. That was just impossible.

KROGSTAD: Then it would have been better if you'd given up the trip abroad.

NORA: I couldn't possibly. The trip was to save my husband's life. I couldn't give that up.

KROGSTAD: But didn't you ever consider that this was a fraud against me?

NORA: I couldn't let myself be bothered by that. You weren't any concern of mine. I couldn't stand you, with all those cold complications you made, even though you knew how badly off my husband was.

KROGSTAD: Mrs. Helmer, obviously you haven't the vaguest idea of what you've involved yourself in. But I can tell you this: it was nothing more and nothing worse that I once did—and it wrecked my whole reputation.

NORA: You? Do you expect me to believe that you ever acted bravely to save your wife's life?

KROGSTAD: Laws don't inquire into motives.

NORA: Then they must be very poor laws.

KROGSTAD: Poor or not—if I introduce this paper in court, you'll be judged according to law.

NORA: This I refuse to believe. A daughter hasn't a right to protect her dying father from anxiety and care? A wife hasn't a right to save her husband's life? I don't know much about laws, but I'm sure that somewhere in the books these things are allowed. And you don't know anything about it—you who practice the law? You must be an awful lawyer, Mr. Krogstad.

KROGSTAD: Could be. But business—the kind of business we two are mixed up in—don't you think I know about that? All right. Do what you want now. But I'm telling you *this*: if I get shoved down a second time, you're going to keep me company. [*He bows and goes out through the hall.*]

NORA: [*Pensive for a moment, then tossing her head.*] Oh, really! Trying to frighten me! I'm not so silly as all that. [*Begins gathering up the children's clothes, but soon stops.*] But—? No, but that's impossible! I did it out of love.

THE CHILDREN: [*In the doorway, left.*] Mama, that strange man's gone out the door.

NORA: Yes, yes, I know it. But don't tell anyone about the strange man. Do you hear? Not even Papa!

THE CHILDREN: No, Mama. But now will you play again?

NORA: No, not now.

THE CHILDREN: Oh, but Mama, you promised.

NORA: Yes, but I can't now. Go inside; I have too much to do. Go in, go in, my sweet darlings. [*She herds them gently back in the room and shuts the door after them. Settling on the sofa, she takes up a piece of embroidery and makes some stitches, but soon stops abruptly.*] No! [*Throws the work aside, rises, goes to the hall door and calls out.*] Helene! Let me have the tree in here. [*Goes to the table, left, opens the table drawer, and stops again.*] No, but that's utterly impossible!

MAID: [*With the Christmas tree.*] Where should I put it, ma'am?

NORA: There. The middle of the floor.

MAID: Should I bring anything else?

NORA: No, thanks. I have what I need.

[*The* MAID, *who has set the tree down, goes out.*]

NORA: [*Absorbed in trimming the tree.*] Candles here—and flowers here. That terrible creature! Talk, talk, talk! There's nothing to it at all. The tree's going to be lovely. I'll do anything to please you, Torvald. I'll sing for you, dance for you—

[HELMER *comes in from the hall, with a sheaf of papers under his arm.*]

NORA: Oh! You're back so soon?

HELMER: Yes. Has anyone been here?

NORA: Here? No.

HELMER: That's odd. I saw Krogstad leaving the front door.

NORA: So? Oh yes, that's true. Krogstad was here a moment.

HELMER: Nora, I can see by your face that he's been here, begging you to put in a good word for him.

NORA: Yes.

HELMER: And it was supposed to seem like your own idea? You were to hide it from me that he'd been here. He asked you that, too, didn't he?

NORA: Yes, Torvald, but—

HELMER: Nora, Nora, and you could fall for that? Talk with that sort of person and promise him anything? And then in the bargain, tell me an untruth.

NORA: An untruth—?

HELMER: Didn't you say that no one had been here? [*Wagging his finger.*] My little songbird must never do that again. A songbird needs a clean beak to warble with. No false notes. [*Putting his arm about her waist.*] That's the way it should be, isn't it? Yes, I'm sure of it. [*Releasing her.*] And so, enough of that. [*Sitting by the stove.*] Ah, how snug and cozy it is here. [*Leafing among his papers.*]

NORA: [*Busy with the tree, after a short pause.*] Torvald!

HELMER: Yes.

NORA: I'm so much looking forward to the Stenborgs' costume party, day after tomorrow.

HELMER: And I can't wait to see what you'll surprise me with.

NORA: Oh, that stupid business!

HELMER: What?

NORA: I can't find anything that's right. Everything seems so ridiculous, so inane.

HELMER: So my little Nora's come to *that* recognition?

NORA: [*Going behind his chair, her arms resting on its back.*] Are you very busy, Torvald?

HELMER: Oh—

NORA: What papers are those?

HELMER: Bank matters.

NORA: Already?

HELMER: I've gotten full authority from the retiring management to make all necessary changes in personnel and procedure. I'll need Christmas week for that. I want to have everything in order by New Year's.

NORA: So that was the reason this poor Krogstad—

HELMER: Hm.

NORA: [*Still leaning on the chair and slowly stroking the nape of his neck.*] If you weren't so very busy, I would have asked you an enormous favor, Torvald.

HELMER: Let's hear. What is it?

NORA: You know, there isn't anyone who has your good taste—and I want so much to look well at the costume party. Torvald, couldn't you take over and decide what I should be and plan my costume?

HELMER: Ah, is my stubborn little creature calling for a lifeguard?

NORA: Yes, Torvald, I can't get anywhere without your help.

HELMER: All right—I'll think it over. We'll hit on something.

NORA: Oh, how sweet of you. [*Goes to the tree again. Pause.*] Aren't the red flowers pretty—? But tell me, was it really such a crime that this Krogstad committed?

HELMER: Forgery. Do you have any idea what that means?

NORA: Couldn't he have done it out of need?

HELMER: Yes, or thoughtlessness, like so many others. I'm not so heartless that I'd condemn a man categorically for just one mistake.

NORA: No, of course not, Torvald!

HELMER: Plenty of men have redeemed themselves by openly confessing their crimes and taking their punishment.

NORA: Punishment—?

HELMER: But now Krogstad didn't go that way. He got himself out by sharp practices, and that's the real cause of his moral breakdown.

NORA: Do you really think that would—?

HELMER: Just imagine how a man with that sort of guilt in him has to lie and cheat and deceive on all sides, has to wear a mask even with the nearest and dearest he has, even with his own wife and children. And with the children, Nora—that's where it's most horrible.

NORA: Why?

HELMER: Because that kind of atmosphere of lies infects the whole life of a home. Every breath the children take in is filled with the germs of something degenerate.

NORA: [*Coming closer behind him.*] Are you sure of that?

HELMER: Oh, I've seen it often enough as a lawyer. Almost everyone who goes bad early in life has a mother who's a chronic liar.

NORA: Why just—the mother?

HELMER: It's usually the mother's influence that's dominant, but the father's works in the same way, of course. Every lawyer is quite familiar with it. And still this Krogstad's been going home year in, year out, poisoning his own children with lies and pretense; that's why I call him morally lost. [*Reaching his hands out toward her.*] So my sweet little Nora must promise me never to plead his cause. Your hand on it. Come, come, what's this? Give me your hand. There, now. All settled. I can tell you it'd be impossible for me to work alongside of him. I literally feel physically revolted when I'm anywhere near such a person.

NORA: [*Withdraws her hand and goes to the other side of the Christmas tree.*] How hot it is here! And I've got so much to do.

HELMER: [*Getting up and gathering his papers.*] Yes, and I have to think about getting some of these read through before dinner. I'll think about your costume, too. And something to hang on the tree in gilt paper, I may even see about that. [*Putting his hand on her head.*] Oh you, my darling little songbird. [*He goes into his study and closes the door after him.*]

NORA: [*Softly, after a silence.*] Oh, really! It isn't so. It's impossible. It must be impossible.

ANNE-MARIE: [*In the doorway, left.*] The children are begging so hard to come in to Mama.

NORA: No, no, no, don't let them in to me! You stay with them, Anne-Marie.

ANNE-MARIE: Of course, ma'am. [*Closes the door.*]

NORA: [*Pale with terror.*] Hurt my children—! Poison my home? [*A moment's pause; then she tosses her head.*] That's not true. Never. Never in all the world.

ACT TWO

Same room. Beside the piano the Christmas tree now stands stripped of ornament, burned-down candle stubs on its ragged branches. NORA's *street clothes lie on the sofa.* NORA, *alone in the room, moves restlessly about; at last she stops at the sofa and picks up her coat.*

NORA: [*Dropping the coat again.*] Someone's coming! [*Goes toward the door, listens.*] No—there's no one. Of course—nobody's coming today, Christmas Day—or tomorrow, either. But maybe— [*Opens the door and looks out.*] No, nothing in the mailbox. Quite empty. [*Coming forward.*] What nonsense! He won't do anything serious. Nothing terrible could happen. It's impossible. Why, I have three small children.

[ANNE-MARIE, *with a large carton, comes in from the room to the left.*]

ANNE-MARIE: Well, at last I found the box with the masquerade clothes.

NORA: Thanks. Put it on the table.

ANNE-MARIE: [*Does so.*] But they're all pretty much of a mess.

NORA: Ahh! I'd love to rip them in a million pieces!

ANNE-MARIE: Oh, mercy, they can be fixed right up. Just a little patience.

NORA: Yes, I'll go get Mrs. Linde to help me.

ANNE-MARIE: Out again now? In this nasty weather? Miss Nora will catch cold—get sick.

NORA: Oh, worse things could happen— How are the children?

ANNE-MARIE: The poor mites are playing with their Christmas presents, but—

NORA: Do they ask for me much?

ANNE-MARIE: They're so used to having Mama around, you know.

NORA: Yes, but Anne-Marie, I *can't* be together with them as much as I was.

ANNE-MARIE: Well, small children get used to anything.

NORA: You think so? Do you think they'd forget their mother if she was gone for good?

ANNE-MARIE: Oh, mercy—gone for good!

NORA: Wait, tell me, Anne-Marie—I've wondered so often—how could you ever have the heart to give your child over to strangers?

ANNE-MARIE: But I had to, you know, to become little Nora's nurse.

NORA: Yes, but how could you *do* it?

ANNE-MARIE: When I could get such a good place? A girl who's poor and who's gotten in trouble is glad enough for that. Because that slippery fish, he didn't do a thing for me, you know.

NORA: But your daughter's surely forgotten you.

ANNE-MARIE: Oh, she certainly has not. She's written to me, both when she was confirmed and when she was married.

NORA: [*Clasping her about the neck.*] You old Anne-Marie, you were a good mother for me when I was little.

ANNE-MARIE: Poor little Nora, with no other mother but me.

NORA: And if the babies didn't have one, then I know that you'd— What silly talk! [*Opening the carton.*] Go in to them. Now I'll have to— Tomorrow you can see how lovely I'll look.

ANNE-MARIE: Oh, there won't be anyone at the party as lovely as Miss Nora. [*She goes off into the room, left.*]

NORA: [*Begins unpacking the box, but soon throws it aside.*] Oh, if I dared to go out. If only nobody would come. If only nothing would happen here while I'm out. What craziness—nobody's coming. Just don't think. This muff—needs a brushing. Beautiful gloves, beautiful gloves. Let it go. Let it go! One, two, three, four, five, six— [*With a cry.*] Oh, there they are! [*Poises to move toward the door, but remains irresolutely standing.* MRS. LINDE *enters from the hall, where she has removed her street clothes.*]

NORA: Oh, it's you, Kristine. There's no one else out there? How good that you've come.

MRS. LINDE: I hear you were up asking for me.

NORA: Yes, I just stopped by. There's something you really can help me with. Let's get settled on the sofa. Look, there's going to be a costume party tomorrow evening at the Stenborgs' right above us, and now Torvald wants me to go as a Neapolitan peasant girl and dance the tarantella that I learned in Capri.

MRS. LINDE: Really, are you giving a whole performance?

NORA: Torvald says yes, I should. See, here's the dress. Torvald had it made for me down there; but now it's all so tattered that I just don't know—

MRS. LINDE: Oh, we'll fix that up in no time. It's nothing more than the trimmings—they're a bit loose here and there. Needle and thread? Good, now we have what we need.

NORA: Oh, how sweet of you!

MRS. LINDE: [*Sewing.*] So you'll be in disguise tomorrow, Nora. You know what? I'll stop by then for a moment and have a look at you all dressed up. But listen, I've absolutely forgotten to thank you for that pleasant evening yesterday.

NORA: [*Getting up and walking about.*] I don't think it was as pleasant as usual yesterday. You should have come to town a bit sooner, Kristine— Yes, Torvald really knows how to give a home elegance and charm.

MRS. LINDE: And you do, too, if you ask me. You're not your father's daughter for nothing. But tell me, is Dr. Rank always so down in the mouth as yesterday?

NORA: No, that was quite an exception. But he goes around critically ill all the time—tuberculosis of the spine, poor man. You know, his father was a disgusting thing who kept mistresses and so on—and that's why the son's been sickly from birth.[1]

MRS. LINDE: [*Lets her sewing fall to her lap.*] But my dearest Nora, how do you know about such things?

NORA: [*Walking more jauntily.*] Hmp! When you've had three children, then you've had a few visits from—from women who know something of medicine, and they tell you this and that.

MRS. LINDE: [*Resumes sewing; a short pause.*] Does Dr. Rank come here every day?

NORA: Every blessed day. He's Torvald's best friend from childhood, and *my* good friend, too. Dr. Rank almost belongs to this house.

MRS. LINDE: But tell me—is he quite sincere? I mean, doesn't he rather enjoy flattering people?

NORA: Just the opposite. Why do you think that?

MRS. LINDE: When you introduced us yesterday, he was proclaiming that he'd often heard my name in this house; but later I noticed that your husband hadn't the slightest idea who I really was. So how could Dr. Rank—?

NORA: But it's all true, Kristine. You see, Torvald loves me beyond words, and, as he puts it, he'd like to keep me all to himself. For a

---

1. Dr. Rank suffers from congenital syphilis.

long time he'd almost be jealous if I even mentioned any of my old friends back home. So of course I dropped that. But with Dr. Rank I talk a lot about such things, because he likes hearing about them.

MRS. LINDE: Now listen, Nora; in many ways you're still like a child. I'm a good deal older than you, with a little more experience. I'll tell you something: you ought to put an end to all this with Dr. Rank.

NORA: What should I put an end to?

MRS. LINDE: Both parts of it, I think. Yesterday you said something about a rich admirer who'd provide you with money—

NORA: Yes, one who doesn't exist—worse luck. So?

MRS. LINDE: Is Dr. Rank well off?

NORA: Yes, he is.

MRS. LINDE: With no dependents?

NORA: No, no one. But—

MRS. LINDE: And he's over here every day?

NORA: Yes, I told you that.

MRS. LINDE: How can a man of such refinement be so grasping?

NORA: I don't follow you at all.

MRS. LINDE: Now don't try to hide it, Nora. You think I can't guess who loaned you the forty-eight hundred crowns?

NORA: Are you out of your mind? How could you think such a thing! A friend of ours, who comes here every single day. What an intolerable situation that would have been!

MRS. LINDE: Then it really wasn't him.

NORA: No, absolutely not. It never even crossed my mind for a moment— And he had nothing to lend in those days; his inheritance came later.

MRS. LINDE: Well, I think that was a stroke of luck for you, Nora dear.

NORA: No, it never would have occurred to me to ask Dr. Rank— Still, I'm quite sure that if I had asked him—

MRS. LINDE: Which you won't, of course.

NORA: No, of course not. I can't see that I'd ever need to. But I'm quite positive that if I talked to Dr. Rank—

MRS. LINDE: Behind your husband's back?

NORA: I've got to clear up this other thing; *that's* also behind his back. I've *got* to clear it all up.

MRS. LINDE: Yes, I was saying that yesterday, but—

NORA: [*Pacing up and down.*] A man handles these problems so much better than a woman—

MRS. LINDE: One's husband does, yes.

NORA: Nonsense. [*Stopping.*] When you pay everything you owe, then you get your note back, right?

MRS. LINDE: Yes, naturally.

NORA: And can rip it into a million pieces and burn it up—that filthy scrap of paper!

MRS. LINDE: [*Looking hard at her, laying her sewing aside, and rising slowly.*] Nora, you're hiding something from me.

NORA: You can see it in my face?

MRS. LINDE: Something's happened to you since yesterday morning. Nora, what is it?

NORA: [*Hurrying toward her.*] Kristine! [*Listening.*] Shh! Torvald's home. Look, go in with the children a while. Torvald can't bear all this snipping and stitching. Let Anne-Marie help you.

MRS. LINDE: [*Gathering up some of the things.*] All right, but I'm not leaving here until we've talked this out. [*She disappears into the room, left, as* TORVALD *enters from the hall.*]

NORA: Oh, how I've been waiting for you, Torvald dear.

HELMER: Was that the dressmaker?

NORA: No, that was Kristine. She's helping me fix up my costume. You know, it's going to be quite attractive.

HELMER: Yes, wasn't that a bright idea I had?

NORA: Brilliant! But then wasn't I good as well to give in to you?

HELMER: Good—because you give in to your husband's judgment? All right, you little goose, I know you didn't mean it like that. But I won't disturb you. You'll want to have a fitting, I suppose.

NORA: And you'll be working?

HELMER: Yes. [*Indicating a bundle of papers.*] See. I've been down to the bank. [*Starts toward his study.*]

NORA: Torvald.

HELMER: [*Stops.*] Yes.

NORA: If your little squirrel begged you, with all her heart and soul, for something—?

HELMER: What's that?

NORA: Then would you do it?

HELMER: First, naturally, I'd have to know what it was.

NORA: Your squirrel would scamper about and do tricks, if you'd only be sweet and give in.

HELMER: Out with it.

NORA: Your lark would be singing high and low in every room—

HELMER: Come on, she does that anyway.

NORA: I'd be a wood nymph[2] and dance for you in the moonlight.

HELMER: Nora—don't tell me it's that same business from this morning?

NORA: [*Coming closer.*] Yes, Torvald, I beg you, please!

HELMER: And you actually have the nerve to drag that up again?

NORA: Yes, yes, you've got to give in to me; you *have* to let Krogstad keep his job in the bank.

HELMER: My dear Nora, I've slated his job for Mrs. Linde.

NORA: That's awfully kind of you. But you could just fire another clerk instead of Krogstad.

HELMER: This is the most incredible stubbornness! Because you go and give an impulsive promise to speak up for him, I'm expected to—

NORA: That's not the reason, Torvald. It's for your own sake. That man does writing for the worst papers; you said it yourself. He could do you any amount of harm. I'm scared to death of him—

HELMER: Ah, I understand. It's the old memories haunting you.

NORA: What do you mean by that?

HELMER: Of course, you're thinking about your father.

NORA: Yes, all right. Just remember how those nasty gossips wrote in the papers about Papa and slandered him so cruelly. I think they'd have had him dismissed if the department hadn't sent you up to investigate, and if you hadn't been so kind and open-minded toward him.

HELMER: My dear Nora, there's a notable difference between your father and me. Your father's official career was hardly above reproach. But mine is; and I hope it'll stay that way as long as I hold my position.

NORA: Oh, who can ever tell what vicious minds can invent? We

2. In Greek mythology, a maiden goddess who lives in nature.

could be so snug and happy now in our quiet, carefree home—
you and I and the children, Torvald! That's why I'm pleading
with you so—

HELMER: And just by pleading for him you make it impossible for
me to keep him on. It's already known at the bank that I'm firing
Krogstad. What if it's rumored around now that the new bank
manager was vetoed by his wife—

NORA: Yes, what then—?

HELMER: Oh yes—as long as our little bundle of stubbornness
gets her way—! I should go and make myself ridiculous in front
of the whole office—give people the idea I can be swayed by
all kinds of outside pressure. Oh, you can bet I'd feel the effects
of that soon enough! Besides—there's something that rules
Krogstad right out at the bank as long as I'm the manager.

NORA: What's that?

HELMER: His moral failings I could maybe overlook if I had to—

NORA: Yes, Torvald, why not?

HELMER: And I hear he's quite efficient on the job. But he was a
crony of mine back in my teens—one of those rash friendships
that crop up again and again to embarrass you later in life. Well,
I might as well say it straight out: we're on a first-name basis.
And that tactless fool makes no effort at all to hide it in front of
others. Quite the contrary—he thinks that entitles him to take a
familiar air around me, and so every other second he comes
booming out with his "Yes, Torvald!" and "Sure thing, Torvald!"
I tell you, it's been excruciating for me. He's out to make my
place in the bank unbearable.

NORA: Torvald, you can't be serious about all this.

HELMER: Oh no? Why not?

NORA: Because these are such petty considerations.

HELMER: What are you saying? Petty? You think I'm petty!

NORA: No, just the opposite, Torvald dear. That's exactly why—

HELMER: Never mind. You call my motives petty; then I might as
well be just that. Petty! All right! We'll put a stop to this for good.
[*Goes to the hall door and calls.*] Helene!

NORA: What do you want?

HELMER: [*Searching among his papers.*] A decision. [*The* MAID *comes in.*] Look here; take this letter; go out with it at once. Get hold of a messenger and have him deliver it. Quick now. It's already addressed. Wait, here's some money.

MAID: Yes, sir. [*She leaves with the letter.*]

HELMER: [*Straightening his papers.*] There, now, little Miss Willful.

NORA: [*Breathlessly.*] Torvald, what was that letter?

HELMER: Krogstad's notice.

NORA: Call it back, Torvald! There's still time. Oh, Torvald, call it back! Do it for my sake—for your sake, for the children's sake! Do you hear, Torvald; do it! You don't know how this can harm us.

HELMER: Too late.

NORA: Yes, too late.

HELMER: Nora dear, I can forgive you this panic, even though basically you're insulting me. Yes, you are! Or isn't it an insult to think that *I* should be afraid of a courtroom hack's revenge? But I forgive you anyway, because this shows so beautifully how much you love me. [*Takes her in his arms.*] This is the way it should be, my darling Nora. Whatever comes, you'll see: when it really counts, I have strength and courage enough as a man to take on the whole weight myself.

NORA: [*Terrified.*] What do you mean by that?

HELMER: The whole weight, I said.

NORA: [*Resolutely.*] No, never in all the world.

HELMER: Good. So we'll share it, Nora, as man and wife. That's as it should be. [*Fondling her.*] Are you happy now? There, there, there—not these frightened dove's eyes. It's nothing at all but empty fantasies— Now you should run through your tarantella and practice your tambourine. I'll go to the inner office and shut both doors, so I won't hear a thing; you can make all the noise you like. [*Turning in the doorway.*] And when Rank comes, just tell him where he can find me. [*He nods to her and goes with his papers into the study, closing the door.*]

NORA: [*Standing as though rooted, dazed with fright, in a whisper.*] He really could do it. He will do it. He'll do it in spite of everything. No, not that, never, never! Anything but that! Escape! A way out— [*The doorbell rings.*] Dr. Rank! Anything but that! *Anything*, whatever it is! [*Her hands pass over her face, smoothing it; she*

pulls herself together, goes over and opens the hall door. DR. RANK
*stands outside, hanging his fur coat up. During the following scene,
it begins getting dark.*]

NORA: Hello, Dr. Rank. I recognized your ring. But you mustn't go
in to Torvald yet; I believe he's working.

RANK: And you?

NORA: For you, I always have an hour to spare—you know that. [*He
has entered, and she shuts the door after him.*]

RANK: Many thanks. I'll make use of these hours while I can.

NORA: What do you mean by that? While you can?

RANK: Does that disturb you?

NORA: Well, it's such an odd phrase. Is anything going to happen?

RANK: What's going to happen is what I've been expecting so long—
but I honestly didn't think it would come so soon.

NORA: [*Gripping his arm.*] What is it you've found out? Dr. Rank,
you have to tell me!

RANK: [*Sitting by the stove.*] It's all over with me. There's nothing to
be done about it.

NORA: [*Breathing easier.*] Is it you—then—?

RANK: Who else? There's no point in lying to one's self. I'm the most
miserable of all my patients, Mrs. Helmer. These past few days
I've been auditing my internal accounts. Bankrupt! Within a
month I'll probably be laid out and rotting in the churchyard.

NORA: Oh, what a horrible thing to say.

RANK: The thing itself is horrible. But the worst of it is all the other
horror before it's over. There's only one final examination left;
when I'm finished with that, I'll know about when my disinte-
gration will begin. There's something I want to say. Helmer with
his sensitivity has such a sharp distaste for anything ugly. I don't
want him near my sickroom.

NORA: Oh, but Dr. Rank—

RANK: I won't have him in there. Under no condition. I'll lock my
door to him— As soon as I'm completely sure of the worst, I'll
send you my calling card marked with a black cross, and you'll
know then the wreck has started to come apart.

NORA: No, today you're completely unreasonable. And I wanted you
so much to be in a really good humor.

RANK: With death up my sleeve? And then to suffer this way for somebody else's sins. Is there any justice in that? And in every single family, in some way or another, this inevitable retribution of nature goes on—

NORA: [*Her hands pressed over her ears.*] Oh, stuff! Cheer up! Please—be gay!

RANK: Yes, I'd just as soon laugh at it all. My poor, innocent spine, serving time for my father's gay army days.

NORA: [*By the table, left.*] He was so infatuated with asparagus tips and *pâté de foie gras*, wasn't that it?

RANK: Yes—and with truffles.

NORA: Truffles, yes. And then with oysters, I suppose?

RANK: Yes, tons of oysters, naturally.

NORA: And then the port and champagne to go with it. It's so sad that all these delectable things have to strike at our bones.

RANK: Especially when they strike at the unhappy bones that never shared in the fun.

NORA: Ah, that's the saddest of all.

RANK: [*Looks searchingly at her.*] Hm.

NORA: [*After a moment.*] Why did you smile?

RANK: No, it was you who laughed.

NORA: No, it was you who smiled, Dr. Rank!

RANK: [*Getting up.*] You're even a bigger tease than I'd thought.

NORA: I'm full of wild ideas today.

RANK: That's obvious.

NORA: [*Putting both hands on his shoulders.*] Dear, dear Dr. Rank, you'll never die for Torvald and me.

RANK: Oh, that loss you'll easily get over. Those who go away are soon forgotten.

NORA: [*Looks fearfully at him.*] You believe that?

RANK: One makes new connections, and then—

NORA: Who makes new connections?

RANK: Both you and Torvald will when I'm gone. I'd say you're well under way already. What was that Mrs. Linde doing here last evening?

NORA: Oh, come—you can't be jealous of poor Kristine?

RANK: Oh yes, I am. She'll be my successor here in the house. When I'm down under, that woman will probably—

NORA: Shh! Not so loud. She's right in there.

RANK: Today as well. So you see.

NORA: Only to sew on my dress. Good gracious, how unreasonable you are. [*Sitting on the sofa.*] Be nice now, Dr. Rank. Tomorrow you'll see how beautifully I'll dance; and you can imagine then that I'm dancing only for you—yes, and of course for Torvald, too—that's understood. [*Takes various items out of the carton.*] Dr. Rank, sit over here and I'll show you something.

RANK: [*Sitting.*] What's that?

NORA: Look here. Look.

RANK: Silk stockings.

NORA: Flesh-colored. Aren't they lovely? Now it's so dark here, but tomorrow— No, no, no, just look at the feet. Oh well, you might as well look at the rest.

RANK: Hm—

NORA: Why do you look so critical? Don't you believe they'll fit?

RANK: I've never had any chance to form an opinion on that.

NORA: [*Glancing at him a moment.*] Shame on you. [*Hits him lightly on the ear with the stockings.*] That's for you. [*Puts them away again.*]

RANK: And what other splendors am I going to see now?

NORA: Not the least bit more, because you've been naughty. [*She hums a little and rummages among her things.*]

RANK: [*After a short silence.*] When I sit here together with you like this, completely easy and open, then I don't know—I simply can't imagine—whatever would have become of me if I'd never come into this house.

NORA: [*Smiling.*] Yes, I really think you feel completely at ease with us.

RANK: [*More quietly, staring straight ahead.*] And then to have to go away from it all—

NORA: Nonsense, you're not going away.

RANK: [*His voice unchanged.*] —and not even be able to leave some poor show of gratitude behind, scarcely a fleeting regret—no more than a vacant place that anyone can fill.

NORA: And if I asked you now for—? No—

RANK: For what?

NORA: For a great proof of your friendship—

RANK: Yes, yes?

NORA: No, I mean—for an exceptionally big favor—

RANK: Would you really, for once, make me so happy?

NORA: Oh, you haven't the vaguest idea what it is.

RANK: All right, then tell me.

NORA: No, but I can't, Dr. Rank—it's all out of reason. It's advice and help, too—and a favor—

RANK: So much the better. I can't fathom what you're hinting at. Just speak out. Don't you trust me?

NORA: Of course. More than anyone else. You're my best and truest friend, I'm sure. That's why I want to talk to you. All right, then, Dr. Rank: there's something you can help me prevent. You know how deeply, how inexpressibly dearly Torvald loves me; he'd never hesitate a second to give up his life for me.

RANK: [*Leaning close to her.*] Nora—do you think he's the only one—

NORA: [*With a slight start.*] Who—?

RANK: Who'd gladly give up his life for you.

NORA: [*Heavily.*] I see.

RANK: I swore to myself you should know this before I'm gone. I'll never find a better chance. Yes, Nora, now you know. And also you know now that you can trust me beyond anyone else.

NORA: [*Rising, natural and calm.*] Let me by.

RANK: [*Making room for her, but still sitting.*] Nora—

NORA: [*In the hall doorway.*] Helene, bring the lamp in. [*Goes over to the stove.*] Ah, dear Dr. Rank, that was really mean of you.

RANK: [*Getting up.*] That I've loved you just as deeply as somebody else? Was *that* mean?

NORA: No, but that you came out and told me. That was quite unnecessary—

RANK: What do you mean? Have you known—?

[*The* MAID *comes in with the lamp, sets it on the table, and goes out again.*]

RANK: Nora—Mrs. Helmer—I'm asking you: have you known about it?

NORA: Oh, how can I tell what I know or don't know? Really, I don't know what to say— Why did you have to be so clumsy, Dr. Rank! Everything was so good.

RANK: Well, in any case, you now have the knowledge that my body and soul are at your command. So won't you speak out?

NORA: [*Looking at him.*] After that?

RANK: Please, just let me know what it is.

NORA: You can't know anything now.

RANK: I have to. You mustn't punish me like this. Give me the chance to do whatever is humanly possible for you.

NORA: Now there's nothing you can do for me. Besides, actually, I don't need any help. You'll see—it's only my fantasies. That's what it is. Of course! [*Sits in the rocker, looks at him, and smiles.*] What a nice one you are, Dr. Rank. Aren't you a little bit ashamed, now that the lamp is here?

RANK: No, not exactly. But perhaps I'd better go—for good?

NORA: No, you certainly can't do that. You must come here just as you always have. You know Torvald can't do without you.

RANK: Yes, but *you*?

NORA: You know how much I enjoy it when you're here.

RANK: That's precisely what threw me off. You're a mystery to me. So many times I've felt you'd almost rather be with me than with Helmer.

NORA: Yes—you see, there are some people that one loves most and other people that one would almost prefer being with.

RANK: Yes, there's something to that.

NORA: When I was back home, of course I loved Papa most. But I always thought it was so much fun when I could sneak down to the maids' quarters, because they never tried to improve me, and it was always so amusing, the way they talked to each other.

RANK: Aha, so it's *their* place that I've filled.

NORA: [*Jumping up and going to him.*] Oh, dear, sweet Dr. Rank, that's not what I meant at all. But you can understand that with Torvald it's just the same as with Papa—

[*The* MAID *enters from the hall.*]

MAID: Ma'am—please! [*She whispers to* NORA *and hands her a calling card.*]

NORA: [*Glancing at the card.*] Ah! [*Slips it into her pocket.*]

RANK: Anything wrong?

NORA: No, no, not at all. It's only some—it's my new dress—

RANK: Really? But—there's your dress.

NORA: Oh, that. But this is another one—I ordered it—Torvald mustn't know—

RANK: Ah, now we have the big secret.

NORA: That's right. Just go in with him—he's back in the inner study. Keep him there as long as—

RANK: Don't worry. He won't get away. [*Goes into the study.*]

NORA: [*To the* MAID.] And he's standing waiting in the kitchen?

MAID: Yes, he came up by the back stairs.

NORA: But didn't you tell him somebody was here?

MAID: Yes, but that didn't do any good.

NORA: He won't leave?

MAID: No, he won't go till he's talked with you, ma'am.

NORA: Let him come in, then—but quietly. Helene, don't breathe a word about this. It's a surprise for my husband.

MAID: Yes, yes, I understand— [*Goes out.*]

NORA: This horror—it's going to happen. No, no, no, it can't happen, it mustn't. [*She goes and bolts* HELMER's *door. The* MAID *opens the hall door for* KROGSTAD *and shuts it behind him. He is dressed for travel in a fur coat, boots, and a fur cap.*]

NORA: [*Going toward him.*] Talk softly. My husband's home.

KROGSTAD: Well, good for him.

NORA: What do you want?

KROGSTAD: Some information.

NORA: Hurry up, then. What is it?

KROGSTAD: You know, of course, that I got my notice.

NORA: I couldn't prevent it, Mr. Krogstad. I fought for you to the bitter end, but nothing worked.

KROGSTAD: Does your husband's love for you run so thin? He knows everything I can expose you to, and all the same he dares to—

NORA: How can you imagine he knows anything about this?

KROGSTAD: Ah, no—I can't imagine it either, now. It's not at all like my fine Torvald Helmer to have so much guts—

NORA: Mr. Krogstad, I demand respect for my husband!

KROGSTAD: Why, of course—all due respect. But since the lady's keeping it so carefully hidden, may I presume to ask if you're also a bit better informed than yesterday about what you've actually done?

NORA: More than you ever could teach me.

KROGSTAD: Yes, I *am* such an awful lawyer.

NORA: What is it you want from me?

KROGSTAD: Just a glimpse of how you are, Mrs. Helmer. I've been thinking about you all day long. A cashier, a night-court scribbler, a—well, a type like me also has a little of what they call a heart, you know.

NORA: Then show it. Think of my children.

KROGSTAD: Did you or your husband ever think of mine? But never mind. I simply wanted to tell you that you don't need to take this thing too seriously. For the present, I'm not proceeding with any action.

NORA: Oh no, really! Well—I knew that.

KROGSTAD: Everything can be settled in a friendly spirit. It doesn't have to get around town at all; it can stay just among us three.

NORA: My husband must never know anything of this.

KROGSTAD: How can you manage that? Perhaps you can pay me the balance?

NORA: No, not right now.

KROGSTAD: Or you know some way of raising the money in a day or two?

NORA: No way that I'm willing to use.

KROGSTAD: Well, it wouldn't have done you any good, anyway. If you stood in front of me with a fistful of bills, you still couldn't buy your signature back.

NORA: Then tell me what you're going to do with it.

KROGSTAD: I'll just hold onto it—keep it on file. There's no outsider who'll even get wind of it. So if you've been thinking of taking some desperate step—

NORA: I have.

KROGSTAD: Been thinking of running away from home—

NORA: I have!

KROGSTAD: Or even of something worse—

NORA: How could you guess that?

KROGSTAD: You can drop those thoughts.

NORA: How could you guess I was thinking of *that*?

KROGSTAD: Most of us think about *that* at first. I thought about it too, but I discovered I hadn't the courage—

NORA: [*Lifelessly.*] I don't either.

KROGSTAD: [*Relieved.*] That's true, you haven't the courage? You too?

NORA: I don't have it—I don't have it.

KROGSTAD: It would be terribly stupid, anyway. After that first storm at home blows out, why, then— I have here in my pocket a letter for your husband—

NORA: Telling everything?

KROGSTAD: As charitably as possible.

NORA: [*Quickly.*] He mustn't ever get that letter. Tear it up. I'll find some way to get money.

KROGSTAD: Beg pardon, Mrs. Helmer, but I think I just told you—

NORA: Oh, I don't mean the money I owe you. Let me know how much you want from my husband, and I'll manage it.

KROGSTAD: I don't want any money from your husband.

NORA: What do you want, then?

KROGSTAD: I'll tell you what. I want to recoup, Mrs. Helmer; I want to get on in the world—and there's where your husband can help me. For a year and a half I've kept myself clean of anything disreputable—all that time struggling with the worst conditions; but I was satisfied, working my way up step by step. Now I've been written right off, and I'm just not in the mood to come crawling back. I tell you, I want to move on. I want to get back in the bank—in a better position. Your husband can set up a job for me—

NORA: He'll never do that!

KROGSTAD: He'll do it. I know him. He won't dare breathe a word of protest. And once I'm in there together with him, you just wait and see! Inside of a year, I'll be the manager's right-hand man. It'll be Nils Krogstad, not Torvald Helmer, who runs the bank.

NORA: You'll never see the day!

KROGSTAD: Maybe you think you can—

NORA: I have the courage now—for *that.*

KROGSTAD: Oh, you don't scare me. A smart, spoiled lady like you—

NORA: You'll see; you'll see!

KROGSTAD: Under the ice, maybe? Down in the freezing, coal-black water? There, till you float up in the spring, ugly, unrecognizable, with your hair falling out—

NORA: You don't frighten me.

KROGSTAD: Nor do you frighten me. One doesn't do these things, Mrs. Helmer. Besides, what good would it be? I'd still have him safe in my pocket.

NORA: Afterwards? When I'm no longer—?

KROGSTAD: Are you forgetting that *I'll* be in control then over your final reputation? [NORA *stands speechless, staring at him.*] Good; now I've warned you. Don't do anything stupid. When Helmer's read my letter, I'll be waiting for his reply. And bear in mind that it's your husband himself who's forced me back to my old ways. I'll never forgive him for that. Good-bye, Mrs. Helmer. [*He goes out through the hall.*]

NORA: [*Goes to the hall door, opens it a crack, and listens.*] He's gone. Didn't leave the letter. Oh no, no, that's impossible too! [*Opening the door more and more.*] What's that? He's standing outside—not going downstairs. He's thinking it over? Maybe he'll—? [*A letter falls in the mailbox; then* KROGSTAD's *footsteps are heard, dying away down a flight of stairs.* NORA *gives a muffled cry and runs over toward the sofa table. A short pause.*] In the mailbox. [*Slips warily over to the hall door.*] It's lying there. Torvald, Torvald—now we're lost!

MRS. LINDE: [*Entering with the costume from the room, left.*] There now, I can't see anything else to mend. Perhaps you'd like to try—

NORA: [*In a hoarse whisper.*] Kristine, come here.

MRS. LINDE: [*Tossing the dress on the sofa.*] What's wrong? You look upset.

NORA: Come here. See that letter? *There!* Look—through the glass in the mailbox.

MRS. LINDE: Yes, yes, I see it.

NORA: That letter's from Krogstad—

MRS. LINDE: Nora—it's Krogstad who loaned you the money!

NORA: Yes, and now Torvald will find out everything.

MRS. LINDE: Believe me, Nora, it's best for both of you.

NORA: There's more you don't know. I forged a name.

MRS. LINDE: But for heaven's sake—?

NORA: I only want to tell you that, Kristine, so that you can be my witness.

MRS. LINDE: Witness? Why should I—?

NORA: If I should go out of my mind—it could easily happen—

MRS. LINDE: Nora!

NORA: Or anything else occurred—so I couldn't be present here—

MRS. LINDE: Nora, Nora, you aren't yourself at all!

NORA: And someone should try to take on the whole weight, all of the guilt, you follow me—

MRS. LINDE: Yes, of course, but why do you think—?

NORA: Then you're the witness that it isn't true, Kristine. I'm very much myself; my mind right now is perfectly clear; and I'm telling you: nobody else has known about this; I alone did everything. Remember that.

MRS. LINDE: I will. But I don't understand all this.

NORA: Oh, how could you ever understand it? It's the miracle now that's going to take place.

MRS. LINDE: The miracle?

NORA: Yes, the miracle. But it's so awful, Kristine. It mustn't take place, not for anything in the world.

MRS. LINDE: I'm going right over and talk with Krogstad.

NORA: Don't go near him; he'll do you some terrible harm!

MRS. LINDE: There was a time once when he'd gladly have done anything for me.

NORA: He?

MRS. LINDE: Where does he live?

NORA: Oh, how do I know? Yes. [*Searches in her pocket.*] Here's his card. But the letter, the letter—!

HELMER: [*From the study, knocking on the door.*] Nora!

NORA: [*With a cry of fear.*] Oh! What is it? What do you want?

HELMER: Now, now, don't be so frightened. We're not coming in. You locked the door—are you trying on the dress?

NORA: Yes, I'm trying it. I'll look just beautiful, Torvald.

MRS. LINDE: [*Who has read the card.*] He's living right around the corner.

NORA: Yes, but what's the use? We're lost. The letter's in the box.

MRS. LINDE: And your husband has the key?

NORA: Yes, always.

MRS. LINDE: Krogstad can ask for his letter back unread; he can find some excuse—

NORA: But it's just this time that Torvald usually—

MRS. LINDE: Stall him. Keep him in there. I'll be back as quick as I can. [*She hurries out through the hall entrance.*]

NORA: [*Goes to* HELMER's *door, opens it, and peers in.*] Torvald!

HELMER: [*From the inner study.*] Well—does one dare set foot in one's own living room at last? Come on, Rank, now we'll get a look— [*In the doorway.*] But what's this?

NORA: What, Torvald dear?

HELMER: Rank had me expecting some grand masquerade.

RANK: [*In the doorway.*] That was my impression, but I must have been wrong.

NORA: No one can admire me in my splendor—not till tomorrow.

HELMER: But Nora dear, you look so exhausted. Have you practiced too hard?

NORA: No, I haven't practiced at all yet.

HELMER: You know, it's necessary—

NORA: Oh, it's absolutely necessary, Torvald. But I can't get anywhere without your help. I've forgotten the whole thing completely.

HELMER: Ah, we'll soon take care of that.

NORA: Yes, take care of me, Torvald, please! Promise me that? Oh, I'm so nervous. That big party— You must give up everything this evening for me. No business—don't even touch your pen. Yes? Dear Torvald, promise?

HELMER: It's a promise. Tonight I'm totally at your service—you little helpless thing. Hm—but first there's one thing I want to— [*Goes toward the hall door.*]

NORA: What are you looking for?

HELMER: Just to see if there's any mail.

NORA: No, no, don't do that, Torvald!

HELMER: Now what?

NORA: Torvald, please. There isn't any.

HELMER: Let me look, though. [*Starts out.* NORA, *at the piano, strikes the first notes of the tarantella.* HELMER, *at the door, stops.*] Aha!

NORA: I can't dance tomorrow if I don't practice with you.

HELMER: [*Going over to her.*] Nora dear, are you really so frightened?

NORA: Yes, so terribly frightened. Let me practice right now; there's still time before dinner. Oh, sit down and play for me, Torvald. Direct me. Teach me, the way you always have.

HELMER: Gladly, if it's what you want. [*Sits at the piano.*]

NORA: [*Snatches the tambourine up from the box, then a long, varicolored shawl, which she throws around herself, whereupon she springs forward and cries out.*] Play for me now! Now I'll dance!

[HELMER *plays and* NORA *dances.* RANK *stands behind* HELMER *at the piano and looks on.*]

HELMER: [*As he plays.*] Slower. Slow down.

NORA: Can't change it.

HELMER: Not so violent, Nora!

NORA: Has to be just like this.

HELMER: [*Stopping.*] No, no, that won't do at all.

NORA: [*Laughing and swinging her tambourine.*] Isn't that what I told you?

RANK: Let me play for her.

HELMER: [*Getting up.*] Yes, go on. I can teach her more easily then.
[RANK *sits at the piano and plays;* NORA *dances more and more wildly.* HELMER *has stationed himself by the stove and repeatedly gives her directions; she seems not to hear them; her hair loosens and falls over her shoulders; she does not notice, but goes on dancing.* MRS. LINDE *enters.*]

MRS. LINDE: [*Standing dumbfounded at the door.*] Ah—!

NORA: [*Still dancing.*] See what fun, Kristine!

HELMER: But Nora darling, you dance as if your life were at stake.

NORA: And it is.

HELMER: Rank, stop! This is pure madness. Stop it, I say!
[RANK *breaks off playing, and* NORA *halts abruptly.*]

HELMER: [*Going over to her.*] I never would have believed it. You've forgotten everything I taught you.

NORA: [*Throwing away the tambourine.*] You see for yourself.

HELMER: Well, there's certainly room for instruction here.

NORA: Yes, you see how important it is. You've got to teach me to the very last minute. Promise me that, Torvald?

HELMER: You can bet on it.

NORA: You mustn't, either today or tomorrow, think about anything else but me; you mustn't open any letters—or the mailbox—

HELMER: Ah, it's still the fear of that man—

NORA: Oh yes, yes, that too.

HELMER: Nora, it's written all over you—there's already a letter from him out there.

NORA: I don't know. I guess so. But you mustn't read such things now; there mustn't be anything ugly between us before it's all over.

RANK: [*Quietly to* HELMER.] You shouldn't deny her.

HELMER: [*Putting his arm around her.*] The child can have her way.
But tomorrow night, after you've danced—

NORA: Then you'll be free.

MAID: [*In the doorway, right.*] Ma'am, dinner is served.

NORA: We'll be wanting champagne, Helene.

MAID: Very good, ma'am. [*Goes out.*]

HELMER: So—a regular banquet, hm?

NORA: Yes, a banquet—champagne till daybreak! [*Calling out.*] And
some macaroons, Helene. Heaps of them—just this once.

HELMER: [*Taking her hands.*] Now, now, now—no hysterics. Be my
own little lark again.

NORA: Oh, I will soon enough. But go on in—and you, Dr. Rank.
Kristine, help me put up my hair.

RANK: [*Whispering, as they go.*] There's nothing wrong—really
wrong, is there?

HELMER: Oh, of course not. It's nothing more than this childish
anxiety I was telling you about. [*They go out, right.*]

NORA: Well?

MRS. LINDE: Left town.

NORA: I could see by your face.

MRS. LINDE: He'll be home tomorrow evening. I wrote him a note.

NORA: You shouldn't have. Don't try to stop anything now. After all,
it's a wonderful joy, this waiting here for the miracle.

MRS. LINDE: What is it you're waiting for?

NORA: Oh, you can't understand that. Go in to them; I'll be along in
a moment.

[MRS. LINDE *goes into the dining room.* NORA *stands a short
while as if composing herself; then she looks at her watch.*]

NORA: Five. Seven hours to midnight. Twenty-four hours to the
midnight after, and then the tarantella's done. Seven and twenty-
four? Thirty-one hours to live.

HELMER: [*In the doorway, right.*] What's become of the little lark?

NORA: [*Going toward him with open arms.*] Here's your lark!

ACT THREE

*Same scene. The table, with chairs around it, has been moved to the
center of the room. A lamp on the table is lit. The hall door stands open.*

Dance music drifts down from the floor above. MRS. LINDE *sits at the table, absently paging through a book, trying to read, but apparently unable to focus her thoughts. Once or twice she pauses, tensely listening for a sound at the outer entrance.*

MRS. LINDE: [*Glancing at her watch.*] Not yet—and there's hardly any time left. If only he's not— [*Listening again.*] Ah, there he is. [*She goes out in the hall and cautiously opens the outer door. Quiet footsteps are heard on the stairs. She whispers.*] Come in. Nobody's here.

KROGSTAD: [*In the doorway.*] I found a note from you at home. What's back of all this?

MRS. LINDE: I just *had* to talk to you.

KROGSTAD: Oh? And it just *had* to be here in this house?

MRS. LINDE: At my place it was impossible; my room hasn't a private entrance. Come in; we're all alone. The maid's asleep, and the Helmers are at the dance upstairs.

KROGSTAD: [*Entering the room.*] Well, well, the Helmers are dancing tonight? Really?

MRS. LINDE: Yes, why not?

KROGSTAD: How true—why not?

MRS. LINDE: All right, Krogstad, let's talk.

KROGSTAD: Do we two have anything more to talk about?

MRS. LINDE: We have a great deal to talk about.

KROGSTAD: I wouldn't have thought so.

MRS. LINDE: No, because you've never understood me, really.

KROGSTAD: Was there anything more to understand—except what's all too common in life? A calculating woman throws over a man the moment a better catch comes by.

MRS. LINDE: You think I'm so thoroughly calculating? You think I broke it off lightly?

KROGSTAD: Didn't you?

MRS. LINDE: Nils—is that what you really thought?

KROGSTAD: If you cared, then why did you write me the way you did?

MRS. LINDE: What else could I do? If I had to break off with you, then it was my job as well to root out everything you felt for me.

KROGSTAD: [*Wringing his hands.*] So that was it. And this—all this, simply for money!

MRS. LINDE: Don't forget I had a helpless mother and two small brothers. We couldn't wait for you, Nils; you had such a long road ahead of you then.

KROGSTAD: That may be; but you still hadn't the right to abandon me for somebody else's sake.

MRS. LINDE: Yes—I don't know. So many, many times I've asked myself if I did have that right.

KROGSTAD: [*More softly.*] When I lost you, it was as if all the solid ground dissolved from under my feet. Look at me; I'm a half-drowned man now, hanging onto a wreck.

MRS. LINDE: Help may be near.

KROGSTAD: It was near—but then you came and blocked it off.

MRS. LINDE: Without my knowing it, Nils. Today for the first time I learned that it's you I'm replacing at the bank.

KROGSTAD: All right—I believe you. But now that you know, will you step aside?

MRS. LINDE: No, because that wouldn't benefit you in the slightest.

KROGSTAD: Not "benefit" me, hm! I'd step aside anyway.

MRS. LINDE: I've learned to be realistic. Life and hard, bitter necessity have taught me that.

KROGSTAD: And life's taught me never to trust fine phrases.

MRS. LINDE: Then life's taught you a very sound thing. But you do have to trust in actions, don't you?

KROGSTAD: What does that mean?

MRS. LINDE: You said you were hanging on like a half-drowned man to a wreck.

KROGSTAD: I've good reason to say that.

MRS. LINDE: I'm also like a half-drowned woman on a wreck. No one to suffer with; no one to care for.

KROGSTAD: You made your choice.

MRS. LINDE: There wasn't any choice then.

KROGSTAD: So—what of it?

MRS. LINDE: Nils, if only we two shipwrecked people could reach across to each other.

KROGSTAD: What are you saying?

MRS. LINDE: Two on one wreck are at least better off than each on his own.

KROGSTAD: Kristine!

MRS. LINDE: Why do you think I came into town?

KROGSTAD: Did you really have some thought of me?

MRS. LINDE: I have to work to go on living. All my born days, as long as I can remember, I've worked, and it's been my best and my only joy. But now I'm completely alone in the world; it frightens me to be so empty and lost. To work for yourself—there's no joy in that. Nils, give me something—someone to work for.

KROGSTAD: I don't believe all this. It's just some hysterical feminine urge to go out and make a noble sacrifice.

MRS. LINDE: Have you ever found me to be hysterical?

KROGSTAD: Can you honestly mean this? Tell me—do you know everything about my past?

MRS. LINDE: Yes.

KROGSTAD: And you know what they think I'm worth around here.

MRS. LINDE: From what you were saying before, it would seem that with me you could have been another person.

KROGSTAD: I'm positive of that.

MRS. LINDE: Couldn't it happen still?

KROGSTAD: Kristine—you're saying this in all seriousness? Yes, you are! I can see it in you. And do you really have the courage, then—?

MRS. LINDE: I need to have someone to care for; and your children need a mother. We both need each other. Nils, I have faith that you're good at heart—I'll risk everything together with you.

KROGSTAD: [*Gripping her hands.*] Kristine, thank you, thank you— Now I know I can win back a place in their eyes. Yes—but I forgot—

MRS. LINDE: [*Listening.*] Shh! The tarantella. Go now! Go on!

KROGSTAD: Why? What is it?

MRS. LINDE: Hear the dance up there? When that's over, they'll be coming down.

KROGSTAD: Oh, then I'll go. But—it's all pointless. Of course, you don't know the move I made against the Helmers.

MRS. LINDE: Yes, Nils, I know.

KROGSTAD: And all the same, you have the courage to—?

MRS. LINDE: I know how far despair can drive a man like you.

KROGSTAD: Oh, if I only could take it all back.

MRS. LINDE: You easily could—your letter's still lying in the mailbox.

KROGSTAD: Are you sure of that?

MRS. LINDE: Positive. But—

KROGSTAD: [*Looks at her searchingly.*] Is that the meaning of it, then? You'll save your friend at any price. Tell me straight out. Is that it?

MRS. LINDE: Nils—anyone who's sold herself for somebody else once isn't going to do it again.

KROGSTAD: I'll demand my letter back.

MRS. LINDE: No, no.

KROGSTAD: Yes, of course. I'll stay here till Helmer comes down; I'll tell him to give me my letter again—that it only involves my dismissal—that he shouldn't read it—

MRS. LINDE: No, Nils, don't call the letter back.

KROGSTAD: But wasn't that exactly why you wrote me to come here?

MRS. LINDE: Yes, in that first panic. But it's been a whole day and night since then, and in that time I've seen such incredible things in this house. Helmer's got to learn everything; this dreadful secret has to be aired; those two have to come to a full understanding; all these lies and evasions can't go on.

KROGSTAD: Well, then, if you want to chance it. But at least there's one thing I can do, and do right away—

MRS. LINDE: [*Listening.*] Go now, go, quick! The dance is over. We're not safe another second.

KROGSTAD: I'll wait for you downstairs.

MRS. LINDE: Yes, please do; take me home.

KROGSTAD: I can't believe it; I've never been so happy. [*He leaves by way of the outer door; the door between the room and the hall stays open.*]

MRS. LINDE: [*Straightening up a bit and getting together her street clothes.*] How different now! How different! Someone to work for, to live for—a home to build. Well, it is worth the try! Oh, if they'd only come! [*Listening.*] Ah, there they are. Bundle up. [*She picks up her hat and coat. NORA's and HELMER's voices can be heard outside; a key turns in the lock, and HELMER brings NORA into the hall almost by force. She is wearing the Italian costume with a large black shawl about her; he has on evening dress, with a black domino[1] open over it.*]

---

1. A loose cloak fitted with a mask, used at masquerades.

NORA: [*Struggling in the doorway.*] No, no, no, not inside! I'm going up again. I don't want to leave so soon.

HELMER: But Nora dear—

NORA: Oh, I beg you, please, Torvald. From the bottom of my heart, *please*—only an hour more!

HELMER: Not a single minute, Nora darling. You know our agreement. Come on, in we go; you'll catch cold out here. [*In spite of her resistance, he gently draws her into the room.*]

MRS. LINDE: Good evening.

NORA: Kristine!

HELMER: Why, Mrs. Linde—are you here so late?

MRS. LINDE: Yes, I'm sorry, but I did want to see Nora in costume.

NORA: Have you been sitting here, waiting for me?

MRS. LINDE: Yes. I didn't come early enough; you were all upstairs; and then I thought I really couldn't leave without seeing you.

HELMER: [*Removing* NORA'*s shawl.*] Yes, take a good look. She's worth looking at, I can tell you that, Mrs. Linde. Isn't she lovely?

MRS. LINDE: Yes, I should say—

HELMER: A dream of loveliness, isn't she? That's what everyone thought at the party, too. But she's horribly stubborn—this sweet little thing. What's to be done with her? Can you imagine, I almost had to use force to pry her away.

NORA: Oh, Torvald, you're going to regret you didn't indulge me, even for just a half hour more.

HELMER: There, you see. She danced her tarantella and got a tumultuous hand—which was well earned, although the performance may have been a bit too naturalistic—I mean it rather overstepped the proprieties of art. But never mind—what's important is, she made a success, an overwhelming success. You think I could let her stay on after that and spoil the effect? Oh no; I took my lovely little Capri girl—my capricious little Capri girl, I should say—took her under my arm; one quick tour of the ballroom, a curtsy to every side, and then—as they say in novels—the beautiful vision disappeared. An exit should always be effective, Mrs. Linde, but that's what I can't get Nora to grasp. Phew, it's hot in here. [*Flings the domino on a chair and opens the door to his room.*] Why's it dark in here? Oh yes, of course. Excuse me. [*He goes in and lights a couple of candles.*]

NORA: [*In a sharp, breathless whisper.*] So?

MRS. LINDE: [*Quietly.*] I talked with him.

NORA: And—?

MRS. LINDE: Nora—you must tell your husband everything.

NORA: [*Dully.*] I knew it.

MRS. LINDE: You've got nothing to fear from Krogstad, but you have to speak out.

NORA: I won't tell.

MRS. LINDE: Then the letter will.

NORA: Thanks, Kristine. I know now what's to be done. Shh!

HELMER: [*Reentering.*] Well, then, Mrs. Linde—have you admired her?

MRS. LINDE: Yes, and now I'll say good night.

HELMER: Oh, come, so soon? Is this yours, this knitting?

MRS. LINDE: Yes, thanks. I nearly forgot it.

HELMER: Do you knit, then?

MRS. LINDE: Oh yes.

HELMER: You know what? You should embroider instead.

MRS. LINDE: Really? Why?

HELMER: Yes, because it's a lot prettier. See here, one holds the embroidery so, in the left hand, and then one guides the needle with the right—so—in an easy, sweeping curve—right?

MRS. LINDE: Yes, I guess that's—

HELMER: But, on the other hand, knitting—it can never be anything but ugly. Look, see here, the arms tucked in, the knitting needles going up and down—there's something Chinese about it. Ah, that was really a glorious champagne they served.

MRS. LINDE: Yes, good night, Nora, and don't be stubborn anymore.

HELMER: Well put, Mrs. Linde!

MRS. LINDE: Good night, Mr. Helmer.

HELMER: [*Accompanying her to the door.*] Good night, good night. I hope you get home all right. I'd be very happy to—but you don't have far to go. Good night, good night. [*She leaves. He shuts the door after her and returns.*] There, now, at last we got her out the door. She's a deadly bore, that creature.

NORA: Aren't you pretty tired, Torvald?

HELMER: No, not a bit.

NORA: You're not sleepy?

HELMER: Not at all. On the contrary, I'm feeling quite exhilarated. But you? Yes, you really look tired and sleepy.

NORA: Yes, I'm very tired. Soon now I'll sleep.

HELMER: See! You see! I was right all along that we shouldn't stay longer.

NORA: Whatever you do is always right.

HELMER: [*Kissing her brow.*] Now my little lark talks sense. Say, did you notice what a time Rank was having tonight?

NORA: Oh, was he? I didn't get to speak with him.

HELMER: I scarcely did either, but it's a long time since I've seen him in such high spirits. [*Gazes at her a moment, then comes nearer her.*] Hm—it's marvelous, though, to be back home again—to be completely alone with you. Oh, you bewitchingly lovely young woman!

NORA: Torvald, don't look at me like that!

HELMER: Can't I look at my richest treasure? At all that beauty that's mine, mine alone—completely and utterly.

NORA: [*Moving around to the other side of the table.*] You mustn't talk to me that way tonight.

HELMER: [*Following her.*] The tarantella is still in your blood, I can see—and it makes you even more enticing. Listen. The guests are beginning to go. [*Dropping his voice.*] Nora—it'll soon be quiet through this whole house.

NORA: Yes, I hope so.

HELMER: You do, don't you, my love? Do you realize—when I'm out at a party like this with you—do you know why I talk to you so little, and keep such a distance away; just send you a stolen look now and then—you know why I do it? It's because I'm imagining then that you're my secret darling, my secret young bride-to-be, and that no one suspects there's anything between us.

NORA: Yes, yes; oh, yes, I know you're always thinking of me.

HELMER: And then when we leave and I place the shawl over those fine young rounded shoulders—over that wonderful curving neck—then I pretend that you're my young bride, that we're just coming from the wedding, that for the first time I'm bringing you into my house—that for the first time I'm alone with you— completely alone with you, your trembling young beauty! All this evening I've longed for nothing but you. When I saw you turn and sway in the tarantella—my blood was pounding till I couldn't stand it—that's why I brought you down here so early—

NORA: Go away, Torvald! Leave me alone. I don't want all this.

HELMER: What do you mean? Nora, you're teasing me. You will, won't you? Aren't I your husband—?

[*A knock at the outside door.*]

NORA: [*Startled.*] What's that?

HELMER: [*Going toward the hall.*] Who is it?

RANK: [*Outside.*] It's me. May I come in a moment?

HELMER: [*With quiet irritation.*] Oh, what does he want now? [*Aloud.*] Hold on. [*Goes and opens the door.*] Oh, how nice that you didn't just pass us by!

RANK: I thought I heard your voice, and then I wanted so badly to have a look in. [*Lightly glancing about.*] Ah, me, these old familiar haunts. You have it snug and cozy in here, you two.

HELMER: You seemed to be having it pretty cozy upstairs, too.

RANK: Absolutely. Why shouldn't I? Why not take in everything in life? As much as you can, anyway, and as long as you can. The wine was superb—

HELMER: The champagne especially.

RANK: You noticed that too? It's amazing how much I could guzzle down.

NORA: Torvald also drank a lot of champagne this evening.

RANK: Oh?

NORA: Yes, and that always makes him so entertaining.

RANK: Well, why shouldn't one have a pleasant evening after a well-spent day?

HELMER: Well spent? I'm afraid I can't claim that.

RANK: [*Slapping him on the back.*] But I can, you see!

NORA: Dr. Rank, you must have done some scientific research today.

RANK: Quite so.

HELMER: Come now—little Nora talking about scientific research!

NORA: And can I congratulate you on the results?

RANK: Indeed you may.

NORA: Then they were good?

RANK: The best possible for both doctor and patient—certainty.

NORA: [*Quickly and searchingly.*] Certainty?

RANK: Complete certainty. So don't I owe myself a gay evening afterwards?

NORA: Yes, you're right, Dr. Rank.

HELMER: I'm with you—just so long as you don't have to suffer for it in the morning.

RANK: Well, one never gets something for nothing in life.

NORA: Dr. Rank—are you very fond of masquerade parties?

RANK: Yes, if there's a good array of odd disguises—

NORA: Tell me, what should we two go as at the next masquerade?

HELMER: You little featherhead—already thinking of the next!

RANK: We two? I'll tell you what: you must go as Charmed Life—

HELMER: Yes, but find a costume for *that*!

RANK: Your wife can appear just as she looks every day.

HELMER: That was nicely put. But don't you know what you're going to be?

RANK: Yes, Helmer, I've made up my mind.

HELMER: Well?

RANK: At the next masquerade I'm going to be invisible.

HELMER: That's a funny idea.

RANK: They say there's a hat—black, huge—have you never heard of the hat that makes you invisible? You put it on, and then no one on earth can see you.

HELMER: [*Suppressing a smile.*] Ah, of course.

RANK: But I'm quite forgetting what I came for. Helmer, give me a cigar, one of the dark Havanas.

HELMER: With the greatest pleasure. [*Holds out his case.*]

RANK: Thanks. [*Takes one and cuts off the tip.*]

NORA: [*Striking a match.*] Let me give you a light.

RANK: Thank you. [*She holds the match for him; he lights the cigar.*] And now good-bye.

HELMER: Good-bye, good-bye, old friend.

NORA: Sleep well, Doctor.

RANK: Thanks for that wish.

NORA: Wish me the same.

RANK: You? All right, if you like— Sleep well. And thanks for the light. [*He nods to them both and leaves.*]

HELMER: [*His voice subdued.*] He's been drinking heavily.

NORA: [*Absently.*] Could be. [HELMER *takes his keys from his pocket and goes out in the hall.*] Torvald—what are you after?

HELMER: Got to empty the mailbox; it's nearly full. There won't be room for the morning papers.

NORA: Are you working tonight?

HELMER: You know I'm not. Why—what's this? Someone's been at the lock.

NORA: At the lock—?

HELMER: Yes, I'm positive. What do you suppose—? I can't imagine one of the maids—? Here's a broken hairpin. Nora, it's yours—

NORA: [*Quickly.*] Then it must be the children—

HELMER: You'd better break them of that. Hm, hm—well, opened it after all. [*Takes the contents out and calls into the kitchen.*] Helene! Helene, would you put out the lamp in the hall. [*He returns to the room, shutting the hall door, then displays the handful of mail.*] Look how it's piled up. [*Sorting through them.*] Now what's this?

NORA: [*At the window.*] The letter! Oh, Torvald, no!

HELMER: Two calling cards—from Rank.

NORA: From Dr. Rank?

HELMER: [*Examining them.*] "Dr. Rank, Consulting Physician." They were on top. He must have dropped them in as he left.

NORA: Is there anything on them?

HELMER: There's a black cross over the name. See? That's a gruesome notion. He could almost be announcing his own death.

NORA: That's just what he's doing.

HELMER: What! You've heard something? Something he's told you?

NORA: Yes. That when those cards came, he'd be taking his leave of us. He'll shut himself in now and die.

HELMER: Ah, my poor friend! Of course I knew he wouldn't be here much longer. But so soon— And then to hide himself away like a wounded animal.

NORA: If it has to happen, then it's best it happens in silence—don't you think so, Torvald?

HELMER: [*Pacing up and down.*] He'd grown right into our lives. I simply can't imagine him gone. He with his suffering and loneliness—like a dark cloud setting off our sunlit happiness. Well, maybe it's best this way. For him, at least. [*Standing still.*] And maybe for us too, Nora. Now we're thrown back on each other, completely. [*Embracing her.*] Oh you, my darling wife, how can I hold you close enough? You know what, Nora—time and again I've wished you were in some terrible danger, just so I could stake my life and soul and everything, for your sake.

NORA: [*Tearing herself away, her voice firm and decisive.*] Now you must read your mail, Torvald.

HELMER: No, no, not tonight. I want to stay with you, dearest.

NORA: With a dying friend on your mind?

HELMER: You're right. We've both had a shock. There's ugliness between us—these thoughts of death and corruption. We'll have to get free of them first. Until then—we'll stay apart.

NORA: [*Clinging about his neck.*] Torvald—good night! Good night!

HELMER: [*Kissing her on the cheek.*] Good night, little songbird. Sleep well, Nora. I'll be reading my mail now. [*He takes the letters into his room and shuts the door after him.*]

NORA: [*With bewildered glances, groping about, seizing* HELMER's *domino, throwing it around her, and speaking in short, hoarse, broken whispers.*] Never see him again. Never, never. [*Putting her shawl over her head.*] Never see the children either—them, too. Never, never. Oh, the freezing black water! The depths—down— Oh, I wish it were over— He has it now; he's reading it—now. Oh no, no, not yet. Torvald, good-bye, you and the children— [*She starts for the hall; as she does,* HELMER *throws open his door and stands with an open letter in his hand.*]

HELMER: Nora!

NORA: [*Screams.*] Oh—!

HELMER: What is this? You know what's in this letter?

NORA: Yes, I know. Let me go! Let me out!

HELMER: [*Holding her back.*] Where are you going?

NORA: [*Struggling to break loose.*] You can't save me, Torvald!

HELMER: [*Slumping back.*] True! Then it's true what he writes? How horrible! No, no, it's impossible—it can't be true.

NORA: It *is* true. I've loved you more than all this world.

HELMER: Ah, none of your slippery tricks.

NORA: [*Taking one step toward him.*] Torvald—!

HELMER: What *is* this you've blundered into!

NORA: Just let me loose. You're not going to suffer for my sake. You're not going to take on my guilt.

HELMER: No more playacting. [*Locks the hall door.*] You stay right
here and give me a reckoning. You understand what you've done?
Answer! You understand?

NORA: [*Looking squarely at him, her face hardening.*] Yes. I'm beginning to understand everything now.

HELMER: [*Striding about.*] Oh, what an awful awakening! In all these
eight years—she who was my pride and joy—a hypocrite, a
liar—worse, worse—a criminal! How infinitely disgusting it all
is! The shame! [NORA *says nothing and goes on looking straight at
him. He stops in front of her.*] I should have suspected something
of the kind. I should have known. All your father's flimsy values— Be still! All your father's flimsy values have come out in
you. No religion, no morals, no sense of duty— Oh, how I'm
punished for letting him off! I did it for your sake, and you repay
me like this.

NORA: Yes, like this.

HELMER: Now you've wrecked all my happiness—ruined my whole
future. Oh, it's awful to think of. I'm in a cheap little grafter's[2]
hands; he can do anything he wants with me, ask for anything,
play with me like a puppet—and I can't breathe a word. I'll be
swept down miserably into the depths on account of a feather-
brained woman.

NORA: When I'm gone from this world, you'll be free.

HELMER: Oh, quit posing. Your father had a mess of those speeches
too. What good would that ever do me if you were gone from
this world, as you say? Not the slightest. He can still make the
whole thing known; and if he does, I could be falsely suspected
as your accomplice. They might even think that I was behind
it—that I put you up to it. And all that I can thank you for—
you that I've coddled the whole of our marriage. Can you see
now what you've done to me?

NORA: [*Icily calm.*] Yes.

HELMER: It's so incredible, I just can't grasp it. But we'll have to
patch up whatever we can. Take off the shawl. I said, take it off!
I've got to appease him somehow or other. The thing has to be
hushed up at any cost. And as for you and me, it's got to seem

---

2. Swindler's; in this usage, blackmailer's.

like everything between us is just as it was—to the outside world, that is. You'll go right on living in this house, of course. But you can't be allowed to bring up the children; I don't dare trust you with them— Oh, to have to say this to someone I've loved so much, and that I still—! Well, that's done with. From now on happiness doesn't matter; all that matters is saving the bits and pieces, the appearance— [*The doorbell rings.* HELMER *starts.*] What's that? And so late. Maybe the worst—? You think he'd—? Hide, Nora! Say you're sick. [NORA *remains standing motionless.* HELMER *goes and opens the door.*]

MAID: [*Half dressed, in the hall.*] A letter for Mrs. Helmer.

HELMER: I'll take it. [*Snatches the letter and shuts the door.*] Yes, it's from him. You don't get it; I'm reading it myself.

NORA: Then read it.

HELMER: [*By the lamp.*] I hardly dare. We may be ruined, you and I. But—I've got to know. [*Rips open the letter, skims through a few lines, glances at an enclosure, then cries out joyfully.*] Nora! [NORA *looks inquiringly at him.*] Nora! Wait—better check it again— Yes, yes, it's true. I'm saved. Nora, I'm saved!

NORA: And I?

HELMER: You too, of course. We're both saved, both of us. Look. He's sent back your note. He says he's sorry and ashamed—that a happy development in his life—oh, who cares what he says! Nora, we're saved! No one can hurt you. Oh, Nora, Nora—but first, this ugliness all has to go. Let me see— [*Takes a look at the note.*] No, I don't want to see it; I want the whole thing to fade like a dream. [*Tears the note and both letters to pieces, throws them into the stove and watches them burn.*] There—now there's nothing left— He wrote that since Christmas Eve you— Oh, they must have been three terrible days for you, Nora.

NORA: I fought a hard fight.

HELMER: And suffered pain and saw no escape but— No, we're not going to dwell on anything unpleasant. We'll just be grateful and keep on repeating: it's over now, it's over! You hear me, Nora? You don't seem to realize—it's over. What's it mean—that frozen look? Oh, poor little Nora, I understand. You can't believe I've forgiven you. But I have, Nora; I swear I have. I know that what you did, you did out of love for me.

NORA: That's true.

HELMER: You loved me the way a wife ought to love her husband. It's simply the means that you couldn't judge. But you think I love you any the less for not knowing how to handle your affairs? No, no—just lean on me; I'll guide you and teach you. I wouldn't be a man if this feminine helplessness didn't make you twice as attractive to me. You mustn't mind those sharp words I said—that was all in the first confusion of thinking my world had collapsed. I've forgiven you, Nora; I swear I've forgiven you.

NORA: My thanks for your forgiveness. [*She goes out through the door, right.*]

HELMER: No, wait— [*Peers in.*] What are you doing in there?

NORA: [*Inside.*] Getting out of my costume.

HELMER: [*By the open door.*] Yes, do that. Try to calm yourself and collect your thoughts again, my frightened little songbird. You can rest easy now; I've got wide wings to shelter you with. [*Walking about close by the door.*] How snug and nice our home is, Nora. You're safe here; I'll keep you like a hunted dove I've rescued out of a hawk's claws. I'll bring peace to your poor, shuddering heart. Gradually it'll happen, Nora; you'll see. Tomorrow all this will look different to you; then everything will be as it was. I won't have to go on repeating I forgive you; you'll feel it for yourself. How can you imagine I'd ever conceivably want to disown you—or even blame you in any way? Ah, you don't know a man's heart, Nora. For a man there's something indescribably sweet and satisfying in knowing he's forgiven his wife—and forgiven her out of a full and open heart. It's as if she belongs to him in two ways now: in a sense he's given her fresh into the world again, and she's become his wife and his child as well. From now on that's what you'll be to me—you little, bewildered, helpless thing. Don't be afraid of anything, Nora; just open your heart to me, and I'll be conscience and will to you both— [NORA *enters in her regular clothes.*] What's this? Not in bed? You've changed your dress?

NORA: Yes, Torvald, I've changed my dress.

HELMER: But why now, so late?

NORA: Tonight I'm not sleeping.

HELMER: But Nora dear—

NORA: [*Looking at her watch.*] It's still not so very late. Sit down, Torvald; we have a lot to talk over. [*She sits at one side of the table.*]

HELMER: Nora—what is this? That hard expression—

NORA: Sit down. This'll take some time. I have a lot to say.

HELMER: [*Sitting at the table directly opposite her.*] You worry me, Nora. And I don't understand you.

NORA: No, that's exactly it. You don't understand me. And I've never understood you either—until tonight. No, don't interrupt. You can just listen to what I say. We're closing out accounts, Torvald.

HELMER: How do you mean that?

NORA: [*After a short pause.*] Doesn't anything strike you about our sitting here like this?

HELMER: What's that?

NORA: We've been married now eight years. Doesn't it occur to you that this is the first time we two, you and I, man and wife, have ever talked seriously together?

HELMER: What do you mean—seriously?

NORA: In eight whole years—longer even—right from our first acquaintance, we've never exchanged a serious word on any serious thing.

HELMER: You mean I should constantly go and involve you in problems you couldn't possibly help me with?

NORA: I'm not talking of problems. I'm saying that we've never sat down seriously together and tried to get to the bottom of anything.

HELMER: But dearest, what good would that ever do you?

NORA: That's the point right there: you've never understood me. I've been wronged greatly, Torvald—first by Papa, and then by you.

HELMER: What! By us—the two people who've loved you more than anyone else?

NORA: [*Shaking her head.*] You never loved me. You've thought it fun to be in love with me, that's all.

HELMER: Nora, what a thing to say!

NORA: Yes, it's true now, Torvald. When I lived at home with Papa, he told me all his opinions, so I had the same ones too; or if they were different I hid them, since he wouldn't have cared for that. He used to call me his doll-child, and he played with me the way I played with my dolls. Then I came into your house—

HELMER: How can you speak of our marriage like that?

NORA: [*Unperturbed.*] I mean, then I went from Papa's hands into yours. You arranged everything to your own taste, and so I got the same taste as you—or I pretended to; I can't remember. I guess a little of both, first one, then the other. Now when I look back, it seems as if I'd lived here like a beggar—just from hand to mouth. I've lived by doing tricks for you, Torvald. But that's the way you wanted it. It's a great sin what you and Papa did to me. You're to blame that nothing's become of me.

HELMER: Nora, how unfair and ungrateful you are! Haven't you been happy here?

NORA: No, never. I thought so—but I never have.

HELMER: Not—not happy!

NORA: No, only lighthearted. And you've always been so kind to me. But our home's been nothing but a playpen. I've been your doll-wife here, just as at home I was Papa's doll-child. And in turn the children have been my dolls. I thought it was fun when you played with me, just as they thought it fun when I played with them. That's been our marriage, Torvald.

HELMER: There's some truth in what you're saying—under all the raving exaggeration. But it'll all be different after this. Playtime's over; now for the schooling.

NORA: Whose schooling—mine or the children's?

HELMER: Both yours and the children's, dearest.

NORA: Oh, Torvald, you're not the man to teach me to be a good wife to you.

HELMER: And you can say that?

NORA: And I—how am I equipped to bring up children?

HELMER: Nora!

NORA: Didn't you say a moment ago that that was no job to trust me with?

HELMER: In a flare of temper! Why fasten on that?

NORA: Yes, but you were so very right. I'm not up to the job. There's another job I have to do first. I have to try to educate myself. You can't help me with that. I've got to do it alone. And that's why I'm leaving you now.

HELMER: [*Jumping up.*] What's that?

NORA: I have to stand completely alone, if I'm ever going to discover myself and the world out there. So I can't go on living with you.

HELMER: Nora, Nora!

NORA: I want to leave right away. Kristine should put me up for the night—

HELMER: You're insane! You've no right! I forbid you!

NORA: From here on, there's no use forbidding me anything. I'll take with me whatever is mine. I don't want a thing from you, either now or later.

HELMER: What kind of madness is this!

NORA: Tomorrow I'm going home—I mean, home where I came from. It'll be easier up there to find something to do.

HELMER: Oh, you blind, incompetent child!

NORA: I must learn to be competent, Torvald.

HELMER: Abandon your home, your husband, your children! And you're not even thinking what people will say.

NORA: I can't be concerned about that. I only know how essential this is.

HELMER: Oh, it's outrageous. So you'll run out like this on your most sacred vows.

NORA: What do you think are my most sacred vows?

HELMER: And I have to tell you that! Aren't they your duties to your husband and children?

NORA: I have other duties equally sacred.

HELMER: That isn't true. What duties are they?

NORA: Duties to myself.

HELMER: Before all else, you're a wife and a mother.

NORA: I don't believe in that anymore. I believe that, before all else, I'm a human being, no less than you—or anyway, I ought to try to become one. I know the majority thinks you're right, Torvald, and plenty of books agree with you, too. But I can't go on believing what the majority says, or what's written in books. I have to think over these things myself and try to understand them.

HELMER: Why can't you understand your place in your own home? On a point like that, isn't there one everlasting guide you can turn to? Where's your religion?

NORA: Oh, Torvald, I'm really not sure what religion is.

HELMER: What—?

NORA: I only know what the minister said when I was confirmed. He told me religion was this thing and that. When I get clear and away by myself, I'll go into that problem too. I'll see if what the minister said was right, or, in any case, if it's right for me.

HELMER: A young woman your age shouldn't talk like that. If religion can't move you, I can try to rouse your conscience. You do have some moral feeling? Or, tell me—has that gone too?

NORA: It's not easy to answer that, Torvald. I simply don't know. I'm all confused about these things. I just know I see them so differently from you. I find out, for one thing, that the law's not at all what I'd thought—but I can't get it through my head that the law is fair. A woman hasn't a right to protect her dying father or save her husband's life! I can't believe that.

HELMER: You talk like a child. You don't know anything of the world you live in.

NORA: No, I don't. But now I'll begin to learn for myself. I'll try to discover who's right, the world or I.

HELMER: Nora, you're sick; you've got a fever. I almost think you're out of your head.

NORA: I've never felt more clearheaded and sure in my life.

HELMER: And—clearheaded and sure—you're leaving your husband and children?

NORA: Yes.

HELMER: Then there's only one possible reason.

NORA: What?

HELMER: You no longer love me.

NORA: No. That's exactly it.

HELMER: Nora! You can't be serious!

NORA: Oh, this is so hard, Torvald—you've been so kind to me always. But I can't help it. I don't love you anymore.

HELMER: [*Struggling for composure.*] Are you also clearheaded and sure about that?

NORA: Yes, completely. That's why I can't go on staying here.

HELMER: Can you tell me what I did to lose your love?

NORA: Yes, I can tell you. It was this evening when the miraculous thing didn't come—then I knew you weren't the man I'd imagined.

HELMER: Be more explicit; I don't follow you.

NORA: I've waited now so patiently eight long years—for, my Lord, I know miracles don't come every day. Then this crisis broke over me, and such a certainty filled me: *now* the miraculous event would occur. While Krogstad's letter was lying out there, I never for an instant dreamed that you could give in to his terms. I was so utterly sure you'd say to him: go on, tell your tale to the whole wide world. And when he'd done that—

HELMER: Yes, what then? When I'd delivered my own wife into shame and disgrace—!

NORA: When he'd done that, I was so utterly sure that you'd step forward, take the blame on yourself and say: I am the guilty one.

HELMER: Nora—!

NORA: You're thinking I'd never accept such a sacrifice from you? No, of course not. But what good would my protests be against you? That was the miracle I was waiting for, in terror and hope. And to stave that off, I would have taken my life.

HELMER: I'd gladly work for you day and night, Nora—and take on pain and deprivation. But there's no one who gives up honor for love.

NORA: Millions of women have done just that.

HELMER: Oh, you think and talk like a silly child.

NORA: Perhaps. But you neither think nor talk like the man I could join myself to. When your big fright was over—and it wasn't from any threat against me, only for what might damage you— when all the danger was past, for you it was just as if nothing had happened. I was exactly the same, your little lark, your doll, that you'd have to handle with double care now that I'd turned out so brittle and frail. [*Gets up.*] Torvald—in that instant it dawned on me that for eight years I've been living here with a stranger, and that I'd even conceived three children—oh, I can't stand the thought of it! I could tear myself to bits.

HELMER: [*Heavily.*] I see. There's a gulf that's opened between us— that's clear. Oh, but Nora, can't we bridge it somehow?

NORA: The way I am now, I'm no wife for you.

HELMER: I have the strength to make myself over.

NORA: Maybe—if your doll gets taken away.

HELMER: But to part! To part from you! No, Nora, no—I can't imagine it.

NORA: [*Going out, right.*] All the more reason why it has to be. [*She reenters with her coat and a small overnight bag, which she puts on a chair by the table.*]

HELMER: Nora, Nora, not now! Wait till tomorrow.

NORA: I can't spend the night in a strange man's room.

HELMER: But couldn't we live here like brother and sister—

NORA: You know very well how long that would last. [*Throws her shawl about her.*] Good-bye, Torvald. I won't look in on the children. I know they're in better hands than mine. The way I am now, I'm no use to them.

HELMER: But someday, Nora—someday—?

NORA: How can I tell? I haven't the least idea what'll become of me.

HELMER: But you're my wife, now and wherever you go.

NORA: Listen, Torvald—I've heard that when a wife deserts her husband's house just as I'm doing, then the law frees him from all responsibility. In any case, I'm freeing you from being responsible. Don't feel yourself bound, any more than I will. There has to be absolute freedom for us both. Here, take your ring back. Give me mine.

HELMER: That too?

NORA: That too.

HELMER: There it is.

NORA: Good. Well, now it's all over. I'm putting the keys here. The maids know all about keeping up the house—better than I do. Tomorrow, after I've left town, Kristine will stop by to pack up everything that's mine from home. I'd like those things shipped up to me.

HELMER: Over! All over! Nora, won't you ever think about me?

NORA: I'm sure I'll think of you often, and about the children and the house here.

HELMER: May I write you?

NORA: No—never. You're not to do that.

HELMER: Oh, but let me send you—

NORA: Nothing. Nothing.

HELMER: Or help you if you need it.

NORA: No. I accept nothing from strangers.

HELMER: Nora—can I never be more than a stranger to you?

NORA: [*Picking up the overnight bag.*] Ah, Torvald—it would take the greatest miracle of all—

HELMER: Tell me the greatest miracle!

NORA: You and I both would have to transform ourselves to the point that— Oh, Torvald, I've stopped believing in miracles.

HELMER: But I'll believe. Tell me! Transform ourselves to the point that—?

NORA: That our living together could be a true marriage. [*She goes out down the hall.*]

HELMER: [*Sinks down on a chair by the door, face buried in his hands.*] Nora! Nora! [*Looking about and rising.*] Empty. She's gone. [*A sudden hope leaps in him.*] The greatest miracle—?

[*From below, the sound of a door slamming shut.*]

1878   1879

Oscar Wilde
1854–1900

THE IMPORTANCE OF BEING EARNEST

Oscar Wilde, an Irishman schooled at Oxford and living in London, embodied the Aesthetic movement, which made its way through English literary society in the 1880s and 1890s. Based on the epicurean philosophy of the essayist and critic Walter Pater, the movement promoted a cult of the beautiful. Its slogan, "Art for art's sake," repudiated the more characteristically Victorian notion that art ought to serve a good and edifying purpose.

This undercutting of values is evident in the title of Wilde's best-known play. Victorians prized "earnestness" in their men more than nearly any other virtue. This old and complex word betokens bravery in battle, a seriousness in demeanor (and, of course, an aversion to tomfoolery), zeal in religious convictions, and confidence in one's purpose. The English generally associated these traits with the middle class, which rose to economic and political power in the nineteenth century. Indeed, the English middle class relied on "earnestness" and its accompanying traits for so many accomplishments in that century—the erection of elaborate systems of railroads, the building of the world's greatest fleets of steam-powered ships, extraordinary feats of engineering (bridges, canals), in short, the whole might and energy and work ethic of the industrial age.

The industrial age had replaced the antiquated structures of an agricultural society, and so the earnest bourgeoisie disdained the lifestyle and ideology of the landed aristocracy. To the prudish Victorians, the old aristocracy often seemed not only obsolete but lazy and decadent.

Wilde deflated this high tide of stuffy and self-important Victorianism through **satire**, a comedic genre that encourages audiences to laugh at and even ridicule human (and societal) vices and follies. Indeed, this play helped generate a cultural shift in England, a shift that undermined the "truths" and values on which the sense of proper Victorian behavior had been erected. Wilde also made fun of himself and the aristocrats he found so congenial. Audiences would have recognized the playwright in the characterization of Algernon: the cynical, effeminate aesthete who cannot take anything seriously. And the portrait of Lady Bracknell exposes how ready the old aristocrats were to sell their sense of exclusivity for a few thousand pounds.

If he did not introduce the English to the well-made play (at that time in vogue in France), Wilde succeeded with the form better than anyone else. His plays delighted in the plot intrigues and the devices of mistaken identity that were codified in the French theater. His characters, drawn from types, seem less like real people than do the characters in other plays. But audiences approach comedy with different expectations than they bring to serious drama, and satire works by exaggeration. The Importance of Being Earnest presents cynicism, craven greed, and vacuousness in proportions not likely to be found in real life. In fact, the one characteristic not exaggerated in the play is earnestness, which often comes in greater concentrations than it does in Jack.

Wilde wanted to make his audiences laugh, and the London public proved happy to oblige. The play was a hit in the early months of 1895. As in all great comedies, though, the laughs came not just for their own sake—the jokes bit like hyenas. In fact, just months after the premiere, audiences viewed the play in light of Wilde's dramatic, scandalous private life, which suddenly became public. Though married with two children, Wilde had conducted a homosexual affair with an aristocrat, whose father, upset by the re-

lationship, publicly accused Wilde of being a sodomite. Wilde, encouraged by his lover, sued for libel. The result of the suit was Wilde's conviction for homosexuality. To many contemporaries, London's profligate society, and much of the sentiment expressed in his play, was tried and convicted also. Certainly, the trial chilled the increasingly libertine late-Victorian Londoners and dampened the play's accomplishments.

To some extent, because it satirizes its time, The Importance of Being Earnest *is a period piece. The Victorians it mocks are no longer with us, nor do we have the vestige of even an obsolescent aristocracy. But we, like the Victorians, live in an age dominated by middle-class values and morality, in a society that still attaches importance to earnestness. To what extent is this play apropos today? Is it irrelevant to your life, or do its bites still sting?*

The Importance of Being Earnest

CHARACTERS

JOHN WORTHING, J.P.   LADY BRACKNELL
ALGERNON MONCRIEFF   HON. GWENDOLEN FAIRFAX
REV. CANON CHASUBLE, D.D.   CECILY CARDEW
MERRIMAN (*Butler*)   MISS PRISM (*Governess*)
LANE (*Manservant*)

THE SCENES OF THE PLAY

ACT I. *Algernon Moncrieff's Flat in Half-Moon Street, W.*
ACT II. *The Garden at the Manor House, Woolton.*
ACT III. *Drawing-Room of the Manor House, Woolton.*

TIME.—*The Present.* PLACE.—*London.*

ACT I

SCENE.—*Morning-room in* ALGERNON'S *flat in Half-Moon Street. The room is luxuriously and artistically furnished. The sound of a piano is heard in the adjoining room.* LANE *is arranging afternoon tea on the table, and after the music has ceased,* ALGERNON *enters.*

ALGERNON: Did you hear what I was playing, Lane?

LANE: I didn't think it polite to listen, sir.

ALGERNON: I'm sorry for that, for your sake. I don't play accurately—anyone can play accurately—but I play with wonderful expression. As far as the piano is concerned, sentiment is my forte. I keep science for Life.

LANE: Yes, sir.

ALGERNON: And, speaking of the science of Life, have you got the cucumber sandwiches cut for Lady Bracknell?

LANE: Yes, sir. [*Hands them on a salver.*]

ALGERNON: [*Inspects them, takes two, and sits down on the sofa.*] Oh! . . . by the way, Lane, I see from your book that on Thursday night, when Lord Shoreman and Mr. Worthing were dining with me, eight bottles of champagne are entered as having been consumed.

LANE: Yes, sir; eight bottles and a pint.

ALGERNON: Why is it that at a bachelor's establishment the servants invariably drink the champagne? I ask merely for information.

LANE: I attribute it to the superior quality of the wine, sir. I have often observed that in married households the champagne is rarely of a first-rate brand.

ALGERNON: Good Heavens! Is marriage so demoralizing as that?

LANE: I believe it *is* a very pleasant state, sir. I have had very little experience of it myself up to the present. I have only been married once. That was in consequence of a misunderstanding between myself and a young woman.

ALGERNON: [*Languidly.*] I don't know that I am much interested in your family life, Lane.

LANE: No, sir; it is not a very interesting subject. I never think of it myself.

ALGERNON: Very natural, I am sure. That will do, Lane, thank you.

LANE: Thank you, sir. [LANE *goes out.*]

ALGERNON: Lane's views on marriage seem somewhat lax. Really, if the lower orders don't set us a good example, what on earth is the use of them? They seem, as a class, to have absolutely no sense of moral responsibility.

[*Enter* LANE.]

LANE: Mr. Ernest Worthing.

[*Enter* JACK. LANE *goes out.*]

ALGERNON: How are you, my dear Ernest? What brings you up to town?

JACK: Oh, pleasure, pleasure! What else should bring one anywhere? Eating as usual, I see, Algy!

ALGERNON: [*Stiffly.*] I believe it is customary in good society to take some slight refreshment at five o'clock. Where have you been since last Thursday?

JACK: [*Sitting down on the sofa.*] In the country.

ALGERNON: What on earth do you do there?

JACK: [*Pulling off his gloves.*] When one is in town one amuses oneself. When one is in the country one amuses other people. It is excessively boring.

ALGERNON: And who are the people you amuse?

JACK: [*Airily.*] Oh, neighbours, neighbours.

ALGERNON: Got nice neighbours in your part of Shropshire?[1]

JACK: Perfectly horrid! Never speak to one of them.

ALGERNON: How immensely you must amuse them! [*Goes over and takes sandwich.*] By the way, Shropshire is your county, is it not?

JACK: Eh? Shropshire? Yes, of course. Hallo! Why all these cups? Why cucumber sandwiches? Why such reckless extravagance in one so young? Who is coming to tea?

ALGERNON: Oh! merely Aunt Augusta and Gwendolen.

JACK: How perfectly delightful!

ALGERNON: Yes, that is all very well; but I am afraid Aunt Augusta won't quite approve of your being here.

JACK: May I ask why?

ALGERNON: My dear fellow, the way you flirt with Gwendolen is perfectly disgraceful. It is almost as bad as the way Gwendolen flirts with you.

JACK: I am in love with Gwendolen. I have come up to town expressly to propose to her.

ALGERNON: I thought you had come up for pleasure? . . . I call that business.

JACK: How utterly unromantic you are!

ALGERNON: I really don't see anything romantic in proposing. It is

1. Rural county in the west of England, remote from metropolitan London.

very romantic to be in love. But there is nothing romantic about a definite proposal. Why, one may be accepted. One usually is, I believe. Then the excitement is all over. The very essence of romance is uncertainty. If ever I get married, I'll certainly try to forget the fact.

JACK: I have no doubt about that, dear Algy. The Divorce Court was specially invented for people whose memories are so curiously constituted.

ALGERNON: Oh! there is no use speculating on that subject. Divorces are made in Heaven— [JACK *puts out his hand to take a sandwich.* ALGERNON *at once interferes.*] Please don't touch the cucumber sandwiches. They are ordered specially for Aunt Augusta. [*Takes one and eats it.*]

JACK: Well, you have been eating them all the time.

ALGERNON: That is quite a different matter. She is my aunt. [*Takes plate from below.*] Have some bread and butter. The bread and butter is for Gwendolen. Gwendolen is devoted to bread and butter.

JACK: [*Advancing to table and helping himself.*] And very good bread and butter it is, too.

ALGERNON: Well, my dear fellow, you need not eat as if you were going to eat it all. You behave as if you were married to her already. You are not married to her already, and I don't think you ever will be.

JACK: Why on earth do you say that?

ALGERNON: Well, in the first place girls never marry the men they flirt with. Girls don't think it right.

JACK: Oh, that is nonsense!

ALGERNON: It isn't. It is a great truth. It accounts for the extraordinary number of bachelors that one sees all over the place. In the second place, I don't give my consent.

JACK: Your consent!

ALGERNON: My dear fellow, Gwendolen is my first cousin. And before I allow you to marry her, you will have to clear up the whole question of Cecily. [*Rings bell.*]

JACK: Cecily! What on earth do you mean? What do you mean, Algy, by Cecily? I don't know anyone of the name of Cecily.

[*Enter* LANE.]

ALGERNON: Bring me that cigarette case Mr. Worthing left in the smoking-room the last time he dined here.

LANE: Yes, sir. [LANE *goes out.*]

JACK: Do you mean to say you have had my cigarette case all this time? I wish to goodness you had let me know. I have been writing frantic letters to Scotland Yard about it. I was very nearly offering a large reward.

ALGERNON: Well, I wish you would offer one. I happen to be more than usually hard up.

JACK: There is no good offering a large reward now that the thing is found.

[*Enter* LANE *with the cigarette case on a salver.* ALGERNON *takes it at once.* LANE *goes out.*]

ALGERNON: I think that is rather mean of you, Ernest, I must say. [*Opens case and examines it.*] However, it makes no matter, for, now that I look at the inscription, I find that the thing isn't yours after all.

JACK: Of course it's mine. [*Moving to him.*] You have seen me with it a hundred times, and you have no right whatsoever to read what is written inside. It is a very ungentlemanly thing to read a private cigarette case.

ALGERNON: Oh! it is absurd to have a hard-and-fast rule about what one should read and what one shouldn't. More than half of modern culture depends on what one shouldn't read.

JACK: I am quite aware of the fact, and I don't propose to discuss modern culture. It isn't the sort of thing one should talk of in private. I simply want my cigarette case back.

ALGERNON: Yes; but this isn't your cigarette case. This cigarette case is a present from someone of the name of Cecily, and you said you didn't know anyone of that name.

JACK: Well, if you want to know, Cecily happens to be my aunt.

ALGERNON: Your aunt!

JACK: Yes. Charming old lady she is, too. Lives at Tunbridge Wells. Just give it back to me, Algy.

ALGERNON: [*Retreating to back of sofa.*] But why does she call herself little Cecily if she is your aunt and lives at Tunbridge Wells? [*Reading.*] "From little Cecily with her fondest love."

JACK: [*Moving to sofa and kneeling upon it.*] My dear fellow, what on earth is there in that? Some aunts are tall, some aunts are not tall. That is a matter that surely an aunt may be allowed to decide for herself. You seem to think that every aunt should be exactly like your aunt! That is absurd! For Heaven's sake give me back my cigarette case. [*Follows* ALGERNON *round the room.*]

ALGERNON: Yes. But why does your aunt call you her uncle? "From little Cecily, with her fondest love to her dear Uncle Jack." There is no objection, I admit, to an aunt being a small aunt, but why an aunt, no matter what her size may be, should call her own nephew her uncle, I can't quite make out. Besides, your name isn't Jack at all; it is Ernest.

JACK: It isn't Ernest; it's Jack.

ALGERNON: You have always told me it was Ernest. I have introduced you to everyone as Ernest. You answer to the name of Ernest. You look as if your name was Ernest. You are the most ernest looking person I ever saw in my life. It is perfectly absurd your saying that your name isn't Ernest. It's on your cards. Here is one of them. [*Taking it from case.*] "Mr. Ernest Worthing, B 4, The Albany." I'll keep this as a proof your name is Ernest if ever you attempt to deny it to me, or to Gwendolen, or to anyone else. [*Puts the card in his pocket.*]

JACK: Well, my name is Ernest in town and Jack in the country, and the cigarette case was given to me in the country.

ALGERNON: Yes, but that does not account for the fact that your small Aunt Cecily, who lives at Tumbridge Wells, calls you her dear uncle. Come, old boy, you had much better have the thing out at once.

JACK: My dear Algy, you talk exactly as if you were a dentist. It is very vulgar to talk like a dentist when one isn't a dentist. It produces a false impression.

ALGERNON: Well, that is exactly what dentists always do. Now, go on! Tell me the whole thing. I may mention that I have always suspected you of being a confirmed and secret Bunburyist; and I am quite sure of it now.

JACK: Bunburyist? What on earth do you mean by a Bunburyist?

ALGERNON: I'll reveal to you the meaning of that incomparable expression as soon as you are kind enough to inform me why you are Ernest in town and Jack in the country.

JACK: Well, produce my cigarette case first.

ALGERNON: Here it is. [*Hands cigarette case.*] Now produce your explanation, and pray make it improbable. [*Sits on sofa.*]

JACK: My dear fellow, there is nothing improbable about my explanation at all. In fact it's perfectly ordinary. Old Mr. Thomas Cardew, who adopted me when I was a little boy, made me in his will guardian to his granddaughter, Miss Cecily Cardew. Cecily, who addresses me as her uncle from motives of respect that you could not possibly appreciate, lives at my place in the country under the charge of her admirable governess, Miss Prism.

ALGERNON: Where is that place in the country, by the way?

JACK: That is nothing to you, dear boy. You are not going to be invited. . . . I may tell you candidly that the place is not in Shropshire.

ALGERNON: I suspected that, my dear fellow! I have Bunburyed all over Shropshire on two separate occasions. Now, go on. Why are you Ernest in town and Jack in the country?

JACK: My dear Algy, I don't know whether you will be able to understand my real motives. You are hardly serious enough. When one is placed in the position of guardian, one has to adopt a very high moral tone on all subjects. It's one's duty to do so. And as a high moral tone can hardly be said to conduce very much to either one's health or one's happiness, in order to get up to town I have always pretended to have a younger brother of the name of Ernest, who lives in the Albany, and gets into the most dreadful scrapes. That, my dear Algy, is the whole truth pure and simple.

ALGERNON: The truth is rarely pure and never simple. Modern life would be very tedious if it were either, and modern literature a complete impossibility!

JACK: That wouldn't be at all a bad thing.

ALGERNON: Literary criticism is not your forte, my dear fellow. Don't try it. You should leave that to people who haven't been at a University. They do it so well in the daily papers. What you really are is a Bunburyist. I was quite right in saying you were a Bunburyist. You are one of the most advanced Bunburyists I know.

JACK: What on earth do you mean?

ALGERNON: You have invented a very useful younger brother called

Ernest, in order that you may be able to come up to town as often as you like. I have invented an invaluable permanent invalid called Bunbury, in order that I may be able to go down into the country whenever I choose. Bunbury is perfectly invaluable. If it wasn't for Bunbury's extraordinary bad health, for instance, I wouldn't be able to dine with you at Willis's to-night, for I have been really engaged to Aunt Augusta for more than a week.

JACK: I haven't asked you to dine with me anywhere tonight.

ALGERNON: I know. You are absolutely careless about sending out invitations. It is very foolish of you. Nothing annoys people so much as not receiving invitations.

JACK: You had much better dine with your Aunt Augusta.

ALGERNON: I haven't the smallest intention of doing anything of the kind. To begin with, I dined there on Monday, and once a week is quite enough to dine with one's own relatives. In the second place, whenever I do dine there I am always treated as a member of the family, and sent down with either no woman at all, or two. In the third place, I know perfectly well whom she will place me next to, to-night. She will place me next Mary Farquhar, who always flirts with her own husband across the dinner-table. That is not very pleasant. Indeed, it is not even decent . . . and that sort of thing is enormously on the increase. The amount of women in London who flirt with their own husbands is perfectly scandalous. It looks so bad. It is simply washing one's clean linen in public. Besides, now that I know you to be a confirmed Bunburyist I naturally want to talk to you about Bunburying. I want to tell you the rules.

JACK: I'm not a Bunburyist at all. If Gwendolen accepts me, I am going to kill my brother, indeed I think I'll kill him in any case. Cecily is a little too much interested in him. It is rather a bore. So I am going to get rid of Ernest. And I strongly advise you to do the same with Mr. . . . with your invalid friend who has the absurd name.

ALGERNON: Nothing will induce me to part with Bunbury, and if you ever get married, which seems to me extremely problematic, you will be very glad to know Bunbury. A man who marries without knowing Bunbury has a very tedious time of it.

JACK: That is nonsense. If I marry a charming girl like Gwendolen, and she is the only girl I ever saw in my life that I would marry, I certainly won't want to know Bunbury.

ALGERNON: Then your wife will. You don't seem to realize, that in married life three is company and two is none.

JACK: [*Sententiously.*] That, my dear young friend, is the theory that the corrupt French Drama[2] has been propounding for the last fifty years.

ALGERNON: Yes; and that the happy English home has proved in half the time.

JACK: For heaven's sake, don't try to be cynical. It's perfectly easy to be cynical.

ALGERNON: My dear fellow, it isn't easy to be anything now-a-days. There's such a lot of beastly competition about. [*The sound of an electric bell is heard.*] Ah! that must be Aunt Augusta. Only relatives, or creditors, ever ring in that Wagnerian manner. Now, if I get her out of the way for ten minutes, so that you can have an opportunity for proposing to Gwendolen, may I dine with you to-night at Willis's?

JACK: I suppose so if you want to.

ALGERNON: Yes, but you must be serious about it. I hate people who are not serious about meals. It is so shallow of them.

    [*Enter* LANE.]

LANE: Lady Bracknell and Miss Fairfax.

    [ALGERNON *goes forward to meet them. Enter* LADY BRACKNELL *and* GWENDOLEN.]

LADY BRACKNELL: Good afternoon, dear Algernon, I hope you are behaving very well.

ALGERNON: I'm feeling very well, Aunt Augusta.

LADY BRACKNELL: That's not quite the same thing. In fact the two things rarely go together. [*Sees* JACK *and bows to him with icy coldness.*]

ALGERNON: [*To* GWENDOLEN.] Dear me, you are smart!

GWENDOLEN: I am always smart! Aren't I, Mr. Worthing?

JACK: You're quite perfect, Miss Fairfax.

GWENDOLEN: Oh! I hope I am not that. It would leave no room

2. With its irreverent and often comical treatment of real life, the French theater seemed libertine to the English.

for developments, and I intend to develop in *many directions*.
[GWENDOLEN *and* JACK *sit down together in the corner.*]

LADY BRACKNELL: I'm sorry if we are a little late, Algernon, but I was
obliged to call on dear Lady Harbury. I hadn't been there since
her poor husband's death. I never saw a woman so altered; she
looks quite twenty years younger. And now I'll have a cup of tea,
and one of those nice cucumber sandwiches you promised me.

ALGERNON: Certainly, Aunt Augusta. [*Goes over to tea-table.*]

LADY BRACKNELL: Won't you come and sit here, Gwendolen?

GWENDOLEN: Thanks, mamma, I'm quite comfortable where I am.

ALGERNON: [*Picking up empty plate in horror.*] Good heavens!
Lane! Why are there no cucumber sandwiches? I ordered them
specially.

LANE: [*Gravely.*] There were no cucumbers in the market this morning, sir. I went down twice.

ALGERNON: No cucumbers!

LANE: No, sir. Not even for ready money.

ALGERNON: That will do, Lane, thank you.

LANE: Thank you sir. [*Goes out.*]

ALGERNON: I am greatly distressed, Aunt Augusta, about there being
no cucumbers, not even for ready money.

LADY BRACKNELL: It really makes no matter, Algernon. I had some
crumpets with Lady Harbury, who seems to me to be living entirely for pleasure now.

ALGERNON: I hear her hair has turned quite gold from grief.

LADY BRACKNELL: It certainly has changed its colour. From what
cause I, of course, cannot say. [ALGERNON *crosses and hands tea.*]
Thank you. I've quite a treat for you to-night, Algernon. I am
going to send you down with Mary Farquhar. She is such a nice
woman, and so attentive to her husband. It's delightful to watch
them.

ALGERNON: I am afraid, Aunt Augusta, I shall have to give up the
pleasure of dining with you to-night after all.

LADY BRACKNELL: [*Frowning.*] I hope not, Algernon. It would put
my table completely out. Your uncle would have to dine upstairs.
Fortunately he is accustomed to that.

ALGERNON: It is a great bore, and, I need hardly say, a terrible disappointment to me, but the fact is I have just had a telegram to say

that my poor friend Bunbury is very ill again. [*Exchanges glances with* JACK.] They seem to think I should be with him.

LADY BRACKNELL: It is very strange. This Mr. Bunbury seems to suffer from curiously bad health.

ALGERNON: Yes; poor Bunbury is a dreadful invalid.

LADY BRACKNELL: Well, I must say, Algernon, that I think it is high time that Mr. Bunbury made up his mind whether he was going to live or to die. This shilly-shallying with the question is absurd. Nor do I in any way approve of the modern sympathy with invalids. I consider it morbid. Illness of any kind is hardly a thing to be encouraged in others. Health is the primary duty of life. I am always telling that to your poor uncle, but he never seems to take much notice . . . as far as any improvement in his ailments goes. I should be much obliged if you would ask Mr. Bunbury, from me, to be kind enough not to have a relapse on Saturday, for I rely on you to arrange my music for me. It is my last reception and one wants something that will encourage conversation, particularly at the end of the season when everyone has practically said whatever they had to say, which, in most cases, was probably not much.

ALGERNON: I'll speak to Bunbury, Aunt Augusta, if he is still conscious, and I think I can promise you he'll be all right by Saturday. You see, if one plays good music, people don't listen, and if one plays bad music people don't talk. But I'll run over the programme I've drawn out, if you will kindly come into the next room for a moment.

LADY BRACKNELL: Thank you, Algernon. It is very thoughtful of you. [*Rising, and following* ALGERNON.] I'm sure the programme will be delightful, after a few expurgations. French songs I cannot possibly allow. People always seem to think that they are improper, and either look shocked, which is vulgar, or laugh, which is worse. But German sounds a thoroughly respectable language, and indeed, I believe is so.[3] Gwendolen, you will accompany me.

GWENDOLEN: Certainly, mamma.

[LADY BRACKNELL *and* ALGERNON *go into the music-room*, GWENDOLEN *remains behind.*]

3. To the English, French culture seemed racy; German culture, staid.

JACK: Charming day it has been, Miss Fairfax.

GWENDOLEN: Pray don't talk to me about the weather, Mr. Worthing. Whenever people talk to me about the weather, I always feel quite certain that they mean something else. And that makes me so nervous.

JACK: I do mean something else.

GWENDOLEN: I thought so. In fact, I am never wrong.

JACK: And I would like to be allowed to take advantage of Lady Bracknell's temporary absence . . .

GWENDOLEN: I would certainly advise you to do so. Mamma has a way of coming back suddenly into a room that I have often had to speak to her about.

JACK: [*Nervously.*] Miss Fairfax, ever since I met you I have admired you more than any girl . . . I have ever met since . . . I met you.

GWENDOLEN: Yes, I am quite aware of the fact. And I often wish that in public, at any rate, you had been more demonstrative. For me you have always had an irresistible fascination. Even before I met you I was far from indifferent to you. [JACK *looks at her in amazement.*] We live, as I hope you know, Mr. Worthing, in an age of ideals. The fact is constantly mentioned in the more expensive monthly magazines, and has reached the provincial pulpits I am told: and my ideal has always been to love some one of the name of Ernest. There is something in that name that inspires absolute confidence. The moment Algernon first mentioned to me that he had a friend called Ernest, I knew I was destined to love you.

JACK: You really love me, Gwendolen?

GWENDOLEN: Passionately!

JACK: Darling! You don't know how happy you've made me.

GWENDOLEN: My own Ernest!

JACK: But you don't really mean to say that you couldn't love me if my name wasn't Ernest?

GWENDOLEN: But your name is Ernest.

JACK: Yes, I know it is. But supposing it was something else? Do you mean to say you couldn't love me then?

GWENDOLEN: [*Glibly.*] Ah! that is clearly a metaphysical speculation, and like most metaphysical speculations has very little reference at all to the actual facts of real life, as we know them.

JACK: Personally, darling, to speak quite candidly, I don't much care about the name of Ernest . . . I don't think that name suits me at all.

GWENDOLEN: It suits you perfectly. It is a divine name. It has a music of its own. It produces vibrations.

JACK: Well, really, Gwendolen, I must say that I think there are lots of other much nicer names. I think, Jack, for instance, a charming name.

GWENDOLEN: Jack? . . . No, there is very little music in the name Jack, if any at all, indeed. It does not thrill. It produces absolutely no vibration. . . . I have known several Jacks, and they all, without exception, were more than usually plain. Besides, Jack is a notorious domesticity for John! And I pity any woman who is married to a man called John. She would probably never be allowed to know the entrancing pleasure of a single moment's solitude. The only really safe name is Ernest.

JACK: Gwendolen, I must get christened at once—I mean we must get married at once. There is no time to be lost.

GWENDOLEN: Married, Mr. Worthing?

JACK: [*Astounded.*] Well . . . surely. You know that I love you, and you led me to believe, Miss Fairfax, that you were not absolutely indifferent to me.

GWENDOLEN: I adore you. But you haven't proposed to me yet. Nothing has been said at all about marriage. The subject has not even been touched on.

JACK: Well . . . may I propose to you now?

GWENDOLEN: I think it would be an admirable opportunity. And to spare you any possible disappointment, Mr. Worthing, I think it only fair to tell you quite frankly beforehand that I am fully determined to accept you.

JACK: Gwendolen!

GWENDOLEN: Yes, Mr. Worthing, what have you got to say to me?

JACK: You know what I have got to say to you.

GWENDOLEN: Yes, but you don't say it.

JACK: Gwendolen, will you marry me? [*Goes on his knees.*]

GWENDOLEN: Of course I will, darling. How long you have been about it! I am afraid you have had very little experience in how to propose.

JACK: My own one, I have never loved anyone in the world but you.

GWENDOLEN: Yes, but men often propose for practice. I know my brother Gerald does. All my girl-friends tell me so. What wonderfully blue eyes you have, Ernest! They are quite, quite blue. I hope you will always look at me just like that, especially when there are other people present.

[*Enter* LADY BRACKNELL.]

LADY BRACKNELL: Mr. Worthing! Rise, sir, from this semi-recumbent posture. It is most indecorous.

GWENDOLEN: Mamma! [*He tries to rise; she restrains him.*] I must beg you to retire. This is no place for you, besides, Mr. Worthing has not quite finished yet.

LADY BRACKNELL: Finished what, may I ask?

GWENDOLEN: I am engaged to Mr. Worthing, mamma. [*They rise together.*]

LADY BRACKNELL: Pardon me, you are not engaged to anyone. When you do become engaged to some one, I, or your father, should his health permit him, will inform you of the fact. An engagement should come on a young girl as a surprise, pleasant or unpleasant, as the case may be. It is hardly a matter that she could be allowed to arrange for herself[4] . . . And now I have a few questions to put to you, Mr. Worthing. While I am making these inquiries, you, Gwendolen, will wait for me below in the carriage.

GWENDOLEN: [*Reproachfully.*] Mamma!

LADY BRACKNELL: In the carriage, Gwendolen! [GWENDOLEN *goes to the door. She and* JACK *blow kisses to each other behind* LADY BRACKNELL's *back.* LADY BRACKNELL *looks vaguely about as if she could not understand what the noise was. Finally turns round.*] Gwendolen, the carriage!

GWENDOLEN: Yes, mamma. [*Goes out, looking back at* JACK.]

LADY BRACKNELL: [*Sitting down.*] You can take a seat, Mr. Worthing. [*Looks in her pocket for note-book and pencil.*]

JACK: Thank you, Lady Bracknell, I prefer standing.

LADY BRACKNELL: [*Pencil and notebook in hand.*] I feel bound to tell you that you are not down on my list of eligible young men, al-

---

4. By the 1890s, marriages in England, even among the aristocracy, were no longer "arranged."

though I have the same list as the dear Duchess of Bolton has. We work together, in fact. However, I am quite ready to enter your name, should your answers be what a really affectionate mother requires. Do you smoke?

JACK: Well, yes, I must admit I smoke.

LADY BRACKNELL: I am glad to hear it. A man should always have an occupation of some kind.[5] There are far too many idle men in London as it is. How old are you?

JACK: Twenty-nine.

LADY BRACKNELL: A very good age to be married at. I have always been of opinion that a man who desires to get married should know either everything or nothing. Which do you know?

JACK: [*After some hesitation.*] I know nothing, Lady Bracknell.

LADY BRACKNELL: I am pleased to hear it. I do not approve of anything that tampers with natural ignorance. Ignorance is like a delicate exotic fruit; touch it and the bloom is gone. The whole theory of modern education is radically unsound. Fortunately in England, at any rate, education produces no effect whatsoever. If it did, it would prove a serious danger to the upper classes, and probably lead to acts of violence in Grosvenor Square.[6] What is your income?

JACK: Between seven and eight thousand a year.

LADY BRACKNELL: [*Makes a note in her book.*] In land, or in investments?

JACK: In investments, chiefly.[7]

LADY BRACKNELL: That is satisfactory. What between the duties expected of one during one's life-time, and the duties exacted from one after one's death, land has ceased to be either a profit or a pleasure. It gives one position, and prevents one from keeping it up.[8] That's all that can be said about land.

JACK: I have a country house with some land, of course, attached to

5. Not having to work for a living often distinguished true aristocrats from pretenders; even so, the rise of middle-class ethics in the Victorian age promoted a work ethic even among the rich.

6. Wealthy residential district in London.

7. Jack's income is considerable, and its deriving from investments links him with the newly rich rather than the landed aristocracy.

8. Land was the mark of an old family, but by the 1890s it was already obsolete as a source of wealth—in fact, owning a lot of land drained one's finances.

it, about fifteen hundred acres, I believe; but I don't depend on that for my real income. In fact, as far as I can make out, the poachers are the only people who make anything out of it.

LADY BRACKNELL: A country house! How many bedrooms? Well, that point can be cleared up afterwards. You have a town house, I hope? A girl with a simple, unspoiled nature, like Gwendolen, could hardly be expected to reside in the country.

JACK: Well, I own a house in Belgrave Square, but it is let by the year to Lady Bloxham. Of course, I can get it back whenever I like, at six months' notice.

LADY BRACKNELL: Lady Bloxham? I don't know her.

JACK: Oh, she goes about very little. She is a lady considerably advanced in years.

LADY BRACKNELL: Ah, now-a-days that is no guarantee of respectability of character. What number in Belgrave Square?

JACK: 149.

LADY BRACKNELL: [*Shaking her head.*] The unfashionable side. I thought there was something. However, that could easily be altered.

JACK: Do you mean the fashion, or the side?

LADY BRACKNELL: [*Sternly.*] Both, if necessary, I presume. What are your politics?

JACK: Well, I am afraid I really have none. I am a Liberal Unionist.[9]

LADY BRACKNELL: Oh, they count as Tories.[1] They dine with us. Or come in the evening, at any rate. Now to minor matters. Are your parents living?

JACK: I have lost both my parents.

LADY BRACKNELL: Both? . . . That seems like carelessness. Who was your father? He was evidently a man of some wealth. Was he born in what the Radical papers call the purple of commerce, or did he rise from the ranks of the aristocracy?

JACK: I am afraid I really don't know. The fact is, Lady Bracknell, I said I had lost my parents. It would be nearer the truth to say that my parents seem to have lost me . . . I don't actually know who I am by birth. I was . . . well, I was found.

9. An English political party that split from the Liberal Party in 1886 and, by the turn of the century, effectively merged with the Conservative Party.

1. A political party linked to the landed aristocracy; forerunner of the Conservative Party.

LADY BRACKNELL: Found!

JACK: The late Mr. Thomas Cardew, an old gentleman of a very charitable and kindly disposition, found me, and gave me the name of Worthing, because he happened to have a first-class ticket for Worthing in his pocket at the time. Worthing is a place in Sussex. It is a seaside resort.

LADY BRACKNELL: Where did the charitable gentleman who had a first-class ticket for this seaside resort find you?

JACK: [*Gravely.*] In a hand-bag.

LADY BRACKNELL: A hand-bag?

JACK: [*Very seriously.*] Yes, Lady Bracknell. I was in a hand-bag—a somewhat large, black leather hand-bag, with handles to it—an ordinary hand-bag in fact.

LADY BRACKNELL: In what locality did Mr. James, or Thomas, Cardew come across this ordinary hand-bag?

JACK: In the cloak-room at Victoria Station. It was given to him in mistake for his own.

LADY BRACKNELL: The cloak-room at Victoria Station?

JACK: Yes. The Brighton line.

LADY BRACKNELL: The line is immaterial. Mr. Worthing, I confess I feel somewhat bewildered by what you have just told me. To be born, or at any rate bred, in a hand-bag, whether it had handles or not, seems to me to display a contempt for the ordinary decencies of family life that remind one of the worst excesses of the French Revolution.[2] And I presume you know what that unfortunate movement led to? As for the particular locality in which the hand-bag was found, a cloak-room at a railway station might serve to conceal a social indiscretion—has probably, indeed, been used for the purpose before now—but it could hardly be regarded as an assured basis for a recognized position in good society.

JACK: May I ask you then what you would advise me to do? I need hardly say I would do anything in the world to ensure Gwendolen's happiness.

LADY BRACKNELL: I would strongly advise you, Mr. Worthing, to try and acquire some relations as soon as possible, and to make a

---

2. The French Revolution dissolved many of the legal privileges given aristocrats by virtue of their "noble" blood.

definite effort to produce at any rate one parent, of either sex, before the season is quite over.

JACK: Well, I don't see how I could possibly manage to do that. I can produce the hand-bag at any moment. It is in my dressing-room at home. I really think that should satisfy you, Lady Bracknell.

LADY BRACKNELL: Me, sir! What has it to do with me? You can hardly imagine that I and Lord Bracknell would dream of allowing our only daughter—a girl brought up with the utmost care—to marry into a cloak-room, and form an alliance with a parcel? Good morning, Mr. Worthing! [LADY BRACKNELL *sweeps out in majestic indignation.*]

JACK: Good morning! [ALGERNON, *from the other room, strikes up the Wedding March.* JACK *looks perfectly furious, and goes to the door.*] For goodness' sake don't play that ghastly tune, Algy! How idiotic you are!

[*The music stops, and* ALGERNON *enters cheerily.*]

ALGERNON: Didn't it go off all right, old boy? You don't mean to say Gwendolen refused you? I know it is a way she has. She is always refusing people. I think it is most ill-natured of her.

JACK: Oh, Gwendolen is as right as a trivet. As far as she is concerned, we are engaged. Her mother is perfectly unbearable. Never met such a Gorgon[3] . . . I don't really know what a Gorgon is like, but I am quite sure that Lady Bracknell is one. In any case, she is a monster, without being a myth, which is rather unfair. . . . I beg your pardon, Algy, I suppose I shouldn't talk about your own aunt in that way before you.

ALGERNON: My dear boy, I love hearing my relations abused. It is the only thing that makes me put up with them at all. Relations are simply a tedious pack of people, who haven't got the remotest knowledge of how to live, nor the smallest instinct about when to die.

JACK: Oh, that is nonsense!

ALGERNON: It isn't!

JACK: Well, I won't argue about the matter. You always want to argue about things.

ALGERNON: That is exactly what things were originally made for.

---

3. One of three snake-haired sisters in Greek mythology; to look at a Gorgon would turn a person to stone.

JACK: Upon my word, if I thought that, I'd shoot myself . . . [*A pause.*] You don't think there is any chance of Gwendolen becoming like her mother in about a hundred and fifty years, do you, Algy?

ALGERNON: All women become like their mothers. That is their tragedy. No man does. That's his.

JACK: Is that clever?

ALGERNON: It is perfectly phrased! and quite as true as any observation in civilized life should be.

JACK: I am sick to death of cleverness. Everybody is clever now-a-days. You can't go anywhere without meeting clever people. The thing has become an absolute public nuisance. I wish to goodness we had a few fools left.

ALGERNON: We have.

JACK: I should extremely like to meet them. What do they talk about?

ALGERNON: The fools? Oh! about the clever people, of course.

JACK: What fools!

ALGERNON: By the way, did you tell Gwendolen the truth about your being Ernest in town, and Jack in the country?

JACK: [*In a very patronising manner.*] My dear fellow, the truth isn't quite the sort of thing one tells to a nice, sweet, refined girl. What extraordinary ideas you have about the way to behave to a woman!

ALGERNON: The only way to behave to a woman is to make love to[4] her, if she is pretty, and to someone else if she is plain.

JACK: Oh, that is nonsense.

ALGERNON: What about your brother? What about the profligate Ernest?

JACK: Oh, before the end of the week I shall have got rid of him. I'll say he died in Paris of apoplexy. Lots of people die of apoplexy, quite suddenly, don't they?

ALGERNON: Yes, but it's hereditary, my dear fellow. It's a sort of thing that runs in families. You had much better say a severe chill.

JACK: You are sure a severe chill isn't hereditary, or anything of that kind?

---

4. *Make love to:* court.

ALGERNON: Of course it isn't!

JACK: Very well, then. My poor brother Ernest is carried off suddenly in Paris, by a severe chill. That gets rid of him.

ALGERNON: But I thought you said that . . . Miss Cardew was a little too much interested in your poor brother Ernest? Won't she feel his loss a good deal?

JACK: Oh, that is all right. Cecily is not a silly, romantic girl, I am glad to say. She has got a capital appetite, goes for long walks, and pays no attention at all to her lessons.

ALGERNON: I would rather like to see Cecily.

JACK: I will take very good care you never do. She is excessively pretty, and she is only just eighteen.

ALGERNON: Have you told Gwendolen yet that you have an excessively pretty ward who is only just eighteen?

JACK: Oh! one doesn't blurt these things out to people. Cecily and Gwendolen are perfectly certain to be extremely great friends. I'll bet you anything you like that half an hour after they have met, they will be calling each other sister.

ALGERNON: Women only do that when they have called each other a lot of other things first. Now, my dear boy, if we want to get a good table at Willis's, we really must go and dress. Do you know it is nearly seven?

JACK: [*Irritably.*] Oh! it always is nearly seven.

ALGERNON: Well, I'm hungry.

JACK: I never knew you when you weren't. . . .

ALGERNON: What shall we do after dinner? Go to a theatre?

JACK: Oh, no! I loathe listening.

ALGERNON: Well, let us go to the Club?

JACK: Oh, no! I hate talking.

ALGERNON: Well, we might trot round to the Empire[5] at ten?

JACK: Oh, no! can't bear looking at things. It is so silly.

ALGERNON: Well, what shall we do?

JACK: Nothing!

ALGERNON: It is awfully hard work doing nothing. However, I don't mind hard work where there is no definite object of any kind.

5. The Empire Theatre of Varieties, a music hall.

[*Enter* LANE.]

LANE: Miss Fairfax.

[*Enter* GWENDOLEN. LANE *goes out.*]

ALGERNON: Gwendolen, upon my word!

GWENDOLEN: Algy, kindly turn your back. I have something very particular to say to Mr. Worthing.

ALGERNON: Really, Gwendolen, I don't think I can allow this at all.

GWENDOLEN: Algy, you always adopt a strictly immoral attitude towards life. You are not quite old enough to do that.

[ALGERNON *retires to the fireplace.*]

JACK: My own darling!

GWENDOLEN: Ernest, we may never be married. From the expression on mamma's face I fear we never shall. Few parents now-a-days pay any regard to what their children say to them. The old-fashioned respect for the young is fast dying out. Whatever influence I ever had over mamma, I lost at the age of three. But although she may prevent us from becoming man and wife, and I may marry someone else, and marry often, nothing that she can possibly do can alter my eternal devotion to you.

JACK: Dear Gwendolen.

GWENDOLEN: The story of your romantic origin, as related to me by mamma, with unpleasing comments, has naturally stirred the deeper fibers of my nature. Your Christian name has an irresistible fascination. The simplicity of your character makes you exquisitely incomprehensible to me. Your town address at the Albany I have. What is your address in the country?

JACK: The Manor House, Woolton, Hertfordshire.

[ALGERNON, *who has been carefully listening, smiles to himself, and writes the address on his shirt-cuff. Then picks up the Railway Guide.*]

GWENDOLEN: There is a good postal service, I suppose? It may be necessary to do something desperate. That, of course, will require serious consideration. I will communicate with you daily.

JACK: My own one!

GWENDOLEN: How long do you remain in town?

JACK: Till Monday.

GWENDOLEN: Good! Algy, you may turn round now.

ALGERNON: Thanks, I've turned round already.

GWENDOLEN: You may also ring the bell.

JACK: You will let me see you to your carriage, my own darling?

GWENDOLEN: Certainly.

JACK: [*To* LANE, *who now enters.*] I will see Miss Fairfax out.

LANE: Yes, sir.

> [JACK *and* GWENDOLEN *go off.* LANE *presents several letters on a salver to* ALGERNON. *It is to be surmised that they are bills, as* ALGERNON, *after looking at the envelopes, tears them up.*]

ALGERNON: A glass of sherry, Lane.

LANE: Yes, sir.

ALGERNON: To-morrow, Lane, I'm going Bunburying.

LANE: Yes, sir.

ALGERNON: I shall probably not be back till Monday. You can put up my dress clothes, my smoking jacket, and all the Bunbury suits . . .

LANE: Yes, sir. [*Handing sherry.*]

ALGERNON: I hope to-morrow will be a fine day, Lane.

LANE: It never is, sir.

ALGERNON: Lane, you're a perfect pessimist.

LANE: I do my best to give satisfaction, sir.

> [*Enter* JACK. LANE *goes off.*]

JACK: There's a sensible, intellectual girl! the only girl I ever cared for in my life. [ALGERNON *is laughing immoderately.*] What on earth are you so amused at?

ALGERNON: Oh, I'm a little anxious about poor Bunbury, that's all.

JACK: If you don't take care, your friend Bunbury will get you into a serious scrape some day.

ALGERNON: I love scrapes. They are the only things that are never serious.

JACK: Oh, that's nonsense, Algy. You never talk anything but nonsense.

ALGERNON: Nobody ever does.

> [JACK *looks indignantly at him, and leaves the room.* ALGERNON *lights a cigarette, reads his shirt-cuff and smiles.*]

[*Curtain.*]

ACT II

SCENE.—*Garden at the Manor House. A flight of gray stone steps leads up to the house. The garden, an old-fashioned one, full of roses. Time of year, July. Basket chairs, and a table covered with books are set under a large yew tree.* MISS PRISM *discovered seated at the table.* CECILY *is at the back watering flowers.*

MISS PRISM: [*Calling.*] Cecily, Cecily! Surely such a utilitarian occupation as the watering of flowers is rather Moulton's duty than yours? Especially at a moment when intellectual pleasures await you. Your German grammar is on the table. Pray open it at page fifteen. We will repeat yesterday's lesson.

CECILY: [*Coming over very slowly.*] But I don't like German. It isn't at all a becoming language. I know perfectly well that I look quite plain after my German lesson.

MISS PRISM: Child, you know how anxious your guardian is that you should improve yourself in every way. He laid particular stress on your German, as he was leaving for town yesterday. Indeed, he always lays stress on your German when he is leaving for town.

CECILY: Dear Uncle Jack is so very serious! Sometimes he is so serious that I think he cannot be quite well.

MISS PRISM: [*Drawing herself up.*] Your guardian enjoys the best of health, and his gravity of demeanour is especially to be commended in one so comparatively young as he is. I know no one who has a higher sense of duty and responsibility.

CECILY: I suppose that is why he often looks a little bored when we three are together.

MISS PRISM: Cecily! I am surprised at you. Mr. Worthing has many troubles in his life. Idle merriment and triviality would be out of place in his conversation. You must remember his constant anxiety about that unfortunate young man, his brother.

CECILY: I wish Uncle Jack would allow the unfortunate young man, his brother, to come down here sometimes. We might have a good influence over him, Miss Prism. I am sure you certainly would. You know German, and geology, and things of that kind influence a man very much. [CECILY *begins to write in her diary.*]

MISS PRISM: [*Shaking her head.*] I do not think that even I could produce any effect on a character that, according to his own brother's admission, is irretrievably weak and vacillating. Indeed, I am not sure that I would desire to reclaim him. I am not in favour of this modern mania for turning bad people into good people at a moment's notice. As a man sows so let him reap. You must put away your diary, Cecily. I really don't see why you should keep a diary at all.

CECILY: I keep a diary in order to enter the wonderful secrets of my life. If I didn't write them down I should probably forget all about them.

MISS PRISM: Memory, my dear Cecily, is the diary that we all carry about with us.

CECILY: Yes, but it usually chronicles the things that have never happened, and couldn't possibly have happened. I believe that Memory is responsible for nearly all the three-volume novels that Mudie sends us.[1]

MISS PRISM: Do not speak slightingly of the three-volume novel, Cecily. I wrote one myself in earlier days.

CECILY: Did you really, Miss Prism? How wonderfully clever you are! I hope it did not end happily? I don't like novels that end happily. They depress me so much.

MISS PRISM: The good ended happily, and the bad unhappily. That is what Fiction means.

CECILY: I suppose so. But it seems very unfair. And was your novel ever published?

MISS PRISM: Alas! no. The manuscript unfortunately was abandoned. I use the word in the sense of lost or mislaid. To your work, child, these speculations are profitless.

CECILY: [*Smiling.*] But I see dear Dr. Chasuble coming up through the garden.

MISS PRISM: [*Rising and advancing.*] Dr. Chasuble! This is indeed a pleasure.

[*Enter* CANON CHASUBLE.]

CHASUBLE: And how are we this morning? Miss Prism, you are, I trust, well?

---

1. Three-volume novels were the standard format for novelists of an earlier generation, like Dickens and Thackeray, but people like Wilde considered them old-fashioned and their contents unrealistic. *Mudie:* Mudie's, a lending library.

CECILY: Miss Prism has just been complaining of a slight headache. I think it would do her so much good to have a short stroll with you in the park, Dr. Chasuble.

MISS PRISM: Cecily, I have not mentioned anything about a headache.

CECILY: No, dear Miss Prism, I know that, but I felt instinctively that you had a headache. Indeed I was thinking about that, and not about my German lesson, when the Rector came in.

CHASUBLE: I hope, Cecily, you are not inattentive.

CECILY: Oh, I am afraid I am.

CHASUBLE: That is strange. Were I fortunate enough to be Miss Prism's pupil, I would hang upon her lips. [MISS PRISM *glares*.] I spoke metaphorically.—My metaphor was drawn from bees. Ahem! Mr. Worthing, I suppose, has not returned from town yet?

MISS PRISM: We do not expect him till Monday afternoon.

CHASUBLE: Ah, yes, he usually likes to spend his Sunday in London. He is not one of those whose sole aim is enjoyment, as by all accounts, that unfortunate young man, his brother, seems to be. But I must not disturb Egeria[2] and her pupil any longer.

MISS PRISM: Egeria? My name is Lætitia, Doctor.

CHASUBLE: [*Bowing*.] A classical allusion merely, drawn from the Pagan authors. I shall see you both no doubt at Evensong.

MISS PRISM: I think, dear Doctor, I will have a stroll with you. I find I have a headache after all, and a walk might do it good.

CHASUBLE: With pleasure, Miss Prism, with pleasure. We might go as far as the schools and back.

MISS PRISM: That would be delightful. Cecily, you will read your Political Economy in my absence. The chapter on the Fall of the Rupee[3] you may omit. It is somewhat too sensational. Even these metallic problems have their melodramatic side. [*Goes down the garden with* DR. CHASUBLE.]

CECILY: [*Picks up books and throws them back on table.*] Horrid Political Economy! Horrid Geography! Horrid, horrid German!

[*Enter* MERRIMAN *with a card on a salver.*]

2. In Roman mythology, a wood nymph (maiden goddess) who advised a king of Rome until his death, after which she pined for him.

3. Standard coin of India; in the early 1890s, it suffered such a devaluation that the mints were closed to try to break its fall.

MERRIMAN: Mr. Ernest Worthing has just driven over from the station. He has brought his luggage with him.

CECILY: [*Takes the card and reads it.*] "Mr. Ernest Worthing, B 4 The Albany, W." Uncle Jack's brother! Did you tell him Mr. Worthing was in town?

MERRIMAN: Yes, Miss. He seemed very much disappointed. I mentioned that you and Miss Prism were in the garden. He said he was anxious to speak to you privately for a moment.

CECILY: Ask Mr. Ernest Worthing to come here. I suppose you had better talk to the housekeeper about a room for him.

MERRIMAN: Yes, Miss. [MERRIMAN *goes off.*]

CECILY: I have never met any really wicked person before. I feel rather frightened. I am so afraid he will look just like everyone else.

[*Enter* ALGERNON, *very gay and debonair.*]

He does!

ALGERNON: [*Raising his hat.*] You are my little cousin Cecily, I'm sure.

CECILY: You are under some strange mistake. I am not little. In fact, I am more than usually tall for my age. [ALGERNON *is rather taken aback.*] But I am your cousin Cecily. You, I see from your card, are Uncle Jack's brother, my cousin Ernest, my wicked cousin Ernest.

ALGERNON: Oh! I am not really wicked at all, cousin Cecily. You mustn't think that I am wicked.

CECILY: If you are not, then you have certainly been deceiving us all in a very inexcusable manner. I hope you have not been leading a double life, pretending to be wicked and being really good all the time. That would be hypocrisy.

ALGERNON: [*Looks at her in amazement.*] Oh! of course I have been rather reckless.

CECILY: I am glad to hear it.

ALGERNON: In fact, now you mention the subject, I have been very bad in my own small way.

CECILY: I don't think you should be so proud of that, though I am sure it must have been very pleasant.

ALGERNON: It is much pleasanter being here with you.

CECILY: I can't understand how you are here at all. Uncle Jack won't be back till Monday afternoon.

ALGERNON: That is a great disappointment. I am obliged to go up by the first train on Monday morning. I have a business appointment that I am anxious . . . to miss.

CECILY: Couldn't you miss it anywhere but in London?

ALGERNON: No; the appointment is in London.

CECILY: Well, I know, of course, how important it is not to keep a business engagement, if one wants to retain any sense of the beauty of life, but still I think you had better wait till Uncle Jack arrives. I know he wants to speak to you about your emigrating.

ALGERNON: About my what?

CECILY: Your emigrating. He has gone up to buy your outfit.

ALGERNON: I certainly wouldn't let Jack buy my outfit. He has no taste in neckties at all.

CECILY: I don't think you will require neckties. Uncle Jack is sending you to Australia.

ALGERNON: Australia! I'd sooner die.

CECILY: Well, he said at dinner on Wednesday night, that you would have to choose between this world, the next world, and Australia.

ALGERNON: Oh, well! The accounts I have received of Australia and the next world are not particularly encouraging. This world is good enough for me, cousin Cecily.

CECILY: Yes, but are you good enough for it?

ALGERNON: I'm afraid I'm not that. That is why I want you to reform me. You might make that your mission, if you don't mind, cousin Cecily.

CECILY: I'm afraid I've not time, this afternoon.

ALGERNON: Well, would you mind my reforming myself this afternoon?

CECILY: That is rather Quixotic of you. But I think you should try.

ALGERNON: I will. I feel better already.

CECILY: You are looking a little worse.

ALGERNON: That is because I am hungry.

CECILY: How thoughtless of me. I should have remembered that when one is going to lead an entirely new life, one requires regular and wholesome meals. Won't you come in?

ALGERNON: Thank you. Might I have a button-hole first? I never have any appetite unless I have a button-hole first.

CECILY: A Maréchal Niel?[4] [*Picks up scissors.*]

ALGERNON: No, I'd sooner have a pink rose.

CECILY: Why? [*Cuts a flower.*]

ALGERNON: Because you are like a pink rose, cousin Cecily.

CECILY: I don't think it can be right for you to talk to me like that. Miss Prism never says such things to me.

ALGERNON: Then Miss Prism is a short-sighted old lady. [CECILY *puts the rose in his button-hole.*] You are the prettiest girl I ever saw.

CECILY: Miss Prism says that all good looks are a snare.

ALGERNON: They are a snare that every sensible man would like to be caught in.

CECILY: Oh! I don't think I would care to catch a sensible man. I shouldn't know what to talk to him about.

[*They pass into the house.* MISS PRISM *and* DR. CHASUBLE *return.*]

MISS PRISM: You are too much alone, dear Dr. Chasuble. You should get married. A misanthrope I can understand—a womanthrope, never!

CHASUBLE: [*With a scholar's shudder.*] Believe me, I do not deserve so neologistic a phrase. The precept as well as the practice of the Primitive Church was distinctly against matrimony.

MISS PRISM: [*Sententiously.*] That is obviously the reason why the Primitive Church has not lasted up to the present day. And you do not seem to realize, dear Doctor, that by persistently remaining single, a man converts himself into a permanent public temptation. Men should be careful; this very celibacy leads weaker vessels astray.

CHASUBLE: But is a man not equally attractive when married?

MISS PRISM: No married man is ever attractive except to his wife.

CHASUBLE: And often, I've been told, not even to her.

MISS PRISM: That depends on the intellectual sympathies of the woman. Maturity can always be depended on. Ripeness can be trusted. Young women are green. [DR. CHASUBLE *starts.*] I spoke horticulturally. My metaphor was drawn from fruits. But where is Cecily?

CHASUBLE: Perhaps she followed us to the schools.

4. A popular yellow rose of the period, here to be worn on Algernon's lapel.

[*Enter* JACK *slowly from the back of the garden. He is dressed in the deepest mourning, with crepe hatband and black gloves.*]

MISS PRISM: Mr. Worthing!

CHASUBLE: Mr. Worthing?

MISS PRISM: This is indeed a surprise. We did not look for you till Monday afternoon.

JACK: [*Shakes* MISS PRISM'*s hand in a tragic manner.*] I have returned sooner than I expected. Dr. Chasuble, I hope you are well?

CHASUBLE: Dear Mr. Worthing, I trust this garb of woe does not betoken some terrible calamity?

JACK: My brother.

MISS PRISM: More shameful debts and extravagance?

CHASUBLE: Still leading his life of pleasure?

JACK: [*Shaking his head.*] Dead!

CHASUBLE: Your brother Ernest dead?

JACK: Quite dead.

MISS PRISM: What a lesson for him! I trust he will profit by it.

CHASUBLE: Mr. Worthing, I offer you my sincere condolence. You have at least the consolation of knowing that you were always the most generous and forgiving of brothers.

JACK: Poor Ernest! He had many faults, but it is a sad, sad blow.

CHASUBLE: Very sad indeed. Were you with him at the end?

JACK: No. He died abroad; in Paris, in fact. I had a telegram last night from the manager of the Grand Hotel.

CHASUBLE: Was the cause of death mentioned?

JACK: A severe chill, it seems.

MISS PRISM: As a man sows, so shall he reap.

CHASUBLE: [*Raising his hand.*] Charity, dear Miss Prism, charity! None of us are perfect. I myself am peculiarly susceptible to draughts. Will the interment take place here?

JACK: No. He seems to have expressed a desire to be buried in Paris.

CHASUBLE: In Paris! [*Shakes his head.*] I fear that hardly points to any very serious state of mind at the last. You would no doubt wish me to make some slight allusion to this tragic domestic affliction next Sunday. [JACK *presses his hand convulsively.*] My sermon on the meaning of the manna in the wilderness can be adapted to almost any occasion, joyful, or, as in the present case, distressing. [*All sigh.*] I have preached it at harvest celebrations, christenings, confirmations, on days of humiliation and festal days. The last time I delivered it was in the Cathedral, as a charity sermon on behalf of the Society for the Prevention of Discontentment among the Upper Orders. The Bishop, who was present, was much struck by some of the analogies I drew.

JACK: Ah, that reminds me, you mentioned christenings I think, Dr. Chasuble? I suppose you know how to christen all right? [DR. CHASUBLE *looks astounded.*] I mean, of course, you are continually christening, aren't you?

MISS PRISM: It is, I regret to say, one of the Rector's most constant duties in this parish. I have often spoken to the poorer classes on the subject. But they don't seem to know what thrift is.

CHASUBLE: But is there any particular infant in whom you are interested, Mr. Worthing? Your brother was, I believe, unmarried, was he not?

JACK: Oh, yes.

MISS PRISM: [*Bitterly.*] People who live entirely for pleasure usually are.

JACK: But it is not for any child, dear Doctor. I am very fond of children. No! the fact is, I would like to be christened myself, this afternoon, if you have nothing better to do.

CHASUBLE: But surely, Mr. Worthing, you have been christened already?

JACK: I don't remember anything about it.

CHASUBLE: But have you any grave doubts on the subject?

JACK: I certainly intend to have. Of course, I don't know if the thing would bother you in any way, or if you think I am a little too old now.

CHASUBLE: Not at all. The sprinkling, and, indeed, the immersion of adults is a perfectly canonical practice.

JACK: Immersion!

CHASUBLE: You need have no apprehensions. Sprinkling is all that is necessary, or indeed I think advisable. Our weather is so changeable. At what hour would you wish the ceremony performed?

JACK: Oh, I might trot around about five if that would suit you.

CHASUBLE: Perfectly, perfectly! In fact I have two similar ceremonies to perform at that time. A case of twins that occurred recently in one of the outlying cottages on your own estate. Poor Jenkins the carter, a most hard-working man.

JACK: Oh! I don't see much fun in being christened along with other babies. It would be childish. Would half-past five do?

CHASUBLE: Admirably! Admirably! [*Takes out watch.*] And now, dear Mr. Worthing, I will not intrude any longer into a house of sorrow. I would merely beg you not to be too much bowed down by grief. What seem to us bitter trials at the moment are often blessings in disguise.

MISS PRISM: This seems to me a blessing of an extremely obvious kind.

[*Enter* CECILY *from the house.*]

CECILY: Uncle Jack! Oh, I am pleased to see you back. But what horrid clothes you have on! Do go and change them.

MISS PRISM: Cecily!

CHASUBLE: My child! my child!

[CECILY *goes towards* JACK; *he kisses her brow in a melancholy manner.*]

CECILY: What is the matter, Uncle Jack? Do look happy! You look as if you had a toothache and I have such a surprise for you. Who do you think is in the dining-room? Your brother!

JACK: Who?

CECILY: Your brother Ernest. He arrived about half an hour ago.

JACK: What nonsense! I haven't got a brother.

CECILY: Oh, don't say that. However badly he may have behaved to you in the past he is still your brother. You couldn't be so heartless as to disown him. I'll tell him to come out. And you will shake hands with him, won't you, Uncle Jack? [*Runs back into the house.*]

CHASUBLE: There are very joyful tidings.

MISS PRISM: After we had all been resigned to his loss, his sudden return seems to me peculiarly distressing.

JACK: My brother is in the dining-room? I don't know what it all means. I think it is perfectly absurd.

[*Enter* ALGERNON *and* CECILY *hand in hand. They come slowly up to* JACK.]

JACK: Good heavens! [*Motions* ALGERNON *away.*]

ALGERNON: Brother John, I have come down from town to tell you that I am very sorry for all the trouble I have given you, and that I intend to lead a better life in the future. [JACK *glares at him and does not take his hand.*]

CECILY: Uncle Jack, you are not going to refuse your own brother's hand.

JACK: Nothing will induce me to take his hand. I think his coming down here disgraceful. He knows perfectly well why.

CECILY: Uncle Jack, do be nice. There is good in everyone. Ernest has just been telling me about his poor invalid friend, Mr. Bunbury, whom he goes to visit so often. And surely there must be much good in one who is kind to an invalid, and leaves the pleasures of London to sit by a bed of pain.

JACK: Oh, he has been talking about Bunbury, has he?

CECILY: Yes, he has told me all about poor Mr. Bunbury, and his terrible state of health.

JACK: Bunbury! Well, I won't have him talk to you about Bunbury or about anything else. It is enough to drive one perfectly frantic.

ALGERNON: Of course I admit that the faults were all on my side. But I must say that I think that Brother John's coldness to me is peculiarly painful. I expected a more enthusiastic welcome, especially considering it is the first time I have come here.

CECILY: Uncle Jack, if you don't shake hands with Ernest I will never forgive you.

JACK: Never forgive me?

CECILY: Never, never, never!

JACK: Well, this is the last time I shall ever do it. [*Shakes hands with* ALGERNON *and glares.*]

CHASUBLE: It's pleasant, is it not, to see so perfect a reconciliation? I think we might leave the two brothers together.

MISS PRISM: Cecily, you will come with us.

CECILY: Certainly, Miss Prism. My little task of reconciliation is over.

CHASUBLE: You have done a beautiful action to-day, dear child.

MISS PRISM: We must not be premature in our judgments.

CECILY: I feel very happy. [*They all go off.*]

JACK: You young scoundrel, Algy, you must get out of this place as soon as possible. I don't allow any Bunburying here.

[*Enter* MERRIMAN.]

MERRIMAN: I have put Mr. Ernest's things in the room next to yours, sir. I suppose that is all right?

JACK: What?

MERRIMAN: Mr. Ernest's luggage, sir. I have unpacked it and put it in the room next to your own.

JACK: His luggage?

MERRIMAN: Yes, sir. Three portmanteaus, a dressing-case, two hat-boxes, and a large luncheon-basket.

ALGERNON: I am afraid I can't stay more than a week this time.

JACK: Merriman, order the dog-cart at once. Mr. Ernest has been suddenly called back to town.

MERRIMAN: Yes, sir. [*Goes back into the house.*]

ALGERNON: What a fearful liar you are, Jack. I have not been called back to town at all.

JACK: Yes, you have.

ALGERNON: I haven't heard anyone call me.

JACK: Your duty as a gentleman calls you back.

ALGERNON: My duty as a gentleman has never interfered with my pleasures in the smallest degree.

JACK: I can quite understand that.

ALGERNON: Well, Cecily is a darling.

JACK: You are not to talk of Miss Cardew like that. I don't like it.

ALGERNON: Well, I don't like your clothes. You look perfectly ridiculous in them. Why on earth don't you go up and change? It is perfectly childish to be in deep mourning for a man who is actually staying for a whole week with you in your house as a guest. I call it grotesque.

JACK: You are certainly not staying with me for a whole week as a guest or anything else. You have got to leave . . . by the four-five train.

ALGERNON: I certainly won't leave you so long as you are in mourning. It would be most unfriendly. If I were in mourning you would stay with me, I suppose. I should think it very unkind if you didn't.

JACK: Well, will you go if I change my clothes?

ALGERNON: Yes, if you are not too long. I never saw anybody take so long to dress, and with such little result.

JACK: Well, at any rate, that is better than being always over-dressed as you are.

ALGERNON: If I am occasionally a little over-dressed, I make up for it by being always immensely over-educated.

JACK: Your vanity is ridiculous, your conduct an outrage, and your presence in my garden utterly absurd. However, you have got to catch the four-five, and I hope you will have a pleasant journey back to town. This Bunburying, as you call it, has not been a great success for you. [*Goes into the house.*]

ALGERNON: I think it has been a great success. I'm in love with Cecily, and that is everything. [*Enter* CECILY *at the back of the garden. She picks up the can and begins to water the flowers.*] But I must see her before I go, and make arrangements for another Bunbury. Ah, there she is.

CECILY: Oh, I merely came back to water the roses. I thought you were with Uncle Jack.

ALGERNON: He's gone to order the dog-cart for me.

CECILY: Oh, is he going to take you for a nice drive?

ALGERNON: He's going to send me away.

CECILY: Then have we got to part?

ALGERNON: I am afraid so. It's a very painful parting.

CECILY: It is always painful to part from people whom one has known for a very brief space of time. The absence of old friends one can endure with equanimity. But even a momentary separation from anyone to whom one has just been introduced is almost unbearable.

ALGERNON: Thank you.

  [*Enter* MERRIMAN.]

MERRIMAN: The dog-cart is at the door, sir. [ALGERNON *looking appealingly at* CECILY.]

CECILY: It can wait, Merriman . . . for . . . five minutes.

MERRIMAN: Yes, miss. [*Exit* MERRIMAN.]

ALGERNON: I hope, Cecily, I shall not offend you if I state quite frankly and openly that you seem to me to be in every way the visible personification of absolute perfection.

CECILY: I think your frankness does you great credit, Ernest. If you will allow me I will copy your remarks into my diary. [*Goes over to table and begins writing in diary.*]

ALGERNON: Do you really keep a diary? I'd give any thing to look at it. May I?

CECILY: Oh, no. [*Puts her hand over it.*] You see, it is simply a very young girl's record of her own thoughts and impressions, and consequently meant for publication. When it appears in volume form I hope you will order a copy. But pray, Ernest, don't stop. I delight in taking down from dictation. I have reached "absolute perfection." You can go on. I am quite ready for more.

ALGERNON: [*Somewhat taken aback.*] Ahem! Ahem!

CECILY: Oh, don't cough, Ernest. When one is dictating one should speak fluently and not cough. Besides, I don't know how to spell a cough. [*Writes as* ALGERNON *speaks.*]

ALGERNON: [*Speaking very rapidly.*] Cecily, ever since I first looked upon your wonderful and incomparable beauty, I have dared to love you wildly, passionately, devotedly, hopelessly.

CECILY: I don't think that you should tell me that you love me wildly, passionately, devotedly, hopelessly. Hopelessly doesn't seem to make much sense, does it?

ALGERNON: Cecily!

[*Enter* MERRIMAN.]

MERRIMAN: The dog-cart is waiting, sir.

ALGERNON: Tell it to come round next week, at the same hour.

MERRIMAN: [*Looks at* CECILY, *who makes no sign.*] Yes, sir. [MERRIMAN *retires.*]

CECILY: Uncle Jack would be very much annoyed if he knew you were staying on till next week, at the same hour.

ALGERNON: Oh, I don't care about Jack. I don't care for anybody in the whole world but you. I love you, Cecily. You will marry me, won't you?

CECILY: You silly you! Of course. Why, we have been engaged for the last three months.

ALGERNON: For the last three months?

CECILY: Yes, it will be exactly three months on Thursday.

ALGERNON: But how did we become engaged?

CECILY: Well, ever since dear Uncle Jack first confessed to us that he had a younger brother who was very wicked and bad, you of course have formed the chief topic of conversation between myself and Miss Prism. And of course a man who is much talked

about is always very attractive. One feels there must be something in him after all. I daresay it was foolish of me, but I fell in
love with you, Ernest.

ALGERNON: Darling! And when was the engagement actually
settled?

CECILY: On the 14th of February last. Worn out by your entire ignorance of my existence, I determined to end the matter one way or
the other, and after a long struggle with myself I accepted you
under this dear old tree here. The next day I bought this little
ring in your name, and this is the little bangle with the true
lovers' knot I promised you always to wear.

ALGERNON: Did I give you this? It's very pretty, isn't it?

CECILY: Yes, you've wonderfully good taste, Ernest. It's the excuse
I've always given for your leading such a bad life. And this is the
box in which I keep all your dear letters. [*Kneels at table, opens
box, and produces letters tied up with blue ribbon.*]

ALGERNON: My letters! But my own sweet Cecily, I have never written you any letters.

CECILY: You need hardly remind me of that, Ernest. I remember
only too well that I was forced to write your letters for you. I
wrote always three times a week, and sometimes oftener.

ALGERNON: Oh, do let me read them, Cecily?

CECILY: Oh, I couldn't possibly. They would make you far too conceited. [*Replaces box.*] The three you wrote me after I had broken
off the engagement are so beautiful, and so badly spelled, that
even now I can hardly read them without crying a little.

ALGERNON: But was our engagement ever broken off?

CECILY: Of course it was. On the 22nd of last March. You can see
the entry if you like. [*Shows diary.*] "Today I broke off my engagement with Ernest. I feel it is better to do so. The weather still
continues charming."

ALGERNON: But why on earth did you break it off? What had I
done? I had done nothing at all, Cecily. I am very much hurt indeed to hear you broke it off. Particularly when the weather was
so charming.

CECILY: It would hardly have been a really serious engagement if it
hadn't been broken off at least once. But I forgave you before the
week was out.

ALGERNON: [*Crossing to her, and kneeling.*] What a perfect angel you
   are, Cecily.

CECILY: You dear romantic boy. [*He kisses her, she puts her fingers
   through his hair.*] I hope your hair curls naturally, does it?

ALGERNON: Yes, darling, with a little help from others.

CECILY: I am so glad.

ALGERNON: You'll never break off our engagement again, Cecily?

CECILY: I don't think I could break it off now that I have actually
   met you. Besides, of course, that is the question of your name.

ALGERNON: Yes, of course. [*Nervously.*]

CECILY: You must not laugh at me, darling, but it had always been a
   girlish dream of mine to love some one whose name was Ernest.
   [ALGERNON *rises*, CECILY *also.*] There is something in that name
   that seems to inspire absolute confidence. I pity any poor married woman whose husband is not called Ernest.

ALGERNON: But, my dear child, do you mean to say you could not
   love me if I had some other name?

CECILY: But what name?

ALGERNON: Oh, any name you like—Algernon, for instance. . . .

CECILY: But I don't like the name of Algernon.

ALGERNON: Well, my own dear, sweet, loving little darling, I really
   can't see why you should object to the name of Algernon. It is
   not at all a bad name. In fact, it is rather an aristocratic name.
   Half of the chaps who get into the Bankruptcy Court are called
   Algernon. But seriously, Cecily . . . [*Moving to her*] . . . if my
   name was Algy, couldn't you love me?

CECILY: [*Rising.*] I might respect you, Ernest, I might admire your
   character, but I fear that I should not be able to give you my un-
   divided attention.

ALGERNON: Ahem! Cecily! [*Picking up hat.*] Your Rector here is, I
   suppose, thoroughly experienced in the practice of all the rites
   and ceremonials of the church?

CECILY: Oh, yes. Dr. Chasuble is a most learned man. He has never
   written a single book, so you can imagine how much he knows.

ALGERNON: I must see him at once on a most important christening—I mean on most important business.

CECILY: Oh!

ALGERNON: I sha'n't be away more than half an hour.

CECILY: Considering that we have been engaged since February the 14th, and that I only met you to-day for the first time, I think it is rather hard that you should leave me for so long a period as half an hour. Couldn't you make it twenty minutes?

ALGERNON: I'll be back in no time. [*Kisses her and rushes down the garden.*]

CECILY: What an impetuous boy he is. I like his hair so much. I must enter his proposal in my diary.

[*Enter* MERRIMAN.]

MERRIMAN: A Miss Fairfax has just called to see Mr. Worthing. On very important business, Miss Fairfax states.

CECILY: Isn't Mr. Worthing in his library?

MERRIMAN: Mr. Worthing went over in the direction of the Rectory some time ago.

CECILY: Pray ask the lady to come out here; Mr. Worthing is sure to be back soon. And you can bring tea.

MERRIMAN: Yes, miss. [*Goes out.*]

CECILY: Miss Fairfax! I suppose one of the many good elderly women who are associated with Uncle Jack in some of his philanthropic work in London. I don't quite like women who are interested in philanthropic work. I think it is so forward of them.

[*Enter* MERRIMAN.]

MERRIMAN: Miss Fairfax.

[*Enter* GWENDOLEN. *Exit* MERRIMAN.]

CECILY: [*Advancing to meet her.*] Pray let me introduce myself to you. My name is Cecily Cardew.

GWENDOLEN: Cecily Cardew? [*Moving to her and shaking hands.*] What a very sweet name! Something tells me that we are going to be great friends. I like you already more than I can say. My first impressions of people are never wrong.

CECILY: How nice of you to like me so much after we have known each other such a comparatively short time. Pray sit down.

GWENDOLEN: [*Still standing up.*] I may call you Cecily, may I not?

CECILY: With pleasure!

GWENDOLEN: And you will always call me Gwendolen, won't you?

CECILY: If you wish.

GWENDOLEN: Then that is all quite settled, is it not?

CECILY: I hope so. [*A pause. They both sit down together.*]

GWENDOLEN: Perhaps this might be a favourable opportunity for my mentioning who I am. My father is Lord Bracknell. You have never heard of papa, I suppose?

CECILY: I don't think so.

GWENDOLEN: Outside the family circle, papa, I am glad to say, is entirely unknown. I think that is quite as it should be. The home seems to me to be the proper sphere for the man. And certainly once a man begins to neglect his domestic duties he becomes painfully effeminate, does he not? And I don't like that. It makes men so very attractive. Cecily, mamma, whose views on education are remarkably strict, has brought me up to be extremely short-sighted; it is part of her system; so do you mind my looking at you through my glasses?

CECILY: Oh, not at all, Gwendolen. I am very fond of being looked at.

GWENDOLEN: [*After examining* CECILY *carefully through a lorgnette.*] You are here on a short visit, I suppose.

CECILY: Oh, no, I live here.

GWENDOLEN: [*Severely.*] Really? Your mother, no doubt, or some female relative of advanced years, resides here also?

CECILY: Oh, no. I have no mother, nor, in fact, any relations.

GWENDOLEN: Indeed?

CECILY: My dear guardian, with the assistance of Miss Prism, has the arduous task of looking after me.

GWENDOLEN: Your guardian?

CECILY: Yes, I am Mr. Worthing's ward.

GWENDOLEN: Oh! It is strange he never mentioned to me that he had a ward. How secretive of him! He grows more interesting hourly. I am not sure, however, that the news inspires me with feelings of unmixed delight. [*Rising and going to her.*] I am very fond of you, Cecily; I have liked you ever since I met you. But I am bound to state that now that I know that you are Mr. Worthing's ward, I cannot help expressing a wish you were— well, just a little older than you seem to be—and not quite so very alluring in appearance. In fact, if I may speak candidly—

CECILY: Pray do! I think that whenever one has anything unpleasant to say, one should always be quite candid.

GWENDOLEN: Well, to speak with perfect candour, Cecily, I wish that you were fully forty-two, and more than usually plain for your age. Ernest has a strong upright nature. He is the very soul of truth and honour. Disloyalty would be as impossible to him as deception. But even men of the noblest possible moral character are extremely susceptible to the influence of the physical charms of others. Modern, no less than Ancient History, supplies us with many most painful examples of what I refer to. If it were not so, indeed, History would be quite unreadable.

CECILY: I beg your pardon, Gwendolen, did you say Ernest?

GWENDOLEN: Yes.

CECILY: Oh, but it is not Mr. Ernest Worthing who is my guardian. It is his brother—his elder brother.

GWENDOLEN: [*Sitting down again.*] Ernest never mentioned to me that he had a brother.

CECILY: I am sorry to say they have not been on good terms for a long time.

GWENDOLEN: Ah! that accounts for it. And now that I think of it I have never heard any man mention his brother. The subject seems distasteful to most men. Cecily, you have lifted a load from my mind. I was growing almost anxious. It would have been terrible if any cloud had come across a friendship like ours, would it not? Of course you are quite, quite sure that it is not Mr. Ernest Worthing who is your guardian?

CECILY: Quite sure. [*A pause.*] In fact, I am going to be his.

GWENDOLEN: [*Enquiringly.*] I beg your pardon?

CECILY: [*Rather shy and confidingly.*] Dearest Gwendolen, there is no reason why I should make a secret of it to you. Our little county newspaper is sure to chronicle the fact next week. Mr. Ernest Worthing and I are engaged to be married.

GWENDOLEN: [*Quite politely, rising.*] My darling Cecily, I think there must be some slight error. Mr. Ernest Worthing is engaged to me. The announcement will appear in the *Morning Post* on Saturday at the latest.

CECILY: [*Very politely, rising.*] I am afraid you must be under some misconception. Ernest proposed to me exactly ten minutes ago. [*Shows diary.*]

GWENDOLEN: [*Examines diary through her lorgnette carefully.*] It is certainly very curious, for he asked me to be his wife yesterday afternoon at 5.30. If you would care to verify the incident, pray do so. [*Produces diary of her own.*] I never travel without my diary. One should always have something sensational to read in the train. I am so sorry, dear Cecily, if it is any disappointment to you, but I am afraid *I* have the prior claim.

CECILY: It would distress me more than I can tell you, dear Gwendolen, if it caused you any mental or physical anguish, but I feel. bound to point out that since Ernest proposed to you he clearly has changed his mind.

GWENDOLEN: [*Meditatively.*] If the poor fellow has been entrapped into any foolish promise I shall consider it my duty to rescue him at once, and with a firm hand.

CECILY: [*Thoughtfully and sadly.*] Whatever unfortunate entanglement my dear boy may have got into, I will never reproach him with it after we are married.

GWENDOLEN: Do you allude to me, Miss Cardew, as an entanglement? You are presumptuous. On an occasion of this kind it becomes more than a moral duty to speak one's mind. It becomes a pleasure.

CECILY: Do you suggest, Miss Fairfax, that I entrapped Ernest into an engagement? How dare you? This is no time for wearing the shallow mask of manners. When I see a spade I call it a spade.

GWENDOLEN: [*Satirically.*] I am glad to say that I have never seen a spade. It is obvious that our social spheres have been widely different.

> [*Enter* MERRIMAN, *followed by the footman. He carries a salver, tablecloth, and plate-stand.* CECILY *is about to retort. The presence of the servants exercises a restraining influence, under which both girls chafe.*]

MERRIMAN: Shall I lay tea here as usual, miss?

CECILY: [*Sternly, in a calm voice.*] Yes, as usual.

> [MERRIMAN *begins to clear and lay cloth. A long pause.* CECILY *and* GWENDOLYN *glare at each other.*]

GWENDOLEN: Are there many interesting walks in the vicinity, Miss Cardew?

CECILY: Oh, yes, a great many. From the top of one of the hills quite close one can see five counties.

GWENDOLEN: Five counties! I don't think I should like that. I hate crowds.

CECILY: [*Sweetly.*] I suppose that is why you live in town?

    [GWENDOLEN *bites her lip, and beats her foot nervously with her parasol.*]

GWENDOLEN: [*Looking round.*] Quite a well-kept garden this is, Miss Cardew.

CECILY: So glad you like it, Miss Fairfax.

GWENDOLEN: I had no idea there were any flowers in the country.

CECILY: Oh, flowers are as common here, Miss Fairfax, as people are in London.

GWENDOLEN: Personally I cannot understand how anybody manages to exist in the country, if anybody who is anybody does. The country always bores me to death.

CECILY: Ah! This is what the newspapers call agricultural depression, is it not? I believe the aristocracy are suffering very much from it just at present. It is almost an epidemic amongst them, I have been told. May I offer you some tea, Miss Fairfax?

GWENDOLEN: [*With elaborate politeness.*] Thank you. [*Aside.*] Detestable girl! But I require tea!

CECILY: [*Sweetly.*] Sugar?

GWENDOLEN: [*Superciliously.*] No, thank you. Sugar is not fashionable any more.

    [CECILY *looks angrily at her, takes up the tongs and puts four lumps of sugar into the cup.*]

CECILY: [*Severely.*] Cake or bread and butter?

GWENDOLEN: [*In a bored manner.*] Bread and butter, please. Cake is rarely seen at the best houses nowadays.

CECILY: [*Cuts a very large slice of cake, and puts it on the tray.*] Hand that to Miss Fairfax.

    [MERRIMAN *does so, and goes out with footman.* GWENDOLEN *drinks the tea and makes a grimace. Puts down cup at once, reaches out her hand to the bread and butter, looks at it, and finds it is cake. Rises in indignation.*]

GWENDOLEN: You have filled my tea with lumps of sugar, and though I asked most distinctly for bread and butter, you have given me cake. I am known for the gentleness of my disposition, and the extraordinary sweetness of my nature, but I warn you, Miss Cardew, you may go too far.

CECILY: [*Rising.*] To save my poor, innocent, trusting boy from the machinations of any other girl there are no lengths to which I would not go.

GWENDOLEN: From the moment I saw you I distrusted you. I felt that you were false and deceitful. I am never deceived in such matters. My first impressions of people are invariably right.

CECILY: It seems to me, Miss Fairfax, that I am trespassing on your valuable time. No doubt you have many other calls of a similar character to make in the neighbourhood.

[*Enter* JACK.]

GWENDOLEN: [*Catching sight of him.*] Ernest! My own Ernest!

JACK: Gwendolen! Darling! [*Offers to kiss her.*]

GWENDOLEN: [*Drawing back.*] A moment! May I ask if you are engaged to be married to this young lady? [*Points to* CECILY.]

JACK: [*Laughing.*] To dear little Cecily! Of course not! What could have put such an idea into your pretty little head?

GWENDOLEN: Thank you. You may. [*Offers her cheek.*]

CECILY: [*Very sweetly.*] I knew there must be some misunderstanding, Miss Fairfax. The gentleman whose arm is at present around your waist is my dear guardian, Mr. John Worthing.

GWENDOLEN: I beg your pardon?

CECILY: This is Uncle Jack.

GWENDOLEN: [*Receding.*] Jack! Oh!

[*Enter* ALGERNON.]

CECILY: Here is Ernest.

ALGERNON: [*Goes straight over to* CECILY *without noticing anyone else.*] My own love! [*Offers to kiss her.*]

CECILY: [*Drawing back.*] A moment, Ernest! May I ask you—are you engaged to be married to this young lady?

ALGERNON: [*Looking round.*] To what young lady? Good heavens! Gwendolen!

CECILY: Yes, to good heavens, Gwendolen, I mean to Gwendolen.

ALGERNON: [*Laughing.*] Of course not! What could have put such an idea into your pretty little head?

CECILY: Thank you. [*Presenting her cheek to be kissed.*] You may. [AL-GERNON *kisses her.*]

GWENDOLEN: I felt there was some slight error, Miss Cardew. The gentleman who is now embracing you is my cousin, Mr. Algernon Moncrieff.

CECILY: [*Breaking away from* ALGERNON.] Algernon Moncrieff! Oh! [*The two girls move towards each other and put their arms round each other's waists as if for protection.*] Are you called Algernon?

ALGERNON: I cannot deny it.

CECILY: Oh!

GWENDOLEN: Is your name really John?

JACK: [*Standing rather proudly.*] I could deny it if I liked. I could deny anything if I liked. But my name certainly is John. It has been John for years.

CECILY: [*To* GWENDOLEN.] A gross deception has been practised on both of us.

GWENDOLEN: My poor wounded Cecily!

CECILY: My sweet, wronged Gwendolen!

GWENDOLEN: [*Slowing and seriously.*] You will call me sister, will you not?

[*They embrace.* JACK *and* ALGERNON *groan and walk up and down.*]

CECILY: [*Rather brightly.*] There is just one question I would like to be allowed to ask my guardian.

GWENDOLEN: An admirable idea! Mr. Worthing, there is just one question I would like to be permitted to put to you. Where is your brother Ernest? We are both engaged to be married to your brother Ernest, so it is a matter of some importance to us to know where your brother Ernest is at present.

JACK: [*Slowly and hesitatingly.*] Gwendolen—Cecily—it is very painful for me to be forced to speak the truth. It is the first time in my life that I have ever been reduced to such a painful position, and I am really quite inexperienced in doing anything of the kind. However I will tell you quite frankly that I have no brother Ernest. I have no brother at all. I never had a brother in my life, and I certainly have not the smallest intention of ever having one in the future.

CECILY: [*Surprised.*] No brother at all?

JACK: [*Cheerily.*] None!

GWENDOLEN: [*Severely.*] Had you never a brother of any kind?

JACK: [*Pleasantly.*] Never. Not even of any kind.

GWENDOLEN: I am afraid it is quite clear, Cecily, that neither of us is engaged to be married to anyone.

CECILY: It is not a very pleasant position for a young girl suddenly to find herself in. Is it?

GWENDOLEN: Let us go into the house. They will hardly venture to come after us there.

CECILY: No, men are so cowardly, aren't they?

[*They retire into the house with scornful looks.*]

JACK: This ghastly state of things is what you call Bunburying, I suppose?

ALGERNON: Yes, and a perfectly wonderful Bunbury it is. The most wonderful Bunbury I have ever had in my life.

JACK: Well, you've no right whatsoever to Bunbury here.

ALGERNON: That is absurd. One has a right to Bunbury anywhere one chooses. Every serious Bunburyist knows that.

JACK: Serious Bunburyist! Good heavens!

ALGERNON: Well, one must be serious about something, if one wants to have any amusement in life. I happen to be serious about Bunburying. What on earth you are serious about I haven't got the remotest idea. About everything, I should fancy. You have such an absolutely trivial nature.

JACK: Well, the only small satisfaction I have in the whole of this wretched business is that your friend Bunbury is quite exploded. You won't be able to run down to the country quite so often as you used to do, dear Algy. And a very good thing, too.

ALGERNON: Your brother is a little off colour, isn't he, dear Jack? You won't be able to disappear to London quite so frequently as your wicked custom was. And not a bad thing, either.

JACK: As for your conduct towards Miss Cardew, I must say that your taking in a sweet, simple, innocent girl like that is quite inexcusable. To say nothing of the fact that she is my ward.

ALGERNON: I can see no possible defence at all for your deceiving a brilliant, clever, thoroughly experienced young lady like Miss Fairfax. To say nothing of the fact that she is my cousin.

JACK: I wanted to be engaged to Gwendolen, that is all. I love her.

ALGERNON: Well, I simply wanted to be engaged to Cecily. I adore her.

JACK: There is certainly no chance of your marrying Miss Cardew.

ALGERNON: I don't think there is much likelihood, Jack, of you and Miss Fairfax being united.

JACK: Well, that is no business of yours.

ALGERNON: If it was my business, I wouldn't talk about it. [*Begins to eat muffins.*] It is very vulgar to talk about one's business. Only people like stock-brokers do that, and then merely at dinner parties.

JACK: How you can sit there, calmly eating muffins, when we are in this horrible trouble, I can't make out. You seem to me to be perfectly heartless.

ALGERNON: Well, I can't eat muffins in an agitated manner. The butter would probably get on my cuffs. One should always eat muffins quite calmly. It is the only way to eat them.

JACK: I say it's perfectly heartless your eating muffins at all, under the circumstances.

ALGERNON: When I am in trouble, eating is the only thing that consoles me. Indeed, when I am in really great trouble, as anyone who knows me intimately will tell you, I refuse everything except food and drink. At the present moment I am eating muffins because I am unhappy. Besides, I am particularly fond of muffins. [*Rising.*]

JACK: [*Rising.*] Well, that is no reason why you should eat them all in that greedy way. [*Takes muffin from* ALGERNON.]

ALGERNON: [*Offering tea-cake.*] I wish you would have tea-cake instead. I don't like tea-cake.

JACK: Good heavens! I suppose a man may eat his own muffins in his own garden.

ALGERNON: But you have just said it was perfectly heartless to eat muffins.

JACK: I said it was perfectly heartless of you, under the circumstances. That is a very different thing.

ALGERNON: That may be. But the muffins are the same. [*He seizes the muffin dish from* JACK.]

JACK: Algy, I wish to goodness you would go.

ALGERNON: You can't possibly ask me to go without having some dinner. It's absurd. I never go without my dinner. No one ever does, except vegetarians and people like that. Besides I have just made arrangements with Dr. Chasuble to be christened at a quarter to six under the name of Ernest.

JACK: My dear fellow, the sooner you give up that nonsense the better. I made arrangements this morning with Chasuble to be christened myself at 5.30, and I naturally will take the name of Ernest. Gwendolen would wish it. We can't both be christened Ernest. It's absurd. Besides, I have a perfect right to be christened if I like. There is no evidence at all that I ever have been christened by anybody. I should think it extremely probable I never was, and so does Dr. Chasuble. It is entirely different in your case. You have been christened already.

ALGERNON: Yes, but I have not been christened for years.

JACK: Yes, but you have been christened. That is the important thing.

ALGERNON: Quite so. So I know my constitution can stand it. If you are not quite sure about your ever having been christened, I must say I think it rather dangerous your venturing on it now. It might make you very unwell. You can hardly have forgotten that someone very closely connected with you was very nearly carried off this week in Paris by a severe chill.

JACK: Yes, but you said yourself that a severe chill was not hereditary.

ALGERNON: It usedn't to be, I know—but I daresay it is now. Science is always making wonderful improvements in things.

JACK: [*Picking up the muffin-dish.*] Oh, that is nonsense; you are always talking nonsense.

ALGERNON: Jack, you are at the muffins again! I wish you wouldn't. There are only two left. [*Takes them.*] I told you I was particularly fond of muffins.

JACK: But I hate tea-cake.

ALGERNON: Why on earth then do you allow tea-cake to be served up for your guests? What ideas you have of hospitality!

JACK: Algernon! I have already told you to go. I don't want you here. Why don't you go?

ALGERNON: I haven't quite finished my tea yet, and there is still one muffin left.

[JACK *groans, and sinks into a chair.* ALGERNON *still continues eating.*]

[*Curtain.*]

ACT III

SCENE.—*Morning-room at the Manor House.* GWENDOLEN *and* CECILY *are at the window, looking out into the garden.*

GWENDOLEN: The fact that they did not follow us at once into the house, as anyone else would have done, seems to me to show that they have some sense of shame left.

CECILY: They have been eating muffins. That looks like repentance.

GWENDOLEN: [*After a pause.*] They don't seem to notice us at all. Couldn't you cough?

GWENDOLEN: They're looking at us. What effrontery!

CECILY: They're approaching. That's very forward of them.

GWENDOLEN: Let us preserve a dignified silence.

CECILY: Certainly, it's the only thing to do now.

[*Enter* JACK, *followed by* ALGERNON. *They whistle some dreadful popular air from a British opera.*]

GWENDOLEN: This dignified silence seems to produce an unpleasant effect.

CECILY: A most distasteful one.

GWENDOLEN: But we will not be the first to speak.

CECILY: Certainly not.

GWENDOLEN: Mr. Worthing, I have something very particular to ask you. Much depends on your reply.

CECILY: Gwendolen, your common sense is invaluable. Mr. Moncrieff, kindly answer me the following question. Why did you pretend to be my guardian's brother?

ALGERNON: In order that I might have an opportunity of meeting you.

CECILY: [*To* GWENDOLEN.] That certainly seems a satisfactory explanation, does it not?

GWENDOLEN: Yes, dear, if you can believe him.

CECILY: I don't. But that does not affect the wonderful beauty of his answer.

GWENDOLEN: True. In matters of grave importance, style, not sincerity, is the vital thing. Mr. Worthing, what explanation can you offer to me for pretending to have a brother? Was it in order that you might have an opportunity of coming up to town to see me as often as possible?

JACK: Can you doubt it, Miss Fairfax?

GWENDOLEN: I have the gravest doubts upon the subject. But I intend to crush them. This is not the moment for German scepticism.[1] [*Moving to* CECILY.] Their explanations appear to be quite satisfactory, especially Mr. Worthing's. That seems to me to have the stamp of truth upon it.

CECILY: I am more than content with what Mr. Moncrieff said. His voice alone inspires one with absolute credulity.

GWENDOLEN: Then you think we should forgive them?

CECILY: Yes. I mean no.

GWENDOLEN: True! I had forgotten. There are principles at stake that one cannot surrender. Which of us should tell them? The task is not a pleasant one.

CECILY: Could we not both speak at the same time?

GWENDOLEN: An excellent ideal I nearly always speak at the same time as other people. Will you take the time from me?

CECILY: Certainly. [GWENDOLEN *beats time with uplifted finger.*]

GWENDOLEN *and* CECILY: [*Speaking together.*] Your Christian names are still an insuperable barrier. That is all!

JACK *and* ALGERNON: [*Speaking together.*] Our Christian names! Is that all? But we are going to be christened this afternoon.

GWENDOLEN: [*To* JACK.] For my sake you are prepared to do this terrible thing?

JACK: I am.

CECILY: [*To* ALGERNON.] To please me you are ready to face this fearful ordeal?

ALGERNON: I am!

GWENDOLEN: How absurd to talk of the equality of the sexes! Where questions of self-sacrifice are concerned, men are infinitely beyond us.

JACK: We are. [*Clasps hands with* ALGERNON.]

CECILY: They have moments of physical courage of which we women know absolutely nothing.

GWENDOLEN: [*To* JACK.] Darling!

ALGERNON: [*To* CECILY.] Darling! [*They fall into each other's arms.*]

---

1. A reference to theological movements such as the "Higher Criticism," which subjected the Bible to the kind of study accorded other books.

[*Enter* MERRIMAN. *When he enters he coughs loudly seeing the situation.*]

MERRIMAN: Ahem! Ahem! Lady Bracknell!

JACK: Good heavens!

[*Enter* LADY BRACKNELL. *The couples separate in alarm. Exit* MERRIMAN.]

LADY BRACKNELL: Gwendolen! What does this mean?

GWENDOLEN: Merely that I am engaged to be married to Mr. Worthing, Mamma.

LADY BRACKNELL: Come here. Sit down. Sit down immediately. Hesitation of any kind is a sign of mental decay in the young, of physical weakness in the old. [*Turns to* JACK.] Apprised, sir, of my daughter's sudden flight by her trusty maid, whose confidence I purchased by means of a small coin, I followed her at once by a luggage train. Her unhappy father is, I am glad to say, under the impression that she is attending a more than usually lengthy lecture by the University Extension Scheme on the Influence of a Permanent Income on Thought. I do not propose to undeceive him. Indeed I have never undeceived him on any question. I would consider it wrong. But of course, you will clearly understand that all communication between yourself and my daughter must cease immediately from this moment. On this point, as indeed on all points, I am firm.

JACK: I am engaged to be married to Gwendolen, Lady Bracknell!

LADY BRACKNELL: You are nothing of the kind, sir. And now, as regards Algernon! . . . Algernon!

ALGERNON: Yes, Aunt Augusta.

LADY BRACKNELL: May I ask if it is in this house that your invalid friend Mr. Bunbury resides?

ALGERNON: [*Stammering.*] Oh no! Bunbury doesn't live here. Bunbury is somewhere else at present. In fact, Bunbury is dead.

LADY BRACKNELL: Dead! When did Mr. Bunbury die? His death must have been extremely sudden.

ALGERNON: [*Airily.*] Oh, I killed Bunbury this afternoon. I mean poor Bunbury died this afternoon.

LADY BRACKNELL: What did he die of?

ALGERNON: Bunbury? Oh, he was quite exploded.

LADY BRACKNELL: Exploded! Was he the victim of a revolutionary

outrage? I was not aware that Mr. Bunbury was interested in social legislation. If so, he is well punished for his morbidity.

ALGERNON: My dear Aunt Augusta, I mean he was found out! The
doctors found out that Bunbury could not live, that is what I
mean—so Bunbury died.

LADY BRACKNELL: He seems to have had great confidence in the
opinion of his physicians. I am glad, however, that he made up
his mind at the last to some definite course of action, and acted
under proper medical advice. And now that we have finally got
rid of this Mr. Bunbury, may I ask, Mr. Worthing, who is that
young person whose hand my nephew Algernon is now holding
in what seems to me a peculiarly unnecessary manner?

JACK: That lady is Miss Cecily Cardew, my ward.

[LADY BRACKNELL *bows coldly to* CECILY.]

ALGERNON: I am engaged to be married to Cecily, Aunt Augusta.

LADY BRACKNELL: I beg your pardon?

CECILY: Mr. Moncrieff and I are engaged to be married, Lady
Bracknell.

LADY BRACKNELL: [*With a shiver, crossing to the sofa and sitting
down.*] I do not know whether there is anything peculiarly exciting in the air of this particular part of Hertfordshire, but the
number of engagements that go on seems to me considerably above the proper average that statistics have laid down for
our guidance. I think some preliminary enquiry on my part
would not be out of place. Mr. Worthing, is Miss Cardew at
all connected with any of the larger railway stations in London? I merely desire information. Until yesterday I had no idea
that there were any families or persons whose origin was a
Terminus.

[JACK *looks perfectly furious, but restrains himself.*]

JACK: [*In a clear, cold voice.*] Miss Cardew is the granddaughter
of the late Mr. Thomas Cardew of 149, Belgrave Square, S.W.;
Gervase Park, Dorking, Surrey; and the Sporran, Fifeshire,
N.B.

LADY BRACKNELL: That sounds not unsatisfactory. Three addresses
always inspire confidence, even in tradesmen. But what proof
have I of their authenticity?

JACK: I have carefully preserved the Court Guide[2] of the period. They are open to your inspection, Lady Bracknell.

LADY BRACKNELL: [*Grimly.*] I have known strange errors in that publication.

JACK: Miss Cardews's family solicitors are Messrs. Markby, Markby, and Markby.

LADY BRACKNELL: Markby, Markby, and Markby? A firm of the very highest position in their profession. Indeed I am told that one of the Mr. Markbys is occasionally to be seen at dinner parties. So far I am satisfied.

JACK: [*Very irritably.*] How extremely kind of you, Lady Bracknell! I have also in my possession, you will be pleased to hear, certificates of Miss Cardew's birth, baptism, whooping cough, registration, vaccination, confirmation, and the measles; both the German and the English variety.

LADY BRACKNELL: Ah! A life crowded with incident, I see; though perhaps somewhat too exciting for a young girl. I am not myself in favor of premature experiences. [*Rises, looks at her watch.*] Gwendolen! the time approaches for our departure. We have not a moment to lose. As a matter of form, Mr. Worthing, I had better ask you if Miss Cardew has any little fortune?

JACK: Oh, about a hundred and thirty thousand pounds in the Funds.[3] That is all. Good-bye, Lady Bracknell. So pleased to have seen you.

LADY BRACKNELL: [*Sitting down again.*] A moment, Mr. Worthing. A hundred and thirty thousand pounds! And in the Funds! Miss Cardew seems to me a most attractive young lady, now that I look at her. Few girls of the present day have any really solid qualities, any of the qualities that last, and improve with time. We live, I regret to say, in an age of surfaces. [*To* CECILY.] Come over here, dear. [CECILY *goes across.*] Pretty child! your dress is sadly simple, and your hair seems almost as Nature might have left it. But we can soon alter all that. A thoroughly experienced French maid produces a really marvellous result in a very brief

2. A registry of aristocratic genealogy.
3. Government stocks.

space of time. I remember recommending one to young Lady Lancing, and after three months her own husband did not know her.

JACK: [*Aside.*] And after six months nobody knew her.

LADY BRACKNELL: [*Glares at* JACK *for a few moments. Then bends, with a practised smile, to* CECILY.] Kindly turn round, sweet child. [CECILY *turns completely round.*] No, the side view is what I want. [CECILY *presents her profile.*] Yes, quite as I expected. There are distinct social possibilities in your profile. The two weak points in our age are its want of principle and its want of profile. The chin a little higher, dear. Style largely depends on the way the chin is worn. They are worn very high, just at present. Algernon!

ALGERNON: Yes, Aunt Augusta!

LADY BRACKNELL: There are distinct social possibilities in Miss Cardew's profile.

ALGERNON: Cecily is the sweetest, dearest, prettiest girl in the whole world. And I don't care twopence about social possibilities.

LADY BRACKNELL: Never speak disrespectfully of society,[4] Algernon. Only people who can't get into it do that. [*To* CECILY.] Dear child, of course you know that Algernon has nothing but his debts to depend upon. But I do not approve of mercenary marriages. When I married Lord Bracknell I had no fortune of any kind. But I never dreamed for a moment of allowing that to stand in my way. Well, I suppose I must give my consent.

ALGERNON: Thank you, Aunt Augusta.

LADY BRACKNELL: Cecily, you may kiss me!

CECILY: [*Kisses her.*] Thank you, Lady Bracknell.

LADY BRACKNELL: You may also address me as Aunt Augusta for the future.

CECILY: Thank you, Aunt Augusta.

LADY BRACKNELL: The marriage, I think, had better take place quite soon.

ALGERNON: Thank you, Aunt Augusta.

CECILY: Thank you, Aunt Augusta.

LADY BRACKNELL: To speak frankly, I am not in favour of long engagements. They give people the opportunity of finding out

---

4. The exclusive circle of the aristocracy.

each other's character before marriage, which I think is never advisable.

JACK: I beg your pardon for interrupting you, Lady Bracknell, but this engagement is quite out of the question. I am Miss Cardew's guardian, and she cannot marry without my consent until she comes of age. That consent I absolutely decline to give.

LADY BRACKNELL: Upon what grounds, may I ask? Algernon is an extremely, I may almost say an ostentatiously, eligible young man. He has nothing, but he looks everything. What more can one desire?

JACK: It pains me very much to have to speak frankly to you, Lady Bracknell, about your nephew, but the fact is that I do not approve at all of his moral character. I suspect him of being untruthful.

[ALGERNON *and* CECILY *look at him in indignant amazement.*]

LADY BRACKNELL: Untruthful! My nephew Algernon? Impossible! He is an Oxonian.[5]

JACK: I fear there can be no possible doubt about the matter. This afternoon, during my temporary absence in London on an important question of romance, he obtained admission to my house by means of the false pretence of being my brother. Under an assumed name he drank, I've just been informed by my butler, an entire pint bottle of my Perrier-Jouet, Brut, '89; a wine I was specially reserving for myself. Continuing his disgraceful deception, he succeeded in the course of the afternoon in alienating the affections of my only ward. He subsequently stayed to tea, and devoured every single muffin. And what makes his conduct all the more heartless is, that he was perfectly well aware from the first that I have no brother, that I never had a brother, and that I don't intend to have a brother, not even of any kind. I distinctly told him so myself yesterday afternoon.

LADY BRACKNELL: Ahem! Mr. Worthing, after careful consideration I have decided entirely to overlook my nephew's conduct to you.

JACK: That is very generous of you, Lady Bracknell. My own decision, however, is unalterable. I decline to give my consent.

---

5. Someone who has attended Oxford University.

LADY BRACKNELL: [*To* CECILY.] Come here, sweet child. [CECILY *goes over.*] How old are you, dear?

CECILY: Well, I am really only eighteen, but I always admit to twenty when I go to evening parties.

LADY BRACKNELL: You are perfectly right in making some slight alteration. Indeed, no woman should ever be quite accurate about her age. It looks so calculating. . . . [*In meditative manner.*] Eighteen, but admitting to twenty at evening parties. Well, it will not be very long before you are of age and free from the restraints of tutelage. So I don't think your guardian's consent is, after all, a matter of any importance.

JACK: Pray excuse me, Lady Bracknell, for interrupting you again, but it is only fair to tell you that according to the terms of her grandfather's will Miss Cardew does not come legally of age till she is thirty-five.

LADY BRACKNELL: That does not seem to me to be a grave objection. Thirty-five is a very attractive age. London society is full of women of the very highest birth who have, of their own free choice, remained thirty-five for years. Lady Dumbleton is an instance in point. To my own knowledge she has been thirty-five ever since she arrived at the age of forty, which was many years ago now. I see no reason why our dear Cecily should not be even still more attractive at the age you mention than she is at present. There will be a large accumulation of property.

CECILY: Algy, could you wait for me till I was thirty-five?

ALGERNON: Of course I could, Cecily. You know I could.

CECILY: Yes, I felt it instinctively, but I couldn't wait all that time. I hate waiting even five minutes for anybody. It always makes me rather cross. I am not punctual myself, I know, but I do like punctuality in others, and waiting, even to be married, is quite out of the question.

ALGERNON: Then what is to be done, Cecily?

CECILY: I don't know, Mr. Moncrieff.

LADY BRACKNELL: My dear Mr. Worthing, as Miss Cardew states positively that she cannot wait till she is thirty-five—a remark which I am bound to say seems to me to show a somewhat impatient nature—I would beg of you to reconsider your decision.

JACK: But my dear Lady Bracknell, the matter is entirely in your own hands. The moment you consent to my marriage with Gwendolen, I will most gladly allow your nephew to form an alliance with my ward.

LADY BRACKNELL: [*Rising and drawing herself up.*] You must be quite aware that what you propose is out of the question.

JACK: Then a passionate celibacy is all that any of us can look forward to.

LADY BRACKNELL: That is not the destiny I propose for Gwendolen. Algernon, of course, can choose for himself. [*Pulls out her watch.*] Come, dear; [GWENDOLEN *rises.*] we have already missed five, if not six, trains. To miss any more might expose us to comment on the platform.

[*Enter* DR. CHASUBLE.]

CHASUBLE: Everything is quite ready for the christenings.

LADY BRACKNELL: The christenings, sir! Is not that somewhat premature?

CHASUBLE: [*Looking rather puzzled, and pointing to* JACK *and* ALGERNON.] Both these gentlemen have expressed a desire for immediate baptism.

LADY BRACKNELL: At their age? The idea is grotesque and irreligious! Algernon, I forbid you to be baptised. I will not hear of such excesses. Lord Bracknell would be highly displeased if he learned that that was the way in which you wasted your time and money.

CHASUBLE: Am I to understand then that there are to be no christenings at all this afternoon?

JACK: I don't think that, as things are now, it would be of much practical value to either of us, Dr. Chasuble.

CHASUBLE: I am grieved to hear such sentiments from you, Mr. Worthing. They savour of the heretical views of the Anabaptists,[6] views that I have completely refuted in four of my unpublished sermons. However, as your present mood seems to be one peculiarly secular, I will return to the church at once. Indeed, I have just been informed by the pew-opener that for the last hour and a half Miss Prism has been waiting for me in the vestry.

---

6. A Christian sect distinguished by its opposition to baptism.

LADY BRACKNELL: [*Starting.*] Miss Prism! Did I hear you mention a
Miss Prism?

CHASUBLE: Yes, Lady Bracknell. I am on my way to join her.

LADY BRACKNELL: Pray allow me to detain you for a moment. This
matter may prove to be one of vital importance to Lord Bracknell and myself. Is this Miss Prism a female of repellent aspect,
remotely connected with education?

CHASUBLE: [*Somewhat indignantly.*] She is the most cultivated of
ladies, and the very picture of respectability.

LADY BRACKNELL: It is obviously the same person. May I ask what
position she holds in your household?

CHASUBLE: [*Severely.*] I am a celibate, madam.

JACK: [*Interposing.*] Miss Prism, Lady Bracknell, has been for the last
three years Miss Cardew's esteemed governess and valued companion.

LADY BRACKNELL: In spite of what I hear of her, I must see her at
once. Let her be sent for.

CHASUBLE: [*Looking off.*] She approaches; she is nigh.

[*Enter* MISS PRISM *hurriedly.*]

MISS PRISM: I was told you expected me in the vestry, dear Canon. I
have been waiting for you there for an hour and three-quarters.
[*Catches sight of* LADY BRACKNELL, *who has fixed her with a stony
glare.* MISS PRISM *grows pale and quails. She looks anxiously round
as if desirous to escape.*]

LADY BRACKNELL: [*In a severe, judicial voice.*] Prism! [MISS PRISM
bows her head in shame.] Come here, Prism! [MISS PRISM *approaches in a humble manner.*] Where is that baby? [*General con-
sternation. The Canon starts back in horror.* ALGERNON *and* JACK
pretend to be anxious to shield CECILY *and* GWENDOLEN *from hearing the details of a terrible public scandal.*] Twenty-eight years ago,
Prism, you left Lord Bracknell's house, Number 104, Upper
Grosvenor Street, in charge of a perambulator that contained a
baby, of the male sex. You never returned. A few weeks later,
through the elaborate investigations of the Metropolitan police,
the perambulator was discovered at midnight, standing by itself
in a remote corner of Bayswater. It contained the manuscript of a
three-volume novel of more than usually revolting sentimentality.
[MISS PRISM *starts in involuntary indignation.*] But the baby was

not there! [*Everyone looks at* MISS PRISM.] Prism, where is that baby? [*A pause.*]

MISS PRISM: Lady Bracknell, I admit with shame that I do not know. I only wish I did. The plain facts of the case are these. On the morning of the day you mention, a day that is forever branded on my memory, I prepared as usual to take the baby out in its perambulator. I had also with me a somewhat old but capacious hand-bag in which I had intended to place the manuscript of a work of fiction that I had written during my few unoccupied hours. In a moment of mental abstraction, for which I never can forgive myself, I deposited the manuscript in the bassinette, and placed the baby in the hand-bag.

JACK: [*Who had been listening attentively.*] But where did you deposit the hand-bag?

MISS PRISM: Do not ask me, Mr. Worthing.

JACK: Miss Prism, this is a matter of no small importance to me. I insist on knowing where you deposited the hand-bag that contained that infant.

MISS PRISM: I left it in the cloak-room of one of the larger railway stations in London.

JACK: What railway station?

MISS PRISM: [*Quite crushed.*] Victoria. The Brighton line. [*Sinks into a chair.*]

JACK: I must retire to my room for a moment. Gwendolen, wait here for me.

GWENDOLEN: If you are not too long, I will wait here for you all my life.

[*Exit* JACK *in great excitement.*]

CHASUBLE: What do you think this means, Lady Bracknell?

LADY BRACKNELL: I dare not even suspect, Dr. Chasuble. I need hardly tell you that in families of high position strange coincidences are not supposed to occur. They are hardly considered the thing.

[*Noises heard overhead as if someone was throwing trunks about. Everybody looks up.*]

CECILY: Uncle Jack seems strangely agitated.

CHASUBLE: Your guardian has a very emotional nature.

LADY BRACKNELL: This noise is extremely unpleasant. It sounds as if he was having an argument. I dislike arguments of any kind. They are always vulgar, and often convincing.

CHASUBLE: [*Looking up.*] It has stopped now.

    [*The noise is redoubled.*]

LADY BRACKNELL: I wish he would arrive at some conclusion.

GWENDOLEN: The suspense is terrible. I hope it will last.

    [*Enter* JACK *with a hand-bag of black leather in his hand.*]

JACK: [*Rushing over to* MISS PRISM.] Is this the hand-bag, Miss Prism? Examine it carefully before you speak. The happiness of more than one life depends on your answers.

MISS PRISM: [*Calmly.*] It seems to be mine. Yes, here is the injury it received through the upsetting of a Gower Street omnibus in younger and happier days. Here is the stain on the lining caused by the explosion of a temperance beverage,[1] an incident that occurred at Leamington. And here, on the lock, are my initials. I had forgotten that in an extravagant mood I had had them placed there. The bag is undoubtedly mine. I am delighted to have it so unexpectedly restored to me. It has been a great inconvenience being without it all these years.

JACK: [*In a pathetic voice.*] Miss Prism, more is restored to you than this hand-bag. I was the baby you placed in it.

MISS PRISM: [*Amazed.*] You?

JACK: [*Embracing her.*] Yes . . . mother!

MISS PRISM: [*Recoiling in indignant astonishment.*] Mr. Worthing! I am unmarried!

JACK: Unmarried! I do not deny that is a serious blow. But after all, who has the right to cast a stone against one who has suffered? Cannot repentance wipe out an act of folly? Why should there be one law for men and another for women? Mother, I forgive you. [*Tries to embrace her again.*]

MISS PRISM: [*Still more indignant.*] Mr. Worthing, there is some error. [*Pointing to* LADY BRACKNELL.] There is the lady who can tell you who you really are.

JACK: [*After a pause.*] Lady Bracknell, I hate to seem inquisitive, but would you kindly inform me who I am?

LADY BRACKNELL: I am afraid that the news I have to give you will

---

[1] Soft drink.

not altogether please you. You are the son of my poor sister, Mrs. Moncrieff, and consequently Algernon's elder brother.

JACK: Algy's elder brother! Then I have a brother after all. I knew I had a brother! I always said I had a brother! Cecily,—how could you have ever doubted that I had a brother? [*Seizes hold of* AL-GERNON.] Dr. Chasuble, my unfortunate brother. Miss Prism, my unfortunate brother. Gwendolen, my unfortunate brother. Algy, you young scoundrel, you will have to treat me with more respect in the future. You have never behaved to me like a brother in all your life.

ALGERNON: Well, not till to-day, old boy, I admit. I did my best, however, though I was out of practice. [*Shakes hands.*]

GWENDOLEN: [*To* JACK.] My own! But what own are you? What is your Christian name, now that you have become someone else?

JACK: Good heavens! . . . I had quite forgotten that point. Your decision on the subject of my name is irrevocable, I suppose?

GWENDOLEN: I never change, except in my affections.

CECILY: What a noble nature you have, Gwendolen!

JACK: Then the question had better be cleared up at once. Aunt Augusta, a moment. At the time when Miss Prism left me in the hand-bag, had I been christened already?

LADY BRACKNELL: Every luxury that money could buy, including christening, had been lavished on you by your fond and doting parents.

JACK: Then I was christened! That is settled. Now, what name was I given? Let me know the worst.

LADY BRACKNELL: Being the eldest son you were naturally christened after your father.

JACK: [*Irritably.*] Yes, but what was my father's Christian name?

LADY BRACKNELL: [*Meditatively.*] I cannot at the present moment recall what the General's Christian name was. But I have no doubt he had one. He was eccentric, I admit. But only in later years. And that was the result of the Indian climate, and marriage, and indigestion, and other things of that kind.

JACK: Algy! Can't you recollect what our father's Christian name was?

ALGERNON: My dear boy, we were never even on speaking terms. He died before I was a year old.

JACK: His name would appear in the Army Lists of the period, I suppose, Aunt Augusta?

LADY BRACKNELL: The general was essentially a man of peace, except in his domestic life. But I have no doubt his name would appear in any military directory.

JACK: The Army Lists of the last forty years are here. These delightful records should have been my constant study. [*Rushes to bookcase and tears the books out.*] M. Generals . . . Mallham, Maxbohm, Magley, what ghastly names they have— Markby, Migsby, Mobbs, Moncrieff! Lieutenant 1840, Captain, Lieutenant-Colonel, Colonel, General 1869, Christian names, Ernest John. [*Puts book very quietly down and speaks quite calmly.*] I always told you, Gwendolen, my name was Ernest, didn't I? Well, it is Ernest after all, I mean it naturally is Ernest.

LADY BRACKNELL: Yes, I remember the General was called Ernest. I knew I had some particular reason for disliking the name.

GWENDOLEN: Ernest! My own Ernest! I felt from the first that you could have no other name!

JACK: Gwendolen, it is a terrible thing for a man to find out suddenly that all his life he has been speaking nothing but the truth. Can you forgive me?

GWENDOLEN: I can. For I feel sure that you are sure to change.

JACK: My own one!

CHASUBLE: [*To* MISS PRISM.] Lætitia! [*Embraces her.*]

MISS PRISM: [*Enthusiastically.*] Frederick! At last!

ALGERNON: Cecily! [*Embraces her.*] At last!

JACK: Gwendolen! [*Embraces her.*] At last!

LADY BRACKNELL: My nephew, you seem to be displaying signs of triviality.

JACK: On the contrary, Aunt Augusta, I've now realized for the first time in my life the vital Importance of Being Earnest.

[*Tableau.*]

[*Curtain.*]

1895

Susan Glaspell
1882–1948

TRIFLES

Trifles *is based on a real-life murder. On a cold December night, in an Iowa farmhouse, John Hossack was sleeping in his bed when someone struck him in the head with an axe. His wife, Margaret, claimed she was awakened by the noise of the blows, which sounded like one block of wood striking another one, but evidence suggested she was the murderer. Her motive, according to the authorities, was unhappiness within a bad marriage.*

Susan Glaspell, a young reporter for the Des Moines Daily News, *covered the case. At first, she led readers down a familiar, lurid path of indignation and outrage, appealing to her readers' prejudices, sensationalizing the crime, and portraying Margaret Hossack as a monster. But after visiting the Hossacks' kitchen in the company of investigators, she came to regard the wife not as a criminal but as a victim, and her newspaper stories began to describe the horrific life Margaret Hossack suffered during thirty-three years of marriage to an oppressive and abusive husband. The trial proved a great public entertainment; the courthouse was packed to overflowing, with more women in attendance than men. Although Hossack was convicted of murder and sentenced to life at hard labor, her lawyers appealed the verdict and won; in a retrial, the jury couldn't reach a consensus, so Hossack was released.*

The story lay dormant in Glaspell's imagination for a dozen years. When her husband, the writer George Cook, announced to their friends that Glaspell would provide a new play for the 1916 "season" of the Provincetown Players, a modest theatrical company the couple had cofounded in Provincetown, Massachusetts, Glaspell, who was really a fiction writer, settled down to write a play. In the heat of summer days, she sat in the empty space of the Wharf Theater until, as she put it, the "bare little stage" began to take on the features of Margaret Hossack's kitchen. She wrote the play in two weeks, and it opened on August 8, 1916, with Cook and Glaspell in the roles of Mr. and Mrs. Hale. Some critics have seen features of the young Glaspell, as she was when she reported the Hossack case, in Mrs. Hale.

The play was picked up by New York City's Washington Square Players, a group midway between the Provincetown Players and the mainstream, commercial theaters on Broadway. The New York production gave Glaspell a wider audience, and soon she was a famous figure in the New York theater world, with The New York Times *printing feature stories about her.*

Like her fellow Provincetowners, including playwright Eugene O'Neill, Glaspell sought to give America a serious theater predicated on a repudiation of the melodrama and sentimentality that dominated the popular stage. She did not, however, disdain common theatergoers or think that her proper audience was the elite intellectuals among whom she worked and lived. A socialist, Glaspell wanted her work to affect people beyond her circle, to entertain a popular audience at the same time that it improved Americans' lives.

Within Trifles, *you'll find many insights into relations between men and women in America. If you look carefully, you'll also detect Glaspell's social commentary on class distinctions, in the different characterizations of Mrs. Hale and Mrs. Peters, who have different class status.*

Trifles

CHARACTERS

SHERIFF   MRS. PETERS, *Sheriff's wife*

COUNTY ATTORNEY   MRS. HALE

HALE

SCENE: *The kitchen in the now abandoned farmhouse of* JOHN WRIGHT, *a gloomy kitchen, and left without having been put in order—unwashed pans under the sink, a loaf of bread outside the bread-box, a dish-towel on the table—other signs of incompleted work. At the rear the outer door opens and the* SHERIFF *comes in followed by the* COUNTY ATTORNEY *and* HALE. *The* SHERIFF *and* HALE *are men in middle life, the* COUNTY ATTORNEY *is a young man; all are much bundled up and go at once to the stove. They are followed by the two women—the* SHERIFF's *wife first; she is a slight wiry woman, a thin nervous face.* MRS. HALE *is larger and would ordinarily be called more comfortable looking, but she is disturbed now and looks fearfully about as she enters. The women have come in slowly, and stand close together near the door.*

COUNTY ATTORNEY: [*Rubbing his hands.*] This feels good. Come up to the fire, ladies.

MRS. PETERS: [*After taking a step forward.*] I'm not—cold.

SHERIFF: [*Unbuttoning his overcoat and stepping away from the stove as if to mark the beginning of official business.*] Now, Mr. Hale, before we move things about, you explain to Mr. Henderson just what you saw when you came here yesterday morning.

COUNTY ATTORNEY: By the way, has anything been moved? Are things just as you left them yesterday?

SHERIFF: [*Looking about.*] It's just the same. When it dropped below zero last night I thought I'd better send Frank out this morning to make a fire for us—no use getting pneumonia with a big case on, but I told him not to touch anything except the stove—and you know Frank.

COUNTY ATTORNEY: Somebody should have been left here yesterday.

SHERIFF: Oh—yesterday. When I had to send Frank to Morris Center for that man who went crazy—I want you to know I had my hands full yesterday. I knew you could get back from Omaha by today and as long as I went over everything here myself—

COUNTY ATTORNEY: Well, Mr. Hale, tell just what happened when you came here yesterday morning.

HALE: Harry and I had started to town with a load of potatoes. We came along the road from my place and as I got here I said, "I'm going to see if I can't get John Wright to go in with me on a party telephone."[1] I spoke to Wright about it once before and he put me off, saying folks talked too much anyway, and all he asked was peace and quiet—I guess you know about how much he talked himself; but I thought maybe if I went to the house and talked about it before his wife, though I said to Harry that I didn't know as what his wife wanted made much difference to John—

---

1. One telephone line shared by a number of houses.

COUNTY ATTORNEY: Let's talk about that later, Mr. Hale. I do want to talk about that, but tell now just what happened when you got to the house.

HALE: I didn't hear or see anything; I knocked at the door, and still it was all quiet inside. I knew they must be up, it was past eight o'clock. So I knocked again, and I thought I heard somebody say, "Come in." I wasn't sure, I'm not sure yet, but I opened the door— this door [*Indicating the door by which the two women are still standing.*] and there in that rocker— [*Pointing to it.*] sat Mrs. Wright.

   [*They all look at the rocker.*]

COUNTY ATTORNEY: What—was she doing?

HALE: She was rockin' back and forth. She had her apron in her hand and was kind of—pleating it.

COUNTY ATTORNEY: And how did she—look?

HALE: Well, she looked queer.

COUNTY ATTORNEY: How do you mean—queer?

HALE: Well, as if she didn't know what she was going to do next. And kind of done up.

COUNTY ATTORNEY: How did she seem to feel about your coming?

HALE: Why, I don't think she minded—one way or other. She didn't pay much attention. I said, "How do, Mrs. Wright, it's cold, ain't it?" And she said, "Is it?"—and went on kind of pleating at her apron. Well, I was surprised; she didn't ask me to come up to the stove, or to set down, but just sat there, not even looking at me, so I said, "I want to see John." And then she—laughed. I guess you would call it a laugh. I thought of Harry and the team outside, so I said a little sharp: "Can't I see John?" "No," she says, kind o' dull like. "Ain't he home?" says I. "Yes," says she, "he's home." "Then why can't I see him?" I asked her, out of patience. " 'Cause he's dead," says she. "*Dead?*" says I. She just nodded her head, not getting a bit excited, but rockin' back and forth. "Why—where is he?" says I, not knowing what to say. She just pointed upstairs—like that. [*Himself pointing to the room above.*] I got up, with the idea of going up there. I walked from there to here—then I says, "Why, what did he die of?" "He died of a rope round his neck," says she, and just went on pleatin' at her apron. Well, I went out and called Harry. I thought I might—need help. We went upstairs and there he was lyin'—

COUNTY ATTORNEY: I think I'd rather have you go into that upstairs, where you can point it all out. Just go on now with the rest of the story.

HALE: Well, my first thought was to get that rope off. It looked . . . [*Stops, his face twitches.*] . . . but Harry, he went up to him, and he said, "No, he's dead all right, and we'd better not touch anything." So we went back down stairs. She was still sitting that same way. "Has anybody been notified?" I asked. "No," says she unconcerned. "Who did this, Mrs. Wright?" said Harry. He said it business-like—and she stopped pleatin' of her apron. "I don't know," she says. "You don't *know?*" says Harry. "No," says she. "Weren't you sleepin' in the bed with him?" says Harry. "Yes," says she, "but I was on the inside." "Somebody slipped a rope round his neck and strangled him and you didn't wake up?" says Harry. "I didn't wake up," she said after him. We must 'a looked as if we didn't see how that could be, for after a minute she said, "I sleep sound." Harry was going to ask her more questions but I said maybe we ought to let her tell her story first to the coroner, or the sheriff, so Harry went fast as he could to Rivers' place, where there's a telephone.

COUNTY ATTORNEY: And what did Mrs. Wright do when she knew that you had gone for the coroner?

HALE: She moved from that chair to this one over here [*Pointing to a small chair in the corner.*] and just sat there with her hands held together and looking down. I got a feeling that I ought to make some conversation, so I said I had come in to see if John wanted to put in a telephone, and at that she started to laugh, and then she stopped and looked at me—scared. [*The* COUNTY ATTORNEY, *who has had his notebook out, makes a note.*] I dunno, maybe it wasn't scared. I wouldn't like to say it was. Soon Harry got back, and then Dr. Lloyd came, and you, Mr. Peters, and so I guess that's all I know that you don't.

COUNTY ATTORNEY: [*Looking around.*] I guess we'll go upstairs first—and then out to the barn and around there. [*To the* SHERIFF.] You're convinced that there was nothing important here—nothing that would point to any motive?

SHERIFF: Nothing here but kitchen things.

[*The* COUNTY ATTORNEY, *after again looking around the kitchen, opens the door of a cupboard closet. He gets up on a chair and looks on a shelf. Pulls his hand away, sticky.*]

COUNTY ATTORNEY: Here's a nice mess.

[*The women draw nearer.*]

MRS. PETERS: [*To the other woman.*] Oh, her fruit; it did freeze. [*To the* LAWYER.] She worried about that when it turned so cold. She said the fire'd go out and her jars would break.

SHERIFF: Well, can you beat the women! Held for murder and worryin' about her preserves.

COUNTY ATTORNEY: I guess before we're through she may have something more serious than preserves to worry about.

HALE: Well, women are used to worrying over trifles.

[*The two women move a little closer together.*]

COUNTY ATTORNEY: [*With the gallantry of a young politician.*] And yet, for all their worries, what would we do without the ladies? [*The women do not unbend. He goes to the sink, takes a dipperful of water from the pail, and pouring it into a basin, washes his hands. Starts to wipe them on the roller-towel, turns it for a cleaner place.*] Dirty towels! [*Kicks his foot against the pans under the sink.*] Not much of a housekeeper, would you say, ladies?

MRS. HALE: [*Stiffly.*] There's a great deal of work to be done on a farm.

COUNTY ATTORNEY: To be sure. And yet [*With a little bow to her.*] I know there are some Dickson county farmhouses which do not have such roller towels. [*He gives it a pull to expose its length again.*]

MRS. HALE: Those towels get dirty awful quick. Men's hands aren't always as clean as they might be.

COUNTY ATTORNEY: Ah, loyal to your sex, I see. But you and Mrs. Wright were neighbors. I suppose you were friends, too.

MRS. HALE: [*Shaking her head.*] I've not seen much of her of late years. I've not been in this house—it's more than a year.

COUNTY ATTORNEY: And why was that? You didn't like her?

MRS. HALE: I liked her all well enough. Farmers' wives have their hands full, Mr. Henderson. And then—

COUNTY ATTORNEY: Yes—?

MRS. HALE: [*Looking about.*] It never seemed a very cheerful place.

COUNTY ATTORNEY: No—it's not cheerful. I shouldn't say she had the homemaking instinct.

MRS. HALE: Well, I don't know as Wright had, either.

COUNTY ATTORNEY: You mean that they didn't get on very well?

MRS. HALE: No, I don't mean anything. But I don't think a place'd be any cheerfuller for John Wright's being in it.

COUNTY ATTORNEY: I'd like to talk more of that a little later. I want to get the lay of things upstairs now. [*He goes to the left, where three steps lead to a stair door.*]

SHERIFF: I suppose anything Mrs. Peters does'll be all right. She was to take in some clothes for her, you know, and a few little things. We left in such a hurry yesterday.

COUNTY ATTORNEY: Yes, but I would like to see what you take, Mrs. Peters, and keep an eye out for anything that might be of use to us.

MRS. PETERS: Yes, Mr. Henderson. [*The women listen to the men's steps on the stairs, then look about the kitchen.*]

MRS. HALE: I'd hate to have men coming into my kitchen, snooping around and criticizing. [*She arranges the pans under sink which the* LAWYER *had shoved out of place.*]

MRS. PETERS: Of course it's no more than their duty.

MRS. HALE: Duty's all right, but I guess that deputy sheriff that came out to make the fire might have got a little of this on. [*Gives the roller towel a pull.*] Wish I'd thought of that sooner. Seems mean to talk about her for not having things slicked up when she had to come away in such a hurry.

MRS. PETERS: [*Who has gone to a small table in the left rear corner of the room, and lifted one end of a towel that covers a pan.*] She had bread set. [*Stands still.*]

MRS. HALF: [*Eyes fixed on a loaf of bread beside the bread box, which is on a low shelf at the other side of the room. Moves slowly toward it.*] She was going to put this in there. [*Picks up loaf, then abruptly drops it. In a manner of returning to familiar things.*] It's a shame about her fruit. I wonder if it's all gone. [*Gets up on the chair and looks.*] I think there's some here that's all right, Mrs. Peters. Yes— here; [*Holding it toward the window.*] this is cherries, too. [*Looking again.*] I declare I believe that's the only one. [*Gets down,*

bottle in her hand. Goes to the sink and wipes it off on the outside.]
She'll feel awful bad after all her hard work in the hot weather. I
remember the afternoon I put up my cherries last summer. [*She
puts the bottle on the big kitchen table, center of the room. With a
sigh, is about to sit down in the rocking-chair. Before she is seated re-
alizes what chair it is; with a slow look at it, steps back. The chair,
which she has touched, rocks back and forth.*]

MRS. PETERS: Well, I must get those things from the front room
closet. [*She goes to the door at the right, but after looking into the
other room, steps back.*] You coming with me, Mrs. Hale? You
could help me carry them. [*They go in the other room; reappear,*
MRS. PETERS *carrying a dress and skirt,* MRS. HALE *following with a
pair of shoes.*] My, it's cold in there. [*She puts the clothes on the big
table, and hurries to the stove.*]

MRS. HALE: [*Examining the skirt.*] Wright was close. I think maybe
that's why she kept so much to herself. She didn't even belong to
the Ladies Aid.[2] I suppose she felt she couldn't do her part, and
then you don't enjoy things when you feel shabby. She used to
wear pretty clothes and be lively, when she was Minnie Foster,
one of the town girls singing in the choir. But that—oh, that was
thirty years ago. This all you was to take in?

MRS. PETERS: She said she wanted an apron. Funny thing to want,
for there isn't much to get you dirty in jail, goodness knows. But
I suppose just to make her feel more natural. She said they was in
the top drawer in this cupboard. Yes, here. And then her little
shawl that always hung behind the door. [*Opens stair door and
looks.*] Yes, here it is. [*Quickly shuts door leading upstairs.*]

MRS. HALE: [*Abruptly moving toward her.*] Mrs. Peters?

MRS. PETERS: Yes, Mrs. Hale?

MRS. HALE: Do you think she did it?

MRS. PETERS: [*In a frightened voice.*] Oh, I don't know.

MRS. HALE: Well, I don't think she did. Asking for an apron and her
little shawl. Worrying about her fruit.

MRS. PETERS: [*Starts to speak, glances up, where footsteps are heard in
the room above. In a low voice.*] Mr. Peters says it looks bad for

2. A volunteer benevolence society.

her. Mr. Henderson is awful sarcastic in a speech and he'll make fun of her sayin' she didn't wake up.

MRS. HALE: Well, I guess John Wright didn't wake when they was slipping that rope under his neck.

MRS. PETERS: No, it's strange. It must have been done awful crafty and still. They say it was such a—funny way to kill a man, rigging it all up like that.

MRS. HALE: That's just what Mr. Hale said. There was a gun in the house. He says that's what he can't understand.

MRS. PETERS: Mr. Henderson said coming out that what was needed for the case was a motive; something to show anger, or—sudden feeling.

MRS. HALE: [*Who is standing by the table.*] Well, I don't see any signs of anger around here. [*She puts her hand on the dish towel which lies on the table, stands looking down at table, one half of which is clean, the other half messy.*] It's wiped to here. [*Makes a move as if to finish work, then turns and looks at loaf of bread outside the bread box. Drops towel. In that voice of coming back to familiar things.*] Wonder how they are finding things upstairs. I hope she had it a little more red-up[3] up there. You know, it seems kind of *sneaking*. Locking her up in town and then coming out here and trying to get her own house to turn against her!

MRS. PETERS: But Mrs. Hale, the law is the law.

MRS. HALE: I s'pose 'tis. [*Unbuttoning her coat.*] Better loosen up your things, Mrs. Peters. You won't feel them when you go out.

[MRS. PETERS *takes off her fur tippet,[4] goes to hang it on hook at back of room, stands looking at the under part of the small corner table.*]

MRS. PETERS: She was piecing a quilt. [*She brings the large sewing basket and they look at the bright pieces.*]

MRS. HALE: It's log cabin pattern. Pretty, isn't it? I wonder if she was goin' to quilt it or just knot it?[5]

[*Footsteps have been heard coming down the stairs. The* SHERIFF *enters followed by* HALE *and the* COUNTY ATTORNEY.]

3. Tidied up.
4. Shoulder covering, like a full scarf.
5. The top of a quilt can be attached to the backing by sewing, which is a laborious process, or by knotting thick yarn, which is much quicker and easier.

SHERIFF: They wonder if she was going to quilt it or just knot it!
[*The men laugh, the women look abashed.*]

COUNTY ATTORNEY: [*Rubbing his hands over the stove.*] Frank's fire
didn't do much up there, did it? Well, let's go out to the barn and
get that cleared up.
[*The men go outside.*]

MRS. HALE: [*Resentfully.*] I don't know as there's anything so strange,
our takin' up our time with little things while we're waiting for
them to get the evidence. [*She sits down at the big table smoothing
out a block with decision.*] I don't see as it's anything to laugh about.

MRS. PETERS: [*Apologetically.*] Of course they've got awful important
things on their minds. [*Pulls up a chair and joins* MRS. HALE *at the
table.*]

MRS. HALE: [*Examining another block.*] Mrs. Peters, look at this one.
Here, this is the one she was working on, and look at the sewing!
All the rest of it has been so nice and even. And look at this! It's
all over the place! Why, it looks as if she didn't know what she
was about! [*After she has said this they look at each other, then start
to glance back at the door. After an instant* MRS. HALE *has pulled at
a knot and ripped the sewing.*]

MRS. PETERS: Oh, what are you doing, Mrs. Hale?

MRS. HALE: [*Mildly.*] Just pulling out a stitch or two that's not sewed
very good. [*Threading the needle.*] Bad sewing always made me
fidgety.

MRS. PETERS: [*Nervously.*] I don't think we ought to touch things.

MRS. HALE: I'll just finish up this end. [*Suddenly stopping and leaning
forward.*] Mrs. Peters?

MRS. PETERS: Yes, Mrs. Hale?

MRS. HALE: What do you suppose she was so nervous about?

MRS. PETERS: Oh—I don't know. I don't know as she was nervous. I
sometimes sew awful queer when I'm just tired. [MRS. HALE *starts
to say something, looks at* MRS. PETERS, *then goes on sewing.*] Well I
must get these things wrapped up. They may be through sooner
than we think. [*Putting apron and other things together.*] I wonder
where I can find a piece of paper, and string.

MRS. HALE: In that cupboard, maybe.

MRS. PETERS: [*Looking in cupboard.*] Why, here's a bird-cage. [*Holds
it up.*] Did she have a bird, Mrs. Hale?

MRS. HALE: Why, I don't know whether she did or not—I've not been here for so long. There was a man around last year selling canaries cheap, but I don't know as she took one; maybe she did. She used to sing real pretty herself.

MRS. PETERS: [*Glancing around.*] Seems funny to think of a bird here. But she must have had one, or why would she have a cage? I wonder what happened to it.

MRS. HALE: I s'pose maybe the cat got it.

MRS. PETERS: No, she didn't have a cat. She's got that feeling some people have about cats—being afraid of them. My cat got in her room and she was real upset and asked me to take it out.

MRS. HALE: My sister Bessie was like that. Queer, ain't it?

MRS. PETERS: [*Examining the cage.*] Why, look at this door. It's broke. One hinge is pulled apart.

MRS. HALE: [*Looking too.*] Looks as if someone must have been rough with it.

MRS. PETERS: Why, yes. [*She brings the cage forward and puts it on the table.*]

MRS. HALE: I wish if they're going to find any evidence they'd be about it. I don't like this place.

MRS. PETERS: But I'm awful glad you came with me, Mrs. Hale. It would be lonesome for me sitting here alone.

MRS. HALE: It would, wouldn't it? [*Dropping her sewing.*] But I tell you what I do wish, Mrs. Peters. I wish I had come over sometimes when *she* was here. I— [*Looking around the room.*] —wish I had.

MRS. PETERS: But of course you were awful busy, Mrs. Hale—your house and your children.

MRS. HALE: I could've come. I stayed away because it weren't cheerful—and that's why I ought to have come. I—I've never liked this place. Maybe because it's down in a hollow and you don't see the road. I dunno what it is, but it's a lonesome place and always was. I wish I had come over to see Minnie Foster sometimes. I can see now— [*Shakes her head.*]

MRS. PETERS: Well, you mustn't reproach yourself, Mrs. Hale. Somehow we just don't see how it is with other folks until—something comes up.

MRS. HALE: Not having children makes less work—but it makes a quiet house, and Wright out to work all day, and no company when he did come in. Did you know John Wright, Mrs. Peters?

MRS. PETERS: Not to know him; I've seen him in town. They say he was a good man.

MRS. HALE: Yes—good; he didn't drink, and kept his word as well as most, I guess, and paid his debts. But he was a hard man, Mrs. Peters. Just to pass the time of day with him— [*Shivers.*] Like a raw wind that gets to the bone. [*Pauses, her eye falling on the cage.*] I should think she would 'a wanted a bird. But what do you suppose went with it?

MRS. PETERS: I don't know, unless it got sick and died. [*She reaches over and swings the broken door, swings it again, both women watch it.*]

MRS. HALE: You weren't raised round here, were you? [MRS. PETERS *shakes her head.*] You didn't know—her?

MRS. PETERS: Not till they brought her yesterday.

MRS. HALE: She—come to think of it, she was kind of like a bird herself—real sweet and pretty, but kind of timid and—fluttery. How—she—did—change. [*Silence; then as if struck by a happy thought and relieved to get back to everyday things.*] Tell you what, Mrs. Peters, why don't you take the quilt in with you? It might take up her mind.

MRS. PETERS: Why, I think that's a real nice idea, Mrs. Hale. There couldn't possibly be any objection to it, could there? Now, just what would I take? I wonder if her patches are in here—and her things. [*They look in the sewing basket.*]

MRS. HALE: Here's some red. I expect this has got sewing things in it. [*Brings out a fancy box.*] What a pretty box. Looks like something somebody would give you. Maybe her scissors are in here. [*Opens box. Suddenly puts her hand to her nose.*] Why— [MRS. PETERS *bends nearer, then turns her face away.*] There's something wrapped up in this piece of silk.

MRS. PETERS: Why, this isn't her scissors.

MRS. HALE: [*Lifting the silk.*] Oh, Mrs. Peters—it's—
    [MRS. PETERS *bends closer.*]

MRS. PETERS: It's the bird.

MRS. HALE: [*Jumping up.*] But, Mrs. Peters—look at it! Its neck! Look at its neck! It's all—other side *to.*

MRS. PETERS: Somebody—wrung—its—neck.

[*Their eyes meet. A look of growing comprehension, of horror. Steps are heard outside.* MRS. HALE *slips box under quilt pieces, and sinks into her chair. Enter* SHERIFF *and* COUNTY ATTORNEY. MRS. PETERS *rises.*]

COUNTY ATTORNEY: [*As one turning from serious things to little pleasantries.*] Well ladies, have you decided whether she was going to quilt it or knot it?

MRS. PETERS: We think she was going to—knot it.

COUNTY ATTORNEY: Well, that's interesting, I'm sure. [*Seeing the bird-cage.*] Has the bird flown?

MRS. HALE: [*Putting more quilt pieces over the box.*] We think the—cat got it.

COUNTY ATTORNEY: [*Preoccupied.*] Is there a cat?

[MRS. HALE *glances in a quick covert way at* MRS. PETERS.]

MRS. PETERS: Well not *now.* They're superstitious, you know. They leave.

COUNTY ATTORNEY: [*To* SHERIFF PETERS, *continuing an interrupted conversation.*] No sign at all of anyone having come from the outside. Their own rope. Now let's go up again and go over it piece by piece. [*They start upstairs.*] It would have to have been someone who knew just the—

[MRS. PETERS *sits down. The two women sit there not looking at one another, but as if peering into something and at the same time holding back. When they talk now it is in the manner of feeling their way over strange ground, as if afraid of what they are saying, but as if they cannot help saying it.*]

MRS. HALE: She liked the bird. She was going to bury it in that pretty box.

MRS. PETERS: [*In a whisper.*] When I was a girl—my kitten—there was a boy took a hatchet, and before my eyes—and before I could get there— [*Covers her face an instant.*] If they hadn't held me back I would have— [*Catches herself, looks upstairs where steps are heard, falters weakly.*] —hurt him.

MRS. HALE: [*With a slow look around her.*] I wonder how it would seem never to have had any children around. [*Pause.*] No, Wright wouldn't like the bird—a thing that sang. She used to sing. He killed that, too.

MRS. PETERS: [*Moving uneasily.*] We don't know who killed the bird.

MRS. HALE: I knew John Wright.

MRS. PETERS: It was an awful thing was done in this house that night, Mrs. Hale. Killing a man while he slept, slipping a rope around his neck that choked the life out of him.

MRS. HALE: His neck. Choked the life out of him. [*Her hand goes out and rests on the bird-cage.*]

MRS. PETERS: [*With rising voice.*] We don't know who killed him. We don't *know*.

MRS. HALE: [*Her own feeling not interrupted.*] If there's been years and years of nothing, then a bird to sing to you, it would be awful—still, after the bird was still.

MRS. PETERS: [*Something within her speaking.*] I know what stillness is. When we homesteaded in Dakota, and my first baby died—after he was two years old, and me with no other then—

MRS. HALE: [*Moving.*] How soon do you suppose they'll be through, looking for the evidence?

MRS. PETERS: I know what stillness is. [*Pulling herself back.*] The law has got to punish crime, Mrs. Hale.

MRS. HALE: [*Not as if answering that.*] I wish you'd seen Minnie Foster when she wore a white dress with blue ribbons and stood up there in the choir and sang. [*A look around the room.*] Oh, I *wish* I'd come over here once in a while! That was a crime! That was a crime! Who's going to punish that?

MRS. PETERS: [*Looking upstairs.*] We mustn't—take on.

MRS. HALE: I might have known she needed help! I know how things can be—for women. I tell you, it's queer, Mrs. Peters. We live close together and we live far apart. We all go through the same things—it's all just a different kind of the same thing. [*Brushes her eyes, noticing the bottle of fruit, reaches out for it.*] If I was you, I wouldn't tell her her fruit was gone. Tell her it *ain't*. Tell her it's all right. Take this in to prove it to her. She—she may never know whether it was broke or not.

MRS. PETERS: [*Takes the bottle, looks about for something to wrap it in; takes petticoat from the clothes brought from the other room, very nervously begins winding this around the bottle. In a false voice.*] My, it's a good thing the men couldn't hear us. Wouldn't they just laugh! Getting all stirred up over a little thing like a—dead canary. As if that could have anything to do with—with—wouldn't they *laugh!*

[*The men are heard coming down stairs.*]

MRS. HALE: [*Under her breath.*] Maybe they would—maybe they wouldn't.

COUNTY ATTORNEY: No, Peters, it's all perfectly clear except a reason for doing it. But you know juries when it comes to women. If there was some definite thing. Something to show—something to make a story about—a thing that would connect up with this strange way of doing it—

[*The women's eyes meet for an instant. Enter* HALE *from outer door.*]

HALE: Well, I've got the team around. Pretty cold out there.

COUNTY ATTORNEY: I'm going to stay here a while by myself. [*To the* SHERIFF.] You can send Frank out for me, can't you? I want to go over everything. I'm not satisfied that we can't do better.

SHERIFF: Do you want to see what Mrs. Peters is going to take in?

[*The* LAWYER *goes to the table, picks up the apron, laughs.*]

COUNTY ATTORNEY: Oh, I guess they're not very dangerous things the ladies have picked out. [*Moves a few things about, disturbing the quilt pieces which cover the box. Steps back.*] No, Mrs. Peters doesn't need supervising. For that matter, a sheriff's wife is married to the law. Ever think of it that way, Mrs. Peters?

MRS. PETERS: Not—just that way.

SHERIFF: [*Chuckling.*] Married to the law. [*Moves toward the other room.*] I just want you to come in here a minute, George. We ought to take a look at these windows.

COUNTY ATTORNEY: [*Scoffingly.*] Oh, windows!

SHERIFF: We'll be right out, Mr. Hale.

[HALE *goes outside. The* SHERIFF *follows the* COUNTY ATTORNEY *into the other room. Then* MRS. HALE *rises, hands tight together, looking intensely at* MRS. PETERS, *whose eyes make a slow turn, finally meeting* MRS. HALE'*s. A moment* MRS. HALE *holds her, then her own eyes point the way to where the box is concealed. Suddenly* MRS. PETERS *throws back quilt pieces and tries to put the box in the bag she is wearing. It is too big. She opens box, starts to take bird out, cannot touch it, goes to pieces, stands there helpless. Sound of a knob turning in the other room.* MRS. HALE *snatches*

the box and puts it in the pocket of her big coat. Enter COUNTY
ATTORNEY *and* SHERIFF.]

COUNTY ATTORNEY: [*Facetiously.*] Well, Henry, at least we found out
that she was not going to quilt it. She was going to—what is it
you call it, ladies?

MRS. HALE: [*Her hand against her pocket.*] We call it—knot it, Mr.
Henderson.

[*Curtain.*]

1916   *1920*

Lorraine Hansberry
1930–1965

A RAISIN IN THE SUN

*This play takes its title from a line in a Langston Hughes poem that
asks, "What happens to a dream deferred?" In the 1950s, many
African Americans felt their claim on the American dream had
been deferred because "separate but equal," the dominant ideology
governing race relations in the United States at that time, was really a formula for white supremacy. Hughes wrote his poem in 1951,
when Hansberry was just twenty-one, a student who left college at
University of Wisconsin, Madison, to launch her career as a writer
in New York.*

*The play draws upon Hansberry's personal experiences. For ex-
ample, in 1938, Lorraine's father, Carl, decided to fight segregation
by moving his family into an all-white community in Chicago. At
the time, restrictive residential covenants made such actions illegal,
but the Hansberry family fought the law all the way to the U.S.
Supreme Court, where they won a landmark decision. Along the
way, the eight-year-old Lorraine witnessed an angry white mob
gathering outside their house and was nearly hit by a piece of concrete thrown through their window. Nevertheless, Hansberry's own
circumstances provided better prospects than those of the Younger
family in the play. Her father, successful in real estate, was a mem-*

ber of the NAACP and was politically active, once running (unsuccessfully) for Congress. Her mother was a progressive committeewoman in their neighborhood ward. And an uncle, a professor of African American history at Howard University, often brought African visitors, like Joseph Asagai in the play, to the Hansberrys' Chicago home. In addition, many prominent African Americans visited their home, including Paul Robeson, Jesse Owens, and Joe Louis. When she came to New York in 1950, Hansberry went to work for Robeson's newspaper, Freedom.

Not long after the publication of Hughes's poem, Rosa Parks committed her famous act of civil disobedience, sparking the Montgomery bus boycott and the modern civil rights movement; and the U.S. Supreme Court struck down segregated schools in Brown v. the Board of Education. Hansberry participated in this active challenging of American segregation, often taking part in demonstrations herself. She wrote in an age of greater promise than that of her parents' generation, and her play might be considered a cultural parallel to legal and extra-legal methods of social reform. Her work belongs in the tradition of realists, initiated by Henrik Ibsen, who wrote "problem" plays. It is certainly logical to think of A Raisin in the Sun as a descendant of A Doll House, not only stylistically but also thematically. Though more attention has been paid—not only by audiences but also by Hansberry herself—to the racial issues in the play, it is also about women in American society and the special burdens put upon women of color.

Hansberry was unknown as a creative writer in 1957 when a friend, Philip Rose, read the script of Raisin and announced he wanted to produce it on Broadway. He secured Sidney Poitier for the role of Walter, and they toured New Haven, Connecticut, Philadelphia, and Chicago before opening on Broadway in March 1959 to excellent reviews. Though the play conformed to many of the conventions of realistic theater, the fact that it portrayed a black family made it revolutionary, and it revolutionized audiences as well, drawing far more African Americans to Broadway theater than ever before. Most literary historians credit the play with launching African American theater in the United States, as have several generations of black writers, actors, directors, and producers. A few did dissent from the general praise, however. According to these critics, the Youngers aspired to nothing more than the crass materialistic prosperity that white Americans enjoyed, which was a rather shallow goal.

Today we view the civil rights movement mostly through the lens of Martin Luther King Jr.'s dream of an integrated society, but in the 1950s it was not at all clear that this would be the goal of reform. While the play obviously advocates the better treatment of African Americans, it also participates in a debate among reform-minded African Americans, a debate that can be exemplified by the contrast between Martin Luther King Jr. and Malcolm X, who advocated an anti-assimilationist black "nationalism." This alternative to integration celebrated black culture, often looking to Africa for a cultural inspiration unashamedly different from mainstream white culture.

If the 1950s were dynamic years for race relations in the United States, they were revolutionary in Africa. In the twenty years between 1950 and 1970, nearly forty African nations gained their independence from European powers. Most of these changes came within a few years of the first (1959) production of A Raisin in the Sun. As is typical in any de-colonization, these independence movements spurred revivals of native culture—in dress, music, and the arts. But also typical of de-colonization are internal conflicts that often lead to bloodshed. For example, Nigeria won its independence from Great Britain in 1960, but during the next ten years a million people would die in civil war. Though such consequences are alluded to in the play, in 1959 they were still mostly a dark cloud below the horizon of independence.

A Raisin in the Sun

What happens to a dream deferred?

Does it dry up
Like a raisin in the sun?
Or fester like a sore—
And then run?
Does it stink like rotten meat?

Or crust and sugar over—
Like a syrupy sweet?
Maybe it just sags
Like a heavy load.

Or does it explode?
—LANGSTON HUGHES[1]

CAST OF CHARACTERS

RUTH YOUNGER

TRAVIS YOUNGER

WALTER LEE YOUNGER (BROTHER)

BENEATHA YOUNGER

LENA YOUNGER (MAMA)

JOSEPH ASAGAI

GEORGE MURCHISON

KARL LINDNER

BOBO

MOVING MEN

The action of the play is set in Chicago's Southside, sometime between World War II and the present.

ACT I
SCENE ONE

The Younger living room would be a comfortable and well-ordered room if it were not for a number of indestructible contradictions to this state of being. Its furnishings are typical and undistinguished and their primary feature now is that they have clearly had to accommodate the living of too many people for too many years—and they are tired. Still, we can see that at some time, a time probably no longer remembered by the family (except perhaps for MAMA*), the furnishings of this room were actually selected with care and love and even hope—and brought to this apartment and arranged with taste and pride.*

That was a long time ago. Now the once loved pattern of the couch upholstery has to fight to show itself from under acres of crocheted doilies and couch covers which have themselves finally come to be more important than the upholstery. And here a table or a chair has been moved to disguise the worn places in the carpet; but the carpet has fought back by showing its weariness, with depressing uniformity, elsewhere on its surface.

Weariness has, in fact, won in this room. Everything has been pol-

---

1. The title of this 1951 poem is "Harlem (A Dream Deferred)."

ished, washed, sat on, used, scrubbed too often. All pretenses but living itself have long since vanished from the very atmosphere of this room.

Moreover, a section of this room, for it is not really a room unto itself, though the landlord's lease would make it seem so, slopes backward to provide a small kitchen area, where the family prepares the meals that are eaten in the living room proper, which must also serve as dining room. The single window that has been provided for these "two" rooms is located in this kitchen area. The sole natural light the family may enjoy in the course of a day is only that which fights its way through this little window.

At left, a door leads to a bedroom which is shared by MAMA *and her daughter,* BENEATHA. *At right, opposite, is a second room (which in the beginning of the life of this apartment was probably a breakfast room) which serves as a bedroom for* WALTER *and his wife,* RUTH.

Time: Sometime between World War II and the present.[2]

Place: Chicago's Southside.

At Rise: It is morning dark in the living room. TRAVIS *is asleep on the make-down bed at center. An alarm clock sounds from within the bedroom at right, and presently* RUTH *enters from that room and closes the door behind her. She crosses sleepily toward the window. As she passes her sleeping son she reaches down and shakes him a little. At the window she raises the shade and a dusky Southside morning light comes in feebly. She fills a pot with water and puts it on to boil. She calls to the boy, between yawns, in a slightly muffled voice.*

RUTH *is about thirty. We can see that she was a pretty girl, even exceptionally so, but now it is apparent that life has been little that she expected, and disappointment has already begun to hang in her face. In a few years, before thirty-five even, she will be known among her people as a "settled woman."*

She crosses to her son and gives him a good, final, rousing shake.

RUTH: Come on now, boy, it's seven thirty! [*Her son sits up at last, in a stupor of sleepiness.*] I say hurry up, Travis! You ain't the only person in the world got to use a bathroom! [*The child, a sturdy, handsome little boy of ten or eleven, drags himself out of the bed and*

2. 1959.

*almost blindly takes his towels and "today's clothes" from drawers and
a closet and goes out to the bathroom, which is in an outside hall
and which is shared by another family or families on the same floor.*
RUTH *crosses to the bedroom door at right and opens it and calls in
to her husband.*] Walter Lee! . . . It's after seven thirty! Lemme see
you do some waking up in there now! [*She waits.*] You better get
up from there, man! It's after seven thirty I tell you. [*She waits
again.*] All right, you just go ahead and lay there and next thing
you know Travis be finished and Mr. Johnson'll be in there and
you'll be fussing and cussing round here like a mad man! And be
late too! [*She waits, at the end of patience.*] Walter Lee—it's time
for you to get up!

> [*She waits another second and then starts to go into the bedroom,
> but is apparently satisfied that her husband has begun to get up.
> She stops, pulls the door to, and returns to the kitchen area. She
> wipes her face with a moist cloth and runs her fingers through her
> sleep-disheveled hair in a vain effort and ties an apron around
> her housecoat. The bedroom door at right opens and her husband
> stands in the doorway in his pajamas, which are rumpled and
> mismated. He is a lean, intense young man in his middle thirties,
> inclined to quick nervous movements and erratic speech habits—
> and always in his voice there is a quality of indictment.*]

WALTER: Is he out yet?

RUTH: What you mean *out*? He ain't hardly got in there good yet.

WALTER: [*Wandering in, still more oriented to sleep than to a new day.*]
Well, what was you doing all that yelling for if I can't even get in
there yet? [*Stopping and thinking.*] Check coming today?

RUTH: They *said* Saturday and this is just Friday and I hopes to God
you ain't going to get up here first thing this morning and start
talking to me 'bout no money—'cause I 'bout don't want to hear
it.

WALTER: Something the matter with you this morning?

RUTH: No—I'm just sleepy as the devil. What kind of eggs you want?

WALTER: Not scrambled. [RUTH *starts to scramble eggs.*] Paper come?
[RUTH *points impatiently to the rolled up* Tribune *on the table, and
he gets it and spreads it out and vaguely reads the front page.*] Set off
another bomb yesterday.

RUTH: [*Maximum indifference.*] Did they?

WALTER: [*Looking up.*] What's the matter with you?

RUTH: Ain't nothing the matter with me. And don't keep asking me that this morning.

WALTER: Ain't nobody bothering you. [*Reading the news of the day absently again.*] Say Colonel McCormick[3] is sick.

RUTH: [*Affecting tea-party interest.*] Is he now? Poor thing.

WALTER: [*Sighing and looking at his watch.*] Oh, me. [*He waits.*] Now what is that boy doing in that bathroom all this time? He just going to have to start getting up earlier. I can't be late to work on account of him fooling around in there.

RUTH: [*Turning on him.*] Oh, no he ain't going to be getting up no earlier no such thing! It ain't his fault that he can't get to bed no earlier nights 'cause he got a bunch of crazy good-for-nothing clowns sitting up running their mouths in what is supposed to be his bedroom after ten o'clock at night . . .

WALTER: That's what you mad about, ain't it? The things I want to talk about with my friends just couldn't be important in your mind, could they?

[*He rises and finds a cigarette in her handbag on the table and crosses to the little window and looks out, smoking and deeply enjoying this first one.*]

RUTH: [*Almost matter of factly, a complaint too automatic to deserve emphasis.*] Why you always got to smoke before you eat in the morning?

WALTER: [*At the window.*] Just look at 'em down there . . . Running and racing to work . . . [*He turns and faces his wife and watches her a moment at the stove, and then, suddenly.*] You look young this morning, baby.

RUTH: [*Indifferently.*] Yeah?

WALTER: Just for a second—stirring them eggs. It's gone now—just for a second it was—you looked real young again. [*Then, drily.*] It's gone now—you look like yourself again.

RUTH: Man, if you don't shut up and leave me alone.

WALTER: [*Looking out to the street again.*] First thing a man ought to

3. Robert Rutherford McCormick (1880–1955), long–time publisher, editor, and owner of the *Chicago Tribune*. He championed conservative causes his whole life.

learn in life is not to make love to no colored woman first thing in the morning. You all some evil people at eight o'clock in the morning.

[TRAVIS *appears in the hall doorway, almost fully dressed and quite wide awake now, his towels and pajamas across his shoulders. He opens the door and signals for his father to make the bathroom in a hurry.*]

TRAVIS: [*Watching the bathroom.*] Daddy, come on!

[WALTER *gets his bathroom utensils and flies out to the bathroom.*]

RUTH: Sit down and have your breakfast, Travis.

TRAVIS: Mama, this is Friday. [*Gleefully.*] Check coming tomorrow, huh?

RUTH: You get your mind off money and eat your breakfast.

TRAVIS: [*Eating.*] This is the morning we supposed to bring the fifty cents to school.

RUTH: Well, I ain't got no fifty cents this morning.

TRAVIS: Teacher say we have to.

RUTH: I don't care what teacher say. I ain't got it. Eat your breakfast, Travis.

TRAVIS: I *am* eating.

RUTH: Hush up now and just eat!

[*The boy gives her an exasperated look for her lack of understanding, and eats grudgingly.*]

TRAVIS: You think Grandmama would have it?

RUTH: No! And I want you to stop asking your grandmother for money, you hear me?

TRAVIS: [*Outraged.*] Gaaaleee! I don't ask her, she just gimme it sometimes!

RUTH: Travis Willard Younger—I got too much on me this morning to be—

TRAVIS: Maybe Daddy—

RUTH: *Travis!*

[*The boy hushes abruptly. They are both quiet and tense for several seconds.*]

TRAVIS: [*Presently.*] Could I maybe go carry some groceries in front of the supermarket for a little while after school then?

RUTH: Just hush, I said. [TRAVIS *jabs his spoon into his cereal bowl vi-*

ciously, and rests his head in anger upon his fists.] If you through eating, you can get over there and make up your bed.

[*The boy obeys stiffly and crosses the room, almost mechanically, to the bed and more or less carefully folds the covering. He carries the bedding into his mother's room and returns with his books and cap.*]

TRAVIS: [*Sulking and standing apart from her unnaturally.*] I'm gone.

RUTH: [*Looking up from the stove to inspect him automatically.*] Come here. [*He crosses to her and she studies his head.*] If you don't take this comb and fix this here head, you better! [TRAVIS *puts down his books with a great sigh of oppression, and crosses to the mirror. His mother mutters under her breath about his "slubbornness."*] 'Bout to march out of here with that head looking just like chickens slept in it! I just don't know where you get your slub-born ways . . . And get your jacket, too. Looks chilly out this morning.

TRAVIS: [*With conspicuously brushed hair and jacket.*] I'm gone.

RUTH: Get carfare and milk money—[*Waving one finger.*]—and not a single penny for no caps, you hear me?

TRAVIS: [*With sullen politeness.*] Yes'm.

[*He turns in outrage to leave. His mother watches after him as in his frustration he approaches the door almost comically. When she speaks to him, her voice has become a very gentle tease.*]

RUTH: [*Mocking; as she thinks he would say it.*] Oh, Mama makes me so mad sometimes, I don't know what to do! [*She waits and continues to his back as he stands stock-still in front of the door.*] I wouldn't kiss that woman good-bye for nothing in this world this morning! [*The boy finally turns around and rolls his eyes at her, knowing the mood has changed and he is vindicated; he does not, however, move toward her yet.*] Not for nothing in this world! [*She finally laughs aloud at him and holds out her arms to him and we see that it is a way between them, very old and practiced. He crosses to her and allows her to embrace him warmly but keeps his face fixed with masculine rigidity. She holds him back from her presently and looks at him and runs her fingers over the features of his face. With utter gentleness—*] Now—whose little old angry man are you?

TRAVIS: [*The masculinity and gruffness start to fade at last.*] Aw gaalee—Mama . . .

RUTH: [*Mimicking.*] Aw—gaaaaalleeeee, Mama! [*She pushes him, with rough playfulness and finality, toward the door.*] Get on out of here or you going to be late.

TRAVIS: [*In the face of love, new aggressiveness.*] Mama, could I *please* go carry groceries?

RUTH: Honey, it's starting to get so cold evenings.

WALTER: [*Coming in from the bathroom and drawing a make-believe gun from a make-believe holster and shooting at his son.*] What is it he wants to do?

RUTH: Go carry groceries after school at the supermarket.

WALTER: Well, let him go . . .

TRAVIS: [*Quickly, to the ally.*] I *have* to—she won't gimme the fifty cents . . .

WALTER: [*To his wife only.*] Why not?

RUTH: [*Simply, and with flavor.*] 'Cause we don't have it.

WALTER: [*To* RUTH *only.*] What you tell the boy things like that for? [*Reaching down into his pants with a rather important gesture.*] Here, son—
[*He hands the boy the coin, but his eyes are directed to his wife's.* TRAVIS *takes the money happily.*]

TRAVIS: Thanks, Daddy.
[*He starts out.* RUTH *watches both of them with murder in her eyes.* WALTER *stands and stares back at her with defiance, and suddenly reaches into his pocket again on an afterthought.*]

WALTER: [*Without even looking at his son, still staring hard at his wife.*] In fact, here's another fifty cents . . . Buy yourself some fruit to-day—or take a taxicab to school or something!

TRAVIS: Whoopee—
[*He leaps up and clasps his father around the middle with his legs, and they face each other in mutual appreciation; slowly* WAL-TER LEE *peeks around the boy to catch the violent rays from his wife's eyes and draws his head back as if shot.*]

WALTER: You better get down now—and get to school, man.

TRAVIS: [*At the door.*] O.K. Good-bye.
[*He exits.*]

WALTER: [*After him, pointing with pride.*] That's *my* boy. [*She looks at him in disgust and turns back to her work.*] You know what I was thinking 'bout in the bathroom this morning?

RUTH: No.

WALTER: How come you always try to be so pleasant!

RUTH: What is there to be pleasant 'bout!

WALTER: You want to know what I was thinking 'bout in the bathroom or not!

RUTH: I know what you thinking 'bout.

WALTER: [*Ignoring her.*] 'Bout what me and Willy Harris was talking about last night.

RUTH: [*Immediately—a refrain.*] Willy Harris is a good-for-nothing loud mouth.

WALTER: Anybody who talks to me has got to be a good-for-nothing loud mouth, ain't he? And what you know about who is just a good-for-nothing loud mouth? Charlie Atkins was just a "good-for-nothing loud mouth" too, wasn't he! When he wanted me to go in the dry-cleaning business with him. And now—he's grossing a hundred thousand a year. A hundred thousand dollars a year! You still call *him* a loud mouth!

RUTH: [*Bitterly.*] Oh, Walter Lee . . .

[*She folds her head on her arms over the table.*]

WALTER: [*Rising and coming to her and standing over her.*] You tired, ain't you? Tired of everything. Me, the boy, the way we live—this beat-up hole—everything. Ain't you? [*She doesn't look up, doesn't answer.*] So tired—moaning and groaning all the time, but you wouldn't do nothing to help, would you? You couldn't be on my side that long for nothing, could you?

RUTH: Walter, please leave me alone.

WALTER: A man needs for a woman to back him up . . .

RUTH: Walter—

WALTER: Mama would listen to you. You know she listen to you more than she do me and Bennie. She think more of you. All you have to do is just sit down with her when you drinking your coffee one morning and talking 'bout things like you do and— [*He sits down beside her and demonstrates graphically what he thinks her methods and tone should be.*] —you just sip your coffee, see, and say easy like that you been thinking 'bout that deal Walter Lee is so interested in, 'bout the store and all, and sip some more coffee, like what you saying ain't really that important to you—And the next thing you know, she be listening good and asking you questions and when I come home—I can tell her the details. This ain't no fly-by-night proposition, baby. I mean we figured it out, me and Willy and Bobo.

RUTH: [*With a frown.*] Bobo?

WALTER: Yeah. You see, this little liquor store we got in mind cost seventy-five thousand and we figured the initial investment on the place be 'bout thirty thousand, see. That be ten thousand each. Course, there's a couple of hundred you got to pay so's you don't spend your life just waiting for them clowns to let your license get approved—

RUTH: You mean graft?

WALTER: [*Frowning impatiently.*] Don't call it that. See there, that just goes to show you what women understand about the world. Baby, don't *nothing* happen for you in this world 'less you pay *somebody* off!

RUTH: Walter, leave me alone! [*She raises her head and stares at him vigorously—then says, more quietly.*] Eat your eggs, they gonna be cold.

WALTER: [*Straightening up from her and looking off.*] That's it. There you are. Man say to his woman: I got me a dream. His woman say: Eat your eggs. [*Sadly, but gaining in power.*] Man say: I got to take hold of this here world, baby! And a woman will say: Eat your eggs and go to work. [*Passionately now.*] Man say: I got to change my life, I'm choking to death, baby! And his woman say— [*In utter anguish as he brings his fists down on his thighs.*] — Your eggs is getting cold!

RUTH: [*Softly.*] Walter, that ain't none of our money.

WALTER: [*Not listening at all or even looking at her.*] This morning, I was lookin' in the mirror and thinking about it . . . I'm thirty-five years old; I been married eleven years and I got a boy who sleeps in the living room— [*Very, very quietly.*] —and all I got to give him is stories about how rich white people live . . .

RUTH: Eat your eggs, Walter.

WALTER: *Damn my eggs . . . damn all the eggs that ever was!*

RUTH: Then go to work.

WALTER: [*Looking up at her.*] See—I'm trying to talk to you 'bout myself— [*Shaking his head with the repetition.*] —and all you can say is eat them eggs and go to work.

RUTH: [*Wearily.*] Honey, you never say nothing new. I listen to you every day, every night and every morning, and you never say nothing new. [*Shrugging.*] So you would rather *be* Mr. Arnold than be his chauffeur. So—I would *rather* be living in Buckingham Palace.[4]

WALTER: That is just what is wrong with the colored woman in this world . . . Don't understand about building their men up and making 'em feel like they somebody. Like they can do something.

RUTH: [*Drily, but to hurt.*] There *are* colored men who do things.

WALTER: No thanks to the colored woman.

RUTH: Well, being a colored woman, I guess I can't help myself none.

[*She rises and gets the ironing board and sets it up and attacks a huge pile of rough-dried clothes, sprinkling them in preparation for the ironing and then rolling them into tight fat balls.*]

WALTER: [*Mumbling.*] We one group of men tied to a race of women with small minds.

[*His sister* BENEATHA *enters. She is about twenty, as slim and intense as her brother. She is not as pretty as her sister-in-law, but her lean, almost intellectual face has a handsomeness of its own. She wears a bright-red flannel nightie, and her thick hair stands wildly about her head. Her speech is a mixture of many things; it is different from the rest of the family's insofar as education has permeated her sense of English—and perhaps the Midwest rather than the South has finally—at last—won out in her inflection; but not altogether, because over all of it is a soft slurring and transformed use of vowels which is the decided influence of the Southside. She passes through the room without looking at either* RUTH *or* WALTER *and goes to the outside door and looks, a little blindly, out to the bathroom. She sees that it has been lost to the Johnsons. She closes the door with a sleepy vengeance and crosses to the table and sits down a little defeated.*]

BENEATHA: I am going to start timing those people.

WALTER: You should get up earlier.

---

4. The lavish London residence of British royalty.

BENEATHA: [*Her face in her hands. She is still fighting the urge to go back to bed.*] Really—would you suggest dawn? Where's the paper?

WALTER: [*Pushing the paper across the table to her as he studies her almost clinically, as though he has never seen her before.*] You a horrible-looking chick at this hour.

BENEATHA: [*Drily.*] Good morning, everybody.

WALTER: [*Senselessly.*] How is school coming?

BENEATHA: [*In the same spirit.*] Lovely. Lovely. And you know, biology is the greatest. [*Looking up at him.*] I dissected something that looked just like you yesterday.

WALTER: I just wondered if you've made up your mind and everything.

BENEATHA: [*Gaining in sharpness and impatience.*] And what did I answer yesterday morning—and the day before that?

RUTH: [*From the ironing board, like someone disinterested and old.*] Don't be so nasty, Bennie.

BENEATHA: [*Still to her brother.*] And the day before that and the day before that!

WALTER: [*Defensively.*] I'm interested in you. Something wrong with that? Ain't many girls who decide—

WALTER AND BENEATHA: [*In unison.*] —"to be a doctor."
   [*Silence.*]

WALTER: Have we figured out yet just exactly how much medical school is going to cost?

RUTH: Walter Lee, why don't you leave that girl alone and get out of here to work?

BENEATHA: [*Exits to the bathroom and bangs on the door.*] Come on out of there, please!
   [*She comes back into the room.*]

WALTER: [*Looking at his sister intently.*] You know the check is coming tomorrow.

BENEATHA: [*Turning on him with a sharpness all her own.*] That money belongs to Mama, Walter, and it's for her to decide how she wants to use it. I don't care if she wants to buy a house or a rocket ship or just nail it up somewhere and look at it. It's hers. Not ours—*hers*.

WALTER: [*Bitterly.*] Now ain't that fine! You just got your mother's interest at heart, ain't you, girl? You such a nice girl—but if Mama got that money she can always take a few thousand and help you through school too—can't she?

BENEATHA: I have never asked anyone around here to do anything for me.

WALTER: No! And the line between asking and just accepting when the time comes is big and wide—ain't it!

BENEATHA: [*With fury.*] What do you want from me, Brother—that I quit school or just drop dead, which!

WALTER: I don't want nothing but for you to stop acting holy 'round here. Me and Ruth done made some sacrifices for you—why can't you do something for the family?

RUTH: Walter, don't be dragging me in it.

WALTER: You are in it—Don't you get up and go work in somebody's kitchen for the last three years to help put clothes on her back?

RUTH: Oh, Walter—that's not fair . . .

WALTER: It ain't that nobody expects you to get on your knees and say thank you, Brother; thank you, Ruth; thank you, Mama— and thank you, Travis, for wearing the same pair of shoes for two semesters—

BENEATHA: [*Dropping to her knees.*] Well—I *do*—all right?—thank everybody . . . and forgive me for ever wanting to be anything at all . . . forgive me, forgive me!

RUTH: Please stop it! Your mama'll hear you.

WALTER: Who the hell told you you had to be a doctor? If you so crazy 'bout messing 'round with sick people—then go be a nurse like other women—or just get married and be quiet . . .

BENEATHA: Well—you finally got it said . . . it took you three years but you finally got it said. Walter, give up; leave me alone—it's Mama's money.

WALTER: *He was my father, too!*

BENEATHA: So what? He was mine, too—and Travis' grandfather— but the insurance money belongs to Mama. Picking on me is not going to make her give it to you to invest in any liquor stores— [*Underbreath, dropping into a chair.*]—and I for one say, God bless Mama for that!

WALTER: [*To* RUTH.] See—did you hear? Did you hear!

RUTH: Honey, please go to work.

WALTER: Nobody in this house is ever going to understand me.

BENEATHA: Because you're a nut.

WALTER: Who's a nut?

BENEATHA: You—you are a nut. Thee is mad, boy.

WALTER: [*Looking at his wife and his sister from the door, very sadly.*] The world's most backward race of people, and that's a fact.

BENEATHA: [*Turning slowly in her chair.*] And then there are all those prophets who would lead us out of the wilderness— [WALTER *slams out of the house.*] —into the swamps!

RUTH: Bennie, why you always gotta be pickin' on your brother? Can't you be a little sweeter sometimes? [*Door opens.* WALTER *walks in.*]

WALTER: [*To* RUTH.] I need some money for carfare.

RUTH: [*Looks at him, then warms; teasing, but tenderly.*] Fifty cents? [*She goes to her bag and gets money.*] Here, take a taxi.

[WALTER *exits.* MAMA *enters. She is a woman in her early sixties, full-bodied and strong. She is one of those women of a certain grace and beauty who wear it so unobtrusively that it takes a while to notice. Her dark-brown face is surrounded by the total whiteness of her hair, and, being a woman who has adjusted to many things in life and overcome many more, her face is full of strength. She has, we can see, wit and faith of a kind that keep her eyes lit and full of interest and expectancy. She is, in a word, a beautiful woman. Her bearing is perhaps most like the noble bearing of the women of the Hereros of Southwest Africa—rather as if she imagines that as she walks she still bears a basket or a vessel upon her head. Her speech, on the other hand, is as careless as her carriage is precise—she is inclined to slur everything—but her voice is perhaps not so much quiet as simply soft.*]

MAMA: Who that 'round here slamming doors at this hour?

[*She crosses through the room, goes to the window, opens it, and brings in a feeble little plant growing doggedly in a small pot on the window sill. She feels the dirt and puts it back out.*]

RUTH: That was Walter Lee. He and Bennie was at it again.

MAMA: My children and they tempers. Lord, if this little old plant don't get more sun than it's been getting it ain't never going to see spring again. [*She turns from the window.*] What's the matter with you this morning, Ruth? You looks right peaked. You aiming to iron all them things? Leave some for me. I'll get to 'em this afternoon. Bennie honey, it's too drafty for you to be sitting 'round half dressed. Where's your robe?

BENEATHA: In the cleaners.

MAMA: Well, go get mine and put it on.

BENEATHA: I'm not cold, Mama, honest.

MAMA: I know—but you so thin . . .

BENEATHA: [*Irritably.*] Mama, I'm not cold.

MAMA: [*Seeing the make-down bed as* TRAVIS *has left it.*] Lord have mercy, look at that poor bed. Bless his heart—he tries, don't he?

[*She moves to the bed* TRAVIS *has sloppily made up.*]

RUTH: No—he don't half try at all 'cause he knows you going to come along behind him and fix everything. That's just how come he don't know how to do nothing right now—you done spoiled that boy so.

MAMA: Well—he's a little boy. Ain't supposed to know 'bout housekeeping. My baby, that's what he is. What you fix for his breakfast this morning?

RUTH: [*Angrily.*] I feed my son, Lena!

MAMA: I ain't meddling— [*Underbreath; busy-bodyish.*] I just noticed all last week he had cold cereal, and when it starts getting this chilly in the fall a child ought to have some hot grits or something when he goes out in the cold—

RUTH: [*Furious.*] I gave him hot oats—is that all right!

MAMA: I ain't meddling. [*Pause.*] Put a lot of nice butter on it? [RUTH *shoots her an angry look and does not reply.*] He likes lots of butter.

RUTH: [*Exasperated.*] Lena—

MAMA: [*To* BENEATHA. MAMA *is inclined to wander conversationally sometimes.*] What was you and your brother fussing 'bout this morning?

BENEATHA: It's not important, Mama.

[*She gets up and goes to look out at the bathroom, which is apparently free, and she picks up her towels and rushes out.*]

MAMA: What was they fighting about?

RUTH: Now you know as well as I do.

MAMA: [*Shaking her head.*] Brother still worrying hisself sick about that money?

RUTH: You know he is.

MAMA: You had breakfast?

RUTH: Some coffee.

MAMA: Girl, you better start eating and looking after yourself better. You almost thin as Travis.

RUTH: Lena—

MAMA: Un-hunh?

RUTH: What are you going to do with it?

MAMA: Now don't you start, child. It's too early in the morning to be talking about money. It ain't Christian.

RUTH: It's just that he got his heart set on that store—

MAMA: You mean that liquor store that Willy Harris want him to invest in?

RUTH: Yes—

MAMA: We ain't no business people, Ruth. We just plain working folks.

RUTH: Ain't nobody business people till they go into business. Walter Lee say colored people ain't never going to start getting ahead till they start gambling on some different kinds of things in the world—investments and things.

MAMA: What done got into you, girl? Walter Lee done finally sold you on investing.

RUTH: No. Mama, something is happening between Walter and me. I don't know what it is—but he needs something—something I can't give him anymore. He needs this chance, Lena.

MAMA: [*Frowning deeply.*] But liquor, honey—

RUTH: Well—like Walter say—I spec people going to always be drinking themselves some liquor.

MAMA: Well—whether they drinks it or not ain't none of my business. But whether I go into business selling it to 'em *is,* and I don't want that on my ledger this late in life. [*Stopping suddenly and studying her daughter-in-law.*] Ruth Younger, what's the matter with you today? You look like you could fall over right there.

RUTH: I'm tired.

MAMA: Then you better stay home from work today.

RUTH: I can't stay home. She'd be calling up the agency and screaming at them, "My girl didn't come in today—send me somebody! My girl didn't come in!" Oh, she just have a fit . . .

MAMA: Well, let her have it. I'll just call her up and say you got the flu—

RUTH: [*Laughing.*] Why the flu?

MAMA: 'Cause it sounds respectable to 'em. Something white people get, too. They know 'bout the flu. Otherwise they think you been cut up or something when you tell 'em you sick.

RUTH: I got to go in. We need the money.

MAMA: Somebody would of thought my children done all but starved to death the way they talk about money here late. Child, we got a great big old check coming tomorrow.

RUTH: [*Sincerely, but also self-righteously.*] Now that's your money. It ain't got nothing to do with me. We all feel like that—Walter and Bennie and me—even Travis.

MAMA: [*Thoughtfully, and suddenly very far away.*] Ten thousand dollars—

RUTH: Sure is wonderful.

MAMA: Ten thousand dollars.

RUTH: You know what you should do, Miss Lena? You should take yourself a trip somewhere. To Europe or South America or someplace—

MAMA: [*Throwing up her hands at the thought.*] Oh, child!

RUTH: I'm serious. Just pack up and leave! Go on away and enjoy yourself some. Forget about the family and have yourself a ball for once in your life—

MAMA: [*Drily.*] You sound like I'm just about ready to die. Who'd go with me? What I look like wandering 'round Europe by myself?

RUTH: Shoot—these here rich white women do it all the time. They don't think nothing of packing up they suitcases and piling on one of them big steamships and—swoosh!—they gone, child.

MAMA: Something always told me I wasn't no rich white woman.

RUTH: Well—what are you going to do with it then?

MAMA: I ain't rightly decided. [*Thinking. She speaks now with emphasis.*] Some of it got to be put away for Beneatha and her schoolin'—and ain't nothing going to touch that part of it. Nothing. [*She waits several seconds, trying to make up her mind about something, and looks at* RUTH *a little tentatively before going on.*] Been thinking that we maybe could meet the notes on a little old two-story somewhere, with a yard where Travis could play in the summertime, if we use part of the insurance for a down payment and everybody kind of pitch in. I could maybe take on a little day work again, few days a week—

RUTH: [*Studying her mother-in-law furtively and concentrating on her ironing, anxious to encourage without seeming to.*] Well, Lord knows, we've put enough rent into this here rat trap to pay for four houses by now . . .

MAMA: [*Looking up at the words "rat trap" and then looking around and leaning back and sighing—in a suddenly reflective mood—*] "Rat trap"—yes, that's all it is. [*Smiling.*] I remember just as well the day me and Big Walter moved in here. Hadn't been married but two weeks and wasn't planning on living here no more than a year. [*She shakes her head at the dissolved dream.*] We was going to set away, little by little, don't you know, and buy a little place out in Morgan Park.[5] We had even picked out the house. [*Chuckling a little.*] Looks right dumpy today. But Lord, child, you should know all the dreams I had 'bout buying that house and fixing it up and making me a little garden in the back— [*She waits and stops smiling.*] And didn't none of it happen.

[*Dropping her hands in a futile gesture.*]

RUTH: [*Keeps her head down, ironing.*] Yes, life can be a barrel of disappointments, sometimes.

MAMA: Honey, Big Walter would come in here some nights back then and slump down on that couch there and just look at the rug, and look at me and look at the rug and then back at me— and I'd know he was down then . . . really down. [*After a second very long and thoughtful pause; she is seeing back to times that only she can see.*] And then, Lord, when I lost that baby—little Claude—I almost thought I was going to lose Big Walter too. Oh, that man grieved hisself! He was one man to love his children.

RUTH: Ain't nothin' can tear at you like losin' your baby.

MAMA: I guess that's how come that man finally worked hisself to death like he done. Like he was fighting his own war with this here world that took his baby from him.

RUTH: He sure was a fine man, all right. I always liked Mr. Younger.

---

5. Respectable neighborhood on the extreme Southside of Chicago, largely populated with Irish and African Americans.

MAMA: Crazy 'bout his children! God knows there was plenty wrong with Walter Younger—hard-headed, mean, kind of wild with women—plenty wrong with him. But he sure loved his children. Always wanted them to have something—be something. That's where Brother gets all these notions, I reckon. Big Walter used to say, he'd get right wet in the eyes sometimes, lean his head back with the water standing in his eyes and say, "Seem like God didn't see fit to give the black man nothing but dreams—but He did give us children to make them dreams seem worthwhile." [*She smiles.*] He could talk like that, don't you know.

RUTH: Yes, he sure could. He was a good man, Mr. Younger.

MAMA: Yes, a fine man—just couldn't never catch up with his dreams, that's all.

[BENEATHA *comes in, brushing her hair and looking up to the ceiling, where the sound of a vacuum cleaner has started up.*]

BENEATHA: What could be so dirty on that woman's rugs that she has to vacuum them every single day?

RUTH: I wish certain young women 'round here who I could name would take inspiration about certain rugs in a certain apartment I could also mention.

BENEATHA: [*Shrugging.*] How much cleaning can a house need, for Christ's sakes.

MAMA: [*Not liking the Lord's name used thus.*] Bennie!

RUTH: Just listen to her—just listen!

BENEATHA: Oh, God!

MAMA: If you use the Lord's name just one more time—

BENEATHA: [*A bit of a whine.*] Oh, Mama—

RUTH: Fresh—just fresh as salt, this girl!

BENEATHA: [*Drily.*] Well—if the salt loses its savor—[6]

MAMA: Now that will do. I just ain't going to have you 'round here reciting the scriptures in vain—you hear me?

BENEATHA: How did I manage to get on everybody's wrong side by just walking into a room?

RUTH: If you weren't so fresh—

BENEATHA: Ruth, I'm twenty years old.

6. See Matthew 5:13: "You are the salt of the earth. But if the salt loses its taste, with what can it be seasoned? It is no longer good for anything but to be thrown out and trampled underfoot."

MAMA: What time you be home from school today?

BENEATHA: Kind of late. [*With enthusiasm.*] Madeline is going to start my guitar lessons today.

> [MAMA *and* RUTH *look up with the same expression.*]

MAMA: Your *what* kind of lessons?

BENEATHA: Guitar.

RUTH: Oh, Father!

MAMA: How come you done taken it in your mind to learn to play the guitar?

BENEATHA: I just want to, that's all.

MAMA: [*Smiling.*] Lord, child, don't you know what to do with yourself? How long it going to be before you get tired of this now—like you got tired of that little play-acting group you joined last year? [*Looking at* RUTH.] And what was it the year before that?

RUTH: The horseback-riding club for which she bought that fifty-five-dollar riding habit that's been hanging in the closet ever since!

MAMA: [*To* BENEATHA.] Why you got to flit so from one thing to another, baby?

BENEATHA: [*Sharply.*] I just want to learn to play the guitar. Is there anything wrong with that?

MAMA: Ain't nobody trying to stop you. I just wonders sometimes why you has to flit so from one thing to another all the time. You ain't never done nothing with all that camera equipment you brought home—

BENEATHA: I don't flit! I—I experiment with different forms of expression—

RUTH: Like riding a horse?

BENEATHA: —People have to express themselves one way or another.

MAMA: What is it you want to express?

BENEATHA: [*Angrily.*] Me! [MAMA *and* RUTH *look at each other and burst into raucous laughter.*] Don't worry—I don't expect you to understand.

MAMA: [*To change the subject.*] Who you going out with tomorrow night?

BENEATHA: [*With displeasure.*] George Murchison again.

MAMA: [*Pleased.*] Oh—you getting a little sweet on him?

RUTH: You ask me, this child ain't sweet on nobody but herself—[*Underbreath.*] Express herself!

[*They laugh.*]

BENEATHA: Oh—I like George all right, Mama. I mean I like him enough to go out with him and stuff, but—

RUTH: [*For devilment.*] What does *and stuff* mean?

BENEATHA: Mind your own business.

MAMA: Stop picking at her now, Ruth. [*A thoughtful pause, and then a suspicious sudden look at her daughter as she turns in her chair for emphasis.*] What *does* it mean?

BENEATHA: [*Wearily.*] Oh, I just mean I couldn't ever really be serious about George. He's—he's so shallow.

RUTH: Shallow—what do you mean he's shallow? He's *rich!*

MAMA: Hush, Ruth.

BENEATHA: I know he's rich. He knows he's rich, too.

RUTH: Well—what other qualities a man got to have to satisfy you, little girl?

BENEATHA: You wouldn't even begin to understand. Anybody who married Walter could not possibly understand.

MAMA: [*Outraged.*] What kind of way is that to talk about your brother?

BENEATHA: Brother is a flip—let's face it.

MAMA: [*To* RUTH, *helplessly.*] What's a flip?

RUTH: [*Glad to add kindling.*] She's saying he's crazy.

BENEATHA: Not crazy. Brother isn't really crazy yet—he—he's an elaborate neurotic.

MAMA: Hush your mouth!

BENEATHA: As for George. Well. George looks good—he's got a beautiful car and he takes me to nice places and, as my sister-in-law says, he is probably the richest boy I will ever get to know and I even like him sometimes—but if the Youngers are sitting around waiting to see if their little Bennie is going to tie up the family with the Murchisons, they are wasting their time.

RUTH: You mean you wouldn't marry George Murchison if he asked you someday? That pretty, rich thing? Honey, I knew you was odd—

BENEATHA: No I would not marry him if all I felt for him was what I feel now. Besides, George's family wouldn't really like it.

MAMA: Why not?

BENEATHA: Oh, Mama—The Murchisons are honest-to-God-real-*live*-rich colored people, and the only people in the world who are more snobbish than rich white people are rich colored people. I thought everybody knew that. I've met Mrs. Murchison. She's a scene!

MAMA: You must not dislike people 'cause they well off, honey.

BENEATHA: Why not? It makes just as much sense as disliking people 'cause they are poor, and lots of people do that.

RUTH: [*A wisdom-of-the-ages manner. To* MAMA.] Well, she'll get over some of this—

BENEATHA: Get over it? What are you talking about, Ruth? Listen, I'm going to be a doctor. I'm not worried about who I'm going to marry yet—if I ever get married.

MAMA AND RUTH: *If!*

MAMA: Now, Bennie—

BENEATHA: Oh, I probably will . . . but first I'm going to be a doctor, and George, for one, still thinks that's pretty funny. I couldn't be bothered with that. I am going to be a doctor and everybody around here better understand that!

MAMA: [*Kindly.*] 'Course you going to be a doctor, honey, God willing.

BENEATHA: [*Drily.*] God hasn't got a thing to do with it.

MAMA: Beneatha—that just wasn't necessary.

BENEATHA: Well—neither is God. I get sick of hearing about God.

MAMA: Beneatha!

BENEATHA: I mean it! I'm just tired of hearing about God all the time. What has He got to do with anything? Does He pay tuition?

MAMA: You 'bout to get your fresh little jaw slapped!

RUTH: That's just what she needs, all right!

BENEATHA: Why? Why can't I say what I want to around here, like everybody else?

MAMA: It don't sound nice for a young girl to say things like that—you wasn't brought up that way. Me and your father went to trouble to get you and Brother to church every Sunday.

BENEATHA: Mama, you don't understand. It's all a matter of ideas, and God is just one idea I don't accept. It's not important. I am not going out and be immoral or commit crimes because I don't believe in God. I don't even think about it. It's just that I get tired of Him getting credit for all the things the human race achieves through its own stubborn effort. There simply is no blasted God—there is only man and it is he who makes miracles!

[MAMA *absorbs this speech, studies her daughter and rises slowly and crosses to* BENEATHA *and slaps her powerfully across the face. After, there is only silence and the daughter drops her eyes from her mother's face, and* MAMA *is very tall before her.*]

MAMA: Now—you say after me, in my mother's house there is still God. [*There is a long pause and* BENEATHA *stares at the floor wordlessly.* MAMA *repeats the phrase with precision and cool emotion.*] In my mother's house there is still God.

BENEATHA: In my mother's house there is still God.

[*A long pause.*]

MAMA: [*Walking away from* BENEATHA, *too disturbed for triumphant posture. Stopping and turning back to her daughter.*] There are some ideas we ain't going to have in this house. Not long as I am at the head of this family.

BENEATHA: Yes, ma'am.

[MAMA *walks out of the room.*]

RUTH: [*Almost gently, with profound understanding.*] You think you a woman, Bennie—but you still a little girl. What you did was childish—so you got treated like a child.

BENEATHA: I see. [*Quietly.*] I also see that everybody thinks it's all right for Mama to be a tyrant. But all the tyranny in the world will never put a God in the heavens!

[*She picks up her books and goes out.*]

RUTH: [*Goes to* MAMA'*s door.*] She said she was sorry.

MAMA: [*Coming out, going to her plant.*] They frightens me, Ruth. My children.

RUTH: You got good children, Lena. They just a little off sometimes—but they're good.

MAMA: No—there's something come down between me and them that don't let us understand each other and I don't know what it is. One done almost lost his mind thinking 'bout money all the time and the other done commence to talk about things I can't seem to understand in no form or fashion. What is it that's changing, Ruth?

RUTH: [*Soothingly, older than her years.*] Now . . . you taking it all too seriously. You just got strong-willed children and it takes a strong woman like you to keep 'em in hand.

MAMA: [*Looking at her plant and sprinkling a little water on it.*] They spirited all right, my children. Got to admit they got spirit— Bennie and Walter. Like this little old plant that ain't never had enough sunshine or nothing—and look at it . . .

[*She has her back to* RUTH, *who has had to stop ironing and lean against something and put the back of her hand to her forehead.*]

RUTH: [*Trying to keep* MAMA *from noticing.*] You . . . sure . . . loves that little old thing, don't you? . . .

MAMA: Well, I always wanted me a garden like I used to see sometimes at the back of the houses down home. This plant is close as I ever got to having one. [*She looks out of the window as she replaces the plant.*] Lord, ain't nothing as dreary as the view from this window on a dreary day, is there? Why ain't you singing this morning, Ruth? Sing that "No Ways Tired."[7] That song always lifts me up so— [*She turns at last to see that* RUTH *has slipped quietly into a chair, in a state of semiconsciousness.*] Ruth! Ruth honey—what's the matter with you . . . Ruth!

[*Curtain.*]

SCENE TWO

It is the following morning; a Saturday morning, and house cleaning is in progress at the Youngers. Furniture has been shoved hither and yon and MAMA *is giving the kitchen-area walls a washing down.* BENEATHA, *in dungarees, with a handkerchief tied around her face, is spraying insecticide into the cracks in the walls. As they work, the radio is on and a Southside disk-jockey program is inappropriately filling the house with a rather exotic saxophone blues.* TRAVIS, *the sole idle one, is leaning on his arms, looking out of the window.*

TRAVIS: Grandmama, that stuff Bennie is using smells awful. Can I go downstairs, please?

---

7. "I Don't Feel No Ways Tired," a gospel song by the Reverend James Cleveland (1931–1991).

MAMA: Did you get all them chores done already? I ain't seen you doing much.

TRAVIS: Yes'm—finished early. Where did Mama go this morning?

MAMA: [*Looking at* BENEATHA.] She had to go on a little errand.

TRAVIS: Where?

MAMA: To tend to her business.

TRAVIS: Can I go outside then?

MAMA: Oh, I guess so. You better stay right in front of the house, though . . . and keep a good lookout for the postman.

TRAVIS: Yes'm. [*He starts out and decides to give his aunt* BENEATHA *a good swat on the legs as he passes her.*] Leave them poor little old cockroaches alone, they ain't bothering you none.

[*He runs as she swings the spray gun at him both viciously and playfully.* WALTER *enters from the bedroom and goes to the phone.*]

MAMA: Look out there, girl, before you be spilling some of that stuff on that child!

TRAVIS: [*Teasing.*] That's right—look out now!

[*He exits.*]

BENEATHA: [*Drily.*] I can't imagine that it would hurt him—it has never hurt the roaches.

MAMA: Well, little boys' hides ain't as tough as Southside roaches.

WALTER: [*Into phone.*] Hello—Let me talk to Willy Harris.

MAMA: You better get over there behind the bureau. I seen one marching out of there like Napoleon yesterday.

WALTER: Hello, Willy? It ain't come yet. It'll be here in a few minutes. Did the lawyer give you the papers?

BENEATHA: There's really only one way to get rid of them, Mama—

MAMA: How?

BENEATHA: Set fire to this building.

WALTER: Good. Good. I'll be right over.

BENEATHA: Where did Ruth go, Walter?

WALTER: I don't know.

[*He exits abruptly.*]

BENEATHA: Mama, where did Ruth go?

MAMA: [*Looking at her with meaning.*] To the doctor, I think.

BENEATHA: The doctor? What's the matter? [*They exchange glances.*] You don't think—

MAMA: [*With her sense of drama.*] Now I ain't saying what I think. But I ain't never been wrong 'bout a woman neither.

[*The phone rings.*]

BENEATHA: [*At the phone.*] Hay-lo . . . [*Pause, and a moment of recognition.*] Well— when did you get back! . . . And how was it? . . . Of course I've missed you—in my way . . . This morning? No . . . house cleaning and all that and Mama hates it if I let people come over when the house is like this . . . You *have?* Well, that's different . . . What is it—Oh, what the hell, come on over . . . Right, see you then.

[*She hangs up.*]

MAMA: [*Who has listened vigorously, as is her habit.*] Who is that you inviting over here with this house looking like this? You ain't got the pride you was born with!

BENEATHA: Asagai doesn't care how houses look, Mama—he's an intellectual.

MAMA: *Who?*

BENEATHA: Asagai—Joseph Asagai. He's an African boy I met on campus. He's been studying in Canada all summer.

MAMA: What's his name?

BENEATHA: Asagai, Joseph. Ah-sah-guy . . . He's from Nigeria.

MAMA: Oh, that's the little country that was founded by slaves way back . . .

BENEATHA: No, Mama—that's Liberia.

MAMA: I don't think I never met no African before.

BENEATHA: Well, do me a favor and don't ask him a whole lot of ignorant questions about Africans. I mean, do they wear clothes and all that—

MAMA: Well, now, I guess if you think we so ignorant 'round here maybe you shouldn't bring your friends here—

BENEATHA: It's just that people ask such crazy things. All anyone seems to know about when it comes to Africa is Tarzan—

MAMA: [*Indignantly.*] Why should I know anything about Africa?

BENEATHA: Why do you give money at church for the missionary work?

MAMA: Well, that's to help save people.

BENEATHA: You mean save them from *heathenism*—

MAMA: [*Innocently.*] Yes.

BENEATHA: I'm afraid they need more salvation from the British and the French.[8]

> [RUTH *comes in forlornly and pulls off her coat with dejection. They both turn to look at her.*]

RUTH: [*Dispiritedly.*] Well, I guess from all the happy faces—everybody knows.

BENEATHA: You pregnant?

MAMA: Lord have mercy, I sure hope it's a little old girl. Travis ought to have a sister.

> [BENEATHA *and* RUTH *give her a hopeless look for this grandmotherly enthusiasm.*]

BENEATHA: How far along are you?

RUTH: Two months.

BENEATHA: Did you mean to? I mean did you plan it or was it an accident?

MAMA: What do you know about planning or not planning?

BENEATHA: Oh, Mama.

RUTH: [*Wearily.*] She's twenty years old, Lena.

BENEATHA: Did you plan it, Ruth?

RUTH: Mind your own business.

BENEATHA: It is my business—where is he going to live, on the roof? [*There is silence following the remark as the three women react to the sense of it.*] Gee—I didn't mean that, Ruth, honest. Gee, I don't feel like that at all. I—I think it is wonderful.

RUTH: [*Dully.*] Wonderful.

BENEATHA: Yes—really.

MAMA: [*Looking at* RUTH, *worried.*] Doctor say everything going to be all right?

RUTH: [*Far away.*] Yes—she says everything is going to be fine . . .

MAMA: [*Immediately suspicious.*] "She"—What doctor you went to?

> [RUTH *folds over, near hysteria.*]

MAMA: [*Worriedly hovering over* RUTH.] Ruth honey—what's the matter with you— you sick?

---

8. In the 1950s, seven African nations won their independence from European colonizers. In 1959, over forty other countries were still controlled by foreign powers, mostly France and Great Britain.

[RUTH *has her fists clenched on her thighs and is fighting hard to suppress a scream that seems to be rising in her.*]

BENEATHA: What's the matter with her, Mama?

MAMA: [*Working her fingers in* RUTH'*s shoulder to relax her.*] She be all right. Women gets right depressed sometimes when they get her way. [*Speaking softly, expertly, rapidly.*] Now you just relax. That's right . . . just lean back, don't think 'bout nothing at all . . . nothing at all—

RUTH: I'm all right . . .

[*The glassy-eyed look melts and then she collapses into a fit of heavy sobbing. The bell rings.*]

BENEATHA: Oh, my God—that must be Asagai.

MAMA: [*To* RUTH.] Come on now, honey. You need to lie down and rest awhile . . . then have some nice hot food.

[*They exit,* RUTH'*s weight on her mother-in-law.* BENEATHA, *herself profoundly disturbed, opens the door to admit a rather dramatic-looking young man with a large package.*]

ASAGAI: Hello, Alaiyo—

BENEATHA: [*Holding the door open and regarding him with pleasure.*] Hello . . . [*Long pause.*] Well—come in. And please excuse everything. My mother was very upset about my letting anyone come here with the place like this.

ASAGAI: [*Coming into the room.*] You look disturbed too . . . Is something wrong?

BENEATHA: [*Still at the door, absently.*] Yes . . . we've all got acute ghettoitus. [*She smiles and comes toward him, finding a cigarette and sitting.*] So—sit down! How was Canada?

ASAGAI: [*A sophisticate.*] Canadian.

BENEATHA: [*Looking at him.*] I'm very glad you are back.

ASAGAI: [*Looking back at her in turn.*] Are you really?

BENEATHA: Yes—very.

ASAGAI: Why—you were quite glad when I went away. What happened?

BENEATHA: You went away.

ASAGAI: Ahhhhhhhh.

BENEATHA: Before you wanted to be so serious before there was time.

ASAGAI: How much time must there be before one knows what one feels?

BENEATHA: [*Stalling this particular conversation. Her hands pressed together, in a deliberately childish gesture.*] What did you bring me?

ASAGAI: [*Handing her the package.*] Open it and see.

BENEATHA: [*Eagerly opening the package and drawing out some records and the colorful robes of a Nigerian woman.*] Oh, Asagai! . . . You got them for me! . . . How beautiful . . . and the records too! [*She lifts out the robes and runs to the mirror with them and holds the drapery up in front of herself.*]

ASAGAI: [*Coming to her at the mirror.*] I shall have to teach you how to drape it properly. [*He flings the material about her for the moment and stands back to look at her.*] Ah—*Oh-pay-gay-day, oh-gbah-mu-shay.* [*A Yoruba exclamation for admiration.*] You wear it well . . . very well . . . mutilated hair and all.

BENEATHA: [*Turning suddenly.*] My hair—what's wrong with my hair?

ASAGAI: [*Shrugging.*] Were you born with it like that?

BENEATHA: [*Reaching up to touch it.*] No . . . of course not.
[*She looks back to the mirror, disturbed.*]

ASAGAI: [*Smiling.*] How then?

BENEATHA: You know perfectly well how . . . as crinkly as yours . . . that's how.

ASAGAI: And it is ugly to you that way?

BENEATHA: [*Quickly.*] Oh, no—not ugly . . . [*More slowly, apologetically.*] But it's so hard to manage when it's, well—raw.

ASAGAI: And so to accommodate that—you mutilate it every week?

BENEATHA: It's not mutilation!

ASAGAI: [*Laughing aloud at her seriousness.*] Oh . . . please! I am only teasing you because you are so very serious about these things. [*He stands back from her and folds his arms across his chest as he watches her pulling at her hair and frowning in the mirror.*] Do you remember the first time you met me at school? . . . [*He laughs.*] You came up to me and you said—and I thought you were the most serious little thing I had ever seen—you said: [*He imitates her.*] "Mr. Asagai—I want very much to talk with you. About Africa. You see, Mr. Asagai, I am looking for my *identity!*"
[*He laughs.*]

BENEATHA: [*Turning to him, not laughing.*] Yes—
[*Her face is quizzical, profoundly disturbed.*]

ASAGAI: [*Still teasing and reaching out and taking her face in his hands and turning her profile to him.*] Well . . . it is true that this is not so much a profile of a Hollywood queen as perhaps a queen of the Nile— [*A mock dismissal of the importance of the question.*] But what does it matter? Assimilationism[9] is so popular in your country.

BENEATHA: [*Wheeling, passionately, sharply.*] I am not an assimilationist!

ASAGAI: [*The protest hangs in the room for a moment and* ASAGAI *studies her, his laughter fading.*] Such a serious one. [*There is a pause.*] So—you like the robes? You must take excellent care of them— they are from my sister's personal wardrobe.

BENEATHA: [*With incredulity.*] You—you sent all the way home—for me?

ASAGAI: [*With charm.*] For you—I would do much more . . . Well, that is what I came for. I must go.

BENEATHA: Will you call me Monday?

ASAGAI: Yes . . . We have a great deal to talk about. I mean about identity and time and all that.

BENEATHA: Time?

ASAGAI: Yes. About how much time one needs to know what one feels.

BENEATHA: You never understood that there is more than one kind of feeling which can exist between a man and a woman—or, at least, there should be.

ASAGAI: [*Shaking his head negatively but gently.*] No. Between a man and a woman there need be only one kind of feeling. I have that for you . . . Now even . . . right this moment . . .

BENEATHA: I know—and by itself—it won't do. I can find that anywhere.

ASAGAI: For a woman it should be enough.

BENEATHA: I know—because that's what it says in all the novels that men write. But it isn't. Go ahead and laugh—but I'm not interested in being someone's little episode in America or— [*With feminine vengeance.*] —one of them! [ASAGAI *has burst into laughter again.*] That's funny as hell, huh!

9. A minority or marginalized culture molding itself into the majority or mainstream culture.

ASAGAI: It's just that every American girl I have known has said that to me. White—black—in this you are all the same. And the same speech, too!

BENEATHA: [*Angrily.*] Yuk, yuk, yuk!

ASAGAI: It's how you can be sure that the world's most liberated women are not liberated at all. You all talk about it too much!

[MAMA *enters and is immediately all social charm because of the presence of a guest.*]

BENEATHA: Oh—Mama—this is Mr. Asagai.

MAMA: How do you do?

ASAGAI: [*Total politeness to an elder.*] How do you do, Mrs. Younger. Please forgive me for coming at such an outrageous hour on a Saturday.

MAMA: Well, you are quite welcome. I just hope you understand that our house don't always look like this. [*Chatterish.*] You must come again. I would love to hear all about— [*Not sure of the name.*] —your country. I think it's so sad the way our American Negroes don't know nothing about Africa 'cept Tarzan and all that. And all that money they pour into these churches when they ought to be helping you people over there drive out them French and Englishmen done taken away your land.

[*The mother flashes a slightly superior look at her daughter upon completion of the recitation.*]

ASAGAI: [*Taken aback by this sudden and acutely unrelated expression of sympathy.*] Yes . . . yes . . .

MAMA: [*Smiling at him suddenly and relaxing and looking him over.*] How many miles is it from here to where you come from?

ASAGAI: Many thousands.

MAMA: [*Looking at him as she would* WALTER.] I bet you don't half look after yourself, being away from your mama either. I spec you better come 'round here from time to time and get yourself some decent home-cooked meals . . .

ASAGAI: [*Moved.*] Thank you. Thank you very much. [*They are all quiet, then—*] Well . . . I must go. I will call you Monday, Alaiyo.

MAMA: What's that he call you?

ASAGAI: Oh—"Alaiyo." I hope you don't mind. It is what you would call a nickname, I think. It is a Yoruba word. I am a Yoruba.

MAMA: [*Looking at* BENEATHA.] I—I thought he was from—

ASAGAI: [*Understanding.*] Nigeria is my country. Yoruba is my tribal origin—

BENEATHA: You didn't tell us what Alaiyo means . . . for all I know, you might be calling me Little Idiot or something . . .

ASAGAI: Well . . . let me see . . . I do not know how just to explain it . . . The sense of a thing can be so different when it changes languages.

BENEATHA: You're evading.

ASAGAI: No—really it is difficult . . . [*Thinking.*] It means . . . it means One for Whom Bread—Food—Is Not Enough. [*He looks at her.*] Is that all right?

BENEATHA: [*Understanding, softly.*] Thank you.

MAMA: [*Looking from one to the other and not understanding any of it.*] Well . . . that's nice . . . You must come see us again— Mr.—

ASAGAI: Ah-sah-guy . . .

MAMA: Yes . . . Do come again.

ASAGAI: Good-bye.

[*He exits.*]

MAMA: [*After him.*] Lord, that's a pretty thing just went out here! [*Insinuatingly, to her daughter.*] Yes, I guess I see why we done commence to get so interested in Africa 'round here. Missionaries my aunt Jenny!

[*She exits.*]

BENEATHA: Oh, Mama! . . .

[*She picks up the Nigerian dress and holds it up to her in front of the mirror again. She sets the headdress on haphazardly and then notices her hair again and clutches at it and then replaces the headdress and frowns at herself. Then she starts to wriggle in front of the mirror as she thinks a Nigerian woman might.* TRAVIS *enters and regards her.*]

TRAVIS: You cracking up?

BENEATHA: Shut up.

[*She pulls the headdress off and looks at herself in the mirror and clutches at her hair again and squinches her eyes as if trying to imagine something. Then, suddenly, she gets her raincoat and kerchief and hurriedly prepares for going out.*]

MAMA: [*Coming back into the room.*] She's resting now. Travis, baby, run next door and ask Miss Johnson to please let me have a little kitchen cleanser. This here can is empty as Jacob's kettle.

TRAVIS: I just came in.

MAMA: Do as you told. [*He exits and she looks at her daughter.*] Where you going?

BENEATHA: [*Halting at the door.*] To become a queen of the Nile!

[*She exits in a breathless blaze of glory.* RUTH *appears in the bedroom doorway.*]

MAMA: Who told you to get up?

RUTH: Ain't nothing wrong with me to be lying in no bed for. Where did Bennie go?

MAMA: [*Drumming her fingers.*] Far as I could make out—to Egypt. [RUTH *just looks at her.*] What time is it getting to?

RUTH: Ten twenty. And the mailman going to ring that bell this morning just like he done every morning for the last umpteen years.

[TRAVIS *comes in with the cleanser can.*]

TRAVIS: She say to tell you that she don't have much.

MAMA: [*Angrily.*] Lord, some people I could name sure is tight-fisted! [*Directing her grandson.*] Mark two cans of cleanser down on the list there. If she that hard up for kitchen cleanser, I sure don't want to forget to get her none!

RUTH: Lena—maybe the woman is just short on cleanser—

MAMA: [*Not listening.*] —Much baking powder as she done borrowed from me all these years, she could of done gone into the baking business!

[*The bell sounds suddenly and sharply and all three are stunned—serious and silent— mid-speech. In spite of all the other conversations and distractions of the morning, this is what they have been waiting for, even* TRAVIS, *who looks helplessly from his mother to his grandmother.* RUTH *is the first to come to life again.*]

RUTH: [*To* TRAVIS.] *Get down them steps, boy!*

[TRAVIS *snaps to life and flies out to get the mail.*]

MAMA: [*Her eyes wide, her hand to her breast.*] You mean it done really come?

RUTH: [*Excited.*] Oh, Miss Lena!

MAMA: [*Collecting herself.*] Well . . . I don't know what we all so excited about 'round here for. We known it was coming for months.

RUTH: That's a whole lot different from having it come and being able to hold it in your hands . . . a piece of paper worth ten thousand dollars . . . [TRAVIS *bursts back into the room. He holds the envelope high above his head, like a little dancer, his face is radiant and he is breathless. He moves to his grandmother with sudden slow ceremony and puts the envelope into her hands. She accepts it, and then merely holds it and looks at it.*] Come on! Open it . . . Lord have mercy, I wish Walter Lee was here!

TRAVIS: Open it, Grandmama!

MAMA: [*Staring at it.*] Now you all be quiet. It's just a check.

RUTH: Open it . . .

MAMA: [*Still staring at it.*] Now don't act silly . . . We ain't never been no people to act silly 'bout no money—

RUTH: [*Swiftly.*] We ain't never had none before—*open it!*

[MAMA *finally makes a good strong tear and pulls out the thin blue slice of paper and inspects it closely. The boy and his mother study it raptly over* MAMA's *shoulders.*]

MAMA: *Travis!* [*She is counting off with doubt.*] Is that the right number of zeros.

TRAVIS: Yes'm . . . ten thousand dollars. Gaalee, Grandmama, you rich.

MAMA: [*She holds the check away from her, still looking at it. Slowly her face sobers into a mask of unhappiness.*] Ten thousand dollars. [*She hands it to* RUTH.] Put it away somewhere, Ruth. [*She does not look at* RUTH; *her eyes seem to be seeing something somewhere very far off.*] Ten thousand dollars they give you. Ten thousand dollars.

TRAVIS: [*To his mother, sincerely.*] What's the matter with Grandmama—don't she want to be rich?

RUTH: [*Distractedly.*] You go on out and play now, baby. [TRAVIS *exits.* MAMA *starts wiping dishes absently, humming intently to herself.* RUTH *turns to her, with kind exasperation.*] You've gone and got yourself upset.

MAMA: [*Not looking at her.*] I spec if it wasn't for you all . . . I would just put that money away or give it to the church or something.

RUTH: Now what kind of talk is that. Mr. Younger would just be plain mad if he could hear you talking foolish like that.

MAMA: [*Stopping and staring off.*] Yes . . . he sure would. [*Sighing.*] We got enough to do with that money, all right. [*She halts then, and turns and looks at her daughter-in-law hard;* RUTH *avoids her eyes and* MAMA *wipes her hands with finality and starts to speak firmly to* RUTH.] Where did you go today, girl?

RUTH: To the doctor.

MAMA: [*Impatiently.*] Now, Ruth . . . you know better than that. Old Doctor Jones is strange enough in his way but there ain't nothing 'bout him make somebody slip and call him "she"—like you done this morning.

RUTH: Well, that's what happened—my tongue slipped.

MAMA: You went to see that woman, didn't you?

RUTH: [*Defensively, giving herself away.*] What woman you talking about?

MAMA: [*Angrily.*] That woman who—
        [WALTER *enters in great excitement.*]

WALTER: Did it come?

MAMA: [*Quietly.*] Can't you give people a Christian greeting before you start asking about money?

WALTER: [*To* RUTH.] Did it come? [RUTH *unfolds the check and lays it quietly before him, watching him intently with thoughts of her own.* WALTER *sits down and grasps it close and counts off the zeros.*] Ten thousand dollars— [*He turns suddenly, frantically to his mother and draws some papers out of his breast pocket.*] Mama—look. Old Willy Harris put everything on paper—

MAMA: Son—I think you ought to talk to your wife . . . I'll go on out and leave you alone if you want—

WALTER: I can talk to her later—Mama, look—

MAMA: Son—

WALTER: WILL SOMEBODY PLEASE LISTEN TO ME TODAY!

MAMA: [*Quietly.*] I don't 'low no yellin' in this house, Walter Lee, and you know it— [WALTER *stares at them in frustration and starts to speak several times.*] And there ain't going to be no investing in no liquor stores. I don't aim to have to speak on that again.
        [*A long pause.*]

WALTER: Oh—so you don't aim to have to speak on that again? So you have decided . . . [*Crumpling his papers.*] Well, *you* tell that to my boy tonight when you put him to sleep on the living-room couch . . . [*Turning to* MAMA *and speaking directly to her.*] Yeah—and tell it to my wife, Mama, tomorrow when she has to go out of here to look after somebody else's kids. And tell it to *me,* Mama, every time we need a new pair of curtains and I have to watch *you* go out and work in somebody's kitchen. Yeah, you tell me then!

[WALTER *starts out.*]

RUTH: Where you going?

WALTER: I'm going out!

RUTH: Where?

WALTER: Just out of this house somewhere—

RUTH: [*Getting her coat.*] I'll come too.

WALTER: I don't want you to come!

RUTH: I got something to talk to you about, Walter.

WALTER: That's too bad.

MAMA: [*Still quietly.*] Walter Lee— [*She waits and he finally turns and looks at her.*] Sit down.

WALTER: I'm a grown man, Mama.

MAMA: Ain't nobody said you wasn't grown. But you still in my house and my presence. And as long as you are—you'll talk to your wife civil. Now sit down.

RUTH: [*Suddenly.*] Oh, let him go on out and drink himself to death! He makes me sick to my stomach! [*She flings her coat against him.*]

WALTER: [*Violently.*] And you turn mine too, baby! [RUTH *goes into their bedroom and slams the door behind her.*] That was my greatest mistake—

MAMA: [*Still quietly.*] Walter, what is the matter with you?

WALTER: Matter with me? Ain't nothing the matter with *me!*

MAMA: Yes there is. Something eating you up like a crazy man. Something more than me not giving you this money. The past few years I been watching it happen to you. You get all nervous acting and kind of wild in the eyes— [WALTER *jumps up impatiently at her words.*] I said sit there now, I'm talking to you!

WALTER: Mama—I don't need no nagging at me today.

MAMA: Seem like you getting to a place where you always tied up in some kind of knot about something. But if anybody ask you 'bout it you just yell at 'em and bust out the house and go out and drink somewheres. Walter Lee, people can't live with that. Ruth's a good, patient girl in her way—but you getting to be too much. Boy, don't make the mistake of driving that girl away from you.

WALTER: Why—what she do for me?

MAMA: She loves you.

WALTER: Mama—I'm going out. I want to go off somewhere and be by myself for a while.

MAMA: I'm sorry 'bout your liquor store, son. It just wasn't the thing for us to do. That's what I want to tell you about—

WALTER: I got to go out, Mama—

[*He rises.*]

MAMA: It's dangerous, son.

WALTER: What's dangerous?

MAMA: When a man goes outside his home to look for peace.

WALTER: [*Beseechingly.*] Then why can't there never be no peace in this house then?

MAMA: You done found it in some other house?

WALTER: No—there ain't no woman! Why do women always think there's a woman somewhere when a man gets restless. [*Coming to her.*] Mama—Mama—I want so many things . . .

MAMA: Yes, son—

WALTER: I want so many things that they are driving me kind of crazy . . . Mama— look at me.

MAMA: I'm looking at you. You a good-looking boy. You got a job, a nice wife, a fine boy and—

WALTER: A job. [*Looks at her.*] Mama, a job? I open and close car doors all day long. I drive a man around in his limousine and I say, "Yes, sir; no, sir; very good, sir; shall I take the Drive, sir?" Mama, that ain't no kind of job . . . that ain't nothing at all. [*Very quietly.*] Mama, I don't know if I can make you understand.

MAMA: Understand what, baby?

WALTER: [*Quietly.*] Sometimes it's like I can see the future stretched out in front of me—just plain as day. The future, Mama. Hanging over there at the edge of my days. Just waiting for me—a big, looming blank space—full of *nothing.* Just waiting for *me.* [*Pause.*] Mama—sometimes when I'm downtown and I pass them cool, quiet-looking restaurants where them white boys are sitting back and talking 'bout things . . . sitting there turning deals worth millions of dollars . . . sometimes I see guys don't look much older than me—

MAMA: Son—how come you talk so much 'bout money?

WALTER: [*With immense passion.*] Because it is life, Mama!

MAMA: [*Quietly.*]Oh— [*Very quietly.*] So now it's life. Money is life. Once upon a time freedom used to be life—now it's money. I guess the world really do change . . .

WALTER: No—it was always money, Mama. We just didn't know about it.

MAMA: No . . . something has changed. [*She looks at him.*] You something new, boy. In my time we was worried about not being lynched and getting to the North if we could and how to stay alive and still have a pinch of dignity too . . . Now here come you and Beneatha—talking 'bout things we ain't never even thought about hardly, me and your daddy. You ain't satisfied or proud of nothing we done. I mean that you had a home; that we kept you out of trouble till you was grown; that you don't have to ride to work on the back of nobody's streetcar—You my children—but how different we done become.

WALTER: You just don't understand, Mama, you just don't understand.

MAMA: Son—do you know your wife is expecting another baby? [WALTER *stands, stunned, and absorbs what his mother has said.*] That's what she wanted to talk to you about. [WALTER *sinks down into a chair.*] This ain't for me to be telling—but you ought to know. [*She waits.*] I think Ruth is thinking 'bout getting rid of that child.[1]

WALTER: [*Slowly understanding.*] No—no—Ruth wouldn't do that.

MAMA: When the world gets ugly enough—a woman will do anything for her family. *The part that's already living.*

WALTER: You don't know Ruth, Mama, if you think she would do that.

[RUTH *opens the bedroom door and stands there a little limp.*]

RUTH: [*Beaten.*] Yes I would too, Walter. [*Pause.*] I gave her a five-dollar down payment.

---

1. Though abortions were readily available in the 1940s and 1950s, the procedure was illegal and often dangerous.

372 * LORRAINE HANSBERRY

[*There is total silence as the man stares at his wife and the mother stares at her son.*]

MAMA: [*Presently.*] Well— [*Tightly.*] Well—son, I'm waiting to hear you say something . . . I'm waiting to hear how you be your father's son. Be the man he was . . . [*Pause.*] Your wife say she going to destroy your child. And I'm waiting to hear you talk like him and say we a people who give children life, not who destroys them— [*She rises.*] I'm waiting to see you stand up and look like your daddy and say we done give up one baby to poverty and that we ain't going to give up nary another one . . . I'm waiting.

WALTER: Ruth—

MAMA: If you a son of mine, tell her! [*WALTER turns, looks at her and can say nothing. She continues, bitterly.*] You . . . you are a disgrace to your father's memory. Somebody get me my hat.

[*Curtain.*]

ACT II

SCENE ONE

Time: Later the same day.

At rise: RUTH *is ironing again. She has the radio going. Presently* BE-NEATHA'*s bedroom door opens and* RUTH'*s mouth falls and she puts down the iron in fascination.*

RUTH: What have we got on tonight!

BENEATHA: [*Emerging grandly from the doorway so that we can see her thoroughly robed in the costume* ASAGAI *brought.*] You are looking at what a well-dressed Nigerian woman wears— [*She parades for* RUTH, *her hair completely hidden by the headdress; she is coquettishly fanning herself with an ornate oriental fan, mistakenly more like Butterfly[2] than any Nigerian that ever was.*] Isn't it beautiful? [*She promenades to the radio and, with an arrogant flourish, turns off the good*

---

2. Perhaps Madame Butterfly, the titular heroine and tragic victim of Giacomo Puccini's 1907 opera about a love affair between a Japanese woman and an American naval officer. Or Butterfly McQueen (1911–1995), the African American actor most famous for her role as Prissy in the 1938 *Gone with the Wind*. Prissy speaks the notorious line, "I don't know nuthin' 'bout birthin' babies," a line that came to exemplify Hollywood's stereotyping of African Americans.

loud blues that is playing.] Enough of this assimilationist junk! [RUTH *follows her with her eyes as she goes to the phonograph and puts on a record and turns and waits ceremoniously for the music to come up. Then, with a shout—*] OCOMOGOSIAY!

    [RUTH *jumps. The music comes up, a lovely Nigerian melody.* BE-NEATHA *listens, enraptured, her eyes far away—"back to the past." She begins to dance.* RUTH *is dumbfounded.*]

RUTH: What kind of dance is that?

BENEATHA: A folk dance.

RUTH: [*Pearl Bailey.*]³ What kind of folks do that, honey?

BENEATHA: It's from Nigeria. It's a dance of welcome.

RUTH: Who you welcoming?

BENEATHA: The men back to the village.

RUTH: Where they been?

BENEATHA: How should I know—out hunting or something. Anyway, they are coming back now . . .

RUTH: Well, that's good.

BENEATHA: [*With the record.*]

Alundi, alundi
Alundi alunya
Jop pu a jeepua
Ang gu sooooooooooo

Ai yai yae . . .
Ayehaye—alundi . . .

    [WALTER *comes in during this performance; he has obviously been drinking. He leans against the door heavily and watches his sister, at first with distaste. Then his eyes look off—"back to the past"—as he lifts both his fists to the roof, screaming.*]

WALTER: YEAH . . . AND ETHIOPIA STRETCH FORTH HER HANDS AGAIN! . . .⁴

---

3. In other words, in imitation of the singer and actor Pearl Bailey (1918–1990).

4. A loose translation of the sixty-eighth Psalm, these lines were often invoked as a hopeful prediction of the restoration of in-dependence to black nations. Ethiopia, which largely resisted European coloniza-tion, was unique among African nations and therefore enjoyed a special point of pride in the black cultural movement.

RUTH: [*Drily, looking at him.*] Yes—and Africa sure is claiming her own tonight. [*She gives them both up and starts ironing again.*]

WALTER: [*All in a drunken, dramatic shout.*] Shut up! . . . I'm digging them drums . . . them drums move me! . . . [*He makes his weaving way to his wife's face and leans in close to her.*] In my *heart of hearts*—[*He thumps his chest.*] —I am much warrior!

RUTH: [*Without even looking up.*] In your heart of hearts you are much drunkard.

WALTER: [*Coming away from her and starting to wander around the room, shouting.*] Me and Jomo . . . [*Intently, in his sister's face. She has stopped dancing to watch him in this unknown mood.*] That's my man, Kenyatta.[5] [*Shouting and thumping his chest.*] FLAMING SPEAR! HOT DAMN! [*He is suddenly in possession of an imaginary spear and actively spearing enemies all over the room.*] OCOMOGOSIAY . . . THE LION IS WAKING . . . OWIMOWEH![6] [*He pulls his shirt open and leaps up on a table and gestures with his spear. The bell rings.* RUTH *goes to answer.*]

BENEATHA: [*To encourage* WALTER, *thoroughly caught up with this side of him.*] OCOMOGOSIAY, FLAMING SPEAR!

WALTER: [*On the table, very far gone, his eyes pure glass sheets. He sees what we cannot, that he is a leader of his people, a great chief, a descendant of Chaka,[7] and that the hour to march has come.*] Listen, my black brothers—

BENEATHA: OCOMOGOSIAY!

WALTER: —Do you hear the waters rushing against the shores of the coastlands—

BENEATHA: OCOMOGOSIAY!

5. Jomo Kenyatta (1893–1978) would become the first president of the independent nation of Kenya (1964–78). In the late 1940s, he was a leader in the independence movement. The British incarcerated him on trumped-up charges in 1952, and he was still in prison when this play was written.

6. Walter and Beneatha are making up words that have plausible African sounds. "THE LION IS WAKING" might reference the song "Wimoweh" or "The Lion Sleeps Tonight." Pete Seeger popularized this song,

a bastardization of a 1930s Zulu song, in the 1950s. According to Seeger, the song is about Chaka the Lion, who did not die but went to sleep when Europeans took over South Africa.

7. Chaka or Shaka (1786–1828) was also a Zulu chief, known as the Black Napoleon. He was widely credited with revolutionizing African warfare and organizing a number of tribes into a nation. The British did not conquer the Zulus until 1879.

WALTER: —Do you hear the screeching of the cocks in yonder hills beyond where the chiefs meet in council for the coming of the mighty war—

BENEATHA: OCOMOGOSIAY!

WALTER: —Do you hear the beating of the wings of the birds flying low over the mountains and the low places of our land—

[RUTH *opens the door.* GEORGE MURCHISON *enters.*]

BENEATHA: OCOMOGOSIAY!

WALTER: —Do you hear the singing of the women, singing the war songs of our fathers to the babies in the great houses . . . singing the sweet war songs? OH, DO YOU HEAR, MY BLACK BROTHERS!

BENEATHA: [*Completely gone.*] We hear you, Flaming Spear—

WALTER: Telling us to prepare for the greatness of the time— [*To* GEORGE.] Black Brother!

[*He extends his hand for the fraternal clasp.*]

GEORGE: Black Brother, hell!

RUTH: [*Having had enough, and embarrassed for the family.*] Beneatha, you got company—what's the matter with you? Walter Lee Younger, get down off that table and stop acting like a fool . . .

[WALTER *comes down off the table suddenly and makes a quick exit to the bathroom.*]

RUTH: He's had a little to drink . . . I don't know what her excuse is.

GEORGE: [*To* BENEATHA.] Look honey, we're going *to* the theatre— we're not going to be *in* it . . . so go change, huh?

RUTH: You expect this boy to go out with you looking like that?

BENEATHA: [*Looking at* GEORGE.] That's up to George. If he's ashamed of his heritage—

GEORGE: Oh, don't be so proud of yourself, Bennie—just because you look eccentric.

BENEATHA: How can something that's natural be eccentric?

GEORGE: That's what being eccentric means—being natural. Get dressed.

BENEATHA: I don't like that, George.

RUTH: Why must you and your brother make an argument out of everything people say?

BENEATHA: Because I hate assimilationist Negroes!

RUTH: Will somebody please tell me what assimila-who-ever means!

GEORGE: Oh, it's just a college girl's way of calling people Uncle Toms[8]—but that isn't what it means at all.

RUTH: Well, what does it mean?

BENEATHA: [*Cutting* GEORGE *off and staring at him as she replies to* RUTH.] It means someone who is willing to give up his own culture and submerge himself completely in the dominant, and in this case, *oppressive* culture!

GEORGE: Oh, dear, dear, dear! Here we go! A lecture on the African past! On our Great West African Heritage! In one second we will hear all about the great Ashanti empires; the great Songhay civilizations; and the great sculpture of Bénin—and then some poetry in the Bantu—and the whole monologue will end with the word *heritage*![9] [*Nastily.*] Let's face it, baby, your heritage is nothing but a bunch of raggedy-assed spirituals and some grass huts!

BENEATHA: *Grass huts!* [RUTH *crosses to her and forcibly pushes her toward the bedroom.*] See there . . . you are standing there in your splendid ignorance talking about people who were the first to smelt iron on the face of the earth! [RUTH *is pushing her through the door.*] The Ashanti were performing surgical operations when the English— [RUTH *pulls the door to, with* BENEATHA *on the other side, and smiles graciously at* GEORGE. BENEATHA *opens the door and shouts the end of the sentence defiantly at* GEORGE.] —were still tattooing themselves with blue dragons . . . [*She goes back inside.*]

RUTH: Have a seat, George. [*They both sit.* RUTH *folds her hands rather primly on her lap, determined to demonstrate the civilization of the family.*] Warm, ain't it? I mean for September. [*Pause.*] Just like they always say about Chicago weather: If it's too hot or cold for you, just wait a minute and it'll change. [*She smiles happily at*

---

8. The black hero of Harriet Beecher Stowe's 1852 *Uncle Tom's Cabin.* Though the novel was anti-slavery, the character Uncle Tom became synonomous with docile acceptance of white supremacy.

9. The Ashanti Empire was a West African nation in what is today Ghana; the British conquered and colonized the country in 1896. The Songhay or Songhai Empire flourished in West Africa in the fifteenth and sixteenth centuries. Bénin, an empire from 1440 to 1897 and located in modern-day Nigeria, is famed for its sculptures in bronze, ivory, and iron. *Bantu* refers to a linguistic and ethnic grouping of peoples in central, eastern, and south Africa. There are over 500 languages in the Bantu grouping.

this cliché of clichés.] Everybody say it's got to do with them bombs and things they keep setting off.[1] [*Pause.*] Would you like a nice cold beer?

GEORGE: No, thank you. I don't care for beer. [*He looks at his watch.*] I hope she hurries up.

RUTH: What time is the show?

GEORGE: It's an eight-thirty curtain. That's just Chicago, though. In New York standard curtain time is eight-forty.

[*He is rather proud of this knowledge.*]

RUTH: [*Properly appreciating it.*] You get to New York a lot?

GEORGE: [*Offhand.*] Few times a year.

RUTH: Oh—that's nice. I've never been to New York.

[WALTER *enters. We feel he has relieved himself, but the edge of unreality is still with him.*]

WALTER: New York ain't got nothing Chicago ain't. Just a bunch of hustling people all squeezed up together—being "Eastern."

[*He turns his face into a screw of displeasure.*]

GEORGE: Oh—you've been?

WALTER: *Plenty* of times.

RUTH: [*Shocked at the lie.*] Walter Lee Younger!

WALTER: [*Staring her down.*] Plenty! [*Pause.*] What we got to drink in this house? Why don't you offer this man some refreshment. [*To* GEORGE.] They don't know how to entertain people in this house, man.

GEORGE: Thank you—I don't really care for anything.

WALTER: [*Feeling his head; sobriety coming.*] Where's Mama?

RUTH: She ain't come back yet.

WALTER: [*Looking* MURCHISON *over from head to toe, scrutinizing his carefully casual tweed sports jacket over cashmere V-neck sweater over soft eyelet shirt and tie, and soft slacks, finished off with white buckskin shoes.*] Why all you college boys wear them fairyish-looking white shoes?

RUTH: Walter Lee!

[GEORGE MURCHISON *ignores the remark.*]

WALTER: [*To* RUTH.] Well, they look crazy as hell—white shoes, cold as it is.

---

1. It was not uncommon in the 1950s to attribute weather anomalies to nuclear weapons testing.

RUTH: [*Crushed.*] You have to excuse him—

WALTER: No he don't! Excuse me for what? What you always excusing me for! I'll excuse myself when I needs to be excused! [*A pause.*] They look as funny as them black knee socks Beneatha wears out of here all the time.

RUTH: It's the college *style*, Walter.

WALTER: Style, hell, she looks like she got burnt legs or something!

RUTH: Oh, Walter—

WALTER: [*An irritable mimic.*] Oh, Walter! Oh, Walter! [*To* MURCHISON.] How's your old man making out? I understand you all going to buy that big hotel on the Drive?[2] [*He finds a beer in the refrigerator, wanders over to* MURCHISON, *sipping and wiping his lips with the back of his hand, and straddling a chair backwards to talk to the other man.*] Shrewd move. Your old man is all right, man. [*Tapping his head and half winking for emphasis.*] I mean he knows how to operate. I mean he thinks *big*, you know what I mean, I mean for a *home*, you know? But I think he's kind of running out of ideas now. I'd like to talk to him. Listen, man, I got some plans that could turn this city upside down. I mean I think like he does. *Big*. Invest big, gamble big, hell, lose *big* if you have to, you know what I mean. It's hard to find a man on this whole South-side who understands my kind of thinking—you dig? [*He scrutinizes* MURCHISON *again, drinks his beer, squints his eyes and leans in close, confidential, man to man.*] Me and you ought to sit down and talk sometimes, man. Man, I got me some ideas . . .

GEORGE: [*With boredom.*] Yeah—sometimes we'll have to do that, Walter.

WALTER: [*Understanding the indifference, and offended.*] Yeah—well, when you get the time, man. I know you a busy little boy.

RUTH: Walter, please—

WALTER: [*Bitterly, hurt.*] I know ain't nothing in this world as busy as you colored college boys with your fraternity pins and white shoes . . .

RUTH: [*Covering her face with humiliation.*] Oh, Walter Lee—

WALTER: I see you all the time—with the books tucked under your

---

2. Lake Shore Drive, a fashionable street along the shore of Lake Michigan.

arms—going to your [*British A—a mimic.*] "clahsses." And for
what! What the hell you learning over there? Filling up your
heads— [*Counting off on his fingers.*] —with the sociology and
the psychology—but they teaching you how to be a man? How
to take over and run the world? They teaching you how to run a
rubber plantation or a steel mill? Naw—just to talk proper and
read books and wear white shoes . . .

GEORGE: [*Looking at him with distaste, a little above it all.*] You're all
wacked up with bitterness, man.

WALTER: [*Intently, almost quietly, between the teeth, glaring at the boy.*]
And you—ain't you bitter, man? Ain't you just about had it yet?
Don't you see no stars gleaming that you can't reach out and
grab? You happy?—You contented son-of-a-bitch—you happy?
You got it made? Bitter? Man, I'm a volcano. Bitter? Here I am a
giant—surrounded by ants! Ants who can't even understand
what it is the giant is talking about.

RUTH: [*Passionately and suddenly.*] Oh, Walter—ain't you with nobody!

WALTER: [*Violently.*] No! 'Cause ain't nobody with me! Not even my
own mother!

RUTH: Walter, that's a terrible thing to say!

[BENEATHA *enters, dressed for the evening in a cocktail dress and
earrings.*]

GEORGE: Well—hey, you look great.

BENEATHA: Let's go, George. See you all later.

RUTH: Have a nice time.

GEORGE: Thanks. Good night. [*To* WALTER, *sarcastically.*] Good
night, *Prometheus.*[3]

[BENEATHA *and* GEORGE *exit.*]

WALTER: [*To* RUTH.] Who is Prometheus?

RUTH: I don't know. Don't worry about it.

WALTER: [*In fury, pointing after* GEORGE.] See there—they get to a
point where they can't insult you man to man—they got to go
talk about something ain't nobody never heard of!

RUTH: How do you know it was an insult? [*To humor him.*] Maybe
Prometheus is a nice fellow.

---

3. Greek god associated with human aspirations and civilization. He gave humanity the
gift of fire.

WALTER: Prometheus! I bet there ain't even no such thing! I bet that simpleminded clown—

RUTH: Walter—

[*She stops what she is doing and looks at him.*]

WALTER: [*Yelling.*] Don't start!

RUTH: Start what?

WALTER: Your nagging! Where was I? Who was I with? How much money did I spend?

RUTH: [*Plaintively.*] Walter Lee—why don't we just try to talk about it . . .

WALTER: [*Not listening.*] I been out talking with people who understand me. People who care about the things I got on my mind.

RUTH: [*Wearily.*] I guess that means people like Willy Harris.

WALTER: Yes, people like Willy Harris.

RUTH: [*With a sudden flash of impatience.*] Why don't you all just hurry up and go into the banking business and stop talking about it!

WALTER: Why? You want to know why? 'Cause we all tied up in a race of people that don't know how to do nothing but moan, pray and have babies!

[*The line is too bitter even for him and he looks at her and sits down.*]

RUTH: Oh, Walter . . . [*Softly.*] Honey, why can't you stop fighting me?

WALTER: [*Without thinking.*] Who's fighting you? Who even cares about you?

[*This line begins the retardation of his mood.*]

RUTH: Well— [*She waits a long time, and then with resignation starts to put away her things.*] I guess I might as well go on to bed . . . [*More or less to herself.*] I don't know where we lost it . . . but we have . . . [*Then, to him.*] I—I'm sorry about this new baby, Walter. I guess maybe I better go on and do what I started . . . I guess I just didn't realize how bad things was with us . . . I guess I just didn't really realize— [*She starts out to the bedroom and stops.*] You want some hot milk?

WALTER: Hot milk?

RUTH: Yes—hot milk.

WALTER: Why hot milk?

RUTH: 'Cause after all that liquor you come home with you ought to have something hot in your stomach.

WALTER: I don't want no milk.

RUTH: You want some coffee then?

WALTER: No, I don't want no coffee. I don't want nothing hot to drink. [*Almost plaintively.*] Why you always trying to give me something to eat?

RUTH: [*Standing and looking at him helplessly.*] What else can I give you, Walter Lee Younger?

[*She stands and looks at him and presently turns to go out again. He lifts his head and watches her going away from him in a new mood which began to emerge when he asked her "Who cares about you?"*]

WALTER: It's been rough, ain't it, baby? [*She hears and stops but does not turn around and he continues to her back.*] I guess between two people there ain't never as much understood as folks generally thinks there is. I mean like between me and you— [*She turns to face him.*] How we gets to the place where we scared to talk softness to each other. [*He waits, thinking hard himself.*] Why you think it got to be like that? [*He is thoughtful, almost as a child would be.*] Ruth, what is it gets into people ought to be close?

RUTH: I don't know, honey. I think about it a lot.

WALTER: On account of you and me, you mean? The way things are with us. The way something done come down between us.

RUTH: There ain't so much between us, Walter . . . Not when you come to me and try to talk to me. Try to be with me . . . a little even.

WALTER: [*Total honesty.*] Sometimes . . . sometimes . . . I don't even know how to try.

RUTH: Walter—

WALTER: Yes?

RUTH: [*Coming to him, gently and with misgiving, but coming to him.*] Honey . . . life don't have to be like this. I mean sometimes people can do things so that things are better . . . You remember how we used to talk when Travis was born . . . about the way we were going to live . . . the kind of house . . . [*She is stroking his head.*] Well, it's all starting to slip away from us . . .

[MAMA *enters, and* WALTER *jumps up and shouts at her.*]

WALTER: Mama, where have you been?

MAMA: My—them steps is longer than they used to be. Whew! [*She sits down and ignores him.*] How you feeling this evening, Ruth?

[RUTH *shrugs, disturbed some at having been prematurely interrupted and watching her husband knowingly.*]

WALTER: Mama, where have you been all day?

MAMA: [*Still ignoring him and leaning on the table and changing to more comfortable shoes.*] Where's Travis?

RUTH: I let him go out earlier and he ain't come back yet. Boy, is he going to get it!

WALTER: Mama!

MAMA: [*As if she has heard him for the first time.*] Yes, son?

WALTER: Where did you go this afternoon?

MAMA: I went downtown to tend to some business that I had to tend to.

WALTER: What kind of business?

MAMA: You know better than to question me like a child, Brother.

WALTER: [*Rising and bending over the table.*] Where were you, Mama? [*Bringing his fists down and shouting.*] Mama, you didn't go do something with that insurance money, something crazy?

[*The front door opens slowly, interrupting him, and* TRAVIS *peeks his head in, less than hopefully.*]

TRAVIS: [*To his mother.*] Mama, I—

RUTH: "Mama I" nothing! You're going to get it, boy! Get on in that bedroom and get yourself ready!

TRAVIS: But I—

MAMA: Why don't you all never let the child explain hisself.

RUTH: Keep out of it now, Lena.

[MAMA *clamps her lips together, and* RUTH *advances toward her son menacingly.*]

RUTH: A thousand times I have told you not to go off like that—

MAMA: [*Holding out her arms to her grandson.*] Well—at least let me tell him something. I want him to be the first one to hear . . . Come here, Travis. [*The boy obeys, gladly.*] Travis— [*She takes him by the shoulder and looks into his face.*] —you know that money we got in the mail this morning?

TRAVIS: Yes'm—

MAMA: Well—what you think your grandmama gone and done with that money?

TRAVIS: I don't know, Grandmama.

MAMA: [*Putting her finger on his nose for emphasis.*] She went out and she bought you a house! [*The explosion comes from* WALTER *at the end of the revelation and he jumps up and turns away from all of them in a fury.* MAMA *continues, to* TRAVIS.] You glad about the house? It's going to be yours when you get to be a man.

TRAVIS: Yeah—I always wanted to live in a house.

MAMA: All right, gimme some sugar then— [TRAVIS *puts his arms around her neck as she watches her son over the boy's shoulder. Then, to* TRAVIS, *after the embrace.*] Now when you say your prayers tonight, you thank God and your grandfather—'cause it was him who give you the house—in his way.

RUTH: [*Taking the boy from* MAMA *and pushing him toward the bedroom.*] Now you get out of here and get ready for your beating.

TRAVIS: Aw, Mama—

RUTH: Get on in there— [*Closing the door behind him and turning radiantly to her mother-in-law.*] So you went and did it!

MAMA: [*Quietly, looking at her son with pain.*] Yes, I did.

RUTH: [*Raising both arms classically.*] Praise God! [*Looks at* WALTER *a moment, who says nothing. She crosses rapidly to her husband.*] Please, honey—let me be glad . . . you be glad too. [*She has laid her hands on his shoulders, but he shakes himself free of her roughly, without turning to face her.*] Oh, Walter . . . a home . . . *a home.* [*She comes back to* MAMA.] Well—where is it? How big is it? How much it going to cost?

MAMA: Well—

RUTH: When we moving?

MAMA: [*Smiling at her.*] First of the month.

RUTH: [*Throwing back her head with jubilance.*] Praise God!

MAMA: [*Tentatively, still looking at her son's back turned against her and* RUTH.] It's— it's a nice house too . . . [*She cannot help speaking directly to him. An imploring quality in her voice, her manner, makes her almost like a girl now.*] Three bedrooms— nice big one for you and Ruth . . . Me and Beneatha still have to share our room, but Travis have one of his own—and [*With difficulty.*] I figure if the—new baby—is a boy, we could get one of them double-decker outfits . . . And there's a yard with a little patch of dirt where I could maybe get to grow me a few flowers . . . And a nice big basement . . .

RUTH: Walter honey, be glad—

MAMA: [*Still to his back, fingering things on the table.*] 'Course I don't want to make it sound fancier than it is . . . It's just a plain little old house—but it's made good and solid—and it will be *ours*. Walter Lee—it makes a difference in a man when he can walk on floors that belong to *him* . . .

RUTH: Where is it?

MAMA: [*Frightened at this telling.*] Well—well—it's out there in Clybourne Park—[4]

[RUTH's *radiance fades abruptly, and* WALTER *finally turns slowly to face his mother with incredulity and hostility.*]

RUTH: Where?

MAMA: [*Matter-of-factly.*] Four o six Clybourne Street, Clybourne Park.

RUTH: Clybourne Park? Mama, there ain't no colored people living in Clybourne Park.

MAMA: [*Almost idiotically.*] Well, I guess there's going to be some now.

WALTER: [*Bitterly.*] So that's the peace and comfort you went out and bought for us today!

MAMA: [*Raising her eyes to meet his finally.*] Son—I just tried to find the nicest place for the least amount of money for my family.

RUTH: [*Trying to recover from the shock.*] Well—well—'course I ain't one never been 'fraid of no crackers[5] mind you—but—well, wasn't there no other houses nowhere?

MAMA: Them houses they put up for colored in them areas way out all seem to cost twice as much as other houses. I did the best I could.

RUTH: [*Struck senseless with the news, in its various degrees of goodness and trouble, she sits a moment, her fists propping her chin in thought, and then she starts to rise, bringing her fists down with vigor, the radiance spreading from cheek to cheek again.*] Well—

---

4. Neighborhood in the Lincoln Park section of Chicago.
5. Insulting term for poor whites.

well!—All I can say is—if this is my time in life—*my time*—to say good-bye— [*And she builds with momentum as she starts to circle the room with an exuberant, almost tearfully happy release.*] —to these Goddamned cracking walls!— [*She pounds the walls.*] —and these marching roaches!— [*She wipes at an imaginary army of marching roaches.*] —and this cramped little closet which ain't now or never was no kitchen! . . . then I say it loud and good, *Hallelujah! and good-bye misery . . . I don't never want to see your ugly face again!* [*She laughs joyously, having practically destroyed the apartment, and flings her arms up and lets them come down happily, slowly, reflectively, over her abdomen, aware for the first time perhaps that the life therein pulses with happiness and not despair.*] Lena?

MAMA: [*Moved, watching her happiness.*] Yes, honey?

RUTH: [*Looking off.*] Is there—is there a whole lot of sunlight?

MAMA: [*Understanding.*] Yes, child, there's a whole lot of sunlight.

[*Long pause.*]

RUTH: [*Collecting herself and going to the door of the room* TRAVIS *is in.*] Well—I guess I better see 'bout Travis. [*To* MAMA.] Lord, I sure don't feel like whipping nobody today!

[*She exits.*]

MAMA: [*The mother and son are left alone now and the mother waits a long time, considering deeply, before she speaks.*] Son—you—you understand what I done, don't you? [WALTER *is silent and sullen.*] I—I just seen my family falling apart today . . . just falling to pieces in front of my eyes . . . We couldn't of gone on like we was today. We was going backwards 'stead of forwards—talking 'bout killing babies and wishing each other was dead . . . When it gets like that in life—you just got to do something different, push on out and do something bigger . . . [*She waits.*] I wish you say something, son . . . I wish you'd say how deep inside you you think I done the right thing—

WALTER: [*Crossing slowly to his bedroom door and finally turning there and speaking measuredly.*] What you need me to say you done right for? *You* the head of this family. You run our lives like you want to. It was your money and you did what you wanted with it. So what you need for me to say it was all right for? [*Bitterly, to hurt her as deeply as he knows is possible.*] So you butchered up a

dream of mine—you—who always talking 'bout your children's
dreams . . .

MAMA: Walter Lee—

[*He just closes the door behind him.* MAMA *sits alone, thinking
heavily.*]

[*Curtain.*]

SCENE TWO

Time: Friday night. A few weeks later.

At rise: Packing crates mark the intention of the family to move. BE-
NEATHA *and* GEORGE *come in, presumably from an evening out again.*

GEORGE: O.K. . . . O.K., whatever you say . . . [*They both sit on the
couch. He tries to kiss her. She moves away.*] Look, we've had a nice
evening; let's not spoil it, huh? . . .

[*He again turns her head and tries to nuzzle in and she turns
away from him, not with distaste but with momentary lack of interest; in a mood to pursue what they were talking about.*]

BENEATHA: I'm *trying* to talk to you.

GEORGE: We always talk.

BENEATHA: Yes—and I love to talk.

GEORGE: [*Exasperated; rising.*] I know it and I don't mind it sometimes . . . I want you to cut it out, see—The moody stuff, I
mean. I don't like it. You're a nice-looking girl . . . all over. That's
all you need, honey, forget the atmosphere. Guys aren't going to
go for the atmosphere—they're going to go for what they see. Be
glad for that. Drop the Garbo[6] routine. It doesn't go with you. As
for myself, I want a nice— [*Groping.*] —simple [*Thoughtfully.*]
—sophisticated girl . . . not a poet—O.K.?

[*She rebuffs him again and he starts to leave.*]

BENEATHA: Why are you angry?

GEORGE: Because this is stupid! I don't go out with you to discuss
the nature of "quiet desperation"[7] or to hear all about your
thoughts—because the world will go on thinking what it thinks
regardless—

6. Greta Garbo (1905–1990), American
movie star, sex symbol, celebrity noted for
her moodiness.

7. Part of Henry David Thoreau's famous line from *Walden* (1852): "the mass of
men lead lives of quiet desperation."

BENEATHA: Then why read books? Why go to school?

GEORGE: [*With artificial patience, counting on his fingers.*] It's simple. You read books—to learn facts—to get grades—to pass the course—to get a degree. That's all—it has nothing to do with thoughts.

[*A long pause.*]

BENEATHA: I see. [*A longer pause as she looks at him.*] Good night, George.

[GEORGE *looks at her a little oddly, and starts to exit. He meets* MAMA *coming in.*]

GEORGE: Oh—hello, Mrs. Younger.

MAMA: Hello, George, how you feeling?

GEORGE: Fine—fine, how are you?

MAMA: Oh, a little tired. You know them steps can get you after a day's work. You all have a nice time tonight?

GEORGE: Yes—a fine time. Well, good night.

MAMA: Good night. [*He exits.* MAMA *closes the door behind her.*] Hello, honey. What you sitting like that for?

BENEATHA: I'm just sitting.

MAMA: Didn't you have a nice time?

BENEATHA: No.

MAMA: No? What's the matter?

BENEATHA: Mama, George is a fool—honest. [*She rises.*]

MAMA: [*Hustling around unloading the packages she has entered with. She stops.*] Is he, baby?

BENEATHA: Yes.

[BENEATHA *makes up* TRAVIS' *bed as she talks.*]

MAMA: You sure?

BENEATHA: Yes.

MAMA: Well—I guess you better not waste your time with no fools.

[BENEATHA *looks up at her mother, watching her put groceries in the refrigerator. Finally she gathers up her things and starts into the bedroom. At the door she stops and looks back at her mother.*]

BENEATHA: Mama—

MAMA: Yes, baby—

BENEATHA: Thank you.

MAMA: For what?

BENEATHA: For understanding me this time.

[*She exits quickly and the mother stands, smiling a little, looking at the place where* BENEATHA *just stood.* RUTH *enters.*]

RUTH: Now don't you fool with any of this stuff, Lena—

MAMA: Oh, I just thought I'd sort a few things out.

[*The phone rings.* RUTH *answers.*]

RUTH: [*At the phone.*] Hello—Just a minute. [*Goes to door.*] Walter, it's Mrs. Arnold. [*Waits. Goes back to the phone. Tense.*] Hello. Yes, this is his wife speaking . . . He's lying down now. Yes . . . well, he'll be in tomorrow. He's been very sick. Yes—I know we should have called, but we were so sure he'd be able to come in today. Yes—yes, I'm very sorry. Yes . . . Thank you very much. [*She hangs up.* WALTER *is standing in the doorway of the bedroom behind her.*] That was Mrs. Arnold.

WALTER: [*Indifferently.*] Was it?

RUTH: She said if you don't come in tomorrow that they are getting a new man . . .

WALTER: Ain't that sad—ain't that crying sad.

RUTH: She said Mr. Arnold has had to take a cab for three days . . . Walter, you ain't been to work for three days! [*This is a revelation to her.*] Where you been, Walter Lee Younger? [WALTER *looks at her and starts to laugh.*] You're going to lose your job.

WALTER: That's right . . .

RUTH: Oh, Walter, and with your mother working like a dog every day—

WALTER: That's sad too—Everything is sad.

MAMA: What you been doing for these three days, son?

WALTER: Mama—you don't know all the things a man what got leisure can find to do in this city . . . What's this—Friday night? Well—Wednesday I borrowed Willy Harris' car and I went for a drive . . . just me and myself and I drove and drove . . . Way out . . . way past South Chicago, and I parked the car and I sat and looked at the steel mills all day long. I just sat in the car and looked at them big black chimneys for hours. Then I drove back and I went to the Green Hat. [*Pause.*] And Thursday—Thursday I borrowed the car again and I got in it and I pointed it the other way and I drove the other way—for hours— way, way up to Wisconsin, and I looked at the farms. I just drove and looked at the farms. Then I drove back and I went to the Green Hat.

[*Pause.*] And today—today I didn't get the car. Today I just walked. All over the Southside. And I looked at the Negroes and they looked at me and finally I just sat down on the curb at Thirty-ninth and South Parkway and I just sat there and watched the Negroes go by. And then I went to the Green Hat. You all sad? You all depressed? And you know where I am going right now—

    [RUTH *goes out quietly.*]

MAMA: Oh, Big Walter, is this the harvest of our days?

WALTER: You know what I like about the Green Hat? [*He turns the radio on and a steamy, deep blues pours into the room.*] I like this little cat they got there who blows a sax . . . He blows. He talks to me. He ain't but 'bout five feet tall and he's got a conked head[8] and his eyes is always closed and he's all music—

MAMA: [*Rising and getting some papers out of her handbag.*] Walter—

WALTER: And there's this other guy who plays the piano . . . and they got a sound. I mean they can work on some music . . . They got the best little combo in the world in the Green Hat . . . You can just sit there and drink and listen to them three men play and you realize that don't nothing matter worth a damn, but just being there—

MAMA: I've helped do it to you, haven't I, son? Walter, I been wrong.

WALTER: Naw—you ain't never been wrong about nothing, Mama.

MAMA: Listen to me, now. I say I been wrong, son. That I been doing to you what the rest of the world been doing to you. [*She stops and he looks up slowly at her and she meets his eyes pleadingly.*] Walter—what you ain't never understood is that I ain't got nothing, don't own nothing, ain't never really wanted nothing that wasn't for you. There ain't nothing as precious to me . . . There ain't nothing worth holding on to, money, dreams, nothing else—if it means—if it means it's going to destroy my boy. [*She puts her papers in front of him and he watches her without speaking or moving.*] I paid the man thirty-five hundred dollars down on the house. That leaves sixty-five hundred dollars. Monday morning I want you to take this money and take three thousand dollars and put it in a savings account for Beneatha's medical

---

8. Straightened hair popular with African American musicians in the mid-twentieth century.

schooling. The rest you put in a checking account—with your name on it. And from now on any penny that come out of it or that go in it is for you to look after. For you to decide. [*She drops her hands a little helplessly.*] It ain't much, but it's all I got in the world and I'm putting it in your hands. I'm telling you to be the head of this family from now on like you supposed to be.

WALTER: [*Stares at the money.*] You trust me like that, Mama?

MAMA: I ain't never stop trusting you. Like I ain't never stop loving you.

> [*She goes out, and* WALTER *sits looking at the money on the table as the music continues in its idiom, pulsing in the room. Finally, in a decisive gesture, he gets up, and, in mingled joy and desperation, picks up the money. At the same moment,* TRAVIS *enters for bed.*]

TRAVIS: What's the matter, Daddy? You drunk?

WALTER: [*Sweetly, more sweetly than we have ever known him.*] No, Daddy ain't drunk. Daddy ain't going to never be drunk again. . . .

TRAVIS: Well, good night, Daddy.

> [*The father has come from behind the couch and leans over, embracing his son.*]

WALTER: Son, I feel like talking to you tonight.

TRAVIS: About what?

WALTER: Oh, about a lot of things. About you and what kind of man you going to be when you grow up . . . Son—son, what do you want to be when you grow up?

TRAVIS: A bus driver.

WALTER: [*Laughing a little.*] A what? Man, that ain't nothing to want to be!

TRAVIS: Why not?

WALTER: 'Cause, man—it ain't big enough—you know what I mean.

TRAVIS: I don't know then. I can't make up my mind. Sometimes Mama asks me that too. And sometimes when I tell you I just want to be like you—she says she don't want me to be like that and sometimes she says she does . . .

WALTER: [*Gathering him up in his arms.*] You know what, Travis? In seven years you going to be seventeen years old. And things is going to be very different with us in seven years, Travis . . . One day when you are seventeen I'll come home— home from my office downtown somewhere—

TRAVIS: You don't work in no office, Daddy.

WALTER: No—but after tonight. After what your daddy gonna do tonight, there's going to be offices—a whole lot of offices . . .

TRAVIS: What you gonna do tonight, Daddy?

WALTER: You wouldn't understand yet, son, but your daddy's gonna make a transaction . . . a business transaction that's going to change our lives . . . That's how come one day when you 'bout seventeen years old I'll come home and I'll be pretty tired, you know what I mean, after a day of conferences and secretaries getting things wrong the way they do . . . 'cause an executive's life is hell, man— [*The more he talks the farther away he gets.*] And I'll pull the car up on the driveway . . . just a plain black Chrysler, I think, with white walls—no—black tires. More elegant. Rich people don't have to be flashy . . . though I'll have to get something a little sportier for Ruth—maybe a Cadillac convertible to do her shopping in . . . And I'll come up the steps to the house and the gardener will be clipping away at the hedges and he'll say, "Good evening, Mr. Younger." And I'll say, "Hello, Jefferson, how are you this evening?" And I'll go inside and Ruth will come downstairs and meet me at the door and we'll kiss each other and she'll take my arm and we'll go up to your room to see you sitting on the floor with the catalogues of all the great schools in America around you . . . All the great schools in the world. And—and I'll say, all right son—it's your seventeenth birthday, what is it you've decided? . . . Just tell me where you want to go to school and you'll *go.* Just tell me, what it is you want to be— and you'll *be* it . . . Whatever you want to be—Yessir! [*He holds his arms open for* TRAVIS.] You just name it, son . . . [TRAVIS *leaps into them.*] and I hand you the world!

[WALTER*'s voice has risen in pitch and hysterical promise and on the last line he lifts* TRAVIS *high.*]

[*BLACKOUT.*]

SCENE THREE

Time: Saturday, moving day, one week later.

Before the curtain rises, RUTH*'s voice, a strident, dramatic church alto, cuts through the silence.*

It is, in the darkness, a triumphant surge, a penetrating statement of expectation: "Oh, Lord, I don't feel no ways tired! Children, oh, glory hallelujah!"

As the curtain rises we see that RUTH *is alone in the living room, finishing up the family's packing. It is moving day. She is nailing crates and tying cartons.* BENEATHA *enters, carrying a guitar case, and watches her exuberant sister-in-law.*

RUTH: Hey!

BENEATHA: [*Putting away the case.*] Hi.

RUTH: [*Pointing at a package.*] Honey—look in that package there and see what I found on sale this morning at the South Center. [RUTH *gets up and moves to the package and draws out some curtains.*] Lookahere—hand-turned hems!

BENEATHA: How do you know the window size out there?

RUTH: [*Who hadn't thought of that.*] Oh—Well, they bound to fit something in the whole house. Anyhow, they was too good a bargain to pass up. [RUTH *slaps her head, suddenly remembering something.*] Oh, Bennie—I meant to put a special note on that carton over there. That's your mama's good china and she wants 'em to be very careful with it.

BENEATHA: I'll do it.

[BENEATHA *finds a piece of paper and starts to draw large letters on it.*]

RUTH: You know what I'm going to do soon as I get in that new house?

BENEATHA: What?

RUTH: Honey—I'm going to run me a tub of water up to here . . . [*With her fingers practically up to her nostrils.*] And I'm going to get in it—and I am going to sit . . . and sit . . . and sit in that hot water and the first person who knocks to tell *me* to hurry up and come out—

BENEATHA: Gets shot at sunrise.

RUTH: [*Laughing happily.*] You said it, sister! [*Noticing how large* BENEATHA *is absentmindedly making the note.*] Honey, they ain't going to read that from no airplane.

BENEATHA: [*Laughing herself.*] I guess I always think things have more emphasis if they are big, somehow.

RUTH: [*Looking up at her and smiling.*] You and your brother seem to have that as a philosophy of life. Lord, that man—done changed so 'round here. You know—you know what we did last night? Me and Walter Lee?

BENEATHA: What?

RUTH: [*Smiling to herself.*] We went to the movies. [*Looking at BE-NEATHA to see if she understands.*] We went to the movies. You know the last time me and Walter went to the movies together?

BENEATHA: No.

RUTH: Me neither. That's how long it been. [*Smiling again.*] But we went last night. The picture wasn't much good, but that didn't seem to matter. We went—and we held hands.

BENEATHA: Oh, Lord!

RUTH: We held hands—and you know what?

BENEATHA: What?

RUTH: When we come out of the show it was late and dark and all the stores and things was closed up . . . and it was kind of chilly and there wasn't many people on the streets . . . and we was still holding hands, me and Walter.

BENEATHA: You're killing me.

[WALTER *enters with a large package. His happiness is deep in him; he cannot keep still with his new-found exuberance. He is singing and wiggling and snapping his fingers. He puts his package in a corner and puts a phonograph record, which he has brought in with him, on the record player. As the music comes up he dances over to* RUTH *and tries to get her to dance with him. She gives in at last to his raunchiness and in a fit of giggling allows herself to be drawn into his mood and together they deliberately burlesque an old social dance of their youth.*]

BENEATHA: [*Regarding them a long time as they dance, then drawing in her breath for a deeply exaggerated comment which she does not particularly mean.*] Talk about—olddddddddddd-fashioneddddddddd—Negroes!

WALTER: [*Stopping momentarily.*] What kind of Negroes?

[*He says this in fun. He is not angry with her today, nor with anyone. He starts to dance with his wife again.*]

BENEATHA: Old-fashioned.

WALTER: [*As he dances with* RUTH.] You know, when these *New Ne-*

groes have their convention— [*Pointing at his sister.*] —that is going to be the chairman of the Committee on Unending Agitation. [*He goes on dancing, then stops.*] Race, race, race! . . . Girl, I
do believe you are the first person in the history of the entire human race to successfully brainwash yourself. [BENEATHA *breaks up
and he goes on dancing. He stops again, enjoying his tease.*] Damn,
even the N double A C P[9] *takes a holiday sometimes!* [BENEATHA
and RUTH *laugh. He dances with* RUTH *some more and starts to
laugh and stops and pantomimes someone over an operating table.*] I
can just see that chick someday looking down at some poor cat
on an operating table before she starts to slice him, saying . . .
[*Pulling his sleeves back maliciously.*] "By the way, what are your
views on civil rights down there? . . . "

> [*He laughs at her again and starts to dance happily. The bell
> sounds.*]

BENEATHA: Sticks and stones may break my bones but . . . words
will never hurt me!

> [BENEATHA *goes to the door and opens it as* WALTER *and* RUTH *go
> on with the clowning.* BENEATHA *is somewhat surprised to see a
> quiet-looking middle-aged white man in a business suit holding
> his hat and a briefcase in his hand and consulting a small piece of
> paper.*]

MAN: Uh—how do you do, miss. I am looking for a Mrs.— [*He
looks at the slip of paper.*] Mrs. Lena Younger?

BENEATHA: [*Smoothing her hair with slight embarrassment.*] Oh—yes,
that's my mother. Excuse me [*She closes the door and turns to quiet
the other two.*] Ruth! Brother! Somebody's here. [*Then she opens
the door. The* MAN *casts a curious quick glance at all of them.*] Uh—
come in please.

MAN: [*Coming in.*] Thank you.

BENEATHA: My mother isn't here just now. Is it business?

MAN: Yes . . . well, of a sort.

WALTER: [*Freely, the Man of the House.*] Have a seat. I'm Mrs.
Younger's son. I look after most of her business matters.

> [RUTH *and* BENEATHA *exchange amused glances.*]

---

9. National Association for the Advancement of Colored People, civil rights organization
founded in 1909. In 1955, Rosa Parks, a member of the NAACP, sparked the modern civil
rights movement by refusing to go to the back of the bus in Montgomery, Alabama.

MAN: [*Regarding* WALTER, *and sitting.*] Well—My name is Karl Lindner . . .

WALTER: [*Stretching out his hand.*] Walter Younger. This is my wife—
[RUTH *nods politely.*] —and my sister.

LINDNER: How do you do.

WALTER: [*Amiably, as he sits himself easily on a chair, leaning with interest forward on his knees and looking expectantly into the new-
comer's face.*] What can we do for you, Mr. Lindner!

LINDNER: [*Some minor shuffling of the hat and briefcase on his knees.*]
Well—I am a representative of the Clybourne Park Improvement
Association—

WALTER: [*Pointing.*] Why don't you sit your things on the floor?

LINDNER: Oh—yes. Thank you. [*He slides the briefcase and hat under
the chair.*] And as I was saying—I am from the Clybourne Park
Improvement Association and we have had it brought to our
attention at the last meeting that you people—or at least your
mother—has bought a piece of residential property at— [*He digs
for the slip of paper again.*] —four o six Clybourne Street . . .

WALTER: That's right. Care for something to drink? Ruth, get Mr.
Lindner a beer.

LINDNER: [*Upset for some reason.*] Oh—no, really. I mean thank you
very much, but no thank you.

RUTH: [*Innocently.*] Some coffee?

LINDNER: Thank you, nothing at all.

[BENEATHA *is watching the man carefully.*]

LINDNER: Well, I don't know how much you folks know about our
organization. [*He is a gentle man; thoughtful and somewhat la-
bored in his manner.*] It is one of these community organizations
set up to look after—oh, you know, things like block upkeep and
special projects and we also have what we call our New Neighbors Orientation Committee . . .

BENEATHA: [*Drily.*] Yes—and what do they do?

LINDNER: [*Turning a little to her and then returning the main force to*
WALTER.] Well— it's what you might call a sort of welcoming
committee, I guess. I mean they, we, I'm the chairman of the
committee—go around and see the new people who move into
the neighborhood and sort of give them the lowdown on the way
we do things out in Clybourne Park.

BENEATHA: [*With appreciation of the two meanings, which escape* RUTH *and* WALTER.] Un-huh.

LINDNER: And we also have the category of what the association calls— [*He looks elsewhere.*] —uh—special community problems . . .

BENEATHA: Yes—and what are some of those?

WALTER: Girl, let the man talk.

LINDNER: [*With understated relief.*] Thank you. I would sort of like to explain this thing in my own way. I mean I want to explain to you in a certain way.

WALTER: Go ahead.

LINDNER: Yes. Well. I'm going to try to get right to the point. I'm sure we'll all appreciate that in the long run.

BENEATHA: Yes.

WALTER: Be still now!

LINDNER: Well—

RUTH: [*Still innocently.*] Would you like another chair—you don't look comfortable.

LINDNER: [*More frustrated than annoyed.*] No, thank you very much. Please. Well— to get right to the point I— [*A great breath, and he is off at last.*] I am sure you people must be aware of some of the incidents which have happened in various parts of the city when colored people have moved into certain areas— [BENEATHA *exhales heavily and starts tossing a piece of fruit up and down in the air.*] Well—because we have what I think is going to be a unique type of organization in American community life—not only do we deplore that kind of thing—but we are trying to do something about it. [BENEATHA *stops tossing and turns with a new and quizzical interest to the man.*] We feel— [*Gaining confidence in his mission because of the interest in the faces of the people he is talking to.*] —we feel that most of the trouble in this world, when you come right down to it— [*He hits his knee for emphasis.*] —most of the trouble exists because people just don't sit down and talk to each other.

RUTH: [*Nodding as she might in church, pleased with the remark.*] You can say that again, mister.

LINDNER: [*More encouraged by such affirmation.*] That we don't try hard enough in this world to understand the other fellow's problem. The other guy's point of view.

RUTH: Now that's right.

[BENEATHA *and* WALTER *merely watch and listen with genuine interest.*]

LINDNER: Yes—that's the way we feel out in Clybourne Park. And that's why I was elected to come here this afternoon and talk to you people. Friendly like, you know, the way people should talk to each other and see if we couldn't find some way to work this thing out. As I say, the whole business is a matter of *caring* about the other fellow. Anybody can see that you are a nice family of folks, hard working and honest I'm sure. [BENEATHA *frowns slightly, quizzically, her head tilted regarding him.*] Today everybody knows what it means to be on the outside of something. And of course, there is always somebody who is out to take the advantage of people who don't always understand.

WALTER: What do you mean?

LINDNER: Well—you see our community is made up of people who've worked hard as the dickens for years to build up that little community. They're not rich and fancy people; just hardworking, honest people who don't really have much but those little homes and a dream of the kind of community they want to raise their children in. Now, I don't say we are perfect and there is a lot wrong in some of the things they want. But you've got to admit that a man, right or wrong, has the right to want to have the neighborhood he lives in a certain kind of way. And at the moment the overwhelming majority of our people out there feel that people get along better, take more of a common interest in the life of the community, when they share a common background. I want you to believe me when I tell you that race prejudice simply doesn't enter into it. It is a matter of the people of Clybourne Park believing, rightly or wrongly, as I say, that for the happiness of all concerned that our Negro families are happier when they live in their *own* communities.

BENEATHA: [*With a grand and bitter gesture.*] This, friends, is the Welcoming Committee!

WALTER: [*Dumbfounded, looking at* LINDNER.] Is this what you came marching all the way over here to tell us?

LINDNER: Well, now we've been having a fine conversation. I hope you'll hear me all the way through.

WALTER: [*Tightly.*] Go ahead, man.

LINDNER: You see—in the face of all things I have said, we are prepared to make your family a very generous offer . . .

BENEATHA: Thirty pieces and not a coin less![1]

WALTER: Yeah?

LINDNER: [*Putting on his glasses and drawing a form out of the briefcase.*] Our association is prepared, through the collective effort of our people, to buy the house from you at a financial gain to your family.

RUTH: Lord have mercy, ain't this the living gall!

WALTER: All right, you through?

LINDNER: Well, I want to give you the exact terms of the financial arrangement—

WALTER: We don't want to hear no exact terms of no arrangements. I want to know if you got any more to tell us 'bout getting together?

LINDNER: [*Taking off his glasses.*] Well—I don't suppose that you feel . . .

WALTER: Never mind how I feel—you got any more to say 'bout how people ought to sit down and talk to each other? . . . Get out of my house, man.

[*He turns his back and walks to the door.*]

LINDNER: [*Looking around at the hostile faces and reaching and assembling his hat and briefcase.*] Well—I don't understand why you people are reacting this way. What do you think you are going to gain by moving into a neighborhood where you just aren't wanted and where some elements—well—people can get awful worked up when they feel that their whole way of life and everything they've ever worked for is threatened.

WALTER: Get out.

LINDNER: [*At the door, holding a small card.*] Well—I'm sorry it went like this.

WALTER: Get out.

LINDNER: [*Almost sadly regarding* WALTER.] You just can't force people to change their hearts, son.

---

1. Judas is paid thirty pieces of silver after he betrays Jesus. Matthew 26.15.

[*He turns and put his card on a table and exits.* WALTER *pushes the door to with stinging hatred, and stands looking at it.* RUTH *just sits and* BENEATHA *just stands. They say nothing.* MAMA *and* TRAVIS *enter.*]

MAMA: Well—this all the packing got done since I left out of here this morning. I testify before God that my children got all the energy of the dead. What time the moving men due?

BENEATHA: Four o'clock. You had a caller, Mama.

[*She is smiling, teasingly.*]

MAMA: Sure enough—who?

BENEATHA: [*Her arms folded saucily.*] The Welcoming Committee.

[WALTER *and* RUTH *giggle.*]

MAMA: [*Innocently.*] Who?

BENEATHA: The Welcoming Committee. They said they're sure going to be glad to see you when you get there.

WALTER: [*Devilishly.*] Yeah, they said they can't hardly wait to see your face.

[*Laughter.*]

MAMA: [*Sensing their facetiousness.*] What's the matter with you all?

WALTER: Ain't nothing the matter with us. We just telling you 'bout the gentleman who came to see you this afternoon. From the Clybourne Park Improvement Association.

MAMA: What he want?

RUTH: [*In the same mood as* BENEATHA *and* WALTER.] To welcome you, honey.

WALTER: He said they can't hardly wait. He said the one thing they don't have, that they just *dying* to have out there is a fine family of colored people! [*To* RUTH *and* BENEATHA.] Ain't that right!

RUTH AND BENEATHA: [*Mockingly.*] Yeah! He left his card in case—

[*They indicate the card, and* MAMA *picks it up and throws it on the floor—understanding and looking off as she draws her chair up to the table on which she has put her plant and some sticks and some cord.*]

MAMA: Father, give us strength. [*Knowingly—and without fun.*] Did he threaten us?

BENEATHA: Oh—Mama—they don't do it like that anymore. He

talked Brotherhood. He said everybody ought to learn how to sit down and hate each other with good Christian fellowship.

[*She and* WALTER *shake hands to ridicule the remark.*]

MAMA: [*Sadly.*] Lord, protect us . . .

RUTH: You should hear the money those folks raised to buy the house from us. All we paid and then some.

BENEATHA: What they think we going to do—eat 'em?

RUTH: No, honey, marry 'em.

MAMA: [*Shaking her head.*] Lord, Lord, Lord . . .

RUTH: Well—that's the way the crackers crumble. Joke.

BENEATHA: [*Laughingly noticing what her mother is doing.*] Mama, what are you doing?

MAMA: Fixing my plant so it won't get hurt none on the way . . .

BENEATHA: Mama, you going to take *that* to the new house?

MAMA: Un-huh—

BENEATHA: That raggedy-looking old thing?

MAMA: [*Stopping and looking at her.*] It expresses *me.*

RUTH: [*With delight, to* BENEATHA.] So there, Miss Thing!

[WALTER *comes to* MAMA *suddenly and bends down behind her and squeezes her in his arms with all his strength. She is overwhelmed by the suddenness of it and, though delighted, her manner is like that of* RUTH *with* TRAVIS.]

MAMA: Look out now, boy! You make me mess up my thing here!

WALTER: [*His face lit, he slips down on his knees beside her, his arms still about her.*] Mama . . . you know what it means to climb up in the chariot?

MAMA: [*Gruffly, very happy.*] Get on away from me now . . .

RUTH: [*Near the gift-wrapped package, trying to catch* WALTER's *eye.*] Psst—

WALTER: What the old song say, Mama . . .

RUTH: Walter—Now?

[*She is pointing at the package.*]

WALTER: [*Speaking the lines, sweetly, playfully, in his mother's face.*]

I got wings . . . you got wings . . .
All God's Children got wings . . .

MAMA: Boy—get out of my face and do some work . . .

WALTER:
When I get to heaven gonna put on my wings,
Gonna fly all over God's heaven . . .[2]

BENEATHA: [*Teasingly, from across the room.*] Everybody talking 'bout heaven ain't going there!

WALTER: [*To* RUTH, *who is carrying the box across to them.*] I don't know, you think we ought to give her that . . . Seems to me she ain't been very appreciative around here.

MAMA: [*Eying the box, which is obviously a gift.*] What is that?

WALTER: [*Taking it from* RUTH *and putting it on the table in front of* MAMA.] Well— what you all think? Should we give it to her?

RUTH: Oh—she was pretty good today.

MAMA: I'll good you—
[*She turns her eyes to the box again.*]

BENEATHA: Open it, Mama.
[*She stands up, looks at it, turns and looks at all of them, and then presses her hands together and does not open the package.*]

WALTER: [*Sweetly.*] Open it, Mama. It's for you. [MAMA *looks in his eyes. It is the first present in her life without its being Christmas. Slowly she opens her package and lifts out, one by one, a brand-new sparkling set of gardening tools.* WALTER *continues, prodding.*] Ruth made up the note—read it . . .

MAMA: [*Picking up the card and adjusting her glasses.*] "To our own Mrs. Miniver[3]— Love from Brother, Ruth and Beneatha." Ain't that lovely . . .

TRAVIS: [*Tugging at his father's sleeve.*] Daddy, can I give her mine now?

WALTER: All right, son. [TRAVIS *flies to get his gift.*] Travis didn't want to go in with the rest of us, Mama. He got his own. [*Somewhat amused.*] We don't know what it is . . .

TRAVIS: [*Racing back in the room with a large hatbox and putting it in front of his grandmother.*] Here!

2. Lines from "I Got Shoes," an African American spiritual.

3. Mrs. Miniver is the titular heroine of a popular 1942 film credited with helping to swing American sentiment toward war against Nazi Germany. Mrs. Miniver is a plucky suburban London housewife whose adventures include disarming a Nazi pilot who parachutes into her garden.

MAMA: Lord have mercy, baby. You done gone and bought your grandmother a hat?

TRAVIS: [*Very proud.*] Open it!

[*She does and lifts out an elaborate, but very elaborate, wide gardening hat, and all the adults break up at the sight of it.*]

RUTH: Travis, honey, what is that?

TRAVIS: [*Who thinks it is beautiful and appropriate.*] It's a gardening hat! Like the ladies always have on in the magazines when they work in their gardens.

BENEATHA: [*Giggling fiercely.*] Travis—we were trying to make Mama Mrs. Miniver—not Scarlett O'Hara![4]

MAMA: [*Indignantly.*] What's the matter with you all! This here is a beautiful hat! [*Absurdly.*] I always wanted me one just like it!

[*She pops it on her head to prove it to her grandson, and the hat is ludicrous and considerably oversized.*]

RUTH: Hot dog! Go, Mama!

WALTER: [*Doubled over with laughter.*] I'm sorry, Mama—but you look like you ready to go out and chop you some cotton sure enough!

[*They all laugh except MAMA, out of deference to TRAVIS' feelings.*]

MAMA: [*Gathering the boy up to her.*] Bless your heart—this is the prettiest hat I ever owned— [WALTER, RUTH *and* BENEATHA *chime in—noisily, festively and insincerely congratulating* TRAVIS *on his gift.*] What are we all standing around here for? We ain't finished packin' yet. Bennie, you ain't packed one book.

[*The bell rings.*]

BENEATHA: That couldn't be the movers . . . it's not hardly two good yet—

[BENEATHA *goes into her room.* MAMA *starts for door.*]

WALTER: [*Turning, stiffening.*] Wait—wait—I'll get it.

[*He stands and looks at the door.*]

MAMA: You expecting company, son?

WALTER: [*Just looking at the door.*] Yeah—yeah . . .

---

4. Scarlett O'Hara is the heroine of *Gone with the Wind*, the popular 1939 movie whose romantic depictions of the South promoted the Ku Klux Klan and perpetuated gross racial stereotypes. Scarlett is a self-serving, vain, ingenious survivor, the heiress of a plantation ruined by the Civil War.

[MAMA *looks at* RUTH, *and they exchange innocent and unfrightened glances.*]

MAMA: [*Not understanding.*] Well, let them in, son.

BENEATHA: [*From her room.*] We need some more string.

MAMA: Travis—you run to the hardware and get me some string cord.

[MAMA *goes out and* WALTER *turns and looks at* RUTH. TRAVIS *goes to a dish for money.*]

RUTH: Why don't you answer the door, man?

WALTER: [*Suddenly bounding across the floor to her.*] 'Cause sometimes it hard to let the future begin! [*Stooping down in her face.*]

I got wings! You got wings!
All God's children got wings!

[*He crosses to the door and throws it open. Standing there is a very slight little man in a not too prosperous business suit and with haunted frightened eyes and a hat pulled down tightly, brim up, around his forehead.* TRAVIS *passes between the men and exits.* WALTER *leans deep in the man's face, still in his jubilance.*]

When I get to heaven gonna put on my wings,
Gonna fly all over God's heaven . . .

[*The little man just stares at him.*]

Heaven—

[*Suddenly he stops and looks past the little man into the empty hallway.*] Where's Willy, man?

BOBO: He ain't with me.

WALTER: [*Not disturbed.*] Oh—come on in. You know my wife.

BOBO: [*Dumbly, taking off his hat.*] Yes—h'you, Miss Ruth.

RUTH: [*Quietly, a mood apart from her husband already, seeing* BOBO.] Hello, Bobo.

WALTER: You right on time today . . . Right on time. That's the way! [*He slaps* BOBO *on his back.*] Sit down . . . lemme hear.

[RUTH *stands stiffly and quietly in back of them, as though somehow she senses death, her eyes fixed on her husband.*]

BOBO: [*His frightened eyes on the floor, his hat in his hands.*] Could I please get a drink of water, before I tell you about it, Walter Lee? [WALTER *does not take his eyes off the man.* RUTH *goes blindly to the tap and gets a glass of water and brings it to* BOBO.]

WALTER: There ain't nothing wrong, is there?

BOBO: Lemme tell you—

WALTER: Man—didn't nothing go wrong?

BOBO: Lemme tell you—Walter Lee. [*Looking at* RUTH *and talking to her more than to* WALTER.] You know how it was. I got to tell you how it was. I mean first I got to tell you how it was all the way . . . I mean about the money I put in, Walter Lee . . .

WALTER: [*With taut agitation now.*] What about the money you put in?

BOBO: Well—it wasn't much as we told you—me and Willy— [*He stops.*] I'm sorry, Walter. I got a bad feeling about it. I got a real bad feeling about it . . .

WALTER: Man, what you telling me about all this for? . . . Tell me what happened in Springfield . . .

BOBO: Springfield.

RUTH: [*Like a dead woman.*] What was supposed to happen in Springfield?

BOBO: [*To her.*] This deal that me and Walter went into with Willy—Me and Willy was going to go down to Springfield and spread some money 'round so's we wouldn't have to wait so long for the liquor license . . . That's what we were going to do. Everybody said that was the way you had to do, you understand, Miss Ruth?

WALTER: Man—what happened down there?

BOBO: [*A pitiful man, near tears.*] I'm trying to tell you, Walter.

WALTER: [*Screaming at him suddenly.*] THEN TELL ME, GOD-DAMMIT . . . WHAT'S THE MATTER WITH YOU?

BOBO: Man . . . I didn't go to no Springfield, yesterday.

WALTER: [*Halted, life hanging in the moment.*] Why not?

BOBO: [*The long way, the hard way to tell.*] 'Cause I didn't have no reasons to . . .

WALTER: Man, what are you talking about!

BOBO: I'm talking about the fact that when I got to the train station yesterday morning—eight o'clock like we planned . . . Man— *Willy didn't never show up.*

WALTER: Why . . . where was he . . . where is he?

BOBO: That's what I'm trying to tell you . . . I don't know . . . I waited six hours . . . I called his house . . . and I waited . . . six hours . . . I waited in that train station six hours . . . [*Breaking into tears.*] That was all the extra money I had in the world . . . [*Looking up at* WALTER *with the tears running down his face.*] Man, *Willy is gone.*

WALTER: Gone, what you mean Willy is gone? Gone where? You mean he went by himself. You mean he went off to Springfield by himself—to take care of getting the license— [*Turns and looks anxiously at* RUTH.] You mean maybe he didn't want too many people in on the business down there? [*Looks to* RUTH *again, as before.*] You know Willy got his own ways. [*Looks back to* BOBO.] Maybe you was late yesterday and he just went on down there without you. Maybe— maybe—he's been callin' you at home tryin' to tell you what happened or something. Maybe— maybe—he just got sick. He's somewhere—he's got to be somewhere. We just got to find him—me and you got to find him. [*Grabs* BOBO *senselessly by the collar and starts to shake him.*] We got to!

BOBO: [*In sudden angry, frightened agony.*] What's the matter with you, Walter! *When a cat take off with your money he don't leave you no maps!*

WALTER: [*Turning madly, as though he is looking for* WILLY *in the very room.*] Willy! . . . Willy . . . don't do it . . . Please don't do it . . . Man, not with that money . . . Man, please, not with that money . . . Oh, God . . . Don't let it be true . . . [*He is wandering around, crying out for* WILLY *and looking for him or perhaps for help from God.*] Man . . . I trusted you . . . Man, I put my life in your hands . . . [*He starts to crumple down on the floor as* RUTH *just covers her face in horror.* MAMA *opens the door and comes into the room, with* BENEATHA *behind her.*] Man . . . [*He starts to pound the floor with his fists, sobbing wildly.*] *That money is made out of my father's flesh* . . .

BOBO: [*Standing over him helplessly.*] I'm sorry, Walter . . . [*Only*

WALTER's *sobs reply.* BOBO *puts on his hat.*] I had my life staked on this deal, too . . .

[*He exits.*]

MAMA: [*To* WALTER.] Son— [*She goes to him, bends down to him, talks to his bent head.*] Son . . . Is it gone? Son, I gave you sixty-five hundred dollars. Is it gone? All of it? Beneatha's money too?

WALTER: [*Lifting his head slowly.*] Mama . . . I never . . . went to the bank at all . . .

MAMA: [*Not wanting to believe him.*] You mean . . . your sister's school money . . . you used that too . . . Walter? . . .

WALTER: Yessss! . . . All of it . . . It's all gone . . . [*There is total silence.* RUTH *stands with her face covered with her hands;* BENEATHA *leans forlornly against a wall, fingering a piece of red ribbon from the mother's gift.* MAMA *stops and looks at her son without recognition and then, quite without thinking about it, starts to beat him senselessly in the face.* BENEATHA *goes to them and stops it.*]

BENEATHA: Mama!

[MAMA *stops and looks at both of her children and rises slowly and wanders vaguely, aimlessly away from them.*]

MAMA: I seen . . . him . . . night after night . . . come in . . . and look at that rug . . . and then look at me . . . the red showing in his eyes . . . the veins moving in his head . . . I seen him grow thin and old before he was forty . . . working and working and working like somebody's old horse . . . killing himself . . . and you— you give it all away in a day . . .

BENEATHA: Mama—

MAMA: Oh, God . . . [*She looks up to Him.*] Look down here—and show me the strength.

BENEATHA: Mama—

MAMA: [*Folding over.*] Strength . . .

BENEATHA: [*Plaintively.*] Mama . . .

MAMA: Strength!

[*Curtain.*]

ACT III

An hour later.

At curtain, there is a sullen light of gloom in the living room, gray light not unlike that which began the first scene of Act I. At left we can see WALTER *within his room, alone with himself. He is stretched out on the bed, his shirt out and open, his arms under his head. He does not smoke, he does not cry out, he merely lies there, looking up at the ceiling, much as if he were alone in the world.*

In the living room BENEATHA *sits at the table, still surrounded by the now almost ominous packing crates. She sits looking off. We feel that this is a mood struck perhaps an hour before, and it lingers now, full of the empty sound of profound disappointment. We see on a line from her brother's bedroom the sameness of their attitudes. Presently the bell rings and* BENEATHA *rises without ambition or interest in answering. It is* ASAGAI, *smiling broadly, striding into the room with energy and happy expectation and conversation.*

ASAGAI: I came over . . . I had some free time. I thought I might help with the packing. Ah, I like the look of packing crates! A household in preparation for a journey! It depresses some people . . . but for me . . . it is another feeling. Something full of the flow of life, do you understand? Movement, progress . . . It makes me think of Africa.

BENEATHA: Africa!

ASAGAI: What kind of a mood is this? Have I told you how deeply you move me?

BENEATHA: He gave away the money, Asagai . . .

ASAGAI: Who gave away what money?

BENEATHA: The insurance money. My brother gave it away.

ASAGAI: Gave it away?

BENEATHA: He made an investment! With a man even Travis wouldn't have trusted.

ASAGAI: And it's gone?

BENEATHA: Gone!

ASAGAI: I'm very sorry . . . And you, now?

BENEATHA: Me? . . . Me? . . . Me, I'm nothing . . . Me. When I was very small . . . we used to take our sleds out in the wintertime and the only hills we had were the ice-covered stone steps of some houses down the street. And we used to fill them in with snow and make them smooth and slide down them all day . . . and it was very dangerous you know . . . far too steep . . . and sure enough one day a kid named Rufus came down too fast and hit the sidewalk . . . and we saw his face just split open right there in front of us . . . And I remember standing there looking at his bloody open face thinking that was the end of Rufus. But the ambulance came and they took him to the hospital and they fixed the broken bones and they sewed it all up . . . and the next time I saw Rufus he just had a little line down the middle of his face . . . I never got over that . . .

> [WALTER *sits up, listening on the bed. Throughout this scene it is important that we feel his reaction at all times, that he visibly respond to the words of his sister and* ASAGAI.]

ASAGAI: What?

BENEATHA: That that was what one person could do for another, fix him up— sew up the problem, make him all right again. That was the most marvelous thing in the world . . . I wanted to do that. I always thought it was the one concrete thing in the world that a human being could do. Fix up the sick, you know—and make them whole again. This was truly being God . . .

ASAGAI: You wanted to be God?

BENEATHA: No—I wanted to cure. It used to be so important to me. I wanted to cure. It used to matter. I used to care. I mean about people and how their bodies hurt . . .

ASAGAI: And you've stopped caring?

BENEATHA: Yes—I think so.

ASAGAI: Why?

> [WALTER *rises, goes to the door of his room and is about to open it, then stops and stands listening, leaning on the door jamb.*]

BENEATHA: Because it doesn't seem deep enough, close enough to what ails mankind—I mean this thing of sewing up bodies or administering drugs. Don't you understand? It was a child's reaction to the world. I thought that doctors had the secret to all the hurts . . . That's the way a child sees things—or an idealist.

ASAGAI: Children see things very well sometimes—and idealists even better.

BENEATHA: I know that's what you think. Because you are still where I left off— you still care. This is what you see for the world, for Africa. You with the dreams of the future will patch up all Africa—you are going to cure the Great Sore of colonialism with Independence——

ASAGAI: Yes!

BENEATHA: Yes—and you think that one word is the penicillin of the human spirit: "Independence!" But then what?

ASAGAI: That will be the problem for another time. First we must get there.

BENEATHA: And where does it end?

ASAGAI: End? Who even spoke of an end? To life? To living?

BENEATHA: An end to misery!

ASAGAI: [*Smiling.*] You sound like a French intellectual.

BENEATHA: No! I sound like a human being who just had her future taken right out of her hands! While I was sleeping in my bed in there, things were happening in this world that directly concerned me—and nobody asked me, consulted me—they just went out and did things—and changed my life. Don't you see there isn't any real progress, Asagai, there is only one large circle that we march in, around and around, each of us with our own little picture—in front of us—our own little mirage that we think is the future.

ASAGAI: That is the mistake.

BENEATHA: What?

ASAGAI: What you just said—about the circle. It isn't a circle—it is simply a long line—as in geometry, you know, one that reaches into infinity. And because we cannot see the end—we also cannot see how it changes. And it is very odd but those who see the changes are called "idealists"—and those who cannot, or refuse to think, they are the "realists." It is very strange, and amusing too, I think.

BENEATHA: You—you are almost religious.

ASAGAI: Yes . . . I think I have the religion of doing what is necessary in the world— and of worshipping man—because he is so marvelous, you see.

BENEATHA: Man is foul! And the human race deserves its misery!

ASAGAI: You see: *you* have become the religious one in the old sense. Already, and after such a small defeat, you are worshipping despair.

BENEATHA: From now on, I worship the truth—and the truth is that people are puny, small and selfish . . .

ASAGAI: Truth? Why is it that you despairing ones always think that only you have the truth? I never thought to see *you* like that. You! Your brother made a stupid, childish mistake—and you are grateful to him. So that now you can give up the ailing human race on account of it. You talk about what good is struggle; what good is anything? Where are we all going? And why are we bothering?

BENEATHA: *And you cannot answer it!* All your talk and dreams about Africa and Independence. Independence and then what? What about all the crooks and petty thieves and just plain idiots who will come into power to steal and plunder the same as before— only now they will be black and do it in the name of the new Independence—You cannot answer that.

ASAGAI: [*Shouting over her.*] *I live the answer!* [*Pause.*] In my village at home it is the exceptional man who can even read a newspaper . . . or who ever *sees* a book at all. I will go home and much of what I will have to say will seem strange to the people of my village . . . But I will teach and work and things will happen, slowly and swiftly. At times it will seem that nothing changes at all . . . and then again . . . the sudden dramatic events which make history leap into the future. And then quiet again. Retrogression even. Guns, murder, revolution. And I even will have moments when I wonder if the quiet was not better than all that death and hatred. But I will look about my village at the illiteracy and disease and ignorance and I will not wonder long. And perhaps . . . perhaps I will be a great man . . . I mean perhaps I will hold on to the substance of truth and find my way always with the right course . . . and perhaps for it I will be butchered in my bed some night by the servants of empire . . .

BENEATHA: *The martyr!*

ASAGAI: . . . or perhaps I shall live to be a very old man, respected and esteemed in my new nation . . . And perhaps I shall hold office and this is what I'm trying to tell you, Alaiyo; perhaps the things I believe now for my country will be wrong and outmoded, and I will not understand and do terrible things to have things my way or merely to keep my power. Don't you see that there will be young men and women, not British soldiers then, but my own black countrymen . . . to step out of the shadows some evening and slit my then useless throat? Don't you see they have always been there . . . that they always will be. And that such a thing as my own death will be an advance? They who might kill me even . . . actually replenish me!

BENEATHA: Oh, Asagai, I know all that.

ASAGAI: Good! Then stop moaning and groaning and tell me what you plan to do.

BENEATHA: Do?

ASAGAI: I have a bit of a suggestion.

BENEATHA: What?

ASAGAI: [*Rather quietly for him.*] That when it is all over—that you come home with me—

BENEATHA: [*Slapping herself on the forehead with exasperation born of misunderstanding.*] Oh—Asagai—at this moment you decide to be romantic!

ASAGAI: [*Quickly understanding the misunderstanding.*] My dear, young creature of the New World—I do not mean across the city—I mean across the ocean; home—to Africa.

BENEATHA: [*Slowly understanding and turning to him with murmured amazement.*] To—to Nigeria?

ASAGAI: Yes! . . . [*Smiling and lifting his arms playfully.*] Three hundred years later the African Prince rose up out of the seas and swept the maiden back across the middle passage over which her ancestors had come—

BENEATHA: [*Unable to play.*] Nigeria?

ASAGAI: Nigeria. Home. [*Coming to her with genuine romantic flippancy.*] I will show you our mountains and our stars; and give you cool drinks from gourds and teach you the old songs and the ways of our people—and, in time, we will pretend that— [*Very softly.*] —you have only been away for a day—

[*She turns her back to him, thinking. He swings her around and takes her full in his arms in a long embrace which proceeds to passion.*]

BENEATHA: [*Pulling away.*] You're getting me all mixed up—

ASAGAI: Why?

BENEATHA: Too many things—too many things have happened today. I must sit down and think. I don't know what I feel about anything right this minute.

[*She promptly sits down and props her chin on her fist.*]

ASAGAI: [*Charmed.*] All right, I shall leave you. No—don't get up. [*Touching her, gently, sweetly.*] Just sit awhile and think . . . Never be afraid to sit awhile and think. [*He goes to door and looks at her.*] How often I have looked at you and said, "Ah—so this is what the New World hath finally wrought . . . "

> [*He exits.* BENEATHA *sits on alone. Presently* WALTER *enters from his room and starts to rummage through things, feverishly looking for something. She looks up and turns in her seat.*]

BENEATHA: [*Hissingly.*] Yes—just look at what the New World hath wrought! . . . Just look! [*She gestures with bitter disgust.*] There he is! *Monsieur le petit bourgeois noir*—himself! There he is—Symbol of a Rising Class! Entrepreneur! Titan of the system! [WALTER *ignores her completely and continues frantically and destructively looking for something and hurling things to the floor and tearing things out of their place in his search.* BENEATHA *ignores the eccentricity of his actions and goes on with the monologue of insult.*] Did you dream of yachts on Lake Michigan, Brother? Did you see yourself on that Great Day sitting down at the Conference Table, surrounded by all the mighty bald-headed men in America? All halted, waiting, breathless, waiting for your pronouncements on industry? Waiting for you—Chairman of the Board? [WALTER *finds what he is looking for—a small piece of white paper—and pushes it in his pocket and puts on his coat and rushes out without ever having looked at her. She shouts after him.*] I look at you and I see the final triumph of stupidity in the world!

> [*The door slams and she returns to just sitting again.* RUTH *comes quickly out of* MAMA's *room.*]

RUTH: Who was that?

BENEATHA: Your husband.

RUTH: Where did he go?

BENEATHA: Who knows—maybe he has an appointment at U.S. Steel.

RUTH: [*Anxiously, with frightened eyes.*] You didn't say nothing bad to him, did you?

BENEATHA: Bad? Say anything bad to him? No—I told him he was a sweet boy and full of dreams and everything is strictly peachy keen, as the ofay[5] kids say!

---

5. White.

[MAMA *enters from her bedroom. She is lost, vague, trying to catch hold, to make some sense of her former command of the world, but it still eludes her. A sense of waste overwhelms her gait; a measure of apology rides on her shoulders. She goes to her plant, which has remained on the table, looks at it, picks it up and takes it to the window sill and sits it outside, and she stands and looks at it a long moment. Then she closes the window, straightens her body with effort and turns around to her children.*]

MAMA: Well—ain't it a mess in here, though? [*A false cheerfulness, a beginning of something.*] I guess we all better stop moping around and get some work done. All this unpacking and everything we got to do. [RUTH *raises her head slowly in response to the sense of the line; and* BENEATHA *in similar manner turns very slowly to look at her mother.*] One of you all better call the moving people and tell 'em not to come.

RUTH: Tell 'em not to come?

MAMA: Of course, baby. Ain't no need in 'em coming all the way here and having to go back. They charges for that too. [*She sits down, fingers to her brow, thinking.*] Lord, ever since I was a little girl, I always remembers people saying, "Lena— Lena Eggleston, you aims too high all the time. You needs to slow down and see life a little more like it is. Just slow down some." That's what they always used to say down home—"Lord, that Lena Eggleston is a high-minded thing. She'll get her due one day!"

RUTH: No, Lena . . .

MAMA: Me and Big Walter just didn't never learn right.

RUTH: Lena, no! We gotta go. Bennie—tell her . . . [*She rises and crosses to* BENEATHA *with her arms outstretched.* BENEATHA *doesn't respond.*] Tell her we can still move . . . the notes ain't but a hundred and twenty-five a month. We got four grown people in this house—we can work . . .

MAMA: [*To herself.*] Just aimed too high all the time—

RUTH: [*Turning and going to* MAMA *fast—the words pouring out with urgency and desperation.*] Lena—I'll work . . . I'll work twenty hours a day in all the kitchens in Chicago . . . I'll strap my baby on my back if I have to and scrub all the floors in America and wash all the sheets in America if I have to—but we got to move . . . We got to get out of here . . .

[MAMA *reaches out absently and pats* RUTH*'s hand.*]

MAMA: No—I sees things differently now. Been thinking 'bout some of the things we could do to fix this place up some. I seen a second-hand bureau over on Maxwell Street just the other day that could fit right there. [*She points to where the new furniture might go.* RUTH *wanders away from her.*] Would need some new handles on it and then a little varnish and then it look like something brand-new. And—we can put up them new curtains in the kitchen . . . Why this place be looking fine. Cheer us all up so that we forget trouble ever came . . . [*To* RUTH.] And you could get some nice screens to put up in your room round the baby's bassinet . . . [*She looks at both of them, pleadingly.*] Sometimes you just got to know when to give up some things . . . and hold on to what you got.

[WALTER *enters from the outside, looking spent and leaning against the door, his coat hanging from him.*]

MAMA: Where you been, son?

WALTER: [*Breathing hard.*] Made a call.

MAMA: To who, son?

WALTER: To The Man.

MAMA: What man, baby?

WALTER: The Man, Mama. Don't you know who The Man is?

RUTH: Walter Lee?

WALTER: *The Man.* Like the guys in the streets say—The Man. Captain Boss—Mistuh Charley . . . Old Captain Please Mr. Bossman . . .

BENEATHA: [*Suddenly.*] Lindner!

WALTER: That's right! That's good. I told him to come right over.

BENEATHA: [*Fiercely, understanding.*] For what? What do you want to see him for!

WALTER: [*Looking at his sister.*] We going to do business with him.

MAMA: What you talking 'bout, son?

WALTER: Talking 'bout life, Mama. You all always telling me to see life like it is. Well—I laid in there on my back today . . . and I figured it out. Life just like it is. Who gets and who don't get. [*He sits down with his coat on and laughs.*] Mama, you know it's all divided up. Life is. Sure enough. Between the takers and the "tooken." [*He laughs.*] I've figured it out finally. [*He looks around at them.*] Yeah. Some of us always getting "tooken." [*He laughs.*] People like Willy Harris, they don't never get "tooken." And you know why the rest of us do? 'Cause we all mixed up. Mixed up bad. We get to looking 'round for the right and the wrong, and we worry about it and cry about it and stay up nights trying to figure out 'bout the wrong and the right of things all the time . . . And all the time, man, them takers is out there operating, just taking and taking. Willy Harris? Shoot—Willy Harris don't even count. He don't even count in the big scheme of things. But I'll say one thing for old Willy Harris . . . he's taught me something. He's taught me to keep my eye on what counts in this world. Yeah— [*Shouting out a little.*] Thanks, Willy!

RUTH: What did you call that man for, Walter Lee?

WALTER: Called him to tell him to come on over to the show. Gonna put on a show for the man. Just what he wants to see. You see, Mama, the man came here today and he told us that them people out there where you want us to move—well they so upset they willing to pay us not to move out there. [*He laughs again.*] And—and oh, Mama—you would of been proud of the way me and Ruth and Bennie acted. We told him to get out . . . Lord have mercy! We told the man to get out. Oh, we was some proud folks this afternoon, yeah. [*He lights a cigarette.*] We were still full of that old-time stuff . . .

RUTH: [*Coming toward him slowly.*] You talking 'bout taking them people's money to keep us from moving in that house?

WALTER: I ain't just talking 'bout it, baby—I'm telling you that's what's going to happen.

BENEATHA: Oh, God! Where is the bottom! Where is the real honest-to-God bottom so he can't go any farther!

WALTER: See—that's the old stuff. You and that boy that was here today. You all want everybody to carry a flag and a spear and sing some marching songs, huh? You wanna spend your life looking into things and trying to find the right and the wrong part, huh? Yeah. You know what's going to happen to that boy someday—he'll find himself sitting in a dungeon, locked in forever—and the takers will have the key! Forget it, baby! There ain't no causes—there ain't nothing but taking in this world, and he who takes most is smartest—and it don't make a damn bit of difference *how.*

MAMA: You making something inside me cry, son. Some awful pain inside me.

WALTER: Don't cry, Mama. Understand. That white man is going to walk in that door able to write checks for more money than we ever had. It's important to him and I'm going to help him . . . I'm going to put on the show, Mama.

MAMA: Son—I come from five generations of people who was slaves and share-croppers—but ain't nobody in my family never let nobody pay 'em no money that was a way of telling us we wasn't fit to walk the earth. We ain't never been that poor. [*Raising her eyes and looking at him.*] We ain't never been that dead inside.

BENEATHA: Well—we are dead now. All the talk about dreams and sunlight that goes on in this house. All dead.

WALTER: What's the matter with you all! I didn't make this world! It was give to me this way! Hell, yes, I want me some yachts someday! Yes, I want to hang some real pearls 'round my wife's neck. Ain't she supposed to wear no pearls? Somebody tell me—tell me, who decides which women is suppose to wear pearls in this world. I tell you I am a *man*—and I think my wife should wear some pearls in this world!

[*This last line hangs a good while and* WALTER *begins to move about the room. The word "Man" has penetrated his consciousness; he mumbles it to himself repeatedly between strange agitated pauses as he moves about.*]

MAMA: Baby, how you going to feel on the inside?

WALTER: Fine! . . . Going to feel fine . . . a man . . .

MAMA: You won't have nothing left then, Walter Lee.

WALTER: [*Coming to her.*] I'm going to feel fine, Mama. I'm going to look that son-of-a-bitch in the eyes and say— [*He falters.*] —and say, "All right, Mr. Lindner— [*He falters even more.*] —that's your neighborhood out there. You got the right to keep it like you want. You got the right to have it like you want. Just write the check and—the house is yours." And, and I am going to say— [*His voice almost breaks.*] And you—you people just put the money in my hand and you won't have to live next to this bunch of stinking niggers! . . . [*He straightens up and moves away from his mother, walking around the room.*] Maybe—maybe I'll just get down on my black knees . . . [*He does so;* RUTH *and* BENNIE *and* MAMA *watch him in frozen horror.*] Captain, Mistuh, Bossman. [*He starts crying.*] A-hee-hee-hee! [*Wringing his hands in profoundly anguished imitation.*] Yassss-suh! Great White Father, just gi' ussen de money, fo' God's sake, and we's ain't gwine come out deh and dirty up yo' white folks neighborhood . . .

> [*He breaks down completely, then gets up and goes into the bedroom.*]

BENEATHA: That is not a man. That is nothing but a toothless rat.

MAMA: Yes—death done come in this here house. [*She is nodding, slowly, reflectively.*] Done come walking in my house. On the lips of my children. You what supposed to be my beginning again. You—what supposed to be my harvest. [*To* BENEATHA.] You—you mourning your brother?

BENEATHA: He's no brother of mine.

MAMA: What you say?

BENEATHA: I said that that individual in that room is no brother of mine.

MAMA: That's what I thought you said. You feeling like you better than he is today? [BENEATHA *does not answer.*] Yes? What you tell him a minute ago? That he wasn't a man? Yes? You give him up for me? You done wrote his epitaph too—like the rest of the world? Well, who give you the privilege?

BENEATHA: Be on my side for once! You saw what he just did, Mama! You saw him—down on his knees. Wasn't it you who taught me—to despise any man who would do that. Do what he's going to do.

MAMA: Yes—I taught you that. Me and your daddy. But I thought I taught you something else too . . . I thought I taught you to love him.

BENEATHA: Love him? There is nothing left to love.

MAMA: There is always something left to love. And if you ain't learned that, you ain't learned nothing. [*Looking at her.*] Have you cried for that boy today? I don't mean for yourself and for the family 'cause we lost the money. I mean for him; what he been through and what it done to him. Child, when do you think is the time to love somebody the most; when they done good and made things easy for everybody? Well then, you ain't through learning—because that ain't the time at all. It's when he's at his lowest and can't believe in hisself 'cause the world done whipped him so. When you starts measuring somebody, measure him right, child, measure him right. Make sure you done taken into account what hills and valleys he come through before he got to wherever he is.

[TRAVIS *bursts into the room at the end of the speech, leaving the door open.*]

TRAVIS: Grandmama—the moving men are downstairs! The truck just pulled up. MAMA: [*Turning and looking at him.*] Are they, baby? They downstairs?

[*She sighs and sits.* LINDNER *appears in the doorway. He peers in and knocks lightly, to gain attention, and comes in. All turn to look at him.*]

LINDNER: [*Hat and briefcase in hand.*] Uh—hello . . . [RUTH *crosses mechanically to the bedroom door and opens it and lets it swing open freely and slowly as the lights come up on* WALTER *within, still in his coat, sitting at the far corner of the room. He looks up and out through the room to* LINDNER.]

RUTH: He's here.

[*A long minute passes and* WALTER *slowly gets up.*]

LINDNER: [*Coming to the table with efficiency, putting his briefcase on the table and starting to unfold papers and unscrew fountain pens.*] Well, I certainly was glad to hear from you people. [WALTER *has begun the trek out of the room, slowly and awkwardly, rather like a small boy, passing the back of his sleeve across his mouth from time to time.*] Life can really be so much simpler than people let it be most of the time. Well—with whom do I negotiate? You, Mrs. Younger, or your son here? [MAMA *sits with her hands folded on her lap and her eyes closed as* WALTER *advances.* TRAVIS *goes close to* LINDNER *and looks at the papers curiously.*] Just some official papers, sonny.

RUTH: Travis, you go downstairs.

MAMA: [*Opening her eyes and looking into* WALTER'*s.*] No. Travis, you stay right here. And you make him understand what you doing, Walter Lee. You teach him good. Like Willy Harris taught you. You show where our five generations done come to. Go ahead, son—

WALTER: [*Looks down into his boy's eyes.* TRAVIS *grins at him merrily and* WALTER *draws him beside him with his arm lightly around his shoulders.*] Well, Mr. Lindner. [BENEATHA *turns away.*] We called you— [*There is a profound, simple groping quality in his speech.*] —because, well, me and my family [*He looks around and shifts from one foot to the other.*] Well—we are very plain people . . .

LINDNER: Yes—

WALTER: I mean—I have worked as a chauffeur most of my life— and my wife here, she does domestic work in people's kitchens. So does my mother. I mean—we are plain people . . .

LINDNER: Yes, Mr. Younger—

WALTER: [*Really like a small boy, looking down at his shoes and then up at the man.*] And—uh—well, my father, well, he was a laborer most of his life.

LINDNER: [*Absolutely confused.*] Uh, yes—

WALTER: [*Looking down at his toes once again.*] My father almost beat a man to death once because this man called him a bad name or something, you know what I mean?

LINDNER: No, I'm afraid I don't.

WALTER: [*Finally straightening up.*] Well, what I mean is that we come from people who had a lot of pride. I mean—we are very proud people. And that's my sister over there and she's going to be a doctor—and we are very proud—

LINDNER: Well—I am sure that is very nice, but—

WALTER: [*Starting to cry and facing the man eye to eye.*] What I am telling you is that we called you over here to tell you that we are very proud and that this is—this is my son, who makes the sixth generation of our family in this country, and that we have all thought about your offer and we have decided to move into our house because my father—my father—he earned it. [MAMA *has her eyes closed and is rocking back and forth as though she were in church, with her head nodding the amen yes.*] We don't want to make no trouble for nobody or fight no causes—but we will try to be good neighbors. That's all we got to say. [*He looks the man absolutely in the eyes.*] We don't want your money.

[*He turns and walks away from the man.*]

LINDNER: [*Looking around at all of them.*] I take it then that you have decided to occupy.

BENEATHA: That's what the man said.

LINDNER: [*To* MAMA *in her reverie.*] Then I would like to appeal to you, Mrs. Younger. You are older and wiser and understand things better I am sure . . .

MAMA: [*Rising.*] I am afraid you don't understand. My son said we was going to move and there ain't nothing left for me to say. [*Shaking her head with double meaning.*] You know how these young folks is nowadays, mister. Can't do a thing with 'em. Good-bye.

LINDNER: [*Folding up his materials.*] Well—if you are that final about it . . . There is nothing left for me to say. [*He finishes. He is almost ignored by the family, who are concentrating on* WALTER LEE. *At the door* LINDNER *halts and looks around.*] I sure hope you people know what you're doing.

[*He shakes his head and exits.*]

RUTH: [*Looking around and coming to life.*] Well, for God's sake—if the moving men are here—LET'S GET THE HELL OUT OF HERE!

MAMA: [*Into action.*] Ain't it the truth! Look at all this here mess. Ruth, put Travis' good jacket on him . . . Walter Lee, fix your tie and tuck your shirt in, you look just like somebody's hoodlum. Lord have mercy, where is my plant? [*She flies to get it amid the general bustling of the family, who are deliberately trying to ignore the nobility of the past moment.*] You all start on down . . . Travis child, don't go empty-handed . . . Ruth, where did I put that box with my skillets in it? I want to be in charge of it myself . . . I'm going to make us the biggest dinner we ever ate tonight . . . Beneatha, what's the matter with them stockings? Pull them things up, girl . . .

[*The family starts to file out as two moving men appear and begin to carry out the heavier pieces of furniture, bumping into the family as they move about.*]

BENEATHA: Mama, Asagai—asked me to marry him today and go to Africa—

MAMA: [*In the middle of her getting-ready activity.*] He did? You ain't old enough to marry nobody— [*Seeing the moving men lifting one of her chairs precariously.*] Darling, that ain't no bale of cotton, please handle it so we can sit in it again. I had that chair twenty-five years . . .

[*The movers sigh with exasperation and go on with their work.*]

BENEATHA: [*Girlishly and unreasonably trying to pursue the conversation.*] To go to Africa, Mama—be a doctor in Africa . . .

MAMA: [*Distracted.*] Yes, baby—

WALTER: Africa! What he want you to go to Africa for?

BENEATHA: To practice there . . .

WALTER: Girl, if you don't get all them silly ideas out your head! You better marry yourself a man with some loot . . .

BENEATHA: [*Angrily, precisely as in the first scene of the play.*] What have you got to do with who I marry!

WALTER: Plenty. Now I think George Murchison—

[*He and* BENEATHA *go out yelling at each other vigorously;* BENEATHA *is heard saying that she would not marry* GEORGE MURCHISON *if he were Adam and she were Eve, etc. The anger is loud and real till their voices diminish.* RUTH *stands at the door and turns to* MAMA *and smiles knowingly.*]

MAMA: [*Fixing her hat at last.*] Yeah—they something all right, my children . . .

RUTH: Yeah—they're something. Let's go, Lena.

MAMA: [*Stalling, starting to look around at the house.*] Yes—I'm coming. Ruth—

RUTH: Yes?

MAMA: [*Quietly, woman to woman.*] He finally come into his manhood today, didn't he? Kind of like a rainbow after the rain . . .

RUTH: [*Biting her lip lest her own pride explode in front of* MAMA.] Yes, Lena.

[WALTER's *voice calls for them raucously.*]

MAMA: [*Waving* RUTH *out vaguely.*] All right, honey—go on down. I be down directly.

[RUTH *hesitates, then exits.* MAMA *stands, at last alone in the living room, her plant on the table before her as the lights start to* come down. *She looks around at all the walls and ceilings and suddenly, despite herself, while the children call below, a great heaving thing rises in her and she puts her fist to her mouth, takes a final desperate look, pulls her coat about her, pats her hat and goes out. The lights dim down. The door opens and she comes back in, grabs her plant, and goes out for the last time.*]

[*CURTAIN.*]

Arthur Miller
1915–2005

DEATH OF A SALESMAN

Miller's play melds two types of drama generally thought to be antithetical—Realism and Expressionism. Realistic drama, pioneered by such playwrights as Henrik Ibsen in the late nineteenth century, often exposes theatergoers to problems in society, sometimes pointing toward ways to reform. Lorraine Hansberry's A Raisin in the Sun *is a good example of a play written with this social purpose in mind. During the Great Depression, when so many suffered horrible poverty, there was obviously a lot to criticize about western capitalist countries, and Realism dominated not only serious drama but serious literature of all genres. The United States' involvement in World War II, from 1941 to 1945, is often seen as the turning point in the economic crisis, but even as late as 1949 the prosperity that we now associate with the postwar period was neither secured nor universal. Major strikes revealed problems in the American economy into the early 1950s, and many people decried a corporate heartlessness that treated employees not like human beings but like commodities. According to Miller, Americans in 1949 still had the mentality "of a depression people." In his own memoir, Miller proudly tells the tale of how Bernard Gimbel (of Gimbel's department stores) saw the play and immediately decided to never again fire anyone for being too old. That is the kind of social reform that a Realist often intends. Miller saw the play as a "severe" criticism of capitalism, the kind that could not have been written a couple of* years later, in the early 1950s, after the "anti-communist tempest," what we often call the Red Scare, had begun.

A salesman, with his characteristic showmanship and bravura, is an appropriate "everyman" to put on stage to examine the problems inherent in a modern consumer society. In a consumer economy, products take on symbolic value beyond their functional qualities. We buy things in pursuit of the images and dreams that salesmen teach us to associate with them. Naturally, then, through the years many critics have thought the play criticizes the American dream that still animates us today.

More recently, historical-minded critics have come to believe that Miller's play is not so universally applicable, that instead the play records a transition in the American economy from an industrial to a post-industrial age. In this view, Willy's problem is that he is a relic of an earlier, less technological age, when his type of selling worked. Whether Miller himself recognized this transition is beside the point. Because Realism attempts to reflect real life, we can use plays like this almost the same way a historian examines other types of evidence. For example, if Miller succeeded in reproducing realistic characters, a feminist approach could detect in the play evidence about the place of women in middle-class American society in the mid-twentieth century, whether or not Miller meant to criticize the role of women in mid-century American life.

Miller's own theory of Realism had another dimension unrelated to social criticism. He thought that Realism was the proper format for a "family" drama. During our daily lives, at work and in public spaces, we put on masks or fake versions of ourselves. But at home we are no longer performing, and in the company of our families we have a sense of our real selves. We speak in a revealing, mundane, unadorned, and prosaic language. And the conflicts in our families are battles between psychologically individuated personalities— which can best be depicted in realistic terms. In this sense, Miller's realism does not comment on an economic system so much as it dramatizes the problems and dynamics within a particular American family. It is interesting to note that Miller himself claimed that he never intended any "heavy-handed symbolism" through Willy's surname ("Low-man"). Willy is not a "type" but an individual with as much idiosyncratic, psychological depth as you and me.

Nevertheless, it is impossible to deny the mythic character of the play, and since its first production readers and critics and audiences have always asserted that Death of a Salesman *brilliantly adapts the principles of Greek tragedy, which dealt in myth, to a modern, democratic society. To the degree that the play succeeds as tragedy, it resists the thrust of Realism and tends toward Expressionism. Expressionism deals less with the nuances of the individual psyche than with universals. In Miller's own words, Expressionism dramatizes "the conflict of either social, religious, ethical, or moral forces per se." In other words, Expressionism does not depict conflicts between individuals, but between "forces." An example would be Greek drama.* Oedipus *is not so much about an individual person (Oedipus) as it is about the human struggle against fate. You might ask yourself, then, to what degree Miller's play follows Aristotle's description of tragedy? For example, is anyone "fated" like Oedipus? If someone is fated, what "force" in twentieth-century America takes the place of the gods in Greek drama? Miller claimed that the pathos of tragedy came easily to him, and he almost regretted how pathetic he made Willy Loman, thinking it almost ruined his tragic character. But what he meant by "pathetic" is a little different than our common usage. In his "Tragedy and the Common Man," Miller claimed that "the pathetic is achieved when the protagonist is, by virtue of witlessness, his insensitivity or the very air he gives off, incapable of grappling with a much superior force." In that same essay Miller wrote that the so-called tragic flaw "or crack in the character, is really nothing—and need be nothing—but his inherent unwillingness to remain passive in the face of what he conceives to be a challenge to his dignity, his image of his rightful status."*

In the visual arts, such as painting, Expressionists wanted to depict objects not as they "really" are but imbued with the emotional force they aroused in the artist. On the canvas, objects look distorted and unreal, filtered through a dreamlike—often a nightmarish—lens. Vincent Van Gogh's Starry Night *and Edward Munch's* The Scream *are good examples of this style. On the stage, Expressionism sketches mythic characters with little realistic detail. While Expressionist playwrights did intend to revolt against the stifling boundaries imposed by bourgeois, middle-class society, they were not interested in sociological analysis and practical reform. They con-*

cerned themselves with timeless, universal themes, like the struggle of youth against age, and visions of apocalypse, and they often used the external aspects of stagecraft—lighting, sound, sets—to express internal states of mind. Consequently, Expressionist theater did not look like "real" life. The audience was not looking at the lives of real people through an invisible "fourth wall." Sets are often minimal or distorted. Dialogue makes no attempt to mimic real-life speech. Instead, characters make unrealistic speeches and use poetic constructions. Expressionism flowered in the German theater in the early decades of the twentieth century and had an influence on American playwrights like Eugene O'Neill in the 1920s.

Ironically, Miller borrowed some of the techniques of Expressionism to convey the inner life of Willy Loman. But those characteristics also lend a mythical atmosphere to the play. Miller expressed his own surprise at how universal the play seems, resonating even in cultures extremely different from our own, such as communist China.

Death of a Salesman

Certain Private Conversations in Two Acts and a Requiem

CHARACTERS

WILLY LOMAN	THE WOMAN	STANLEY
LINDA	CHARLEY	MISS FORSYTHE
BIFF	UNCLE BEN	LETTA
HAPPY	HOWARD WAGNER	
BERNARD	JENNY	

The action takes place in WILLY LOMAN's *house and yard and in various places he visits in the New York and Boston of today.*[1]

ACT I
A melody is heard, playing upon a flute. It is small and fine, telling of grass and trees and the horizon. The curtain rises.

1. Circa 1949.

Before us is the Salesman's house. We are aware of towering angular shapes behind it, surrounding it on all sides. Only the blue light of the sky falls upon the house and forestage; the surrounding area shows an angry flow of orange. As more light appears, we see a solid vault of apartment houses around the small, fragile-seeming home. An air of the dream clings to the place, a dream rising out of reality. The kitchen at center seems actual enough, for there is a kitchen table with three chairs, and a refrigerator. But no other fixtures are seen. At the back of the kitchen there is a draped entrance, which leads to the living-room. To the right of the kitchen, on a level raised two feet, is a bedroom furnished only with a brass bedstead and a straight chair. On a shelf over the bed a silver athletic trophy stands. A window opens onto the apartment house at the side.

Behind the kitchen, on a level raised six and a half feet, is the boys' bedroom, at present barely visible. Two beds are dimly seen, and at the back of the room a dormer window. (This bedroom is above the unseen living-room.) At the left a stairway curves up to it from the kitchen.

The entire setting is wholly or, in some places, partially transparent. The roof-line of the house is one-dimensional; under and over it we see the apartment buildings. Before the house lies an apron, curving beyond the forestage into the orchestra. This forward area serves as the back yard as well as the locale of all WILLY*'s imaginings and of his city scenes. Whenever the action is in the present the actors observe the imaginary wall-lines, entering the house only through its door at the left. But in the scenes of the past these boundaries are broken, and characters enter or leave a room by stepping "through" a wall onto the forestage.*

From the right, WILLY LOMAN, *the Salesman, enters, carrying two large sample cases. The flute plays on. He hears but is not aware of it. He is past sixty years of age, dressed quietly. Even as he crosses the stage to the doorway of the house, his exhaustion is apparent. He unlocks the door, comes into the kitchen, and thankfully lets his burden down, feeling the soreness of his palms. A word-sigh escapes his lips—it might be "Oh, boy, oh, boy." He closes the door, then carries his cases out into the living-room, through the draped kitchen doorway.*

LINDA, *his wife, has stirred in her bed at the right. She gets out and puts on a robe, listening. Most often jovial, she has developed an iron repression of her exceptions to* WILLY*'s behavior—she more than loves him,*

*she admires him, as though his mercurial nature, his temper, his massive
dreams and little cruelties, served her only as sharp reminders of the turbulent longings within him, longings which she shares but lacks the
temperament to utter and follow to their end.*

LINDA: [*Hearing* WILLY *outside the bedroom, calls with some trepida-
tion.*] Willy!

WILLY: It's all right. I came back.

LINDA: Why? What happened? [*Slight pause.*] Did something happen, Willy?

WILLY: No, nothing happened.

LINDA: You didn't smash the car, did you?

WILLY: [*With casual irritation.*] I said nothing happened. Didn't you
hear me?

LINDA: Don't you feel well?

WILLY: I'm tired to the death. [*The flute has faded away. He sits on the
bed beside her, a little numb.*] I couldn't make it. I just couldn't
make it, Linda.

LINDA: [*Very carefully, delicately.*] Where were you all day? You look
terrible.

WILLY: I got as far as a little above Yonkers. I stopped for a cup of
coffee. Maybe it was the coffee.

LINDA: What?

WILLY: [*After a pause.*] I suddenly couldn't drive any more. The car
kept going off onto the shoulder, y'know?

LINDA: [*Helpfully.*] Oh. Maybe it was the steering again. I don't
think Angelo knows the Studebaker.[2]

WILLY: No, it's me, it's me. Suddenly I realize I'm goin' sixty miles an
hour and I don't remember the last five minutes. I'm—I can't
seem to—keep my mind to it.

LINDA: Maybe it's your glasses. You never went for your new glasses.

WILLY: No, I see everything. I came back ten miles an hour. It took
me nearly four hours from Yonkers.

LINDA: [*Resigned.*] Well, you'll just have to take a rest, Willy, you
can't continue this way.

2. The Studebaker Corporation manufactured cars from 1902 to 1963. It targeted middle-
class buyers.

WILLY: I just got back from Florida.

LINDA: But you didn't rest your mind. Your mind is overactive, and the mind is what counts, dear.

WILLY: I'll start out in the morning. Maybe I'll feel better in the morning. [*She is taking off his shoes.*] These goddam arch supports are killing me.

LINDA: Take an aspirin. Should I get you an aspirin? It'll soothe you.

WILLY: [*With wonder.*] I was driving along, you understand? And I was fine. I was even observing the scenery. You can imagine, me looking at scenery, on the road every week of my life. But it's so beautiful up there, Linda, the trees are so thick, and the sun is warm. I opened the windshield and just let the warm air bathe over me. And then all of a sudden I'm goin' off the road! I'm tellin' ya, I absolutely forgot I was driving. If I'd've gone the other way over the white line I might've killed somebody. So I went on again—and five minutes later I'm dreamin' again, and I nearly— [*He presses two fingers against his eyes.*] I have such thoughts, I have such strange thoughts.

LINDA: Willy, dear. Talk to them again. There's no reason why you can't work in New York.

WILLY: They don't need me in New York. I'm the New England man. I'm vital in New England.

LINDA: But you're sixty years old. They can't expect you to keep traveling every week.

WILLY: I'll have to send a wire[3] to Portland. I'm supposed to see Brown and Morrison tomorrow morning at ten o'clock to show the line. Goddammit, I could sell them! [*He starts putting on his jacket.*]

LINDA: [*Taking the jacket from him.*] Why don't you go down to the place tomorrow and tell Howard you've simply got to work in New York? You're too accommodating, dear.

WILLY: If old man Wagner was alive I'da been in charge of New York now! That man was a prince, he was a masterful man. But that boy of his, that Howard, he don't appreciate. When I went north the first time, the Wagner Company didn't know where New England was!

---

3. Telegram.

LINDA: Why don't you tell those things to Howard, dear?

WILLY: [*Encouraged.*] I will, I definitely will. Is there any cheese?

LINDA: I'll make you a sandwich.

WILLY: No, go to sleep. I'll take some milk. I'll be up right away. The boys in?

LINDA: They're sleeping. Happy took Biff on a date tonight.

WILLY: [*Interested.*] That so?

LINDA: It was so nice to see them shaving together, one behind the other, in the bathroom. And going out together. You notice? The whole house smells of shaving lotion.

WILLY: Figure it out. Work a lifetime to pay off a house. You finally own it, and there's nobody to live in it.

LINDA: Well, dear, life is a casting off. It's always that way.

WILLY: No, no, some people—some people accomplish something. Did Biff say anything after I went this morning?

LINDA: You shouldn't have criticized him, Willy, especially after he just got off the train. You mustn't lose your temper with him.

WILLY: When the hell did I lose my temper? I simply asked him if he was making any money. Is that a criticism?

LINDA: But, dear, how could he make any money?

WILLY: [*Worried and angered.*] There's such an undercurrent in him. He became a moody man. Did he apologize when I left this morning?

LINDA: He was crestfallen, Willy. You know how he admires you. I think if he finds himself, then you'll both be happier and not fight any more.

WILLY: How can he find himself on a farm? Is that a life? A farmhand? In the beginning, when he was young, I thought, well, a young man, it's good for him to tramp around, take a lot of different jobs. But it's more than ten years now and he has yet to make thirty-five dollars a week!

LINDA: He's finding himself, Willy.

WILLY: Not finding yourself at the age of thirty-four is a disgrace!

LINDA: Shh!

WILLY: The trouble is he's lazy, goddammit!

LINDA: Willy, please!

WILLY: Biff is a lazy bum!

LINDA: They're sleeping. Get something to eat. Go on down.

WILLY: Why did he come home? I would like to know what brought him home.

LINDA: I don't know. I think he's still lost, Willy. I think he's very lost.

WILLY: Biff Loman is lost. In the greatest country in the world a young man with such—personal attractiveness, gets lost. And such a hard worker. There's one thing about Biff—he's not lazy.

LINDA: Never.

WILLY: [*With pity and resolve.*] I'll see him in the morning; I'll have a nice talk with him. I'll get him a job selling. He could be big in no time. My God! Remember how they used to follow him around in high school? When he smiled at one of them their faces lit up. When he walked down the street . . . [*He loses himself in reminiscences.*]

LINDA: [*Trying to bring him out of it.*] Willy, dear, I got a new kind of American-type cheese today. It's whipped.

WILLY: Why do you get American when I like Swiss?

LINDA: I just thought you'd like a change—

WILLY: I don't want a change! I want Swiss cheese. Why am I always being contradicted?

LINDA: [*With a covering laugh.*] I thought it would be a surprise.

WILLY: Why don't you open a window in here, for God's sake?

LINDA: [*With infinite patience.*] They're all open, dear.

WILLY: The way they boxed us in here. Bricks and windows, windows and bricks.

LINDA: We should've bought the land next door.

WILLY: The street is lined with cars. There's not a breath of fresh air in the neighborhood. The grass don't grow any more, you can't raise a carrot in the back yard. They should've had a law against apartment houses. Remember those two beautiful elm trees out there? When I and Biff hung the swing between them?

LINDA: Yeah, like being a million miles from the city.

WILLY: They should've arrested the builder for cutting those down. They massacred the neighborhood. [*Lost.*] More and more I think of those days, Linda. This time of year it was lilac and wisteria. And then the peonies would come out, and the daffodils. What fragrance in this room!

LINDA: Well, after all, people had to move somewhere.

WILLY: No, there's more people now.

LINDA: I don't think there's more people. I think—

WILLY: There's more people! That's what ruining this country! Population is getting out of control. The competition is maddening! Smell the stink from that apartment house! And another one on the other side . . . How can they whip cheese?

> [On WILLY's *last line,* BIFF *and* HAPPY *raise themselves up in their beds, listening.*]

LINDA: Go down, try it. And be quiet.

WILLY: [*Turning to* LINDA, *guiltily.*] You're not worried about me, are you, sweetheart?

BIFF: What's the matter?

HAPPY: Listen!

LINDA: You've got too much on the ball to worry about.

WILLY: You're my foundation and my support, Linda.

LINDA: Just try to relax, dear. You make mountains out of molehills.

WILLY: I won't fight with him anymore. If he wants to go back to Texas, let him go.

LINDA: He'll find his way.

WILLY: Sure. Certain men just don't get started till later in life. Like Thomas Edison, I think. Or B. F. Goodrich. One of them was deaf. [*He starts for the bedroom doorway.*] I'll put my money on Biff.

LINDA: And Willy—if it's warm Sunday we'll drive in the country. And we'll open the windshield, and take lunch.

WILLY: No, the windshields don't open on the new cars.

LINDA: But you opened it today.

WILLY: Me? I didn't. [*He stops.*] Now isn't that peculiar! Isn't that a remarkable— [*He breaks off in amazement and fright as the flute is heard distantly.*]

LINDA: What, darling?

WILLY: That is the most remarkable thing.

LINDA: What, dear?

WILLY: I was thinking of the Chevvy.[4] [*Slight pause.*] Nineteen twenty-eight . . . when I had that red Chevvy—[*Breaks off.*] That funny? I coulda sworn I was driving that Chevvy today.

---

4. Chevrolet, a division of General Motors since 1916, has been making cars since 1911.

LINDA: Well, that's nothing. Something must've reminded you.

WILLY: Remarkable. *Ts.*[5] Remember those days? The way Biff used to simonize that car?[6] The dealer refused to believe there was eighty thousand miles on it. [*He shakes his head.*] Heh! [*To* LINDA.] Close your eyes, I'll be right up. [*He walks out of the bedroom.*]

HAPPY: [*To* BIFF.] Jesus, maybe he smashed up the car again!

LINDA: [*Calling after* WILLY.] Be careful on the stairs, dear! The cheese is on the middle shelf! [*She turns, goes over to the bed, takes his jacket, and goes out of the bedroom.*]

> [*Light has risen on the boys' room. Unseen,* WILLY *is heard talking to himself,* "Eighty thousand miles," *and a little laugh.* BIFF *gets out of bed, comes downstage a bit, and stands attentively.* BIFF *is two years older than his brother,* HAPPY, *well built, but in these days bears a worn air and seems less self-assured. He has succeeded less, and his dreams are stronger and less acceptable than* HAPPY's. HAPPY *is tall, powerfully made. Sexuality is like a visible color on him, or a scent that many women have discovered. He, like his brother, is lost, but in a different way, for he has never allowed himself to turn his face toward defeat and is thus more confused and hard-skinned, although seemingly more content.*]

HAPPY: [*Getting out of bed.*] He's going to get his license taken away if he keeps that up. I'm getting nervous about him, y'know, Biff?

BIFF: His eyes are going.

HAPPY: No, I've driven with him. He sees all right. He just doesn't keep his mind on it. I drove into the city with him last week. He stops at a green light and then it turns red and he goes. [*He laughs.*]

BIFF: Maybe he's color-blind.

HAPPY: Pop? Why he's got the finest eye for color in the business. You know that.

BIFF: [*Sitting down on his bed.*] I'm going to sleep.

HAPPY: You're not still sour on Dad, are you Biff?

---

5. Between 1908 and 1928, Ford manufactured the inexpensive and popular Model T automobile.

6. *Simonize*: polish with Simoniz Paste Wax.

BIFF: He's all right, I guess.

WILLY: [*Underneath them, in the living-room.*] Yes, sir, eighty thousand miles—eighty-two thousand!

BIFF: You smoking?

HAPPY: [*Holding out a pack of cigarettes.*] Want one?

BIFF: [*Taking a cigarette.*] I can never sleep when I smell it.

WILLY: What a simonizing job, heh!

HAPPY: [*With deep sentiment.*] Funny, Biff, y'know? Us sleeping in here again? The old beds. [*He pats his bed affectionately.*] All the talk that went across those two beds, huh? Our whole lives.

BIFF: Yeah. Lotta dreams and plans.

HAPPY: [*With a deep and masculine laugh.*] About five hundred women would like to know what was said in this room.

 [*They share a soft laugh.*]

BIFF: Remember that big Betsy something—what the hell was her name—over on Bushwick Avenue?

HAPPY: [*Combing his hair.*] With the collie dog!

BIFF: That's the one. I got you in there, remember?

HAPPY: Yeah, that was my first time—I think. Boy, there was a pig! [*They laugh, almost crudely.*] You taught me everything I know about women. Don't forget that.

BIFF: I bet you forgot how bashful you used to be. Especially with girls.

HAPPY: Oh, I still am, Biff.

BIFF: Oh, go on.

HAPPY: I just control it, that's all. I think I got less bashful and you got more so. What happened, Biff? Where's the old humor, the old confidence? [*He shakes BIFF's knee. BIFF gets up and moves restlessly about the room.*] What's the matter?

BIFF: Why does Dad mock me all the time?

HAPPY: He's not mocking you, he—

BIFF: Everything I say there's a twist of mockery on his face. I can't get near him.

HAPPY: He just wants you to make good, that's all. I wanted to talk to you about Dad for a long time, Biff. Something's—happening to him. He—talks to himself.

BIFF: I noticed that this morning. But he always mumbled.

HAPPY: But not so noticeable. It got so embarrassing I sent him to
Florida. And you know something? Most of the time he's talking
to you.

BIFF: What's he say about me?

HAPPY: I can't make it out.

BIFF: What's he say about me?

HAPPY: I think the fact that you're not settled, that you're still kind
of up in the air . . .

BIFF: There's one or two things depressing him, Happy.

HAPPY: What do you mean?

BIFF: Never mind. Just don't lay it all to me.

HAPPY: But I think if you just got started—I mean—is there any future for you out there?

BIFF: I tell ya, Hap, I don't know what the future is. I don't know—
what I'm supposed to want.

HAPPY: What do you mean?

BIFF: Well, I spent six or seven years after high school trying to work
myself up. Shipping clerk, salesman, business of one kind or another. And it's a measly manner of existence. To get on that subway on the hot mornings in summer. To devote your whole life
to keeping stock, or making phone calls, or selling or buying. To
suffer fifty weeks of the year for the sake of a two-week vacation,
when all you really desire is to be outdoors, with your shirt off.
And always to have to get ahead of the next fella. And still—
that's how you build a future.

HAPPY: Well, you really enjoy it on a farm? Are you content out
there?

BIFF: [*With rising agitation.*] Hap, I've had twenty or thirty different kinds of jobs since I left home before the war, and it always
turns out the same. I just realized it lately. In Nebraska when I
herded cattle, and the Dakotas, and Arizona, and now in Texas.
It's why I came home now, I guess, because I realized it. This
farm I work on, it's spring there now, see? And they've got about
fifteen new colts. There's nothing more inspiring or—beautiful
than the sight of a mare and a new colt. And it's cool there now,
see? Texas is cool now, and it's spring. And whenever spring
comes to where I am, I suddenly get the feeling, my God, I'm
not gettin' anywhere! What the hell am I doing, playing around

with horses, twenty-eight dollars a week! I'm thirty-four years old. I oughta be makin' my future. That's when I come running home. And now, I get there, and I don't know what to do with myself. [*After a pause.*] I've always made a point of not wasting my life, and everytime I come back here I know that all I've done is to waste my life.

HAPPY: You're a poet, you know that, Biff? You're a—you're an idealist!

BIFF: No, I'm mixed up very bad. Maybe I oughta get married. Maybe I oughta get stuck into something. Maybe that's my trouble. I'm like a boy. I'm not married. I'm not in business, I just— I'm like a boy. Are you content, Hap? You're a success, aren't you? Are you content?

HAPPY: Hell, no!

BIFF: Why? You're making money, aren't you?

HAPPY: [*Moving about with energy, expressiveness.*] All I can do now is wait for the merchandise manager to die. And suppose I get to be merchandise manager? He's a good friend of mine, and he just built a terrific estate on Long Island. And he lived there about two months and sold it, and now he's building another one. He can't enjoy it once it's finished. And I know that's just what I would do. I don't know what the hell I'm workin' for. Sometimes I sit in my apartment—all alone. And I think of the rent I'm paying. And it's crazy. But then, it's what I always wanted. My own apartment, a car, and plenty of women. And still, goddammit, I'm lonely.

BIFF: [*With enthusiasm.*] Listen, why don't you come out West with me?

HAPPY: You and I, heh?

BIFF: Sure, maybe we could buy a ranch. Raise cattle, use our muscles. Men built like we are should be working out in the open.

HAPPY: [*Avidly.*] The Loman Brothers, heh?

BIFF: [*With vast affection.*] Sure, we'd be known all over the counties!

HAPPY: [*Enthralled.*] That's what I dream about, Biff. Sometimes I want to just rip my clothes off in the middle of the store and outbox that goddam merchandise manager. I mean I can outbox, outrun, and outlift anybody in that store, and I have to take orders from those common, petty sons-of-bitches till I can't stand it any more.

BIFF: I'm tellin' you, kid, if you were with me I'd be happy out there.

HAPPY: [*Enthused.*] See, Biff, everybody around me is so false that I'm constantly lowering my ideals . . .

BIFF: Baby, together we'd stand up for one another, we'd have someone to trust.

HAPPY: If I were around you—

BIFF: Hap, the trouble is we weren't brought up to grub for money. I don't know how to do it.

HAPPY: Neither can I!

BIFF: Then let's go!

HAPPY: The only thing is—what can you make out there?

BIFF: But look at your friend. Builds an estate and then hasn't the peace of mind to live in it.

HAPPY: Yeah, but when he walks into the store the waves part in front of him. That's fifty-two thousand dollars a year coming through the revolving door, and I got more in my pinky finger than he's got in his head.

BIFF: Yeah, but you just said—

HAPPY: I gotta show some of those pompous, self-important executives over there that Hap Loman can make the grade. I want to walk into the store the way he walks in. Then I'll go with you, Biff. We'll be together yet, I swear. But take those two we had tonight. Now weren't they gorgeous creatures?

BIFF: Yeah, yeah, most gorgeous I've had in years.

HAPPY: I get that any time I want, Biff. Whenever I feel disgusted. The only trouble is, it gets like bowling or something. I just keep knockin' them over and it doesn't mean anything. You still run around a lot?

BIFF: Naa. I'd like to find a girl—steady, somebody with substance.

HAPPY: That's what I long for.

BIFF: Go on! You'd never come home.

HAPPY: I would! Somebody with character, with resistance! Like Mom, y'know? You're gonna call me a bastard when I tell you this. That girl Charlotte I was with tonight is engaged to be married in five weeks. [*He tries on his new hat.*]

BIFF: No kiddin'!

HAPPY: Sure, the guy's in line for the vice-presidency of the store. I don't know what gets into me, maybe I just have an overdeveloped sense of competition or something, but I went and ruined her, and furthermore I can't get rid of her. And he's the third executive I've done that to. Isn't that a crummy characteristic? And to top it all, I go to their weddings! [*Indignantly, but laughing.*] Like I'm not supposed to take bribes. Manufacturers offer me a hundred-dollar bill now and then to throw an order their way. You know how honest I am, but it's like this girl, see. I hate myself for it. Because I don't want the girl, and, still, I take it and—I love it!

BIFF: Let's go to sleep.

HAPPY: I guess we didn't settle anything, heh?

BIFF: I just got one idea that I'm going to try.

HAPPY: What's that?

BIFF: Remember Bill Oliver?

HAPPY: Sure, Oliver is very big now. You want to work for him again?

BIFF: No, but when I quit he said something to me. He put his arm on my shoulder, and he said, "Biff, if you ever need anything, come to me."

HAPPY: I remember that. That sounds good.

BIFF: I think I'll go to see him. If I could get ten thousand or even seven or eight thousand dollars I could buy a beautiful ranch.

HAPPY: I bet he'd back you. 'Cause he thought highly of you, Biff. I mean, they all do. You're well liked, Biff. That's why I say to come back here, and we both have the apartment. And I'm tellin' you, Biff, any babe you want . . .

BIFF: No, with a ranch I could do the work I like and still be something. I just wonder though. I wonder if Oliver still thinks I stole that carton of basketballs.

HAPPY: Oh, he probably forgot that long ago. It's almost ten years. You're too sensitive. Anyway, he didn't really fire you.

BIFF: Well, I think he was going to. I think that's why I quit. I was never sure whether he knew or not. I know he thought the world of me, though. I was the only one he'd let lock up the place.

WILLY: [*Below.*] You gonna wash the engine, Biff?

HAPPY: Shh! [BIFF *looks at* HAPPY, *who is gazing down, listening.* WILLY *is mumbling in the parlor.*] You hear that?

  [*They listen.* WILLY *laughs warmly.*]

BIFF: [*Growing angry.*] Doesn't he know Mom can hear that?

WILLY: Don't get your sweater dirty, Biff!

[*A look of pain crosses* BIFF*'s face.*]

HAPPY: Isn't that terrible? Don't leave again, will you? You'll find a job here. You gotta stick around. I don't know what to do about him, it's getting embarrassing.

WILLY: What a simonizing job!

BIFF: Mom's hearing that!

WILLY: No kiddin', Biff, you got a date? Wonderful!

HAPPY: Go on to sleep. But talk to him in the morning, will you?

BIFF: [*Reluctantly getting into bed.*] With her in the house. Brother!

HAPPY: [*Getting into bed.*] I wish you'd have a good talk with him.

[*The light on their room begins to fade.*]

BIFF: [*To himself in bed.*] That selfish, stupid . . .

HAPPY: Sh . . . Sleep, Biff.

[*Their light is out. Well before they have finished speaking,* WILLY*'s form is dimly seen below in the darkened kitchen. He opens the refrigerator, searches in there, and takes out a bottle of milk. The apartment houses are fading out, and the entire house and surroundings become covered with leaves. Music insinuates itself as the leaves appear.*]

WILLY: Just wanna be careful with those girls, Biff, that's all. Don't make any promises. No promises of any kind. Because a girl, y'know, they always believe what you tell 'em, and you're very young, Biff, you're too young to be talking seriously to girls. [*Light rises on the kitchen.* WILLY, *talking, shuts the refrigerator door and comes downstage to the kitchen table. He pours milk into a glass. He is totally immersed in himself, smiling faintly.*] Too young entirely, Biff. You want to watch your schooling first. Then when you're all set, there'll be plenty of girls for a boy like you. [*He smiles broadly at a kitchen chair.*] That so? The girls pay for you? [*He laughs.*] Boy, you must really be makin' a hit. [WILLY *is gradually addressing—physically—a point offstage, speaking through the wall of the kitchen, and his voice has been rising in volume to that of a normal conversation.*] I been wondering why you polish the car so careful. Ha! Don't leave the hubcaps, boys. Get the chamois to the hubcaps. Happy, use newspaper on the windows, it's the easiest thing. Show him how to do it, Biff! You see, Happy? Pad it up, use it like a pad. That's it, that's it, good work. You're doin' all right, Hap. [*He pauses, then nods in approbation for a few seconds, then looks upward.*] Biff, first thing we gotta do when we get time is clip that big branch over the house. Afraid it's gonna fall in a storm and hit the roof. Tell you what. We get a rope and sling her around, and then we climb up there with a couple of saws and take her down. Soon as you finish the car, boys, I wanna see ya. I got a surprise for you, boys.

BIFF: [*Offstage.*] Whatta ya got, Dad?

WILLY: No, you finish first. Never leave a job till you're finished—remember that. [*Looking toward the "big trees."*] Biff, up in Albany I saw a beautiful hammock. I think I'll buy it next trip, and we'll hang it right between those two elms. Wouldn't that be something? Just swingin' there under those branches. Boy, that would be . . .

[YOUNG BIFF *and* YOUNG HAPPY *appear from the direction* WILLY *was addressing.* HAPPY *carries rags and a pail of water.* BIFF, *wearing a sweater with a block "S," carries a football.*]

BIFF: [*Pointing in the direction of the car offstage.*] How's that, Pop, professional?

WILLY: Terrific. Terrific job, boys. Good work, Biff.

HAPPY: Where's the surprise, Pop?

WILLY: In the back seat of the car.

HAPPY: Boy! [*He runs off.*]

BIFF: What is it, Dad? Tell me, what'd you buy?

WILLY: [*Laughing, cuffs him.*] Never mind, something I want you to have.

BIFF: [*Turns and starts off.*] What is it, Hap?

HAPPY: [*Offstage.*] It's a punching bag!

BIFF: Oh, Pop!

WILLY: It's got Gene Tunney's[7] signature on it!

[HAPPY *runs onstage with a punching bag.*]

BIFF: Gee, how'd you know we wanted a punching bag?

WILLY: Well, it's the finest thing for the timing.

HAPPY: [*Lies down on his back and pedals with his feet.*] I'm losing weight, you notice, Pop?

---

7. James Joseph "Gene" Tunney (1897–1978), skilled and thoughtful heavyweight boxer, defeated Jack Dempsy twice and was champion from 1926 to 1928.

WILLY: [*To* HAPPY.] Jumping rope is good too.

BIFF: Did you see the new football I got?

WILLY: [*Examining the ball.*] Where'd you get a new ball?

BIFF: The coach told me to practice my passing.

WILLY: That so? And he gave you the ball, heh?

BIFF: Well, I borrowed it from the locker room. [*He laughs confidentially.*]

WILLY: [*Laughing with him at the theft.*] I want you to return that.

HAPPY: I told you he wouldn't like it!

BIFF: [*Angrily.*] Well, I'm bringing it back!

WILLY: [*Stopping the incipient argument, to* HAPPY.] Sure, he's gotta practice with a regulation bail, doesn't he? [*To* BIFF.] Coach'll probably congratulate you on your initiative!

BIFF: Oh, he keeps congratulating my initiative all the time, Pop.

WILLY: That's because he likes you. If somebody else took that ball there'd be an uproar. So what's the report, boys, what's the report?

BIFF: Where'd you go this time, Dad? Gee we were lonesome for you.

WILLY: [*Pleased, puts an arm around each boy and they come down to the apron.*] Lonesome, heh?

BIFF: Missed you every minute.

WILLY: Don't say? Tell you a secret, boys. Don't breathe it to a soul. Someday I'll have my own business, and I'll never have to leave home anymore.

HAPPY: Like Uncle Charley, heh?

WILLY: Bigger than Uncle Charley! Because Charley is not—liked. He's liked, but he's not—well liked.

BIFF: Where'd you go this time, Dad?

WILLY: Well, I got on the road, and I went north to Providence. Met the mayor.

BIFF: The mayor of Providence!

WILLY: He was sitting in the hotel lobby.

BIFF: What'd he say?

WILLY: He said, "Morning!" And I said, "You got a fine city here, Mayor." And then he had coffee with me. And then I went to Waterbury. Waterbury is a fine city. Big clock city, the famous Waterbury clock. Sold a nice bill there. And then Boston—

Boston is the cradle of the Revolution. A fine city. And a couple of other towns in Mass., and on to Portland and Bangor and straight home!

BIFF: Gee, I'd love to go with you sometime, Dad.

WILLY: Soon as summer comes.

HAPPY: Promise?

WILLY: You and Hap and I, and I'll show you all the towns. America is full of beautiful towns and fine, upstanding people. And they know me, boys, they know me up and down New England. The finest people. And when I bring you fellas up, there'll be open sesame for all of us, 'cause one thing, boys: I have friends. I can park my car in any street in New England, and the cops protect it like their own. This summer, heh?

BIFF and HAPPY: [*Together.*] Yeah! You bet!

WILLY: We'll take our bathing suits.

HAPPY: We'll carry your bags, Pop!

WILLY: Oh, won't that be something! Me comin' into the Boston stores with you boys carryin' my bags. What a sensation! [BIFF *is prancing around, practicing passing the ball.*] You nervous, Biff, about the game?

BIFF: Not if you're gonna be there.

WILLY: What do they say about you in school, now that they made you captain?

HAPPY: There's a crowd of girls behind him everytime the classes change.

BIFF: [*Taking* WILLY's *hand.*] This Saturday, Pop, this Saturday—just for you, I'm going to break through for a touchdown.

HAPPY: You're supposed to pass.

BIFF: I'm takin' one play for Pop. You watch me, Pop, and when I take off my helmet, that means I'm breakin' out. Then you watch me crash through that line!

WILLY: [*Kisses* BIFF.] Oh, wait'll I tell this in Boston!

[BERNARD *enters in knickers. He is younger than* BIFF, *earnest and loyal, a worried boy.*]

BERNARD: Biff, where are you? You're supposed to study with me today.

WILLY: Hey, looka Bernard. What're you lookin' so anemic about, Bernard?

BERNARD: He's gotta study, Uncle Willy. He's got Regents[8] next week.

HAPPY: [*Tauntingly, spinning* BERNARD *around.*] Let's box, Bernard!

BERNARD: Biff! [*He gets away from* HAPPY.] Listen, Biff, I heard Mr. Birnbaum say that if you don't start studyin' math he's gonna flunk you, and you won't graduate. I heard him!

WILLY: You better study with him, Biff. Go ahead now.

BERNARD: I heard him!

BIFF: Oh, Pop, you didn't see my sneakers! [*He holds up a foot for* WILLY *to look at.*]

WILLY: Hey, that's a beautiful job of printing!

BERNARD: [*Wiping his glasses.*] Just because he printed University of Virginia on his sneakers doesn't mean they've got to graduate him, Uncle Willy!

WILLY: [*Angrily.*] What're you talking about? With scholarships to three universities they're gonna flunk him?

BERNARD: But I heard Mr. Birnbaum say—

WILLY: Don't be a pest, Bernard! [*To his boys.*] What an anemic!

BERNARD: Okay, I'm waiting for you in my house, Biff.

[BERNARD *goes off. The* LOMANS *laugh.*]

WILLY: Bernard is not well liked, is he?

BIFF: He's liked, but he's not well liked.

HAPPY: That's right, Pop.

WILLY: That's just what I mean. Bernard can get the best marks in school, y'understand, but when he gets out in the business world, y'understand, you are going to be five times ahead of him. That's why I thank Almighty God you're both built like Adonises. Because the man who makes an appearance in the business world, the man who creates personal interest, is the man who gets ahead. Be liked and you will never want. You take me, for instance. I never have to wait in line to see a buyer. "Willy Loman is here!" That's all they have to know, and I go right through.

BIFF: Did you knock them dead, Pop?

WILLY: Knocked 'em cold in Providence, slaughtered 'em in Boston.

---

8. Exams given under the authority of the Board of Regents to high school students in New York State. To earn a Regents diploma, students must pass not only their classes but the Regents exams in each subject area.

HAPPY: [*On his back, pedaling again.*] I'm losing weight, you notice, Pop?

[LINDA *enters, as of old, a ribbon in her hair, carrying a basket of washing.*]

LINDA: [*With youthful energy.*] Hello, dear!

WILLY: Sweetheart!

LINDA: How'd the Chevvy run?

WILLY: Chevrolet, Linda, is the greatest car ever built. [*To the boys.*] Since when do you let your mother carry wash up the stairs?

BIFF: Grab hold there, boy!

HAPPY: Where to, Mom?

LINDA: Hang them up on the line. And you better go down to your friends, Biff. The cellar is full of boys. They don't know what to do with themselves.

BIFF: Ah, when Pop comes home they can wait!

WILLY: [*Laughs appreciatively.*] You better go down and tell them what to do, Biff.

BIFF: I think I'll have them sweep out the furnace room.

WILLY: Good work, Biff.

BIFF: [*Goes through wall-line of kitchen to doorway at back and calls down.*] Fellas! Everybody sweep out the furnace room! I'll be right down!

VOICES: All right! Okay, Biff.

BIFF: George and Sam and Frank, come out back! We're hangin' up the wash! Come on, Hap, on the double!

[*He and* HAPPY *carry out the basket.*]

LINDA: The way they obey him!

WILLY: Well, that training, the training. I'm tellin' you, I was sellin' thousands and thousands, but I had to come home.

LINDA: Oh, the whole block'll be at that game. Did you sell anything?

WILLY: I did five hundred gross in Providence and seven hundred gross in Boston.

LINDA: No! Wait a minute, I've got a pencil. [*She pulls pencil and paper out of her apron pocket.*] That makes your commission . . . Two hundred—my God! Two hundred and twelve dollars!

WILLY: Well, I didn't figure it yet, but . . .

LINDA: How much did you do?

WILLY: Well, I—I did—about a hundred and eighty gross in Providence. Well, no—it came to—roughly two hundred gross on the whole trip.

LINDA: [*Without hesitation.*] Two hundred gross. That's . . . [*She figures.*]

WILLY: The trouble was that three of the stores were half closed for inventory in Boston. Otherwise I woulda broke records.

LINDA: Well, it makes seventy dollars and some pennies. That's very good.

WILLY: What do we owe?

LINDA: Well, on the first there's sixteen dollars on the refrigerator—

WILLY: Why sixteen?

LINDA: Well, the fan belt broke, so it was a dollar eighty.

WILLY: But it's brand new.

LINDA: Well, the man said that's the way it is. Till they work themselves in, y'know.

[*They move through the wall-line into the kitchen.*]

WILLY: I hope we didn't get stuck on that machine.

LINDA: They got the biggest ads of any of them!

WILLY: I know, it's a fine machine. What else?

LINDA: Well, there's nine-sixty for the washing machine. And for the vacuum cleaner there's three and a half due on the fifteenth. Then the roof, you got twenty-one dollars remaining.

WILLY: It don't leak, does it?

LINDA: No, they did a wonderful job. Then you owe Frank for the carburetor.

WILLY: I'm not going to pay that man! That goddam Chevrolet, they ought to prohibit the manufacture of that car!

LINDA: Well, you owe him three and a half. And odds and ends, comes to around a hundred and twenty dollars by the fifteenth.

WILLY: A hundred and twenty dollars! My God, if business don't pick up I don't know what I'm gonna do!

LINDA: Well, next week you'll do better.

WILLY: Oh, I'll knock 'em dead next week. I'll go to Hartford. I'm very well liked in Hartford. You know, the trouble is, Linda, people don't seem to take to me.

[*They move onto the forestage.*]

LINDA: Oh, don't be foolish.

WILLY: I know it when I walk in. They seem to laugh at me.

LINDA: Why? Why would they laugh at you? Don't talk that way, Willy.

> [WILLY *moves to the edge of the stage.* LINDA *goes into the kitchen and starts to darn stockings.*]

WILLY: I don't know the reason for it, but they just pass me by. I'm not noticed.

LINDA: But you're doing wonderful, dear. You're making seventy to a hundred dollars a week.

WILLY: But I gotta be at it ten, twelve hours a day. Other men—I don't know—they do it easier. I don't know why—I can't stop myself—I talk too much. A man oughta come in with a few words. One thing about Charley. He's a man of few words, and they respect him.

LINDA: You don't talk too much, you're just lively.

WILLY: [*Smiling.*] Well, I figure, what the hell, life is short, a couple of jokes. [*To himself.*] I joke too much! [*The smile goes.*]

LINDA: Why? You're—

WILLY: I'm fat. I'm very—foolish to look at, Linda. I didn't tell you, but Christmas time I happened to be calling on F. H. Stewarts, and a salesman I know, as I was going in to see the buyer I heard him say something about—walrus. And I—I cracked him right across the face. I won't take that. I simply will not take that. But they do laugh at me. I know that.

LINDA: Darling . . .

WILLY: I gotta overcome it. I know I gotta overcome it. I'm not dressing to advantage, maybe.

LINDA: Willy, darling, you're the handsomest man in the world—

WILLY: Oh, no, Linda.

LINDA: To me you are. [*Slight pause.*] The handsomest. [*From the darkness is heard the laughter of a woman.* WILLY *doesn't turn to it, but it continues through* LINDA's *lines.*] And the boys, Willy. Few men are idolized by their children the way you are.

> [*Music is heard as behind a scrim, to the left of the house,* THE WOMAN, *dimly seen, is dressing.*]

WILLY: [*With great feeling.*] You're the best there is, Linda, you're a pal, you know that? On the road—on the road I want to grab you sometimes and just kiss the life outa you. [*The laughter is loud now, and he moves into a brightening area at the left, where* THE WOMAN *has come from behind the scrim and is standing, putting on her hat, looking into a "mirror" and laughing.*] 'Cause I get so lonely—especially when business is bad and there's nobody to talk to. I get the feeling that I'll never sell anything again, that I won't make a living for you, or a business, a business for the boys. [*He talks through* THE WOMAN's *subsiding laughter.* THE WOMAN *primps at the "mirror."*] There's so much I want to make for—

THE WOMAN: Me? You didn't make me, Willy. I picked you.

WILLY: [*Pleased.*] You picked me?

THE WOMAN: [*Who is quite proper-looking,* WILLY's *age.*] I did. I've been sitting at that desk watching all the salesmen go by, day in, day out. But you've got such a sense of humor, and we do have such a good time together, don't we?

WILLY: Sure, sure. [*He takes her in his arms.*] Why do you have to go now?

THE WOMAN: It's two o'clock . . .

WILLY: No, come on in! [*He pulls her.*]

THE WOMAN: . . . my sisters'll be scandalized. When'll you be back?

WILLY: Oh, two weeks about. Will you come up again?

THE WOMAN: Sure thing. You do make me laugh. It's good for me. [*She squeezes his arm, kisses him.*] And I think you're a wonderful man.

WILLY: You picked me, heh?

THE WOMAN: Sure. Because you're so sweet. And such a kidder.

WILLY: Well, I'll see you next time I'm in Boston.

THE WOMAN: I'll put you right through to the buyers.

WILLY: [*Slapping her bottom.*] Right. Well, bottoms up!

THE WOMAN: [*Slaps him gently and laughs.*] You just kill me, Willy. [*He suddenly grabs her and kisses her roughly.*] You kill me. And thanks for the stockings. I love a lot of stockings. Well, good night.

WILLY: Good night. And keep your pores open!

THE WOMAN: Oh, Willy!

　　　[THE WOMAN *bursts out laughing, and* LINDA's *laughter blends in.* THE WOMAN *disappears into the dark. Now the area at the kitchen table brightens.* LINDA *is sitting where she was at the kitchen table, but now is mending a pair of her silk stockings.*]

LINDA: You are, Willy. The handsomest man. You've got no reason to feel that—

WILLY: [*Coming out of* THE WOMAN*'s dimming area and going over to* LINDA.] I'll make it all up to you, Linda. I'll—

LINDA: There's nothing to make up, dear. You're doing fine, better than—

WILLY: [*Noticing her mending.*] What's that?

LINDA: Just mending my stockings. They're so expensive—

WILLY: [*Angrily, taking them from her.*] I won't have you mending stockings in this house! Now throw them out!

[LINDA *puts the stockings in her pocket.*]

BERNARD: [*Entering on the run.*] Where is he? If he doesn't study!

WILLY: [*Moving to the forestage, with great agitation.*] You'll give him the answers!

BERNARD: I do, but I can't on a Regents! That's a state exam! They're liable to arrest me!

WILLY: Where is he? I'll whip him, I'll whip him!

LINDA: And he'd better give back that football, Willy, it's not nice.

WILLY: Biff! Where is he? Why is he taking everything?

LINDA: He's too rough with the girls, Willy. All the mothers are afraid of him!

WILLY: I'll whip him!

BERNARD: He's driving the car without a license!

[THE WOMAN*'s laugh is heard.*]

WILLY: Shut up!

LINDA: All the mothers—

WILLY: Shut up!

BERNARD: [*Backing quietly away and out.*] Mr. Birnbaum says he's stuck up.

WILLY: Get outa here!

BERNARD: If he doesn't buckle down he'll flunk math! [*He goes off.*]

LINDA: He's right, Willy, you've gotta—

WILLY: [*Exploding at her.*] There's nothing the matter with him! You want him to be a worm like Bernard? He's got spirit, personality . . . [*As he speaks,* LINDA, *almost in tears, exits into the living room.*

WILLY *is alone in the kitchen, wilting and staring. The leaves are gone. It is night again, and the apartment houses look down from behind.*] Loaded with it. Loaded! What is he stealing? He's giving it back, isn't he? Why is he stealing? What did I tell him? I never in my life told him anything but decent things.

> [HAPPY *in pajamas has come down the stairs;* WILLY *suddenly becomes aware of* HAPPY's *presence.*]

HAPPY: Let's go now, come on.

WILLY: [*Sitting down at the kitchen table.*] Huh! Why did she have to wax the floors herself? Everytime she waxes the floors she keels over. She knows that!

HAPPY: Shh! Take it easy. What brought you back tonight?

WILLY: I got an awful scare. Nearly hit a kid in Yonkers. God! Why didn't I go to Alaska with my brother Ben that time! Ben! That man was a genius, that man was success incarnate! What a mistake! He begged me to go.

HAPPY: Well, there's no use in—

WILLY: You guys! There was a man started with the clothes on his back and ended up with diamond mines!

HAPPY: Boy, someday I'd like to know how he did it.

WILLY: What's the mystery? The man knew what he wanted and went out and got it! Walked into a jungle, and comes out, the age of twenty-one, and he's rich! The world is an oyster, but you don't crack it open on a mattress!

HAPPY: Pop, I told you I'm gonna retire you for life.

WILLY: You'll retire me for life on seventy goddam dollars a week? And your women and your car and your apartment, and you'll retire me for life! Christ's sake, I couldn't get past Yonkers today! Where are you guys, where are you? The woods are burning! I can't drive a car!

> [CHARLEY *has appeared in the doorway. He is a large man, slow of speech, laconic, immovable. In all he says, despite what he says, there is pity, and now, trepidation. He has a robe over pajamas, slippers on his feet. He enters the kitchen.*]

CHARLEY: Everything all right?

HAPPY: Yeah, Charley, everything's . . .

WILLY: What's the matter?

CHARLEY: I heard some noise. I thought something happened. Can't we do something about the walls? You sneeze in here, and in my house hats blow off.

HAPPY: Let's go to bed, Dad. Come on.

[CHARLEY *signals to* HAPPY *to go.*]

WILLY: You go ahead, I'm not tired at the moment.

HAPPY: [*To* WILLY.] Take it easy, huh? [*He exits.*]

WILLY: What're you doin' up?

CHARLEY: [*Sitting down at the kitchen table opposite* WILLY.] Couldn't sleep good. I had a heartburn.

WILLY: Well, you don't know how to eat.

CHARLEY: I eat with my mouth.

WILLY: No, you're ignorant. You gotta know about vitamins and things like that.

CHARLEY: Come on, let's shoot. Tire you out a little.

WILLY: [*Hesitantly.*] All right. You got cards?

CHARLEY: [*Taking a deck from his pocket.*] Yeah, I got them. Someplace. What is it with those vitamins?

WILLY: [*Dealing.*] They build up your bones. Chemistry.

CHARLEY: Yeah, but there's no bones in a heartburn.

WILLY: What are you talkin' about? Do you know the first thing about it?

CHARLEY: Don't get insulted.

WILLY: Don't talk about something you don't know anything about.

[*They are playing. Pause.*]

CHARLEY: What're you doin' home?

WILLY: A little trouble with the car.

CHARLEY: Oh. [*Pause.*] I'd like to take a trip to California.

WILLY: Don't say.

CHARLEY: You want a job?

WILLY: I got a job, I told you that. [*After a slight pause.*] What the hell are you offering me a job for?

CHARLEY: Don't get insulted.

WILLY: Don't insult me.

CHARLEY: I don't see no sense in it. You don't have to go on this way.

WILLY: I got a good job. [*Slight pause.*] What do you keep comin' in here for?

CHARLEY: You want me to go?

WILLY: [*After a pause, withering.*] I can't understand it. He's going back to Texas again. What the hell is that?

CHARLEY: Let him go.

WILLY: I got nothin' to give him, Charley, I'm clean, I'm clean.

CHARLEY: He won't starve. None a them starve. Forget about him.

WILLY: Then what have I got to remember?

CHARLEY: You take it too hard. To hell with it. When a deposit bottle is broken you don't get your nickel back.

WILLY: That's easy enough for you to say.

CHARLEY: That ain't easy for me to say.

WILLY: Did you see the ceiling I put up in the living-room?

CHARLEY: Yeah, that's a piece of work. To put up a ceiling is a mystery to me. How do you do it?

WILLY: What's the difference?

CHARLEY: Well, talk about it.

WILLY: You gonna put up a ceiling?

CHARLEY: How could I put up a ceiling?

WILLY: Then what the hell are you bothering me for?

CHARLEY: You're insulted again.

WILLY: A man who can't handle tools is not a man. You're disgusting.

CHARLEY: Don't call me disgusting, Willy.

[UNCLE BEN, *carrying a valise and an umbrella, enters the forestage from around the right corner of the house. He is a stolid man, in his sixties, with a mustache and an authoritative air. He is utterly certain of his destiny, and there is an aura of far places about him. He enters exactly as* WILLY *speaks.*]

WILLY: I'm getting awfully tired, Ben.

[BEN's *music is heard.* BEN *looks around at everything.*]

CHARLEY: Good, keep playing; you'll sleep better. Did you call me Ben?

[BEN *looks at his watch.*]

WILLY: That's funny. For a second there you reminded me of my brother Ben.

BEN: I only have a few minutes. [*He strolls, inspecting the place.* WILLY *and* CHARLEY *continue playing.*]

CHARLEY: You never heard from him again, heh? Since that time?

WILLY: Didn't Linda tell you? Couple of weeks ago we got a letter from his wife in Africa. He died.

CHARLEY: That so.

BEN: [*Chuckling.*] So this is Brooklyn, eh?

CHARLEY: Maybe you're in for some of his money.

WILLY: Naa, he had seven sons. There's just one opportunity I had with that man . . .

BEN: I must make a train, William. There are several properties I'm looking at in Alaska.

WILLY: Sure, sure! If I'd gone with him to Alaska that time, everything would've been totally different.

CHARLEY: Go on, you'da froze to death up there.

WILLY: What're you talking about?

BEN: Opportunity is tremendous in Alaska, William. Surprised you're not up there.

WILLY: Sure, tremendous.

CHARLEY: Heh?

WILLY: There was the only man I ever met who knew the answers.

CHARLEY: Who?

BEN: How are you all?

WILLY: [*Taking a pot, smiling.*] Fine, fine.

CHARLEY: Pretty sharp tonight.

BEN: Is Mother living with you?

WILLY: No, she died a long time ago.

CHARLEY: Who?

BEN: That's too bad. Fine specimen of a lady, Mother.

WILLY: [*To* CHARLEY.] Heh?

BEN: I'd hoped to see the old girl.

CHARLEY: Who died?

BEN: Heard anything from Father, have you?

WILLY: [*Unnerved.*] What do you mean, who died?

CHARLEY: [*Taking a pot.*] What're you talkin' about?

BEN: [*Looking at his watch.*] William, it's half-past eight!

WILLY: [*As though to dispel his confusion he angrily stops* CHARLEY'S *hand.*] That's my build!

CHARLEY: I put the ace—

WILLY: If you don't know how to play the game I'm not gonna throw my money away on you!

CHARLEY: [*Rising.*] It was my ace, for God's sake!

WILLY: I'm through, I'm through!

BEN: When did Mother die?

WILLY: Long ago. Since the beginning you never knew how to play cards.

CHARLEY: [*Picks up the cards and goes to the door.*] All right! Next time I'll bring a deck with five aces.

WILLY: I don't play that kind of game!

CHARLEY: [*Turning to him.*] You ought to be ashamed of yourself!

WILLY: Yeah?

CHARLEY: Yeah! [*He goes out.*]

WILLY: [*Slamming the door after him.*] Ignoramus!

BEN: [*As* WILLY *comes toward him through the wall-line of the kitchen.*] So you're William.

WILLY: [*Shaking* BEN's *hand.*] Ben! I've been waiting for you so long! What's the answer? How did you do it?

BEN: Oh, there's a story in that.

[LINDA *enters the forestage, as of old, carrying the wash basket.*]

LINDA: Is this Ben?

BEN: [*Gallantly.*] How do you do, my dear.

LINDA: Where've you been all these years? Willy's always wondered why you—

WILLY: [*Pulling* BEN *away from her impatiently.*] Where is Dad? Didn't you follow him? How did you get started?

BEN: Well, I don't know how much you remember.

WILLY: Well, I was just a baby, of course, only three or four years old—

BEN: Three years and eleven months.

WILLY: What a memory, Ben!

BEN: I have many enterprises, William, and I have never kept books.

WILLY: I remember I was sitting under the wagon in—was it Nebraska?

BEN: It was South Dakota, and I gave you a bunch of wild flowers.

WILLY: I remember you walking away down some open road.

BEN: [*Laughing.*] I was going to find Father in Alaska.

WILLY: Where is he?

BEN: At that age I had a very faulty view of geography, William. I discovered after a few days that I was heading due south, so instead of Alaska, I ended up in Africa.

LINDA: Africa!

WILLY: The Gold Coast!

BEN: Principally diamond mines.

LINDA: Diamond mines!

BEN: Yes, my dear. But I've only a few minutes—

WILLY: No! Boys! Boys! [*Young* BIFF *and* HAPPY *appear.*] Listen to this. This is your Uncle Ben, a great man! Tell my boys, Ben!

BEN: Why, boys, when I was seventeen I walked into the jungle, and when I was twenty-one I walked out. [*He laughs.*] And by God I was rich.

WILLY: [*To the boys.*] You see what I been talking about? The greatest things can happen!

BEN: [*Glancing at his watch.*] I have an appointment in Ketchikan Tuesday week.

WILLY: No, Ben! Please tell about Dad. I want my boys to hear. I want them to know the kind of stock they spring from. All I remember is a man with a big beard, and I was in Mamma's lap, sitting around a fire, and some kind of high music.

BEN: His flute. He played the flute.

WILLY: Sure, the flute, that's right!

[*New music is heard, a high, rollicking tune.*]

BEN: Father was a very great and a very wild-hearted man. We would start in Boston, and he'd toss the whole family into the wagon, and then he'd drive the team right across the country; through Ohio, and Indiana, Michigan, Illinois, and all the Western states. And we'd stop in the towns and sell the flutes that he'd made on the way. Great inventor, Father. With one gadget he made more in a week than a man like you could make in a lifetime.

WILLY: That's just the way I'm bringing them up, Ben—rugged, well liked, all-around.

BEN: Yeah? [*To* BIFF.] Hit that, boy—hard as you can. [*He pounds his stomach.*]

BIFF: Oh, no, sir!

BEN: [*Taking boxing stance.*] Come on, get to me! [*He laughs.*]

WILLY: Go to it, Biff! Go ahead, show him!

BIFF: Okay! [*He cocks his fist and starts in.*]

LINDA: [*To* WILLY.] Why must he fight, dear?

BEN: [*Sparring with* BIFF.] Good boy! Good boy!

WILLY: How's that, Ben, heh?

HAPPY: Give him the left, Biff!

LINDA: Why are you fighting?

BEN: Good boy! [*Suddenly comes in, trips* BIFF, *and stands over him, the point of his umbrella poised over* BIFF'S *eye.*]

LINDA: Look out, Biff!

BIFF: Gee!

BEN: [*Patting* BIFF'S *knee.*] Never fight fair with a stranger, boy. You'll never get out of the jungle that way. [*Taking* LINDA'S *hand and bowing.*] It was an honor and a pleasure to meet you, Linda.

LINDA: [*Withdrawing her hand coldly, frightened.*] Have a nice—trip.

BEN: [*To* WILLY.] And good luck with your—what do you do?

WILLY: Selling.

BEN: Yes. Well . . . [*He raises his hand in farewell to all.*]

WILLY: No, Ben, I don't want you to think . . . [*He takes* BEN'S *arm to show him.*] It's Brooklyn, I know, but we hunt too.

BEN: Really, now.

WILLY: Oh, sure, there's snakes and rabbits and—that's why I moved out here. Why, Biff can fell any one of these trees in no time! Boys! Go right over to where they're building the apartment house and get some sand. We're gonna rebuild the entire front stoop right now! Watch this, Ben!

BIFF: Yes, sir! On the double, Hap!

HAPPY: [*As he and* BIFF *run off.*] I lost weight, Pop, you notice?

[CHARLEY *enters in knickers, even before the boys are gone.*]

CHARLEY: Listen, if they steal any more from that building the watchman'll put the cops on them!

LINDA: [*To* WILLY.] Don't let Biff . . .

[BEN *laughs lustily.*]

WILLY: You shoulda seen the lumber they brought home last week. At least a dozen six-by-tens worth all kinds a money.

CHARLEY: Listen, if that watchman—

WILLY: I gave them hell, understand. But I got a couple of fearless characters there.

CHARLEY: Willy, the jails are full of fearless characters.

BEN: [*Clapping* WILLY *on the back, with a laugh at* CHARLEY.] And the stock exchange, friend!

WILLY: [*Joining in* BEN's *laughter.*] Where are the rest of your pants?

CHARLEY: My wife bought them.

WILLY: Now all you need is a golf club and you can go upstairs and go to sleep. [*To* BEN.] Great athlete! Between him and his son Bernard they can't hammer a nail!

BERNARD: [*Rushing in.*] The watchman's chasing Biff!

WILLY: [*Angrily.*] Shut up! He's not stealing anything!

LINDA: [*Alarmed, hurrying off left.*] Where is he? Biff, dear! [*She exits.*]

WILLY: [*Moving toward the left, away from* BEN.] There's nothing wrong. What's the matter with you?

BEN: Nervy boy. Good!

WILLY: [*Laughing.*] Oh, nerves of iron, that Biff!

CHARLEY: Don't know what it is. My New England man comes back and he's bleedin', they murdered him up there.

WILLY: It's contacts, Charley, I got important contacts!

CHARLEY: [*Sarcastically.*] Glad to hear it, Willy. Come in later, we'll shoot a little casino. I'll take some of your Portland money. [*He laughs at* WILLY *and exits.*]

WILLY: [*Turning to* BEN.] Business is bad, it's murderous. But not for me, of course.

BEN: I'll stop by on my way back to Africa.

WILLY: [*Longingly.*] Can't you stay a few days? You're just what I need, Ben, because I—I have a fine position here, but I—well, Dad left when I was such a baby and I never had a chance to talk to him and I still feel—kind of temporary about myself.

BEN: I'll be late for my train.

[*They are at opposite ends of the stage.*]

WILLY: Ben, my boys—can't we talk? They'd go into the jaws of hell for me, see, but I—

BEN: William, you're being first-rate with your boys. Outstanding, manly chaps!

WILLY: [*Hanging on to his words.*] Oh, Ben, that's good to hear! Because sometimes I'm afraid that I'm not teaching them the right kind of—Ben, how should I teach them?

BEN: [*Giving great weight to each word, and with a certain vicious audacity.*] William, when I walked into the jungle, I was seventeen. When I walked out I was twenty-one. And, by God, I was rich! [*He goes off into darkness around the right corner of the house.*]

WILLY: . . . was rich! That's just the spirit I want to imbue them with! To walk into a jungle! I was right! I was right! I was right!

[BEN *is gone, but* WILLY *is still speaking to him as* LINDA, *in nightgown and robe, enters the kitchen, glances around for* WILLY, *then goes to the door of the house, looks out and sees him. Comes down to his left. He looks at her.*]

LINDA: Willy, dear? Willy?

WILLY: I was right!

LINDA: Did you have some cheese? [*He can't answer.*] It's very late, darling. Come to bed, heh?

WILLY: [*Looking straight up.*] Gotta break your neck to see a star in this yard.

LINDA: You coming in?

WILLY: Whatever happened to that diamond watch fob? Remember? When Ben came from Africa that time? Didn't he give me a watch fob with a diamond in it?

LINDA: You pawned it, dear. Twelve, thirteen years ago. For Biff's radio correspondence course.

WILLY: Gee, that was a beautiful thing. I'll take a walk.

LINDA: But you're in your slippers.

WILLY: [*Starting to go around the house at the left.*] I was right! I was! [*Half to* LINDA, *as he goes, shaking his head.*] What a man! There was a man worth talking to. I was right!

LINDA: [*Calling after* WILLY.] But in your slippers, Willy!

[WILLY *is almost gone when* BIFF, *in his pajamas, comes down the stairs and enters the kitchen.*]

BIFF: What is he doing out there?

LINDA: Sh!

BIFF: God Almighty, Mom, how long has he been doing this?

LINDA: Don't, he'll hear you.

BIFF: What the hell is the matter with him?

LINDA: It'll pass by morning.

BIFF: Shouldn't we do anything?

LINDA: Oh, my dear, you should do a lot of things, but there's nothing to do, so go to sleep.

[HAPPY *comes down the stairs and sits on the steps.*]

HAPPY: I never heard him so loud, Mom.

LINDA: Well, come around more often; you'll hear him. [*She sits down at the table and mends the lining of* WILLY'S *jacket.*]

BIFF: Why didn't you ever write me about this, Mom?

LINDA: How would I write to you? For over three months you had no address.

BIFF: I was on the move. But you know I thought of you all the time. You know that, don't you, pal?

LINDA: I know, dear, I know. But he likes to have a letter. Just to know that there's still a possibility for better things.

BIFF: He's not like this all the time, is he?

LINDA: It's when you come home he's always the worst.

BIFF: When I come home?

LINDA: When you write you're coming, he's all smiles, and talks about the future, and—he's just wonderful. And then the closer you seem to come, the more shaky he gets, and then, by the time you get here, he's arguing, and he seems angry at you. I think it's just that maybe he can't bring himself to—to open up to you. Why are you so hateful to each other? Why is that?

BIFF: [*Evasively.*] I'm not hateful, Mom.

LINDA: But you no sooner come in the door than you're fighting!

BIFF: I don't know why. I mean to change. I'm tryin', Mom, you understand?

LINDA: Are you home to stay now?

BIFF: I don't know. I want to look around, see what's doin'.

LINDA: Biff, you can't look around all your life, can you?

BIFF: I just can't take hold, Mom. I can't take hold of some kind of a life.

LINDA: Biff, a man is not a bird, to come and go with the springtime.

BIFF: Your hair . . . [*He touches her hair.*] Your hair got so gray.

LINDA: Oh, it's been gray since you were in high school. I just stopped dyeing it, that's all.

BIFF: Dye it again, will ya? I don't want my pal looking old. [*He smiles.*]

LINDA: You're such a boy! You think you can go away for a year and . . . You've got to get it into your head now that one day you'll knock on this door and there'll be strange people here—

BIFF: What are you talking about? You're not even sixty, Mom.

LINDA: But what about your father?

BIFF: [*Lamely.*] Well, I meant him too.

HAPPY: He admires Pop.

LINDA: Biff, dear, if you don't have any feeling for him, then you can't have any feeling for me.

BIFF: Sure I can, Mom.

LINDA: No. You can't just come to see me, because I love him. [*With a threat, but only a threat, of tears.*] He's the dearest man in the world to me, and I won't have anyone making him feel unwanted and low and blue. You've got to make up your mind now, darling, there's no leeway anymore. Either he's your father and you pay him that respect, or else you're not to come here, I know he's not easy to get along with—nobody knows that better than me—but . . .

WILLY: [*From the left, with a laugh.*] Hey, hey, Biffo!

BIFF: [*Starting to go out after* WILLY.] What the hell is the matter with him? [HAPPY *stops him.*]

LINDA: Don't—don't go near him!

BIFF: Stop making excuses for him! He always, always wiped the floor with you. Never had an ounce of respect for you.

HAPPY: He's always had respect for—

BIFF: What the hell do you know about it?

HAPPY: [*Surlily.*] Just don't call him crazy!

BIFF: He's got no character—Charley wouldn't do this. Not in his own house—spewing out that vomit from his mind.

HAPPY: Charley never had to cope with what he's got to.

BIFF: People are worse off than Willy Loman. Believe me, I've seen them!

LINDA: Then make Charley your father, Biff. You can't do that, can you? I don't say he's a great man. Willy Loman never made a lot of money. His name was never in the paper. He's not the finest character that ever lived. But he's a human being, and a terrible thing is happening to him. So attention must be paid. He's not to be allowed to fall into his grave like an old dog. Attention, attention must be finally paid to such a person. You called him crazy—

BIFF: I didn't mean—

LINDA: No, a lot of people think he's lost his—balance. But you don't have to be very smart to know what his trouble is. The man is exhausted.

HAPPY: Sure!

LINDA: A small man can be just as exhausted as a great man. He works for a company thirty-six years this March, opens up un-heard-of territories to their trademark, and now in his old age they take his salary away.

HAPPY: [*Indignantly.*] I didn't know that, Mom.

LINDA: You never asked, my dear! Now that you get your spending money someplace else you don't trouble your mind with him.

HAPPY: But I gave you money last—

LINDA: Christmas time, fifty dollars! To fix the hot water it cost ninety-seven fifty! For five weeks he's been on straight commis-sion, like a beginner, an unknown!

BIFF: Those ungrateful bastards!

LINDA: Are they any worse than his sons? When he brought them business, when he was young, they were glad to see him. But now his old friends, the old buyers that loved him so and always found some order to hand him in a pinch—they're all dead, re-tired. He used to be able to make six, seven calls a day in Boston. Now he takes his valises out of the car and puts them back and takes them out again and he's exhausted. Instead of walking he talks now. He drives seven hundred miles, and when he gets there no one knows him anymore, no one welcomes him. And what goes through a man's mind, driving seven hundred miles home without having earned a cent? Why shouldn't he talk to himself? Why? When he has to go to Charley and borrow fifty dollars a week and pretend to me that it's his pay? How long can that go on? How long? You see what I'm sitting here and waiting for? And you tell me he has no character? The man who never worked a day but for your benefit? When does he get the medal for that? Is this his reward—to turn around at the age of sixty-three and find his sons, who he loved better than his life, one a philandering bum—

HAPPY: Mom!

LINDA: That's all you are, my baby! [*To* BIFF.] And you! What happened to the love you had for him? You were such pals! How you used to talk to him on the phone every night! How lonely he was till he could come home to you!

BIFF: All right, Mom. I'll live here in my room, and I'll get a job. I'll keep away from him, that's all.

LINDA: No, Biff. You can't stay here and fight all the time.

BIFF: He threw me out of this house, remember that.

LINDA: Why did he do that? I never knew why.

BIFF: Because I know he's a fake and he doesn't like anybody around who knows!

LINDA: Why a fake? In what way? What do you mean?

BIFF: Just don't lay it all at my feet. It's between me and him—that's all I have to say. I'll chip in from now on. He'll settle for half my paycheck. He'll be all right. I'm going to bed. [*He starts for the stairs.*]

LINDA: He won't be all right.

BIFF: [*Turning on the stairs, furiously.*] I hate this city and I'll stay here. Now what do you want?

LINDA: He's dying, BIFF.

    [HAPPY *turns quickly to her, shocked.*]

BIFF: [*After a pause.*] Why is he dying?

LINDA: He's been trying to kill himself.

BIFF: [*With great horror.*] How?

LINDA: I live from day to day.

BIFF: What're you talking about?

LINDA: Remember I wrote you that he smashed up the car again? In February?

BIFF: Well?

LINDA: The insurance inspector came. He said that they have evidence. That all these accidents in the last year—weren't—weren't—accidents.

HAPPY: How can they tell that? That's a lie.

LINDA: It seems there's a woman . . . [*She takes a breath as. . . .*]

{BIFF: [*Sharply but contained.*] What woman?

 LINDA: [*Simultaneously.*] . . . and this woman . . .

LINDA: What?

BIFF: Nothing. Go ahead.

LINDA: What did you say?

BIFF: Nothing. I just said what woman?

HAPPY: What about her?

LINDA: Well, it seems she was walking down the road and saw his car. She says that he wasn't driving fast at all, and that he didn't skid. She says he came to that little bridge, and then deliberately smashed into the railing, and it was only the shallowness of the water that saved him.

BIFF: Oh, no, he probably just fell asleep again.

LINDA: I don't think he fell asleep.

BIFF: Why not?

LINDA: Last month . . . [*With great difficulty.*] Oh, boys, it's so hard to say a thing like this! He's just a big stupid man to you, but I tell you there's more good in him than in many other people. [*She chokes, wipes her eyes.*] I was looking for a fuse. The lights blew out, and I went down the cellar. And behind the fuse box—it happened to fall out—was a length of rubber pipe—just short.

HAPPY: No kidding?

LINDA: There's a little attachment on the end of it. I knew right away. And sure enough, on the bottom of the water heater there's a new little nipple on the gas pipe.

HAPPY: [*Angrily.*] That—jerk.

BIFF: Did you have it taken off?

LINDA: I'm—I'm ashamed to. How can I mention it to him? Every day I go down and take away that little rubber pipe. But, when he comes home, I put it back where it was. How can I insult him that way? I don't know what to do. I live from day to day, boys. I tell you, I know every thought in his mind. It sounds so old-fashioned and silly, but I tell you he put his whole life into you and you've turned your backs on him. [*She is bent over in the chair, weeping, her face in her hands.*] Biff, I swear to God! Biff, his life is in your hands!

HAPPY: [*To* BIFF.] How do you like that damned fool!

BIFF: [*Kissing her.*] All right, pal, all right. It's all settled now. I've been remiss. I know that, Mom. But now I'll stay, and I swear to you, I'll apply myself. [*Kneeling in front of her, in a fever of self-*

reproach.] It's just—you see, Mom, I don't fit in business. Not that I won't try. I'll try, and I'll make good.

HAPPY: Sure you will. The trouble with you in business was you never tried to please people.

BIFF: I know, I—

HAPPY: Like when you worked for Harrison's. Bob Harrison said you were tops, and then you go and do some damn fool thing like whistling whole songs in the elevator like a comedian.

BIFF: [*Against* HAPPY.] So what? I like to whistle sometimes.

HAPPY: You don't raise a guy to a responsible job who whistles in the elevator!

LINDA: Well, don't argue about it now.

HAPPY: Like when you'd go off and swim in the middle of the day instead of taking the line around.

BIFF: [*His resentment rising.*] Well, don't you run off? You take off sometimes, don't you? On a nice summer day?

HAPPY: Yeah, but I cover myself!

LINDA: Boys!

HAPPY: If I'm going to take a fade the boss can call any number where I'm supposed to be and they'll swear to him that I just left. I'll tell you something that I hate to say, Biff, but in the business world some of them think you're crazy.

BIFF: [*Angered.*] Screw the business world!

HAPPY: All right, screw it! Great, but cover yourself!

LINDA: Hap, Hap!

BIFF: I don't care what they think! They've laughed at Dad for years, and you know why? Because we don't belong in this nuthouse of a city! We should be mixing cement on some open plain, or—or carpenters. A carpenter is allowed to whistle!

[WILLY *walks in from the entrance of the house, at left.*]

WILLY: Even your grandfather was better than a carpenter. [*Pause. They watch him.*] You never grew up. Bernard does not whistle in the elevator, I assure you.

BIFF: [*As though to laugh* WILLY *out of it.*] Yeah, but you do, Pop.

WILLY: I never in my life whistled in an elevator! And who in the business world thinks I'm crazy?

BIFF: I didn't mean it like that, Pop. Now don't make a whole thing out of it, will ya?

WILLY: Go back to the West! Be a carpenter, a cowboy, enjoy your-self!

LINDA: Willy, he was just saying—

WILLY: I heard what he said!

HAPPY: [*Trying to quiet* WILLY.] Hey, Pop, come on now. . .

WILLY: [*Continuing over* HAPPY's *line.*] They laugh at me, heh? Go to Filene's, go to the Hub, go to Slattery's Boston. Call out the name Willy Loman and see what happens! Big shot!

BIFF: All right, Pop.

WILLY: Big!

BIFF: All right!

WILLY: Why do you always insult me?

BIFF: I didn't say a word. [*To* LINDA.] Did I say a word?

LINDA: He didn't say anything, Willy.

WILLY: [*Going to the doorway of the living-room.*] All right, good night, good night.

LINDA: Willy, dear, he just decided. . .

WILLY: [*To* BIFF.] If you get tired hanging around tomorrow, paint the ceiling I put up in the living-room.

BIFF: I'm leaving early tomorrow.

HAPPY: He's going to see Bill Oliver, Pop.

WILLY: [*Interestedly.*] Oliver? For what?

BIFF: [*With reserve, but trying, trying.*] He always said he'd stake me. I'd like to go into business, so maybe I can take him up on it.

LINDA: Isn't that wonderful?

WILLY: Don't interrupt. What's wonderful about it? There's fifty men in the City of New York who'd stake him. [*To* BIFF.] Sporting goods?

BIFF: I guess so. I know something about it and—

WILLY: He knows something about it! You know sporting goods bet-ter than Spalding,[9] for God's sake! How much is he giving you?

BIFF: I don't know, I didn't even see him yet, but—

WILLY: Then what're you talkin' about?

BIFF: [*Getting angry.*] Well, all I said was I'm gonna see him, that's all!

WILLY: [*Turning away.*] Ah, you're counting your chickens again.

---

9. Sporting goods manufacturer best known for standardizing baseballs and basketballs.

BIFF: [*Starting left for the stairs.*] Oh, Jesus, I'm going to sleep!

WILLY: [*Calling after him.*] Don't curse in this house!

BIFF: [*Turning.*] Since when did you get so clean?

HAPPY: [*Trying to stop them.*] Wait a. . .

WILLY: Don't use that language to me! I won't have it!

HAPPY: [*Grabbing* BIFF, *shouts.*] Wait a minute! I got an idea. I got a feasible idea. Come here, Biff, let's talk this over now, let's talk some sense here. When I was down in Florida last time, I thought of a great idea to sell sporting goods. It just came back to me. You and I, Biff—we have a line, the Loman Line. We train a couple of weeks, and put on a couple of exhibitions, see?

WILLY: That's an idea!

HAPPY: Wait! We form two basketball teams, see? Two water-polo teams. We play each other. It's a million dollars' worth of public-ity. Two brothers, see? The Loman Brothers. Displays in the Royal Palms—all the hotels. And banners over the ring and the basketball court: "Loman Brothers." Baby, we could sell sporting goods!

WILLY: That is a one-million-dollar idea!

LINDA: Marvelous!

BIFF: I'm in great shape as far as that's concerned.

HAPPY: And the beauty of it is, Biff, it wouldn't be like a business. We'd be out playin' ball again . . .

BIFF: [*Enthused.*] Yeah, that's. . .

WILLY: Million-dollar . . .

HAPPY: And you wouldn't get fed up with it, Biff. It'd be the family again. There'd be the old honor, and comradeship, and if you wanted to go off for a swim or somethin'—well, you'd do it! Without some smart cooky gettin' up ahead of you!

WILLY: Lick the world! You guys together could absolutely lick the civilized world.

BIFF: I'll see Oliver tomorrow. Hap, if we could work that out . . .

LINDA: Maybe things are beginning to—

WILLY: [*Wildly enthused, to* LINDA.] Stop interrupting! [*To* BIFF.] But don't wear sport jacket and slacks when you see Oliver.

BIFF: No, I'll—

WILLY: A business suit, and talk as little as possible, and don't crack any jokes.

BIFF: He did like me. Always liked me.

LINDA: He loved you!

WILLY: [*To* LINDA.] Will you stop! [*To* BIFF.] Walk in very serious. You are not applying for a boy's job. Money is to pass. Be quiet, fine, and serious. Everybody likes a kidder, but nobody lends him money.

HAPPY: I'll try to get some myself, Biff. I'm sure I can.

WILLY: I see great things for you kids, I think your troubles are over. But remember, start big and you'll end big. Ask for fifteen. How much you gonna ask for?

BIFF: Gee, I don't know—

WILLY: And don't say "Gee." "Gee" is a boy's word. A man walking in for fifteen thousand dollars does not say "Gee!"

BIFF: Ten, I think, would be top though.

WILLY: Don't be so modest. You always started too low. Walk in with a big laugh. Don't look worried. Start off with a couple of your good stories to lighten things up. It's not what you say, it's how you say it—because personality always wins the day.

LINDA: Oliver always thought the highest of him—

WILLY: Will you let me talk?

BIFF: Don't yell at her, Pop, will ya?

WILLY: [*Angrily.*] I was talking, wasn't I?

BIFF: I don't like you yelling at her all the time, and I'm tellin' you, that's all.

WILLY: What're you, takin' over this house?

LINDA: Willy—

WILLY: [*Turning on her.*] Don't take his side all the time, god-dammit!

BIFF: [*Furiously.*] Stop yelling at her!

WILLY: [*Suddenly pulling on his cheek, beaten down, guilt ridden.*] Give my best to Bill Oliver—he may remember me. [*He exits through the living-room doorway.*]

LINDA: [*Her voice subdued.*] What'd you have to start that for? [BIFF *turns away.*] You see how sweet he was as soon as you talked hopefully? [*She goes over to* BIFF.] Come up and say good night to him. Don't let him go to bed that way.

HAPPY: Come on, Biff, let's buck him up.

LINDA: Please, dear. Just say good night. It takes so little to make him happy. Come. [*She goes through the living-room doorway, calling upstairs from within the living-room.*] Your pajamas are hanging in the bathroom, Willy!

HAPPY: [*Looking toward where* LINDA *went out.*] What a woman! They broke the mold when they made her. You know that, Biff?

BIFF: He's off salary. My God, working on commission!

HAPPY: Well, let's face it: he's no hot-shot selling man. Except that sometimes, you have to admit, he's a sweet personality.

BIFF: [*Deciding.*] Lend me ten bucks, will ya? I want to buy some new ties.

HAPPY: I'll take you to a place I know. Beautiful stuff. Wear one of my striped shirts tomorrow.

BIFF: She got gray. Mom got awful old. Gee, I'm gonna go in to Oliver tomorrow and knock him for a—

HAPPY: Come on up. Tell that to Dad. Let's give him a whirl. Come on.

BIFF: [*Steamed up.*] You know, with ten thousand bucks, boy!

HAPPY: [*As they go into the living-room.*] That's the talk, Biff, that's the first time I've heard the old confidence out of you! [*From within the living-room, fading off.*] You're gonna live with me, kid, and any babe you want just say the word . . .

[*The last lines are hardly heard. They are mounting the stairs to their parents' bedroom.*]

LINDA: [*Entering her bedroom and addressing* WILLY, *who is in the bathroom. She is straightening the bed for him.*] Can you do anything about the shower? It drips.

WILLY: [*From the bathroom.*] All of a sudden everything falls to pieces! Goddam plumbing, oughta be sued, those people. I hardly finished putting it in and the thing . . . [*His words rumble off.*]

LINDA: I'm just wondering if Oliver will remember him. You think he might?

WILLY: [*Coming out of the bathroom in his pajamas.*] Remember him? What's the matter with you, you crazy? If he'd've stayed with Oliver he'd be on top by now! Wait'll Oliver gets a look at him. You don't know the average caliber anymore. The average young man today—[*He is getting into bed.*]—is got a caliber of zero. Greatest thing in the world for him was to burn around. [BIFF and HAPPY *enter the bedroom. Slight pause.* WILLY *stops short, looking at* BIFF.] Glad to hear it, boy.

HAPPY: He wanted to say good night to you, sport.

WILLY: [*To* BIFF.] Yeah. Knock him dead, boy. What'd you want to tell me?

BIFF: Just take it easy, Pop. Good night. [*He turns to go.*]

WILLY: [*Unable to resist.*] And if anything falls off the desk while you're talking to him—like a package or something—don't you pick it up. They have office boys for that.

LINDA: I'll make a big breakfast—

WILLY: Will you let me finish? [*To* BIFF.] Tell him you were in the business in the West. Not farm work.

BIFF: All right, Dad.

LINDA: I think everything—

WILLY: [*Going right through her speech.*] And don't undersell yourself. No less than fifteen thousand dollars.

BIFF: [*Unable to bear him.*] Okay. Good night, Mom. [*He starts moving.*]

WILLY: Because you got a greatness in you, Biff, remember that. You got all kinds of greatness . . . [*He lies back, exhausted.* BIFF *walks out.*]

LINDA: [*Calling after* BIFF.] Sleep well, darling!

HAPPY: I'm gonna get married, Mom. I wanted to tell you.

LINDA: Go to sleep, dear.

HAPPY: [*Going.*] I just wanted to tell you.

WILLY: Keep up the good work. [HAPPY *exits.*] God . . . remember that Ebbets Field[1] game? The championship of the city?

LINDA: Just rest. Should I sing to you?

WILLY: Yeah. Sing to me. [LINDA *hums a soft lullaby.*] When that team came out—he was the tallest, remember?

LINDA: Oh, yes. And in gold.

[BIFF *enters the darkened kitchen, takes a cigarette, and leaves the house. He comes downstage into a golden pool of light. He smokes, staring at the night.*]

WILLY: Like a young god. Hercules—something like that. And the

---

1. Home stadium of the Brooklyn Dodgers from 1913 to 1957. Football games were also played there.

sun, the sun all around him. Remember how he waved to me? Right up from the field, with the representatives of three colleges standing by? And the buyers I brought, and the cheers when he came out—Loman, Loman, Loman! God Almighty, he'll be great yet. A star like that, magnificent, can never really fade away!

[*The light on* WILLY *is fading. The gas heater begins to glow through the kitchen wall, near the stairs, a blue flame beneath red coils.*]

LINDA: [*Timidly.*] Willy dear, what has he got against you?

WILLY: I'm so tired. Don't talk anymore.

[BIFF *slowly returns to the kitchen. He stops, stares toward the heater.*]

LINDA: Will you ask Howard to let you work in New York?

WILLY: First thing in the morning. Everything'll be all right.

[BIFF *reaches behind the heater and draws out a length of rubber tubing. He is horrified and turns his head toward* WILLY's *room, still dimly lit, from which the strains of* LINDA's *desperate but monotonous humming rise.*]

WILLY: [*Staring through the window into the moonlight.*] Gee, look at the moon moving between the buildings!

[BIFF *wraps the tubing around his hand and quickly goes up the stairs.*]

[*CURTAIN*]

ACT II

Music is heard, gay and bright. The curtain rises as the music fades away. WILLY, *in shirt sleeves, is sitting at the kitchen table, sipping coffee, his hat in his lap.* LINDA *is filling his cup when she can.*

WILLY: Wonderful coffee. Meal in itself.

LINDA: Can I make you some eggs?

WILLY: No. Take a breath.

LINDA: You look so rested, dear.

WILLY: I slept like a dead one. First time in months. Imagine, sleeping till ten on a Tuesday morning. Boys left nice and early, heh?

LINDA: They were out of here by eight o'clock.

WILLY: Good work!

LINDA: It was so thrilling to see them leaving together. I can't get over the shaving lotion in this house!

WILLY: [*Smiling.*] Mmm—

LINDA: Biff was very changed this morning. His whole attitude seemed to be hopeful. He couldn't wait to get downtown to see Oliver.

WILLY: He's heading for a change. There's no question, there simply are certain men that take longer to get—solidified. How did he dress?

LINDA: His blue suit. He's so handsome in that suit. He could be a—anything in that suit!

[WILLY *gets up from the table.* LINDA *holds his jacket for him.*]

WILLY: There's no question, no question at all. Gee, on the way home tonight I'd like to buy some seeds.

LINDA: [*Laughing.*] That'd be wonderful. But not enough sun gets back there. Nothing'll grow any more.

WILLY: You wait, kid, before it's all over we're gonna get a little place out in the country, and I'll raise some vegetables, a couple of chickens . . .

LINDA: You'll do it yet, dear.

[WILLY *walks out of his jacket.* LINDA *follows him.*]

WILLY: And they'll get married, and come for a weekend. I'd build a little guest house. 'Cause I got so many fine tools, all I'd need would be a little lumber and some peace of mind.

LINDA: [*Joyfully.*] I sewed the lining . . .

WILLY: I could build two guest houses, so they'd both come. Did he decide how much he's going to ask Oliver for?

LINDA: [*Getting him into the jacket.*] He didn't mention it, but I imagine ten or fifteen thousand. You going to talk to Howard today?

WILLY: Yeah. I'll put it to him straight and simple. He'll just have to take me off the road.

LINDA: And Willy, don't forget to ask for a little advance, because we've got the insurance premium. It's the grace period now.

WILLY: That's a hundred . . . ?

LINDA: A hundred and eight, sixty-eight. Because we're a little short again.

WILLY: Why are we short?

LINDA: Well, you had the motor job on the car . . .

WILLY: That goddam Studebaker!

LINDA: And you got one more payment on the refrigerator . . .

WILLY: But it just broke again!

LINDA: Well, it's old, dear.

WILLY: I told you we should've bought a well-advertised machine. Charley bought a General Electric and it's twenty years old and it's still good, that son-of-a-bitch.

LINDA: But, Willy—

WILLY: Whoever heard of a Hastings refrigerator? Once in my life I would like to own something outright before it's broken! I'm always in a race with the junkyard! I just finished paying for the car and it's on its last legs. The refrigerator consumes belts like a goddam maniac. They time those things. They time them so when you finally paid for them, they're used up.

LINDA: [*Buttoning up his jacket as he unbuttons it.*] All told, about two hundred dollars would carry us, dear. But that includes the last payment on the mortgage. After this payment, Willy, the house belongs to us.

WILLY: It's twenty-five years!

LINDA: Biff was nine years old when we bought it.

WILLY: Well, that's a great thing. To weather a twenty-five year mortgage is—

LINDA: It's an accomplishment.

WILLY: All the cement, the lumber, the reconstruction I put in this house! There ain't a crack to be found in it anymore.

LINDA: Well, it served its purpose.

WILLY: What purpose? Some stranger'll come along, move in, and that's that. If only Biff would take this house, and raise a family . . . [*He starts to go.*] Good-bye, I'm late.

LINDA: [*Suddenly remembering.*] Oh, I forgot! You're supposed to meet them for dinner.

WILLY: Me?

LINDA: At Frank's Chop House on Forty-eighth near Sixth Avenue.

WILLY: Is that so! How about you?

LINDA: No, just the three of you. They're gonna blow you to a big meal!

WILLY: Don't say! Who thought of that?

LINDA: Biff came to me this morning, Willy, and he said, "Tell Dad, we want to blow him to a big meal." Be there six o'clock. You and your two boys are going to have dinner.

WILLY: Gee whiz! That's really somethin'. I'm gonna knock Howard for a loop, kid. I'll get an advance, and I'll come home with a New York job, Goddammit, now I'm gonna do it!

LINDA: Oh, that's the spirit, Willy!

WILLY: I will never get behind a wheel the rest of my life!

LINDA: It's changing, Willy, I can feel it changing!

WILLY: Beyond a question. G'bye, I'm late. [*He starts to go again.*]

LINDA: [*Calling after him as she runs to the kitchen table for a handkerchief.*] You got your glasses?

WILLY: [*Feels for them, then comes back in.*] Yeah, yeah, got my glasses.

LINDA: [*Giving him the handkerchief.*] And a handkerchief.

WILLY: Yeah, handkerchief.

LINDA: And your saccharine?[2]

WILLY: Yeah, my saccharine.

LINDA: Be careful on the subway stairs.

[*She kisses him, and a silk stocking is seen hanging from her hand.* WILLY *notices it.*]

WILLY: Will you stop mending stockings? At least while I'm in the house. It gets me nervous. I can't tell you. Please.

[LINDA *hides the stocking in her hand as she follows* WILLY *across the forestage in front of the house.*]

LINDA: Remember, Frank's Chop House.

WILLY: [*Passing the apron.*] Maybe beets would grow out there.

LINDA: [*Laughing.*] But you tried so many times.

WILLY: Yeah. Well, don't work hard today. [*He disappears around the right corner of the house.*]

LINDA: Be careful! [*As* WILLY *vanishes,* LINDA *waves to him. Suddenly the phone rings. She runs across the stage and into the kitchen and lifts it.*] Hello? Oh, Biff! I'm so glad you called, I just . . . Yes, sure, I just told him. Yes, he'll be there for dinner at six o'clock, I didn't forget. Listen, I was just dying to tell you. You know that little rubber pipe I told you about? That he connected to the gas

---

2. A low-calorie sweetner often substituted for sugar.

heater? I finally decided to go down the cellar this morning and take it away and destroy it. But it's gone! Imagine? He took it away himself, it isn't there! [*She listens.*] When? Oh, then you took it. Oh—nothing, it's just that I'd hoped he'd taken it away himself. Oh, I'm not worried, darling, because this morning he left in such high spirits, it was like the old days! I'm not afraid anymore. Did Mr. Oliver see you? . . . Well, you wait there then. And make a nice impression on him, darling. Just don't perspire too much before you see him. And have a nice time with Dad. He may have big news too! . . . That's right, a New York job. And be sweet to him tonight, dear. Be loving to him. Because he's only a little boat looking for a harbor. [*She is trembling with sorrow and joy.*] Oh, that's wonderful, Biff, you'll save his life. Thanks, darling. Just put your arm around him when he comes into the restaurant. Give him a smile. That's the boy . . . Good-bye, dear . . . You got your comb? . . . That's fine. Good-bye, Biff dear.

[*In the middle of her speech,* HOWARD WAGNER, *thirty-six, wheels on a small typewriter table on which is a wire-recording machine and proceeds to plug it in. This is on the left forestage. Light slowly fades on* LINDA *as it rises on* HOWARD. HOWARD *is intent on threading the machine and only glances over his shoulder as* WILLY *appears.*]

WILLY: Pst! Pst!

HOWARD: Hello, Willy, come in.

WILLY: Like to have a little talk with you, Howard.

HOWARD: Sorry to keep you waiting. I'll be with you in a minute.

WILLY: What's that, Howard?

HOWARD: Didn't you ever see one of these? Wire recorder.

WILLY: Oh. Can we talk a minute?

HOWARD: Records things. Just got delivery yesterday. Been driving me crazy, the most terrific machine I ever saw in my life. I was up all night with it.

WILLY: What do you do with it?

HOWARD: I bought it for dictation, but you can do anything with it. Listen to this. I had it home last night. Listen to what I picked up. The first one is my daughter. Get this. [*He flicks the switch and "Roll out the Barrel" is heard being whistled.*] Listen to that kid whistle.

WILLY: That is lifelike, isn't it?

HOWARD: Seven years old. Get that tone.

WILLY: Ts, ts. Like to ask a little favor if you . . .

[*The whistling breaks off, and the voice of* HOWARD's *daughter is heard.*]

HIS DAUGHTER: "Now you, Daddy."

HOWARD: She's crazy for me! [*Again the same song is whistled.*] That's me! Ha! [*He winks.*]

WILLY: You're very good!

[*The whistling breaks off again. The machine runs silent for a moment.*]

HOWARD: Sh! Get this now, this is my son.

HIS SON: "The capital of Alabama is Montgomery; the capital of Arizona is Phoenix; the capital of Arkansas is Little Rock; the capital of California is Sacramento . . ." [*And on, and on.*]

HOWARD: [*Holding up five fingers.*] Five years old, Willy!

WILLY: He'll make an announcer some day!

HIS SON: [*Continuing.*] "The capital . . ."

HOWARD: Get that—alphabetical order! [*The machine breaks off suddenly.*] Wait a minute. The maid kicked the plug out.

WILLY: It certainly is a—

HOWARD: Sh, for God's sake!

HIS SON: "It's nine o'clock, Bulova watch time.[3] So I have to go to sleep."

WILLY: That really is—

HOWARD: Wait a minute! The next is my wife.

[*They wait.*]

HOWARD'S VOICE: "Go on, say something." [*Pause.*] "Well, you gonna talk?"

HIS WIFE: "I can't think of anything."

HOWARD'S VOICE: "Well, talk—it's turning."

HIS WIFE: [*Shyly, beaten.*] "Hello." [*Silence.*] "Oh, Howard, I can't talk into this . . ."

---

3. Commercial slogan of the Bulova Watch Company often heard on the radio.

HOWARD: [*Snapping the machine off.*] That was my wife.

WILLY: That is a wonderful machine. Can we—

HOWARD: I tell you, Willy, I'm gonna take my camera, and my bandsaw, and all my hobbies, and out they go. This is the most fascinating relaxation I ever found.

WILLY: I think I'll get one myself.

HOWARD: Sure, they're only a hundred and a half. You can't do without it. Supposing you wanna hear Jack Benny,[4] see? But you can't be at home at that hour. So you tell the maid to turn the radio on when Jack Benny comes on, and this automatically goes on with the radio . . .

WILLY: And when you come home you . . .

HOWARD: You can come home twelve o'clock, one o'clock, any time you like, and you get yourself a Coke and sit yourself down, throw the switch, and there's Jack Benny's program in the middle of the night!

WILLY: I'm definitely going to get one. Because lots of time I'm on the road, and I think to myself, what I must be missing on the radio!

HOWARD: Don't you have a radio in the car?

WILLY: Well, yeah, but who ever thinks of turning it on?

HOWARD: Say, aren't you supposed to be in Boston?

WILLY: That's what I want to talk to you about, Howard. You got a minute? [*He draws a chair in from the wing.*]

HOWARD: What happened? What're you doing here?

WILLY: Well . . .

HOWARD: You didn't crack up again, did you?

WILLY: Oh, no. No . . .

HOWARD: Geez, you had me worried there for a minute. What's the trouble?

WILLY: Well, tell you the truth, Howard. I've come to the decision that I'd rather not travel anymore.

HOWARD: Not travel! Well, what'll you do?

WILLY: Remember, Christmas time, when you had the party here? You said you'd try to think of some spot for me here in town.

---

4. Jack Benny (1894–1974) starred in the popular weekly radio show, *The Jack Benny Program*, from 1932 to 1955.

HOWARD: With us?

WILLY: Well, sure.

HOWARD: Oh, yeah, yeah. I remember. Well, I couldn't think of anything for you, Willy.

WILLY: I tell ya, Howard. The kids are all grown up, y'know. I don't need much anymore. If I could take home—well, sixty-five dollars a week, I could swing it.

HOWARD: Yeah, but Willy, see I—

WILLY: I tell ya why, Howard. Speaking frankly and between the two of us, y'know—I'm just a little tired.

HOWARD: Oh, I could understand that, Willy. But you're a road man, Willy, and we do a road business. We've only got a half-dozen salesmen on the floor here.

WILLY: God knows, Howard, I never asked a favor of any man. But I was with the firm when your father used to carry you in here in his arms.

HOWARD: I know that, Willy, but—

WILLY: Your father came to me the day you were born and asked me what I thought of the name of Howard, may he rest in peace.

HOWARD: I appreciate that, Willy, but there just is no spot here for you. If I had a spot I'd slam you right in, but I just don't have a single solitary spot.

[*He looks for his lighter.* WILLY *has picked it up and gives it to him. Pause.*]

WILLY: [*With increasing anger.*] Howard, all I need to set my table is fifty dollars a week.

HOWARD: But where am I going to put you, kid?

WILLY: Look, it isn't a question of whether I can sell merchandise, is it?

HOWARD: No, but it's a business, kid, and everybody's gotta pull his own weight.

WILLY: [*Desperately.*] Just let me tell you a story, Howard—

HOWARD: 'Cause you gotta admit, business is business.

WILLY: [*Angrily.*] Business is definitely business, but just listen for a minute. You don't understand this. When I was a boy—eighteen, nineteen—I was already on the road. And there was a question in my mind as to whether selling had a future for me. Because in those days I had a yearning to go to Alaska. See, there were three gold strikes in one month in Alaska, and I felt like going out. Just for the ride, you might say.

HOWARD: [*Barely interested.*] Don't say.

WILLY: Oh, yeah, my father lived many years in Alaska. He was an adventurous man. We've got quite a little streak of self-reliance in our family. I thought I'd go out with my older brother and try to locate him, and maybe settle in the North with the old man. And I was almost decided to go, when I met a salesman in the Parker House. His name was Dave Singleman. And he was eighty-four years old, and he'd drummed merchandise in thirty-one states. And old Dave, he'd go up to his room, y'understand, put on his green velvet slippers—I'll never forget—and pick up his phone and call the buyers, and without ever leaving his room, at the age of eighty-four, he made a living. And when I saw that, I realized that selling was the greatest career a man could want. 'Cause what could be more satisfying than to be able to go, at the age of eighty-four, into twenty or thirty different cities, and pick up his phone and be remembered and loved and helped by so many different people? Do you know? when he died—and by the way he died the death of a salesman, in his green velvet slippers in the smoker of the New York, New Haven and Hartford, going into Boston[5]—when he died, hundreds of salesmen and buyers were at his funeral. Things were sad on a lotta trains for months after that. [*He stands up.* HOWARD *has not looked at him.*] In those days there was personality in it, Howard. There was respect, and comradeship, and gratitude in it. Today, it's all cut and dried, and there's no chance for bringing friendship to bear—or personality. You see what I mean? They don't know me anymore.

HOWARD: [*Moving away, toward the right.*] That's just the thing, Willy.

WILLY: If I had forty dollars a week—that's all I'd need. Forty dollars, Howard.

HOWARD: Kid, I can't take blood from a stone, I—

WILLY: [*Desperation is on him now.*] Howard, the year Al Smith[6] was nominated, your father came to me and—

5. Smoking lounge on a train running from New York to Boston.

6. In 1928, New Yorker Alfred E. Smith (1873–1944) was the Democratic candidate for president. He lost to Herbert Hoover.

HOWARD: [*Starting to go off.*] I've got to see some people, kid.

WILLY: [*Stopping him.*] I'm talking about your father! There were promises made across this desk! You mustn't tell me you've got people to see—I put thirty-four years into this firm, Howard, and now I can't pay my insurance! You can't eat the orange and throw the peel away—a man is not a piece of fruit! [*After a pause.*] Now pay attention. Your father—in 1928 I had a big year. I averaged a hundred and seventy dollars a week in commissions.

HOWARD: [*Impatiently.*] Now, Willy, you never averaged—

WILLY: [*Banging his hand on the desk.*] I averaged a hundred and seventy dollars a week in the year of 1928! And your father came to me—or rather, I was in the office here—it was right over this desk—and he put his hand on my shoulder—

HOWARD: [*Getting up.*] You'll have to excuse me, Willy, I gotta see some people. Pull yourself together. [*Going out.*] I'll be back in a little while.

[*On* HOWARD's *exit, the light on his chair grows very bright and strange.*]

WILLY: Pull myself together! What the hell did I say to him? My God, I was yelling at him! How could I! [WILLY *breaks off, staring at the light, which occupies the chair, animating it. He approaches this chair, standing across the desk from it.*] Frank, Frank, don't you remember what you told me that time? How you put your hand on my shoulder, and Frank . . . [*He leans on the desk and as he speaks the dead man's name he accidentally switches on the recorder, and instantly.*]

HOWARD's SON: ". . . of New York is Albany. The capital of Ohio is Cincinnati, the capital of Rhode Island is . . ." [*The recitation continues.*]

WILLY: [*Leaping away with fright, shouting.*] Ha! Howard! Howard! Howard!

HOWARD: [*Rushing in.*] What happened?

WILLY: [*Pointing at the machine, which continues nasally, childishly, with the capital cities.*] Shut it off! Shut it off!

HOWARD: [*Pulling the plug out.*] Look, Willy . . .

WILLY: [*Pressing his hands to his eyes.*] I gotta get myself some coffee. I'll get some coffee . . .

[WILLY *starts to walk out.* HOWARD *stops him.*]

HOWARD: [*Rolling up the cord.*] Willy, look . . .

WILLY: I'll go to Boston.

HOWARD: Willy, you can't go to Boston for us.

WILLY: Why can't I go?

HOWARD: I don't want you to represent us. I've been meaning to tell you for a long time now.

WILLY: Howard, are you firing me?

HOWARD: I think you need a good long rest, Willy.

WILLY: Howard—

HOWARD: And when you feel better, come back, and we'll see if we can work something out.

WILLY: But I gotta earn money, Howard. I'm in no position to—

HOWARD: Where are your sons? Why don't your sons give you a hand?

WILLY: They're working on a very big deal.

HOWARD: This is no time for false pride, Willy. You go to your sons and you tell them that you're tired. You've got two great boys, haven't you?

WILLY: Oh, no question, no question, but in the meantime . . .

HOWARD: Then that's that, heh?

WILLY: All right, I'll go to Boston tomorrow.

HOWARD: No, no.

WILLY: I can't throw myself on my sons. I'm not a cripple!

HOWARD: Look, kid, I'm busy, I'm busy this morning.

WILLY: [*Grasping* HOWARD's *arm.*] Howard, you've got to let me go to Boston!

HOWARD: [*Hard, keeping himself under control.*] I've got a line of people to see this morning. Sit down, take five minutes, and pull yourself together, and then go home, will ya? I need the office, Willy. [*He starts to go, turns, remembering the recorder, starts to push off the table holding the recorder.*] Oh, yeah. Whenever you can this week, stop by and drop off the samples. You'll feel better, Willy, and then come back and we'll talk. Pull yourself together, kid, there's people outside.

> [HOWARD *exits, pushing the table off left.* WILLY *stares into space, exhausted. Now the music is heard—*BEN's *music—first distantly, then closer, closer. As* WILLY *speaks,* BEN *enters from the right. He carries valise and umbrella.*]

WILLY: Oh, Ben, how did you do it? What is the answer? Did you wind up the Alaska deal already?

BEN: Doesn't take much time if you know what you're doing. Just a short business trip. Boarding ship in an hour. Wanted to say good-by.

WILLY: Ben, I've got to talk to you.

BEN: [*Glancing at his watch.*] Haven't the time, William.

WILLY: [*Crossing the apron to* BEN.] Ben, nothing's working out. I don't know what to do.

BEN: Now, look here, William. I've bought timberland in Alaska and I need a man to look after things for me.

WILLY: God, timberland! Me and my boys in those grand outdoors!

BEN: You've a new continent at your doorstep, William. Get out of these cities, they're full of talk and time payments and courts of law. Screw on your fists and you can fight for a fortune up there.

WILLY: Yes, yes! Linda, Linda!

[LINDA *enters as of old, with the wash.*]

LINDA: Oh, you're back?

BEN: I haven't much time.

WILLY: No, wait! Linda, he's got a proposition for me in Alaska.

LINDA: But you've got—[*To* BEN.] He's got a beautiful job here.

WILLY: But in Alaska, kid, I could—

LINDA: You're doing well enough, Willy!

BEN: [*To* LINDA.] Enough for what, my dear?

LINDA: [*Frightened of* BEN *and angry at him.*] Don't say those things to him! Enough to be happy right here, right now. [*To* WILLY, *while* BEN *laughs.*] Why must everybody conquer the world? You're well liked, and the boys love you, and someday—[*To* BEN.]—why, old man Wagner told him just the other day that if he keeps it up he'll be a member of the firm, didn't he, Willy?

WILLY: Sure, sure. I am building something with this firm, Ben, and if a man is building something he must be on the right track, mustn't he?

BEN: What are you building? Lay your hand on it. Where is it?

WILLY: [*Hesitantly.*] That's true, Linda, there's nothing.

LINDA: Why? [*To* BEN.] There's a man eighty-four years old—

WILLY: That's right, Ben, that's right. When I look at that man I say, what is there to worry about?

BEN: Bah!

WILLY: It's true, Ben. All he has to do is go into any city, pick up the phone, and he's making his living and you know why?

BEN: [*Picking up his valise.*] I've got to go.

WILLY: [*Holding* BEN *back.*] Look at this boy! [BIFF, *in his high school sweater, enters carrying suitcase.* HAPPY *carries* BIFF's *shoulder guards, gold helmet, and football pants.*] Without a penny to his name, three great universities are begging for him, and from there the sky's the limit, because it's not what you do, Ben. It's who you know and the smile on your face! It's contacts, Ben, contacts! The whole wealth of Alaska passes over the lunch table at the Commodore Hotel, and that's the wonder, the wonder of this country, that a man can end with diamonds here on the basis of being liked! [*He turns to* BIFF.] And that's why when you get out on that field today it's important. Because thousands of people will be rooting for you and loving you. [*To* BEN, *who has again begun to leave.*] And Ben! when he walks into a business office his name will sound out like a bell and all the doors will open to him! I've seen it, Ben, I've seen it a thousand times! You can't feel it with your hand like timber, but it's there!

BEN: Good-by, William.

WILLY: Ben, am I right? Don't you think I'm right? I value your advice.

BEN: There's a new continent at your doorstep, William. You could walk out rich. Rich! [*He is gone.*]

WILLY: We'll do it here, Ben! You hear me? We're gonna do it here!
　　[*Young* BERNARD *rushes in. The gay music of the Boys is heard.*]

BERNARD: Oh, gee, I was afraid you left already!

WILLY: Why? What time is it?

BERNARD: It's half-past one!

WILLY: Well, come on, everybody! Ebbets Field next stop! Where's the pennants? [*He rushes through the wall-line of the kitchen and out into the living room.*]

LINDA: [*To* BIFF.] Did you pack fresh underwear?

BIFF: [*Who has been limbering up.*] I want to go!

BERNARD: Biff, I'm carrying your helmet, ain't I?

HAPPY: No, I'm carrying the helmet.

BERNARD: Oh, Biff, you promised me.

HAPPY: I'm carrying the helmet.

BERNARD: How am I going to get in the locker room?

LINDA: Let him carry the shoulder guards. [*She puts her coat and hat on in the kitchen.*]

BERNARD: Can I, Biff? 'Cause I told everybody I'm going to be in the locker room.

HAPPY: In Ebbets Field it's the clubhouse.

BERNARD: I meant the clubhouse, Biff!

HAPPY: Biff!

BIFF: [*Grandly, after a slight pause.*] Let him carry the shoulder guards.

HAPPY: [*As he gives* BERNARD *the shoulder guards.*] Stay close to us now.

    [WILLY *rushes in with the pennants.*]

WILLY: [*Handing them out.*] Everybody wave when Biff comes out on the field. [HAPPY *and* BERNARD *run off.*] You set now, boy?

    [*The music has died away.*]

BIFF: Ready to go, Pop. Every muscle is ready.

WILLY: [*At the edge of the apron.*] You realize what this means?

BIFF: That's right, Pop.

WILLY: [*Feeling* BIFF'S *muscles.*] You're comin' home this afternoon captain of the All-Scholastic Championship Team of the City of New York.

BIFF: I got it, Pop. And remember, pal, when I take off my helmet, that touchdown is for you.

WILLY: Let's go! [*He is starting out, with his arm around* BIFF, *when* CHARLEY *enters, as of old, in knickers.*] I got no room for you, Charley.

CHARLEY: Room? For what?

WILLY: In the car.

CHARLEY: You goin' for a ride? I wanted to shoot some casino.

WILLY: [*Furiously.*] Casino! [*Incredulously.*] Don't you realize what to-day is?

LINDA: Oh, he knows, Willy. He's just kidding you.

WILLY: That's nothing to kid about!

CHARLEY: No, Linda, what's goin' on?

LINDA: He's playing in Ebbets Field.

CHARLEY: Baseball in this weather?

WILLY: Don't talk to him. Come on, come on! [*He is pushing them out.*]

CHARLEY: Wait a minute, didn't you hear the news?

WILLY: What?

CHARLEY: Don't you listen to the radio? Ebbets Field just blew up.

WILLY: You go to hell! [CHARLEY *laughs. Pushing them out.*] Come on, come on! We're late.

CHARLEY: [*As they go.*] Knock a homer, Biff, knock a homer!

WILLY: [*The last to leave, turning to* CHARLEY.] I don't think that was funny, Charley. This is the greatest day of my life.

CHARLEY: Willy, when are you going to grow up?

WILLY: Yeah, heh? When this game is over, Charley, you'll be laughing out of the other side of your face. They'll be calling him another Red Grange.[7] Twenty-five thousand a year.

CHARLEY: [*Kidding.*] Is that so?

WILLY: Yeah, that's so.

CHARLEY: Well, then, I'm sorry, Willy. But tell me something.

WILLY: What?

CHARLEY: Who is Red Grange?

WILLY: Put up your hands. Goddam you, put up your hands! [CHARLEY, *chuckling, shakes his head and walks away, around the left corner of the stage.* WILLY *follows him. The music rises to a mocking frenzy.*] Who the hell do you think you are, better than everybody else? You don't know everything, you big, ignorant, stupid . . . Put up your hands!

[*Light rises, on the right side of the forestage, on a small table in the reception room of* CHARLEY's *office. Traffic sounds are heard.* BERNARD, *now mature, sits whistling to himself. A pair of tennis rackets and an overnight bag are on the floor beside him.*]

WILLY: [*Offstage.*] What are you walking away for? Don't walk away! If you're going to say something say it to my face! I know you laugh at me behind my back. You'll laugh out of the other side of your goddam face after this game. Touchdown! Touchdown! Eighty thousand people! Touchdown! Right between the goal posts.

---

7. Harold Edward Grange (1903–1991), a college and professional football hall-of-famer, played halfback at the University of Illinois from 1923 to 1925.

[BERNARD *is a quiet, earnest, but self-assured young man.* WILLY's *voice is coming from right upstage now.* BERNARD *lowers his feet off the table and listens.* JENNY, *his father's secretary, enters.*]

JENNY: [*Distressed.*] Say, Bernard, will you go out in the hall?

BERNARD: What is that noise? Who is it?

JENNY: Mr. Loman. He just got off the elevator.

BERNARD: [*Getting up.*] Who's he arguing with?

JENNY: Nobody. There's nobody with him. I can't deal with him anymore, and your father gets all upset everytime he comes. I've got a lot of typing to do, and your father's waiting to sign it. Will you see him?

WILLY: [*Entering.*] Touchdown! Touch—[*He sees* JENNY.] Jenny, Jenny, good to see you. How're ya? Workin'? Or still honest?

JENNY: Fine. How've you been feeling?

WILLY: Not much anymore, Jenny. Ha, ha! [*He is surprised to see the rackets.*]

BERNARD: Hello, Uncle Willy.

WILLY: [*Almost shocked.*] Bernard! Well, look who's here! [*He comes quickly, guiltily to* BERNARD *and warmly shakes his hand.*]

BERNARD: How are you? Good to see you.

WILLY: What are you doing here?

BERNARD: Oh, just stopped by to see Pop. Get off my feet till my train leaves. I'm going to Washington in a few minutes.

WILLY: Is he in?

BERNARD: Yes, he's in his office with the accountant. Sit down.

WILLY: [*Sitting down.*] What're you going to do in Washington?

BERNARD: Oh, just a case I've got there, Willy.

WILLY: That so? [*Indicating the rackets.*] You going to play tennis there?

BERNARD: I'm staying with a friend who's got a court.

WILLY: Don't say. His own tennis court. Must be fine people, I bet.

BERNARD: They are, very nice. Dad tells me Biff's in town.

WILLY: [*With a big smile.*] Yeah, Biff's in. Working on a very big deal, Bernard.

BERNARD: What's Biff doing?

WILLY: Well, he's been doing very big things in the West. But he decided to establish himself here. Very big. We're having dinner. Did I hear your wife had a boy?

BERNARD: That's right. Our second.

WILLY: Two boys! What do you know!

BERNARD: What kind of a deal has Biff got?

WILLY: Well, Bill Oliver—very big sporting-goods man—he wants Biff very badly. Called him in from the West. Long distance, carte blanche, special deliveries. Your friends have their own private tennis court?

BERNARD: You still with the old firm, Willy?

WILLY: [*After a pause.*] I'm—I'm overjoyed to see how you made the grade, Bernard, overjoyed. It's an encouraging thing to see a young man really—really—Looks very good for Biff—very—[*He breaks off, then.*] Bernard—[*He is so full of emotion, he breaks off again.*]

BERNARD: What is it, Willy?

WILLY: [*Small and alone.*] What—what's the secret?

BERNARD: What secret?

WILLY: How—how did you? Why didn't he ever catch on?

BERNARD: I wouldn't know that, Willy.

WILLY: [*Confidentially, desperately.*] You were his friend, his boyhood friend. There's something I don't understand about it. His life ended after that Ebbets Field game. From the age of seventeen nothing good ever happened to him.

BERNARD: He never trained himself for anything.

WILLY: But he did, he did. After high school he took so many correspondence courses. Radio mechanics; television; God knows what, and never made the slightest mark.

BERNARD: [*Taking off his glasses.*] Willy, do you want to talk candidly?

WILLY: [*Rising, faces BERNARD.*] I regard you as a very brilliant man, Bernard. I value your advice.

BERNARD: Oh, the hell with the advice, Willy. I couldn't advise you. There's just one thing I've always wanted to ask you. When he was supposed to graduate, and the math teacher flunked him—

WILLY: Oh, that son-of-a-bitch ruined his life.

BERNARD: Yeah, but, Willy, all he had to do was go to summer school and make up that subject.

WILLY: That's right, that's right.

BERNARD: Did you tell him not to go to summer school?

WILLY: Me? I begged him to go. I ordered him to go!

BERNARD: Then why wouldn't he go?

WILLY: Why? Why! Bernard, that question has been trailing me like a ghost for the last fifteen years. He flunked the subject, and laid down and died like a hammer hit him!

BERNARD: Take it easy, kid.

WILLY: Let me talk to you—I got nobody to talk to. Bernard, Bernard, was it my fault? Y'see? It keeps going around in my mind, maybe I did something to him. I got nothing to give him.

BERNARD: Don't take it so hard.

WILLY: Why did he lay down? What is the story there? You were his friend!

BERNARD: Willy, I remember, it was June, and our grades came out. And he'd flunked math.

WILLY: That son-of-a-bitch!

BERNARD: No, it wasn't right then. Biff just got very angry, I remember, and he was ready to enroll in summer school.

WILLY: [Surprised.] He was?

BERNARD: He wasn't beaten by it at all. But then, Willy, he disappeared from the block for almost a month. And I got the idea that he'd gone up to New England to see you. Did he have a talk with you then? [WILLY stares in silence.] Willy?

WILLY: [With a strong edge of resentment in his voice.] Yeah, he came to Boston. What about it?

BERNARD: Well, just that when he came back—I'll never forget this, it always mystifies me. Because I'd thought so well of Biff, even though he'd always taken advantage of me. I loved him, Willy, y'know? And he came back after that month and took his sneakers—remember those sneakers with "University of Virginia" printed on them? He was so proud of those, wore them every day. And he took them down in the cellar, and burned them up in the furnace. We had a fist fight. It lasted at least half an hour. Just the two of us, punching each other down the cellar, and crying right through it. I've often thought of how strange it was that I knew he'd given up his life. What happened in Boston, Willy? [WILLY looks at him as at an intruder.] I just bring it up because you asked me.

WILLY: [*Angrily.*] Nothing. What do you mean, "What happened?" What's that got to do with anything?

BERNARD: Well, don't get sore.

WILLY: What are you trying to do, blame it on me? If a boy lays down is that my fault?

BERNARD: Now, Willy, don't get—

WILLY: Well, don't—don't talk to me that way! What does that mean, "What happened?"

[CHARLEY *enters. He is in his vest, and he carries a bottle of bourbon.*]

CHARLEY: Hey, you're going to miss that train. [*He waves the bottle.*]

BERNARD: Yeah, I'm going. [*He takes the bottle.*] Thanks, Pop. [*He picks up his rackets and bag.*] Good-bye, Willy, and don't worry about it. You know, "If at first you don't succeed . . ."

WILLY: Yes, I believe in that.

BERNARD: But sometimes, Willy, it's better for a man just to walk away.

WILLY: Walk away?

BERNARD: That's right.

WILLY: But if you can't walk away?

BERNARD: [*After a slight pause.*] I guess that's when it's tough. [*Extending his hand.*] Good-bye, Willy.

WILLY: [*Shaking* BERNARD'*s hand.*] Good-bye, boy.

CHARLEY: [*An arm on* BERNARD'*s shoulder.*] How do you like this kid? Gonna argue a case in front of the Supreme Court.

BERNARD: [*Protesting.*] Pop!

WILLY: [*Genuinely shocked, pained, and happy.*] No! The Supreme Court!

BERNARD: I gotta run. 'Bye, Dad!

CHARLEY: Knock 'em dead, Bernard!

[BERNARD *goes off.*]

WILLY: [*As* CHARLEY *takes out his wallet.*] The Supreme Court! And he didn't even mention it!

CHARLEY: [*Counting out money on the desk.*] He don't have to—he's gonna do it.

WILLY: And you never told him what to do, did you? You never took any interest in him.

CHARLEY: My salvation is that I never took any interest in anything. There's some money—fifty dollars. I got an accountant inside.

WILLY: Charley, look . . . [*With difficulty.*] I got my insurance to pay. If you can manage it—I need a hundred and ten dollars. [CHARLEY *doesn't reply for a moment; merely stops moving.*] I'd draw it from my bank but Linda would know, and I . . .

CHARLEY: Sit down, Willy.

WILLY: [*Moving toward the chair.*] I'm keeping an account of everything, remember. I'll pay every penny back. [*He sits.*]

CHARLEY: Now listen to me, Willy.

WILLY: I want you to know I appreciate . . .

CHARLEY: [*Sitting down on the table.*] Willy, what're you doin'? What the hell is goin' on in your head?

WILLY: Why? I'm simply . . .

CHARLEY: I offered you a job. You can make fifty dollars a week. And I won't send you on the road.

WILLY: I've got a job.

CHARLEY: Without pay? What kind of job is a job without pay? [*He rises.*] Now, look kid, enough is enough. I'm no genius but I know when I'm being insulted.

WILLY: Insulted!

CHARLEY: Why don't you want to work for me?

WILLY: What's the matter with you? I've got a job.

CHARLEY: Then what're you walkin' in here every week for?

WILLY: [*Getting up.*] Well, if you don't want me to walk in here—

CHARLEY: I am offering you a job!

WILLY: I don't want your goddam job!

CHARLEY: When the hell are you going to grow up?

WILLY: [*Furiously.*] You big ignoramus, if you say that to me again I'll rap you one! I don't care how big you are! [*He's ready to fight. Pause.*]

CHARLEY: [*Kindly, going to him.*] How much do you need, Willy?

WILLY: Charley, I'm strapped, I'm strapped. I don't know what to do. I was just fired.

CHARLEY: Howard fired you?

WILLY: That snotnose. Imagine that? I named him. I named him Howard.

CHARLEY: Willy, when're you gonna realize that them things don't mean anything? You named him Howard, but you can't sell that. The only thing you got in this world is what you can sell. And the funny thing is that you're a salesman, and you don't know that.

WILLY: I've always tried to think otherwise, I guess. I always felt that if a man was impressive, and well liked, that nothing—

CHARLEY: Why must everybody like you? Who liked J. P. Morgan?[8] Was he impressive? In a Turkish bath he'd look like a butcher. But with his pockets on he was very well liked. Now listen, Willy, I know you don't like me, and nobody can say I'm in love with you, but I'll give you a job because—just for the hell of it, put it that way. Now what do you say?

WILLY: I—I just can't work for you, Charley.

CHARLEY: What're you, jealous of me?

WILLY: I can't work for you, that's all, don't ask me why.

CHARLEY: [Angered, takes out more bills.] You been jealous of me all your life, you damned fool! Here, pay your insurance. [He puts the money in WILLY's hand.]

WILLY: I'm keeping strict accounts.

CHARLEY: I've got some work to do. Take care of yourself. And pay your insurance.

WILLY: [Moving to the right.] Funny, y'know? After all the highways and the trains, and the appointments, and the years, you end up worth more dead than alive.

CHARLEY: Willy, nobody's worth nothin' dead. [After a slight pause.] Did you hear what I said? [WILLY stands still, dreaming.] Willy!

WILLY: Apologize to Bernard for me when you see him. I didn't mean to argue with him. He's a fine boy. They're all fine boys, and they'll end up big—all of them. Someday they'll all play tennis together. Wish me luck, Charley. He saw Bill Oliver today.

CHARLEY: Good luck.

WILLY: [On the verge of tears.] Charley, you're the only friend I got. Isn't that a remarkable thing? [He goes out.]

CHARLEY: Jesus!

---

8. John Pierpont Morgan (1837–1913), financier who created U.S. Steel, among other companies.

[CHARLEY *stares after him a moment and follows. All light blacks out. Suddenly raucous music is heard, and a red glow rises behind the screen at right.* STANLEY, *a young waiter, appears, carrying a table, followed by* HAPPY, *who is carrying two chairs.*]

STANLEY: [*Putting the table down.*] That's all right, Mr. Loman, I can handle it myself. [*He turns and takes the chairs from* HAPPY *and places them at the table.*]

HAPPY: [*Glancing around.*] Oh, this is better.

STANLEY: Sure, in the front there you're in the middle of all kinds of noise. Whenever you got a party, Mr. Loman, you just tell me and I'll put you back here. Y'know, there's a lotta people they don't like it private, because when they go out they like to see a lotta action around them because they're sick and tired to stay in the house by theirself. But I know you, you ain't from Hackensack.[9] You know what I mean?

HAPPY: [*Sitting down.*] So how's it coming, Stanley?

STANLEY: Ah, it's a dog life. I only wish during the war they'd took me in the Army. I couda been dead by now.

HAPPY: My brother's back, Stanley.

STANLEY: Oh, he come back, heh? From the Far West.

HAPPY: Yeah, big cattle man, my brother, so treat him right. And my father's coming too.

STANLEY: Oh, your father too!

HAPPY: You got a couple of nice lobsters?

STANLEY: Hundred per cent, big.

HAPPY: I want them with the claws.

STANLEY: Don't worry, I don't give you no mice. [HAPPY *laughs.*] How about some wine? It'll put a head on the meal.

HAPPY: No. You remember, Stanley, that recipe I brought you from overseas? With the champagne in it?

STANLEY: Oh, yeah, sure. I still got it tacked up yet in the kitchen. But that'll have to cost a buck apiece anyways.

HAPPY: That's all right.

STANLEY: What'd you, hit a number or somethin'?

HAPPY: No, it's a little celebration. My brother is—I think he pulled off a big deal today. I think we're going into business together.

9. New Jersey city about seven miles west of New York City.

STANLEY: Great! That's the best for you. Because a family business, you know what I mean?—that's the best.

HAPPY: That's what I think.

STANLEY: 'Cause what's the difference? Somebody steals? It's in the family. Know what I mean? [*Sotto voce.*] Like this bartender here. The boss is goin' crazy what kinda leak he's got in the cash register. You put it in but it don't come out.

HAPPY: [*Raising his head.*] Sh!

STANLEY: What?

HAPPY: You notice I wasn't lookin' right or left, was I?

STANLEY: No.

HAPPY: And my eyes are closed.

STANLEY: So what's the—?

HAPPY: Strudel's comin.

STANLEY: [*Catching on, looks around.*] Ah, no, there's no—[*He breaks off as a furred, lavishly dressed* GIRL *enters and sits at the next table. Both follow her with their eyes.*] Geez, how'd ya know?

HAPPY: I got radar or something. [*Staring directly at her profile.*] Oooooooo . . . Stanley.

STANLEY: I think, that's for you, Mr. Loman.

HAPPY: Look at that mouth. Oh, God. And the binoculars.

STANLEY: Geez, you got a life, Mr. Loman.

HAPPY: Wait on her.

STANLEY: [*Going to the* GIRL's *table.*] Would you like a menu, ma'am?

GIRL: I'm expecting someone, but I'd like a—

HAPPY: Why don't you bring her—excuse me, miss, do you mind? I sell champagne, and I'd like you to try my brand. Bring her a champagne, Stanley.

GIRL: That's awfully nice of you.

HAPPY: Don't mention it. It's all company money. [*He laughs.*]

GIRL: That's a charming product to be selling, isn't it?

HAPPY: Oh, gets to be like everything else. Selling is selling, y'know.

GIRL: I suppose.

HAPPY: You don't happen to sell, do you?

GIRL: No, I don't sell.

HAPPY: Would you object to a compliment from a stranger? You ought to be on a magazine cover.

GIRL: [*Looking at him a little archly.*] I have been.

[STANLEY *comes in with a glass of champagne.*]

HAPPY: What'd I say before, Stanley? You see? She's a cover girl.

STANLEY: Oh, I could see, I could see.

HAPPY: [*To the* GIRL.] What magazine?

GIRL: Oh, a lot of them. [*She takes the drink.*] Thank you.

HAPPY: You know what they say in France, don't you? "Champagne is the drink of the complexion"—Hya, Biff!

[BIFF *has entered and sits with* HAPPY.]

BIFF: Hello, kid. Sorry I'm late.

HAPPY: I just got here. Uh, Miss—?

GIRL: Forsythe.

HAPPY: Miss Forsythe, this is my brother.

BIFF: Is Dad here?

HAPPY: His name is Biff. You might've heard of him. Great football player.

GIRL: Really? What team?

HAPPY: Are you familiar with football?

GIRL: No, I'm afraid I'm not.

HAPPY: Biff is quarterback with the New York Giants.

GIRL: Well, that's nice, isn't it? [*She drinks.*]

HAPPY: Good health.

GIRL: I'm happy to meet you.

HAPPY: That's my name, Hap. It's really Harold, but at West Point they called me Happy.

GIRL: [*Now really impressed.*] Oh, I see. How do you do? [*She turns her profile.*]

BIFF: Isn't Dad coming?

HAPPY: You want her?

BIFF: Oh, I could never make that.

HAPPY: I remember the time that idea would never come into your head. Where's the old confidence, Biff?

BIFF: I just saw Oliver—

HAPPY: Wait a minute. I've got to see that old confidence again. Do you want her? She's on call.

BIFF: Oh, no. [*He turns to look at the* GIRL.]

HAPPY: I'm telling you. Watch this. [*Turning to see the* GIRL.] Honey? [*She turns to him.*] Are you busy?

GIRL: Well, I am . . . but I could make a phone call.

HAPPY: Do that, will you, honey? And see if you can get a friend. We'll be here for a while. Biff is one of the greatest football players in the country.

GIRL: [*Standing up.*] Well, I'm certainly happy to meet you.

HAPPY: Come back soon.

GIRL: I'll try.

HAPPY: Don't try, honey, try hard. [*The* GIRL *exits.* STANLEY *follows, shaking his head in bewildered admiration.*] Isn't that a shame now? A beautiful girl like that? That's why I can't get married. There's not a good woman in a thousand. New York is loaded with them, kid!

BIFF: Hap, look—

HAPPY: I told you she was on call!

BIFF: [*Strangely unnerved.*] Cut it out, will ya? I want to say something to you.

HAPPY: Did you see Oliver?

BIFF: I saw him all right. Now look, I want to tell Dad a couple of things and I want you to help me.

HAPPY: What? Is he going to back you?

BIFF: Are you crazy? You're out of your goddam head, you know that?

HAPPY: Why? What happened?

BIFF: [*Breathlessly.*] I did a terrible thing today, Hap. It's been the strangest day I ever went through. I'm all numb, I swear.

HAPPY: You mean he wouldn't see you?

BIFF: Well, I waited six hours for him, see? All day. Kept sending my name in. Even tried to date his secretary so she'd get me to him, but no soap.

HAPPY: Because you're not showin' the old confidence, Biff. He remembered you, didn't he?

BIFF: [*Stopping* HAPPY *with a gesture.*] Finally, about five o'clock, he comes out. Didn't remember who I was or anything. I felt like such an idiot, Hap.

HAPPY: Did you tell him my Florida idea?

BIFF: He walked away. I saw him for one minute. I got so mad I could've torn the walls down! How the hell did I ever get the idea I was a salesman there? I even believed myself that I'd been a salesman for him! And then he gave me one look and—I realized what a ridiculous lie my whole life has been! We've been talking in a dream for fifteen years. I was a shipping clerk.

HAPPY: What'd you do?

BIFF: [*With great tension and wonder.*] Well, he left, see. And the secretary went out. I was all alone in the waiting-room. I don't know what came over me, Hap. The next thing I know I'm in his office—paneled walls, everything. I can't explain it. I—Hap, I took his fountain pen.

HAPPY: Geez, did he catch you?

BIFF: I ran out. I ran down all eleven flights. I ran and ran and ran.

HAPPY: That was an awful dumb—what'd you do that for?

BIFF: [*Agonized.*] I don't know, I just—wanted to take something, I don't know. You gotta help me, Hap, I'm gonna tell Pop.

HAPPY: You crazy? What for?

BIFF: Hap, he's got to understand that I'm not the man somebody lends that kind of money to. He thinks I've been spiting him all these years and it's eating him up.

HAPPY: That's just it. You tell him something nice.

BIFF: I can't.

HAPPY: Say you got a lunch date with Oliver tomorrow.

BIFF: So what do I do tomorrow?

HAPPY: You leave the house tomorrow and come back at night and say Oliver is thinking it over. And he thinks it over for a couple of weeks, and gradually it fades away and nobody's the worse.

BIFF: But it'll go on forever!

HAPPY: Dad is never so happy as when he's looking forward to something! [WILLY *enters.*] Hello, scout!

WILLY: Gee, I haven't been here in years!

[STANLEY *has followed* WILLY *in and sets a chair for him.* STANLEY *starts off but* HAPPY *stops him.*]

HAPPY: Stanley!

[STANLEY *stands by, waiting for an order.*]

BIFF: [*Going to* WILLY *with guilt, as to an invalid.*] Sit down, Pop. You want a drink?

WILLY: Sure, I don't mind.

BIFF: Let's get a load on.

WILLY: You look worried.

BIFF: N-no. [*To* STANLEY.] Scotch all around. Make it doubles.

STANLEY: Doubles, right. [*He goes.*]

WILLY: You had a couple already, didn't you?

BIFF: Just a couple, yeah.

WILLY: Well, what happened, boy? [*Nodding affirmatively, with a smile.*] Everything go all right?

BIFF: [*Takes a breath, then reaches out and grasps* WILLY'*s hand.*] Pal . . . [*He is smiling bravely, and* WILLY *is smiling too.*] I had an experience today.

HAPPY: Terrific, Pop.

WILLY: That so? What happened?

BIFF: [*High, slightly alcoholic, above the earth.*] I'm going to tell you everything from first to last. It's been a strange day. [*Silence. He looks around, composes himself as best he can, but his breath keeps breaking the rhythm of his voice.*] I had to wait quite a while for him, and—

WILLY: Oliver?

BIFF: Yeah, Oliver. All day, as a matter of cold fact. And a lot of—instances—facts, Pop, facts about my life came back to me. Who was it, Pop? Who ever said I was a salesman with Oliver?

WILLY: Well, you were.

BIFF: No, Dad, I was shipping clerk.

WILLY: But you were practically—

BIFF: [*With determination.*] Dad, I don't know who said it first, but I was never a salesman for Bill Oliver.

WILLY: What're you talking about?

BIFF: Let's hold on to the facts tonight, Pop. We're not going to get anywhere bullin' around. I was a shipping clerk.

WILLY: [*Angrily.*] All right, now listen to me—

BIFF: Why don't you let me finish?

WILLY: I'm not interested in stories about the past or any crap of that kind because the woods are burning, boys, you understand? There's a big blaze going on all around. I was fired today.

BIFF: [*Shocked.*] How could you be?

WILLY: I was fired, and I'm looking for a little good news to tell your mother, because the woman has waited and the woman has suffered. The gist of it is that I haven't got a story left in my head, Biff. So don't give me a lecture about facts and aspects. I am not interested. Now what've you got to say to me? [STANLEY *enters with three drinks. They wait until he leaves.*] Did you see Oliver?

BIFF: Jesus, Dad!

WILLY: You mean you didn't go up there?

HAPPY: Sure he went up there.

BIFF: I did. I—saw him. How could they fire you?

WILLY: [*On the edge of his chair.*] What kind of a welcome did he give you?

BIFF: He won't even let you work on commission?

WILLY: I'm out. [*Driving.*] So tell me, he gave you a warm welcome?

HAPPY: Sure, Pop, sure!

BIFF: [*Driven.*] Well, it was kind of—

WILLY: I was wondering if he'd remember you. [*To* HAPPY.] Imagine, man doesn't see him for ten, twelve years and gives him that kind of a welcome!

HAPPY: Damn right!

BIFF: [*Trying to return to the offensive.*] Pop, look—

WILLY: You know why he remembered you, don't you? Because you impressed him in those days.

BIFF: Let's talk quietly and get this down to the facts, huh?

WILLY: [*As though* BIFF *had been interrupting.*] Well, what happened? It's great news, Biff. Did he take you into his office or'd you talk in the waiting-room?

BIFF: Well, he came in, see and—

WILLY: [*With a big smile.*] What'd he say? Betcha he threw his arm around you.

BIFF: Well, he kinda—

WILLY: He's a fine man. [*To* HAPPY.] Very hard man to see, y'know.

HAPPY: [*Agreeing.*] Oh, I know.

WILLY: [*To* BIFF.] Is that where you had the drinks?

BIFF: Yeah, he gave me a couple of—no, no!

HAPPY: [*Cutting in.*] He told him my Florida idea.

WILLY: Don't interrupt. [*To* BIFF.] How'd he react to the Florida idea?

BIFF: Dad, will you give me a minute to explain?

WILLY: I've been waiting for you to explain since I sat down here! What happened? He took you into his office and what?

BIFF: Well—I talked. And—he listened, see.

WILLY: Famous for the way he listens, y'know. What was his answer?

BIFF: His answer was—[*He breaks off, suddenly angry.*] Dad, you're not letting me tell you what I want to tell you!

WILLY: [*Accusing, angered.*] You didn't see him, did you?

BIFF: I did see him!

WILLY: What'd you insult him or something? You insulted him, didn't you?

BIFF: Listen, will you let me out of it, will you just let me out of it!

HAPPY: What the hell!

WILLY: Tell me what happened!

BIFF: [*To* HAPPY.] I can't talk to him!

[*A single trumpet note jars the ear. The light of green leaves stains the house, which holds the air of night and a dream.* YOUNG BERNARD *enters and knocks on the door of the house.*]

YOUNG BERNARD: [*Frantically.*] Mrs. Loman, Mrs. Loman!

HAPPY: Tell him what happened!

BIFF: [*To* HAPPY.] Shut up and leave me alone!

WILLY: No, no. You had to go and flunk math!

BIFF: What math? What're you talking about?

YOUNG BERNARD: Mrs. Loman, Mrs. Loman!

[LINDA *appears in the house, as of old.*]

WILLY: [*Wildly.*] Math, math, math!

BIFF: Take it easy, Pop!

YOUNG BERNARD: Mrs. Loman!

WILLY: [*Furiously.*] If you hadn't flunked you'd've been set by now!

BIFF: Now, look, I'm gonna tell you what happened, and you're going to listen to me.

YOUNG BERNARD: Mrs. Loman!

BIFF: I waited six hours—

HAPPY: What the hell are you saying?

BIFF: I kept sending in my name but he wouldn't see me. So finally he . . . [*He continues unheard as light fades low on the restaurant.*]

YOUNG BERNARD: Biff flunked math!

LINDA: No!

YOUNG BERNARD: Birnbaum flunked him! They won't graduate him!

LINDA: But they have to. He's gotta go to the university. Where is he? Biff! Biff!

YOUNG BERNARD: No, he left. He went to Grand Central.

LINDA: Grand—You mean he went to Boston!

YOUNG BERNARD: Is Uncle Willy in Boston?

LINDA: Oh, maybe Willy can talk to the teacher. Oh, the poor, poor boy!

> [*Light on house area snaps out.*]

BIFF: [*At the table, now audible, holding up a gold fountain pen.*] . . . so I'm washed up with Oliver, you understand? Are you listening to me?

WILLY: [*At a loss.*] Yeah, sure. If you hadn't flunked—

BIFF: Flunked what? What're you talking about?

WILLY: Don't blame everything on me! I didn't flunk math—you did! What pen?

HAPPY: That was awful dumb, Biff, a pen like that is worth—

WILLY: [*Seeing the pen for the first time.*] You took Oliver's pen?

BIFF: [*Weakening.*] Dad, I just explained it to you.

WILLY: You stole Bill Oliver's fountain pen!

BIFF: I didn't exactly steal it! That's just what I've been explaining to you!

HAPPY: He had it in his hand and just then Oliver walked in, so he got nervous and stuck it in his pocket!

WILLY: My God, Biff!

BIFF: I never intended to do it, Dad!

OPERATOR'S VOICE: Standish Arms, good evening!

WILLY: [*Shouting.*] I'm not in my room!

BIFF: [*Frightened.*] Dad, what's the matter? [*He and* HAPPY *stand up.*]

OPERATOR: Ringing Mr. Loman for you!

BIFF: [*Horrified, gets down on one knee before* WILLY.] Dad, I'll make good, I'll make good. [WILLY *tries to get to his feet.* BIFF *holds him down.*] Sit down now.

WILLY: No, you're no good, you're no good for anything.

BIFF: I am, Dad, I'll find something else, you understand? Now don't worry about anything. [*He holds up* WILLY's *face.*] Talk to me, Dad.

OPERATOR: Mr. Loman does not answer. Shall I page him?

WILLY: [*Attempting to stand, as though to rush and silence the* OPERATOR.] No, no, no!

HAPPY: He'll strike something, Pop.

WILLY: No, no . . .

BIFF: [*Desperately, standing over* WILLY.] Pop, listen! Listen to me! I'm telling you something good. Oliver talked to his partner about the Florida idea. You listening? He—he talked to his partner, and he came to me . . . I'm going to be all right, you hear? Dad, listen to me, he said it was just a question of the amount!

WILLY: Then you . . . got it?

HAPPY: He's gonna be terrific, Pop!

WILLY: [*Trying to stand.*] Then you got it, haven't you? You got it! You got it!

BIFF: [*Agonized, holds* WILLY *down.*] No, no. Look, Pop. I'm supposed to have lunch with them tomorrow. I'm just telling you this so you'll know that I can still make an impression, Pop. And I'll make good somewhere, but I can't go tomorrow, see?

WILLY: Why not? You simply—

BIFF: But the pen, Pop!

WILLY: You give it to him and tell him it was an oversight!

HAPPY: Sure, have lunch tomorrow!

BIFF: I can't say that—

WILLY: You were doing a crossword puzzle and accidentally used his pen!

BIFF: Listen, kid, I took those balls years ago, now I walk in with his fountain pen? That clinches it, don't you see? I can't face him like that! I'll try elsewhere.

PAGE'S VOICE: Paging Mr. Loman!

WILLY: Don't you want to be anything?

BIFF: Pop, how can I go back?

WILLY: You don't want to be anything, is that what's behind it?

BIFF: [*Now angry at* WILLY *for not crediting his sympathy.*] Don't take it that way! You think it was easy walking into that office after what I'd done to him? A team of horses couldn't have dragged me back to Bill Oliver!

WILLY: Then why'd you go?

BIFF: Why did I go? Why did I go! Look at you! Look at what's become of you!

[*Off left,* THE WOMAN *laughs.*]

WILLY: Biff, you're going to go to that lunch tomorrow, or—

BIFF: I can't go. I've got an appointment!

HAPPY: Biff, for . . . !

WILLY: Are you spiting me?

BIFF: Don't take it that way! Goddammit!

WILLY: [*Strikes* BIFF *and falters away from the table.*] You rotten little louse! Are you spiting me?

THE WOMAN: Someone's at the door, Willy!

BIFF: I'm no good, can't you see what I am?

HAPPY: [*Separating them.*] Hey, you're in a restaurant! Now cut it out, both of you! [*The* GIRLS *enter.*] Hello, girls, sit down.

[THE WOMAN *laughs, off left.*]

MISS FORSYTHE: I guess we might as well. This is Letta.

THE WOMAN: Willy, are you going to wake up?

BIFF: [*Ignoring* WILLY.] How're ya, miss, sit down. What do you drink?

MISS FORSYTHE: Letta might not be able to stay long.

LETTA: I gotta get up early tomorrow. I got jury duty. I'm so excited! Were you fellows ever on a jury?

BIFF: No, but I been in front of them! [*The* GIRLS *laugh.*] This is my father.

LETTA: Isn't he cute? Sit down with us, Pop.

HAPPY: Sit him down, Biff!

BIFF: [*Going to him.*] Come on, slugger, drink us under the table. To hell with it! Come on, sit down, pal.

[*On* BIFF's *last insistence,* WILLY *is about to sit.*]

THE WOMAN: [*Now urgently.*] Willy, are you going to answer the door!

[THE WOMAN's *call pulls* WILLY *back. He starts right, befuddled.*]

BIFF: Hey, where are you going?

WILLY: Open the door.

BIFF: The door?

WILLY: The washroom . . . the door . . . where's the door?

BIFF: [*Leading* WILLY *to the left.*] Just go straight down.

[WILLY *moves left.*]

THE WOMAN: Willy, Willy, are you going to get up, get up, get up, get up?

[WILLY *exits left.*]

LETTA: I think it's sweet you bring your daddy along.

MISS FORSYTHE: Oh, he isn't really your father!

BIFF: [*At left, turning to her resentfully.*] Miss Forsythe, you've just seen a prince walk by. A fine, troubled prince. A hardworking, unappreciated prince. A pal, you understand? A good companion. Always for his boys.

LETTA: That's so sweet.

HAPPY: Well, girls, what's the program? We're wasting time. Come on, Biff. Gather round. Where would you like to go?

BIFF: Why don't you do something for him?

HAPPY: Me!

BIFF: Don't you give a damn for him, Hap?

HAPPY: What're you talking about? I'm the one who—

BIFF: I sense it, you don't give a good goddam about him. [*He takes the rolled-up hose from his pocket and puts it on the table in front of* HAPPY.] Look what I found in the cellar, for Christ's sake. How can you bear to let it go on?

HAPPY: Me? Who goes away? Who runs off and—

BIFF: Yeah, but he doesn't mean anything to you. You could help him—I can't! Don't you understand what I'm talking about? He's going to kill himself, don't you know that?

HAPPY: Don't I know it! Me!

BIFF: Hap, help him! Jesus . . . help him . . . Help me, help me, I can't bear to look at his face! [*Ready to weep, he hurries out, up right.*]

HAPPY: [*Starting after him.*] Where are you going?

MISS FORSYTHE: What's he so mad about?

HAPPY: Come on, girls, we'll catch up with him.

MISS FORSYTHE: [*As* HAPPY *pushes her out.*] Say, I don't like that temper of his!

HAPPY: He's just a little overstrung, he'll be all right!

WILLY: [*Off left, as* THE WOMAN *laughs.*] Don't answer! Don't answer!

LETTA: Don't you want to tell your father—

HAPPY: No, that's not my father. He's just a guy. Come on, we'll catch Biff, and, honey, we're going to paint this town! Stanley, where's the check! Hey, Stanley!

[*They exit.* STANLEY *looks toward left.*]

STANLEY: [*Calling to* HAPPY *indignantly.*] Mr. Loman! Mr. Loman!

[STANLEY *picks up a chair and follows them off. Knocking is heard off left.* THE WOMAN *enters, laughing.* WILLY *follows her.*

She is in a black slip; he is buttoning his shirt. Raw, sensuous music accompanies their speech.]

WILLY: Will you stop laughing? Will you stop?

THE WOMAN: Aren't you going to answer the door? He'll wake the whole hotel.

WILLY: I'm not expecting anybody.

THE WOMAN: Whyn't you have another drink, honey, and stop being so damn self-centered?

WILLY: I'm so lonely.

THE WOMAN: You know you ruined me, Willy? From now on, whenever you come to the office, I'll see that you go right through to the buyers. No waiting at my desk anymore, Willy. You ruined me.

WILLY: That's nice of you to say that.

THE WOMAN: Gee, you are self-centered! Why so sad? You are the saddest, self-centeredest soul I ever did see-saw. [*She laughs. He kisses her.*] Come on inside, drummer boy. It's silly to be dressing in the middle of the night. [*As knocking is heard.*] Aren't you going to answer the door?

WILLY: They're knocking on the wrong door.

THE WOMAN: But I felt the knocking. And he heard us talking in here. Maybe the hotel's on fire!

WILLY: [*His terror rising.*] It's a mistake.

THE WOMAN: Then tell them to go away!

WILLY: There's nobody there.

THE WOMAN: It's getting on my nerves, Willy. There's somebody standing out there and it's getting on my nerves!

WILLY: [*Pushing her away from him.*] All right, stay in the bathroom here, and don't come out. I think there's a law in Massachusetts about it, so don't come out. It may be that new room clerk. He looked very mean. So don't come out. It's a mistake, there's no fire.

[*The knocking is heard again. He takes a few steps away from her, and she vanishes into the wing. The light follows him, and now he is facing* YOUNG BIFF, *who carries a suitcase.* BIFF *steps toward him. The music is gone.*]

BIFF: Why didn't you answer?

WILLY: Biff! What are you doing in Boston?

BIFF: Why didn't you answer? I've been knocking for five minutes, I called you on the phone—

WILLY: I just heard you. I was in the bathroom and had the door shut. Did anything happen home?

BIFF: Dad—I let you down.

WILLY: What do you mean?

BIFF: Dad . . .

WILLY: Biffo, what's this about? [*Putting his arm around* BIFF.] Come on, let's go downstairs and get you a malted.

BIFF: Dad, I flunked math.

WILLY: Not for the term?

BIFF: The term. I haven't got enough credits to graduate.

WILLY: You mean to say Bernard wouldn't give you the answers?

BIFF: He did, he tried, but I only got a sixty-one.

WILLY: And they wouldn't give you four points?

BIFF: Birnbaum refused absolutely. I begged him, Pop, but he won't give me those points. You gotta talk to him before they close the school. Because if he saw the kind of man you are, and you just talked to him in your way, I'm sure he'd come through for me. The class came right before practice, see, and I didn't go enough. Would you talk to him? He'd like you, Pop. You know the way you could talk.

WILLY: You're on. We'll drive right back.

BIFF: Oh, Dad, good work! I'm sure he'll change for you!

WILLY: Go downstairs and tell the clerk I'm checkin' out. Go right down.

BIFF: Yes, sir! See, the reason he hates me, Pop—one day he was late for class so I got up at the blackboard and imitated him. I crossed my eyes and talked with a lithp.

WILLY: [*Laughing.*] You did? The kids like it?

BIFF: They nearly died laughing!

WILLY: Yeah? What'd you do?

BIFF: The thquare root of thixty twee is . . . [WILLY *bursts out laughing;* BIFF *joins him.*] And in the middle of it he walked in!

　　[WILLY *laughs and* THE WOMAN *joins in offstage.*]

WILLY: [*Without hesitation.*] Hurry downstairs and—

BIFF: Somebody in there?

WILLY: No, that was next door.

[THE WOMAN *laughs offstage.*]

BIFF: Somebody got in your bathroom!

WILLY: No, it's the next room, there's a party—

THE WOMAN: [*Enters laughing. She lisps this.*] Can I come in? There's something in the bathtub, Willy, and it's moving!

[WILLY *looks at* BIFF, *who is staring open-mouthed and horrified at* THE WOMAN.]

WILLY: Ah—you better go back to your room. They must be finished painting by now. They're painting her room so I let her take a shower here. Go back, go back . . . [*He pushes her.*]

THE WOMAN: [*Resisting.*] But I've got to get dressed, Willy, I can't—

WILLY: Get out of here! Go back, go back . . . [*Suddenly striving for the ordinary.*] This is Miss Francis, Biff, she's a buyer. They're painting her room. Go back, Miss Francis, go back . . .

THE WOMAN: But my clothes, I can't go out naked in the hall!

WILLY: [*Pushing her offstage.*] Get outa here! Go back, go back!

[BIFF *slowly sits down on his suitcase as the argument continues offstage.*]

THE WOMAN: Where's my stockings? You promised me stockings, Willy!

WILLY: I have no stockings here!

THE WOMAN: You had two boxes of size nine sheers for me, and I want them!

WILLY: Here, for God's sake, will you get outa here!

THE WOMAN: [*Enters holding a box of stockings.*] I just hope there's nobody in the hall. That's all I hope. [*To* BIFF.] Are you football or baseball?

BIFF: Football.

THE WOMAN: [*Angry, humiliated.*] That's me too. G'night. [*She snatches her clothes from* WILLY, *and walks out.*]

WILLY: [*After a pause.*] Well, better get going. I want to get to the school first thing in the morning. Get my suits out of the closet. I'll get my valise. [BIFF *doesn't move.*] What's the matter? [BIFF *remains motionless, tears falling.*] She's a buyer. Buys for J. H. Simmons. She lives down the hall—they're painting. You don't imagine—[*He breaks off. After a pause.*] Now listen, pal, she's just a buyer. She sees merchandise in her room and they have to keep it looking just so . . . [*Pause. Assuming command.*] All right, get my suits. [BIFF *doesn't move.*] Now stop crying and do as I say. I gave you an order. Biff, I gave you an order! Is that what you do when I give you an order? How dare you cry! [*Putting his arm around* BIFF.] Now look, Biff, when you grow up you'll understand about these things. You mustn't—you mustn't overemphasize a thing like this. I'll see Birnbaum first thing in the morning.

BIFF: Never mind.

WILLY: [*Getting down beside* BIFF.] Never mind! He's going to give you those points. I'll see to it.

BIFF: He wouldn't listen to you.

WILLY: He certainly will listen to me. You need those points for the U. of Virginia.

BIFF: I'm not going there.

WILLY: Heh? If I can't get him to change that mark you'll make it up in summer school. You've got all summer to—

BIFF: [*His weeping breaking from him.*] Dad . . .

WILLY: [*Infected by it.*] Oh, my boy . . .

BIFF: Dad . . .

WILLY: She's nothing to me, Biff. I was lonely, I was terribly lonely.

BIFF: You—you gave her Mama's stockings! [*His tears break through and he rises to go.*]

WILLY: [*Grabbing for* BIFF.] I gave you an order!

BIFF: Don't touch me, you—liar!

WILLY: Apologize for that!

BIFF: You fake! You phony little fake! You fake!
    [*Overcome, he turns quickly and weeping fully goes out with his suitcase.* WILLY *is left on the floor on his knees.*]

WILLY: I gave you an order! Biff, come back here or I'll beat you! Come back here! I'll whip you! [STANLEY *comes quickly in from the right and stands in front of* WILLY. WILLY *shouts at* STANLEY.] I gave you an order . . .

STANLEY: Hey, let's pick it up, pick it up, Mr. Loman. [*He helps* WILLY *to his feet.*] Your boys left with the chippies. They said they'll see you home.
    [*A* SECOND WAITER *watches some distance away.*]

WILLY: But we were supposed to have dinner together.
    [*Music is heard,* WILLY*'s theme.*]

STANLEY: Can you make it?

WILLY: I'll—sure, I can make it. [*Suddenly concerned about his clothes.*] Do I—I look all right?

STANLEY: Sure, you look all right. [*He flicks a speck off* WILLY's *lapel.*]

WILLY: Here—here's a dollar.

STANLEY: Oh, your son paid me. It's all right.

WILLY: [*Putting it in* STANLEY's *hand.*] No, take it. You're a good boy.

STANLEY: Oh, no, you don't have to . . .

WILLY: Here—here's some more, I don't need it anymore. [*After a slight pause.*] Tell me—is there a seed store in the neighborhood?

STANLEY: Seeds? You mean like to plant?

[*As* WILLY *turns,* STANLEY *slips the money back into his jacket pocket.*]

WILLY: Yes. Carrots, peas . . .

STANLEY: Well, there's hardware stores on Sixth Avenue, but it may be too late now.

WILLY: [*Anxiously.*] Oh, I'd better hurry. I've got to get some seeds. [*He starts off to the right.*] I've got to get some seeds, right away. Nothing's planted. I don't have a thing in the ground.

[WILLY *hurries out as the light goes down.* STANLEY *moves over to the right after him, watches him off. The other* WAITER *has been staring at* WILLY.]

STANLEY: [*To the* WAITER.] Well, whatta you looking at?

[*The* WAITER *picks up the chairs and moves off right.* STANLEY *takes the table and follows him. The light fades on this area. There is a long pause, the sound of the flute coming over. The light gradually rises on the kitchen, which is empty.* HAPPY *appears at the door of the house, followed by* BIFF. HAPPY *is carrying a large bunch of long-stemmed roses. He enters the kitchen, looks around for* LINDA. *Not seeing her, he turns to* BIFF, *who is just outside the house door, and makes a gesture with his hands, indicating "Not here, I guess." He looks into the living-room and freezes. Inside,* LINDA, *unseen, is seated,* WILLY's *coat on her lap. She rises ominously and quietly and moves toward* HAPPY, *who backs up into the kitchen, afraid.*]

HAPPY: Hey, what're you doing up? [LINDA *says nothing but moves toward him implacably.*] Where's Pop? [*He keeps backing to the right, and now* LINDA *is in full view in the doorway to the living-room.*] Is he sleeping?

LINDA: Where were you?

HAPPY: [*Trying to laugh it off.*] We met two girls, Mom, very fine types. Here, we brought you some flowers. [*Offering them to her.*] Put them in your room, Ma. [*She knocks them to the floor at* BIFF'*s feet. He has now come inside and closed the door behind him. She stares at* BIFF, *silent.*] Now what'd you do that for? Mom, I want you to have some flowers—

LINDA: [*Cutting* HAPPY *off, violently to* BIFF.] Don't you care whether he lives or dies?

HAPPY: [*Going to the stairs.*] Come upstairs, Biff.

BIFF: [*With a flare of disgust, to* HAPPY.] Go away from me! [*To* LINDA.] What do you mean, lives or dies? Nobody's dying around here, pal.

LINDA: Get out of my sight! Get out of here!

BIFF: I wanna see the boss.

LINDA: You're not going near him!

BIFF: Where is he? [*He moves into the living-room and* LINDA *follows.*]

LINDA: [*Shouting after* BIFF.] You invite him for dinner. He looks forward to it all day—[BIFF *appears in his parents' bedroom, looks around and exits.*]—and then you desert him there. There's no stranger you'd do that to!

HAPPY: Why? He had a swell time with us. Listen, when I—[LINDA *comes back into the kitchen.*]—desert him I hope I don't outlive the day!

LINDA: Get out of here!

HAPPY: Now look, Mom . . .

LINDA: Did you have to go to women tonight? You and your lousy rotten whores!

[BIFF *re-enters the kitchen.*]

HAPPY: Mom, all we did was follow Biff around trying to cheer him up! [*To* BIFF.] Boy, what a night you gave me!

LINDA: Get out of here, both of you, and don't come back! I don't want you tormenting him anymore. Go on now, get your things together! [*To* BIFF.] You can sleep in his apartment. [*She starts to pick up the flowers and stops herself.*] Pick up this stuff, I'm not your maid anymore. Pick it up, you bum, you! [HAPPY *turns his back to her in refusal.* BIFF *slowly moves over and gets down on his knees, picking up the flowers.*] You're a pair of animals! Not one, not another living soul would have had the cruelty to walk out on that man in a restaurant!

BIFF: [*Not looking at her.*] Is that what he said?

LINDA: He didn't have to say anything. He was so humiliated he nearly limped when he came in.

HAPPY: But, Mom, he had a great time with us—

BIFF: [*Cutting him off violently.*] Shut up!

[*Without another word,* HAPPY *goes upstairs.*]

LINDA: You! You didn't even go in to see if he was all right!

BIFF: [*Still on the floor in front of* LINDA, *the flowers in his hand; with self-loathing.*] No. Didn't. Didn't do a damned thing. How do you like that, heh? Left him babbling in a toilet.

LINDA: You louse. You . . .

BIFF: Now you hit it on the nose! [*He gets up, throws the flowers in the wastebasket.*] The scum of the earth, and you're looking at him!

LINDA: Get out of here!

BIFF: I gotta talk to the boss, Mom. Where is he?

LINDA: You're not going near him. Get out of this house!

BIFF: [*With absolute assurance, determination.*] No. We're gonna have an abrupt conversation, him and me.

LINDA: You're not talking to him! [*Hammering is heard from outside the house, off right.* BIFF *turns toward the noise. Suddenly pleading.*] Will you please leave him alone?

BIFF: What's he doing out there?

LINDA: He's planting the garden!

BIFF: [*Quietly.*] Now? Oh, my God!

[BIFF *moves outside,* LINDA *following. The light dies down on them and comes up on the center of the apron as* WILLY *walks into it. He is carrying a flashlight, a hoe, and a handful of seed packets. He raps the top of the hoe sharply to fix it firmly, and then moves to the left, measuring off the distance with his foot. He holds the flashlight to look at the seed packets, reading off the instructions. He is in the blue of night.*]

WILLY: Carrots . . . quarter-inch apart. Rows . . . one-foot rows. [*He measures it off.*] One foot. [*He puts down a package and measures off.*] Beets. [*He puts down another package and measures again.*] Lettuce. [*He reads the package, puts it down.*] One foot—[*He breaks off as* BEN *appears at the right and moves slowly down to him.*] What a proposition, ts, ts. Terrific, terrific. 'Cause she's suffered, Ben, the woman has suffered. You understand me? A man can't go out the way he came in, Ben, a man has got to add up to something. You can't, you can't—[BEN *moves toward him as though to interrupt.*] You gotta consider, now. Don't answer so quick. Remember, it's a guaranteed twenty-thousand-dollar proposition. Now look, Ben, I want you to go through the ins and outs of this thing with me. I've got nobody to talk to, Ben, and the woman has suffered, you hear me?

BEN: [*Standing still, considering.*] What's the proposition?

WILLY: It's twenty thousand dollars on the barrelhead. Guaranteed, gilt-edged, you understand?

BEN: You don't want to make a fool of yourself. They might not honor the policy.

WILLY: How can they dare refuse? Didn't I work like a coolie to meet every premium on the nose? And now they don't pay off! Impossible!

BEN: It's called a cowardly thing, William.

WILLY: Why? Does it take more guts to stand here the rest of my life ringing up a zero?

BEN: [*Yielding.*] That's a point, William. [*He moves, thinking, turns.*] And twenty thousand—that *is* something one can feel with the hand, it is there.

WILLY: [*Now assured, with rising power.*] Oh, Ben, that's the whole beauty of it! I see it like a diamond, shining in the dark, hard and rough, that I can pick up and touch in my hand. Not like—like an appointment! This would not be another damned-fool appointment, Ben, and it changes all the aspects. Because he thinks I'm nothing, see, and so he spites me. But the funeral—[*Straightening up.*] Ben, that funeral will be massive! They'll come from Maine, Massachusetts, Vermont, New Hampshire! All the old-timers with the strange license plates—that boy will be thunderstruck, Ben, because he never realized—I am known! Rhode Island, New York, New Jersey—I am known, Ben, and he'll see it with his eyes once and for all. He'll see what I am, Ben! He's in for a shock, that boy!

BEN: [*Coming down to the edge of the garden.*] He'll call you a coward.

WILLY: [*Suddenly fearful.*] No, that would be terrible.

BEN: Yes. And a damned fool.

WILLY: No, no, he mustn't, I won't have that! [*He is broken and desperate.*]

BEN: He'll hate you, William.

[*The gay music of the Boys is heard.*]

WILLY: Oh, Ben, how do we get back to all the great times? Used to be so full of light, and comradeship, the sleigh-riding in winter, and the ruddiness on his cheeks. And always some kind of good news coming up, always something nice coming up ahead. And never even let me carry the valises in the house, and simonizing, simonizing that little red car! Why, why can't I give him something and not have him hate me?

BEN: Let me think about it. [*He glances at his watch.*] I still have a little time. Remarkable proposition, but you've got to be sure you're not making a fool of yourself.

[BEN *drifts off upstage and goes out of sight.* BIFF *comes down from the left.*]

WILLY: [*Suddenly conscious of* BIFF, *turns and looks up at him, then begins picking up the packages of seeds in confusion.*] Where the hell is that seed? [*Indignantly.*] You can't see nothing out here! They boxed in the whole goddam neighborhood!

BIFF: There are people all around here. Don't you realize that?

WILLY: I'm busy. Don't bother me.

BIFF: [*Taking the hoe from* WILLY.] I'm saying good-bye to you, Pop. [WILLY *looks at him, silent, unable to move.*] I'm not coming back anymore.

WILLY: You're not going to see Oliver tomorrow?

BIFF: I've got no appointment, Dad.

WILLY: He put his arm around you, and you've got no appointment?

BIFF: Pop, get this now, will you? Everytime I've left it's been a fight that sent me out of here. Today I realized something about myself and I tried to explain it to you and I—I think I'm just not smart enough to make any sense out of it for you. To hell with whose fault it is or anything like that. [*He takes* WILLY's *arm.*]

Let's just wrap it up, heh? Come on in, we'll tell Mom. [*He gently tries to pull* WILLY *to left.*]

WILLY: [*Frozen, immobile, with guilt in his voice.*] No, I don't want to see her.

BIFF: Come on! [*He pulls again, and* WILLY *tries to pull away.*]

WILLY: [*Highly nervous.*] No, no, I don't want to see her.

BIFF: [*Tries to look into* WILLY's *face, as if to find the answer there.*] Why don't you want to see her?

WILLY: [*More harshly now.*] Don't bother me, will you?

BIFF: What do you mean, you don't want to see her? You don't want them calling you yellow, do you? This isn't your fault; it's me, I'm a bum. Now come inside! [WILLY *strains to get away.*] Did you hear what I said to you?

[WILLY *pulls away and quickly goes by himself into the house.* BIFF *follows.*]

LINDA: [*To* WILLY.] Did you plant, dear?

BIFF: [*At the door, to* LINDA.] All right, we had it out. I'm going and I'm not writing anymore.

LINDA: [*Going to* WILLY *in the kitchen.*] I think that's the best way, dear. 'Cause there's no use drawing it out, you'll just never get along.

[WILLY *doesn't respond.*]

BIFF: People ask where I am and what I'm doing, you don't know, and you don't care. That way it'll be off your mind and you can start brightening up again. All right? That clears it, doesn't it? [WILLY *is silent, and* BIFF *goes to him.*] You gonna wish me luck, scout? [*He extends his hand.*] What do you say?

LINDA: Shake his hand, Willy.

WILLY: [*Turning to her, seething with hurt.*] There's no necessity to mention the pen at all, y'know.

BIFF: [*Gently.*] I've got no appointment, Dad.

WILLY: [*Erupting fiercely.*] He put his arm around . . . ?

BIFF: Dad, you're never going to see what I am, so what's the use of arguing? If I strike oil I'll send you a check. Meantime forget I'm alive.

WILLY: [*To* LINDA.] Spite, see?

BIFF: Shake hands, Dad.

WILLY: Not my hand.

BIFF: I was hoping not to go this way.

WILLY: Well, this is the way you're going. Good-bye. [BIFF *looks at him a moment, then turns sharply and goes to the stairs.* WILLY *stops him with.*] May you rot in hell if you leave this house!

BIFF: [*Turning.*] Exactly what is it that you want from me?

WILLY: I want you to know, on the train, in the mountains, in the valleys, wherever you go, that you cut down your life for spite!

BIFF: No, no.

WILLY: Spite, spite, is the word of your undoing! And when you're down and out, remember what did it. When you're rotting somewhere beside the railroad tracks, remember, and don't you dare blame it on me!

BIFF: I'm not blaming it on you!

WILLY: I won't take the rap for this, you hear?

[HAPPY *comes down the stairs and stands on the bottom step, watching.*]

BIFF: That's just what I'm telling you!

WILLY: [*Sinking into a chair at the table, with full accusation.*] You're trying to put a knife in me—don't think I don't know what you're doing!

BIFF: All right, phony! Then let's lay it on the line. [*He whips the rubber tube out of his pocket and puts it on the table.*]

HAPPY: You crazy—

LINDA: Biff!

[*She moves to grab the hose, but* BIFF *holds it down with his hand.*]

BIFF: Leave it there! Don't move it!

WILLY: [*Not looking at it.*] What is that?

BIFF: You know goddam well what that is.

WILLY: [*Caged, wanting to escape.*] I never saw that.

BIFF: You saw it. The mice didn't bring it into the cellar! What is this supposed to do, make a hero out of you? This supposed to make me sorry for you?

WILLY: Never heard of it.

BIFF: There'll be no pity for you, you hear it? No pity!

WILLY: [*To* LINDA.] You hear the spite!

BIFF: No, you're going to hear the truth—what you are and what I am!

LINDA: Stop it!

WILLY: Spite!

HAPPY: [*Coming down toward* BIFF.] You cut it now!

BIFF: [*To* HAPPY.] The man don't know who we are! The man is
gonna know! [*To* WILLY.] We never told the truth for ten minutes
in this house!

HAPPY: We always told the truth!

BIFF: [*Turning on him.*] You big blow, are you the assistant buyer?
You're one of the two assistants to the assistant, aren't you?

HAPPY: Well, I'm practically—

BIFF: You're practically full of it! We all are! And I'm through with it.
[*To* WILLY.] Now hear this, Willy, this is me.

WILLY: I know you!

BIFF: You know why I had no address for three months? I stole a suit
in Kansas City and I was in jail. [*To* LINDA, *who is sobbing.*] Stop
crying. I'm through with it.

[LINDA *turns away from them, her hands covering her face.*]

WILLY: I suppose that's my fault!

BIFF: I stole myself out of every good job since high school!

WILLY: And whose fault is that?

BIFF: And I never got anywhere because you blew me so full of hot
air I could never stand taking orders from anybody! That's whose
fault it is!

WILLY: I hear that!

LINDA: Don't, Biff!

BIFF: It's goddam time you heard that! I had to be boss big shot in
two weeks, and I'm through with it!

WILLY: Then hang yourself! For spite, hang yourself!

BIFF: No! Nobody's hanging himself, Willy! I ran down eleven
flights with a pen in my hand today. And suddenly I stopped,
you hear me? And in the middle of that office building, do you
hear this? I stopped in the middle of that building and I saw—
the sky. I saw the things that I love in this world. The work and
the food and time to sit and smoke. And I looked at the pen and
said to myself, what the hell am I grabbing this for? Why am I
trying to become what I don't want to be? What am I doing in an
office, making a contemptuous, begging fool of myself, when all

I want is out there, waiting for me the minute I say I know who I am! Why can't I say that, Willy? [*He tries to make* WILLY *face him, but* WILLY *pulls away and moves to the left.*]

WILLY: [*With hatred, threateningly.*] The door of your life is wide open!

BIFF: Pop! I'm a dime a dozen, and so are you!

WILLY: [*Turning on him now in an uncontrolled outburst.*] I am not a dime a dozen! I am Willy Loman, and you are Biff Loman!

[BIFF *starts for* WILLY, *but is blocked by* HAPPY. *In his fury,* BIFF *seems on the verge of attacking his father.*]

BIFF: I am not a leader of men, Willy, and neither are you. You were never anything but a hard-working drummer who landed in the ash can like all the rest of them! I'm one dollar an hour, Willy![1] I tried seven states and couldn't raise it. A buck an hour! Do you gather my meaning? I'm not bringing home any prizes anymore, and you're going to stop waiting for me to bring them home!

WILLY: [*Directly to* BIFF.] You vengeful, spiteful mut!

[BIFF *breaks from* HAPPY. WILLY, *in fright, starts up the stairs.* BIFF *grabs him.*]

BIFF: [*At the peak of his fury.*] Pop, I'm nothing! I'm nothing, Pop. Can't you understand that? There's no spite in it anymore. I'm just what I am, that's all.

[BIFF's *fury has spent itself, and he breaks down, sobbing, holding on to* WILLY, *who dumbly fumbles for* BIFF's *face.*]

WILLY: [*Astonished.*] What're you doing? What're you doing? [*To* LINDA.] Why is he crying?

BIFF: [*Crying, broken.*] Will you let me go, for Christ's sake? Will you take that phony dream and burn it before something happens? [*Struggling to contain himself, he pulls away and moves to the stairs.*] I'll go in the morning. Put him—put him to bed. [*Exhausted,* BIFF *moves up the stairs to his room.*]

WILLY: [*After a long pause, astonished, elevated.*] Isn't that—isn't that remarkable? Biff—he likes me!

LINDA: He loves you, Willy!

HAPPY: [*Deeply moved.*] Always did, Pop.

---

1. In 1949, Congress raised the minimum wage from 40 to 75 cents per hour.

WILLY: Oh, Biff! [*Staring wildly.*] He cried! Cried to me. [*He is choking with his love, and now cries out his promise.*] That boy—that boy is going to be magnificent!

[BEN *appears in the light just outside the kitchen.*]

BEN: Yes, outstanding, with twenty thousand behind him.

LINDA: [*Sensing the racing of his mind, fearfully, carefully.*] Now come to bed, Willy. It's all settled now.

WILLY: [*Finding it difficult not to rush out of the house.*] Yes, we'll sleep. Come on. Go to sleep, Hap.

BEN: And it does take a great kind of man to crack the jungle.

[*In accents of dread,* BEN'*s idyllic music starts up.*]

HAPPY: [*His arm around* LINDA.] I'm getting married, Pop, don't forget it. I'm changing everything. I'm gonna run that department before the year is up. You'll see, Mom. [*He kisses her.*]

BEN: The jungle is dark but full of diamonds, Willy.

[WILLY *turns, moves, listening to* BEN.]

LINDA: Be good. You're both good boys, just act that way, that's all.

HAPPY: 'Night, Pop. [*He goes upstairs.*]

LINDA: [*To* WILLY.] Come, dear.

BEN: [*With greater force.*] One must go in to fetch a diamond out.

WILLY: [*To* LINDA, *as he moves slowly along the edge of the kitchen, toward the door.*] I just want to get settled down, Linda. Let me sit alone for a little.

LINDA: [*Almost uttering her fear.*] I want you upstairs.

WILLY: [*Taking her in his arms.*] In a few minutes, Linda. I couldn't sleep right now. Go on, you look awful tired. [*He kisses her.*]

BEN: Not like an appointment at all. A diamond is rough and hard to the touch.

WILLY: Go on now. I'll be right up.

LINDA: I think this is the only way, Willy.

WILLY: Sure, it's the best thing.

BEN: Best thing!

WILLY: The only way. Everything is gonna be—go on, kid, get to bed. You look so tired.

LINDA: Come right up.

WILLY: Two minutes. [LINDA *goes into the living-room, then reappears in her bedroom.* WILLY *moves just outside the kitchen door.*] Loves me. [*Wonderingly.*] Always loved me. Isn't that a remarkable thing? Ben, he'll worship me for it!

BEN: [*With promise.*] It's dark there, but full of diamonds.

WILLY: Can you imagine that magnificence with twenty thousand dollars in his pocket?

LINDA: [*Calling from her room.*] Willy! Come up!

WILLY: [*Calling into the kitchen.*] Yes! Yes. Coming! It's very smart, you realize that, don't you, sweetheart? Even Ben sees it. I gotta go, baby. 'Bye! 'Bye! [*Going over to* BEN, *almost dancing.*] Imagine? When the mail comes he'll be ahead of Bernard again!

BEN: A perfect proposition all around.

WILLY: Did you see how he cried to me? Oh, if I could kiss him, Ben!

BEN: Time, William, time!

WILLY: Oh, Ben, I always knew one way or another we were gonna make it, Biff and I!

BEN: [*Looking at his watch.*] The boat. We'll be late. [*He moves slowly off into the darkness.*]

WILLY: [*Elegiacally, turning to the house.*] Now when you kick off, boy, I want a seventy-yard boot, and get right down the field under the ball, and when you hit, hit low and hit hard, because it's important, boy. [*He swings around and faces the audience.*] There's all kinds of important people in the stands, and the first thing you know . . . [*Suddenly realizing he is alone.*] Ben! Ben, where do I . . . ? [*He makes a sudden movement of search.*] Ben, how do I . . . ?

LINDA: [*Calling.*] Willy, you coming up?

WILLY: [*Uttering a gasp of fear, whirling about as if to quiet her.*] Sh! [*He turns around as if to find his way; sounds, faces, voices, seem to be swarming in upon him and he flicks at them, crying!*] Sh! Sh! [*Suddenly music, faint and high, stops him. It rises in intensity, almost to an unbearable scream. He goes up and down on his toes, and rushes off around the house.*] Shhh!

LINDA: Willy? [*There is no answer.* LINDA *waits.* BIFF *gets up off his bed. He is still in his clothes.* HAPPY *sits up.* BIFF *stands listening.*] [*With real fear.*] Willy, answer me! Willy! [*There is the sound of a car starting and moving away at full speed.*] No!

BIFF: [*Rushing down the stairs.*] Pop!

[*As the car speeds off, the music crashes down in a frenzy of sound, which becomes the soft pulsation of a single cello string.* BIFF *slowly returns to his bedroom. He and* HAPPY *gravely don their jackets.* LINDA *slowly walks out of her room. The music has developed into a dead march. The leaves of day are appearing over everything.* CHARLEY *and* BERNARD, *somberly dressed, appear and knock on the kitchen door.* BIFF *and* HAPPY *slowly descend the stairs to the kitchen as* CHARLEY *and* BERNARD *enter. All stop a moment when* LINDA, *in clothes of mourning, bearing a little bunch of roses, comes through the draped doorway into the kitchen. She goes to* CHARLEY *and takes his arm. Now all move toward the audience, through the wall-line of the kitchen. At the limit of the apron,* LINDA *lays down the flowers, kneels, and sits back on her heels. All stare down at the grave.*]

REQUIEM

CHARLEY: It's getting dark, Linda.

[LINDA *doesn't react. She stares at the grave.*]

BIFF: How about it, Mom? Better get some rest, heh? They'll be closing the gate soon.

[LINDA *makes no move. Pause.*]

HAPPY: [*Deeply angered.*] He had no right to do that. There was no necessity for it. We would've helped him.

CHARLEY: [*Grunting.*] Hmmm.

BIFF: Come along, Mom.

LINDA: Why didn't anybody come?

CHARLEY: It was a very nice funeral.

LINDA: But where are all the people he knew? Maybe they blame him.

CHARLEY: Naa. It's a rough world, Linda. They wouldn't blame him.

LINDA: I can't understand it. At this time especially. First time in thirty-five years we were just about free and clear. He only needed a little salary. He was even finished with the dentist.

CHARLEY: No man only needs a little salary.

LINDA: I can't understand it.

BIFF: There were a lot of nice days. When he'd come home from a trip; or on Sundays, making the stoop; finishing the cellar; putting on the new porch; when he built the extra bathroom; and put up the garage. You know something, Charley, there's more of him in that front stoop than in all the sales he ever made.

CHARLEY: Yeah. He was a happy man with a batch of cement.

LINDA: He was so wonderful with his hands.

BIFF: He had the wrong dreams. All, all, wrong.

HAPPY: [*Almost ready to fight* BIFF.] Don't say that!

BIFF: He never knew who he was.

CHARLEY: [*Stopping* HAPPY'*s movement and reply. To* BIFF.] Nobody dast blame this man. You don't understand: Willy was a salesman. And for a salesman, there is no rock bottom to the life. He don't put a bolt to a nut, he don't tell you the law or give you medicine. He's a man way out there in the blue, riding on a smile and a shoeshine. And when they start not smiling back—that's an earthquake. And then you get yourself a couple of spots on your hat, and you're finished. Nobody dast blame this man. A salesman is got to dream, boy. It comes with the territory.

BIFF: Charley, the man didn't know who he was.

HAPPY: [*Infuriated.*] Don't say that!

BIFF: Why don't you come with me, Happy?

HAPPY: I'm not licked that easily. I'm staying right in this city, and I'm gonna beat this racket! [*He looks at* BIFF, *his chin set.*] The Loman Brothers!

BIFF: I know who I am, kid.

HAPPY: All right, boy. I'm gonna show you and everybody else that Willy Loman did not die in vain. He had a good dream. It's the only dream you can have—to come out number-one-man. He fought it out here, and this is where I'm gonna win it for him.

BIFF: [*With a hopeless glance at* HAPPY, *bends towards his mother.*] Let's go, Mom.

LINDA: I'll be with you in a minute. Go on, Charley. [*He hesitates.*] I want to, just for a minute. I never had a chance to say good-bye. [CHARLEY *moves away, followed by* HAPPY, BIFF *remains a slight distance up and left of* LINDA. *She sits there, summoning herself. The flute begins, not far away, playing behind her speech.*] Forgive me, dear. I can't cry. I don't know what it is, but I can't cry. I don't understand it. Why did you ever do that? Help me, Willy, I can't cry. It seems to me that you're just on another trip. I keep expecting you. Willy, dear, I can't cry. Why did you do it? I search and search and I search, and I can't understand it, Willy. I made the last payment on the house today. Today, dear. And there'll be nobody home. [*A sob rises in her throat.*] We're free and clear. [*Sobbing more fully, released.*] We're free. [BIFF *comes slowly toward her.* We're free . . . We're free . . .

> [BIFF *lifts her to her feet and moves out up right with her in his arms.* LINDA *sobs quietly.* BERNARD *and* CHARLEY *come together and follow them, followed by* HAPPY. *Only the music of the flute is left on the darkening stage as over the house the hard towers of the apartment buildings rise into sharp focus.*]

[*CURTAIN*]   1949

August Wilson
1945–2005

FENCES

All of August Wilson's plays dramatize the experiences of African Americans in a racist society. Most of them focus on life in an African American neighborhood of Pittsburgh, the "Hill," during particular decades of the twentieth century. Fences, the second play in this historical cycle, takes place during the 1950s and derives partly from Wilson's family history. Like the play's main character, Troy Maxson, Wilson's stepfather, David Bedford, had been an exceptional high school athlete in the 1930s. He was poor, however, and at that time few colleges would offer a scholarship to a black man. Bedford turned to crime, and in a robbery gone wrong he killed someone. He served over two decades in prison before he was released and married Wilson's mother.

While he drew on Bedford for some details of Maxson's biography, Wilson's portrait of a proud soul battered by racism needed no model other than himself. As an African American growing up in a largely white suburb, he saw and experienced the effects of an envi-

ronment hostile to its inhabitants' success, especially to their intellectual success. In response, Wilson later affiliated himself with the Nation of Islam, especially with the civil rights leader Malcolm X and his message of black self-reliance and independence.

Another model for Troy Maxson is the baseball legend Josh Gibson. Born in Georgia in 1911, Gibson moved with his family to Pittsburgh, Pennsylvania, in the early 1920s. He studied to be an electrician, but had to drop out of school after the ninth grade to work in a factory. He started playing for a Negro League baseball team, the Pittsburgh Crawfords, in 1929, and for the next seventeen years he played for the Crawfords, for the Homestead Grays (also in Pittsburgh), and in the Mexican League. He was a prodigious slugger, the black Babe Ruth (as many called him, though it might have been more accurate to call Ruth the white Josh Gibson). His accomplishments are incredible: 962 home runs, a lifetime batting average of .354, and an amazing 84 home runs in one season in 1936.

In the mid-1940s, the Washington Senators (a Major League team) flirted with the idea of signing Gibson, but the owner, Clark Griffith, lacked the courage to break the color barrier. Gibson's last season was 1946. He died of a stroke in early 1947. His health had been declining for four years, and he was always a hard drinker, but legend contends that he died of a broken heart, for by 1946, Jackie Robinson was headed for the Major Leagues and Gibson knew that he was too old to join him. Though Gibson made decent money in the Negro Leagues and even more in the Mexican League, he was so poor when he died that donations had to be collected to pay for his funeral. You might consider Troy Maxson to be a portrait of Josh Gibson had he lived another ten years.

Maxson's experience as a garbage man, especially his fights with the sanitation workers' union, reflects Wilson's interest in the rise of the American labor movement. Of all American cities, Pittsburgh probably has been the most important to the political cause of labor, and Homestead, on the outskirts of the city, was the battleground of the most notorious assault on workers in American history. In 1892, industrialist Andrew Carnegie, assiduously denying steel workers the right to unionize and refusing them a decent wage, triggered a long and bloody battle between labor and capital.

Until fairly recently, however, unions were just as racist as the rest of American society. Though all laborers had the same interest in wresting decent pay and humane working conditions from corporations, whites typically refused to close ranks with their black coworkers. African Americans had to fight for equal treatment by the labor movement just as they fought for equal treatment by the law. In fact, Martin Luther King Jr. was helping black sanitation workers unionize when he was assassinated in Memphis in 1968.

As he chronicles such changes, Wilson also notes what the black communities lost when America integrated. Though few people today would argue for the ghettoizing of any single race of Americans, such enforced isolation fostered a sense of community and allowed for an economic independence that integration undermined. For example, integrating the Major Leagues destroyed the Negro Leagues, and with the Negro Leagues went the only black-owned ball clubs in America. Only now, more than half a century after Jackie Robinson started to play for the Dodgers, are African Americans breaking into the upper ranks of management and ownership in the Major Leagues.

The first generation of integrated minorities must experience a sense of loss even as it gains so much. Wilson was accused of sentimentalizing that loss and even of supporting separatism, the belief that African Americans must sustain their own communities and cultural institutions apart from the white-dominated mainstream. Certainly, he worked to improve opportunities for black actors, black theaters, and black directors, staunchly supporting regional theaters that cater to black audiences. Indeed, Paramount Pictures' plans to make a movie out of Fences stalled because of Wilson's insistence on using a black director.

Even as you read the play in light of these issues, however, don't forget that it is also about family—about fathers and sons, wives and husbands. Like the best "problem" plays in the Ibsen tradition, Fences can stand as well outside as it stands inside its historical and cultural context.

Fences

CHARACTERS

TROY MAXSON
JIM BONO   TROY's *friend*
ROSE   TROY's *wife*
LYONS   TROY's *oldest son by previous marriage*
GABRIEL   TROY's *brother*
CORY   TROY *and* ROSE's *son*
RAYNELL   TROY's *daughter*

SETTING

The setting is the yard which fronts the only entrance to the MAX-SON household, an ancient two-story brick house set back off a small alley in a big-city neighborhood. The entrance to the house is gained by two or three steps leading to a wooden porch badly in need of paint.

A relatively recent addition to the house and running its full width, the porch lacks congruence. It is a sturdy porch with a flat roof. One or two chairs of dubious value sit at one end where the kitchen window opens onto the porch. An old-fashioned icebox stands silent guard at the opposite end.

The yard is a small dirt yard, partially fenced, except for the last scene, with a wooden sawhorse, a pile of lumber, and other fence-building equipment set off to the side. Opposite is a tree from which hangs a ball made of rags. A baseball bat leans against the tree. Two oil drums serve as garbage receptacles and sit near the house at right to complete the setting.

THE PLAY

Near the turn of the century, the destitute of Europe sprang on the city with tenacious claws and an honest and solid dream. The city devoured them. They swelled its belly until it burst into a thousand furnaces and sewing machines, a thousand butcher shops and bakers' ovens, a thousand churches and hospitals and funeral parlors and moneylenders. The city grew. It nourished itself and offered each man a partnership limited only by his talent, his guile, and his willingness and capacity for hard work. For the immigrants of Europe, a dream dared and won true.

The descendants of African slaves were offered no such welcome or participation. They came from places called the Carolinas and the Virginias, Georgia, Alabama, Mississippi, and Tennessee. They came strong, eager, searching. The city rejected them and they fled and settled along the riverbanks and under bridges in shallow, ramshackle houses made of sticks and tar-paper. They collected rags and wood. They sold the use of their muscles and their bodies. They cleaned houses and washed clothes, they shined shoes, and in quiet desperation and vengeful pride, they stole, and lived in pursuit of their own dream. That they could breathe free, finally, and stand to meet life with the force of dignity and whatever eloquence the heart could call upon.

By 1957, the hard-won victories of the European immigrants had solidified the industrial might of America. War had been confronted and won with new energies that used loyalty and patriotism as its fuel. Life was rich, full, and flourishing. The Milwaukee Braves won the World Series, and the hot winds of change that would make the sixties a turbulent, racing, dangerous, and provocative decade had not yet begun to blow full.

ACT ONE
Scene One

It is 1957. TROY *and* BONO *enter the yard, engaged in conversation.* TROY *is fifty-three years old, a large man with thick, heavy hands; it is this largeness that he strives to fill out and make an accommodation with. Together with his blackness, his largeness informs his sensibilities and the choices he has made in his life.*

Of the two men, BONO *is obviously the follower. His commitment to their friendship of thirty-odd years is rooted in his admiration of* TROY's *honesty, capacity for hard work, and strength, which* BONO *seeks to emulate.*

It is Friday night, payday, and the one night of the week the two men engage in a ritual of talk and drink. TROY *is usually the most talkative and at times he can be crude and almost vulgar, though he is capable of rising to profound heights of expression. The men carry lunch buckets and wear or carry burlap aprons and are dressed in clothes suitable to their jobs as garbage collectors.*

BONO: Troy, you ought to stop that lying!

TROY: I ain't lying! The nigger had a watermelon this big. [*He indicates with his hands.*] Talking about . . . "What watermelon, Mr. Rand?" I liked to fell out! "What watermelon, Mr. Rand?" . . . And it sitting there big as life.

BONO: What did Mr. Rand say?

TROY: Ain't said nothing. Figure if the nigger too dumb to know he carrying a watermelon, he wasn't gonna get much sense out of him. Trying to hide that great big old watermelon under his coat. Afraid to let the white man see him carry it home.

BONO: I'm like you. . . . I ain't got no time for them kind of people.

TROY: Now what he look like getting mad cause he see the man from the union talking to Mr. Rand?

BONO: He come to me talking about . . . "Maxson gonna get us fired." I told him to get away from me with that. He walked away from me calling you a troublemaker. What Mr. Rand say?

TROY: Ain't said nothing. He told me to go down the Commissioner's office next Friday. They called me down there to see them.

BONO: Well, as long as you got your complaint filed, they can't fire you. That's what one of them white fellows tell me.

TROY: I ain't worried about them firing me. They gonna fire me cause I asked a question? That's all I did. I went to Mr. Rand and asked him, "Why? Why you got the white mens driving and the colored lifting?" Told him, "What's the matter, don't I count? You think only white fellows got sense enough to drive a truck. That ain't no paper job! Hell, anybody can drive a truck. How come you got all whites driving and the colored lifting? He told me "take it to the union." Well, hell, that's what I done! Now they wanna come up with this pack of lies.

BONO: I told Brownie if the man come and ask him any questions . . . just tell the truth! It ain't nothing but something they done trumped up on you cause you filed a complaint on them.

TROY: Brownie don't understand nothing. All I want them to do is change the job description. Give everybody a chance to drive the truck. Brownie can't see that. He ain't got that much sense.

BONO: How you figure he be making out with that gal be up at Taylors' all the time . . . that Alberta gal?

TROY: Same as you and me. Getting just as much as we is. Which is to say, nothing.

BONO: It is, huh? I figure you doing a little better than me . . . and I ain't saying what I'm doing.

TROY: Aw, nigger, look here . . . I know you. If you had got anywhere near that gal, twenty minutes later you be looking to tell somebody. And the first one you gonna tell . . . that you gonna want to brag to . . . is gonna be me.

BONO: I ain't saying that. I see where you be eyeing her.

TROY: I eye all the women. I don't miss nothing. Don't never let nobody tell you Troy Maxson don't eye the women.

BONO: You been doing more than eyeing her. You done bought her a drink or two.

TROY: Hell yeah, I bought her a drink! What that mean? I bought you one, too. What that mean cause I buy her a drink? I'm just being polite.

BONO: It's alright to buy her one drink. That's what you call being polite. But when you wanna be buying two or three . . . that's what you call eyeing her.

TROY: Look here, as long as you known me . . . you ever known me to chase after women?

BONO: Hell yeah! Long as I done known you. You forgetting I knew you when.

TROY: Naw, I'm talking about since I been married to Rose?

BONO: Oh, not since you been married to Rose. Now, that's the truth, there. I can say that.

TROY: Alright then! Case closed.

BONO: I see you be walking up around Alberta's house. You supposed to be at Taylors' and you be walking up around there.

TROY: What you watching where I'm walking for? I ain't watching after you.

BONO: I seen you walking around there more than once.

TROY: Hell, you liable to see me walking anywhere! That don't mean nothing cause you see me walking around there.

BONO: Where she come from anyway? She just kinda showed up one day.

TROY: Tallahassee. You can look at her and tell she one of them Florida gals. They got some big healthy women down there. Grow them right up out the ground. Got a little bit of Indian in her. Most of them niggers down in Florida got some Indian in them.

BONO: I don't know about that Indian part. But she damn sure big and healthy. Woman wear some big stockings. Got them great big old legs and hips as wide as the Mississippi River.

TROY: Legs don't mean nothing. You don't do nothing but push them out of the way. But them hips cushion the ride!

BONO: Troy, you ain't got no sense.

TROY: It's the truth! Like you riding on Goodyears!

[ROSE *enters from the house. She is ten years younger than* TROY, *her devotion to him stems from her recognition of the possibilities of her life without him: a succession of abusive men and their babies, a life of partying and running the streets, the Church, or aloneness with its attendant pain and frustration. She recognizes* TROY's *spirit as a fine and illuminating one and she either ignores or forgives his faults, only some of which she recognizes. Though she doesn't drink, her presence is an integral part of the Friday night rituals. She alternates between the porch and the kitchen, where supper preparations are under way.*]

ROSE: What you all out here getting into?

TROY: What you worried about what we getting into for? This is men talk, woman.

ROSE: What I care what you all talking about? Bono, you gonna stay for supper?

BONO: No, I thank you, Rose. But Lucille say she cooking up a pot of pigfeet.

TROY: Pigfeet! Hell, I'm going home with you! Might even stay the night if you got some pigfeet. You got something in there to top them pigfeet, Rose?

ROSE: I'm cooking up some chicken. I got some chicken and collard greens.

TROY: Well, go on back in the house and let me and Bono finish what we was talking about. This is men talk. I got some talk for you later. You know what kind of talk I mean. You go on and powder it up.

ROSE: Troy Maxson, don't you start that now!

TROY: [*Puts his arm around her.*] Aw, woman . . . come here. Look here, Bono . . . when I met this woman . . . I got out that place, say, "Hitch up my pony, saddle up my mare . . . there's a woman out there for me somewhere. I looked here. Looked there. Saw Rose and latched on to her." I latched on to her and told her— I'm gonna tell you the truth—I told her, "Baby, I don't wanna marry, I just wanna be your man." Rose told me . . . tell him what you told me, Rose.

ROSE: I told him if he wasn't the marrying kind, then move out the way so the marrying kind could find me.

TROY: That's what she told me. "Nigger, you in my way. You blocking the view! Move out the way so I can find me a husband." I thought it over two or three days. Come back—

ROSE: Ain't no two or three days nothing. You was back the same night.

TROY: Come back, told her . . . "Okay, baby . . . but I'm gonna buy me a banty rooster and put him out there in the backyard . . . and when he see a stranger come, he'll flap his wings and crow . . ." Look here, Bono, I could watch the front door by myself . . . it was that back door I was worried about.

ROSE: Troy, you ought not talk like that. Troy ain't doing nothing but telling a lie.

TROY: Only thing is . . . when we first got married . . . forget the rooster . . . we ain't had no yard!

BONO: I hear you tell it. Me and Lucille was staying down there on Logan Street. Had two rooms with the outhouse in the back. I ain't mind the outhouse none. But when that goddamn wind blow through there in the winter . . . that's what I'm talking about! To this day I wonder why in the hell I ever stayed down there for six long years. But see, I didn't know I could do no better. I thought only white folks had inside toilets and things.

ROSE: There's a lot of people don't know they can do no better than they doing now. That's just something you got to learn. A lot of folks still shop at Bella's.

TROY: Ain't nothing wrong with shopping at Bella's. She got fresh food.

ROSE: I ain't said nothing about if she got fresh food. I'm talking about what she charge. She charge ten cents more than the A&P.

TROY: The A&P ain't never done nothing for me. I spends my money where I'm treated right. I go down to Bella, say, "I need a loaf of bread, I'll pay you Friday." She give it to me. What sense that make when I got money to go and spend it somewhere else and ignore the person who done right by me? That ain't in the Bible.

ROSE: We ain't talking about what's in the Bible. What sense it make to shop there when she overcharge?

TROY: You shop where you want to. I'll do my shopping where the people been good to me.

ROSE: Well, I don't think it's right for her to overcharge. That's all I was saying.

BONO: Look here . . . I got to get on. Lucille going be raising all kind of hell.

TROY: Where you going, nigger? We ain't finished this pint. Come here, finish this pint.

BONO: Well, hell, I am . . . if you ever turn the bottle loose.

TROY: [*Hands him the bottle.*] The only thing I say about the A&P is I'm glad Cory got that job down there. Help him take care of his school clothes and things. Gabe done moved out and things getting tight around here. He got that job. . . . He can start to look out for himself.

ROSE: Cory done went and got recruited by a college football team.

TROY: I told that boy about that football stuff. The white man ain't gonna let him get nowhere with that football. I told him when he first come to me with it. Now you come telling me he done went and got more tied up in it. He ought to go and get recruited in how to fix cars or something where he can make a living.

ROSE: He ain't talking about making no living playing football. It's just something the boys in school do. They gonna send a recruiter by to talk to you. He'll tell you he ain't talking about making no living playing football. It's a honor to be recruited.

TROY: It ain't gonna get him nowhere. Bono'll tell you that.

BONO: If he be like you in the sports . . . he's gonna be alright. Ain't but two men ever played baseball as good as you. That's Babe Ruth and Josh Gibson.[1] Them's the only two men ever hit more home runs than you.

TROY: What it ever get me? Ain't got a pot to piss in or a window to throw it out of.

ROSE: Times have changed since you was playing baseball, Troy. That was before the war.[2] Times have changed a lot since then.

TROY: How in hell they done changed?

ROSE: They got lots of colored boys playing ball now. Baseball and football.

BONO: You right about that, Rose. Times have changed, Troy. You just come along too early.

TROY: There ought not never have been no time called too early! Now you take that fellow . . . what's that fellow they had playing right field for the Yankees back then? You know who I'm talking about, Bono. Used to play right field for the Yankees.

ROSE: Selkirk?

TROY: Selkirk! That's it! Man batting .269, understand? .269. What kind of sense that make? I was hitting .432 with thirty-seven home runs! Man batting .269 and playing right field for the Yankees! I saw Josh Gibson's daughter yesterday. She walking around with raggedy shoes on her feet. Now I bet you Selkirk's daughter ain't walking around with raggedy shoes on her feet! I bet you that!

ROSE: They got a lot of colored baseball players now. Jackie Robinson was the first. Folks had to wait for Jackie Robinson.

TROY: I done seen a hundred niggers play baseball better than Jackie Robinson. Hell, I know some teams Jackie Robinson couldn't even make! What you talking about Jackie Robinson. Jackie Robinson wasn't nobody. I'm talking about if you could play ball then they ought to have let you play. Don't care what color you were. Come telling me I come along too early. If you could play . . . then they ought to have let you play. [TROY *takes a long drink from the bottle.*]

ROSE: You gonna drink yourself to death. You don't need to be drinking like that.

1. See headnote (p. 518) for a discussion of Josh Gibson.   2. World War II, which ended in 1945.

TROY: Death ain't nothing. I done seen him. Done wrassled with him. You can't tell me nothing about death. Death ain't nothing but a fastball on the outside corner. And you know what I'll do to that! Lookee here, Bono . . . am I lying? You get one of them fastballs, about waist high, over the outside corner of the plate where you can get the meat of the bat on it . . . and good God! You can kiss it goodbye. Now, am I lying?

BONO: Naw, you telling the truth there. I seen you do it.

TROY: If I'm lying . . . that 450 feet worth of lying! [*Pause.*] That's all death is to me. A fastball on the outside corner.

ROSE: I don't know why you want to get on talking about death.

TROY: Ain't nothing wrong with talking about death. That's part of life. Everybody gonna die. You gonna die, I'm gonna die. Bono's gonna die. Hell, we all gonna die.

ROSE: But you ain't got to talk about it. I don't like to talk about it.

TROY: You the one brought it up. Me and Bono was talking about baseball . . . you tell me I'm gonna drink myself to death. Ain't that right, Bono? You know I don't drink this but one night out of the week. That's Friday night. I'm gonna drink just enough to where I can handle it. Then I cuts it loose. I leave it alone. So don't you worry about me drinking myself to death. 'Cause I ain't worried about Death. I done seen him. I done wrestled with him.

Look here, Bono . . . I looked up one day and Death was marching straight at me. Like Soldiers on Parade! The Army of Death was marching straight at me. The middle of July, 1941. It got real cold just like it be winter. It seem like Death himself reached out and touched me on the shoulder. He touch me just like I touch you. I got cold as ice and Death standing there grinning at me.

ROSE: Troy, why don't you hush that talk.

TROY: I say . . . What you want, Mr. Death? You be wanting me? You done brought your army to be getting me? I looked him dead in the eye. I wasn't fearing nothing. I was ready to tangle. Just like I'm ready to tangle now. The Bible say be ever vigilant. That's why I don't get but so drunk. I got to keep watch.

ROSE: Troy was right down there in Mercy Hospital. You remember he had pneumonia? Laying there with a fever talking plumb out of his head.

TROY: Death standing there staring at me . . . carrying that sickle in his hand. Finally he say, "You want bound over for another year?" See, just like that . . . "You want bound over for another year?" I told him, "Bound over hell! Let's settle this now!"

It seem like he kinda fell back when I said that, and all the cold went out of me. I reached down and grabbed that sickle and threw it just as far as I could throw it . . . and me and him commenced to wrestling.

We wrestled for three days and three nights. I can't say where I found the strength from. Every time it seemed like he was gonna get the best of me, I'd reach way down deep inside myself and find the strength to do him one better.

ROSE: Every time Troy tell that story he find different ways to tell it. Different things to make up about it.

TROY: I ain't making up nothing. I'm telling you the facts of what happened. I wrestled with Death for three days and three nights and I'm standing here to tell you about it. [*Pause.*] Alright. At the end of the third night we done weakened each other to where we can't hardly move. Death stood up, throwed on his robe . . . had him a white robe with a hood on it. He throwed on that robe and went off to look for his sickle. Say, "I'll be back." Just like that. "I'll be back." I told him, say, "Yeah, but . . . you gonna have to find me!" I wasn't no fool. I wasn't going looking for him. Death ain't nothing to play with. And I know he's gonna get me. I know I got to join his army . . . his camp followers. But as long as I keep my strength and see him coming . . . as long as I keep up my vigilance . . . he's gonna have to fight to get me. I ain't going easy.

BONO: Well, look here, since you got to keep up your vigilance . . . let me have the bottle.

TROY: Aw hell, I shouldn't have told you that part. I should have left out that part.

ROSE: Troy be talking that stuff and half the time don't even know what he be talking about.

TROY: Bono know me better than that.

BONO: That's right. I know you. I know you got some Uncle

Remus[3] in your blood. You got more stories than the devil got
sinners.

TROY: Aw hell, I done seen him too! Done talked with the devil.

ROSE: Troy, don't nobody wanna be hearing all that stuff.

[LYONS *enters the yard from the street. Thirty-four years old,*
TROY's *son by a previous marriage, he sports a neatly trimmed
goatee, sport coat, white shirt, tieless and buttoned at the collar.
Though he fancies himself a musician, he is more caught up in the
rituals and "idea" of being a musician than in the actual practice of the music. He has come to borrow money from* TROY, *and
while he knows he will be successful, he is uncertain as to what
extent his lifestyle will be held up to scrutiny and ridicule.*]

LYONS: Hey, Pop.

TROY: What you come "Hey, Popping" me for?

LYONS: How you doing, Rose? [*He kisses her.*] Mr. Bono. How you
doing?

BONO: Hey, Lyons . . . how you been?

TROY: He must have been doing alright. I ain't seen him around here
last week.

ROSE: Troy, leave your boy alone. He come by to see you and you
wanna start all that nonsense.

TROY: I ain't bothering Lyons. [*Offers him the bottle.*] Here . . . get
you a drink. We got an understanding. I know why he come by
to see me and he know I know.

LYONS: Come on, Pop . . . I just stopped by to say hi . . . see how
you was doing.

TROY: You ain't stopped by yesterday.

ROSE: You gonna stay for supper, Lyons? I got some chicken cooking
in the oven.

LYONS: No, Rose . . . thanks. I was just in the neighborhood and
thought I'd stop by for a minute.

TROY: You was in the neighborhood alright, nigger. You telling
the truth there. You was in the neighborhood cause it's my payday.

---

3. The wise, old, black narrator of a series of stories about Brer Rabbit and Brer Fox, written by Joel Chandler Harris (1848–1908).

LYONS: Well, hell, since you mentioned it . . . let me have ten dollars.

TROY: I'll be damned! I'll die and go to hell and play blackjack with the devil before I give you ten dollars.

BONO: That's what I wanna know about . . . that devil you done seen.

LYONS: What . . . Pop done seen the devil? You too much, Pops.

TROY: Yeah, I done seen him. Talked to him too!

ROSE: You ain't seen no devil. I done told you that man ain't had nothing to do with the devil. Anything you can't understand, you want to call it the devil.

TROY: Look here, Bono . . . I went down to see Hertzberger about some furniture. Got three rooms for two-ninety-eight. That what it say on the radio. "Three rooms . . . two-ninety-eight." Even made up a little song about it. Go down there . . . man tell me I can't get no credit. I'm working every day and can't get no credit. What to do? I got an empty house with some raggedy furniture in it. Cory ain't got no bed. He's sleeping on a pile of rags on the floor. Working every day and can't get no credit. Come back here—Rose'll tell you—madder than hell. Sit down . . . try to figure what I'm gonna do. Come a knock on the door. Ain't been living here but three days. Who know I'm here? Open the door . . . devil standing there bigger than life. White fellow . . . got on good clothes and everything. Standing there with a clipboard in his hand. I ain't had to say nothing. First words come out of his mouth was . . . "I understand you need some furniture and can't get no credit." I liked to fell over. He say "I'll give you all the credit you want, but you got to pay the interest on it." I told him, "Give me three rooms' worth and charge whatever you want." Next day a truck pulled up here and two men unloaded them three rooms. Man what drove the truck give me a book. Say send ten dollars, first of every month to the address in the book and everything will be alright. Say if I miss a payment the devil was coming back and it'll be hell to pay. That was fifteen years ago. To this day . . . the first of the month I send my ten dollars, Rose'll tell you.

ROSE: Troy lying.

TROY: I ain't never seen that man since. Now you tell me who else that could have been but the devil? I ain't sold my soul or nothing like that, you understand. Naw, I wouldn't have truck with the devil about nothing like that. I got my furniture and pays my ten dollars the first of the month just like clockwork.

BONO: How long you say you been paying this ten dollars a month?

TROY: Fifteen years!

BONO: Hell, ain't you finished paying for it yet? How much the man done charged you.

TROY: Aw hell, I done paid for it. I done paid for it ten times over! The fact is I'm scared to stop paying it.

ROSE: Troy lying. We got that furniture from Mr. Glickman. He ain't paying no ten dollars a month to nobody.

TROY: Aw hell, woman. Bono know I ain't that big a fool.

LYONS: I was just getting ready to say . . . I know where there's a bridge for sale.

TROY: Look here, I'll tell you this . . . it don't matter to me if he was the devil. It don't matter if the devil give credit. Somebody has got to give it.

ROSE: It ought to matter. You going around talking about having truck with the devil . . . God's the one you gonna have to answer to. He's the one gonna be at the Judgment.

LYONS: Yeah, well, look here, Pop . . . let me have that ten dollars. I'll give it back to you. Bonnie got a job working at the hospital.

TROY: What I tell you, Bono? The only time I see this nigger is when he wants something. That's the only time I see him.

LYONS: Come on, Pop, Mr. Bono don't want to hear all that. Let me have the ten dollars. I told you Bonnie working.

TROY: What that mean to me? "Bonnie working." I don't care if she working. Go ask her for the ten dollars if she working. Talking about "Bonnie working." Why ain't you working?

LYONS: Aw, Pop, you know I can't find no decent job. Where am I gonna get a job at? You know I can't get no job.

TROY: I told you I know some people down there. I can get you on the rubbish if you want to work. I told you that the last time you came by here asking me for something.

LYONS: Naw, Pop . . . thanks. That ain't for me. I don't wanna be carrying nobody's rubbish. I don't wanna be punching nobody's time clock.

TROY: What's the matter, you too good to carry people's rubbish? Where you think that ten dollars you talking about come from? I'm just supposed to haul people's rubbish and give my money to you cause you too lazy to work. You too lazy to work and wanna know why you ain't got what I got.

ROSE: What hospital Bonnie working at? Mercy?

LYONS: She's down at Passavant working in the laundry.

TROY: I ain't got nothing as it is. I give you that ten dollars and I got to eat beans the rest of the week. Naw . . . you ain't getting no ten dollars here.

LYONS: You ain't got to be eating no beans. I don't know why you wanna say that.

TROY: I ain't got no extra money. Gabe done moved over to Miss Pearl's paying her the rent and things done got tight around here. I can't afford to be giving you every payday.

LYONS: I ain't asked you to give me nothing. I asked you to loan me ten dollars. I know you got ten dollars.

TROY: Yeah, I got it. You know why I got it? Cause I don't throw my money away out there in the streets. You living the fast life . . . wanna be a musician . . . running around in them clubs and things . . . then, you learn to take care of yourself. You ain't gonna find me going and asking nobody for nothing. I done spent too many years without.

LYONS: You and me is two different people, Pop.

TROY: I done learned my mistake and learned to do what's right by it. You still trying to get something for nothing. Life don't owe you nothing. You owe it to yourself. Ask Bono. He'll tell you I'm right.

LYONS: You got your way of dealing with the world . . . I got mine. The only thing that matters to me is the music.

TROY: Yeah, I can see that! It don't matter how you gonna eat . . . where your next dollar is coming from. You telling the truth there.

LYONS: I know I got to eat. But I got to live too. I need something that gonna help me to get out of the bed in the morning. Make me feel like I belong in the world. I don't bother nobody. I just stay with my music cause that's the only way I can find to live in the world. Otherwise there ain't no telling what I might do. Now I don't come criticizing you and how you live. I just come by to ask you for ten dollars. I don't wanna hear all that about how I live.

TROY: Boy, your mama did a hell of a job raising you.

LYONS: You can't change me, Pop. I'm thirty-four years old. If you wanted to change me, you should have been there when I was growing up. I come by to see you . . . ask for ten dollars and you want to talk about how I was raised. You don't know nothing about how I was raised.

ROSE: Let the boy have ten dollars, Troy.

TROY: [*To* LYONS.] What the hell you looking at me for? I ain't got no ten dollars. You know what I do with my money. [*To* ROSE.] Give him ten dollars if you want him to have it.

ROSE: I will. Just as soon as you turn it loose.

TROY: [*Handing* ROSE *the money.*] There it is. Seventy-six dollars and forty-two cents. You see this, Bono? Now, I ain't gonna get but six of that back.

ROSE: You ought to stop telling that lie. Here, Lyons. [*She hands him the money.*]

LYONS: Thanks, Rose. Look . . . I got to run. . . . I'll see you later.

TROY: Wait a minute. You gonna say, "Thanks, Rose" and ain't gonna look to see where she got that ten dollars from? See how they do me, Bono?

LYONS: I know she got it from you, Pop. Thanks. I'll give it back to you.

TROY: There he go telling another lie. Time I see that ten dollars . . . he'll be owing me thirty more.

LYONS: See you, Mr. Bono.

BONO: Take care, Lyons!

LYONS: Thanks, Pop. I'll see you again. [LYONS *exits the yard.*]

TROY: I don't know why he don't go and get him a decent job and take care of that woman he got.

BONO: He'll be alright, Troy. The boy is still young.

TROY: The *boy* is thirty-four years old.

ROSE: Let's not get off into all that.

BONO: Look here . . . I got to be going. I got to be getting on. Lucille gonna be waiting.

TROY: [*Puts his arm around* ROSE.] See this woman, Bono? I love this woman. I love this woman so much it hurts. I love her so much

. . . I done run out of ways of loving her. So I got to go back to basics. Don't you come by my house Monday morning talking about time to go to work . . . 'cause I'm still gonna be stroking!

ROSE: Troy! Stop it now!

BONO: I ain't paying him no mind, Rose. That ain't nothing but gintalk. Go on, Troy. I'll see you Monday.

TROY: Don't you come by my house, nigger! I done told you what I'm gonna be doing.

[*The lights go down to black.*]

SCENE TWO

The lights come up on ROSE *hanging up clothes. She hums and sings softly to herself. It is the following morning.*

ROSE: [*Sings.*] Jesus, be a fence all around me every day.
   Jesus, I want you to protect me as I travel on my way.
   Jesus, be a fence all around me every day.
   [TROY *enters from the house.*]
   Jesus, I want you to protect me
   As I travel on my way.
   [*To* TROY.] 'Morning. You ready for breakfast? I can fix it soon as I finish hanging up these clothes.

TROY: I got the coffee on. That'll be alright. I'll just drink some of that this morning.

ROSE: That 651 hit yesterday. That's the second time this month. Miss Pearl hit for a dollar . . . seem like those that need the least always get lucky. Poor folks can't get nothing.

TROY: Them numbers don't know nobody. I don't know why you fool with them. You and Lyons both.

ROSE: It's something to do.

TROY: You ain't doing nothing but throwing your money away.

ROSE: Troy, you know I don't play foolishly. I just play a nickel here and a nickel there.

TROY: That's two nickels you done thrown away.

ROSE: Now I hit sometimes . . . that makes up for it. It always comes in handy when I do hit. I don't hear you complaining then.

TROY: I ain't complaining now. I just say it's foolish. Trying to guess out of six hundred ways which way the number gonna come. If I

had all the money niggers, these Negroes, throw away on numbers for one week—just one week—I'd be a rich man.

ROSE: Well, you wishing and calling it foolish ain't gonna stop folks
from playing numbers. That's one thing for sure. Besides . . .
some good things come from playing numbers. Look where Pope
done bought him that restaurant off of numbers.

TROY: I can't stand niggers like that. Man ain't had two dimes to rub
together. He walking around with his shoes all run over bum-
ming money for cigarettes. Alright. Got lucky there and hit the
numbers. . . .

ROSE: Troy, I know all about it.

TROY: Had good sense, I'll say that for him. He ain't throwed his
money away. I seen niggers hit the numbers and go through two
thousand dollars in four days. Man brought him that restaurant
down there . . . fixed it up real nice . . . and then didn't want nobody to come in it! A Negro go in there and can't get no kind of
service. I seen a white fellow come in there and order a bowl of
stew. Pope picked all the meat out the pot for him. Man ain't had
nothing but a bowl of meat! Negro come behind him and ain't
got nothing but the potatoes and carrots. Talking about what
numbers do for people, you picked a wrong example. Ain't done
nothing but make a worser fool out of him than he was before.

ROSE: Troy, you ought to stop worrying about what happened at
work yesterday.

TROY: I ain't worried. Just told me to be down there at the Commissioner's office on Friday. Everybody think they gonna fire
me. I ain't worried about them firing me. You ain't got to worry
about that. [*Pause.*] Where's Cory? Cory in the house? [*Calls.*]
Cory?

ROSE: He gone out.

TROY: Out, huh? He gone out 'cause he know I want him to help
me with this fence. I know how he is. That boy scared of work.
[GABRIEL *enters. He comes halfway down the alley and, hearing*
TROY's *voice, stops.*] He ain't done a lick of work in his life.

ROSE: He had to go to football practice. Coach wanted them to get
in a little extra practice before the season start.

TROY: I got his practice . . . running out of here before he get his
chores done.

ROSE: Troy, what is wrong with you this morning? Don't nothing set right with you. Go on back in there and go to bed . . . get up on the other side.

TROY: Why something got to be wrong with me? I ain't said nothing wrong with me.

ROSE: You got something to say about everything. First it's the numbers . . . then it's the way the man runs his restaurant . . . then you done got on Cory. What's it gonna be next? Take a look up there and see if the weather suits you . . . or is it gonna be how you gonna put up the fence with the clothes hanging in the yard.

TROY: You hit the nail on the head then.

ROSE: I know you like I know the back of my hand. Go on in there and get you some coffee . . . see if that straighten you up. 'Cause you ain't right this morning.

[TROY *starts into the house and sees* GABRIEL. GABRIEL *starts singing.* TROY'*s brother, he is seven years younger than* TROY. *Injured in World War II, he has a metal plate in his head. He carries an old trumpet tied around his waist and believes with every fiber of his being that he is the Archangel Gabriel.*[1] *He carries a chipped basket with an assortment of discarded fruits and vegetables he has picked up in the strip district and which he attempts to sell.*]

GABRIEL: [*Singing.*] Yes, ma'am, I got plums
　　You ask me how I sell them
　　Oh ten cents apiece
　　Three for a quarter
　　Come and buy now
　　'Cause I'm here today
　　And tomorrow I'll be gone
　　[GABRIEL *enters.*] Hey, Rose!

ROSE: How you doing, Gabe?

GABRIEL: There's Troy. . . . Hey, Troy!

TROY: Hey, Gabe. [*Exit into kitchen.*]

ROSE: [*To* GABRIEL.] What you got there?

GABRIEL: You know what I got, Rose. I got fruits and vegetables.

---

1. In Christianity, God's messenger who announced the births of John the Baptist and Jesus.

ROSE: [*Looking in basket.*] Where's all these plums you talking about?

GABRIEL: I ain't got no plums today, Rose. I was just singing that. Have some tomorrow. Put me in a big order for plums. Have enough plums tomorrow for St. Peter and everybody. [TROY *re-enters from kitchen, crosses to steps.*] [*To* ROSE.] Troy's mad at me.

TROY: I ain't mad at you. What I got to be mad at you about? You ain't done nothing to me.

GABRIEL: I just moved over to Miss Pearl's to keep out from in your way. I ain't mean no harm by it.

TROY: Who said anything about that? I ain't said anything about that.

GABRIEL: You ain't mad at me, is you?

TROY: Naw . . . I ain't mad at you, Gabe. If I was mad at you I'd tell you about it.

GABRIEL: Got me two rooms. In the basement. Got my own door too. Wanna see my key? [*He holds up a key.*] That's my own key! Ain't nobody else got a key like that. That's my key! My two rooms!

TROY: Well, that's good, Gabe. You got your own key . . . that's good.

ROSE: You hungry, Gabe? I was just fixing to cook Troy his breakfast.

GABRIEL: I'll take some biscuits. You got some biscuits? Did you know when I was in heaven . . . every morning me and St. Peter would sit down by the gate and eat some big fat biscuits? Oh, yeah! We had us a good time. We'd sit there and eat us them biscuits and then St. Peter would go off to sleep and tell me to wake him up when it's time to open the gates for the judgment.

ROSE: Well, come on . . . I'll make up a batch of biscuits. [ROSE *exits into the house.*]

GABRIEL: Troy . . . St. Peter got your name in the book. I seen it. It say . . . Troy Maxson. I say . . . I know him! He got the same name like what I got. That's my brother!

TROY: How many times you gonna tell me that, Gabe?

GABRIEL: Ain't got my name in the book. Don't have to have my name. I done died and went to heaven. He got your name though. One morning St. Peter was looking at his book . . . marking it up for the judgment . . . and he let me see your name.

Got it in there under M. Got Rose's name. . . . I ain't seen it like I seen yours . . . but I know it's in there. He got a great big book. Got everybody's name what was ever been born. That's what he told me. But I seen your name. Seen it with my own eyes.

TROY: Go on in the house there. Rose going to fix you something to eat.

GABRIEL: Oh, I ain't hungry. I done had breakfast with Aunt Jemimah. She come by and cooked me up a whole mess of flapjacks. Remember how we used to eat them flapjacks?

TROY: Go on in the house and get you something to eat now.

GABRIEL: I got to go sell my plums. I done sold some tomatoes. Got me two quarters. Wanna see? [*He shows* TROY *his quarters.*] I'm gonna save them and buy me a new horn so St. Peter can hear me when it's time to open the gates. [GABRIEL *stops suddenly. Listens.*] Hear that? That's the hellhounds. I got to chase them out of here. Go on get out of here! Get out! [GABRIEL *exits singing.*]

>   Better get ready for the judgment
>   Better get ready for the judgment
>   My Lord is coming down
>   [ROSE *enters from the house.*]

TROY: He gone off somewhere.

GABRIEL: [*Offstage.*] Better get ready for the judgment

>   Better get ready for the judgment morning
>   Better get ready for the judgment
>   My God is coming down

ROSE: He ain't eating right. Miss Pearl say she can't get him to eat nothing.

TROY: What you want me to do about it, Rose? I done did everything I can for the man. I can't make him get well. Man got half his head blown away . . . what you expect?

ROSE: Seem like something ought to be done to help him.

TROY: Man don't bother nobody. He just mixed up from that metal plate he got in his head. Ain't no sense for him to go back into the hospital.

ROSE: Least he be eating right. They can help him take care of himself.

TROY: Don't nobody wanna be locked up, Rose. What you wanna lock him up for? Man go over there and fight the war . . . messin' around with them Japs, get half his head blown off . . . and they give him a lousy three thousand dollars. And I had to swoop down on that.

ROSE: Is you fixing to go into that again?

TROY: That's the only way I got a roof over my head . . . 'cause of that metal plate.

ROSE: Ain't no sense you blaming yourself for nothing. Gabe wasn't in no condition to manage that money. You done what was right by him. Can't nobody say you ain't done what was right by him. Look how long you took care of him . . . till he wanted to have his own place and moved over there with Miss Pearl.

TROY: That ain't what I'm saying, woman! I'm just stating the facts. If my brother didn't have that metal plate in his head . . . I wouldn't have a pot to piss in or a window to throw it out of. And I'm fifty-three years old. Now see if you can understand that! [TROY *gets up from the porch and starts to exit the yard.*]

ROSE: Where you going off to? You been running out of here every Saturday for weeks. I thought you was gonna work on this fence?

TROY: I'm gonna walk down to Taylors'. Listen to the ball game. I'll be back in a bit. I'll work on it when I get back. [*He exits the yard. The lights go to black.*]

SCENE THREE

The lights come up on the yard. It is four hours later. ROSE *is taking down the clothes from the line.* CORY *enters carrying his football equipment.*

ROSE: Your daddy like to had a fit with you running out of here this morning without doing your chores.

CORY: I told you I had to go to practice.

ROSE: He say you were supposed to help him with this fence.

CORY: He been saying that the last four or five Saturdays, and then he don't never do nothing, but go down to Taylors'. Did you tell him about the recruiter?

ROSE: Yeah, I told him.

CORY: What he say?

ROSE: He ain't said nothing too much. You get in there and get started on your chores before he gets back. Go on and scrub down them steps before he gets back here hollering and carrying on.

CORY: I'm hungry. What you got to eat, Mama?

ROSE: Go on and get started on your chores. I got some meat loaf in there. Go on and make you a sandwich . . . and don't leave no mess in there. [CORY *exits into the house.* ROSE *continues to take down the clothes.* TROY *enters the yard and sneaks up and grabs her from behind.*] Troy! Go on, now. You liked to scared me to death. What was the score of the game? Lucille had me on the phone and I couldn't keep up with it.

TROY: What I care about the game? Come here, woman. [*He tries to kiss her.*]

ROSE: I thought you went down Taylors' to listen to the game. Go on, Troy! You supposed to be putting up this fence.

TROY: [*Attempting to kiss her again.*] I'll put it up when I finish with what is at hand.

ROSE: Go on, Troy. I ain't studying you.

TROY: [*Chasing after her.*] I'm studying you . . . fixing to do my homework!

ROSE: Troy, you better leave me alone.

TROY: Where's Cory? That boy brought his butt home yet?

ROSE: He's in the house doing his chores.

TROY: [*Calling.*] Cory! Get your butt out here, boy!

[ROSE *exits into the house with the laundry.* TROY *goes over to the pile of wood, picks up a board, and starts sawing.* CORY *enters from the house.*]

TROY: You just now coming in here from leaving this morning?

CORY: Yeah, I had to go to football practice.

TROY: Yeah, what?

CORY: Yessir.

TROY: I ain't but two seconds off you noway. The garbage sitting in there overflowing . . . you ain't done none of your chores . . . and you come in here talking about "Yeah."

CORY: I was just getting ready to do my chores now, Pop. . . .

TROY: Your first chore is to help me with this fence on Saturday. Everything else come after that. Now get that saw and cut them boards.

[CORY *takes the saw and begins cutting the boards.* TROY *continues working. There is a long pause.*]

CORY: Hey, Pop . . . why don't you buy a TV?

TROY: What I want with a TV? What I want one of them for?

CORY: Everybody got one. Earl, Ba Bra . . . Jesse!

TROY: I ain't asked you who had one. I say what I want with one?

CORY: So you can watch it. They got lots of things on TV. Baseball games and everything. We could watch the World Series.

TROY: Yeah . . . and how much this TV cost?

CORY: I don't know. They got them on sale for around two hundred dollars.

TROY: Two hundred dollars, huh?

CORY: That ain't that much, Pop.

TROY: Naw, it's just two hundred dollars. See that roof you got over your head at night? Let me tell you something about that roof. It's been over ten years since that roof was last tarred. See now . . . the snow come this winter and sit up there on that roof like it is . . . and it's gonna seep inside. It's just gonna be a little bit . . . ain't gonna hardly notice it. Then the next thing you know, it's gonna be leaking all over the house. Then the wood rot from all that water and you gonna need a whole new roof. Now, how much you think it cost to get that roof tarred?

CORY: I don't know.

TROY: Two hundred and sixty-four dollars . . . cash money. While you thinking about a TV, I got to be thinking about the roof . . . and whatever else go wrong around here. Now if you had two hundred dollars, what would you do . . . fix the roof or buy a TV?

CORY: I'd buy a TV. Then when the roof started to leak . . . when it needed fixing . . . I'd fix it.

TROY: Where you gonna get the money from? You done spent it for a TV. You gonna sit up and watch the water run all over your brand new TV.

CORY: Aw, Pop. You got money. I know you do.

TROY: Where I got it at, huh?

CORY: You got it in the bank.

TROY: You wanna see my bankbook? You wanna see that seventy-three dollars and twenty-two cents I got sitting up in there.

CORY: You ain't got to pay for it all at one time. You can put a down payment on it and carry it on home with you.

TROY: Not me. I ain't gonna owe nobody nothing if I can help it. Miss a payment and they come and snatch it right out your house. Then what you got? Now, soon as I get two hundred dollars clear, then I'll buy a TV. Right now, as soon as I get two hundred and sixty-four dollars, I'm gonna have this roof tarred.

CORY: Aw . . . Pop!

TROY: You go on and get you two hundred dollars and buy one if ya want it. I got better things to do with my money.

CORY: I can't get no two hundred dollars. I ain't never seen two hundred dollars.

TROY: I'll tell you what . . . you get you a hundred dollars and I'll put the other hundred with it.

CORY: Alright, I'm gonna show you.

TROY: You gonna show me how you can cut them boards right now.

[CORY *begins to cut the boards. There is a long pause.*]

CORY: The Pirates won today. That makes five in a row.

TROY: I ain't thinking about the Pirates. Got an all-white team. Got that boy . . . that Puerto Rican boy . . . Clemente.[1] Don't even half-play him. That boy could be something if they give him a chance. Play him one day and sit him on the bench the next.

CORY: He gets a lot of chances to play.

TROY: I'm talking about playing regular. Playing every day so you can get your timing. That's what I'm talking about.

CORY: They got some white guys on the team that don't play every day. You can't play everybody at the same time.

TROY: If they got a white fellow sitting on the bench . . . you can bet your last dollar he can't play! The colored guy got to be twice as good before he get on the team. That's why I don't want you to get all tied up in them sports. Man on the team and what it get him? They got colored on the team and don't use them. Same as not having them. All them teams the same.

CORY: The Braves got Hank Aaron and Wes Covington.[2] Hank Aaron hit two home runs today. That makes forty-three.

TROY: Hank Aaron ain't nobody. That's what you supposed to do. That's how you supposed to play the game. Ain't nothing to it.

---

1. Roberto Clemente (1934–1972), Hall of Fame right fielder for the Pittsburgh Pirates from 1955 until his death, in a plane crash en route to Nicaragua, where he intended to help victims of an earthquake.

2. John Wesley Covington (1932–1956), outfielder, and Henry Louis Aaron (1934–), infielder and outfielder, helped the Milwaukee Braves win the World Series in 1957. Aaron held the all-time home-run record until it was broken by Barry Bonds in 2007.

It's just a matter of timing . . . getting the right follow-through. Hell, I can hit forty-three home runs right now!

CORY: Not off no major-league pitching, you couldn't.

TROY: We had better pitching in the Negro leagues. I hit seven home runs off of Satchel Paige.[3] You can't get no better than that!

CORY: Sandy Koufax.[4] He's leading the league in strikeouts.

TROY: I ain't thinking of no Sandy Koufax.

CORY: You got Warren Spahn and Lew Burdette.[5] I bet you couldn't hit no home runs off of Warren Spahn.

TROY: I'm through with it now. You go on and cut them boards. [*Pause.*] Your mama tell me you done got recruited by a college football team? Is that right?

CORY: Yeah. Coach Zellman say the recruiter gonna be coming by to talk to you. Get you to sign the permission papers.

TROY: I thought you supposed to be working down there at the A&P. Ain't you suppose to be working down there after school?

CORY: Mr. Stawicki say he gonna hold my job for me until after the football season. Say starting next week I can work weekends.

TROY: I thought we had an understanding about this football stuff? You suppose to keep up with your chores and hold that job down at the A&P. Ain't been around here all day on a Saturday. Ain't none of your chores done . . . and now you telling me you done quit your job.

CORY: I'm gonna be working weekends.

TROY: You damn right you are! And ain't no need for nobody coming around here to talk to me about signing nothing.

CORY: Hey, Pop . . . you can't do that. He's coming all the way from North Carolina.

TROY: I don't care where he coming from. The white man ain't gonna let you get nowhere with that football noway. You go on and get your book-learning so you can work yourself up in that A&P or learn how to fix cars or build houses or something, get you a trade. That way you have something can't nobody take

---

3. Leroy Robert Paige (1906?–1982), considered by many the best pitcher in baseball history, played in the Negro Leagues for over twenty years before the Cleveland Indians hired him in 1948.

4. Sanford Koufax (1935–   ) pitched for the Brooklyn Dodgers in 1957.

5. Selva Lewis Burdette Jr. (1926–   ) and Warren Edward Spahn (1921–2003) were star pitchers for the Braves in 1957.

away from you. You go on and learn how to put your hands to some good use. Besides hauling people's garbage.

CORY: I get good grades, Pop. That's why the recruiter wants to talk with you. You got to keep up your grades to get recruited. This way I'll be going to college. I'll get a chance. . . .

TROY: First you gonna get your butt down there to the A&P and get your job back.

CORY: Mr. Stawicki done already hired somebody else 'cause I told him I was playing football.

TROY: You a bigger fool than I thought . . . to let somebody take away your job so you can play some football. Where you gonna get your money to take out your girlfriend and whatnot? What kind of foolishness is that to let somebody take away your job?

CORY: I'm still gonna be working weekends.

TROY: Naw . . . naw. You getting your butt out of here and finding you another job.

CORY: Come on, Pop! I got to practice. I can't work after school and play football too. The team needs me. That's what Coach Zellman say. . . .

TROY: I don't care what nobody else say. I'm the boss . . . you understand? I'm the boss around here. I do the only saying what counts.

CORY: Come on, Pop!

TROY: I asked you . . . did you understand?

CORY: Yeah . . .

TROY: What?!

CORY: Yessir.

TROY: You go on down there to that A&P and see if you can get your job back. If you can't do both . . . then you quit the football team. You've got to take the crookeds with the straights.

CORY: Yessir. [*Pause.*] Can I ask you a question?

TROY: What the hell you wanna ask me? Mr. Stawicki the one you got the questions for.

CORY: How come you ain't never liked me?

TROY: Liked you? Who the hell say I got to like you? What law is there say I got to like you? Wanna stand up in my face and ask a damn fool-ass question like that. Talking about liking somebody. Come here, boy, when I talk to you. [CORY *comes over to where* TROY *is working. He stands slouched over and* TROY *shoves him on*

his shoulder.] Straighten up, goddammit! I asked you a question
. . . what law is there say I got to like you?

CORY: None.

TROY: Well, alright then! Don't you eat every day? [*Pause.*] Answer
me when I talk to you! Don't you eat every day?

CORY: Yeah.

TROY: Nigger, as long as you in my house, you put that sir on the
end of it when you talk to me!

CORY: Yes . . . sir.

TROY: You eat every day.

CORY: Yessir!

TROY: Got a roof over your head.

CORY: Yessir!

TROY: Got clothes on your back.

CORY: Yessir.

TROY: Why you think that is?

CORY: 'Cause of you.

TROY: Aw, hell I know it's 'cause of me . . . but why do you think
that is?

CORY: [*Hesitant.*] 'Cause you like me.

TROY: Like you? I go out of here every morning . . . bust my butt . . .
putting up with them crackers every day . . . cause I like you? You
about the biggest fool I ever saw. [*Pause.*] It's my job. It's my responsibility! You understand that? A man got to take care of his
family. You live in my house . . . sleep you behind on my bed-
clothes . . . fill you belly up with my food . . . 'cause you my son.
You my flesh and blood. Not 'cause I like you! 'Cause it's my
duty to take care of you. I owe a responsibility to you!

Let's get this straight right here . . . before it go along any further. . . . I ain't got to like you. Mr. Rand don't give me my
money come payday cause he likes me. He gives me cause he owe
me. I done give you everything I had to give you. I gave you your
life! Me and your mama worked that out between us. And liking
your black ass wasn't part of the bargain. Don't you try and go
through life worrying about if somebody like you or not. You
best be making sure they doing right by you. You understand
what I'm saying, boy?

CORY: Yessir.

TROY: Then get the hell out of my face, and get on down to that A&P.

[ROSE *has been standing behind the screen door for much of the scene. She enters as* CORY *exits.*]

ROSE: Why don't you let the boy go ahead and play football, Troy? Ain't no harm in that. He's just trying to be like you with the sports.

TROY: I don't want him to be like me! I want him to move as far away from my life as he can get. You the only decent thing that ever happened to me. I wish him that. But I don't wish him a thing else from my life. I decided seventeen years ago that boy wasn't getting involved in no sports. Not after what they did to me in the sports.

ROSE: Troy, why don't you admit you was too old to play in the major leagues? For once . . . why don't you admit that?

TROY: What do you mean too old? Don't come telling me I was too old. I just wasn't the right color. Hell, I'm fifty-three years old and can do better than Selkirk's .269 right now!

ROSE: How's was you gonna play ball when you were over forty? Sometimes I can't get no sense out of you.

TROY: I got good sense, woman. I got sense enough not to let my boy get hurt over playing no sports. You been mothering that boy too much. Worried about if people like him.

ROSE: Everything that boy do . . . he do for you. He wants you to say "Good job, son." That's all.

TROY: Rose, I ain't got time for that. He's alive. He's healthy. He's got to make his own way. I made mine. Ain't nobody gonna hold his hand when he get out there in that world.

ROSE: Times have changed from when you was young, Troy. People change. The world's changing around you and you can't even see it.

TROY: [*Slow, methodical.*] Woman . . . I do the best I can do. I come in here every Friday. I carry a sack of potatoes and a bucket of lard. You all line up at the door with your hands out. I give you the lint from my pockets. I give you my sweat and my blood. I ain't got no tears. I done spent them. We go upstairs in that room at night . . . and I fall down on you and try to blast a hole into forever. I get up Monday morning . . . find my lunch on the table. I go out. Make my way. Find my strength to carry me through to the next Friday. [*Pause.*] That's all I got, Rose. That's all I got to give. I can't give nothing else. [TROY *exits into the house. The lights go down to black.*]

SCENE FOUR
It is Friday. Two weeks later. CORY *starts out of the house with his football equipment. The phone rings.*

CORY: [*Calling.*] I got it! [*He answers the phone and stands in the screen door talking.*] Hello? Hey, Jesse. Naw . . . I was just getting ready to leave now.
ROSE: [*Calling.*] Cory!
CORY: I told you, man, them spikes is all tore up. You can use them if you want, but they ain't no good. Earl got some spikes.
ROSE: [*Calling.*] Cory!
CORY: [*Calling to* ROSE.] Mam? I'm talking to Jesse. [*Into phone.*] When she say that? [*Pause.*] Aw, you lying, man. I'm gonna tell her you said that.
ROSE: [*Calling.*] Cory, don't you go nowhere!
CORY: I got to go to the game, Ma! [*Into the phone.*] Yeah, hey, look, I'll talk to you later. Yeah, I'll meet you over Earl's house. Later. Bye, Ma. [CORY *exits the house and starts out the yard.*]
ROSE: Cory, where you going off to? You got that stuff all pulled out and thrown all over your room.
CORY: [*In the yard.*] I was looking for my spikes. Jesse wanted to borrow my spikes.
ROSE: Get up there and get that cleaned up before your daddy get back in here.
CORY: I got to go to the game! I'll clean it up *when I get back.* [CORY *exits.*]
ROSE: That's all he need to do is see that room all messed up.
    [ROSE *exits into the house.* TROY *and* BONO *enter the yard.* TROY *is dressed in clothes other than his work clothes.*]
BONO: He told him the same thing he told you. Take it to the union.
TROY: Brownie ain't got that much sense. Man wasn't thinking

about nothing. He wait until I confront them on it . . . then he wanna come crying seniority. [*Calls.*] Hey, Rose!

BONO: I wish I could have seen Mr. Rand's face when he told you.

TROY: He couldn't get it out of his mouth! Liked to bit his tongue! When they called me down there to the Commissioner's office . . . he thought they was gonna fire me. Like everybody else.

BONO: I didn't think they was gonna fire you. I thought they was gonna put you on the warning paper.

TROY: Hey, Rose! [*To* BONO.] Yeah, Mr. Rand like to bit his tongue. [TROY *breaks the seal on the bottle, takes a drink, and hands it to* BONO.]

BONO: I see you run right down to Taylors' and told that Alberta gal.

TROY: [*Calling.*] Hey, Rose! [*To* BONO.] I told everybody. Hey, Rose! I went down there to cash my check.

ROSE: [*Entering from the house.*] Hush all that hollering, man! I know you out here. What they say down there at the Commissioner's office?

TROY: You supposed to come when I call you, woman. Bono'll tell you that. [*To* BONO.] Don't Lucille come when you call her?

ROSE: Man, hush your mouth. I ain't no dog . . . talk about "come when you call me."

TROY: [*Puts his arm around* ROSE.] You hear this, Bono? I had me an old dog used to get uppity like that. You say, "C'mere, Blue!" . . . and he just lay there and look at you. End up getting a stick and chasing him away trying to make him come.

ROSE: I ain't studying you and your dog. I remember you used to sing that old song.

TROY: [*He sings.*] Hear it ring! Hear it ring!
I had a dog his name was Blue.

ROSE: Don't nobody wanna hear you sing that old song.

TROY: [*Sings.*] You know Blue was mighty true.

ROSE: Used to have Cory running around here singing that song.

BONO: Hell, I remember that song myself.

TROY: [*Sings.*] You know Blue was a good old dog.
Blue treed a possum in a hollow log.
That was my daddy's song. My daddy made up that song.

ROSE: I don't care who made it up. Don't nobody wanna hear you sing it.

TROY: [*Makes a song like calling a dog.*] Come here, woman.

ROSE: You come in here carrying on, I reckon they ain't fired you. What they say down there at the Commissioner's office?

TROY: Look here, Rose . . . Mr. Rand called me into his office today when I got back from talking to them people down there . . . it come from up top . . . he called me in and told me they was making me a driver.

ROSE: Troy, you kidding!

TROY: No I ain't. Ask Bono.

ROSE: Well, that's great, Troy. Now you don't have to hassle them people no more.

[LYONS *enters from the street.*]

TROY: Aw hell, I wasn't looking to see you today. I thought you was in jail. Got it all over the front page of the *Courier* about them raiding Sefus' place . . . where you be hanging out with all them thugs.

LYONS: Hey, Pop . . . that ain't got nothing to do with me. I don't go down there gambling. I go down there to sit in with the band. I ain't got nothing to do with the gambling part. They got some good music down there.

TROY: They got some rogues . . . is what they got.

LYONS: How you been, Mr. Bono? Hi, Rose.

BONO: I see where you playing down at the Crawford Grill tonight.

ROSE: How come you ain't brought Bonnie like I told you. You should have brought Bonnie with you, she ain't been over in a month of Sundays.

LYONS: I was just in the neighborhood . . . thought I'd stop by.

TROY: Here he come. . . .

BONO: Your daddy got a promotion on the rubbish. He's gonna be the first colored driver. Ain't got to do nothing but sit up there and read the paper like them white fellows.

LYONS: Hey, Pop . . . if you knew how to read you'd be alright.

BONO: Naw . . . naw . . . you mean if the nigger knew how to *drive* he'd be all right. Been fighting with them people about driving and ain't even got a license. Mr. Rand know you ain't got no driver's license?

TROY: Driving ain't nothing. All you do is point the truck where you want it to go. Driving ain't nothing.

BONO: Do Mr. Rand know you ain't got no driver's license? That's what I'm talking about. I ain't asked if driving was easy. I asked if Mr. Rand know you ain't got no driver's license.

TROY: He ain't got to know. The man ain't got to know my business. Time he find out, I have two or three driver's licenses.

LYONS: [*Going into his pocket.*] Say, look here, Pop . . .

TROY: I knew it was coming. Didn't I tell you, Bono? I know what kind of "Look here, Pop" that was. The nigger fixing to ask me for some money. It's Friday night. It's my payday. All them rogues down there on the avenue . . . the ones that ain't in jail . . . and Lyons is hopping in his shoes to get down there with them.

LYONS: See, Pop . . . if you give somebody else a chance to talk sometime, you'd see that I was fixing to pay you back your ten dollars like I told you. Here . . . I told you I'd pay you when Bonnie got paid.

TROY: Naw . . . you go ahead and keep that ten dollars. Put it in the bank. The next time you feel like you wanna come by here and ask me for something . . . you go on down there and get that.

LYONS: Here's your ten dollars, Pop. I told you I don't want you to give me nothing. I just wanted to borrow ten dollars.

TROY: Naw . . . you go on and keep that for the next time you want to ask me.

LYONS: Come on, Pop . . . here go your ten dollars.

ROSE: Why don't you go on and let the boy pay you back, Troy?

LYONS: Here you go, Rose. If you don't take it I'm gonna have to hear about it for the next six months. [*He hands her the money.*]

ROSE: You can hand yours over here too, Troy.

TROY: You see this, Bono. You see how they do me.

BONO: Yeah, Lucille do me the same way.

[GABRIEL *is heard singing offstage. He enters.*]

GABRIEL: Better get ready for the Judgment! Better get ready for . . . Hey! . . . Hey! . . . There's Troy's boy!

LYONS: How you doing, Uncle Gabe?

GABRIEL: Lyons . . . The King of the Jungle! Rose . . . hey, Rose. Got a flower for you. [*He takes a rose from his pocket.*] Picked it myself. That's the same rose like you is!

ROSE: That's right nice of you, Gabe.

LYONS: What you been doing, Uncle Gabe?

GABRIEL: Oh, I been chasing hellhounds and waiting on the time to tell St. Peter to open the gates.

LYONS: You been chasing hellhounds, huh? Well . . . you doing the right thing, Uncle Gabe. Somebody got to chase them.

GABRIEL: Oh, yeah . . . I know it. The devil's strong. The devil ain't no pushover. Hellhounds snipping at everybody's heels. But I got my trumpet waiting on the judgment time.

LYONS: Waiting on the Battle of Armageddon, huh?

GABRIEL: Ain't gonna be too much of a battle when God get to waving that Judgment sword. But the people's gonna have a hell of a time trying to get into heaven if them gates ain't open.

LYONS: [*Putting his arm around* GABRIEL.] You hear this, Pop. Uncle Gabe, you alright!

GABRIEL: [*Laughing with* LYONS.] Lyons! King of the Jungle.

ROSE: You gonna stay for supper, Gabe. Want me to fix you a plate?

GABRIEL: I'll take a sandwich, Rose. Don't want no plate. Just wanna eat with my hands. I'll take a sandwich.

ROSE: How about you, Lyons? You staying? Got some short ribs cooking.

LYONS: Naw, I won't eat nothing till after we finished playing. [*Pause.*] You ought to come down and listen to me play, Pop.

TROY: I don't like that Chinese music. All that noise.

ROSE: Go on in the house and wash up, Gabe. . . . I'll fix you a sandwich.

GABRIEL: [*To* LYONS, *as he exits.*] Troy's mad at me.

LYONS: What you mad at Uncle Gabe for, Pop.

ROSE: He thinks Troy's mad at him cause he moved over to Miss Pearl's.

TROY: I ain't mad at the man. He can live where he want to live at.

LYONS: What he move over there for? Miss Pearl don't like nobody.

ROSE: She don't mind him none. She treats him real nice. She just don't allow all that singing.

TROY: She don't mind that rent he be paying . . . that's what she don't mind.

ROSE: Troy, I ain't going through that with you no more. He's over there cause he want to have his own place. He can come and go as he please.

TROY: Hell, he could come and go as he please here. I wasn't stopping him. I ain't put no rules on him.

ROSE: It ain't the same thing, Troy. And you know it. [GABRIEL *comes to the door.*] Now, that's the last I wanna hear about that. I don't wanna hear nothing else about Gabe and Miss Pearl. And next week . . .

GABRIEL: I'm ready for my sandwich, Rose.

ROSE: And next week . . . when that recruiter come from that school . . . I want you to sign that paper and go on and let Cory play football. Then that'll be the last I have to hear about that.

TROY: [*To* ROSE *as she exits into the house.*] I ain't thinking about Cory nothing.

LYONS: What . . . Cory got recruited? What school he going to?

TROY: That boy walking around here smelling his piss . . . thinking he's grown. Thinking he's gonna do what he want, irrespective of what I say. Look here, Bono . . . I left the Commissioner's office and went down to the A&P . . . that boy ain't working down there. He lying to me. Telling me he got his job back . . . telling me he working weekends . . . telling me he working after school. . . . Mr. Stawicki tell me he ain't working down there at all!

LYONS: Cory just growing up. He's just busting at the seams trying to fill out your shoes.

TROY: I don't care what he's doing. When he get to the point where he wanna disobey me . . . then it's time for him to move on. Bono'll tell you that. I bet he ain't never disobeyed his daddy without paying the consequences.

BONO: I ain't never had a chance. My daddy came on through . . . but I ain't never knew him to see him . . . or what he had on his mind or where he went. Just moving on through. Searching out the New Land. That's what the old folks used to call it. See a fellow moving around from place to place . . . woman to woman . . . called it searching out the New Land. I can't say if he ever found it. I come along, didn't want no kids. Didn't know if I was gonna be in one place long enough to fix on them right as their daddy. I figured I was going searching too. As it turned out I been hooked up with Lucille near about as long as your daddy been with Rose. Going on sixteen years.

TROY: Sometimes I wish I hadn't known my daddy. He ain't cared nothing about no kids. A kid to him wasn't nothing. All he wanted was for you to learn how to walk so he could start you to working. When it come time for eating . . . he ate first. If there was anything left over, that's what you got. Man would sit down and eat two chickens and give you the wing.

LYONS: You ought to stop that, Pop. Everybody feed their kids. No matter how hard times is . . . everybody care about their kids. Make sure they have something to eat.

TROY: The only thing my daddy cared about was getting them bales of cotton in to Mr. Lubin. That's the only thing that mattered to him. Sometimes I used to wonder why he was living. Wonder why the devil hadn't come and got him. "Get them bales of cotton in to Mr. Lubin" and find out he owe him money. . . .

LYONS: He should have just went on and left when he saw he couldn't get nowhere. That's what I would have done.

TROY: How he gonna leave with eleven kids? And where he gonna go? He ain't knew how to do nothing but farm. No, he was trapped and I think he knew it. But I'll say this for him . . . he felt a responsibility toward us. Maybe he ain't treated us the way I felt he should have . . . but without that responsibility he could have walked off and left us . . . made his own way.

BONO: A lot of them did. Back in those days what you talking about . . . they walk out their front door and just take on down one road or another and keep on walking.

LYONS: There you go! That's what I'm talking about.

BONO: Just keep on walking till you come to something else. Ain't you never heard of nobody having the walking blues? Well, that's what you call it when you just take off like that.

TROY: My daddy ain't had them walking blues! What you talking about? He stayed right there with his family. But he was just as evil as he could be. My mama couldn't stand him. Couldn't stand that evilness. She run off when I was about eight. She sneaked off one night after he had gone to sleep. Told me she was coming back for me. I ain't never seen her no more. All his women run off and left him. He wasn't good for nobody.

When my turn come to head out, I was fourteen and got to sniffing around Joe Canewell's daughter. Had us an old mule we called Greyboy. My daddy sent me out to do some plowing and I tied up Greyboy and went to fooling around with Joe Canewell's daughter. We done found us a nice little spot, got real cozy with each other. She about thirteen and we done figured we was grown anyway . . . so we down there enjoying ourselves . . . ain't thinking about nothing. We didn't know Greyboy had got loose and wandered back to the house and my daddy was looking for me. We down there by the creek enjoying ourselves when my daddy come up on us. Surprised us. He had them leather straps off the mule and commenced to whupping me like there was no tomorrow. I jumped up, mad and embarrassed. I was scared of my daddy. When he commenced to whupping on me . . . quite naturally I run to get out of the way. [*Pause.*]

Now I thought he was mad cause I ain't done my work. But I see where he was chasing me off so he could have the gal for himself. When I see what the matter of it was, I lost all fear of my daddy. Right there is where I become a man . . . at fourteen years of age. [*Pause.*]

Now it was my turn to run him off. I picked up them same reins that he had used on me. I picked up them reins and commenced to whupping on him. The gal jumped up and run off . . . and when my daddy turned to face me, I could see why the devil had never come to get him . . . 'cause he was the devil himself. I don't know what happened. When I woke up, I was laying right there by the creek, and Blue . . . this old dog we had . . . was licking my face. I thought I was blind. I couldn't see nothing. Both my eyes were swollen shut. I layed there and cried. I didn't know what I was gonna do. The only thing I knew was the time had come for me to leave my daddy's house. And right there the world suddenly got big. And it was a long time before I could cut it down to where I could handle it.

Part of that cutting down was when I got to the place where I could feel him kicking in my blood and knew that the only thing that separated us was the matter of a few years.

[GABRIEL *enters from the house with a sandwich.*]

LYONS: What you got there, Uncle Gabe?

GABRIEL: Got me a ham sandwich. Rose gave me a ham sandwich.

TROY: I don't know what happened to him. I done lost touch with everybody except Gabriel. But I hope he's dead. I hope he found some peace.

LYONS: That's a heavy story, Pop. I didn't know you left home when you was fourteen.

TROY: And didn't know nothing. The only part of the world I knew was the forty-two acres of Mr. Lubin's land. That's all I knew about life.

LYONS: Fourteen's kinda young to be out on your own. [*Phone rings.*] I don't even think I was ready to be out on my own at fourteen. I don't know what I would have done.

TROY: I got up from the creek and walked on down to Mobile. I was through with farming. Figured I could do better in the city. So I walked the two hundred miles to Mobile.

LYONS: Wait a minute . . . you ain't walked no two hundred miles, Pop. Ain't nobody gonna walk no two hundred miles. You talking about some walking there.

BONO: That's the only way you got anywhere back in them days.

LYONS: Shhh. Damn if I wouldn't have hitched a ride with somebody!

TROY: Who you gonna hitch it with? They ain't had no cars and things like they got now. We talking about 1918.

ROSE: [*Entering.*] What you all out here getting into?

TROY: [*To* ROSE.] I'm telling Lyons how good he got it. He don't know nothing about this I'm talking.

ROSE: Lyons, that was Bonnie on the phone. She say you supposed to pick her up.

LYONS: Yeah, okay, Rose.

TROY: I walked on down to Mobile and hitched up with some of them fellows that was heading this way. Got up here and found out . . . not only couldn't you get a job . . . you couldn't find no place to live. I thought I was in freedom. Shhh. Colored folks living down there on the riverbanks in whatever kind of shelter they could find for themselves. Right down there under the Brady Street Bridge. Living in shacks made of sticks and tarpaper. Messed around there and went from bad to worse. Started stealing. First it was food. Then I figured, hell, if I steal money I can buy me some food. Buy me some shoes too! One thing led to another. Met your mama. I was young and anxious to be a man. Met your mama and had you. What I do that for? Now I got to worry about feeding you and her. Got to steal three times as much. Went out one day looking for somebody to rob . . . that's what I was, a robber. I'll tell you the truth. I'm ashamed of it today. But it's the truth. Went to rob this fellow . . . pulled out my knife . . . and he pulled out a gun. Shot me in the chest. It felt just like somebody had taken a hot branding iron and laid it on me. When he shot me I jumped at him with my knife. They told me I killed him and they put me in the penitentiary and locked me up for fifteen years. That's where I met Bono. That's where I learned how to play baseball. Got out that place and your mama had taken you and went on to make life without me. Fifteen years was a long time for her to wait. But that fifteen years cured me of that robbing stuff. Rose'll tell you. She asked me when I met her if I had gotten all that foolishness out of my system. And I told her, "Baby, it's you and baseball all what count with me." You hear me, Bono? I meant it too. She say, "Which one comes first?" I told her, "Baby, ain't no doubt it's baseball . . . but you stick and get old with me and we'll both outlive this baseball." Am I right, Rose? And it's true.

ROSE: Man, hush your mouth. You ain't said no such thing. Talking about, "Baby, you know you'll always be number one with me." That's what you was talking.

TROY: You hear that, Bono. That's why I love her.

BONO: Rose'll keep you straight. You get off the track, she'll straighten you up.

ROSE: Lyons, you better get on up and get Bonnie. She waiting on you.

LYONS: [Gets up to go.] Hey, Pop, why don't you come on down to the Grill and hear me play?

TROY: I ain't going down there. I'm too old to be sitting around in them clubs.

BONO: You got to be good to play down at the Grill.

LYONS: Come on, Pop . . .

TROY: I got to get up in the morning.

LYONS: You ain't got to stay long.

TROY: Naw, I'm gonna get my supper and go on to bed.

LYONS: Well, I got to go. I'll see you again.

TROY: Don't you come around my house on my payday.

ROSE: Pick up the phone and let somebody know you coming. And bring Bonnie with you. You know I'm always glad to see her.

LYONS: Yeah, I'll do that, Rose. You take care now. See you, Pop. See you, Mr. Bono. See you, Uncle Gabe.

GABRIEL: Lyons! King of the Jungle!

[LYONS *exits.*]

TROY: Is supper ready, woman? Me and you got some business to take care of. I'm gonna tear it up too.

ROSE: Troy, I done told you now!

TROY: [*Puts his arm around* BONO.] Aw hell, woman . . . this is Bono. Bono like family. I done known this nigger since . . . how long I done know you?

BONO: It's been a long time.

TROY: I done known this nigger since Skippy was a pup. Me and him done been through some times.

BONO: You sure right about that.

TROY: Hell, I done know him longer than I known you. And we still standing shoulder to shoulder. Hey, look here, Bono . . . a man can't ask for no more than that. [*Drinks to him.*] I love you, nigger.

BONO: Hell, I love you too . . . but I got to get home see my woman. You got yours in hand. I got to go get mine.

[BONO *starts to exit as* CORY *enters the yard, dressed in his football uniform. He gives* TROY *a hard, uncompromising look.*]

CORY: What you do that for, Pop? [*He throws his helmet down in the direction of* TROY.]

ROSE: What's the matter? Cory . . . what's the matter?

CORY: Papa done went up to the school and told Coach Zellman I can't play football no more. Wouldn't even let me play the game. Told him to tell the recruiter not to come.

ROSE: Troy . . .

TROY: What you Troying me for. Yeah, I did it. And the boy know why I did it.

CORY: Why you wanna do that to me? That was the one chance I had.

ROSE: Ain't nothing wrong with Cory playing football, Troy.

TROY: The boy lied to me. I told the nigger if he wanna play football . . . to keep up his chores and hold down that job at the A&P. That was the conditions. Stopped down there to see Mr. Stawicki . . .

CORY: I can't work after school during the football season, Pop! I tried to tell you that Mr. Stawicki's holding my job for me. You don't never want to listen to nobody. And then you wanna go and do this to me!

TROY: I ain't done nothing to you. You done it to yourself.

CORY: Just cause you didn't have a chance! You just scared I'm gonna be better than you, that's all.

TROY: Come here.

ROSE: Troy . . .

[CORY *reluctantly crosses over to* TROY.]

TROY: Alright! See. You done made a mistake.

CORY: I didn't even do nothing!

TROY: I'm gonna tell you what your mistake was. See . . . you swung at the ball and didn't hit it. That's strike one. See, you in the batter's box now. You swung and you missed. That's strike one. Don't you strike out!

[*Lights fade to black.*]

ACT TWO
SCENE ONE

The following morning. CORY *is at the tree hitting the ball with the bat. He tries to mimic* TROY, *but his swing is awkward, less sure.* ROSE *enters from the house.*

ROSE: Cory, I want you to help me with this cupboard.

CORY: I ain't quitting the team. I don't care what Poppa say.

ROSE: I'll talk to him when he gets back. He had to go see about your Uncle Gabe. The police done arrested him. Say he was disturbing the peace. He'll be back directly. Come on in here and help me clean out the top of this cupboard. [CORY *exits into the house.* ROSE *sees* TROY *and* BONO *coming down the alley.*] Troy . . . what they say down there?

TROY: Ain't said nothing. I give them fifty dollars and they let him go. I'll talk to you about it. Where's Cory?

ROSE: He's in there helping me clean out these cupboards.

TROY: Tell him to get his butt out here.

[TROY *and* BONO *go over to the pile of wood.* BONO *picks up the saw and begins sawing.*]

TROY: [*To* BONO.] All they want is the money. That makes six or seven times I done went down there and got him. See me coming they stick out their *hands.*

BONO: Yeah. I know what you mean. That's all they care about . . . that money. They don't care about what's right. [*Pause.*] Nigger, why you got to go and get some hard wood? You ain't doing nothing but building a little old fence. Get you some soft pine wood. That's all you need.

TROY: I know what I'm doing. This is outside wood. You put pine wood inside the house. Pine wood is inside wood. This here is outside wood. Now you tell me where the fence is gonna be?

BONO: You don't need this wood. You can put it up with pine wood and it'll stand as long as you gonna be here looking at it.

TROY: How you know how long I'm gonna be here, nigger? Hell, I might just live forever. Live longer than old man Horsely.

BONO: That's what Magee used to say.

TROY: Magee's a damn fool. Now you tell me who you ever heard of gonna pull their own teeth with a pair of rusty pliers.

BONO: The old folks . . . my granddaddy used to pull his teeth with pliers. They ain't had no dentists for the colored folks back then.

TROY: Get clean pliers! You understand? Clean pliers! Sterilize them! Besides we ain't living back then. All Magee had to do was walk over to Doc Goldblums.

BONO: I see where you and that Tallahassee gal . . . that Alberta . . . I see where you all done got tight.

TROY: What you mean "got tight"?

BONO: I see where you be laughing and joking with her all the time.

TROY: I laughs and jokes with all of them, Bono. You know me.

BONO: That ain't the kind of laughing and joking I'm talking about.

[CORY *enters from the house.*]

CORY: How you doing, Mr. Bono?

TROY: Cory? Get that saw from Bono and cut some wood. He talking about the wood's too hard to cut. Stand back there, Jim, and let that young boy show you how it's done.

BONO: He's sure welcome to it. [CORY *takes the saw and begins to cut the wood.*] Whew-e-e! Look at that. Big old strong boy. Look like Joe Louis.[1] Hell, must be getting old the way I'm watching that boy whip through that wood.

CORY: I don't see why Mama want a fence around the yard noways.

TROY: Damn if I know either. What the hell she keeping out with it? She ain't got nothing nobody want.

BONO: Some people build fences to keep people out . . . and other people build fences to keep people in. Rose wants to hold on to you all. She loves you.

TROY: Hell, nigger, I don't need nobody to tell me my wife loves me, Cory . . . go on in the house and see if you can find that other saw.

CORY: Where's it at?

TROY: I said find it! Look for it till you find it! [CORY *exits into the house.*] What's that supposed to mean? Wanna keep us in?

BONO: Troy . . . I done known you seem like damn near my whole life. You and Rose both. I done know both of you all for a long time. I remember when you met Rose. When you was hitting them baseball out the park. A lot of them old gals was after you then. You had the pick of the litter. When you picked Rose, I was happy for you. That was the first time I knew you had any sense. I said . . . My man Troy knows what he's doing . . . I'm gonna follow this nigger . . . he might take me somewhere. I been following you too. I done learned a whole heap of things about life watching you. I done learned how to tell where the shit lies. How to tell it from the alfalfa. You done learned me a lot of things. You showed me how to not make the same mistakes . . . to take life as it comes along and keep putting one foot in front of the other. [*Pause.*] Rose a good woman, Troy.

TROY: Hell, nigger, I know she a good woman. I been married to her for eighteen years. What you got on your mind, Bono?

BONO: I just say she a good woman. Just like I say anything. I ain't got to have nothing on my mind.

TROY: You just gonna say she a good woman and leave it hanging out there like that? Why you telling me she a good woman?

BONO: She loves you, Troy. Rose loves you.

1. Boxer (1914–1981), heavyweight champion of the world from 1937 to 1949.

TROY: You saying I don't measure up. That's what you trying to say. I don't measure up cause I'm seeing this other gal. I know what you trying to say.

BONO: I know what Rose means to you, Troy. I'm just trying to say I don't want to see you mess up.

TROY: Yeah, I appreciate that, Bono. If you was messing around on Lucille I'd be telling you the same thing.

BONO: Well, that's all I got to say. I just say that because I love you both.

TROY: Hell, you know me. . . . I wasn't out there looking for nothing. You can't find a better woman than Rose. I know that. But seems like this woman just stuck onto me where I can't shake her loose. I done wrestled with it, tried to throw her off me . . . but she just stuck on tighter. Now she's stuck on for good.

BONO: You's in control . . . that's what you tell me all the time. You responsible for what you do.

TROY: I ain't ducking the responsibility of it. As long as it sets right in my heart . . . then I'm okay. 'Cause that's all I listen to. It'll tell me right from wrong every time. And I ain't talking about doing Rose no bad turn. I love Rose. She done carried me a long ways and I love and respect her for that.

BONO: I know you do. That's why I don't want to see you hurt her. But what you gonna do when she find out? What you got then? If you try and juggle both of them . . . sooner or later you gonna drop one of them. That's common sense.

TROY: Yeah, I hear what you saying, Bono. I been trying to figure a way to work it out.

BONO: Work it out right, Troy. I don't want to be getting all up between you and Rose's business . . . but work it so it come out right.

TROY: Aw hell, I get all up between you and Lucille's business. When you gonna get that woman that refrigerator she been wanting? Don't tell me you ain't got no money now. I know who your banker is. Mellon don't need that money bad as Lucille want that refrigerator. I'll tell you that.

BONO: Tell you what I'll do . . . when you finish building this fence for Rose . . . I'll buy Lucille that refrigerator.

TROY: You done stuck your foot in your mouth now! [TROY *grabs up a board and begins to saw.* BONO *starts to walk out the yard.*] Hey, nigger . . . where you going?

BONO: I'm going home. I know you don't expect me to help you now. I'm protecting my money. I wanna see you put that fence up by yourself. That's what I want to see. You'll be here another six months without me.

TROY: Nigger, you ain't right.

BONO: When it comes to my money . . . I'm right as fireworks on the Fourth of July.

TROY: Alright, we gonna see now. You better get out your bankbook.
[BONO *exits, and* TROY *continues to work.* ROSE *enters from the house.*]

ROSE: What they say down there? What's happening with Gabe?

TROY: I went down there and got him out. Cost me fifty dollars. Say he was disturbing the peace. Judge set up a hearing for him in three weeks. Say to show cause why he shouldn't be recommitted.

ROSE: What was he doing that cause them to arrest him?

TROY: Some kids was teasing him and he run them off home. Say he was howling and carrying on. Some folks seen him and called the police. That's all it was.

ROSE: Well, what's you say? What'd you tell the judge?

TROY: Told him I'd look after him. It didn't make no sense to recommit the man. He stuck out his big greasy palm and told me to give him fifty dollars and take him on home.

ROSE: Where's he at now? Where'd he go off to?

TROY: He's gone on about his business. He don't need nobody to hold his hand.

ROSE: Well, I don't know. Seem like that would be the best place for him if they did put him into the hospital. I know what you're gonna say. But that's what I think would be best.

TROY: The man done had his life ruined fighting for what? And they wanna take and lock him up. Let him be free. He don't bother nobody.

ROSE: Well, everybody got their own way of looking at it, I guess. Come on and get your lunch. I got a bowl of lima beans and some cornbread in the oven. Come on get something to eat. Ain't no sense you fretting over Gabe. [ROSE *turns to go into the house.*]

TROY: Rose . . . got something to tell you.

ROSE: Well, come on . . . wait till I get this food on the table.

TROY: Rose! [*She stops and turns around.*] I don't know how to say this. [*Pause.*] I can't explain it none. It just sort of grows on you till it gets out of hand. It starts out like a little bush . . . and the next think you know it's a whole forest.

ROSE: Troy . . . what is you talking about?

TROY: I'm talking, woman, let me talk. I'm trying to find a way to tell you . . . I'm gonna be a daddy. I'm gonna be somebody's daddy.

ROSE: Troy . . . you're not telling me this? You're gonna be . . . what?

TROY: Rose . . . now . . . see . . .

ROSE: You telling me you gonna be somebody's daddy? You telling your *wife* this?

[GABRIEL *enters from the street. He carries a rose in his hand.*]

GABRIEL: Hey, Troy! Hey, Rose!

ROSE: I have to wait eighteen years to hear something like this.

GABRIEL: Hey, Rose . . . I got a flower for you. [*He hands it to her.*] That's a rose. Same rose like you is.

ROSE: Thanks, Gabe.

GABRIEL: Troy, you ain't mad at me, is you? Them bad mens come and put me away. You ain't mad at me, is you?

TROY: Naw, Gabe, I ain't mad at you.

ROSE: Eighteen years and you wanna come with this.

GABRIEL: [*Takes a quarter out of his pocket.*] See what I got? Got a brand new quarter.

TROY: Rose . . . it's just . . .

ROSE: Ain't nothing you can say, Troy. Ain't no way of explaining that.

GABRIEL: Fellow that give me this quarter had a whole mess of them. I'm gonna keep this quarter till it stop shining.

ROSE: Gabe, go on in the house there. I got some watermelon in the frigidaire. Go on and get you a piece.

GABRIEL: Say, Rose . . . you know I was chasing hellhounds and them bad mens come and get me and take me away. Troy helped me. He come down there and told them they better let me go before he beat them up. Yeah, he did!

ROSE: You go on and get you a piece of watermelon, Gabe. Them bad mens is gone now.

GABRIEL: Okay, Rose . . . gonna get me some watermelon. The kind with the stripes on it. [GABRIEL *exits into the house.*]

ROSE: Why, Troy? Why? After all these years to come dragging this in to me now. It don't make no sense at your age. I could have expected this ten or fifteen years ago, but not now.

TROY: Age ain't got nothing to do with it, Rose.

ROSE: I done tried to be everything a wife should be. Everything a wife could be. Been married eighteen years and I got to live to see the day you tell me you been seeing another woman and done fathered a child by her. And you know I ain't never wanted no half nothing in my family. My whole family is half. Everybody got different fathers and mothers . . . my two sisters and my brother. Can't hardly tell who's who. Can't never sit down and talk about Papa and Mama. It's your papa and your mama and my papa and my mama . . .

TROY: Rose . . . stop it now.

ROSE: I ain't never wanted that for none of my children. And now you wanna drag your behind in here and tell me something like this.

TROY: You ought to know. It's time for you to know.

ROSE: Well, I don't want to know, goddamn it!

TROY: I can't just make it go away. It's done now. I can't wish the circumstance of the thing away.

ROSE: And you don't want to either. Maybe you want to wish me and my boy away. Maybe that's what you want? Well, you can't wish us away. I've got eighteen years of my life invested in you. You ought to have stayed upstairs in my bed where you belong.

TROY: Rose . . . now listen to me . . . we can get a handle on this thing. We can talk this out . . . come to an understanding.

ROSE: All of a sudden it's "we." Where was "we" at when you was down there rolling around with some godforsaken woman? "We" should have come to an understanding before you started making a damn fool of yourself. You're a day late and a dollar short when it comes to an understanding with me.

TROY: It's just . . . She gives me a different idea . . . a different understanding about myself. I can step out of this house and get away from the pressures and problems . . . be a different man. I ain't got to wonder how I'm gonna pay the bills or get the roof fixed. I can just be a part of myself that I ain't never been.

ROSE: What I want to know . . . is do you plan to continue seeing her. That's all you can say to me.

TROY: I can sit up in her house and laugh. Do you understand what I'm saying. I can laugh out loud . . . and it feels good. It reaches all the way down to the bottom of my shoes. [*Pause.*] Rose, I can't give that up.

ROSE: Maybe you ought to go on and stay down there with her . . . if she a better woman than me.

TROY: It ain't about nobody being a better woman or nothing. Rose, you ain't the blame. A man couldn't ask for no woman to be a better wife than you've been. I'm responsible for it. I done locked myself into a pattern trying to take care of you all that I forgot about myself.

ROSE: What the hell was I there for? That was my job, not somebody else's.

TROY: Rose, I done tried all my life to live decent . . . to live a clean . . . hard . . . useful life. I tried to be a good husband to you. In every way I knew how. Maybe I come into the world backwards, I don't know. But . . . you born with two strikes on you before you come to the plate. You got to guard it closely . . . always looking for the curve-ball on the inside corner. You can't afford to let none get past you. You can't afford a call strike. If you going down . . . you going down swinging. Everything lined up against you. What you gonna do. I fooled them, Rose. I bunted. When I found you and Cory and a halfway decent job . . . I was safe. Couldn't nothing touch me. I wasn't gonna strike out no more. I wasn't going back to the penitentiary. I wasn't gonna lay in the streets with a bottle of wine. I was safe. I had me a family. A job. I wasn't gonna get that last strike. I was on first looking for one of them boys to knock me in. To get me home.

ROSE: You should have stayed in my bed, Troy.

TROY: Then when I saw that gal . . . she firmed up my backbone. And I got to thinking that if I tried . . . I just might be able to steal second. Do you understand after eighteen years I wanted to steal second.

ROSE: You should have held me tight. You should have grabbed me and held on.

TROY: I stood on first base for eighteen years and I thought . . . well, goddamn it . . . go on for it!

ROSE: We're not talking about baseball! We're talking about you going off to lay in bed with another woman . . . and then bring it home to me. That's what we're talking about. We ain't talking about no baseball.

TROY: Rose, you're not listening to me. I'm trying the best I can to explain it to you. It's not easy for me to admit that I been standing in the same place for eighteen years.

ROSE: I been standing with you! I been right here with you, Troy. I got a life too. I gave eighteen years of my life to stand in the same spot with you. Don't you think I ever wanted other things? Don't you think I had dreams and hopes? What about my life? What about me. Don't you think it ever crossed my mind to want to know other men? That I wanted to lay up somewhere and forget about my responsibilities? That I wanted someone to make me laugh so I could feel good? You not the only one who's got wants and needs. But I held on to you, Troy. I took all my feelings, my wants and needs, my dreams . . . and I buried them inside you. I planted a seed and watched and prayed over it. I planted myself inside you and waited to bloom. And it didn't take me no eighteen years to find out the soil was hard and rocky and it wasn't never gonna bloom.

But I held on to you, Troy. I held you tighter. You was my husband. I owed you everything I had. Every part of me I could find to give you. And upstairs in that room . . . with the darkness falling in on me . . . I gave everything I had to try and erase the doubt that you wasn't the finest man in the world. And wherever you was going . . . I wanted to be there with you. 'Cause you was my husband. 'Cause that's the only way I was gonna survive as your wife. You always talking about what you give . . . and what you don't have to give. But you take too. You take . . . and don't even know nobody's giving!

[ROSE *turns to exit into the house;* TROY *grabs her arm.*]

TROY: You say I take and don't give!

ROSE: Troy! You're hurting me!

TROY: You say I take and don't give.

ROSE: Troy . . . you're hurting my arm! Let go!

TROY: I done give you everything I got. Don't you tell that lie on me.

ROSE: Troy!

TROY: Don't you tell that lie on me!

[CORY *enters from the house.*]

CORY: Mama!

ROSE: Troy. You're hurting me.

TROY: Don't you tell me about no taking and giving.

[CORY *comes up behind* TROY *and grabs him.* TROY, *surprised, is thrown off balance just as* CORY *throws a glancing blow that catches him on the chest and knocks him down.* TROY *is stunned, as is* CORY.]

ROSE: Troy. Troy. No! [TROY *gets to his feet and starts at* CORY.] Troy . . . no. Please! Troy! [ROSE *pulls on* TROY *to hold him back.* TROY *stops himself.*]

TROY: [*To* CORY] Alright. That's strike two. You stay away from around me, boy. Don't you strike out. You living with a full count. Don't you strike out. [TROY *exits out the yard as the lights go down.*]

Scene Two

It is six months later, early afternoon. TROY *enters from the house and starts to exit the yard.* ROSE *enters from the house.*

ROSE: Troy, I want to talk to you.

TROY: All of a sudden, after all this time, you want to talk to me, huh? You ain't wanted to talk to me for months. You ain't wanted to talk to me last night. You ain't wanted no part of me then. What you wanna talk to me about now?

ROSE: Tomorrow's Friday.

TROY: I know what day tomorrow is. You think I don't know tomorrow's Friday? My whole life I ain't done nothing but look to see Friday coming and you got to tell me it's Friday.

ROSE: I want to know if you're coming home.

TROY: I always come home, Rose. You know that. There ain't never been a night I ain't come home.

ROSE: That ain't what I mean . . . and you know it. I want to know if you're coming straight home after work.

TROY: I figure I'd cash my check . . . hang out at Taylors' with the boys . . . maybe play a game of checkers. . . .

ROSE: Troy, I can't live like this. I won't live like this. You livin' on borrowed time with me. It's been going on six months now you ain't been coming home.

TROY: I be here every night. Every night of the year. That's 365 days.

ROSE: I want you to come home tomorrow after work.

TROY: Rose . . . I don't mess up my pay. You know that now. I take my pay and I give it to you. I don't have no money but what you give me back. I just want to have a little time to myself . . . a little time to enjoy life.

ROSE: What about me? When's my time to enjoy life?

TROY: I don't know what to tell you, Rose. I'm doing the best I can.

ROSE: You ain't been home from work but time enough to change your clothes and run out . . . and you wanna call that the best you can do?

TROY: I'm going over to the hospital to see Alberta. She went into the hospital this afternoon. Look like she might have the baby early. I won't be gone long.

ROSE: Well, you ought to know. They went over to Miss Pearl's and got Gabe today. She said you told them to go ahead and lock him up.

TROY: I ain't said no such thing. Whoever told you that is telling a lie. Pearl ain't doing nothing but telling a big fat lie.

ROSE: She ain't had to tell me. I read it on the papers.

TROY: I ain't told them nothing of the kind.

ROSE: I saw it right there on the papers.

TROY: What it say, huh?

ROSE: It said you told them to take him.

TROY: Then they screwed that up, just the way they screw up everything. I ain't worried about what they got on the paper.

ROSE: Say the government send part of his check to the hospital and the other part to you.

TROY: I ain't got nothing to do with that if that's the way it works. I ain't made up the rules about how it work.

ROSE: You did Gabe just like you did Cory. You wouldn't sign the paper for Cory . . . but you signed for Gabe. You signed that paper.

[*The telephone is heard ringing inside the house.*]

TROY: I told you I ain't signed nothing, woman! The only thing I signed was the release form. Hell, I can't read, I don't know what they had on that paper! I ain't signed nothing about sending Gabe away.

ROSE: I said send him to the hospital . . . you said let him be free . . . now you done went down there and signed him to the hospital for half his money. You went back on yourself, Troy. You gonna have to answer for that.

TROY: See now . . . you been over there talking to Miss Pearl. She done got mad cause she ain't getting Gabe's rent money. That's all it is. She's liable to say anything.

ROSE: Troy, I seen where you signed the paper.

TROY: You ain't seen nothing I signed. What she doing got papers on my brother anyway? Miss Pearl telling a big fat lie. And I'm gonna tell her about it too! You ain't seen nothing I signed. Say . . . you ain't seen nothing I signed.

[ROSE *exits into the house to answer the telephone. Presently she returns.*]

ROSE: Troy . . . that was the hospital. Alberta had the baby.

TROY: What she have? What is it?

ROSE: It's a girl.

TROY: I better get on down to the hospital to see her.

ROSE: Troy . . .

TROY: Rose . . . I got to go see her now. That's only right . . . what's the matter . . . the baby's alright, ain't it?

ROSE: Alberta died having the baby.

TROY: Died . . . you say she's dead? Alberta's dead?

ROSE: They said they done all they could. They couldn't do nothing for her.

TROY: The baby? How's the baby?

ROSE: They say it's healthy. I wonder who's gonna bury her.

TROY: She had family, Rose. She wasn't living in the world by herself.

ROSE: I know she wasn't living in the world by herself.

TROY: Next thing you gonna want to know if she had any insurance.

ROSE: Troy, you ain't got to talk like that.

TROY: That's the first thing that jumped out your mouth. "Who's gonna bury her?" Like I'm fixing to take on that task for myself.

ROSE: I am your wife. Don't push me away.

TROY: I ain't pushing nobody away. Just give me some space. That's all. Just give me some room to breathe.

[ROSE *exits into the house.* TROY *walks about the yard.*]

TROY: [*With a quiet rage that threatens to consume him.*] Alright . . . Mr. Death. See now . . . I'm gonna tell you what I'm gonna do. I'm gonna take and build me a fence around this yard. See? I'm gonna build me a fence around what belongs to me. And then I want you to stay on the other side. See? You stay over there until you're ready for me. Then you come on. Bring your army. Bring your sickle. Bring your wrestling clothes. I ain't gonna fall down on my vigilance this time. You ain't gonna sneak up on me no more. When you ready for me . . . when the top of your list say Troy Maxson . . . that's when you come around here. You come up and knock on the front door. Ain't nobody else got nothing to do with this. This is between you and me. Man to man. You stay on the other side of that fence until you ready for me. Then you come up and knock on the front door. Anytime you want. I'll be ready for you.

[*The lights go down to black.*]

SCENE THREE

The lights come up on the porch. It is late evening three days later. ROSE *sits listening to the ball game waiting for* TROY. *The final out of the game is made and* ROSE *switches off the radio.* TROY *enters the yard carrying an infant wrapped in blankets. He stands back from the house and calls.*

[ROSE *enters and stands on the porch. There is a long, awkward silence, the weight of which grows heavier with each passing second.*]

TROY: Rose . . . I'm standing here with my daughter in my arms. She ain't but a wee bittie little old thing. She don't know nothing about grownups' business. She innocent . . . and she ain't got no mama.

ROSE: What you telling me for, Troy? [*She turns and exits into the house.*]

TROY: Well . . . I guess we'll just sit out here on the porch. [*He sits down on the porch. There is an awkward indelicateness about the way he handles the baby. His largeness engulfs and seems to swallow it. He speaks loud enough for* ROSE *to hear.*] A man's got to do what's right for him. I ain't sorry for nothing I done. It felt right in my heart.

[*To the baby.*] What you smiling at? Your daddy's a big man. Got these great big old hands. But sometimes he's scared. And right now your daddy's scared cause we sitting out here and ain't got no home. Oh, I been homeless before. I ain't had no little baby with me. But I been homeless. You just be out on the road by your lonesome and you see one of them trains coming and you just kinda go like this . . .

[*He sings as a lullaby.*] Please, Mr. Engineer let a man ride the line

Please, Mr. Engineer let a man ride the line

I ain't got no ticket please let me ride the blinds

[ROSE *enters from the house.* TROY, *hearing her steps behind him, stands and faces her.*]

She's my daughter, Rose. My own flesh and blood. I can't deny her no more than I can deny them boys. [*Pause.*] You and them boys is my family. You and them and this child is all I got in the world. So I guess what I'm saying is . . . I'd appreciate it if you'd help me take care of her.

ROSE: Okay, Troy . . . you're right. I'll take care of your baby for you . . . 'cause . . . like you say . . . she's innocent . . . and you can't visit the sins of the father upon the child. A motherless child has got a hard time. [*She takes the baby from him.*] From right now . . . this child got a mother. But you a womanless man.

[ROSE *turns and exits into the house with the baby. Lights go down to black.*]

SCENE FOUR

It is two months later. LYONS *enters from the street. He knocks on the door and calls.*

LYONS: Hey, Rose! [*Pause.*] Rose!

ROSE: [*From inside the house.*] Stop that yelling. You gonna wake up Raynell. I just got her to sleep.

LYONS: I just stopped by to pay Papa this twenty dollars I owe him. Where's Papa at?

ROSE: He should be here in a minute. I'm getting ready to go down to the church. Sit down and wait on him.

LYONS: I got to go pick up Bonnie over her mother's house.

ROSE: Well, sit it down there on the table. He'll get it.

LYONS: [*Enters the house and sets the money on the table.*] Tell Papa I said thanks. I'll see you again.

ROSE: Alright, Lyons. We'll see you.

[LYONS *starts to exit as* CORY *enters.*]

CORY: Hey, Lyons.

LYONS: What's happening, Cory. Say, man, I'm sorry I missed your graduation. You know I had a gig and couldn't get away. Otherwise, I would have been there, man. So what you doing?

CORY: I'm trying to find a job.

LYONS: Yeah I know how that go, man. It's rough out here. Jobs are scarce.

CORY: Yeah, I know.

LYONS: Look here, I got to run. Talk to Papa . . . he know some people. He'll be able to help get you a job. Talk to him . . . see what he say.

CORY: Yeah . . . alright, Lyons.

LYONS: You take care. I'll talk to you soon. We'll find some time to talk.

[LYONS *exits the yard.* CORY *wanders over to the tree, picks up the bat and assumes a batting stance. He studies an imaginary pitcher and swings. Dissatisfied with the result, he tries again.* TROY *enters. They eye each other for a beat.* CORY *puts the bat down and exits the yard.* TROY *starts into the house as* ROSE *exits with* RAYNELL. *She is carrying a cake.*]

TROY: I'm coming in and everybody's going out.

ROSE: I'm taking this cake down to the church for the bakesale. Lyons was by to see you. He stopped by to pay you your twenty dollars. It's laying in there on the table.

TROY: [*Going into his pocket.*] Well . . . here go this money.

ROSE: Put in there on the table, Troy. I'll get it.

TROY: What time you coming back?

ROSE: Ain't no use in you studying me. It don't matter what time I come back.

TROY: I just asked you a question, woman. What's the matter . . . can't I ask you a question?

ROSE: Troy, I don't want to go into it. Your dinner's in there on the stove. All you got to do is heat it up. And don't you be eating the rest of them cakes in there. I'm coming back for them. We having a bakesale at the church tomorrow.

[ROSE *exits the yard.* TROY *sits down on the steps, takes a pint bottle from his pocket, opens it and drinks. He begins to sing.*]

TROY: Hear it ring! Hear it ring!

Had an old dog his name was Blue
You know Blue was mighty true
You know Blue as a good old dog
Blue trees a possum in a hollow log
You know from that he was a good old dog

[BONO *enters the yard.*]

BONO: Hey, Troy.

TROY: Hey, what's happening, Bono?

BONO: I just thought I'd stop by to see you.

TROY: What you stop by and see me for? You ain't stopped by in a month of Sundays. Hell, I must owe you money or something.

BONO: Since you got your promotion I can't keep up with you. Used to see you everyday. Now I don't even know what route you working.

TROY: They keep switching me around. Got me out in Greentree now . . . hauling white folks' garbage.

BONO: Greentree, huh? You lucky, at least you ain't got to be lifting them barrels. Damn if they ain't getting heavier. I'm gonna put in my two years and call it quits.

TROY: I'm thinking about retiring myself.

BONO: You got it easy. You can *drive* for another five years.

TROY: It ain't the same, Bono. It ain't like working the back of the truck. Ain't got nobody to talk to . . . feel like you working by yourself. Naw, I'm thinking about retiring. How's Lucille?

BONO: She alright. Her arthritis get to acting up on her sometime. Saw Rose on my way in. She going down to the church, huh?

TROY: Yeah, she took up going down there. All them preachers looking for somebody to fatten their pockets. [*Pause.*] Got some gin here.

BONO: Naw, thanks. I just stopped by to say hello.

TROY: Hell, nigger . . . you can take a drink. I ain't never known you to say no to a drink. You ain't got to work tomorrow.

BONO: I just stopped by. I'm fixing to go over to Skinner's. We got us a domino game going over his house every Friday.

TROY: Nigger, you can't play no dominoes. I used to whup you four games out of five.

BONO: Well, that learned me. I'm getting better.

TROY: Yeah? Well, that's alright.

BONO: Look here . . . I got to be getting on. Stop by sometime, huh?

TROY: Yeah, I'll do that, Bono. Lucille told Rose you bought her a new refrigerator.

BONO: Yeah, Rose told Lucille you had finally built your fence . . . so I figured we'd call it even.

TROY: I knew you would.

BONO: Yeah . . . okay. I'll be talking to you.

TROY: Yeah, take care, Bono. Good to see you. I'm gonna stop over.

BONO: Yeah. Okay, Troy. [BONO *exits.* TROY *drinks from the bottle.*]

TROY: Old Blue died and I dig his grave
Let him down with a golden chain
Every night when I hear old Blue bark
I know Blue treed a possum in Noah's Ark.
Hear it ring! Hear it ring!
[CORY *enters the yard. They eye each other for a beat.* TROY *is sitting in the middle of the steps.* CORY *walks over.*]

CORY: I got to get by.

TROY: Say what? What's you say?

CORY: You in my way. I got to get by.

TROY: You got to get by where? This is my house. Bought and paid for. In full. Took me fifteen years. And if you wanna go in my house and I'm sitting on the steps . . . you say excuse me. Like your mama taught you.

CORY: Come on, Pop . . . I got to get by.

[CORY *starts to maneuver his way past* TROY. TROY *grabs his leg and shoves him back.*]

TROY: You just gonna walk over top of me?

CORY: I live here too!

TROY: [*Advancing toward him.*] You just gonna walk over top of me in my own house?

CORY: I ain't scared of you.

TROY: I ain't asked if you was scared of me. I asked you if you was fixing to walk over top of me in my own house? That's the question. You ain't gonna say excuse me? You just gonna walk over top of me?

CORY: If you wanna put it like that.

TROY: How else am I gonna put it?

CORY: I was walking by you to go into the house cause you sitting on the steps drunk, singing to yourself. You can put it like that.

TROY: Without saying excuse me??? [CORY *doesn't respond.*] I asked you a question. Without saying excuse me???

CORY: I ain't got to say excuse me to you. You don't count around here no more.

TROY: Oh, I see, . . . I don't count around here no more. You ain't got to say excuse me to your daddy. All of a sudden you done got so grown that your daddy don't count around here no more. . . . Around here in his own house and yard that he done paid for with the sweat of his brow. You done got so grown to where you gonna take over. You gonna take over my house. Is that right? You gonna wear my pants. You gonna go in there and stretch out on my bed. You ain't got to say excuse me cause I don't count around here no more. Is that right?

CORY: That's right. You always talking this dumb stuff. Now, why don't you just get out my way.

TROY: I guess you got someplace to sleep and something to put in your belly. You got that, huh? You got that? That's what you need. You got that, huh?

CORY: You don't know what I got. You ain't got to worry about what I got.

TROY: You right! You one hundred percent right! I done spent the last seventeen years worrying about what you got. Now it's your turn, see? I'll tell you what to do. You grown . . . we done established that. You a man. Now, let's see you act like one. Turn your behind around and walk out this yard. And when you get out there in the alley . . . you can forget about this house. See? 'Cause this is my house. You go on and be a man and get your own house. You can forget about this. 'Cause this is mine. You go on and get yours 'cause I'm through with doing for you.

CORY: You talking about what you did for me . . . what'd you ever give me?

TROY: Them feet and bones! That pumping heart, nigger! I give you more than anybody else is ever gonna give you.

CORY: You ain't never gave me nothing! You ain't never done nothing but hold me back. Afraid I was gonna be better than you. All you ever did was try and make me scared of you. I used to tremble every time you called my name. Every time I heard your footsteps in the house. Wondering all the time . . . what's Papa gonna say if I do this? . . . What's he gonna say if I do that? . . . What's Papa gonna say if I turn on the radio? And Mama, too . . . she tries . . . but she's scared of you.

TROY: You leave your mama out of this. She ain't got nothing to do with this.

CORY: I don't know how she stand you . . . after what you did to her.

TROY: I told you to leave your mama out of this! [*He advances toward* CORY.]

CORY: What you gonna do . . . give me a whupping? You can't whup me no more. You're too old. You just an old man.

TROY: [*Shoves him on his shoulder.*] Nigger! That's what you are. You just another nigger on the street to me!

CORY: You crazy! You know that?

TROY: Go on now! You got the devil in you. Get on away from me!

CORY: You just a crazy old man . . . talking about I got the devil in me.

TROY: Yeah, I'm crazy! If you don't get on the other side of that yard . . . I'm gonna show you how crazy I am! Go on . . . get the hell out of my yard.

CORY: It ain't your yard. You took Uncle Gabe's money he got from the army to buy this house and then you put him out.

TROY: [TROY *advances on* CORY.] Get your black ass out of my yard!
[TROY's *advance backs* CORY *up against the tree.* CORY *grabs up the bat.*]

CORY: I ain't going nowhere! Come on . . . put me out! I ain't scared of you.

TROY: That's my bat!

CORY: Come on!

TROY: Put my bat down!

CORY: Come on, put me out. [CORY *swings at* TROY, *who backs across the yard.*] What's the matter? You so bad . . . put me out!
[TROY *advances toward* CORY.]

CORY: [*Backing up.*] Come on! Come on!

TROY: You're gonna have to use it! You wanna draw that bat back on me . . . you're gonna have to use it.

CORY: Come on! . . . Come on!
[CORY *swings the bat at* TROY *a second time. He misses.* TROY *continues to advance toward him.*]

TROY: You're gonna have to kill me! You wanna draw that bat back on me. You're gonna have to kill me.
[CORY, *backed up against the tree, can go no farther.* TROY *taunts him. He sticks out his head and offers him a target.*]
Come on! Come on!
[CORY *is unable to swing the bat.* TROY *grabs it.*]

TROY: Then I'll show you.
[CORY *and* TROY *struggle over the bat. The struggle is fierce and fully engaged.* TROY *ultimately is the stronger, and takes the bat from* CORY *and stands over him ready to swing. He stops himself.*]
Go on and get away from around my house.
[CORY, *stung by his defeat, picks himself up, walks slowly out of the yard and up the alley.*]

CORY: Tell Mama I'll be back for my things.

TROY: They'll be on the other side of that fence.
[CORY *exits.*]

TROY: I can't taste nothing. Helluljah! I can't taste nothing no more.
[TROY *assumes a batting posture and begins to taunt Death, the fastball in the outside corner.*] Come on! It's between you and me

now! Come on! Anytime you want! Come on! I be ready for you
. . . but I ain't gonna be easy.
  [*The lights go down on the scene.*]

SCENE FIVE

  The time is 1965. The lights come up in the yard. It is the morning of
TROY's *funeral. A funeral plaque with a light hangs beside the door. There
is a small garden plot off to the side. There is noise and activity in the
house as* ROSE, GABRIEL *and* BONO *have gathered. The door opens and*
RAYNELL, *seven years old, enters dressed in a flannel nightgown. She crosses
to the garden and pokes around with a stick.* ROSE *calls from the house.*

ROSE: Raynell!
RAYNELL: Mam?
ROSE: What you doing out there?
RAYNELL: Nothing.
  [ROSE *comes to the door.*]
ROSE: Girl, get in here and get dressed. What you doing?
RAYNELL: Seeing if my garden growed.
ROSE: I told you it ain't gonna grow overnight. You got to wait.
RAYNELL: It don't look like it never gonna grow. Dag!
ROSE: I told you a watched pot never boils. Get in here and get
  dressed.
RAYNELL: This ain't even no pot, Mama.
ROSE: You just have to give it a chance. It'll grow. Now you come on
  and do what I told you. We got to be getting ready. This ain't no
  morning to be playing around. You hear me?
RAYNELL: Yes, mam.
  [ROSE *exits into the house.* RAYNELL *continues to poke at her gar-
  den with a stick.* CORY *enters. He is dressed in a Marine corporal's
  uniform, and carries a duffel bag. His posture is that of a military
  man, and his speech has a clipped sternness.*]
CORY: [*To* RAYNELL.] Hi. [*Pause.*] I bet your name is Raynell.
RAYNELL: Uh huh.
CORY: Is your mama home?
  [RAYNELL *runs up on the porch and calls through the screendoor.*]
RAYNELL: Mama . . . there's some man out here. Mama?

[ROSE *comes to the door.*]

ROSE: Cory? Lord have mercy! Look here, you all!

[ROSE *and* CORY *embrace in a tearful reunion as* BONO *and* LYONS *enter from the house dressed in funeral clothes.*]

BONO: Aw, looka here . . .

ROSE: Done got all grown up!

CORY: Don't cry, Mama. What you crying about?

ROSE: I'm just so glad you made it.

CORY: Hey, Lyons. How you doing, Mr. Bono.

[LYONS *goes to embrace* CORY.]

LYONS: Look at you, man. Look at you. Don't he look good, Rose. Got them Corporal stripes.

ROSE: What took you so long.

CORY: You know how the Marines are, Mama. They got to get all their paperwork straight before they let you do anything.

ROSE: Well, I'm sure glad you made it. They let Lyons come. Your Uncle Gabe's still in the hospital. They don't know if they gonna let him out or not. I just talked to them a little while ago.

LYONS: A Corporal in the United States Marines.

BONO: Your daddy knew you had it in you. He used to tell me all the time.

LYONS: Don't he look good, Mr. Bono?

BONO: Yeah, he remind me of Troy when I first met him. [*Pause.*] Say, Rose, Lucille's down at the church with the choir. I'm gonna go down and get the pallbearers lined up. I'll be back to get you all.

ROSE: Thanks, Jim.

CORY: See you, Mr. Bono.

LYONS: [*With his arm around* RAYNELL.] Cory . . . look at Raynell. Ain't she precious? She gonna break a whole lot of hearts.

ROSE: Raynell, come and say hello to your brother. This is your brother, Cory. You remember Cory.

RAYNELL: No, Mam.

CORY: She don't remember me, Mama.

ROSE: Well, we talk about you. She heard us talk about you. [*To* RAYNELL.] This is your brother, Cory. Come on and say hello.

RAYNELL: Hi.

CORY: Hi. So you're Raynell. Mama told me a lot about you.

ROSE: You all come on into the house and let me fix you some breakfast. Keep up your strength.

CORY: I ain't hungry, Mama.

LYONS: You can fix me something, Rose. I'll be in there in a minute.

ROSE: Cory, you sure you don't want nothing. I know they ain't feeding you right.

CORY: No, Mama . . . thanks. I don't feel like eating. I'll get something later.

ROSE: Raynell . . . get on upstairs and get that dress on like I told you.

[ROSE *and* RAYNELL *exit into the house.*]

LYONS: So . . . I hear you thinking about getting married.

CORY: Yeah, I done found the right one, Lyons. It's about time.

LYONS: Me and Bonnie been split up about four years now. About the time Papa retired. I guess she just got tired of all them changes I was putting her through. [*Pause.*] I always knew you was gonna make something out yourself. Your head was always in the right direction. So . . . you gonna stay in . . . make it a career . . . put in your twenty years?

CORY: I don't know. I got six already, I think that's enough.

LYONS: Stick with Uncle Sam and retire early. Ain't nothing out here. I guess Rose told you what happened with me. They got me down the workhouse. I thought I was being slick cashing other people's checks.

CORY: How much time you doing?

LYONS: They give me three years. I got that beat now. I ain't got but nine more months. It ain't so bad. You learn to deal with it like anything else. You got to take the crookeds with the straights. That's what Papa used to say. He used to say that when he struck out. I seen him strike out three times in a row . . . and the next time up he hit the ball over the grandstand. Right out there in Homestead Field. He wasn't satisfied hitting in the seats . . . he want to hit it over everything! After the game he had two hundred people standing around waiting to shake his hand. You got to take the crookeds with the straights. Yeah, Papa was something else.

CORY: You still playing?

LYONS: Cory . . . you know I'm gonna do that. There's some fellows down there we got us a band . . . we gonna try and stay together when we get out . . . but yeah, I'm still playing. It still helps me to get out of bed in the morning. As long as it do that I'm gonna be right there playing and trying to make some sense out of it.

ROSE: [*Calling.*] Lyons, I got these eggs in the pan.

LYONS: Let me go on and get these eggs, man. Get ready to go bury Papa. [*Pause.*] How you doing? You doing alright?

[CORY *nods.* LYONS *touches him on the shoulder and they share a moment of silent grief.* LYONS *exits into the house.* CORY *wanders about the yard.* RAYNELL *enters.*]

RAYNELL: Hi.

CORY: Hi.

RAYNELL: Did you used to sleep in my room?

CORY: Yeah . . . that used to be my room.

RAYNELL: That's what Papa call it. "Cory's room." It got your football in the closet.

[ROSE *comes to the door.*]

ROSE: Raynell, get in there and get them good shoes on.

RAYNELL: Mama, can't I wear these. Them other one hurt my feet.

ROSE: Well, they just gonna have to hurt your feet for a while. You ain't said they hurt your feet when you went down to the store and got them.

RAYNELL: They didn't hurt then. My feet done got bigger.

ROSE: Don't you give me no backtalk now. You get in there and get them shoes on. [RAYNELL *exits into the house.*] Ain't too much changed. He still got that piece of rag tied to that tree. He was out here swinging that bat. I was just ready to go back in the house. He swung that bat and then he just fell over. Seem like he swung it and stood there with this grin on his face . . . and then he just fell over. They carried him on down to the hospital, but I knew there wasn't no need . . . why don't you come on in the house?

CORY: Mama . . . I got something to tell you. I don't know how to tell you this . . . but I've got to tell you . . . I'm not going to Papa's funeral.

ROSE: Boy, hush your mouth. That's your daddy you talking about. I don't want hear that kind of talk this morning. I done raised you to come to this? You standing there all healthy and grown talking about you ain't going to your daddy's funeral?

CORY: Mama . . . listen . . .

ROSE: I don't want to hear it, Cory. You just get that thought out of your head.

CORY: I can't drag Papa with me everywhere I go. I've got to say no to him. One time in my life I've got to say no.

ROSE: Don't nobody have to listen to nothing like that. I know you and your daddy ain't seen eye to eye, but I ain't got to listen to that kind of talk this morning. Whatever was between you and your daddy . . . the time has come to put it aside. Just take it and set it over there on the shelf and forget about it. Disrespecting your daddy ain't gonna make you a man, Cory. You got to find a way to come to that on your own. Not going to your daddy's funeral ain't gonna make you a man.

CORY: The whole time I was growing up . . . living in his house . . . Papa was like a shadow that followed you everywhere. It weighed on you and sunk into your flesh. It would wrap around you and lay there until you couldn't tell which one was you anymore. That shadow digging in your flesh. Trying to crawl in. Trying to live through you. Everywhere I looked, Troy Maxson was staring back at me . . . hiding under the bed . . . in the closet. I'm just saying I've got to find a way to get rid of that shadow, Mama.

ROSE: You just like him. You got him in you good.

CORY: Don't tell me that, Mama.

ROSE: You Troy Maxson all over again.

CORY: I don't want to be Troy Maxson. I want to be me.

ROSE: You can't be nobody but who you are, Cory. That shadow wasn't nothing but you growing into yourself. You either got to grow into it or cut it down to fit you. But that's all you got to make life with. That's all you got to measure yourself against that world out there. Your daddy wanted you to be everything he wasn't . . . and at the same time he tried to make you into everything he was. I don't know if he was right or wrong . . . but I do know he meant to do more good than he meant to do harm. He wasn't always right. Sometimes when he touched he bruised. And sometimes when he took me in his arms he cut.

When I first met your daddy I thought . . . Here is a man I can lay down with and make a baby. That's the first thing I thought when I seen him. I was thirty years old and had done seen my share of men. But when he walked up to me and said, "I can dance a waltz that'll make you dizzy," I thought, Rose Lee, here is a man that you can open yourself up to and be filled to bursting. Here is a man that can fill all them empty spaces you been tipping around the edges of. One of them empty spaces was being somebody's mother.

I married your daddy and settled down to cooking his supper and keeping clean sheets on the bed. When your daddy walked through the house he was so big he filled it up. That was my first mistake. Not to make him leave some room for me. For my part in the matter. But at that time I wanted that. I wanted a house that I could sing in. And that's what your daddy gave me. I didn't know to keep up his strength. I had to give up little pieces of mine. I did that. I took on his life as mine and mixed up the pieces so that you couldn't hardly tell which was which anymore. It was my choice. It was my life and I didn't have to live it like that. But that's what life offered me in the way of being a woman and I took it. I grabbed hold of it with both hands.

By the time Raynell came into the house, me and your daddy had done lost touch with one another. I didn't want to make my blessing off of nobody's misfortune . . . but I took on to Raynell like she was all them babies I had wanted and never had. [*The phone rings.*] Like I'd been blessed to relive a part of my life. And if the Lord see fit to keep up my strength . . . I'm gonna do her just like your daddy did you . . . I'm gonna give her the best of what's in me.

RAYNELL: [*Entering, still with her old shoes.*] Mama . . . Reverend Tollivier on the phone.

[ROSE *exits into the house.*]

RAYNELL: Hi.

CORY: Hi.

RAYNELL: You in the Army or the Marines?

CORY: Marines.

RAYNELL: Papa said it was the Army. Did you know Blue?

CORY: Blue? Who's Blue?

RAYNELL: Papa's dog what he sing about all the time.

CORY: [*Singing.*] Hear it ring! Hear it ring!

I had a dog his name was Blue

You know Blue was mighty true
You know Blue was a good old dog
Blue treed a possum in a hollow log
You know from that he was a good old dog.
Hear it ring! Hear it ring!
[RAYNELL *joins in singing.*]

CORY and RAYNELL: Blue treed a possum out on a limb
Blue looked at me and I looked at him
Grabbed that possum and put him in a sack
Blue stayed there till I came back
Old Blue's feets was big and round
Never allowed a possum to touch the ground.

Old Blue died and I dug his grave
I dug his grave with a silver spade
Let him down with a golden chain
And every night I call his name
Go on Blue, you good dog you
Go on Blue, you good dog you

RAYNELL: Blue laid down and died like a man
Blue laid down and died . . .

BOTH: Blue laid down and died like a man
Now he's treeing possums in the Promised Land
I'm gonna tell you this to let you know
Blue's gone where the good dogs go
When I hear old Blue bark
When I hear old Blue bark
Blue treed a possum in Noah's Ark
Blue treed a possum in Noah's Ark.
[ROSE *comes to the screen door.*]

ROSE: Cory, we gonna be ready to go in a minute.

CORY: [*To* RAYNELL.] You go on in the house and change them shoes
like Mama told you so we can go to Papa's funeral.

RAYNELL: Okay, I'll be back.
[RAYNELL *exits into the house.* CORY *gets up and crosses over to the
tree.* ROSE *stands in the screen door watching him.* GABRIEL *enters
from the alley.*]

GABRIEL: [*Calling.*] Hey, Rose!

ROSE: Gabe?

GABRIEL: I'm here, Rose. Hey, Rose, I'm here!

[ROSE *enters from the house.*]

ROSE: Lord . . . Look here, Lyons!

LYONS: See, I told you, Rose . . . I told you they'd let him come.

CORY: How you doing, Uncle Gabe?

LYONS: How you doing, Uncle Gabe?

GABRIEL: Hey, Rose. It's time. It's time to tell St. Peter to open the gates. Troy, you ready? You ready, Troy. I'm gonna tell St. Peter to open the gates. You get ready now. [GABRIEL, *with great fanfare, braces himself to blow. The trumpet is without a mouthpiece. He puts the end of it into his mouth and blows with great force, like a man who has been waiting some twenty-odd years for this single moment. No sound comes out of the trumpet. He braces himself and blows again with the same result. A third time he blows. There is a weight of impossible description that falls away and leaves him bare and exposed to a frightful realization. It is a trauma that a sane and normal mind would be unable to withstand. He begins to dance. A slow, strange dance, eerie and lifegiving. A dance of atavistic signature and ritual.* LYONS *attempts to embrace him.* GABRIEL *pushes* LYONS *away. He begins to howl in what is an attempt at song, or perhaps a song turning back into itself in an attempt at speech. He finishes his dance and the gates of heaven stand open as wide as God's closet.*] That's the way that go!

[*Blackout.*]

1983   1986

Biographical Sketches

Susan Glaspell *(1882–1948)* Glaspell was born in Davenport, Iowa, earned a bachelor's degree in philosophy from Drake University, and started her writing career as a reporter in Des Moines. After a few years, including a period in graduate school at the University of Chicago, she returned to Davenport and wrote short stories for magazines. In 1913, she and George Cook, a writer from a prominent Davenport family, relocated to New York City's Greenwich Village, where they married and became vital figures in the literary, bohemian scene. Each summer they vacationed in Provincetown, Massachusetts, and there, in 1915, they founded the Provincetown Players. A semiprofessional group distinguished by its association with radicals such as the journalist and communist John Reed and the poet Edna St. Vincent Millay, this company launched not only Glaspell's career as a playwright but also Eugene O'Neill's, and it enjoyed success in Greenwich Village. Glaspell and Cook had been living in Greece for two years when Cook died in 1924. Glaspell returned to America, where she wrote mostly fiction and a memoir of Cook's life. She died of cancer in Provincetown.

Lorraine Hansberry *(1930–1965)* Hansberry grew up in Chicago, the daughter of politically active, middle-class African Americans. The household was vibrant, and among the visitors the young Hansberry met were the singer Paul Robeson, the musician Duke Ellington, and the athletes Jesse Owens and Joe Louis. The family had a tradition of attending Howard University, but Hansberry chose to enroll in the University of Wisconsin, though she did not stay long enough to graduate. She moved to New York and began writing for Robeson's newspaper, *Freedom*. She did carry on the family tradition of fighting against the racism in American life and law. In 1952, she stood in for Robeson at the Intercontinental Peace Conference in Montevideo, Chile. Robeson could not attend because the State Department had refused to issue him a passport, and Hansberry's trip was undertaken in a surreptitious manner. After a couple of fitful starts, she wrote *A Raisin in the Sun* in 1957 and read it to her husband's friend, Philip Rose, who so liked it that he immediately embarked on a campaign to get it on Broadway, which he succeeded in doing by 1959. The play was a smash hit, winning the New York Drama Critics Circle Award and running for hundreds of performances. Columbia Pictures made it into a movie, and Hansberry enjoyed instant celebrity as one of the more prominent African American intellectuals. She continued writing plays and worked actively for the Student Nonviolent Coordinating Committee, even after she was diagnosed with cancer in 1963. Within two years she was dead at the age of thirty-four.

Henrik Ibsen (*1828–1906*)   Ibsen was born to a well-to-do family in a lumber town south of Christiana (later called Oslo), Norway. His father's business crashed when Ibsen was six, and the family experienced the humiliations that follow a financial reversal. At fifteen, Ibsen was apprenticed to a druggist; he went to Christiana six years later and, failing to enter the university there, eventually found work in the theater, as an assistant stage manager in Bergen. Here he wrote the plays of his first "period," romantic, mythological works celebrating Norway's national independence. Frustrated and poor, Ibsen left Norway at thirty-six, partly subsidized by government grants, for the warmer climates of Italy and Germany, where he lived for the next three decades. The production of the *League of Youth* in 1869 began the second of Ibsen's periods, this one of realistic drama exemplified by *A Doll House*, which he wrote in 1879. His plays during these twelve or so years revolutionized the European stage, and on the strength of this achievement Ibsen is often called the father of modern theater. During his third period, Ibsen's work remained realistic but made increasing use of symbol and metaphor, and it was preoccupied with the place of the artist in the world. He died after a series of strokes that made him an invalid for his final years, which he spent in Norway.

Arthur Miller *(1915–2005)* Miller's family lived in Manhattan until the Great Depression reversed their fortunes, and they moved to Brooklyn. There Miller graduated from high school, where he excelled more as an athlete than as a student. His grades were good enough for college, but it took him three years of odd jobs before he got accepted to the University of Michigan, where he began writing plays. By the late 1930s, he was writing for radio shows; his first Broadway play, a failure, premiered in 1944. He wrote a successful novel and then the Ibsen-esque play *All My Sons* in 1947, which beat out a play by Eugene O'Neill for the New York Drama Critics Circle Award. In a six-week burst of creativity, he wrote *Death of a Salesman*, abandoning the strict conventions of realism he had used earlier and experimenting with stage design, lighting, music, and the like. The play was an instant success, running for more than two years on Broadway, inspiring a film, and becoming a favorite of local repertoire theaters across the nation. It also won the Pulitzer Prize. Most notable among Miller's subsequent work was *The Crucible* (1953), a play about the Salem witch hunts that allegorizes Senator Joseph McCarthy's persecution of American communists. Miller himself was persecuted by the Catholic War Veterans and the Committee on Un-American Activities, which brought him before Congress to testify about his involvement with communists. He refused to name other writers who had links to the communists and was convicted of contempt of Congress, though the conviction was overturned on appeal. In 1956, Miller married Marilyn Monroe and wrote a film, *The Misfits*, with her in a leading role, but they divorced in 1961. He continued writing plays into the 1990s and lived on a farm in Connecticut until his death from heart failure in 2005.

William Shakespeare *(1564–1616)* Shakespeare was born into an upwardly mobile family in the country town of Stratford-on-Avon, England. His father, the son of a tenant farmer, became a leatherworker, a small businessman, and eventually the mayor of Stratford. His mother came from a fairly prosperous farming family. The Shakespeares' oldest son, William probably went to grammar school, where he would have learned rhetoric and read at least some of the Roman playwrights, but not studied the wider field of classical authors that a university man would have read. At eighteen, he married Anne Hathaway, who was twenty-six and apparently pregnant. They had three children. Shakespeare might have taught school for awhile, but no one knows what he did in the years before history finds him, in 1592, away from his family, living in London, acting, writing plays, and perhaps managing a theater company. During the next twenty-five years, he wrote thirty-eight plays, becoming the unrivaled king of London theater, growing richer every year (in fact, multiplying his fortune many times over), buying property and fine houses back in Stratford and a coat of arms for his family. In 1599, he bought a ten-percent share in the Globe, a new theater on the south bank of the River Thames. He quit the theater in his late forties and retired to the relative quiet and beauty of Stratford, where he died (legend has it) on his birthday, April 23.

Sophocles (*496?–406? B.C.E.*)   Sophocles was born to a wealthy family in a small town outside Athens, Greece, the age's most industrious and intellectual metropolis. Legend holds that he was handsome and a talented public singer. Famous for his companionability, Sophocles held a number of public positions—civic, military, and religious—through his long life. Athens was at the peak of its power and of its culture, and the finest ornaments of that culture were the plays staged in celebration of the annual Dionysian festivals. The playwright Aeschylus had raised the original choral songs and dances to the height of drama, but Sophocles became the master of the Greek stage when, at twenty-eight, he beat Aeschylus in the annual dramatic competition. Over the course of his career he wrote 125 tragedies, including the ever-popular *Antigone*, never finishing worse than second place in the competitions. Only seven plays have survived antiquity, and these all come from the third and most mature period in Sophocles' career, spanning the second fifty years of his life. His last play, *Oedipus at Colonus*, a sequel to *Oedipus the King*, was first performed five years after Sophocles' death.

Oscar Wilde (*1854–1900*)   Wilde was born to a distinguished family in Dublin, Ireland, where he excelled as a student, eventually winning a scholarship to Oxford's Magdalen College. He won numerous prizes at Oxford for his academic work and his poetry. Upon graduation, he began the uncertain life of a man of letters, highlights of which included a successful lecture tour in America in 1882, children's books, works of literary and social criticism, a novel (*The Picture of Dorian Gray*), and editorship of *Women's World* magazine. He achieved his greatest literary success with a rapid succession of comic plays, beginning with *Lady Windermere's Fan* in 1892 and ending with *The Importance of Being Earnest* three years later. During these years, Wilde made himself into a cultural icon, emblemizing in his own person the iconoclastic, droll, disaffected ethos of the late-Victorian esthete. He married in 1884 and had two children, but he never hid his homosexual relationships and by the early 1890s was involved with Lord Alfred Douglas, the son of a prominent English aristocrat. In 1895, he was convicted of homosexuality, and sentenced to two years of hard labor. His wife and children moved to Switzerland in disgrace, and his experience in Reading Gaol broke Wilde's health. Released from jail, bankrupt, he wandered from one cheap European hotel to another. He died of meningitis in Paris.

August Wilson (*1945–2005*)   Wilson was born Frederick August Kittel in "The Hill," the African American community in Pittsburgh, Pennsylvania. His father, a white man, abandoned the family when Wilson was young, and his mother, a black woman whose surname was Wilson, remarried and eventually moved the family to Hazelwood, a predominately white neighborhood. A teacher's racially motivated accusation of plagiarism led Wilson to leave his Catholic high school, and he largely continued his education on his own. In his twenties, Wilson began writing poetry and founded a theater company, Black Horizons, dedicated to voicing the black experience in America and inspiring audiences to political action. In 1978, he moved to St. Paul, Minnesota, where he wrote, among other things, dramatic pieces for the Science Museum. In 1982, his full-length play *Ma Rainey's Black Bottom* was read at the National Playwrights Conference at the O'Neill Theater Center, in Waterford, Connecticut; a production at Yale University went to Broadway two years later. Wilson's first national success began his series of historical plays, each set in a different decade of the twentieth century. *Fences* was read at the O'Neill Theater Center in 1983, and by 1987 it was on Broadway, breaking box-office records for nonmusical dramas. The play also won the New York Drama Critics Circle Award and the Pulitzer Prize, as well as numerous Tony Awards. *Joe Turner's Come and Gone*, *The Piano Lesson*, and subsequent plays in the series enjoyed critical and commercial success.

*

Glossary

antagonist   the character against whom the protagonist struggles; for example, Helmer is the antagonist in *A Doll House.*

atmosphere   the emotional effect or mood produced in an audience, especially by the physical spectacle and the sound of a scene or play: the set, the music, etc.; for example, the atmosphere of *Death of a Salesman* should be claustrophobic or confining.

catharsis   a special effect of tragedy in which the emotions of pity and terror are purged from an audience; according to Aristotle, catharsis accounts for viewers' pleasure in viewing the troubling events of tragedy on stage.

character   most generally, any person represented in a play by an actor; more narrowly, the personality of such a person; Aristotle used the term to refer to the moral temperament of a person.

chorus   a conventional element of ancient-Greek drama, consisting of a group of singers and dancers who participate in or comment on the action; Sophocles used the chorus to represent crowds, such as the citizens of Thebes in *Oedipus the King,* and to voice what might be considered mainstream attitudes toward the characters' interactions.

climax the moment within a plot in which the conflict ends; often (though not necessarily), the emotional high point of the drama.

comedy a subgenre of drama that generally celebrates the human condition; usually, a comedy is funny.

complication an event that sets a conflict in motion; for example, in *Hamlet*, the arrival of the ghost is the complication, because he spurs Hamlet to enmity with Claudius.

conflict the opposition of two people or forces; without this crucial element of plot, there could be no play; for example, in *A Doll House*, Nora, the protagonist, struggles against social conventions and laws, against Helmer, and against her own internalized patterns of behavior.

conventional symbol a thing carrying symbolic meaning only within the context of a particular culture; for example, the maple leaf conventionally symbolizes Canada: that meaning is bestowed on the object by Canadians.

cultural context the nexus of social institutions and beliefs in which a play is produced; for example, the cultural context of *Oedipus the King* is (broadly speaking) democratic Athens and (more narrowly) Athens during a war with Sparta. Although *Fences* is set in 1950s America, its cultural context is the Reagan era, the 1980s, when the play was first produced.

diction the style of language used by a character, especially his or her vocabulary, which can indicate the character's station in life; for example, in *Hamlet*, Polonius's diction marks him as an educated courtier, while the gravediggers' diction indicates their place among the lower classes.

dramatic convention any device habitually used in theater; for example, the closing of a curtain to mark the end of a scene is a convention that arose in the nineteenth-century theater; in Shakespeare's day, playwrights often ended scenes with a rhyming couplet; the use of a chorus is a convention of the Greek theater.

dynamic character a character who changes during the course of the play; usually, the protagonist will be dynamic. For example, Oedipus undergoes a mental and physical transformation by the end of *Oedipus the King*.

equilibrium   the state of relative stability that precedes the introduction of a conflict; for example, Hamlet, though he is unhappy, is in a state of equilibrium until his colloquy with his
father's ghost.

exposition   the revelation, usually by recitation, of events that occurred before the opening scene in a play; for example, in the
opening scene of *Oedipus the King*, the leader of the chorus
recites a list of the plagues that have besieged Thebes and that
occasioned his supplication of Oedipus.

falling action   the events in a play—a sequence of consequences—that occur after the climax; for example, the funeral
scene in *Fences* is part of the falling action.

flashback   a scene interrupting the normal chronological sequence
of a play or film; a flashback enacts events that occurred prior
to the stage "present."

genre   any category into which similar works of literature, film,
and so on, are grouped; for example, speaking broadly, drama
is a genre; tragedy and comedy are genres within that larger
category; satire is a genre within comedy. The hour-long television drama is a genre, and the cop drama and the hospital
drama are genres within that larger category. Genres within
genres are sometimes called *subgenres*.

groundlings   the poorest members of the audience in the Elizabethan theater; the groundlings stood in the open-air yard surrounding the stage.

hubris   excessive pride; it is a common characteristic of tragic
heroes.

identify   to imagine that you are a particular character on the
stage; you identify with a character if the events in a play
trigger the same emotions in you (though perhaps less intensely) as they trigger in the character. For example, someone who identifies with Cory in *Fences* will feel frustrated and
angry and threatened when Troy triggers those emotions in
Cory.

in media res   literally, "in the middle of things"; a story that
begins in media res is already beyond the plot's complication, which then must be divulged to the audience through
exposition.

literary symbol a thing carrying symbolic meaning only within a particular work of literature; the same object in another literary work or in real life does not necessarily carry the same symbolic meaning.

method acting a style of acting developed by the Russian director Konstantin Stanislavsky (1863–1938) and popularized in the United States by Elia Kazan, who directed the first production of *Death of a Salesman*. A method actor tries to take on the identity of the character, identify with the character psychologically, and "act" according to the character's nature.

orchestra in ancient Greek theaters, the circular floor where the chorus danced and sang; in contemporary theaters, the space in front of the stage (used by the orchestra) or the forward section of seats on the main floors.

pity one of the emotions aroused in an audience by tragedy; according to Aristotle, pity comes from feeling that the protagonist's suffering goes beyond what he or she deserves.

plot the events that constitute the story in a play; the plot begins when a conflict is introduced into a state of equilibrium; the events that intensify the conflict are called the rising action; the conflict is ended at the climax; the events following the climax are called the falling action; and the resolution is the final state of equilibrium.

prop any material object handled in a play, such as the swords in the final scene of *Hamlet*.

proscenium arch a decorative arch over the stage and separating it from the auditorium in many nineteenth-century and some twentieth-century theaters; often, the curtain descends from behind this arch.

prosperity in a tragedy, the state of relative success and comfort the protagonist enjoys at the play's beginning.

protagonist the character that the play is about; its central character. The protagonist usually is dynamic and must always be the focus of the primary conflict. For example, Nora is the protagonist in *A Doll House*.

recognition the self-knowledge that a tragic hero gains through the events of the play; usually, this knowledge concerns his or her complicity in the reversal, but it comes too late to mitigate the consequences of that reversal.

resolution in a tragedy, the relatively stable (though often unpleasant) conditions that are the consequence of the working out of the conflict.

revenge tragedy a type of tragedy in which an oath or powerful emotion compels the protagonist to acts of bloody revenge that are often self-destructive; for example, *Hamlet.*

reversal in a tragedy, the moment at which the tragic hero, who has begun the play in a relatively exalted position, falls.

rising action the events that increase the intensity of the conflict.

romantic comedy a drama, usually light and funny, in which the conflict concerns the hindered but eventually successful match of two lovers.

satire a genre of literature that exposes to an audience's laughter or even ridicule the flaws, inconsistencies, or hypocrisies of human character and social institutions; for example, *The Importance of Being Earnest* satirizes Victorian society.

scenery the materials on stage, such as backdrops and structures, that help the audience imagine the setting of a scene or play.

set all the materials, including the scenery, that convey a sense of place to the audience.

spectacle an element in Aristotle's analysis of drama; anything that appeals to the eyes in a play, from costumes to scenery.

static character a character who does not change during the course of the play.

stock character a stereotypical character that reappears in a genre of drama; stock characters are especially prevalent in well-made plays of the nineteenth century; for example, in *The Importance of Being Earnest*, Chasuble is a more or less stereotypical country parson, a parody of the figure familiar to English audiences in the 1890s.

symbol a thing that represents something other than itself. The thing might stand for an object or objects, or it might represent an abstraction or a range of abstractions. For example, a backyard barbecue grill might represent a suburb, or it might represent the American dream.

sympathetic character a character with whom the audience sympathizes; a likeable character.

terror in a tragedy, the emotion the audience feels as a consequence of recognizing that they share the tragic hero's fate.

tiring-house the enclosure at the back of the Elizabethan stage; the inside of the tiring-house was out of the audience's view and thus served for costume changes and other business.

tragedy a genre of drama that traces the fall from prosperity of a heroic, though imperfect, protagonist; for example, *Oedipus the King*.

tragic hero the protagonist in a tragedy; the tragic hero is generally a larger-than-life character, a leader in his or her community, who falls from a state of prosperity to poverty (either material or metaphoric) over the course of the play.

universal symbol a thing carrying the same symbolic meaning in various cultures; for example, the setting sun generally represents death or ending.

unsympathetic character a character with whom the audience does not sympathize; an unlikeable character.

well-made play a type of play popular in the nineteenth-century that drew upon a repertoire of crowd-pleasing plot elements and stock characters; the term became synonymous with superficiality; *The Importance of Being Earnest* profits from, by spoofing, the "well-made" tradition.

*

Permissions Acknowledgments

Lorraine Hansberry: *A Raisin in the Sun*, from *A Raisin in the Sun* by Lorraine Hansberry, copyright © 1958 by Robert Nemiroff, as an unpublished work. Copyright © 1959, 1966, 1984 by Robert Nemiroff. Copyright renewed 1986, 1987 by Robert Nemiroff. Used by permission of Random House, Inc.

Henrik Ibsen: *A Doll House*, from *The Complete Major Prose Plays of Henrik Ibsen* by Henrik Ibsen, translated by Rolf Fjelde, copyright © 1965, 1970, 1978 by Rolf Fjelde. Used by permission of Dutton Signet, a division of Penguin Group (USA), Inc.

Arthur Miller: *Death of a Salesman*, from *Death of a Salesman* by Arthur Miller, copyright 1949, renewed © 1977 by Arthur Miller. Used by permission of Viking Penguin, a division of Penguin Group (USA), Inc.

Sophocles: *The Oedipus Rex of Sophocles: An English Version* by Dudley Fitts and Robert Fitzgerald, copyright 1949 by Houghton Mifflin Harcourt Publishing Company and renewed 1977 by Cornelia Fitts and Robert Fitzgerald, reprinted by permission of the publisher. CAUTION: All rights, including professional, amateur, motion picture, recitation, lecturing,